MARKETING RESEARCH:

A STRUCTURE FOR DECISION MAKING

MARKETING RESEARCH:

A STRUCTURE FOR DECISION MAKING

F. E. BROWN

PRESIDENT, F. E. BROWN MARKETING RESEARCH

Formerly Professor of Marketing and Statistics
The Wharton School of The University of Pennsylvania

Addison-Wesley Publishing Company

Reading, Massachusetts • Menlo Park, California
London • Amsterdam • Don Mills, Ontario • Sydney

This book is in the
Addison-Wesley Marketing Series
Consulting Editor: Yoram Wind

Library of Congress Cataloging in Publication Data

Brown, Francis Earl, 1923-
  Marketing research.
  (Addison-Wesley series in marketing)
  Includes index.
  1. Marketing research. I. Title. II. Series.
HF5415.2.B69   658.8'3   79-25541
ISBN 0-201-00205-1

ISBN 0-201-00205-1
ABCDEFGHIJ-HA-89876543210

PREFACE

Marketing Research: A Structure for Decision Making is designed for two principal groups: (1) graduate MBA students desiring a working knowledge of marketing research and (2) practicing researchers who wish to upgrade their technical skills. It is primarily a text with an integrated development of the subject, but it can also serve as a reference book for those interested in specialized topics. The book was motivated, as probably all texts are, by satisfactions and frustrations experienced over a number of years in teaching the subject matter.

The frustrations are more easily classified and have been more influential in establishing the coverage and structure for the book. The satisfactions are more subtle and have been incorporated in specifics throughout. The past frustrations are best summarized by quotes from three students:

That sounds very fine, but what good is it to a marketing manager?

I sort of follow what you've done, but I could never do it.

I'm glad I've had a semester of marketing research. Now I can be my own researcher.

The first quote is the result of a failure to communicate the relevance of marketing research and is encountered most often when the class becomes bogged down in formulae and mathematical calculations. Problem definition from the decision maker's perspective and how it is translated into a research question supply the remedy. Part I of the text is designed to emphasize that real-world problems are the foundations for any meaningful marketing research. The point is reiterated throughout the text, and the problems at the end of each chapter reinforce this perspective.

The second quote results from a failure to involve the students in the actual solving of problems, leaving the students in the passive role of observers. This occurs most often when the techniques are talked "about" rather than worked through. It also occurs when the instructor slips into a lecture —"the notes of the instructor become the notes of the student without going through the mind of either." The text demonstrates each specific technique on a step-by-step basis so that the students are required to follow the logic as well as the arithmetic. The exercises at the end of the chapters then require the students to apply the techniques to a different set of data. The instructor should not expect students to develop either competence or confidence unless these exercises are a part of the course.

The third quote results from a failure to convey the true extent of marketing research. The quoted student saw marketing research as a closed set of n analytic techniques to be neatly applied to particular marketing problems. The text develops in some detail selected techniques—techniques of which the students can gain a fairly complete understanding. But it also includes references and examples of other techniques. Neither space nor the prerequisite technical level permits the thorough documentation and development of these techniques. Their inclusion acquaints the student with the broader horizons of marketing research and encourages the more ambitious to pursue them.

The only formal mathematics prerequisite is high school algebra. A basic statistics course is not a prerequisite, but a willingness to work with quantitative material is essential. Marketing research of today, and even more of tomorrow, requires quantitative models. The student or instructor who avoids them fails to cover the subject adequately.

Past satisfactions from teaching marketing research are best summarized by "the seeing of the 'Aha' reaction." It is at this point that the student gains understanding and insight. The whole effort is worthwhile when students comprehend the interrelatedness of marketing research, grasp the significance of some particular subtlety, or see how a new idea or technique has specific applicability.

The text stresses for each technique the proper interpretation of the numerical results. This interpretation refers both to the general meaning of a result and to the specific meaning within a particular problem. This stress is also repeated through the exercises at the end of each chapter.

The interrelatedness of the various steps of marketing research is underlined by constant reminders that the step under study is useless unless it is consistent with decisions at all other steps. Sometimes this requires an abrupt interruption by refocusing attention in a different direction. At other times it can be achieved by a broad question at the close of an example or exercise.

The coverage of the four basic techniques of contingency tables, analysis of variance, regression, and discriminant analysis is structured in order to help the student understand their similarities and differences—particularly with respect to managerial problems and the scaling of variables. The development follows a gradual progression from bivariate to multivariate relationships followed by modifications of the initial structure. A series of summary charts enables the student to compare the different techniques, stressing both their structural natures and the relevant statistics that summarize their results.

A second set of summary charts is provided with respect to alternative sample designs. By comparing them, the student can determine the gains or losses available from stratification and clustering—as opposed to simple random sampling.

Although the text is designed for sequential coverage, it is possible to omit certain sections if a shorter course is desired. This approach can also be used with well-motivated undergraduate students who want a good grasp of analytic techniques and an understanding of how these techniques fit into a total project. Instructors who desire a short basic course can cover the first 12 chapters and finish with Chapter 21. Inclusion of Chapter 13 would add multivariate material, and Chapter 8 could be omitted in order to de-emphasize technical sampling considerations.

Marketing research can be approached from at least four different perspectives: (1) the analytic approach, (2) the conceptual approach, (3) the case approach, or (4) the mathematical approach. The text utilizes a blend of the approaches, but it stresses the analytic and conceptual. The types of exercises and problems assigned and the amount of detail considered in specific examples can be varied to meet each instructor's goals. The emphasis given to detail, problems, derivations, and live cases will of course determine the rate at which material is covered. Instructors can select from Chapters 14 to 20 according to their interest in particular topics, their time constraints, and the depth of coverage desired.

ORGANIZATION OF THE BOOK

The text divides the marketing research process into five steps: problem definition, research design, data collection, data analysis, and interpretation. Part I is addressed to the successive detail required in the first three steps. Quantitative skill and analytic sophistication are at a minimum during these three steps. We are trying to be sure the right questions are posed—that relevant data are generated rather than meaningless numbers. At this stage the distinction between a census and a sample is of small concern. Chapter 2 is addressed to problem definition; Chapter 3, to research design; and Chapters 4 and 5, to data collection. Data collection is further divided into instrument design (Chapter 4) and fieldwork (Chapter 5).

Part II focuses on the problems introduced by using a sample rather than a census. In Chapter 6 the selection of various types of samples and their properties are considered. Chapter 7 deals with how sample results are used in reaching conclusions about the universe. Chapter 8 addresses more directly the problem of deciding how large a sample is needed. Finally, Chapter 9 considers comparisons between two samples. Thus Part II is both a bridge to the fourth step of data analysis and an introduction to it by providing a quick review of the elementary principles of sampling and statistical inference.

The elementary techniques for measuring relationships and their interpretation are considered in Part III. Chapter 10 discusses the general problem of establishing relationships and association. Two variable associations are developed in Chapter 11 (contingency tables and the analysis of variance) and Chapter 12 (regression and discriminant analysis). The four techniques are extended to multivariate problems in Chapter 13, and selected modifications are discussed in Chapter 14. Search techniques, as opposed to hypothesis testing, are introduced in Chapter 15. The special case of time-series data is considered in Chapter 16.

Part IV examines selected analytic techniques that have been of particular significance in more recent marketing research application. The techniques are grouped under the topics of nonpartitioned data with particular emphasis on factor analysis and clustering (Chapter 17), use of multiple dependent variables (Chapter 18), ordinal scales (Chapter 19), and multidimensional scaling and conjoint analysis (Chapter 20). Part IV closes with a look at future directions in marketing research (Chapter 21).

I am grateful to the Literary Executor of the late Sir Ronald A. Fisher, F.R.S., to Dr. Frank Yates, F.R.S., and to Longman Group Ltd., London, for permission to reprint Table III from their book, *Statistical Tables for Biological, Agricultural, and Medical Research* (6th ed., 1974.)

Yardley, Pennsylvania   F. E. B.
January 1980

ACKNOWLEDGMENTS

Any book involves a complex of inputs. Some are recognizable and others are not. Those that are not recognizable are usually more fundamental than those that are. This book is no exception but probably involves a more varied input, bearing the marks of instructors from the author's own graduate training starting with E. Douglass Burdick, J. Parker Bursk, and Donald F. Blankertz—all of the Wharton School.

Input from colleagues over the years in structuring and restructuring problems and models has been diverse. Colleagues and clients have freely shared their insights, and the author is particularly grateful for their willingness to release the databases for many of the examples employed. Alfred R. Oxenfeldt of Columbia University and H. Jay Shaffer of the Sperry and Hutchinson Company were particularly encouraging in the early stages, providing helpful soundingboards and comments as the project took shape.

Both undergraduate and graduate classes at the Wharton School made substantial contributions to the final version of the text by laboring through earlier drafts. Paul E. Green and Yoram Wind were kind enough to read the entire manuscript; the final version is greatly improved because of their suggestions and comments.

My wife, Marge, has been the true driving force behind the book. She read every word of every draft, typed each draft, encouraged me, and persevered through the entire project. It never would have been completed without her.

Chapter 11   Contingency Tables and Analysis of Variance   275

Contingency Tables   275
Analysis of Variance   287
Summary   296
Exercises and Problems   298

Chapter 12   Regression and Discriminant Analysis   305

Regression   306
Discriminant Analysis   323
Summary   337
Exercises and Problems   338

Chapter 13   Associative Data with Several Independent Variables   343

Analysis of Variance   343
Multiple Regression   358
Discriminant Analysis   372
Multivariate Contingency Tables   385
Summary   387
Exercises and Problems   389

Chapter 14   Dummy Variables and Analysis of Covariance   395

The Dummy Variable   395
Analysis of Covariance   401
Summary   410
Exercises and Problems   411

Chapter 15   Search Techniques   415

Stepwise Regression   416
Transformations   420
Automatic Interaction Detector   426
Summary   429
Exercises and Problems   430

Chapter 16   Time Series   435

Time as an Independent Variable   436
Lead-lag Relationships   453
Summary   459
Exercises and Problems   460

PART IV RECENT ANALYTIC
DEVELOPMENTS   467

Chapter 17   Collapsing the Number of Variables   469

Factor Analysis   471
Cluster Analysis   485
Summary   498
Exercises and Problems   500

Chapter 18   Multiple Dependent Variables   507

Canonical Correlation   508
Multivariate Analysis of Variance   519
Multivariate Analysis of Covariance   521
Summary   525
Exercises and Problems   526

Chapter 19   Ordinal Scales—Uses and Transformations   529

The Median   530
Rank Tests   532
Sign and Runs Tests   540
Implicit Interval Scales   543
Summary   547
Exercises and Problems   548

Chapter 20   Multidimensional Scaling and Conjoint Analysis   555

Multidimensional Scaling   556
Conjoint Analysis   575
Summary   585
Exercises and Problems   586

Chapter 21   Future Directions in Marketing Research   591

Past Inadequacies of Marketing Research   591
Technical Developments in Data Handling   596
Availability of Competent Research Personnel   598
Developments in Behavioral Science and Marketing   599
Summary   601
Exercises and Problems   601

Appendix

Table A.1 Random digits   604
Table A.2 Areas of the unit normal distribution   606
Table A.3 Critical values of the t-distribution   608

Table A.4 Values of Chi Square distributions
for critical percentile points   609
Table A.5 Five and one percent significance points
of the F-distribution   610
Table A.6 Critical values of s in the
Kendall coefficient of concordance   612
Table A.7 Critical values of T in the
Wilcoxon matched-pairs, signed-ranks test   613

Index   617

LISTS OF IMPORTANT TABLES

The tables designated in the following lists are of value to the instructor in integrating significant material, and to the researcher who uses this book for reference purposes. Note that the designations in the lists refer to the table *topics* rather than to the precise table *titles* given in the book.

WORKSHEETS FOR DETERMINING SAMPLE SIZES

Worksheets

Simple Random Sampling (Table 8.4)   203

Alternatives to Simple Random Sampling (Table 8.9)   219

Comparison of Two Samples (Table 9.2)   239

Related Tables

Illustrative Sample Sizes for Specified Reliability and Confidence. Sample Percentage Problems (Table 8.2)   199

Reduction in Required Sample Size for Finite Populations (Table 8.3)   200

Loss in Reliability with Cluster Sampling Compared with Simple Random Sampling. Selected Values of δ and $\bar{n}$ (Table 8.8)   217

OVERVIEWS OF ASSOCIATION TECHNIQUES

Bivariate

Contingency Table Analysis (Table 11.6)   287

Analysis of Variance (Table 11.12)   296

Regression/Correlation Analysis (Table 12.5)   322

Discriminant Analysis (Table 12.13)   336

Multiple Independent Variables

Analysis of Variance (Table 13.8)   357

Regression/Correlation Analysis (Table 13.13)   371

Discriminant Analysis (Table 13.20)   385

ILLUSTRATIVE COMPUTER PRINTOUTS

Analysis of Variance (Table 13.7)   356

Multiple Regression Analysis (Table 13.12)   369

Discriminant Analysis (Table 13.19)   382

Regression with Dummy Variable (Table 14.2)   398

Analysis of Covariance (Table 14.4)   403

Stepwise Regression (Table 15.1)   418

Cluster Analysis—Interpoint Distances (Table 17.8)   488

Cluster Analysis—Amalgamation Order (Table 17.9)   489

POSING THE RIGHT
QUESTIONS

GIGO—"garbage in, garbage out!" Sophisticated analysis is to no avail unless the basic data are appropriate. Therefore, the starting point of marketing research must be the specification of the required data and the establishment of procedures for their collection. Part I emphasizes these topics after presenting an overview of marketing research in Chapter 1.

The overview of Chapter 1 includes the introduction of the five-step process of marketing research: problem definition, research design, data collection, data analysis, and interpretation. The remainder of Part I discusses in detail the first three of these steps. Chapter 2 addresses problem definition, the identification of the decision to be made and the criteria on which that decision is to be based. Chapter 3 (Research Design) considers the structuring of experiments, the degree of control required, and the specification of environmental conditions. Chapters 4 and 5 address data collection, dividing the discussion into instrument design (Chapter 4) and fieldwork (Chapter 5).

CHAPTER 1

WHAT IS MARKETING RESEARCH?

PURPOSEFUL INVESTIGATION VERSUS A FISHING EXPEDITION

What is our market share in Denver? Who makes the purchase decision for office supplies? How large is the retail inventory for our product? Does our target market know we have introduced a new model? What is the expected level of industrial construction in the Boston metropolitan area in the next six months? What makes a topnotch medical supplies sales person? How important is package design in toothpaste sales? Which magazines are most effective in reaching our target market? How much profit can we build into our bid price for the J&L contract and still have a good chance of winning? What kind of image does our chain project to young marrieds? Can the typical consumer tell the difference between our product and that of our leading competitor? Which of three potential ads delivers the best name recall? the best message recall? What method of compensation produces the most long-run company profit? All these questions require marketing research. Every area of company activity impinges on marketing research and can benefit from its results.

Marketing research is not an existing bag of techniques; nor is it a restructuring of the marketing mix or the 4 P's. Marketing research must also be differentiated from a fishing expedition or from an encyclopedic gathering of assorted facts. Marketing research is *purposeful investigation*. It provides a structure for decision making.

"We recommend that the new pen be priced at 79¢!" This was the recommendation forwarded to the marketing vice-president by the marketing research manager. The quote focuses on two of the three parts of any investigation: (1) the implicit question posed in the quote and (2) the explicit answer proposed. The third part of the investigation is the collection, analysis, and interpretation of the information leading from the question to the answer. This third part is the defense or documentation that justifies the recommendation and is sometimes viewed as "the research." This view is unfortunate since it allocates the first two parts to the decision maker or line executive and the third to the researcher. With this approach, it is not surprising that much research is completed, presented, filed, and forgotten. Useful and good marketing research requires not only the integration of the three parts but also mutual cooperation between the decision maker and the researcher.

The researcher cannot dictate the *right* questions to the decision maker, but an integrated approach of the three parts can aid in the formulation of the questions so that the right research questions are addressed. Nor can the researcher tell the decision maker which alternatives are admissible as possible answers, but again research can aid in recognizing which alternatives the decision maker might adopt—given the decision maker's present assumptions, predispositions, and quandaries.

The question posed and the answer proposed are ultimately the responsibility of the decision maker. But it is the responsibility of the researcher to translate each into specifics that lend themselves to research procedures. The processing stage—the generation and interpretation of data—is basically the responsibility of the researcher. But it is the responsibility of the decision maker to verify that all substantive issues are defined in ways that are acceptable in the real-world problem. The decision maker must evaluate the definitions of terms such as "user," "market areas," "preference," "potential customer," "principal competitors," "alternative packages," and a multitude of other terms. It is counterproductive for the decision maker to object to the definitions at the conclusion of the study.

Unfortunately, two syndromes are prevalent among decision makers with respect to the processing stage. The first minimizes interest in processing and, perhaps unconsciously, downgrades its importance. If processing is faulty, the research results are no less unacceptable than if either the question posed or the answer proposed is faulty. The second syndrome magnifies the importance of processing, almost to the point of worship. Processing was not placed as the third part of research by accident. It is introduced into the investigation by necessity; operational decisions rely on information. The processing is merely a link; it is not an end in itself.

The processing employed should be no more complex than is necessary to select the appropriate alternative for the question posed. Model building and sophisticated quantitative analyses are appropriate only as required for the problem at hand. The opposite syndrome, disinterest in the processing, invites disaster. A claim that the area is outside of the decision maker's particular discipline is of little consolation if an improper recommendation is implemented. It is similarly unsatisfying to fail to adopt an appropriate recommendation with the excuse that the decision maker did not really understand the processing. It is the joint responsibility of the researcher and the decision maker that each understands enough of the work and needs of the other to implement the proper recommendations.

The marketing manager who uses marketing research must be conversant with research procedures. This familiarity is needed for three distinct but related reasons.

1. The marketing manager must adopt or reject research recommendations. Therefore, *the manager must understand the proper interpretation of research results and the assumptions embodied in them.*

2. The marketing manager poses the initial problem and its environment. Therefore, *the manager must understand the kinds of questions research can handle and the type of structure required to make a problem "researchable."*

3. The marketing manager is a prime target for "snow jobs" from marketing researchers and consultants. Therefore, *the manager must be capable of appraising the feasibility of research proposals.*

Our primary objective is to enable the marketing manager to have the understanding of marketing research required by these three tasks. We shall consider some fairly sophisticated quantitative techniques, but the marketing manager should not become ensnarled in the researcher's mathematical considerations. The manager's focus should be on how the results will be useful, what input will be necessary in order to use the technique, and what the technique will not provide.

DEFINITION OF MARKETING RESEARCH

The term *marketing research* obviously ties together two words. Marketing identifies the substantive field of interest while research specifies a methodology. The substantive field of marketing has been defined in many different ways, the breadth or narrowness of its definition usually depending on whether the individual considers himself or herself to be within the field of marketing. Probably its narrowest definition is "the flow of goods and services from the producer to the consumer." Expansion and modification occur as we add words such as "activities that impinge upon," "activities involved in," "satisfaction of needs and wants," and "at a profit."

Although many marketers consider it too narrow, the official definition of marketing by the American Marketing Association will be quite satisfactory for our purposes: ("The performance of business activities that direct the flow of goods and services from producer to consumer or user.")[1] Those who object that this definition is too narrow have based their objections on the argument that intelligent marketing decisions must consider many variables that are not enumerated in the definition. This objection misses the point; the definition should identify the kinds of problems addressed but not necessarily circumscribe the variables considered in the solution. Our objective is to make intelligent decisions and not to engage in jurisdictional disputes concerning the

---

[1]*Marketing Definitions: A Glossary of Marketing Terms,* 1960, Committee on Definitions of the American Marketing Association, Ralph S. Alexander, Chairman, (Chicago: American Marketing Association), p. 15.

proper classification of them. Where such classification or definition is useful in the solving of the problem, we should be among the first to call for precise delimitations. We believe such delimitation is more helpful in establishing lines of authority and responsibility than it is in discussing research procedures. Therefore, we shall construe the field of marketing broadly, embracing many variables that require cooperation with nonmarketing personnel of the organization.

The *marketing concept* places the consumer at the focus of all decisions by the firm. Any business activity that has the potential to influence the consumer's attitude or behavior toward the firm or its offerings must be incorporated in marketing decisions, regardless of the firm's organization chart and labels. Likewise knowledge of consumer behavior is germane to marketing. New product ideas, research and development activities, and financial constraints or the availability of additional funds all influence the flow of goods and services from the firm to the consumer. External factors such as legislation, general business conditions, competitors' activities, and changes in the social climate are also significant to marketing. Whether these factors should all be construed as a part of marketing is unimportant; all of them (and many others) must be considered by marketing personnel in their decision making.

The second word—*research*—identifies a process by which the firm attempts to supply the information required for intelligent marketing decisions. Research is not synonymous with common sense. The difference revolves principally around words such as "systematic," "objective," and "reproducible." Both research and common sense depend on information; the distinction between them lies in the procedures and criteria by which the information is obtained and used in arriving at conclusions.[2] Research cannot address itself to *all* information on a particular subject. Therefore two secondary characteristics of research specify "relevance" and "control."

A *systematic approach* is mandatory in good research. Each step must be planned so that it yields that which is necessary at the next step. It is usually difficult to go back and correct the mistakes of a prior stage; sometimes it is impossible. Even when it is possible, losses in both time and money are usually involved. Many authors have divided marketing research into a series of steps. Both the number of steps and their names are somewhat arbitrary, but the recognition of a sequence is crucial. Planning and organization are part of this systematic approach with explicit consideration given to the interdependence of the various steps and to the unity of the entire project.

One of the more common errors in planning is the separation of data collection and data analysis. First, we collect the data; then, we decide what analysis is appropriate. This approach invites a disaster like that experienced by a

---

[2]Many of the thoughts expressed in this section are similar to those found in Fred N. Kerlinger, 1973, *Foundations of Behavioral Research* (Amsterdam, Netherlands: Holt, Rinehart and Winston), Chapter 1.

large university a number of years ago. Depth interviews of the freshman class were conducted and tape recorded at a cost of well over $100,000. At last report the data were still unanalyzed because no one knew how to proceed. We are not concerned here with how the data might have been analyzed. Our point is that the question should have been addressed in the planning stage. Only by looking at the total project—*before the fact*—can one determine whether it will satisfy the decision maker's needs.

Objectivity requires an approach that is independent of the researcher's personal views with respect to the proper answer to the problem under investigation. Any selection of data or definitions that is suspect destroys the utility of the results for a true decision-making problem. Honest differences may exist with respect to the proper definition or collection procedure, but the one selected must not be chosen in order to verify a prior position.

Often totally different pictures can be obtained by changing one's perspective. Look at a scene in the morning and then in the evening. Use the naked eye and then tinted glasses. It is the same with marketing research. The time and place of an interview is usually crucial. A high proportion of shoppers in Store A have a positive opinion of Store A. Shoppers in Store B may have a totally different opinion of Store A. Purchase behavior varies with price specials. If one wishes to prove a point, careful selection of respondents, time, and place can usually fulfill one's desires. The challenge for the researcher is to select without biasing the results. An assignment "to prove that a market exists for the new deluxe model" or "to show that J–R is the preferred aspirin" is not a research assignment. True research seeks an unbiased answer to a relevant decision-making problem.

A *reproducible* research procedure is one that an equally competent researcher could duplicate and from it obtain approximately the same results. In order to have reproducibility, all procedures must be stated unambiguously. Precise wording of questions, method of sampling, collection technique, interviewer instructions, and all other details must be clearly stated. Even if the environment changes, the research is at least "conceptually" reproducible in the sense that the steps could be mentally duplicated.

One of the greatest temptations encountered by the inexperienced interviewer is to help the respondent by rephrasing the question. Rephrasing per se is permissible, but it must be neutral. If the rephrasing changes the inquiry or "leads" the respondent, the research results apply to a new question although neither the decision maker nor the research supervisor may be aware of it. A repeat of the research, again with poor execution, would probably yield different results.

Poor or vague sampling procedures can also lead to nonreproducibility. An assignment to conduct personal interviews with "representative female shoppers" in a particular shopping mall invites disaster. Findings from such an investigation are not reproducible. Each interviewer's concept of "representative" and the resulting sample composition will differ. Reliance on a large number of interviewers and a "balancing effect" will not suffice. If procedures are vague and not spelled out carefully, not even the same interviewers would be consistent.

The *relevancy* requirement cuts in two directions. It avoids the collection of unnecessary information with the accompanying unnecessary cost. In the other direction, it forces the comparison of the data collected with the decision maker's criteria for action. A good question to ask before the research is undertaken is "What action would you take if the research answer were _____?" This approach projects both the investigator and the decision maker to the end of the research and forces both to ask whether the planned research is on the correct path. An alternative question to ask is "Would answers of A and B lead to the same or different actions?" If both answers will lead to the same action, the research need not be designed so that it will discriminate between answers of A and B.

Researchers of home insulation contemplated using questions on both characteristics of the home and characteristics of the home owner. All except a few of the home owner questions were classified as nonrelevant or low priority when the issue of action implications was raised. The marketing manager was not considering alternative actions based on age, occupation, education, or any of several other owner characteristics. Unless the marketing manager restructures alternatives or is willing to pay for "potentially useful data sometime," there is no reason to include these questions.

The concept of *control* is particularly elusive in marketing research. We must continually guard against the possibility that our results are due to the presence of some factor other than those we are investigating. It is impossible to control for *all* other factors; the best we can do is to control for those we think are most likely to cause us difficulty. A study of the relationship between shopping behavior and income without controlling for education and age may be the height of folly since our findings may reflect the effect of education or age rather than income.

Control raises extremely difficult issues when research is conducted in a live competitive environment. Many factors other than the ones of principal interest may influence the research results. The danger is that the researcher may attribute changes to one variable when the uncontrolled variables are the causes.

The current economic situation almost always affects the outcome of the investigation. Heightened sensitivity to price appeals or price reductions is more likely to occur in periods of high unemployment than in periods of low unemployment. Receptivity to new products, particularly high-cost consumer durables or heavy equipment for expansion of industrial productive capacity, is also dependent on current economic conditions.

The firm's or researcher's acts influence the research results. This is most obvious in survey work or laboratory experiments in which the mere asking of

a question or presentation of a stimulus makes the respondent more aware of specific aspects of the environment. Research results may also be misleading when extra marketing efforts accompany a market test. Any attempt to "make the new plan succeed" is an additional marketing input, invalidating the accuracy of the research results unless the additional inputs are to be incorporated as part of the total plan.

Advertising campaigns are not conducted in a vacuum. It is difficult to maintain control over your own firm's actions during the experiment; it is impossible to control competitors' actions. Even if competitors maintain particular advertising approaches, their retail prices, out-of-stock conditions, trade deals, and sales force policies are bound to change.

Changes in sales force composition and size occur continuously. This is true of both your own sales force and that of other channel members. A top sales person may be promoted, necessitating the realignment of several other sales people. Territorial sales levels may be affected greatly. Additions or deletions in the size of the sales force may affect both aggregate results and those within specific territories. Your firm cannot and will not submit to a prolonged experiment that results in neglect of current operating modifications. The best you can do is record changes in significant uncontrolled variables, in the hope that appropriate adjustments can be made as part of the analysis.

Control must consider each of two aspects. (1) Those variables that are truly within your control must be varied according to the nature of your inquiry. Usually this means selecting specific levels of activity on several different marketing mix variables during the experiment. (2) Those variables beyond your control should be recorded. Various analytic techniques to be considered later can help you adjust for their effects.

THE MARKETING RESEARCH PROCESS

Marketing research can be conveniently divided into five steps: problem definition, research design, data collection, data analysis, and interpretation of results.[3] In order to illustrate these five steps, let us consider the problem you would face if you were the marketing manager for a direct mail merchandiser. You must decide which of two direct mail pieces to use for a recently purchased list of 5,000 names.

Problem Definition

First, what is your problem? Your decision will be to use either direct mail piece A or direct mail piece B. The researcher should at least verify that these are truly the only two options open to you. Should other mail pieces also be

---

[3]Other authors divide the process more finely. See, for example, Harper W. Boyd, Jr. and Ralph Westfall, 1972, *Marketing Research: Text and Cases* (Homewood, Ill.: Irwin), pp. 192–196.

considered? Is it possible that this list of 5,000 names should not be used at all for the particular merchandise under consideration? Should methods other than direct mail be employed? Should a combination of A and B be used? Perhaps the merchandise is inappropriate. Let us assume that the alternatives have been correctly specified: either A or B will be employed.

We have identified the alternatives available to you, but we have not specified a complete problem definition. The complete problem is also concerned with the criterion that will determine which mailing piece is superior. The criterion may be dollar volume of sales generated, number of persons placing orders, or perhaps some definition of profitability from sales generated. Quite generally the definition of the problem is composed of three aspects: the specification of the unit of analysis for the study, the identification of the particular units within the scope of the study, and the specification of the kind of information sought concerning those units. What would you wish to know if information were free and without error? A complete answer to this question defines the initial research problem. It may later be redefined because of cost or time considerations or because of measurement difficulties, but it establishes a starting point.

The unit of analysis for you is a *person*. You want to know how persons would respond to mail piece A and mail piece B. Which persons? Are you interested in the 5,000 on the mailing list or in some larger group? The answer to this question determines the *universe* (or population) of your problem. If you are interested in the 5,000 on the list, that particular mailing list is the universe of your problem. If you are interested in *more than* the 5,000, you must specify the nature of that larger group. You need not study all persons in that universe. Very rarely would one attempt complete coverage, but you must identify the group for which you wish to reach conclusions—that group is your universe. As we shall see later, one of the central questions of sampling is how to secure representativeness. Unless we can specify the relevant universe, we cannot even address the question of the sample's representativeness.

Assume that the relevant population for you consists of the 5,000 names on the list purchased. The information desired concerning that population is its response to the two alternative mailing pieces, response defined in accordance with your objectives for the mailing. Assume you are satisfied to measure response by dollar volume of sales. As a question, the research problem can be stated as "Will A or B generate a higher dollar volume of sales from the 5,000 names?"

The time dimension is missing; sales for what period of time? A properly defined population must have time and space coordinates. If the mailing is scheduled for October 1, 1980, the relevant time period may be from the beginning of October to the end of November. Alternatively, a much longer time dimension may be in view. This mailing piece may be designed to introduce the company and its products favorably with a goal of generating sales over several years. The relevant time period may then be the calendar years of

1981–1982. Assume that you are concerned with initial response to the mailing.

Discussion of the decision to be made and the appropriate cirterion for that decision has gotten us well removed from any population that can be researched. This is typical, but it should raise a warning flag. If the population researched differs in substantial ways from the population for the decision, the research may be misleading. What population could be subjected to research? Clearly the time dimension will be prior to the mailing: October 1, 1980. Can we assume that results obtained in one time period are equivalent to those that would be obtained in another period? It depends on the stability of the characteristic under investigation.

How about the units included in the research? Should they come from the list of 5,000 or another source? Several possibilities come to mind: names of current customers, previously purchased lists, small groups of people recruited for an experiment, or experts in the art of communication. These are only a few of the possibilities, but the problem with the units studied is precisely the same as the problem with the time dimensions of the universe. Substantial differences might exist between the universe researched and the universe for the decision.

Current customers may be preconditioned to the firm's offerings. A different approach may be more effective with those who have limited knowledge of the firm. Persons from other lists, even from other lists supplied by the same source, may be quite dissimilar from those on the current list in their reaction or preferences with respect to the firm's products. Persons willing to participate in an experiment may have life-styles and personalities different from those of persons who are not likely to participate. Which type, if either, is more similar to the current list?

If you were interested in a larger group than the current 5,000, the problem is further complicated because you must identify the nature of this larger universe. Then you must appraise alternative research universes for their similarity to that decision universe. This is particularly difficult if the decision universe is persons on lists to be supplied by a particular source and specific information concerning such lists is unavailable.

Two additional sources of difficulty in problem definition are not particularly obvious in the decision of a marketing manager for the mail order house: What are the space coordinates and how does the researcher recognize a unit of the population when he or she sees it? Marketing decisions are introduced in specific geographic locations. The backup research preceding the decision is often limited in its geographic scope: e.g., Peoria, Illinois; or Denver, Colorado. The space coordinates of the problem definition are those that pertain to the geographic area in which you contemplate possible actions. In this particular problem, the space coordinates refer back to the nature of the list of 5,000 names. Research based on a different geographic area rests on the assumption that the two areas are "sufficiently similar" *with respect to the question studied*. They need not be similar in all respects—only for what is studied. Almost always it is a leap of faith to assume them similar; it is better to research a universe with the same space coordinates. Geographic coverage poses particular difficulties in market tests, laboratory experiments, and sometimes in personal interviews.

The second difficulty—which units within the specified time and space coordinates are properly within the problem—is perhaps the most troublesome. Marketing managers face this problem continually in their attempts to convert potential customers into actual customers. How can we recognize a "potential customer" when we see one? A definition of "a person who would buy if . . . " is not very helpful. Research would have to apply unique or multiple "ifs" before the problem could even be defined.

"Loyal customers" or "heavy users" pose the same sorts of problems. The problems occur at two distinct levels: (1) the establishment of a defensible measurement criterion and (2) the cost and difficulty of applying the agreed-upon definition. The concept of "loyal customers" suggests repeat patronage and a high probability of purchasing from a particular firm rather than from competitors. What frequency of purchase is required and how high must the probability be? Can a high value on one offset a slightly reduced level on the other? The answers will be arbitrary, but some values must be established if a marketing manager wishes either to study loyal customers alone or to compare loyal customers with all others. At the second stage, it will be a miniresearch task just to identify the units that are part of the research universe.

Specification of the units within the time and space coordinates obviously becomes difficult when a descriptive adjective is applied to the unit designation. The problem is only slightly reduced in other situations. Returning to the mailing list of 5,000 names, suppose you do not have that list in hand at the date for the research. An appropriate research universe would be one that is generated by the same process that will generate the list of 5,000. This is not automatically accomplished by taking another list from the same supplier anymore than the same manufacturer turns out identical lots. In the first place, the manufacturer may not even be trying to turn out identical products: washers versus refrigerators, different models of washers, or different model years. Herein is a recurrent warning—*if nothing is known about the universe of interest, there is no way of checking alternative research populations against it.*

Finally the problem definition must specify the relevant measurements for the decision. Similar measurements must be made in the research. These are the characteristics of interest for the investigation. We have specified that this characteristic is dollar sales for the mail order house.

We have moved back and forth between the decision maker's problem and various possibilities for the research problem. We have done this in order to demonstrate how easy it is to confuse the two and slip from one to the other without recognizing that change. We should always start with the decision maker's problem; after that is firmly established we may, if necessary, make modifications in defining the research problem.

Let us state as clearly as we can the problem definition for the marketing manager of the mail order firm. The manager wants to know whether the application of A or B to the list of 5,000 will generate higher dollar sales between October 1, 1980 and November 30, 1980. That is almost precisely what we said several pages ago. Why all of the intervening discussion? Because we must define a research problem that will be useful to a marketing manager. This problem will identify the units (persons in this case), the time and space coordinates, and what is to be measured with respect to those units. The problem definition must also specify a procedure with respect to the assignment of A and B, including whether any control groups are to be employed. One possible definition of the research problem is to change the time coordinates to "September 10, 1980 to September 20, 1980" and use the 5,000 names as the population. Two small samples could be selected from the population. The A approach would be applied to one sample, and the B approach would be applied to the other. The reader should pause at this point to evaluate this approach. Further, note that this approach is possible only if the list of 5,000 names is currently available.

A question is not complete unless the alternative responses are indicated. Management must inform research of the options it would consider. Thus the first part of the investigation—the question posed—must contain management's admissible alternative actions to the second part—the answer proposed. The answer is constrained by the question, and the research must be designed to facilitate the selection from among those alternatives. We have stated that the marketing manager is considering only two options: use A or use B.

The direct mail example could have been framed in many alternative ways, limited only by management's view of the problem and its existing policies. For example, a very real alternative might be not to use the list. Or another alternative could be to use the two mailing pieces in sequence with a given time interval between them. This alternative could be further modified, testing for the more effective sequence. The number of alternatives is almost limitless. But the cost of the research increases as the number of alternatives increases and as the complexity of the alternatives increases. The marketing researcher and marketing manager must together determine whether the expected value of the information will exceed its cost. Information takes on value only as it reduces uncertainty regarding the appropriate management action.

Research Design

The second step in marketing research is research design—the blueprint for the research. The basic issues addressed in research design are three-fold:

1. Should the research environment be intentionally disturbed by the researcher in specified ways—an experimental design—or should the environment be studied as it exists without such disturbances?

2. How many observations should be made on each unit in the study? when?

3. Should a single sample be chosen from the total population or should a series of samples be chosen from various subgroups of the population?

The experimental design enables the researcher to manipulate the environment in a predetermined manner. The decision maker asks, "What would happen if . . . ?" The researcher says, "Let's try it and see." It is an approach that is usually expensive and may be difficult to implement. The researcher must be both able and willing to exercise a significant degree of control on the environment and the units within that environment. The nonexperimental approach, chiefly a survey or observational method, depends on the researcher's ability to find the appropriate conditions as a natural result in the environment.

Inferences from the nonexperimental approach are based upon what has been observed (or stated to be true) in a natural environment. The method may be beset with the presence of uncontrolled variables and possible "coincidental" results. The experimental approach relies on control by the researcher and the ability to replicate (repeat) the experiment. Recommendations based on nonexperimental designs carry implicit confidence that the relationships that developed in the past will recur in the future. The researcher has not "intervened" in the situations observed. Will the researcher "intervention" (or the intervention of the researcher's firm) represent a departure from the pattern studied and destroy the validity of the researcher's recommendation? In the experimental design, the researcher does intervene. Consequently, the intervention does not represent a new variable, untested in the research.

Within experimental designs, the researcher may choose either a laboratory experiment or a field experiment. The laboratory experiment abstracts certain elements of the real world into a restricted environment in which the researcher can exert better control on the variables. It thus becomes a simplification of reality, often resulting in a highly restricted situation or population. For example, undergraduate students at Oshkosh University may be studied or consumer behavior may be studied when only two brands are available. The researcher is willing to tolerate these restricted conditions in order to secure extremely good measures of the phenomenon studied. Field experiments involve the introduction of disturbances into an actual market environment. The results apply to a more representative situation, but the effects of uncontrolled variables may be poorly measured. Thus the measurement of the effect of the controlled variables is also less certain.

The essence of the true experiment is not only the researcher's ability to control specific variables in the environment but the researcher's control of those variables so that he or she can infer the effect of those variables on the test results. A related issue is the distinction between cross-sectional and longitudinal designs. *Cross-sectional* designs employ a sample of units at a point in time. *Longitudinal* designs also employ a single sample, but they call for more than one observation on each unit—made at different time periods. The cross-sectional design compares *differences among units;* it cannot examine *changes in particular units.*

The cross-sectional design requires only one observation on each unit. It is still an experimental design provided the researcher controls the application of specific variables to units as selected by him or her. It is a nonexperimental design when the researcher does not exercise control over how the individual units are treated.

The longitudinal (or time-series) design requires at least two observations on each unit. It, too, may be either an experimental or nonexperimental design, depending on the presence or absence of control by the researcher. More detailed study of changes over time is of course possible in longitudinal designs as the number of observations on each unit is increased.

Division of the population into subgroups permits the determination of whether the tested marketing actions have differential impacts on various segments. Examples of potential subgroups are men–women, different age groups, retail–wholesale buyers, geographic regions, etc. By establishing these subgroups in the design stage, the researcher and decision maker can assure themselves that the designated subgroups can be compared in the analysis.

What research design is most appropriate for the marketing manager of the mail order firm? First, an experimental design is required if the manager is to use mail piece A for one group and mail piece B for the second. A nonexperimental design would require finding past examples in which A and B had been applied—a most unlikely occurrence, particularly for the population defined.

A cross-sectional design would suffice since only one reading on each unit is required. Tracking behavior over a period of time would produce a longitudinal design, but that is not required in the present problem. Separate analysis of different subgroups is not required; therefore two samples should be selected from the entire population. One sample will receive A and the other will receive B.[4]

Data Collection

The next step is the collection of relevant data.[5] Collection involves the basic definitions for the concepts to be investigated, specific wordings of inquiries to communicate those concepts, delineation of the environment in which the data will be collected, specific field procedures, and the design of instruments for recording the actual data. Data collection looks forward to data analysis; data requirements for various analytic techniques must be anticipated in the

[4]The determination of the sample design and the size of the sample will be postponed until Chapters 6 and 8.

[5]Greater detail on data collection will be developed in Chapters 3 and 4.

data collection phase. Special care must be introduced in the collection phase to avoid sources of understatement or overstatement for the various characteristics. If such biases are feared, the researcher should consider whether there are ways of introducing adjustments. These adjustments would be introduced in the analysis phase, but the data must be generated in the collection phase.

Suppose in the direct mail problem the marketing manager insists on fast results. A laboratory experiment may be faster than an actual mail test. But it would also introduce substantial changes in the nature of the research inquiry. It would not be a mail offer. Would the purchase behavior in the laboratory be different from what it would be in a mail experiment?

Regardless of whether a laboratory test or a field trial were used, the researcher must also decide whether subjects should use their own funds or whether they should be provided with extra purchasing power. The data collection phase may be expanded to include past behavior because future behavior may be influenced by past acts. This past behavior may serve as an adjustment factor in interpreting the results of the experiment. The precise wording of questions concerning past behavior poses difficulties, and it is not clear whether the question should be asked before or after the respondent has been exposed to the mail piece to be tested.

The collection phase must also consider the diverse tasks of assignment and recruitment of staff, ways of increasing response rates, costs and bias sources under alternative collection approaches, and proper training of personnel. The effect of each of these on accuracy, monetary costs, and time constraints must be evaluated. Finally, the collection phase must be supervised as well as planned. Unfortunately, many well-planned research projects have failed because of inadequate supervision. Procedures that sound good but are inadequately administered lead to invalid results just as much as ill-conceived procedures do.

The "operational definition" is a must in any scientific inquiry and is most obvious in the collection phase. The "operational definition" is the nitty-gritty of how the details of collection, measurement, and wording are to be handled in the research. It is the practical counterpart of the concept developed for the decision maker's action problem and includes a variety of issues. Some of the more pervasive issues are the use of check responses versus open-ended questions, the number of alternatives offered the respondent, and whether the respondent is to choose one alternative or whether he or she may select several. These issues are most obvious in survey research that employs questionnaires, but they also extend to observational studies since the relevant data and its measurement must be specified. The direct mail experiment must establish appropriate coding instructions, any differences in the treatment of COD and prepaid sales, and similar details.

Good research demands unambiguous terms. Care must be exercised in the use of modifying adjectives or adverbs. The addition or deletion of single words can produce drastically different results without clarifying the meaning of those results. Compare the following four questions.

Do you use brand X?

Have you ever used brand X?

Do you regularly use brand X?

Is brand X your favorite brand?

What frequency of use corresponds to each of these four questions? Does the fourth correspond to frequency in any way? Frequency has still another aspect. It can be defined in terms of a product's use in contrast to the use of competing products, or it can be defined in terms of its use per unit of time. The appropriate wording depends on the problem at hand, but no wording can be appropriate unless its meaning is clear. If the precise meaning does not really matter, the research doesn't matter either; so why bother?

The researcher and the decision maker desire data that are as free from error as possible. This is two-pronged: (1) the data collection plan—questions, instruments, and procedures—must be appropriate for the decision maker's problem and (2) the data collection plan must be properly implemented. Implementation requires competent personnel plus supervision. It is easier to obtain valid data initially than to make corrections later. Despite this, good research includes verification of data validity on at least a sample basis. This is frequently done by regenerating the data a second time and comparing results. Perfect agreement is not expected since an element of instability and experimental error is present, but no systematic differences should be present. A simple inquiry to determine whether the respondent participated in the study and a verification of one or two responses can be used to identify cases of gross errors.

The researcher should not ignore the possibility that relevant data are already available. The federal government issues a vast amount of historical as well as current statistics, ranging from the various census publications to special purpose surveys of particular industries, products, or groups of people. Trade associations, universities, foundations, state and local governments, and the United Nations are other potential sources. Secondary data—data provided by another source—has an obvious advantage in cost and immediate availability. Its appropriateness for a particular study must be judged separately for each problem. It is almost impossible to find precisely the definitions, population, and subdivisions desired for a particular project, but the disadvantages associated with the differences must be weighed against the cost advantage. Even when definitions are acceptable, careful evaluation of secondary sources for the quality of the data is necessary. The better sources supply a summary of procedures employed; lacking any basis for appraising the quality of the data, the researcher should be extremely reluctant to rely on them.

Primary data—data for which the researcher defines the terms and exercises the supervision of the project—must *not* be automatically construed as "more accurate than secondary data." The secondary source may be more capable of generating the required data. It may have the resources to obtain more representative and larger samples. It may have interviewers and measuring instruments with unique capabilities in specialized fields.

Errors associated with data are typically classified into two categories: sampling and nonsampling errors. *Sampling errors* are differences that arise because a sample rather than a census is employed. Different samples composed of different units would yield different results. The magnitude of the differences among the possible samples is an indication of the amount of sampling error associated with the research plan. *Nonsampling errors* arise because the data collection procedures, question wordings, etc. would not yield the "correct" result even if a census were employed. Biases are introduced. Nonsampling errors cannot be mathematically appraised; their magnitude is more a subjective appraisal resting upon familiarity with the substantive nature of the investigation and data collection within it.

Data may be collected by "unobtrusive" means, techniques in which respondents are unaware that their conduct is being observed. The use of unobtrusive techniques ensures that respondents will not role play—either for the benefit of the observer or the researcher. There is a wide variety of unobtrusive measures. The more common are of the observation type in which a hidden camera or recording device monitors behavior. A human observer, of course, can serve the same function. Even a questionnaire or interview might be construed as unobtrusive when the intent of the investigation is disguised.

Data Analysis

The fourth step in marketing research is the analysis. In this stage the data collected are processed in order to summarize the results, whether they may be statements with respect to single characteristics or relationships among characteristics. Data analysis seeks to determine how the units covered in the research project respond to the items under investigation. This may be for individual questions or it may be for sets of questions—seeking to discern whether any patterns exist.

The marketing manager for the mail order firm has defined the decision: the use of either A or B. In this situation, if the data were available, the manager would simply determine the sum of dollar sales over the 5,000 individuals with each mailing piece—a most elementary analytic process. Alternatively, the manager could have subdivided the population in the research design in order to study possible differences by market segments. The same type of comparison would be required, but the comparison would be for various subgroups rather than for the entire population.

The marketing manager might also wonder whether certain types of individuals are better prospects than others. Information must be obtained from each unit in the study for those characteristics that the marketing manager hypothesizes are indicators of the better prospects. The data must then be analyzed in a manner that is satisfactory for testing the hypothesis. This can be further complicated by asking whether some individuals are "good" prospects regardless of which mailing piece is used, whether others are "good" prospects with only one of the mailing pieces, and finally whether others are not "good" prospects with either mailing piece. This rephrasing would have substantial implications for both data collection and analysis. Much of marketing research consists of choosing and applying different techniques of analysis, techniques that are appropriate for the problem definition and collection procedures.

Data analysis can be conveniently classified along the outline presented in Fig. 1.1. This outline classifies analysis first in terms of the number of variables involved. The simplest analytic technique considers only one variable. Awareness of the firm's brand might be such a variable with the computation of an average awareness level or the determination of the percentage of respondents in each awareness category as summary figures.

As additional variables are added to the analysis, we have the option of partitioning the variables into sets of variables or considering them on a composite or nonpartitioned basis. The simplest is a partitioned set with a single dependent variable and a single independent variable (labeled ② in the figure). The independent variable is typically introduced as a potential explanatory variable; for example, exposure to advertising could serve as a base upon which brand awareness might be predicted.

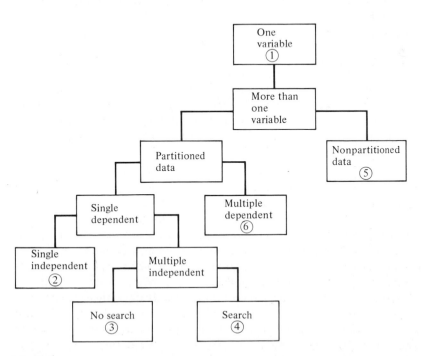

Fig. 1.1
Summary of data analysis techniques to be covered.

Additional independent variables expand the analysis to the single dependent/multiple independent category. Personality type, product usage, and store awareness are examples that might be added in the prediction of brand awareness. If the researcher and decision maker specify which variables are to be included in the relationship established, it is a "no search" analysis (labeled ③). If the analysis examines the data in order to determine which variables to include, it is a "search" routine (labeled ④).

Treatment of the data on a nonpartitioned basis (category ⑤) analyzes for relationships without classifying the variables as dependent and independent. Prediction of a particular variable, based on knowledge of the other variable or variables is not the objective. Nonpartitioned analyses may examine for similarities among units, among variables, or among both.

The final category shown in Fig. 1.1 deals with multiple dependent variables (labeled ⑥). In this type of analysis the task is to predict composites rather than a single variable. The sequence in our treatment of data analysis will be that shown by the sequence in Fig. 1.1. We will start with a single variable, move on to two variables with partitioned data, covering regression, contingency tables, analysis of variance, and discriminant analysis, and then extend our discussion to multiple independent variables without a search involved. Search techniques in connection with the single dependent variable and multiple independent variables will follow. Our discussion of analytic techniques will conclude with the consideration of nonpartitioned data and multiple dependent variables.

Interpretation of Results

Interpretation of results is the "so what?" of research. Research is wasted and useless unless it influences actions. Suppose the two mail pieces being considered by the direct mail marketing manager are submitted to a group of high school English teachers and "lay" readers. Each person is to assign a numerical grade to each composition. Suppose the average score received by A is 89.3, and the average score received by B is 77.4. Should the marketing manager decide to use mail piece A? Only if the manager thinks score in English composition is a good proxy variable for dollar values of sales to be generated. It seems elementary to say that research results must have relevance for the decision to be made. We state it only because it is ignored so much in practice.

Not only must the results be interpreted into action recommendations but the recommendations also must be communicated to the marketing executive in an understandable manner. It is not enough that the executive comprehend the recommendation; the communication must instill confidence that the recommendation is justified. Technical jargon should be avoided except when absolutely essential. Results should be presented in as simple a manner as possible. If the researcher cannot make the results comprehensible to the marketing executive, the researcher may not have sufficient understanding of the problem to warrant adoption of the recommendation.

DECISION MAKING AS HYPOTHESIS TESTING

It is often convenient to structure a research problem in terms of a hypothesis to be tested. The hypothesis (or hypotheses) must be agreed upon by both the manager and the researcher, although the formal statement is primarily the responsibility of the researcher. In this use of the word, a hypothesis is simply a statement about the universe. It may or may not be true; the research is designed to ascertain its truth. Consider the following pair of hypotheses.

H_0: *At least 10 percent of the viewing audience for "children's" TV shows consists of adults.*

H_1: *Less than 10 percent of the viewing audience for "children's" TV shows consists of adults.*

First, it should be noted that these hypotheses are worded in such a way that either one or the other is correct. They cannot both be correct, and they cannot both be incorrect. Second, in order for these two hypotheses to be useful in a research decision-making situation, the decision maker should choose one act if the first is true and a second act if the second is true. Both statements are characteristic of all situations in which a research project is properly structured in terms of hypothesis testing.

The terminology "state of nature" is often used to refer to the true situation in the universe. The advertising manager for a firm selling a product frequently purchased by adults is considering the possibility of advertising the product on children's TV shows. Table 1.1 shows examples of three types of poorly structured research.

In Table 1.1 (a) and (b), the advertising manager will ignore the research. Regardless of its outcome, the manager's mind is made up. The research is useless and should not be pursued. Table 1.1 (c) illustrates futility of a different type. The advertising manager will not know which action to take either before or after the research results are available. The implication of Table 1.1 (c) is that the percentage of adults in the viewing audience is either immaterial or not decisive as far as the manager's decision is concerned. If it is immaterial, why bother to investigate it? If it is not decisive, why not redesign the research so that it will yield specific guidance?

The structures of (d) and (e) are a little better but still not satisfactory. In (d), the advertising manager will be advised against advertising if the percentage of adults in the audience is less than 10 percent. However, the proper advice if the percentage of adults is 10 percent or more is unclear. This is the equivalent of saying that an audience of 10 percent might not be large enough. Apparently 10 percent is not a critical figure in decision making. In (e), the advertising manager believes 10 percent is large enough to warrant advertising. In fact some values less than 10 percent are large enough. Therefore, this structure will never result in a clear recommendation against advertising. Again 10 percent is not a critical value.

Table 1.1
States of Nature versus Recommended Decisions.
Examples of Poorly Structured Research Projects

State of nature	Recommended decision			
	(a)		(b)	
	Advertise	Don't advertise	Advertise	Don't advertise
H_0 true	X			X
H_1 true	X			X

	(c)	
	Advertise	Don't advertise
H_0 true	?	?
H_1 true	?	?

	(d)		(e)	
	Advertise	Don't advertise	Advertise	Don't advertise
H_0 true	?	?	X	
H_1 true		X	?	?

Table 1.2 shows a much better structuring of the hypotheses with respect to decision making. In this case, the hypotheses have been constructed so that if H_0 is true, the recommendation is to advertise while if H_1 is true, the recommendation is not to advertise. This procedure can be extended to any number of alternatives or options. The basic rule is that each hypothesis under test would lead to a specific recommendation if it were true. If any alternatives enumerated would not be adopted regardless of the research findings, those alternatives can be eliminated without any research. If several hypotheses would lead to the same recommendation, there is no need to identify which of these hypotheses be true—all hypotheses leading to the same alternative can be grouped together into a single hypothesis. This is frequently the case when a retail chain is determining if a particular area warrants the opening of a new outlet and what type of outlet, if any, is warranted. The hypotheses refer to broad ranges in total purchasing power; the same recommendation will be forthcoming for dollar figures that differ by considerable amounts.

Consider a retail supermarket chain investigating a particular area as a possible site for a new store. It will base its decision on the total purchasing power of the area. Does this mean it must determine purchasing power as accurately as possible? It depends on the alternatives under consideration. Suppose the chain has reduced the number of options to three: (1) do not open any store, (2) open a medium-size store (10,000 square feet of selling space), or

Table 1.2
States of Nature versus Recommended
Decisions. Properly Structured Research
Project

State of nature	Recommended decision	
	Advertise	Don't advertise
H_0 true	X	
H_1 true		X

(3) open a large store (20,000 square feet). It has established the minimum purchasing power required for the medium and large stores as $100 million and $250 million, respectively. A possible structuring of the three hypotheses is

H_0 : *Total purchasing power is less than $100 million.*

H_1 : *Total purchasing power is between $100 million and $250 million.*

H_2 : *Total purchasing power is greater than $250 million.*

The acceptance of one of these hypotheses leads directly to one of the three actions contemplated. It is not necessary to determine purchasing power more precisely than that indicated in the three hypotheses. A two-stage research project might be indicated. Stage one would establish whether purchasing power were clearly within the values specified by the hypotheses. Only if stage one revealed a figure close to $100 million or $250 million would stage two be undertaken. There is no reason to incur the cost of determining purchasing power with precision unless that precision is required in decision making.

Decision making as hypothesis testing is a two-step process with error possibilities at each step. At step one there is the relationship between the states of nature and the action recommended. The percentage of adults in the audience may not be a proper guide to action. The number of adults may be a better guide. Dollar expenditures on the product category may be still better. At step two there is the possibility that the research result may be erroneous with respect to the state of nature. The sample may indicate that the percentage of adults in the audience is less than 10 percent when the true universe percentage is more than 10 percent. Or the opposite error may occur. Research procedures do not yield certainty with respect to the true state of nature. No matter how careful we are, we may conclude that H_0 is true when H_1 is true or vice versa. This fact means the decision maker and the researcher must evaluate the seriousness of different kinds of errors. The seriousness of the errors can be appraised only in terms of the actions that will be recommended. No harm occurs until the conclusions have an impact on what the firm does.

Table 1.3
True States of Nature versus Conclusions.
Possible Types of Errors

	Conclusion	
True state of nature	H_0 true	H_1 true
H_0 true	No error	Type I error
H_1 true	Type II error	No error

Table 1.3 presents the general situation with two possible states of nature and two alternative actions. Assuming the relationship between the two states of nature and the two actions is valid, no error occurs if we conclude that H_0 is true and it is true; similarly, no error occurs if we conclude that H_1 is true and it is true. Errors occur in each of the other cells.[6]

Consider the format of Table 1.3 in terms of the problem dealing with advertising on children's TV shows. H_0 (at least 10 percent of the audience is composed of adults) leads to a recommendation to advertise. H_1 (less than 10 percent of the audience is composed of adults) leads to a recommendation not to advertise. Under the Type II error we think H_0 is true and recommend in favor of advertising, but less than 10 percent of the audience is composed of adults. The opposite situation exists with the Type I error. We recommend against advertising (thinking H_1 is true), but at least 10 percent of the audience is composed of adults. Which error is more serious—failing to take advantage of an existing opportunity or incurring expenditures when the opportunity does not warrant those expenditures? Placed in those terms, it should be obvious that no general answer can be given to the general question of which error is more serious. The decision maker must carefully evaluate each specific situation with its unique set of potential risks and benefits.

Consider the case of a drug firm contemplating a reformulation of one of its better selling items. Is it a more serious error to switch to the new formula when the present formula should be retained or to retain the present formula when the new should be adopted? If the present formulation is well accepted and profitable, most managers would consider it worse to shift when that action is improper. This is even more likely if unknown health hazards are involved.

What of products or industries that are experiencing declines in sales and profits? Let us consider the chief executive who is torn between (1) an attempt to rejuvenate the product by making substantial marketing expenditures and (2) a "run-out" strategy of cutting costs to the bare minimum, continuing the

---

[6]Table 1.3 uses the terminology Type I and Type II errors in order to be consistent with conventional terminology and later development in the text. The terminology is inconsequential at this point.

CHAPTER 2

PROBLEM DEFINITION

ASKING THE RIGHT QUESTION

A dress manufacturer has been experiencing difficulty in selling to retailers in the Minneapolis–St. Paul area. Sales elsewhere have held up well. The president wants to know what's wrong in the Twin Cities. The general manager of a resort hotel complex is convinced that the hotel must constantly add new attractions and upgrade current facilities. He asks, "What improvement(s) should be scheduled next?" A publisher has recently lost several of its top editors to competitors. It expects this to happen at times but believes the recent exodus is more than "normal attrition." The owner-publisher wants to know what changes, if any, should be instituted. All three cases represent significant and real problems to the respective companies. Each, however, requires further clarification and precision. *The right question must be addressed if marketing research is to aid decision makers.* A correct answer to the wrong question leads either to poor advice or to no advice.

Careful thought before implementation should be the watchword in research. Most of us learn the art of rationalization and the ability to defend our actions at a very early age. It is no different in research. A researcher who has once embarked upon a particular research plan is prone to defend it as the correct approach. This is even more true if the research has been completed. The best time to consider alternative approaches is in the planning stage. The needless cost of false starts and redoing work would dictate the wisdom of careful early examination of alternatives even if our tendency to rationalize did not blind us to our errors. Given this tendency, it is critical.

A good starting point in problem definition is to ask what the decision maker would like to know if the requested information could be obtained without error and without cost. By starting in this make-believe world, the decision maker and researcher avoid unconscious compromises caused by practical situations. Unless the ideal is identified, there is no basis for evaluating the seriousness of the compromises.

Another good general rule in establishing the problem definition is "Never settle on a particular approach without developing and considering at least one alternative." The contest between alternatives enables a finer tuning of the ultimate plan by directing attention to issues that may have been unspecified. Even if the initial problem definition is unchanged (a most unlikely situation), its articulation and communication to the various participants will be improved.

A complete problem definition must specify each of the following:

1. Unit of analysis

2. Time and space boundaries

3. Characteristics of interest—both the "results" that are of concern to management and the variables to be tested for their relationship to those results

4. Specific environmental conditions

Taken together these four aspects identify the who, when, where, and what to be researched.

The units plus the time and space boundaries comprise the universe specification. "Women's Dress Buyers in Chicago Department Stores, January 2, 1981" comprises a particular universe, provided unambiguous definitions are given for "Women's Dress Buyers," "Department Stores," and "Chicago." A quite different universe would be "Women living in the Chicago Standard Metropolitan Statistical Area (SMSA) who are shopping for one or more dresses in January 1981." The *units* of the universe are *buyers* in the first instance and *shoppers* in the second. The units always identify the objects to be studied. The decision maker needs information concerning the designated units or objects in order to make a more intelligent decision.

The precise wording of the universe definition is critical. Note the distinction between the two universes in the placement of the word "women." In the first instance, we are concerned with buyers of women's dresses; the buyer may be either male or female. In the second instance, only women are members of the universe.

The time specification is a precise date, January 2, for the buyer universe, but the entire month of January for the shopper universe. The space specification limits consideration to the city of Chicago in the first problem, but takes in the adjoining counties in the second. A more subtle distinction interacts with the space boundary: the first problem is defined in terms of where the buying is done while the second is defined in terms of place of residence. The first includes buyers who reside outside of Chicago and make a purchase in the city—although only within a department store. The second excludes persons living outside of the Chicago SMSA but the area in which shopping occurs is unlimited.

The characteristics of interest identify the focus of the problem. They might be opinions of various dress manufacturers, budgetary constraints, style and color preferences, personality traits, buying behavior, and any number of other characteristics. In some situations, the decision maker may wish to know only one characteristic. The problem definition must specify not only the various characteristics to be measured, but for which, if any, the nature of relationships are to be determined. For example, a small dressmaker might wish to determine the relationship between style preference and store location (for the buyer universe) or between opinion of manufacturer and disposable income (for the shopper universe).

Problem definition should stress the concepts of interest to the decision maker. If a store manager must decide on radio and TV advertising expenditures, the objective desired from that advertising should be specified. Store traffic, dollar sales from specific merchandise, or some other target should be identified—the variable that comprises the store manager's desired "result" should be clearly defined. Compromises because of practical difficulties have no place in the problem definition. They will come soon enough in making the research "operational." But the ability to appraise the acceptability of the research plan will be unduly handicapped if the problem definition starts out containing compromises.

The environmental conditions indicate the uniqueness or generality of the problem. The decision maker may be interested in how the units respond to certain price changes—changes made by the decision maker or the competitors. The problem definition would then specify the precise prices to be researched. Alternatively, a decision maker may be interested in the behavior of certain types of firms under specific economic or political conditions. These conditions must be spelled out in the problem definition.

The energy crisis, oil and natural gas shortages, and associated political developments have caused many oil companies to review their policies concerning company owned and operated service stations. Research designed to aid in these decisions must specify the precise environment(s) the company is considering. These potential environments include not only the alternatives considered by the company but also a wide variety of other variables that may influence which alternative is most advantageous. Several price strategies by both major oil companies and independents, three levels of general economic activity, and two different antitrust positions by the federal government might be specified as of concern. The problem definition must specify the environments for which the company wants research results. Even if the company is interested in only one set of environmental conditions, the problem definition must specify that set. Then the research must be designed so as to investigate that precise environment.

CENTRAL ROLE OF DECISION MAKER

The problem definition step of marketing research is the determination and structuring of the decision maker's question. It must be the decision maker's question and not the researcher's question. If the research results are viewed as "meaningless" or "too skimpy" by the marketing executive, the researcher should have anticipated this response in the planning stage and made appropriate revisions at that time. The overriding objective of problem definition must always be *to answer the right question.*

Three sometimes embarrassing but crucial questions must be put to the decision maker at the very beginning of the problem definition. (1) What is the decision you face? (2) What are your alternatives? (3) Under what conditions would you view each of these alternatives as the proper action? If the decision maker has no decision to make, there is no research problem. If there are no alternatives from which to choose, again there is no research problem. If the decision maker has no criteria for choosing among alternatives, again there is no research problem. Patient probing by the researcher usually removes these obstacles, and more research problems emerge than can be attacked. At this stage, priorities must be assigned. Then the problem must be constrained and delimited.

The researcher must avoid the acceptance of the the superficial and the obvious. A good guide is to insist that two or more alternatives be considered at every stage, no matter how small a detail is at issue. But the selection must always be determined by whether that alternative is appropriate, given the decision faced by the decision maker.

Consider a recent situation by a supplier of educational materials. A product manager wanted to evaluate a proposed change in visual aids for elementary school mathematics. The first difficulty occurred in identifying the decision. The manager's initial response of "What to do about visual aids" offered no guide whatsoever.

The request for research had arisen because a specific change had been proposed. However, it soon developed that the product manager was much more interested in knowing the characteristics of a "top-flight"visual aid package. Thus, the manager's task was to determine the attributes a new visual aid package should possess rather than to choose between the old visual aid package and the new. The problem definition required extensive development of what attributes were to be tested.

The problem was further complicated when the criteria for conclusions were discussed. Revenue or profit was the ultimate goal, but preference was substituted as a compromise in the research problem. A much more difficult problem arose when the question of universe was posed. "Preference by *those who decide* which visual aids to purchase" was the logical response. Are "those who decide" teachers, principals, supervisors, or some mixture? The product manager ultimately settled for a universe of convention delegates plus a series of group interviews with "influentials" chosen on a highly subjective basis. The problem definition exercise was, however, extremely useful because it forced the product manager to think through the decision problem in terms of alternatives to be considered and the universe of interest to the product manager.

RESEARCH AND THE PHILOSOPHY OF SCIENCE

Research is often viewed as coldly objective; get the facts and let the facts speak for themselves! But how does one recognize a fact when one sees it? How are the facts put together so that they "speak"? Might the story be incorrect? These and many similar questions demand answers from both the researcher and the decision maker. Even if the questions are ignored at the conscious level, the research decisions contain implicit answers.

Two fundamental questions underpin any philosophic position with respect to research. (1) How does one acquire knowledge? (2) Are riskless answers possible? A useful approach is to consider the place of induction and the place of deduction in research. In considering the first question, we ask in what circumstances, if any, research proceeds by deduction and in what circumstances, by induction. In the second question, we ask whether either deduction or induction yields riskless answers—always, sometimes, or never. These are basically questions within the philosophy of science; but since method is at the heart of science and research, we must examine some positions taken within marketing research.[1]

The typical stance articulated in marketing research is that our first step is induction. "Relevant" data are collected and serve as the basis for reaching general conclusions. These general conclusions are applied to a much larger group than just the units examined in the research. That is the purpose of most marketing research: study a limited number of units in order to reach conclusions concerning many units.

The second step of marketing research is usually viewed as deductive. The generalization reached in the first step is used to calculate one or more specifics. If the relationship between number of retail outlets and gross revenue is established (by induction) as the first step, that relationship is then used in the second step to predict gross revenue. This prediction depends on the specific number of retail outlets planned; and several predictions may be generated, each associated with a different plan.

This view that marketing research starts with specifics, moves to generalizations, and then back to specifics is a considerable oversimplification. The general rules for making inductions, the definitions employed for the specific observations, and many similar matters require attention before the sup-

---

[1] Much of the structure followed in this section is taken from C. West Churchman, 1957, *Theory of Experimental Inference* (New York: Macmillan).

posed "first step" of induction is possible. The application of any rule is an example of deduction—using a broad generalization for a specific application. The source of these general rules is usually very vague.

From a research point of view we should be concerned with how any starting points are established. If the generalizations are induced from prior sensory data, we start with specifics, not generalizations. If we start with the generalizations, how are they received? Are they intuitively obvious and not subject to review? Are they received by divine revelation? Both explanations are possible, but they are not subject to analysis by research methodology or the philosophy of science. Ultimately we must either assert that our starting points are "given" and not to be questioned or admit that they may be somewhat arbitrary and subject, sooner or later, to review. Within any given research investigation, we should make these starting points or presuppositions as explicit as possible. They are not to be investigated—at least within the present project.

This problem of presuppositions or starting points is at the base of our earlier statement that several alternatives should be considered for the various definitions and procedures to be employed in the research. By so doing, the researcher obtains a better understanding of how arbritrary his or her plans may be—and how useful the results may be.

The second philosophic issue—whether riskless answers can be obtained—is intricately related to some of the preceding discussion. If the starting point is subject to possible error, the conclusions must also be subject to error. The conclusions can be free of error and risk only if the starting points, the rules employed thereafter, and the ability to apply them are free of error. This situation is most likely to exist in a closed, well-defined mathematical system. Empirical research that asks for verification or testing from the sensory world usually tolerates some margin of error, recognizing that most of its definitions, measurements, and procedures are tentative at best and fraught with numerous sources of error. This is the nature of marketing research. Results—both from induction and deduction—are estimates. We do our best to quantify the results and to quantify the degree of error present, but the marketing manager who wants to know the "true" answer is doomed to failure. Our methods and analyses attempt to reduce the margin of error and to control it—but as yet we do not even aspire to its elimination.[2]

We shall consider research as a continual movement between induction and deduction with neither established as the "correct" initial process. Some-

---

[2]It is quite another question as to whether a "true" answer exists, be it in the mind of God or some impersonal force. Such truth could exist as a limit only to be approached by human beings in their finite attempts. The alternative view, that all is relative, rejects the whole notion of a unique answer to any question. This view basically states that all starting positions are arbitrary, that within a system an element of consistency may be obtained but that the concept of truth is meaningless. The first view has obvious religious overtones concerning the existence and nature of God. The interested reader is referred to Francis A. Schaeffer, 1968, *Escape from Reason* (Downers Grove, Ill.: Inter-Varsity Press).

times one is arbitrarily selected and sometimes the other. We shall also expect nonperfect answers fraught with both measurable and nonmeasurable error. We do not assert that this is the only procedure nor the only result possible. Many value-laden questions and religious issues may be pursued by entirely different approaches, but when they are, the "research approach," as we are using the term, is not being employed.

Within marketing research, when using this combination inductive-deductive approach and settling for nonperfect answers, we are in the category labeled "Experimentalism" by Churchman.[3] Using this approach, the problem definition can be conveniently divided into three specifications: (1) universe, (2) relevant characteristics, and (3) environmental conditions.

UNIVERSE SPECIFICATION

The specification of the universe must identify both the units that comprise it and the desired time and space coordinates. The relevant universe for the decision maker must first be specified. Moving to the research universe too quickly invites the hazard that the research results may be inapplicable.

Units of Analysis

The individuals or objects whose characteristics are to be measured are called the units of analysis. They may be persons, groups of persons, business establishments, inanimate objects, transactions, monetary units, or just about any object or activity a person can name. Some very interesting communication studies have even used words as the units of analysis. Basically, the units answer the question, "What objects am I interested in?" Consideration of several alternatives for units will usually sharpen one's thinking concerning the appropriate universe.

To illustrate the selection of units, consider a manufacturer of small electrical motors that wishes to ascertain the extent to which its potential customers know the company exists. The potential customers are basically business entities. But the units of the universe could also be defined as purchasing departments, production departments, engineering departments, or particular individuals within one or more of these departments. Again we come to the all pervasive question of what alternative actions are being considered by the manufacturer. In terms of these actions, who should be aware of the manufacturer's existence? Is the company considering specific acts that might increase awareness levels for certain groups? These are the sorts of questions that should be considered in specifying the appropriate units of analysis.

Let us go a step further. Is each unit, however defined, equally important? Or does importance vary with the purchasing power of the potential customer? If purchasing power is the critical item, one procedure is to use the

---

[3]Churchman, *op. cit.,* pp. 172–212.

units as established by the prior thought pattern and to weight each by the purchasing power of the entity it represents. With this approach, no difficulty or complexity is introduced in the definition of the universe, but a complexity must be introduced later in the processing.

Alternatively, the basic unit of analysis could be defined in terms of transactions rather than in terms of potential buyers. With buyers as units, the universe consists of persons, groups of persons, or business entities. With transactions as the units, the universe consists of activities as the focus of interest. Typically, in marketing research, we wish to classify or measure the units according to some characteristic. Once more we see the interdependence of research decisions: the selection of universe units is best determined only in conjunction with what is to be measured.

Is the manufacturer interested in finding the percentage of buyers who are aware of the company's existence? Or is the manufacturer more concerned with the percentage of transactions in the marketplace in which the buyer is aware (or unaware) of its existence? The same type of comparison would be required if level of awareness were measured; here it might be average level of awareness of buyers versus average level per transaction.[4]

Dollars would be still another basis for establishing units. These dollars could be dollars expended on small electrical motors of the type made by this manufacturer. The objective would then be to determine the percentage of the total dollar market aware of the company's existence. This was very close to what the president had in mind. In theory the president wanted to classify every dollar spent as coming from a buyer who was or was not aware of the company's existence. The same arithmetic result is obtained if buyers are classified according to awareness with each buyer weighted by the dollar volume he or she generates.

The well-known marketing concept of a "decision-making unit" (DMU) often comes into play in defining the units of the universe. The DMU is crucial in both choosing and evaluating one's marketing mix. But the DMU is usually difficult to define in an unambiguous manner. A purchase that is a wife's decision in one family may be a husband's decision in another and a joint decision in a third. How does one cope with this problem? A two-step procedure is a possibility. The first-stage units are families; within each family the decision maker is identified. The units of the problem universe are the DMU's. Any compromise research universe must be evaluated against that concept, including the possibility that the DMU is a group.

The specification of the appropriate DMU for industrial products is even more difficult than it is for consumer products. The number of persons who have potential involvement is greater. Job titles do not have the same meaning for all organizations. Responsibilities for ultimate decisions vary with size of

---

[4]The entire discussion here assumes that awareness is the proper characteristic to investigate. The selection of the proper characteristic is obviously a critical issue.

organization, organizational structure, philosophy of decentralization, plus the personalities involved. The question is further complicated by the fact that some characteristics of interest refer to the organization—for example, size, geographic location, and past purchases—while others, such as preferences, education, and attitudes, uniquely refer to specific individuals.

The problem definition, whether for a consumer product or an industrial product, must specify the units of analysis. It is better to err at this stage by specifying conceptually correct units that pose difficult problems in implementation. Compromises in the transition to operational definitions can then be better evaluated. This approach also permits the possibility of using different procedures with different market segments or a multistage approach in identifying the relevant DMU's.[5]

Time and Space Coordinates

The time dimension of a decision problem is almost always the future. What should we do the first of next month in order to produce the desired effect the following month? What will consumer response be to our contemplated promotion for the month of November? Marketing managers continually run the risk of making the right decision at the wrong time. Opportunities are transient; the marketing executive who assumes a static environment is doomed to failure. Therefore, it is crucial that the decision maker and researcher establish the appropriate time reference for the decision.

What is the appropriate time dimension for the manufacturer of small electrical motors? The manufacturing company is interested in awareness at the point in time when it contemplates possible actions, either to modify that awareness level or to operate within that constraint. If its decision is to be implemented on January 15, 1981, it would like to know conditions in the universe on that date. If the implementation would be delayed for 5, 10, or 20 years, the company would like to know the state of the universe on those dates. Large time-consuming capital expenditures may be initiated in the near future, but the size of the expenditure is based upon estimates of conditions at a distant point in time. The problem of road construction and the road's ability to handle peak loads are all too familiar examples. Study of the present or past is appropriate only insofar as it can indicate the future.

The space coordinates supply the geographic boundaries within which the action is to be taken. In the problem definition, these lines are rarely neat political divisions or subdivisions. Advertising media do not stop abruptly at city or state lines. Retailers and wholesalers usually welcome customers regardless of where the customers reside. Sales territories may, however, be established along county or state lines. In a similar way, licensing by governmental units may determine the appropriate space coordinates. In the absence of such exter-

---

[5]See Ronald Frank, William F. Massy, and Yoram Wind, 1972, *Market Segmentation* (Englewood Cliffs, N.J.: Prentice-Hall), pp. 91–101.

nally imposed constraints, the problem definition, in theory, often includes the whole earth or the total United States. Recognition of this fact in the problem definition will help evaluate the utility of a research universe that is considerably smaller.

The universe of interest may be defined either conceptually or by enumeration. For example, all current accounts of a service organization can be obtained from current records. These accounts have specific geographic locations, but the specification of location is neither necessary nor germane to the problem definition. The enumerative approach to universe specification is appropriate so long as the decision maker has that group as his or her target and has a list available.

The Kelly Wholesale Company is weighing the advantages and disadvantages of adding the products of the B&O Manufacturing Company. One potential definition of the universe limits the study to Kelly's existing customers—easily defined but not the company's sole concern. A second alternative covers all potential customers in a five-state area. Kelly has some customers in all five states, but over half of its revenues come from its home state (Ohio) and over 90 percent come from Ohio, Michigan, and Indiana. Kelly will make its decision based upon its estimate of the effect of the change in its principal area of operation. The geographic limits ultimately specified by Kelly's president employed county lines, taking in all of Ohio and parts of three other states. The specific counties included were chosen on the basis of Kelly's current market share, subject to the constraint that the geographic coverage be contiguous. Was this a wise decision?

All Units or Specific Units

It is not sufficient to specify that the units of a problem are housewives, or auto owners, or purchasing agents unless the decision maker truly is interested in all such persons within the time and space limits. More often the decision maker is interested in employed housewives, or housewives from households with an automatic washer, or housewives who have tried product X. These examples illustrate three different types of modifications applied to units: (1) a characteristic or present state of the units, (2) a characteristic of an object associated with the unit rather than a more direct characteristic of the unit itself (households with automatic washers), and (3) past behavior of the unit (have tried product X). We will have more to say about types of characteristics later, but these few examples illustrate the vast scope of ways to limit the particular units of concern.

Instead of specifying a universe of auto owners, a tire manufacturer might specify auto owners whose income exceeds a stipulated amount and whose autos are not equipped with radial tires. Any business may select its own target markets, each of which may form a universe worthy of study.

Stipulations of units according to characteristics of objects that are related to the units rather than characteristics of the units themselves sometimes obscure the nature of the units. Are the units *persons* whose autos do not have radial tires or *autos* that do not have radial tires? The proper selection can usually be accomplished by asking what the appropriate base is for calculating percentages or averages. The difference is often critical in the case of industrial products. The percentage of machines leased with maintenance contracts might be much different from the percentage of lessees who lease with maintenance contracts. Failure to distinguish between the two could lead to quite diverse research designs and recommended actions.

PROBLEM UNIVERSE VERSUS RESEARCH UNIVERSE

Proper identification of the problem universe rarely leads to the adoption of the problem universe as the research universe. This applies to all aspects: time and space coordinates, the choice of units, and delimitation among units.

We have already referred to the difficulties experienced with respect to the time dimension. Actions are adopted by the decision maker after the research is completed. The time coordinate cannot be the same; some compromise is required. The seriousness of the compromise depends on both the time lapse and the phenomenon under study. Small time differences for high-style items may be unacceptable. Any example in which large time differences are acceptable will be challenged by someone. But examples in which changes are less likely over a few years are physical characteristics such as height or weight distributions for a specific population, consumption patterns for broad categories, and climatic conditions of a region. Regardless of the time interval or the phenomenon involved, the application of findings for one period to another rests on the assumption that no significant difference exists between the two.

Denotative space coordinates that imply the whole earth or the total United States are typically violated in the selection of the research universe. A Miami hotel studying prospective guests might delimit its research universe to east of the Mississippi River, the east coast, or to an even smaller region despite its willingness to accept guests from anywhere. The same type of compromise occurs whenever a business researches its "principal market" in lieu of its total market. More serious problems may occur when subjectively chosen test regions are substituted in the hope that they are representative.[6]

As long as the general units employed are broad and physically well defined, the stipulation of the general unit does not usually cause a discrepancy between the problem universe and the research universe. Examples of this situ-

---

[6]This approach should be distinguished from the selection of a sample from the problem universe by use of probability methods. In the latter case, the problem universe and the research universe are identical. Potential sources of error arise because a sample, rather than a census, is employed. See Chapters 6 and 8 for sampling considerations.

ation—with various degrees of unanimity in the definitions—are corporations, human beings, stores, cats, and bicycles. The principal discrepancy in these instances occurs either in determining which elements actually exist within the time and space coordinates or in a conscious decision to use some existing list that is known to be less than perfect. The source of imperfection is two-fold and is shown by Fig. 2.1. The unlined portion represents those in the research universe who are a part of the problem and should be studied. The lined (⬚) portion represents those who are a part of the decision maker's problem but have been excluded from the research—those units should be in the research but are not. The crosshatched (⬚) portion represents units in the research that should not be there. The size of these two portions shows the magnitude of the compromises made in going from the problem to the research.

Consumer surveys within an urban community often encounter a situation in which there are differences between the problem universe and the research universe. The telephone directory for the community is often proposed as a readily available and satisfactory approximation of the problem universe. Clearly a large portion of the problem universe is listed in the directory. Are any elements missing? Are there any elements in the directory that are not in the problem universe?

Residences without telephones, unlisted numbers, and new listings since the directory publication cutoff date are three significant groups that are missing from the directory. The important consideration is whether these groups differ from those that are included in the directory—specifically whether they differ with respect to the subject under study. Recent listings usually reflect

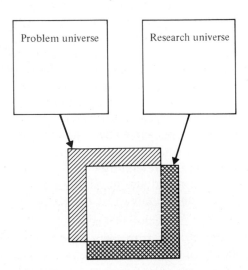

Fig. 2.1
Problem universe versus research universe.

either a change of residence or the formation of a new family unit. Would either be significant for the present study? If yes, use of the telephone directory may introduce biases in the research results. The same general approach should be used in considering the other groups.

Significant economic differences between those with telephones and those without them in 1936 led to one of the worst political forecasts in history. The *Literary Digest* made a rather good study of voting intentions in the 1936 presidential election—but for the wrong universe. It studied telephone subscribers and owners of automobiles, reaching the conclusion that Alfred Landon would defeat Franklin D. Roosevelt. When the election results were in, Landon had carried only two states. Roosevelt of course remained in office, and the *Literary Digest* went into oblivion along with Landon.

Some listings in the telephone directory will reflect individuals who are not properly within the problem universe; for example, business listings and persons outside the appropriate geographic boundaries. It may be possible to eliminate these units from the research by screening procedures, but the cost of the study will be increased by that necessity.[7]

If the problem universe consists of units that have specific characteristics, identification of an acceptable research universe poses additional complications. An urban department store recently defined the "young, single female working in center city" as of particular interest for an image study. Further discussion indicated that life-style and orientation to fashion were more significant than were age and marital status. These revisions helped in seeing the right problem, but they made the implementation more difficult. The research universe was ultimately defined in terms of shoppers (with certain characteristics) at a list of stores and/or departments within stores rather than the workers the store had originally specified. The research universe was considerably smaller than the problem universe, and those involved in the study suspected a bias in the image determined by the research. This bias was attributed to differences between workers (with the life-style and fashion orientation desired) who shop at the stores enumerated and those who did not shop at those stores. Even among the store officials, however, there was considerable debate as to which universe was more relevant. This debate occurred after the research was completed and illustrates that the problem definition was somewhat defective.

The Size of the Universe Is Not Relevant in Problem Definition

Three distinct stages should be identified in problem definition: the problem universe, the research universe, and the research sample. The problem universe is the responsibility of the decision maker. The researcher can help in its identification, but the decision maker must establish what is relevant for the problem. The research universe is more within the domain of the researcher who

---

[7]The use of telephone interviewing with random selection of numbers (apart from directory listings) offers an interesting alternative that will be discussed in Chapter 5.

must determine whether it is defined in a clear and unambiguous manner. The researcher must be able to classify units as being either within the specified universe or not. Still consultation with the decision maker is required; otherwise the decision maker may reject the research as irrelevant because the research universe and problem universe are too diverse. The research sample is almost exclusively the province of the researcher; it must be selected with technical skill in order to avoid bias and to secure adequate reliability. The decision maker rarely has anything to add to this phase.

The size of the problem universe or the research universe rarely limits the feasibility of a research design. The units studied in the research will almost always be a sample from the research universe. Therefore, size becomes a practical consideration at the sampling stage, not at the problem definition stage.

A large aluminum manufacturer wants to know the opinion of United States home owners concerning the use of aluminum siding. The problem universe consists of all home owners in the United States—possibly with time dimension 1980–1989. The research universe may compromise on all home owners registered with a county tax assessor on December 31, 1979. The size of this research universe is not a major concern despite the fact that it runs into tens of millions. The research will be based on a sample selected from that universe. But the research results will be used to make estimates with respect to the research universe; the results will not be limited to the sample.

Practical issues occur at both the research universe and sample stages, but the nature of these practical issues are very different. At the research universe stage the question is whether the definitions are operational. Does the researcher have a procedure for establishing which persons are members of the universe? Depending on the sampling method, it is not usually necessary to enumerate all individuals who are members. Therefore, its size is not usually a practical problem. At the sampling stage, the practical difficulty is how to determine which units should be placed in the sample. This is a technical question that will be discussed later and is not a part of the problem definition.[8]

CHARACTERISTICS OF INTEREST

The characteristics of interest identify what there is about the units that is of concern to the decision maker. These characteristics fall into two categories: the dependent variables and the independent variables. The dependent variables are those of interest for their own sake. In marketing, they often refer to behavior or attitude toward a firm's offering. Examples are purchases, awareness, opinions, or profits associated with consumer behavior or attitudes. The independent variables included in the problem definition are those characteristics thought to be related to the dependent variables. These variables may either be within the control of firm (endogenous)—such as advertising, pricing, or personnel changes—or beyond the control of the firm (exogenous).

---

[8]Technical questions on sample selection and sample size are considered in Chapter 6 and 8.

Exogenous variables of potential interest cover a multitude of possibilities, varying from competitor and government actions to economic conditions to individual consumer characteristics.

It is impossible to give a complete list of the various characteristics that may be of interest to the marketing manager. In order to overcome this impossibility, many marketing practitioners and theorists have suggested a multitude of classification schemes. Indeed it seems that all marketing managers and marketing researchers feel compelled to establish their own classification scheme—and often more than one. No system is optimal for all projects and all discussions; but the 2 × 2 matrix of Frank, Massy, and Wind has two principal merits: simplicity and the highlighting of measurement assumptions.[9] This matrix is presented in Table 2.1.

Market segmentation studies have typically focused on either general characteristics such as age, education, life-style, and personality or on situation-specific variables such as brand loyalty, product usage, and product perceptions. Table 2.1 identifies these two types of variables as the column designations. The row designations distinguish between the variables that are objectively measured and those that are inferred. The 2 × 2 matrix, of course, yields four cells. Discussion of the separate cells with examples helps clarify the general classification scheme.

Cell (1)—General objective measures. Cell (1) contains two different types of variables: demographic and socioeconomic. The demographic are illustrated by age, sex, stage of life cycle, marital status, tenure, geographic location, and race or ethnic group. The socioeconomic variables usually stress income, education, and occupation either singly or in some combination assumed to be a measure of social class.

These variables do not relate to specific products or market activity. They typically enter marketing research projects as potential explanatory variables

Table 2.1
A Classification Scheme for Consumer Characteristics†

	Consumer characteristics	
Measures	General	Situation specific
Objective	(1)	(3)
Inferred	(2)	(4)

†Source: Ronald E. Frank, William F. Massy, and Yoram Wind, 1972, *Market Segmentation,* Englewood Cliffs, N.J.: Prentice-Hall, p. 27.

[9]Frank, Massy, and Wind, *op. cit.,* p. 26 ff.

for the characteristics of direct interest to the marketing manager rather than as variables of direct interest themselves. Does age—a variable of cell (1)—help discriminate between product users and nonusers? At what stage of life cycle are the families who are most interested in condominium living? Neither age nor stage of life cycle would be of interest in these examples apart from its potential relationship to specific products or companies.

The variables in this cell are objectively measured—once defined there is rarely any question of how they should be measured or the establishment of the appropriate measure for the particular unit. The relevance of the variable for the study may be debated, but there is usually little debate concerning its measure. The measurement of chronological age, length of time a family has occupied a particular residence, and number of children under six years of age pose little conceptual difficulties.[10]

Cell (2)—General inferred measures. Variables in this cell are general in character but are not directly measurable. Personality traits, intelligence, and lifestyle are illustrative of these variables. Disagreement concerning the proper or best measures of these characteristics is highly likely. Lack of unanimity is common even with respect to the concepts, even more for the operational definitions. The inclusion of these variables in marketing research projects is usually motivated in the same way as those of cell (1): they may be related to marketing variables of more direct interest. Therefore, the marketing manager is often more concerned with their predictive power than with the purity or defensibility of their definitions. The proper balance between quantitative and qualitative questions in an intelligence test or the relative merits of aptitude and achievement tests are of little concern to the marketing manager except as the various alternatives are related to product use, a sales person's selling ability, or some other characteristic of direct interest to the firm.

Cell (3)—Situation specific objective measures. Variables in this category are typically behavioral with respect to the marketplace. Purchase behavior, brand use, store patronage and loyalty, advertising exposure, and degree of innovativeness are illustrative of these variables. Such behavior is often an ultimate or intermediate goal of the marketing manager. Therefore, variables in this cell may be the dependent variable—the crucial "result"—measured in the research. These variables may also be potential independent variables; prior behavior may aid in understanding or predicting later behavior either for the same variable or a related variable. Store loyalty may be related to trial of new merchandise, heavy usage may be related to brand loyalty, and so forth.

Cell (4)—Situation specific inferred measures. Typical of variables in this category are attitudes, intentions, perceptions, and preferences toward specific

---

[10]The need for precision in its measurement and the degree of refinement in the measuring instrument may be argued. We shall discuss these issues in Chapter 4.

brands, products, and companies. These variables differ from those in cell (3) because they are not directly measurable nor observable. As they may disagree concerning variables in cell (2), researchers may also disagree in either the conceptual definitions or the operational definitions of variables in cell (4). Contrary to the variables in cell (2), the variables in cell (4) may be of direct interest to the marketing manager. Such variables are often viewed as foundations leading to a favorable or unfavorable mental set desired by the marketing manager. These variables may, therefore, be "results" under test in the research; the adequacy of their definitions, in such a situation, is then critical. The familiar advertising ladder concepts incorporate variables from this cell, establishing mental states that are presumed to lead to and precede purchase and repeat purchase.[11]

Characteristics of Interest versus Unit of Analysis

Confusion sometimes arises concerning the difference between the *characteristic of interest* and the *unit of analysis*. A manufacturer of ethical drugs is interested in dollar sales of a particular generic drug. The manufacturer wants to know dollar sales for a group of six states during the period September 1980–April 1981. Thus the time and space coordinates have been defined for the research universe.

"Dollar sales" is the characteristic of interest—this is the measure of concern to the drug company. The unit of analysis identifies "on what" or "on whom" the characteristic of interest is measured. The unit of analysis for the drug company may be the individual drug store. The research may collect dollar sales from the individual drug stores, adding them together in order to determine total sales in the six-state area.

The characteristic of interest is the crucial item to management. Its value will serve as the basis for choosing among alternative actions. The unit of analysis establishes the source for the information. In many cases the unit employed is dictated by convenience rather than the "proper" problem definition. For example, the drug company could generate aggregate sales by using the ultimate consumer as the unit instead of using the drug store. Table 2.2 shows these two alternative approaches.

The drug company wants to know total sales (labeled as $\Sigma\Sigma$). This figure can be generated either by (1) determining sales of each separate drug store and summing these values or (2) determining purchases of each individual customer and summing these values. The first approach is based on the drug store as the unit of analysis, collecting the column totals ($\Sigma 1$, $\Sigma 2$, . . .). The second approach is based on the ultimate customer as the unit of analysis, collecting the row totals (ΣA, ΣB, . . .). Since both approaches yield the target charac-

---

[11]Two models using this concept may be found in Robert J. Lavidge and Gary A. Steiner, 1961, A model for predictive measurements of advertising effectiveness, *Journal of Marketing* 25 (October): 61; and Gail Smith, 1959, Empirical measurement of advertising effectiveness, *Printers Ink* (February): 23–27.

Table 2.2
Two Alternative Units of Analysis for Determining Dollar Sales.
Drug Company Problem

Ultimate customer as unit of analysis	Drug store as unit of analysis			
	Drug store 1	Drug store 2	. . .	Row total
Customer A				ΣA
Customer B				ΣB
.				.
.				.
.				.
Column total	$\Sigma 1$	$\Sigma 2$	. . .	$\Sigma\Sigma$

teristic of interest ($\Sigma\Sigma$), either approach is satisfactory. The choice between the two approaches depends on their respective costs and the extent to which the necessary data can be obtained with accuracy.

Two side issues should also be recognized in choosing between the two alternatives. (1) Purchases by residents of the six-state area may be made outside of the area or from nondrug store outlets. Sales by drug stores in the six-state area may be made to nonresidents. The researcher must decide whether these differences are trivial and, if they aren't, which alternative is a better approximation of the true problem. (2) The company may be interested in the shape and distribution of sales (or purchases) among units. If so, the best way to proceed is to use the unit of analysis corresponding to that interest.

The problem could also be defined with other units of analysis. The individual sales person, counties, or even states are but a few of the possibilities. Again the choice depends on the ease of obtaining the necessary data and the desire for detail concerning the distribution across units.

ENVIRONMENTAL CONDITIONS

Environmental conditions fall within the category of relevant characteristics, but they comprise a special type of relevant characteristic. The characteristics of interest are the target variables. The research is undertaken in order to discover their values. Environmental conditions, however, are of concern because of their possible relationship with the characteristics of interest. What would sales be if price were $169? $149? What would competitor A do if we increased our advertising by 25 percent? decreased it by 25 percent? How would A's action affect our sales and profits? What would happen to the supply of fuel oil if the depletion allowance were cut in half? were removed completely?

The environmental conditions specified in the research problem are of two types: (1) those beyond the firm's control and (2) those within the firm's control. The firm must adjust to the first and choose wisely with respect to the second. Neither is possible without knowing how the particular variables influence the characteristics of interest. Therefore both types of variables must be introduced into the research problem.

Ideally, the decision maker would like to know the precise value of all relevant, uncontrollable variables. He or she would like to know the plans of competitors, the state of the economy, availability of raw material, the international climate, fashion changes, and many other relevant factors. The decision maker cannot obtain all this information, but it is frequently possible to identify the factors that seem most critical to the existing problem. These factors are then incorporated in the problem definition as environmental conditions. They may be specified at a single value—in which case the solution recommended may be inappropriate for other values. Or several values may be specified—in which case alternative recommendations may result, depending on which set of conditions prevail at the decision time.

An example of drastically different environmental conditions now faces companies writing medical insurance. Should they plan for (1) no change in the current federal program, (2) moderate expansion to cover various "disadvantaged" groups, or (3) a comprehensive plan covering the entire population? Practically all decisions currently faced by these companies will be influenced by which of these environments exists at various time periods. Each problem faced should explicitly include one or more of these environments within the problem definition.

The research cannot study every price, every level and type of advertising support, or every sales training program. Only a few alternatives can be researched. The research problem must specify those that seem most promising. These specifications are critical; the research cannot answer unasked questions.

SUMMARY

One of the most frustrating feelings in the world is to have an answer and wonder what the question was. Unless problems are well defined, research may lead to this position. Only slightly less frustrating is the feeling of having the right answer to the wrong question. Proper problem definition can avoid this difficulty, but the difficulty is more likely to be avoided if many alternatives are considered in the early stages of the research project.

Problem definition can be divided into four main aspects: the units of analysis, the time and space boundaries, the characteristics of interest, and the specific environmental conditions. The problem *universe* is identified by the unit of analysis, the time and space boundaries, and the specific designation of which units are to be covered. Here, as in every other aspect of the problem definition, unambiguous delineation is mandatory. The relevant characteristics are the variables of concern to the decision maker in selecting among alternatives. Typical marketing research characteristics can be classified along two dimensions: first, as situation specific or general; and second, as objectively measured or inferred. The environmental conditions are special types of characteristics—variables whose values the decision maker wishes to stipulate. This is in contrast to the typical characteristic whose value is to be determined.

Care must be exercised throughout to distinguish between the problem definition and the research procedure. The first is concerned with the decision maker's action dilemma; the second is the plan (often filled with compromises) of gathering data. Unless a clear separation is maintained between the two, evaluation of the second as a satisfactory approximation for a real-world decision may be extremely difficult.

Research cannot be isolated from the philosophy of science. The basic questions of (1) the relative priorities of induction and deduction and (2) the possibility of riskless answers are interwoven with how one does research and what one thinks can be accomplished through it. The typical stance taken within marketing research—usually at a nonexplicit level—is (1) induction and deduction follow each other with neither given priority (sometimes one comes first and sometimes the other) and (2) marketing research does not yield riskless answers—all conclusions are subject to reevaluation.

EXERCISES AND PROBLEMS

1. Distinguish between the terms within each of the following pairs.
   a) Problem universe and research universe
   b) Research universe and research sample
   c) Endogenous variables and exogenous variables
   d) Characteristic of interest and unit of analysis
   e) Induction and deduction
   f) General consumer characteristics and situation specific characteristics
   g) Objective characteristics and inferred characteristics

2. Name and briefly explain the four basic parts of a problem definition.

3. Give an original example of a problem in which the unit of analysis is a DMU (Decision-making Unit). Discuss the practical difficulties involved in defining the relevant universe and present your recommendations concerning the best procedure to follow. Be sure to include a discussion of how to measure the principal characteristic of interest for DMU's that involve more than a single individual.

4. A local supermarket chain has experienced a decline in unit sales and little change in dollar sales. Profits have almost vanished. The president, in searching for ways to revitalize the operation, was advised to increase the number of hours the stores are open for business. The president is seriously considering this move and comes to you for advice in structuring a research investigation that will provide relevant information for decision making. Define the problem, taking care to

a) state the relevant question,

b) enumerate the alternative answers,

c) specify the universe involved, and

d) clearly define the characteristic of interest.

What are the relevant "states of nature" that would lead to the selection of each alternative answer?

5. Select one of the three problems mentioned in the first paragraph of Chapter 2. Refine and clarify it into an unambiguous question that is acceptable as a problem definition to be researched. Be sure to identify

a) the problem universe,

b) a research universe that does not involve compromises that are unacceptable,

c) two alternative definitions of the principal characteristic of interest,

d) a discussion of the relative merits of the alternatives cited in (c), and

e) suggested bases for establishing subgroups.

6. The drug company problem summarized in Table 2.2 illustrates the determination of a total figure by use of two alternative units of analysis. Is this unique for retail establishments, or does it also apply to manufacturers?

a) Illustrate your answer for General Motors.

b) If alternative approaches are possible for General Motors, which one do you think would pose the least data collection problems?

c) Discuss the possible utility of the subtotals generated by the alternatives.

7. Analyze, criticize, and explain:

a) Specific environmental conditions merely identify the problem situation and would never be subject to control by the researcher.

b) The size of the problem universe will never be less than the size of the research universe which in turn will never be less than the size of the research sample.

c) The unit of analysis for a research problem will usually be either a single physical object or a group of physical objects—recognizing that human beings fall within this concept.

d) There are two general categories within the term "characteristic of interest": (1) the admissible alternative actions (the independent variables) and (2) characteristics that may be related to these alternative actions (the dependent variables).

e) The time and space coordinates of the research universe are easier to cope with when the universe corresponds to an existing list.

f) Since the actual research is applied to the research universe rather than the problem universe, the researcher should be primarily concerned with the specification of the research universe.

CHAPTER 3

RESEARCH DESIGN
MANIPULATION: WHEN AND HOW?

"What will happen if we increase prices by 5 percent?" "Would the proposed new model improve consumer preference?" "Should color advertisements be used in our national promotions?" Many marketing problems are of this type—"What would happen if . . . ?" Research enters the picture as a substitute for full-scale trial and error.

The "What if?" question implies that results will differ depending on the action taken by the marketing manager. Two different types of research designs are available for handling this question: (1) experimental designs through which the researcher intervenes by introducing selected acts for the purpose of observing their effects, and (2) nonexperimental designs through which the researcher intervenes only to the extent necessary to make observations. The first is an experiment designed and conducted by the researcher. The second is an "experiment" observed by the researcher—an experiment that may have been planned by someone else, but more likely a nonexperiment that developed without coordinated planning.

Consider a different set of questions. "How can we improve dealer relations?" "What is the current state of the market for medium-sized autos?" "Why have sales declined?" These questions do not focus on well-defined hypotheses. The issues, relevant variables, and the appropriate universes are not clearly identified. Additional work is necessary before a well-structured research problem can be specified.

The problems faced by marketing managers are of both types, and different research procedures are appropriate for each. Vague, global questions require further "exploration" in order to identify the problem more precisely. The researcher should not force the manager into a narrowly contrained research definition too quickly with such questions. *Exploratory* research—*research designed to identify the decision problem and bring about the formulation of a research problem*—is required.

The opposite of exploratory research is hypothesis testing. The decision problem is sufficiently well defined so that it can be translated into a problem definition that meets the requirements discussed in Chapter 2. Hypothesis testing can in turn be divided into the two categories—experimental designs and nonexperimental designs.[1] The basic distinction between experimental designs and nonexperimental designs centers on whether the researcher manipulates the world being observed. In experimental designs, specific changes are introduced—or changes may be prevented. In nonexperimental designs, the researcher observes the world as it is and does not play the role of the master in the control room deciding the levels at which the various variables should be set.

Explanatory research, regardless of whether it is experimental or nonexperimental, asks the same question: *"If a particular action is taken, what result can be expected?"* Using X to designate the variable under study and Y to designate the result, the question can be posed as "$X_i \overset{?}{\rightarrow} Y_i$." The choice between experimental and nonexperimental designs depends on the ability to control X and the cost of doing so.

An experimental study of the effect of price on sales preselects two or more specific prices for testing. These preselected prices are assigned according to a pattern developed by the researcher, and the resulting sales at each price are recorded. A nonexperimental study records the price and the associated sales as they exist. The researcher may restrict observations to a limited number of prices but no control is exercised in the establishment of the prices. That determination is made by others; the researcher merely finds and records the conditions.

Research design establishes the types of information required and the controls (either physical or conceptual) that are to be introduced. Research design might be considered the first of three phases of data collection. The other two, instrument construction and fieldwork, are covered in the next two chapters. Research design deals with broader questions than the other two, establishing the framework within which the others are considered.

EXPLORATORY RESEARCH VERSUS HYPOTHESIS TESTING

If one does not fully comprehend the questions, how can one plan the research? Indeed an answer proposed to a global or somewhat ambiguous question may misinform rather than inform. Many times a decision maker is grappling with broad and poorly defined problems. Attempts to secure better definitions by analytic thinking may be the wrong approach and may even be

---

[1]Other authors use the terminology of causal instead of experimental, and descriptive instead of nonexperimental. Their discussions usually modify the appropriateness of the word "causal." See, for example, Claire Selltiz, Marie Jahoda, Morton Deitsch, and Stuart W. Cook, 1960, *Research Methods in Social Relations* (New York: Holt).

counterproductive—counterproductive in the sense that this approach may lead to a definitive answer to the wrong question.

Exploratory research uses a less formal approach. It pursues several possibilities simultaneously, and in a sense it is not quite sure of its objective. Exploratory research is designed to provide a background, to familiarize and, as the word implies, just "explore" the general subject. A part of exploratory research is the investigation of relationships between variables without knowing why they are studied. It borders on an idle curiosity approach, differing from it only in that the investigator thinks there may be a payoff in application somewhere in the forest of questions.

Within exploratory research there may be portions that are well structured and other portions that are vague and ephemeral. The distinguishing features are the lack of precise formulation in terms of alternatives and a similar lack of criteria for choosing among them. Its object exists nevertheless; it is to lead to a well-formulated problem definition.

Exploratory research is characterized by flexibility. It searches for insights and leads. When successful, it generates hypotheses to be tested. It does not test them. Consequently, exploratory research does not require representative samples, precision in definitions, or controlled experiments.

Selltiz and her colleagues suggest three typical approaches in exploratory research: (1) the literature search, (2) the experience survey, and (3) the analysis of "insight-stimulating" examples.[2] The literature search is a fast, economical way for researchers to develop a better understanding of a problem area in which they have limited experience. It also familiarizes them with past research results, data sources, and the type of data available. The experience survey concentrates on persons who are particularly knowledgeable in the particular area. Representative samples are not desired. A covering of widely divergent views is better. Researchers are not looking for conclusions; they are looking for ideas. The analysis of specific examples is a sort of case study approach, but again researchers are looking for fresh and possible divergent views.

An Illustration of Exploratory Research

An illustration of exploratory research is a project conducted by a multiline insurance company. The company had a line of credit plus undistributed profits, leading the executive committee to consider expansion of its product line—initially within the insurance field. The research director was given a wide latitude for the investigation, embracing the addition of "new and imaginative" risks, wider geographic coverage, and new channels of distribution.

This exploratory research involved a literature search that included professional journals, trade publications, various government publications, and

---

[2]*Ibid.*, pp. 53–65.

detailed study of several abstracting services—all of this by people who were already knowledgeable in the insurance field. Informal depth interviews with a wide cross section of people in business, government, and the academic world provided a wealth of fresh perspectives. Finally detailed analyses of diversification attempts by other insurance companies, the results of these attempts, and the probable causes of the results were undertaken. This last phase uncovered many ventures that were not in the insurance field.

These explorations generated over 100 ideas, each of which had a certain amount of "hard" or "soft" data useful in a preliminary screening stage. The ideas ranged from a computer service subsidiary and a management consulting firm to a trust and pension venture to diversification into a direct mail insurance operation. The findings from this initial research contained estimates of the magnitude of current sales for the products, opinions concerning market potentials, and various cost estimates. The data were far from precise, but they were sufficient to identify three products that were then subjected to more intensified research. The research in the second phase encompassed hypotheses to be tested. The three products emerging from this exploratory research were highly diverse: a major medical policy, sales of the company's existing line through independent agents in a particular state, and a mutual fund/pension plan combination.

CAUSATION

A marketing manager wants to know what will happen to sales if prices are decreased by 5 percent. It seems to be a problem in prediction. Should the manager also be concerned with causation? Consider the following proposition: "A 5 percent reduction in prices will always be accompanied by a 7 percent increase in sales, but the price reduction does not cause the increase in sales." Assume for the moment that the 5 percent and 7 percent figures are established without error. Does the absence of cause and effect seem reasonable? Does it matter? Three stages can be distinguished in the consideration of prediction problems and the related question of causation: association, producer–product relationship, and cause-and-effect relationship.[3]

Association exists when variables display similar patterns of variation. If high sales tend to occur with low prices and low sales tend to occur with high prices, sales and price are associated with each other. The variables display *co-variation*—they tend to vary together, although in this case in opposite directions. Association is determined by examination of the data; logical analysis of the linkage between the variables is not a part of association.

---

[3]See C. West Churchman, 1957, *Theory of Experimental Inference* (New York: Macmillan), for an extended development and discussion of the difference between producer–product and cause and effect.

A *producer-product relationship* exists when the introduction of one variable (or a change in its level) is followed by a particular result in a second variable, provided the appropriate environmental conditions are present. "A decrease in a product's price will be followed by an increase in its sales, provided management maintains specified levels of advertising and merchandise display." The decrease in price is a "producer" of the sales increase (the "product"). Given the specified environment, the price decrease will be followed by the sales increase. In other environments, the same result might not occur.

A *cause-and-effect relationship* exists if the introduction of one variable (or a change in its level) is followed by a particular result in a second variable, regardless of the environmental conditions. "A decrease in a product's price will be followed by an increase in its sales." No qualifications whatsoever! Qualifications place the relationship in the producer-product category because those qualifications negate the first variable as *the* cause. The stipulated result occurs only under certain conditions; the first variable plus the designated environment together comprise a causal system.

Given this concept of cause and effect and how it differs from association or from a producer-product relationship, how can we demonstrate or prove causation? This is a question that goes back at least to Plato and Aristotle. We shall not attempt to solve it here, but the decision maker and researcher should be aware that their recommendations will implicitly contain their responses to these philosophic issues.

The practical marketing executive may consider the concept of cause and effect as overly theoretical. But the distinction between association and a producer-product relationship is often critical in determining whether to use research results in making predictions. Nonsense associations may be shown if the researcher studies enough different variables. Suppose per capita consumption of orange juice has varied with number of letters in the name of the country. Should a brand manager use such an association as a basis for predicting per capita consumption in a particular country? This finding would come from nonexperimental research. A producer-product relationship can be established only through an experiment in which the researcher has an element of control over both the environment and the variable being tested as a potential "producer" in the specified environment. The marketing executive must also be fully aware that prediction using a producer-product relationship is valid only within the specified environmental conditions.

A slight variation of the producer-product approach uses a probability basis rather than a deterministic basis. Symbolically, a producer-product relationship asserts that a certain act (X_1) is the producer of a specific result (Y_1) in a given environment (N_1). The probability approach modifies the statement to "X_1 produces Y_1 a stated percent of the time in environment N_1." Both lines of reasoning will be prevalent throughout our discussion of research designs and later in the study of more complex relationships.

NONEXPERIMENTAL DESIGNS

Nonexperimental designs exist when the researcher merely observes the situation, intervening only to make the necessary measurements. In some instances, the researcher may use secondary data and not intervene at all. The nonexperimental design is essentially the survey and observation technique: observe the world as it is.

The need to secure observations that coincide with specific environmental conditions causes certain difficulties in nonexperimental research. The researcher must select units with the required characteristics rather than applying the desired treatments to selected units. This difference may lead to a self-selection bias in nonexperimental research. Consumers who have seen a particular TV commercial may differ in other significant characteristics from consumers who have not seen that commercial. Behavior by those who have seen the commercial may have been "produced" by any number of other variables.

Consider the operation of the Wiley Drug Supply company. It sells through its own sales force east of the Mississippi River but sells through other drug houses west of the Mississippi. Sales per capita are much higher in the east than they are in the west. Should the company switch to its own sales force in the west? The company would hardly be justified in assuming that all factors other than the sales force were equal in the two regions. The results observed are probably not the equivalent of applying two different sales force decisions to similar geographic areas.

Research designs attempt to isolate the effects of the variable under investigation from the effects of other variables. We have four basic designs available; the question to ask concerning each is whether the results obtained will reveal the effects of the factor under study or whether other factors might be responsible. If other factors might be responsible, is a better design available that is worth the cost? The four basic designs are

1. After-only,

2. Before-and-after,

3. Cross-sectional, and

4. Before-and-after cross-sectional.

Four Basic Designs

These four designs are generated by time-series and cross-sectional data considerations. Time-series (longitudinal) data involve observations on the same units at different points in time. Cross-sectional data involve observations on different units at the same point in time. The various possibilities are shown by Table 3.1.

Table 3.1
Four Basic Research Designs

Name	Group	Measure before treatment	Treatment	Measure after treatment
After-only	I	No	Yes	Yes (Y_1)
Before-and-after	I	Yes (Y_1)	Yes	Yes (Y_2)
Cross-sectional	I	No	Yes	Yes (Y_2)
	II	No	No	Yes (Y_1)
Before-and-after cross-sectional	I	Yes (Y_1)	Yes	Yes (Y_2)
	II	Yes (Y_3)	No	Yes (Y_4)

Effect measures	
After-only	Y_1 (Dubious!)
Before-and-after	$Y_2 - Y_1$
Cross-sectional	$Y_2 - Y_1$
Before-and-after cross-sectional	$(Y_2 - Y_1) - (Y_4 - Y_3)$

The simplest and most dubious is the after-only design. No attempt is made to adjust for the influence of other variables. If a man who attended our school is successful, our school must be great. The difficulty with that approach is the logical conclusion from a related question: Is our school poor if a person from our school is not successful? Clearly, good research must attempt to "net out" contributions of other variables. A 22 percent return on investment may reflect excellent products, but it may also reflect superiority in other factors. A net loss for a particular store may not reflect poor management. The loss may have been kept to a very low figure by excellent cost controls, effective promotions, and intelligent product selection. An inferior location may make profitability virtually impossible. The after-only design is clearly unacceptable. Something better must be found.

The before-and-after design makes two measurements; one before the application of the test treatment and one after. Any change is assumed to be the result of the treatment. If the researcher wishes to estimate the result of an in-store promotion, he or she measures sales during the two-week period before the promotion and during the two-week period of the promotion. But should the difference in sales be attributed to the promotion? How were the stores selected for the trial? Were weather conditions similar in the two periods? What actions did competitors adopt in each period? In general, how similar were conditions in the two periods; and to what universe, if any, can the results be generalized? The before-and-after design is strong in that observations are made on the same units; it is weak in its failure to assure similar environmental conditions at both points in time.

The cross-sectional design attempts to remove the possible effects of different time periods. The in-store promotion would be evaluated by comparing sales within stores using the promotion against sales within stores not using the promotion, all observations made over the same time periods. Since the time periods are identical, weather, holidays, competitive actions, etc. are assumed to have the same effect on both groups of stores. Observed differences in sales should reflect the effect of the promotion. But should the two groups of stores be equated? Did the more progressive stores elect the promotion? Are the two groups equal in size? The cross-sectional design does a good job on the weak factors of the before-and-after design, but the cross-sectional is weak in areas in which before-and-after is relatively strong. Observed differences may reflect differences in the stores (units) rather than differences due to the promotion.

The before-and-after cross-sectional design attempts to combine the strong points of each design. Sales for the group of stores not using the in-store promotion are measured at two points in time: the two weeks while the promotion is run in the other stores and the preceding two-week period. The change in sales between these two periods is the standard against which the other group is to be evaluated. If the nonpromotion group increases its sales by 50 cases, the effect of the promotion should be judged against an increase of 50 rather than against a "no change" standard. If the promotion group also increased by 50 cases, the promotion should be judged as of "no effect." A larger increase would mean a positive impact, and a smaller increase would mean a negative impact.

Consider the possible measurements shown in Table 3.2, using each of the four designs.[4] The after-only design credits the promotion with producing sales of 570 cases! This is much too high; there must be other factors helping produce these sales. The before-and-after design attributes sales of 75 cases (570 − 495) to the promotion, assuming that no other factors changed and contributed to this increase. From the rest of the table, we doubt that the promotion was the only factor at work since an increase in sales also occurred in the stores not using the promotion. The cross-sectional design estimates an increase of 10 cases (570 − 560) due to the promotion. This approach assumes that sales in the two groups of stores would have been identical except for the presence of the promotion in one group of stores. If this is true, why were sales not the same in the two groups during the two weeks preceding the promotion?

The before-and-after cross-sectional design attempts to adjust for both the differences between the two groups of stores and the differences in time periods. Its estimate of the increase due to the promotion is 25 cases. Although the stores with the promotion experienced an increase of 75 cases, the control

---

[4]All of the numerical examples in this chapter assume that the data are perfectly accurate and refer to the universe. The problem of "When is a sample difference big enough to attach significance to it?" is addressed in Part II and the remainder of the text.

Table 3.2
Number of Cases Sold. Four Basic Research Designs

	Stores with promotion	Stores without promotion
Two weeks preceding promotion	495	510
Two weeks of promotion	570	560
Assumed effect of promotion		
After-only	570 (Extremely dubious!)	
Before-and-after	$570 - 495 = 75$	
Cross-sectional	$570 - 560 = 10$	
Before-and-after cross-sectional	$(570 - 495) - (560 - 510) = 25$	

group of stores experienced an increase of 50 cases. The difference $(75 - 50)$ is attributed to the promotion.

The before-and-after cross-sectional estimate is larger than the cross-sectional estimate because the promotion group of stores had lower sales than the nonpromotion group in the preceding period. It is smaller than the before-and-after estimate because sales in the promotion period increased significantly even for stores not using the promotion. This "natural" increase should not be credited to the promotion.

Suppose the stores opting in favor of the promotion have been experiencing rapid growth in sales of this particular product while the other stores have been relatively stable. The 25 case increase will then be an overestimate; part of this increase should be credited to a time-series component—perhaps trend—rather than the promotion.

Alternatively, the effect of the in-store promotion may have "spilled over" into the nonpromotion stores. The benchmark standard of a 50 case increase would then be inflated. In this instance, the effect of the promotion would be more than 25 cases. From the manufacturer's view, some of the 50 case increase in nonpromotion stores should be credited to the promotion. Both nonexperimental and experimental research must be constantly alert to the possibility that the control group may be affected by the "experimental" treatment. Contamination is always a threat, and the independence of observations must be carefully evaluated. Only the substantive nature of the research can guide the researcher in the problem of independent groups; it is not solved by methodology apart from the subject matter. But the potential for contamination and overlapping effect must not be casually ignored.

Nonexperimental designs encounter the problem of independence in yet another sphere. Marketing decisions are rarely made without reference to support measures from the total marketing mix. A promotion will often generate other in-store activity. Sales clerks may engage in additional personal selling. Out-of-stock conditions may be monitored more closely. If many factors change, attempts to establish their individual contributions rest heavily on assumptions. Settling for an overall evaluation of the total may be equally unacceptable on at least two counts: (1) the precise nature of the total promotion or program may be poorly defined and inconsistent and (2) the decision maker may wish an evaluation and recommendation for the separate parts of the marketing mix.

Components at Work

The forces producing observed changes over time can be classified as: (1) treatment, (2) history, (3) testing, (4) selection, and (5) maturation.[5] The *treatment effect* is the effect under investigation, defined by the problem. It is the "net" effect sought; the others are identified, examined, and adjusted for in order to obtain better estimates of the treatment. As we shall see in complex designs, the treatment may involve several different factors—each of which is to be analyzed separately and in combination with the others.

History deals with those events that affect the research results but are not a part of the research design. These events are extraneous to the interest of the study, but they have influenced the observations. General economic conditions, changes in supply conditions, competitive retaliation, the political climate, weather conditions—there is no end to the list of items that confound the research results. The longer the time interval, the more likely significant events will intervene and affect the research.

The *testing* effect results when the subjects know their behavior is being observed or the results of their activity are being measured. This effect is a frequent problem in both test marketing and before-and-after designs. In test marketing, support is at a higher level and superior performance may result because personnel have been sensitized. The same phenomenon is at work with subjects in a before-and-after design, yielding different and usually superior performance in areas perceived as germane by the subjects. The researcher may attempt to overcome this force by disguising the true nature of the study.

Selection relates to the choice of the units or subjects to study. Any comparison against a benchmark or standard introduces a control group and a test group. The equivalence of the two is always suspect in nonexperimental designs. In experimental designs, random selection is a standard procedure that will yield unbiased estimates with measurable reliability. Subject self-selection is always a potential source of bias in nonexperimental designs. Persons who

---

[5]This classification follows that of Seymour Banks except that Banks adds an instrument effect that refers to changes in the meaning of the unit of measure; for example, different interviewers, fatigue factors, and monetary purchasing power. We prefer to place this factor under the definition of relevant characteristics, stressing the need for unambiguous measuring instruments. See Seymour Banks, 1965, *Experimentation in Marketing,* (New York: McGraw-Hill).

tried your product in the introductory stage are probably different from those who did not try it. An assumption that the two groups may be considered random samples from the same universe is extremely dubious. Assignment of subjects to different groups based on the researcher's "best judgment" may be a slightly better approach, but this procedure may also invite bias.

Maturation refers to natural changes with the passage of time. People age, improve, or deteriorate depending on the subject and the time span involved. Customers gain competence in product use, sales personnel become more familiar with distributors, and the actual physical size of people in a given test may change. The maturation factor is a special case of the time dimension that might be classified under history. It is considered distinct because it focuses on natural changes that occur in the persons or units under study.

Example of Components at Work

A manufacturer of a consumer nondurable wants to compare the relative effectiveness of color advertising and black and white advertising in *Newsweek* magazine. Extensive data are available from Starch Advertising Readership Service on several measures of readership from a number of issues of *Newsweek*.[6] Table 3.3 presents examples of the different components as they apply to this specific problem.

The treatment component is the object of the study. How does readership of an ad in *Newsweek* differ when color is used in contrast to when only black and white is used? This component clearly will be at work if readership is compared for two groups of ads: one using color and the other using black and white. The critical question is whether other components also influence the results.

The history component has to do with timing. The ads did not all appear at the same time. Major news events may have an impact upon both the number of readers of a particular issue of *Newsweek* and the readership of ads within that issue. Heightened interest in news events may increase potential exposure. An interruption of magazine distribution because of labor unrest would tend to have the opposite effect. Publication of a high-interest feature story—for example, an in-depth study of recent assassination attempts—would tend to increase magazine sales and readership.

These sources will cause difficulty only if they have a differential impact on the data for the two groups. Such a differential impact may exist in either of two situations. (1) The relative balance between color and black and white may vary among issues. If color ads appear more often in high-readership

---

[6]See *Starch: Scope, Method, and Use.* 1973 (Mamaroneck, N.Y.: Starch/INRA/Hooper). Three basic measures are employed, but each measure is applied to each distinct part of each ad. We shall discuss these different readership measures in Chapter 4.

Table 3.3
Examples of Components at Work.
Readership of Black and White Ads versus Color Ads in *Newsweek*

Component	Source of influence†
Treatment	Color versus black and white
History	Occurrence of significant news events Interruption of magazine distribution Publication of high-interest feature story
Testing	Sensitizing of respondents to over- or underreport Sensitizing of respondents to change ad readership
Selection	Ads of unequal size, placement within magazine, amount of pictures, etc. Products advertised unequal in overall consumer interest
Maturation	Seasonal, cyclical, or trend changes in magazine readership Changes over time in ad readership

†All of the sources listed will influence the research results only as they have a differential impact on the group of black and white ads in contrast to the group of color ads.

issues, the results will be biased in favor of color ads. If the reverse is true, the results will be biased in the opposite direction. (2) The relative superiority of color may be more (or less) depending on the general news climate and editorial content. If this be true, a general conclusion may be valid on the average but misleading for particular environments.

The testing component depends on the process used to generate the data. If higher readership levels are reflected in the data than would exist without the research, this is a potential source of difficulty. With this particular problem, the testing component—even if present—is a source of bias only if it is different for color ads from what it is for black and white ads. If respondents overstate color ad readership by 50 percent but black and white ad readership by only 20 percent, the testing component is a source of bias. If equal overstatements (or understatements) are made for both ad types, no bias is created in the comparisons.[7]

The selection component must be appraised in terms of the unit of analysis. The unit for this study is the ad. Would readership for the group of ads using color be the same as that for the other group if both were in black and white? if both were in color? If not, the research results may mislead. What is

---

[7]Overstatements or understatements may be expressed in either percentage or absolute terms. In order to maintain comparability, all components should be expressed in the same mode.

thought to be treatment effect may be due to the selection component. If all small ads are black and white while all large ads are in color, measures of readership may reflect a mixture of the effects of size and color rather than a clear measure of either one. Presence of pictures, contrasts, and other factors may also obscure the results thus limiting the utility of the study.

The maturation component influences the data by the natural process of growth or change. This growth or change manifests itself in the dependent variable, "readership" in this case. Normally the growth occurs in the unit of analysis: a person grows physically or mentally, a corporation adds new products, and a city changes in population. All of these changes may influence market results or potential. But does an ad experience maturation? In a certain sense it may—through repeated use, either in the same magazine or in others. Readership (or at least recall of readership) may follow a law of learning model.

Maturation typically follows a pattern of change. This change may be seasonal, cyclical, or a longer growth pattern. If either the readership of *Newsweek* or the readership of ads in *Newsweek* is characterized by such a pattern, maturation may distort the research results. Suppose the data cover a number of years, color use has increased over time, and readership has grown. This combination of factors would lead to an overstatement of any superiority for color.

Nonexperimental designs attempt to deal with the nontreatment factors in two distinct ways. The first concerns the selection of the comparison or "control" group. The second deals with the timing of the observations.

First, the "control" group should be as similar as possible to the "experimental" group. For an in-store promotion study, the two groups of stores might be screened and equated on square feet of selling space, independent–chain status, realized gross margins, advertising policies, and growth patterns. The attempt is to remove differences in factors that might influence research results. It is not always possible to find similar groups in the nonexperimental situation, but researchers do their best to make the control standard as similar as possible. In the *Newsweek* ad study, the "black and white" and "color" ads might be matched on size of ad, product, and placement within the magazine.

Second, observations should be made on both groups at the same instants of time. History and maturation effects are thus minimized. The *Newsweek* study might match ads by week of issue. Occasionally nonexperimental designs may use nonsimultaneous observations. For example, the response rate from a direct mail coupon campaign (for a new product) may be evaluated against past experience with similar campaigns. The same length of time may be involved, but the history effect will be different because different events occur in each setting. Factors such as economic conditions and weather may influence the results even when an attempt is made to follow "essentially similar" procedures.

EXPERIMENTAL DESIGNS

Experimental designs attempt to overcome the self-selection problems of non-experimental designs. In so doing, they require *intervention* by the researcher in two ways. First, the units to be studied are selected by the researcher and each unit is assigned to the group determined by the researcher. The units do not select their groups, thus avoiding the self-selection bias. Second, a necessary consequence of the first, the researcher administers the predetermined treatment or treatments to the units within each group.

The use of a control group is almost mandatory in experimental designs. Without it, the selection component is ignored. The before-and-after design is an attempt to compensate for any selection problems, but it cannot handle the history and maturation components. The inclusion of a control group permits a better isolation of the treatment component either through a simple cross-sectional design or the before-and-after cross-sectional design.

The simple cross-sectional design deletes the before measure. The need for this measure comes primarily from the fear that the two groups are dissimilar. The whole point of random selection and assignment is to overcome this danger. Groups composed by random methods will still exhibit some differences, but the magnitude of such differences decreases as the size of the groups increases.[8] The cross-sectional design has the offsetting advantage of lower cost (two observations versus four) plus elimination of the testing effect produced by a before measure.

The before-and-after cross-sectional experimental design parallels the similar nonexperimental design. Brand preference before and after two types of messages could be compared against a third group that received neither message. This experiment could be performed most easily in a laboratory situation. Brand preference would be determined for all three groups in as unobstrusive a way as possible. All three groups would then be exposed to media presentations—TV, film, magazine, newspaper—that are identical except for some small portion. Group 1 might receive a factual advertisement; group 2, a testimonial advertisement; and group 3, no brand message. Possible results are shown in Table 3.4.

The differences among the three groups in the before measurements are accepted as real differences among the three groups. The slight increase of 1 point $(24 - 23)$ in the control group is the benchmark against which the other two groups are compared. With these results, the factual advertisement is evaluated at a score of $+4$ $[(26 - 21) - (24 - 23)]$ while the testimonial advertisement is evaluated at -3 $[(18 - 20) - (24 - 23)]$. Marketing executives must keep clearly in mind that they are evaluating a particular factual advertisement and a particular testimonial, not factual advertisements in general against testimonials in general. They must also keep in mind that the research is addressed to a particular universe and product.

---

[8]To be technically correct this statement should be framed in terms of probabilities. We postpone these considerations until Chapter 6.

Table 3.4
Before-and-after Brand Preference. Three Groups

	Percentage preferring brand A	
Group	Before	After
Factual advertisement	21	26
Testimonial advertisement	20	18
No brand A advertisement	23	24

Four-group, Six-study Design

The difficulty of measuring the testing effect and the possibility of nonequivalent sample groups have given rise to a four-group, six-study design. This design yields measurements not only for the treatment effect but also for the testing effect and the combined history/maturation effect. The design includes two control groups and two experimental groups with after-only measures for one group of each pair and before-and-after for the other group within the pair.

Table 3.5 illustrates this design for research to test the effect of free trading stamps on consumer saving of trading stamps. One hundred stamps were given each member of the two experimental groups. The number of books of trading stamps saved was determined for one experimental group and one control group both before and after the distribution of the free stamps. Data were collected from the other two groups only after the distribution.

The hypothetical data show observations separated by ten months and also show a decline in stamp saving. Those in experimental group I reduced their stamp saving by .5 book per year ($Y_2 - Y_1 = 1.9 - 2.4$). This decline is produced by all the factors of treatment, history, testing, and maturation. Selection is not involved because the measurements refer to the same group. The decline within control group I is somewhat larger ($Y_4 - Y_3 = -1.1$). This decline is produced by history, testing, and maturation. Again no selection factor enters for within-group changes. It seems that the giving of 100 trading stamps has a positive effect on saving, despite the observed decline. The calculation of the magnitude of its effect is straightforward. The $-.5 - (-1.1)$ indicates a positive effect of .6 book per year.

The second experimental and control groups are supposed to reflect the first two groups aside from the before measures that produced the testing effect. Aside from random fluctuations in the selection process, comparison of the after measures should show this testing effect. The mean after measure for the I groups exceeds the mean for the II groups by .2 ($1.7 - 1.5$)—the estimate of the testing effect.

Finally, an estimate of history and maturation can be found by subtraction. Experimental group I declined by .5. Treatment is estimated at $+.6$, and

Table 3.5
Four-group, Six-study Design. Trading Stamp Saving

Group	Number of books saved per year	
	Before measure	After measure
Experimental I	2.4 (Y_1)	1.9 (Y_2)
Control I	2.6 (Y_3)	1.5 (Y_4)
Experimental II	No observation	1.7 (Y_5)
Control II	No observation	1.3 (Y_6)

Treatment effect: $(Y_2 - Y_1) - (Y_4 - Y_3)$
$(1.9 - 2.4) - (1.5 - 2.6)$
$+.6$

Testing effect: $(Y_2 + Y_4)/2 - (Y_5 + Y_6)/2$
$(1.9 + 1.5)/2 - (1.7 + 1.3)/2$
$+.2$

History + maturation effect: $Y_2 - Y_1 -$ Treatment $-$ Testing
$1.9 - 2.4 - .6 - .2$
-1.3
or $Y_4 - Y_3 -$ Testing
$1.5 - 2.6 - .2$
-1.3

testing is estimated at $+.2$. A total change of $-.5$ can be produced only by a history/maturation effect of -1.3. A similar estimate will result if the observations for control group I are employed.[9]

The experiment permits the trading stamp company to isolate the three separate factors. The announced object of the research was to appraise the effect of giving 100 free stamps. This strategy had a positive effect on the saving of trading stamps, increasing it by .5 book per year on the average. Just doing the research and sensitizing people to trading stamps also had a positive effect—increasing savings by .2 book per year. It would be interesting to follow up on the subjects in the after-only groups to see whether this testing effect were again present. The period covered by the research was one of pronounced decline in trading stamp savings. This is shown by the history/maturation effect that was more than double the treatment effect. Only by adjusting for this factor is it possible to see the positive effects of treatment and testing.

---

[9]Slightly different results will be obtained in estimates of the treatment and testing effects if the analysis is limited to only the after measures. If the before measures are ignored, of course no history or maturation estimates can be made. Restriction to the after-only measures is considered in the next section.

FACTORIAL DESIGNS

The researcher often wishes to investigate the effects of more than one variable; for example, price changes and promotion. If the marketing executive wishes to choose among three different price levels and two different promotional campaigns, six alternatives exist. If the marketing executive complicates the task still further by adding three package designs, 18 alternatives exist. The number of alternatives is readily seen as the product of the number of categories of the different variables. The factorial design specifies that at least one observation must be made for each possible combination. The dummy table (without data) for such an experiment is shown as Table 3.6.

The after-only measures from the four-group, six-study design for the free trading stamp study fit neatly into a factorial design. The first variable is the treatment—either 100 stamps are given or they are not. The second variable is the before measure—although its magnitude is ignored, either such an observation is made or it is not. The factorial design is the 2 × 2 table with four cells, shown as Table 3.7. The effect of receiving free stamps is estimated by comparing the rows, and the effect of the before measure is given by comparing the columns.

The estimate of the treatment effect is $+.4$ (a mean of 1.8 compared with 1.4) with this design; it contrasts to $+.6$ in the prior analysis. The distinction of .2 is explained by and equal to the difference between the two before measures—2.6 for the control group and 2.4 for the experimental group.[10] The

Table 3.6
Dummy Table Showing Observations
Required for Price/Promotion/Package
Experiment†

		Package		
Price	Promotion	X	Y	Z
Level I	A			
	B			
Level II	A			
	B			
Level III	A			
	B			

†Eighteen observations required, one per cell

---

[10]The concept of random variations is not introduced in this chapter for any of the designs. In this chapter we are concerned with the conceptual designs and assume the measures are error-free universe values. Random errors and reliability measures will be added in Part II.

Table 3.7
Factorial Design. Trading Stamp Study

	Before measure	No before measure
Received free stamps	1.9	1.7
Did not receive free stamps	1.5	1.3

Treatment effect: (1.9 + 1.7)/2 − (1.5 + 1.3)/2
+.4
Testing effect: (1.9 + 1.5)/2 − (1.7 + 1.3)/2
+.2

estimate of the testing effect is +.2, similar to the estimate in the previous analysis.

Table 3.7 shows greater consistency than we would normally expect in empirical results. The treatment effect appears at .4 both where a before measure was made and where none was made. The testing effect of .2 also is consistent in both comparisons, where stamps were given and where not given. A slight variation in any one of the four figures would maintain a general consistency but not yield perfect uniformity—a much more typical result.

Reliance on the averages from the factorial design may be misleading. Consider the data in Table 3.8. Mean unit sales are higher with a 79¢ price than with a 99¢ price. When comparing promotions, mean unit sales are higher for the quality image promotion than for the convenience image promotion. Putting the two together is a poor strategy; convenience image at 79¢ or quality image at 99¢ both would be superior to the quality image at 79¢.[11] The two factors interact with each other, and this interaction should not be ignored.[12]

Table 3.8
Factorial Design. Price–Promotion Experiment with Unit Sales

	Promotion		
Unit price	Quality image	Convenience image	Row mean
$.79	236	258	247
.99	252	216	234
Column mean	244	237	

[11]Of course, reliance on high unit sales as a long-run objective would hardly be an appropriate strategy. For this example, we are assuming that management wishes to use unit sales as the criterion for evaluation of alternative actions.

[12]Analytic techniques to test for interaction effects will be developed in Chapter 11 and 13.

Interaction may be either positive or negative. In another setting, the factors producing higher sales might reinforce each other when applied together, thus yielding greater sales than the simple addition of their individual effects would suggest. Friendly sales clerks and wide assortments might both be desirable, but their combined effect might be much greater than would be implied by their separate effects. Lack of either might be devastating.

The data in both Tables 3.7 and 3.8 come from after-only measurements. The factorial design can also be used with data based on differences between the before-and-after measures. Thus the factorial design builds on the basic designs discussed earlier in the chapter; it is not an alternative design to them. Table 3.9 presents the data for a factorial design using the change in opinion of a new product—using before-and-after measures. The distribution of a sample and a telephone campaign were both tested. Four separate groups were employed: (1) a control group receiving neither, (2) a group receiving the sample, (3) a group receiving the telephone call, and (4) a group receiving both. Before-and-after measures were made for all four groups; thus slight differences in the before measures do not affect the results. The data in Table 3.9 indicate that the sample generated higher opinion scores—an increase of $+.55$ versus a slight decrease $(-.05)$ where no sample was received. The telephone campaign seemed to have a slight positive effect ($+.3$ versus $+.2$).

Distribution of a sample plus a telephone call seems to produce a negative interaction rather than reinforcement (for the data in Table 3.9). This is seen most clearly by comparing the figures within columns or within rows. Distribution of the sample raised opinion by .8 points among those that did not receive a telephone call but by only .4 points among those who did receive a telephone call. The row comparison seems even more striking. The telephone call increased opinion by .3 points where no sample was sent, but opinion actually *declined* by .1 when a telephone call was used in conjunction with a sample. A case of oversell?

Table 3.9
Factorial Design. Changes in Opinion of a New Product.† Effects of Distribution of a Sample and a Telephone Call Campaign

Sample received	Telephone call		
	Yes	No	Row mean
Yes	$+.5$	$+.6$	$+.55$
No	$+.1$	$-.2$	$-.05$
Column mean	$+.3$	$+.2$	

†Opinion measured on a 5-point scale.

LATIN SQUARE DESIGNS

The number of units required with a factorial design expands rapidly as additional factors and/or categories are added. A single replication—one observation per cell—with three variables at three levels each would require 27 observations. In order to keep the number of observations manageable, the researcher may move into a Latin square design. This design will reduce the number of observations required but will sacrifice the ability to detect interactions.

The Latin square achieves the objective of estimating the effects of the treatments under investigation by balancing the observations. If three prices are being tested, each price is observed the same number of times with each promotion alternative and the same number of times in each type of store—or each store in the experiment.

Consider an experiment to test three prices and three promotional campaigns. A factorial design would require nine observations. If applied at only one store, the experiment would require nine time periods. To shorten the time span, more stores can be introduced, but the use of several stores introduces a possible store effect. If three stores are introduced, a factorial design would require 27 observations. A Latin square design will yield estimates of all three treatments at each of three levels with only nine observations and will require only three time periods. Table 3.10 shows the layout of the design. The three stores are designated as C_1, C_2, and C_3. Each store is assigned only three of the nine price–promotion combinations, but each store is assigned each price level once and each promotion once. Similar statements pertain to each price level and each promotion. Each price level is assigned to each store once and to each promotion once. The design is "balanced"; aggregate measures for any category of a particular factor will not be distorted by any of the other factors.

Table 3.10
Latin Square Design for Three
Factors, Each at Three Levels

Price level	Promotion		
	B_1	B_2	B_3
A_1	C_1	C_2	C_3
A_2	C_2	C_3	C_1
A_3	C_3	C_1	C_2

C = Store designation

Latin square designs always assume the form of a square: each factor must have the same number of categories. A 5×5 design is shown in Table 3.11. This design investigates the effect of an airline menu on traveler satisfaction. In order to remove extraneous factors, five different flights on five different dates were included in the study. The orderly sequence of the design may suggest nonrandomness. This is easily overcome by a random assignment of the five categories to the various subscripts or by a random transposition of the rows and/or columns.

The actual design for the problem shown in Table 3.11 must specify five different menus, five different dates, and five different flights. The dependent variable would be a measure of satisfaction. Menu, date, and flight are specified in the research design while satisfaction is determined in the research. Twenty-five observations are required. Menu A_1 would be served on date B_1 of flight C_1. Menu A_1 would not be served on any other flight on date B_1 or on flight C_1 on any other date. Each menu would be served once on each flight and once on each date. On which flight would menu A_3 be served on date B_4? Inspection of Table 3.11 reveals the answer to be C_2.

Numerical data and the accompanying analysis for the price–promotion–store design are show in Table 3.12. The data refer to number of sewing machines sold, using three different prices ($159, $189, and $198) and three different promotions—one identified as a manufacturer's deal, the second as a retailer's deal, and a control group of "no special promotion." The price and promotion effects are simply row and column means. The $159 price yields higher sales than either of the other two: 19 units versus 15.3 for the $189 price and 14.3 for the $198 price. The retailer promotion is slightly better than the manufacturer promotion: 17.7 versus 17. It is interesting to note that the $159 price/retailer promotion did not generate the highest sales. The combination

Table 3.11
A 5 $\times$ 5 Latin Square Design for Airline Menu Study

Menu	Date				
	B_1	B_2	B_3	B_4	B_5
A_1	C_1	C_2	C_3	C_4	C_5
A_2	C_5	C_1	C_2	C_3	C_4
A_3	C_4	C_5	C_1	C_2	C_3
A_4	C_3	C_4	C_5	C_1	C_2
A_5	C_2	C_3	C_4	C_5	C_1

C = Flight designation

Table 3.12
Sales for Price-Promotion-Store 3 × 3 Latin Square Design.
Sewing Machine Sales

	Promotion		
Price level	Retailer (B_1)	Manufacturer (B_2)	None (B_3)
$189 ($A_1$)	15 (C_1)	21 (C_2)	10 (C_3)
$198 ($A_2$)	18 (C_2)	12 (C_3)	13 (C_1)
$159 ($A_3$)	20 (C_3)	18 (C_1)	19 (C_2)

Price level effect

$$A_1 = 46 \div 3 = 15.33$$
$$A_2 = 43 \div 3 = 14.33$$
$$A_3 = 57 \div 3 = 19.00$$

Promotion effect

$$B_1 = 53 \div 3 = 17.67$$
$$B_2 = 51 \div 3 = 17.00$$
$$B_3 = 42 \div 3 = 14.00$$

Store effect

$$C_1 = 46 \div 3 = 15.33$$
$$C_2 = 58 \div 3 = 19.33$$
$$C_3 = 42 \div 3 = 14.00$$

was assigned to store C_3, the store with the lowest overall sales. Despite the low sales effect of store C_3, the store recorded 20 sales when combined with the $159 price and the retailer promotion. This result was second only to the 21 sales recorded by store C_2 when using a $189 price and a manufacturer promotion. When store C_2 offered a $159 price, the low price was not accompanied by any promotion, resulting in slightly lower sales of 19 units.[13]

ALTERNATIVE DESIGNS: PRICE STUDY

The experiment that generated the data in Table 3.12 employed only three different stores, but it ran for three months in each store. It investigated not only the effect of different prices but also the effect of different promotions; it also

---

[13]More complex designs involve the sacrifice of some but not all interaction terms, the correction for possible carry-over effects from one period to succeeding ones, implementation for "non-square" problems, etc. Some of these will be discussed in later chapters as we introduce reliability measures with sample data. For in-depth technical development of experimental designs, the reader is referred to William Cochran and Gertrude Cox, *Experimental Designs,* 1957, (New York: Wiley) and Ronald A. Fisher, 1960, *The Design of Experiments* (7th ed.) (Edinburgh, Scotland: Oliver and Boyd, Ltd.).

identified a store effect. What other research designs might be employed to study the price effect?

The marketing manager is concerned at this time primarily with the pricing decision. The promotion and store effects are significant only if they influence the pricing decision or if they must be identified in order to secure a better reading of the price influence. How about a simple before-and-after design with the three stores in question or an even simpler cross-sectional design using the three stores?

First, let us consider the extremely simple cross-sectional design. The three different prices would be tested by applying one in each store. Provided the stores are in reasonably close proximity, the history component might be assumed equal. (Of course such an assumption always runs the risk of not being justified—within-store events and even neighborhood events might not be the same.) The principal difficulties arise because of selection and maturation. The stores do not have equal potentials, and they have arrived at different stages of development. This might be overcome by using three groups of stores rather than three stores. Taking several stores will reduce the significance of both the selection and maturation components. The design is more likely to show price effects without the contamination of other forces. But the more accurate measure of price effect would be achieved only by increasing the cost of running the experiment.

Second, the before-and-after experiment would require two observations from each store. By stressing the change in sales, an attempt is made to adjust for differences in the level of sales associated with each store. Again the researcher assumes that the history component—both during the experiment and prior to the experiment—have been similar. The before measure may be unduly influenced by certain historical events thus producing a misleading base from which to measure changes. As in the cross-sectional design, three groups of stores can be employed rather than three individual stores. The reliability of the findings will be increased but at an increase in cost.

If either the cross-sectional or the before-and-after design is used, what should the researcher do about promotional activity? Should it be the same in all stores? If yes, what promotion? If no, how should the researcher adjust for the effects of the various promotions? Can the researcher simply select three groups of stores, hoping that promotional activity in the three groups will balance? If promotional activity is maintained at a particular level, the research really tests for the effect of price in conjunction with that promotion.

A third alternative might be a Latin square carry-over design. The need for this design can be seen by inspection of the first three rows of Table 3.12. The $198 price would be offered in store C_2 in the first period, store C_3 in the second period, and store C_1 in the third period. In both C_3 and C_1 the $198 price followed the period in which the price was $159. Any carry-over effect of the earlier price—either positive or negative—is not balanced. The carry-over design achieves balance by having each treatment follow every other treatment

SUMMARY

Research design is addressed to that portion of the research plan that specifies the degree of intrusion by the researcher into the research environment. In nonexperimental designs, the researcher merely makes the required observations and measurements. In experimental designs, the researcher intervenes by introducing variables or treatments of prime interest in the decision maker's problem. The measure of the treatment effect is hampered by the potential presence of history, testing, selection, and maturation effects. The use of before-and-after measures plus the inclusion of a control group addresses the problem of measuring these various effects, ending with the four-group, six-study design.

Research is often concerned with measuring the effects of more than one treatment variable. The effects of the separate variables as well as their interactions can be estimated by the factorial design that requires at least one observation for every possible combination of the different variables at their various levels. The Latin square design reduces the number of observations necessary but sacrifices estimates of interactions. The Latin square design may also be extended to overcome possible carry-over effects by a second replication in which the sequence is reversed, and it may be extended to the Greco-Latin square design to accommodate additional factors.

EXERCISES AND PROBLEMS

1. Distinguish between the terms within each of the following sets.
   a) Experimental designs and nonexperimental designs
   b) Association, producer–product relationship, and cause-and-effect relationship
   c) Cross-sectional data and time-series data
   d) Factorial design, Latin square design, and Greco-Latin square design
   e) History component and maturation component
   f) Carry-over design and Greco-Latin square design

2. a) Name and describe the four basic research designs.
   b) Contrast the four-group, six-study design and the four basic designs.

3. Name and describe the five principal components that research designs attempt to identify and measure.

4. A local social work agency wishes to determine the "status of the family" within its relevant geographic area. Discuss, with examples, an appropriate approach to this problem as an exploratory research design. Be sure to address a broad spectrum of data sources and procedures. Why should this be considered "exploratory" research?

5. An international oil company wants to estimate the relationship between the price of home heating oil and the type of heating installed in new homes. Extensive

annual data are available by counties within the entire United States on both variables, extending back for several decades. Assume the data are accurate.

a) Would an experimental design be appropriate? Why?

b) What type research design seems most appropriate to you? Discuss, indicating
its superiority over the most likely alternatives.

c) Discuss the principal substantive factors that would contribute to each of the
five "components at work."

d) How would your design permit the identification of each component?

e) What would be the advantages (and disadvantages) of employing absolute
prices versus various types of relative prices.

6. The American Drug Company, a manufacturer of proprietary drugs, has traditionally placed the bulk of its consumer advertising in local television. The marketing manager is contemplating the allocation of half of the advertising budget to
local radio. The manager has divided the company's market area into two regions,
Northern and Southern, using the old advertising program in the Northern region
and the new program in the Southern region. The data below give sales for the
fourth quarter of last year when both regions used the old program and the first
quarter of the current year when the two regions have followed the different programs. Data are in $1,000.

	Southern region	Northern region
Fourth quarter	245	286
First quarter	305	349

a) Estimate the effect of allocating half the budget to local radio from these figures.

b) Convert the sales data into indices with the fourth quarter for each region set
equal to 100. Estimate the effect of allocating half the budget to local radio,
using the data in index form.

c) Discuss any differences between the estimates in (a) and (b). Which do you
think is a better indicator?

d) Calculate and evaluate the estimates that would have been available had the
design been only
(i) before-and-after
(ii) cross-sectional

e) Would you consider the "selection effect" of any concern in this research?
Discuss.

f) Would a four-group, six-study design have been possible for this problem? Discuss.

g) What, if any, advantages would a four-group, six-study design offer in this
problem?

7. The G&T Maintenance Company has been considering the assignment of "profit responsibility" to some of its middle-management personnel.

   a) Fill in data of the following four-group, six-study design that would indicate a large positive treatment effect, a small negative history plus maturation effect, and an even smaller positive testing effect.

| | Profit | |
Group	Before measure	After measure
Profit responsibility group I		
Control group I		
Profit responsibility group II		
Control group II		

   b) Using your after measures only, analyze the data as a 2 × 2 factorial design.

   c) Are the results of (a) and (b) consistent? Why or why not?

8. The Nelox Candle Company is considering the possibility of adding a line of hand-carved candles. The production manager is afraid the new line will "cannibalize" existing sales. A small factorial experiment is designed in which three salespeople are to call on a sample of their current accounts. Half of each sales person's accounts are offered both the old and new lines while the others are offered only the old line. Dollar sales for the three salespeople were: Bowman—$325 where both offered ($220 old and $105 new) and $275 where only old offered, McNeil—$480 from both ($290 old and $190 new) and $280 from old only, and Simpson—$310 from both ($300 old and $10 new) and $330 old only.

   a) Analyze and interpret the data, focusing on the question of whether the new line seems to "cannibalize" the old line.

   b) Do you have any reservations with respect to either the experimental design or your conclusions? Discuss.

9. A large manufacturing company is revising its billing system. It wants feedback from a sample of its customers concerning various proposals. Each customer selected is asked to compare a specific new format to the current format. Three sizes, two type styles, three layouts for line entries and extensions, and two mailback procedures are to be tested under the new formats.

   a) How many different groups would be required in a factorial design?

   b) Would a Latin square design be a good way to reduce the number of groups? Discuss.

   c) Would a Greco-Latin square design be appropriate? Why?

10. A credit card company wishes to evaluate three direct mail letters and three price offers simultaneously.

a) How many groups would be required in a factorial design?

b) Could the same group be used for more than one treatment? Discuss.

c) Does your answer to (b) affect the possibility of using a Latin square design? Discuss.

11. **a)** Select an original problem that can be tested with a Greco-Latin square design. Identify the variables to be tested and specify the categories of each.

  b) Substitute hypothetical data within the appropriate table, and calculate the effect of each treatment level.

  c) Are any interactions apparent? Discuss.

12. You are the product manager for Something New, a pudding type of dessert. The product was highly rated in laboratory tests but has not done well in the market. You want to design a research project that will simultaneously evaluate its price and name.

  a) Is this exploratory, experimental, or nonexperimental research? Why?

  b) What data would be useful for realizing your objective?

  c) What type of research design would be appropriate for this study? Discuss.

  d) Prepare the table that would be required for recording the necessary data.

  e) Fill in the table from (d) with hypothetical data and perform the appropriate analysis.

  f) What action do you, as brand manager, believe is appropriate? Base your answer on your analysis in (e).

13. Analyze, criticize, and explain:

  a) Exploratory research is usually the result of a poorly conceived research project.

  b) The before-and-after design suffers from its inability to distinguish among the treatment effect, the history effect, and the selection effect.

  c) Manipulation of the environment by the researcher invites disaster because one is never sure which variables to change. Simple observation and recording of variables is a much better approach.

  d) The concept of "producer–product," when modified by probability statements, is just as good for marketing decisions as the nebulous concept of cause and effect.

  e) In most instances the marketing manager is not concerned with the measurement of nontreatment effects. It is the researcher's overly cautious approach that leads to this unnecessary cost in time and money.

  f) The detection of interactions within a factorial design must focus on relationships among cell values rather than on averages for the various categories of the treatment variables.

  g) Testing effects are minimized if both the experimental groups and the control group know that the environment is being monitored. The testing effect is most likely to appear when only the experimental group knows the experiment is being conducted.

h) An experimental design, in contrast to a nonexperimental design, has the disadvantage that the marketing manager can select the units and assign treatments in a way that will allow him or her to "prove" any point.

i) "Self-selection" by units in nonexperimental designs of loyalty is usually offset by the higher degree of cooperation achieved.

j) The "balancing" of the Latin square design is automatically achieved if the same number of observations is made at each level for each variable.

he or she has the technical competence, the time demands ı
of the time available.[1]

The possibility of the observed acting as the observer d
points raised in the preceding paragraph—we shall, for sim
as the UAW test.

1. Will the respondent *understand* the question or task ı

2. Is the respondent *able* to supply a meaningful respon

3. Will the respondent be *willing* to supply that respons

Whether the one observed acts as the observer or not, th
must ultimately be answered in the affirmative. The i
observer as an intermediary and separate party is fundamer
increase the likelihood of affirmative answers to one or ı
questions.

The questions and definitions adopted as part of the
must frequently be modified in the data collection proce
nitions must be translated into language understandable
This may mean that complex concepts are generated by a
questions rather than a single question that is precisely defi
hensible to all except a few. The vocabulary employed mus
the respondent, not to the expert or even to the highly edı

A conglomerate has come on hard times in one of iı
specializes in retirement homes in Florida. It believes tl
between earned income and other income might be cruc
market demand and in selecting appropriate price levels.
questionnaire included the question, "How much of your 1!
earned?" The question is inappropriate on two counts: (1)
will not be familiar with the Internal Revenue Service cono
of "earned income" and (2) the terminology generates anta
tial bias even among those who understand the concept. A
dure is to request data on income from sources other than
services. This is true both as the researcher deals with the oı
observers deal with those observed.[2]

Most exploratory research runs into potential pr
researcher turns over substantial amounts of work to the o
and general guidelines. The same problem exists in the dep
of these situations require that the interviewer be thoroughl

---

[1] In most cases, cost differentials between an observer's wage rate and the
would dictate only a minimum amount of observation by the researcher evo
not prohibitive.

[2] Almost all income concepts are too technical to be used in general populat
as discretionary, disposable, and taxable income are precise concepts that
rectly understood.

DATA COLLECTION—INSTRUMENT DESIGN
DOES THE QUESTION MEAN WHAT IT'S SUPPOSED TO?

The aim of data collection procedures is to get worthwhile data for the problem as defined. The line of demarcation between problem definition and data collection at times seems fuzzy and arbitrary, but a distinction is useful. Problem definition is addressed to the question, "What do I want to know about?" Data collection is addressed to the question, "How can I get the information required?" In the planning stage there will often be recycling and revisions between the two phases; but as long as the distinction is made, the researcher is better able to evaluate the wisdom of the revisions.

When revisions are made in the problem definition because of data collection considerations, one runs the danger of securing a correct answer to a question that is inappropriate for the decision maker. Changes, compromises, and revisions in the problem definition are to be expected; but they must not be permitted to undermine the basic reason for doing the research.

Revisions in data collection procedures because of problem definition requirements are another matter. Here one must consider whether the revised data collection procedures will "work." It is a question of whether the plan can be pulled off as revised. One must ask if the data generated will be worth the effort or whether the procedure will simply generate numbers of dubious quality.

Data collection consists of presenting a stimulus to a respondent or subject and recording his or her response. The stimulus may be a verbal question, a clearly identified task in a laboratory, complex activity in the marketplace, or numerous mixtures or modifications of these situations. The response is typically either behavioral or verbal although a combination of the two is possible. Behavioral responses may be observed in a laboratory situation or in the marketplace, with a multitude of possibilities that could be classified as quasi-laboratory or quasi-marketplace. For verbal responses, the number of possible settings is almost infinite.

Data collection can be divided into two phases: ir
fieldwork. Instrument design deals with the translation
tion into a series of specific questions or tasks for the
research. It encompasses the precise wording and defir
individual questions or tasks, the establishment of the
for the individual inquiries, and the design of forn
sponses—including the delineation of acceptable respo
for completing the form. Fieldwork deals with the proce
data collection process: the communication media used
vision of personnel, methods for securing cooperation,
Chapter 4 covers instrument design, and Chapter 5 cov

The distinguishing features of a well-designed data
are its ability to convey the proper message and its a
message clearly. Since communication depends on the pe
as the message, we must not consider instrument design
fieldwork. The two rely on each other; they are joint c
place of communication in instrument design is best seen
four parties in the overall research plan: decision maker,
and observed. Were it not for the interplay among these i
communication channel, a large portion of marketin;
impossible. However, the existence of these different ro
potential inaccuracy and distortion in communication.

FOUR ROLES IN DATA COLLECTION

All data collection takes the same form: the research
decision maker, asks the observer to record his or her ob;
specific units of the universe. There are always four rc
researcher, observer, and observed—although there nee
separate persons. Communication between the decis
researcher was discussed extensively under problem defin
in this chapter will be on the other three roles.

There may be instances in which the researcher is al
is not usually the case, and the objectivity of the observa
when it occurs. The researcher is, however, frequently f
the observer and the observed should be different
researcher and observer are different individuals, pro
communication and cooperation. Does the observer
question posed? Is he or she willing to obtain the infor
specified? The answers to these two questions tend to ma
researcher to act as the observer. Unfortunately, the rese
sider whether he or she is capable of acting as the observe
not possess the required technical competence in certain
or may not be a well-qualified interviewer for interviewi

subject matter and the goals of the research. A publisher of Sunday school curricular material is currently interested in learning more about how its material is being used, and current users' evaluations of the material. Communication among the parties occupying the four roles is fraught with potential difficulties.

The terms observer and observed are used in a very broad sense. The observer may observe in the restricted sense of "observing" the response to a verbal inquiry. The observed then is simply a respondent whose verbal response is being "observed." True behavior is not being observed in this situation; rather, verbal responses are being observed. The UAW tests are extremely critical when the respondent makes a statement concerning his or her past or expected behavior. Behavior is not objectively measured in this case but is inferred from a verbal response.

Communication in conjunction with nonexperimental research is often a major problem. The researcher (or the observer) is not in control of the environment. He or she enters either a naturally developing environment or an environment controlled by another. The tasks presented and the behavior evoked will vary. Some will be relevant while others will not. The data collection instrument and the accompanying instructions must be clear and precise. The observer must pick and choose among a surplus of activities, selecting the data that apply to the specific research. The situation is best described by the pervasive question, "How do you recognize an observation when you see one?" The answer must come from the wording of the data collection instrument and its instructions.

STRUCTURED VERSUS UNSTRUCTURED QUESTIONS

The issue of structure versus a lack of structure arises in three stages of instrument design: the wording of the individual questions, the provisions of alternative responses to the individual questions, and the overall sequence of questions. A specific question is structured when its wording is to be employed without deviation. Structure is further incorporated when the admissible responses are enumerated. Finally, the overall study is structured when a set sequence of questions is to be followed.

Structure is introduced in order to assure comparability. Changes in wording, sequence, or alternatives presented invite changes in meaning. Unless all respondents reply to the same inquiry, the interpretation of results based on their combination will be uncertain.

Why would anyone intentionally use an unstructured approach? The answer is simply that the researcher may not be sure which structure is most appropriate. In exploratory research the problem has not been fully defined. An unstructured approach is required in order to secure an adequate definition. In other situations, complex relationships may be involved. Motivations and sequence of actions require probing and flexibility. It is possible to attempt to structure the questioning with a series of "If answer to question 3 is A, ask question 4. If answer is B, ask question 7." That approach becomes extremely cumbersome as the number of such instructions increases. It may be impossible to anticipate all of the alternative responses and the appropriate follow-up questions. Insistence on complete structure means that qualifications and additional information are lost.

Unstructured individual questions are recommended in two situations. First, an unstructured overall survey may call for the inclusion of certain enumerated items as well as a general coverage of specified topics. For example, a study of voting behavior may include specific socioeconomic data and past voting record plus a series of open-ended questions concerning the images projected by the current candidates. The appropriate lead-in or precise wording may depend on what has transpired earlier in the interview. In this case, the interviewer should be thoroughly familiar with the concept sought but may choose the wording that seems most appropriate. Second, the objective of a question is to secure information with respect to a particular concept. If different words convey the desired meaning to different respondents, deviation in question wording should be employed. There is no quarrel with this principle; the difficulty is in recognizing it when it is encountered. All too often in practice, the interviewer does not vary the wording to fit the respondent but uses his or her revised question in all interviews.

A study of supermarket image asked respondents to indicate their opinion of the prices charged by different kinds of stores. Short descriptions were presented, and the respondents were to "give the answer that comes to your mind first—very quickly." This is a highly structured approach; departures from the precise wording or the introduction of additional phrases might modify the results considerably. "A store that offers lots of extra services" may bring about an entirely different response from "A store that offers lots of extra services—like the Colonial up the street." Other attempts to explain the concept would be equally poor since they would focus the respondent's attention on a particular store or particular service rather than the more general question. Explanation of the question, "How long have you lived in this neighborhood?", on the other hand, should be possible by specifying the geographic limits or by indicating an approximate distance. Of course, all interviewers must have the same concept of the neighborhood.[3]

The general conclusion to both unstructured individual questions and an overall unstructed approach is two-fold: (1) in exploratory research it is preferable to a structured approach, and (2) for well-defined problems it is acceptable only if the observer or interviewer has both a clear understanding of the concepts sought and the competence to secure responses that conform to those concepts. Otherwise, a well-defined problem degenerates into further explora-

---

[3]For this particular survey the borders of the "neighborhood" were defined in terms of specific streets.

tory research. This additional exploratory research may be required, but the researcher should not fall into the self-deception of believing it to be anything more than that.

The tasks of securing competent interviewers and their cost are strong deterrents to large-scale unstructured projects. Broad but imprecise instructions are given to the interviewers since a routine has not been established. Great skill is needed to implement such an assignment. A further deterrent is the high degree of subjectivity in both guiding the interview and the later interpretation of the data collected. Offsetting these disadvantages is the powerful argument that a well-structured questionnaire for the wrong question is a high price to pay for precision and reliability.

The preceding discussion of unstructured questions and questionnaires has dealt almost exclusively with direct person-to-person interviewing. The discussion could also apply to assignments calling for task completion. Unstructured approaches used in mail questionnaires are even more difficult. Probes to guide the respondents are impossible except through an exchange of correspondence.

Provision for Responses

An unstructured apporoach in dealing with the possible responses is more common than is an unstructured approach to either individual question wording or question sequence. The completely unstructured approach with respect to responses is the open-ended question: "Why did you purchase a Ford?" The structured approach enumerates the admissible alternatives for the respondent: "Do you own an automobile? Yes____ No____." Ambiguity enters when failure to enumerate the alternatives generates possible gradations in the response. Consider the question, "What percentage of your fuel oil did you purchase from McGee Distributors?" The number of potential answers is infinite; the researcher has not structured the admissible alternatives for the respondent. The question is open-ended and unstructured with respect to responses even though the researcher may have expected answers with a specified degree of precision.

There are basically three alternatives available in specifying the form desired for the response: (1) open-ended, (2) multichotomous, and (3) dichotomous. The open-ended form has the advantage of not forcing the respondent into the researcher's mold. Unanticipated responses and the respondent's manner of articulating responses are permitted. An open-ended question concerning ways of using or storing a product would not constrain the respondent by enumerating specific categories. Thus the research would be more likely to reveal unsuspected uses or storage patterns.

The open-ended question has the disadvantage that processing and editing are more difficult. A recent study of sales personnel with respect to training and education asked for the name of the college attended, if any. Over 200 different institutions were named. Two different types of problems ensued in the analysis: (1) how to identify cases in which different designations referred to the same institution and (2) whether the analysis was concerned with types of institutions or their precise identity. For example, some respondents named the Wharton School and others stated the University of Pennsylvania. The researcher had to decide, *after the data were in*, whether these responses should be combined or whether the separate schools within the University of Pennsylvania should be treated as separate institutions. If the latter, a broader category of "University of Pennsylvania" was also needed—although it was not strictly comparable with other data within the tabulations.

The coding of open-ended responses can be evaluated by having two or more judges classify the same answers. Unless a high level of agreement exists, the use and interpretation of the data for the decision problem invites unnecessary risks. Insistence on *interjudge reliability* is a good insurance policy for any form of unstructured approach.

The multichotomous question is a fixed alternative approach with several options available. For example, an income question might specify the following alternatives:

Under $6,000
$6,000–9,999
$10,000–14,999
$15,000–19,999
$20,000–29,999
$30,000 and over

Six alternatives are provided and the respondent is to select one. The number of alternatives and the size of the intervals will vary with the research objectives and the population involved. Multichotomous alternatives may be of the type "select one" or "select as many as are appropriate." Income is obviously in the first category as is a question asking for the "most important reason" or "the most preferred brand." Reasons why, preferred brands, magazines read, etc. may also be placed in a structured format but with permission to select more than one response category. Only the decision maker and researcher can decide which procedure is appropriate for their objectives.

The dichotomous question is also a fixed alternative approach but with only two alternatives available. "Have you ever read *Consumer Reports*?" "Are you presently employed?" Both of these questions offer yes–no alternatives. Another example of a dichotomous question is "Do you prefer gas or electricity for cooking?" Other examples refer to a choice between more and less of a particular ingredient and a choice between two political candidates. Any paired comparison test—choose between two alternatives—falls into this category.

An interesting mixture of structured and unstructured approaches occurs when the interviewer, unknown to the respondent, has been instructed to place each response into one of *n* categories. This procedure is more a matter of strategy than of structure. The researcher has determined the structure; this structure is simply not revealed to the respondent. This procedure may be followed for any one of a number of reasons. The number of categories may be so great that enumeration to the respondent may be tedious and time consuming. The presentation of a list—which must be done in some order—may introduce a bias because of the order in which alternatives are presented. The researcher may have only partial structure in his or her potential responses. The exclusion of some responses from the list is a strong bias against the exclusions. The open-ended presentation avoids this danger.

Research seeking to determine recall rates for ads, familiarity with specific brands, and awareness of product features must choose between *aided* and *unaided* recall approaches. Aided recall shows or names the items for the respondent who is asked to identify those that are "recalled." Unaided recall asks the respondent to list or name items "recalled" without providing any help in the form of a list, pictures, etc. Unaided recall, thus, is an unstructured approach since it does not present the response categories to the respondent. It is simultaneously a structured approach if the interviewer is working with a preestablished set of categories.

The failure to provide structure for the respondent increases the task of respondent, interviewer, and editor. More time, more writing, and more tedious processing are necessary. All increase cost and may decrease the quantity and quality of responses.

Depth Interview

The depth interview is an unstructured approach to a specific subject. The publisher of Sunday school material referred to earlier employed a series of depth interviews in its exploratory research. The depth interview is characterized by the identification of the area of interest, open-ended questions, and a continual probing for further explanations and details. The depth interview may be either on an individual or group basis—with the latter identified as a *focus group interview*.

The Sunday school publisher used both depth interviews and focus group interviews in its project. The individual interviews were conducted with two types of individuals: those making decisions regarding the ordering of curricular material and teachers who were using the material. The focus group interviews were conducted with classes using the material. These group interviews were taped in order to retain all comments without introducing a "note-taking" environment.

Two basic kinds of questions are used in the depth interview: (1) those identifying the subjects of interest and (2) neutral probes to encourage further discussion. Each is introduced in an informal manner, free of the restrictions imposed by a formal list of precisely worded questions. The key to a good depth interview is to get the respondents to talk freely about the subject of interest.

The initial opening for the depth interview is usually constant. For example, "We would like to learn a little more about your views of the proposed cross-town expressway. How do you feel about it?" Such an opening merely identifies the subject. It does not specify any particular aspect—the respondents are free to choose the aspects that are of most concern to them. The interviewer interacts with the respondents but in a neutral way. Comments such as "Isn't that interesting!" "Why do you feel that way?" and "Could you tell me more about that?" are typical. The interviewer has in mind specific aspects or topics to be covered, but the sequence is determined by the issues raised by the respondents and the nature of their remarks.

The focus group interview provides the added dimension of respondent interaction. Individual members can react to the thoughts of other members. The group setting also tends to reduce inhibitions that may exist in a one-on-one individual interview. A good interviewer can establish an environment in which individuals both "piggyback" on the ideas of others and feel free to disagree with others—sometimes rather forcefully. The group interview does possess a possible inhibiting effect if a particular individual is dominant.[4]

DISGUISED VERSUS UNDISGUISED QUESTIONS

Is it ever counterproductive to tell the respondent what you are really investigating? Attitudes or behavior patterns that do not have the complete sanction of society pose major data collection difficulties. Questions must be clear and understandable, but it may be necessary to conceal the deeper implications of the questions.

Psychologists and psychiatrists have recognized for a long time that direct questioning on certain subjects may be of little value. The patient may be either unwilling or unable to supply accurate answers to the direct questions. When the use of a more sympathetic intermediary will not overcome the difficulties, the researcher—following the lead of the psychologist—frequently substitutes indirect methods. L. K. Frank applied the term "projective method" to a group of these indirect methods.[5] In the projective method, the individual's responses are not taken at face value. The approach assumes that the respondent will interpret the given question or situation in terms of his or her own motives or perceptions although the superficial presentation has been nonpersonal.

---

[4]The presence of the teacher in some of the Sunday school class interviews caused less than optimal results because of the teacher's dominant role.

[5]L. K. Frank, 1939, Projective methods for the study of personality, *Journal of Psychology* **8**: 389–413.

Third-person Technique

The simplest projective method is the third-person technique. Respondents are asked about behavior, attitudes, or motivations of their neighbors, friends, or people in general. Respondents can "project" their own answers to others without subjecting themselves to the restraints of social acceptability. Topics such as personal hygiene and racial prejudice are examples of material that may be investigated in this manner.

The technique may also be useful in situations in which respondents are unaware of their own feelings. They may refuse, and indeed may be unable, to respond honestly. If asked to analyze and explain actions of third parties, they can "project" their hitherto unrecognized responses onto the others without feeling threatened.

The third-person technique is particularly appropriate for discovering buying motives. The respondent may be asked to explain the probable reason an acquaintance would purchase a particular product or patronize a particular store. Or a hypothetical situation may be presented; for example, "If a friend of yours were trying to impress a business client, what restaurant would your friend probably choose?"

Several other types of projective techniques may be used for marketing research. Among them are sentence completion, word association, Thematic Apperception Tests (TAT), and story completion. The use of projective techniques assumes that the respondents will "project" themselves into the situation presented. If they answer for others instead of projecting themselves into the situation, the approach has failed. This is the essence of the disguised question: because the researcher believes the respondent is either unable or unwilling to supply the requested information, the researcher changes from a direct to an indirect approach via the disguised question.

Sentence Completion Questions

The sentence completion question requires the respondent to finish sentences that are incomplete. The usual technique is to instruct the respondent to respond with his or her first thought. Some examples taken from different studies are

> *"Crest appeals to people who . . . . "*
>
> *"Our local school board should . . . ."*
>
> *"A man who drives a Buick is . . . . "*
>
> *"The typical shopper at Super Saver is . . . . "*

Responses to these questions may be extremely varied. No single dimension is identified. The respondent supplies his or her own framework and categories. The advantage of the sentence completion question lies in the absence of a "forced fit"—the researcher does not force the respondent into a framework that is at variance with the respondent's thought pattern. Its principal disadvantage is the difficulty experienced in summarizing the data. Should "are concerned with status" be combined with "try to keep up appearances"? Are "be more careful of the budget" and "spend less money" two different categories or the same? The objective with the sentence completion is to secure responses unencumbered by role playing. The difficulty encountered in processing is the price paid.

Word Association Questions

Word association questions are even less structured than are sentence completion questions. The underlying assumption is that the respondent reveals his or her free associations. A time delay in responding to any particular stimulus word casts doubt on the validity of the particular response—consequently, the analysis might be restricted to only those responses obtained instantaneously.

Some of the words presented in a study of mutual funds might be

Stock	*Risk*	*Commission*
Insurance	*Growth*	*Stability*
Broker	*Sales person*	*Income*
Bond	*Dividend*	*Safety*

Depending on how familiar the respondents are with the mutual fund industry, the names of particular funds might be included.

The usual list of words would include both "stimulating" and "neutral" words. The neutral words are mixed throughout the list in order to introduce a control and to minimize a carry-over of a specific mental set. The analysis of word association questions may focus on the specific word responses, but they more commonly classify responses on specific dimensions. Typical dimensions are favorable–unfavorable, pleasant–unpleasant, strong–weak, and male–female. Potential names for a new product might be tested by this approach. The desirable attributes for the name, of course, would depend on the product and the market target.

Image studies often use the quick response approach, mixing neutral stimuli with words or ideas that are of prime concern. The approach is equally appropriate for stores, products, manufacturers, or even political candidates. Responses are usually open-ended although constraints have been introduced successfully. For example, the respondent might be instructed to indicate what vacation spot first comes to mind with each of a number of words. The words are often a mixture of two dimensions: (1) descriptors that imply favorable or unfavorable impressions and (2) descriptors that show the presence or absence of specific features. Examples of such words are glamorous, golf, family, mountains, quiet, expensive, dull, swimming, historic, hot, crowded, luxurious, and fun. The sponsoring community would be interested in appraising its own image and identifying the strongest competition on specific characteristics.

Thematic Apperception Test (TAT)

The Thematic Apperception Test has been used by clinical psychologists for a number of years. A picture or series of pictures is presented to the subject who is to interpret what is happening. The individual's responses serve as the basis for assessing his or her attitude toward a particular product or situation. It is assumed that the respondent will "project" his or her feelings into the situation, thereby revealing his or her attitudes.

Customer reaction to defective merchandise or poor service can be investigated by the TAT approach, using two cartoons. The first cartoon shows the customer becoming aware of the problem. The second is to be completed by the respondent. The picture may simply show a blank "balloon" in which the respondent is to supply the statement made by the customer.

Another version of TAT might show two pictures of women shopping for a dress. The first picture shows a cramped display room filled with pipe racks. The second shows wall-to-wall carpeting and several mannequins displaying current fashions. The respondent is asked to describe (1) the kinds of women shopping in the different establishments and (2) the dresses carried by the two stores. The order of presentation of the two pictures would be randomized—thus adjusting for any possible order effect.

Storytelling

Storytelling is a more general technique than TAT.[6] The respondent is presented a portion of a story—enough to center attention on a particular issue, but not enough to indicate the conclusion. The respondent is then asked to finish the story. Ambiguity must exist in the presentation; otherwise the respondent cannot reflect his or her attitudes and feelings.

The following example shows how storytelling could be used in exploring the response to a proposed new product.

> *As winter approached, Joe Holmes thought he should purchase a pair of snow tires. He inquired about current prices at several tire outlets. A workman at one outlet informed Joe of a new product that could be*

---

[6]TAT might best be considered a projective technique using pictures or cartoons. Stories, in the sense of a continuous flow, may be involved or not. A simple response describing a particular aspect of a picture would still fall into the general projective technique of TAT. Storytelling, whether with or without pictures, involves a continuity and a conclusion supplied by the respondent.

*sprayed on regular tires to improve traction. It was supposed to be ef-
fective for up to five miles, and one can contained enough for three or
four applications. The workman said that at 98¢ a can the spray was a
better buy than snow tires for anyone who drove short distances.*

What was Joe's response?

Why?

A Classic in Disguised Questions

One of the best known applications of the disguised question was made by
Mason Haire in 1950.[7] He constructed two grocery shopping lists, identical except that one contained Nescafé Instant Coffee and the other contained Maxwell House (drip grind). In an unstructured approach, matched samples of
housewives were asked to describe the woman who made up each shopping list.
The housewife with Nescafé Instant on her list was described as lazy by 48 percent of the respondents; only 4 percent described the woman with Maxwell
House as lazy. Other differences appearing between the two referred to failure
to plan, lack of thrift, plus a lower proportion classifying the Nescafé woman
as a "good wife" (4 percent versus 16 percent). Research using an undisguised
approach had failed to disclose these dimensions.

BIAS

Most of the problems associated with data collection are examples of bias.
Bias consists of systematic errors that would be present in the data even if a
complete census of the universe were employed—therefore it is not reduced
with larger samples. The sources of these errors are misunderstood questions,
faulty memory, outright lies, missing data, careless measurements, improperly
calibrated instruments, etc.

Bias is measured by the difference between the "true" value in the universe (according to the problem definition) and the average value that would
be obtained by repeating the specific procedure over all possible applications.
If there is no difference between the two values, the procedure is *unbiased*. The
procedure is evaluated, not a specific result. In order to know whether a procedure is biased, one must know the universe value. Since we practically never
have this kind of information, we rarely *know* whether our procedure is biased. The only practical way of assessing a method for bias is to give careful
consideration to the various phases of the project. Revisions when the proce-

---

[7]Mason Haire, 1950, Projective techniques in marketing research, *Journal of Marketing* **14:**
649–652. The experiment was repeated by Webster and von Pechmann with some of the same results. F. E. Webster and F. von Pechmann, 1970, A replication of the "shopping list" study,
Journal of Marketing **34:** 61–63.

dure seems dubious will decrease the magnitude of the bias, but these revisions cannot be based upon rigorously derived formulas.

There are numerous sources of potential bias in data collection. Each ultimately comes down to the same point: the data as collected, edited, and processed do not correspond to the "truth" in the population of interest. All of the issues raised in our discussion of structured versus unstructured and disguised versus undisguised approaches arise from a desire to reduce bias. Essentially we must ask which procedures are most likely to yield responses that correspond to the characteristics as contained in the problem definition.

Wording of Individual Questions

A few general rules-of-thumb exist for the wording of individual questions, but it is more an art than a science.[8] Some of the more important principles are avoid unnecessary questions, use simple words, avoid "leading" questions, focus on the desired issue, consider alternative wordings, and be sure the question passes the UAW test.

Avoid asking unnecessary questions. A research project is difficult enough when it is limited to the essential matters. The temptation to add related and interesting inquiries is always strong. They might turn out to be significant; why not collect that additional information since its incremental cost will be slight? There is no end to the possible additions, and the incremental cost may not be slight. Interviewer time, editing, and data processing costs are all increased. Rapport may also be sacrificed by the addition of unnecessary questions. The principal exception to the advisability of adding questions is the situation in which transitions are needed and rapport is facilitated. In these cases, the "questions" are more interview procedures than inquiries; and the need to include them in data analysis is dubious.

The first draft of a questionnaire to be used by a pen manufacturer ran five pages. If all of the information was necessary, then the questionnaire had to remain at that length. The objective was to determine the response of prospective buyers to a new type of pen and any differential responses by significant market segments. A whole series of questions on consumer characteristics was deleted because management did not envision differential actions that would be taken for different findings. Some of the characteristics in this category were "handedness" (right- or left-handed), average number of letters written per month, color ink preferred, size of family, and age of children. While these were all interesting or related to pen use "in some way," they were not relevant to the decision involved. Questions on sex, age, and income were retained as potentially significant in market segmentation decisions.

---

[8]One of the better works on questionnaire design is Stanley L. Payne, 1951, *The Art of Asking Questions* (Princeton, N.J.: Princeton University Press).

An example of a transitional question occurred in a survey of alumni of a large college. This particular survey covered only graduates. Despite this limitation of the universe, the question "Did you graduate from _____?" was included as a convenient transition from one topic to another. The question could also serve as a check on whether the respondent was eligible for inclusion although this was not a problem in the particular study.

Use simple words. "Specialty goods," "shopping goods," and "convenience goods" have specific definitions within marketing; but use of the terms in a general survey invites disaster. Technical terms are appropriate only when the universe is composed of technicians. A questionnaire concerning unleaded gasolines that asks about "dieseling" runs the risk of not communicating properly.

Aside from the terms germane to the subject matter of the research, the general vocabulary level should be kept simple. One- and two-syllable words in common usage are best. Nothing is gained by introducing words such as anticipate, innocuous, and emancipate when expect, harmless, and set free will do as well.

Avoid "leading" questions. The specific wording of a question can "lead" the respondent toward certain responses. There are a number of ways of doing this, but they all in effect say, "This is the correct answer, isn't it?" The insertion of highly emotional words will produce large swings in the responses. "Radical" Senator X will receive a lower rating than "Progressive" Senator X. In recent months several politically active groups have conducted public opinion "surveys." The questions have been framed in terms of "Do you think you have the right to choose . . . ?" on the one hand, versus "Do you think government has the duty to help the downtrodden . . . ?" on the other.

Another version of the "leading" question is the presentation of a particular view, asking the extent to which the respondent agrees or disagrees. Different results occur depending on the view presented;[9] the third alternative of a neutral question tends to produce still different results. Even the results from the neutral phrasing may depend on the sequence in which the alternatives are named.

Many marketers want to combine research and promotion. Whenever the product or company is presented in the most favorable light, the respondent is being "led" into favorable responses. Such a simple factor as identification of the sponsor will bias the results. Insertion of introductory remarks run the risk of distorting responses. "Recent investigations by Ralph Nader. . . . " will change the mental set from what it would be without the opening phrase.

---

[9]See, for example, Stephen A. Greyser, 1962, Businessmen re advertising: "Yes, but. . ." *Harvard Business Review* **40**: 28.

The interpretation of results also relates to the issue of the leading question. "What is the audience for a particular TV show?" Define audience! Consider these three questions, all of which refer to "The Waltons" (June 21, 1979).

Did you watch the entire program, including all commercials in their entirety?

Did you watch over half the program?

Did you see any of the program?

The reader can compose other variations. The "leading" nature of the various questions occurs when the results or interpretations gloss over the precise wording employed.

Focus on the desired issue. "What was the total cost of your most recent supermarket order?" Does the researcher want to know about my last purchase regardless of whether it was a "fill-in" or a full-scale shopping trip? Is the researcher asking about my impression of expenditures, or does he or she want as precise a figure as possible? Does he or she really want to know about the last trip, or is he or she interested in a typical trip? The presence of an interviewer could clarify some of these issues, but the researcher should do all he or she can to be sure the respondent's attention is directed toward the dimension of interest.

Questions dealing with buying decisions and motivations often yield dissimilar type responses. "Why did you purchase Del Monte pears at Kroeger's on your last trip?" The article, the place, and the time are all involved. Different respondents may answer in terms of any one of these dimensions or a combination of them. They may also answer in terms of their appraisal of the situation or indicate other parties made the selection—which may or may not be useful information.

The question concerning the purchase of pears also illustrates another frequent source of difficulty. *Are several questions needed instead of one?* If reasons are desired for each aspect of the purchase, a separate question should be introduced for each aspect. "Why did you switch to Dial?" Implicit in this question are assumptions: (1) the respondent used some soap other than Dial at some time in the past and (2) the respondent is now a user of Dial. Both assumptions should be verified by other questions. Only after establishing that a "switch to Dial" has occurred should the research endeavor to ascertain why.

Consider alternative wordings. Many of the biases generated by poorly phrased questions could be avoided by the simple expedient of searching for alternatives. Would it be better to ask about past activities or expected future activities? Should the focus be on a specific event or general behavior? How long a period should be covered for factual information? Should modifying adjectives be employed? The consideration of alternative wordings does not supply an additional criterion for selection; it merely provides the opportunity of applying the various criteria.

Three alternative wordings regarding TV watching of a specific episode of "The Waltons" were given above. The distinction in that illustration stressed the portion of the program that must be watched in order to classify as a "viewer." Consider the following alternative wordings in a study of brand preference.

Which toaster would you prefer to receive as a gift: General Electric, Proctor, or Sunbeam?

Who do you think makes the best toaster: General Electric, Proctor, or Sunbeam?

Which toaster would you be most likely to buy if you were making a purchase today: General Electric, Proctor, or Sunbeam?

"Preference" is recorded in a different context in each case. The appropriate context depends on the definition of the problem.

The UAW test. The question must be *understood* by the respondent—communication must occur. The respondent must be *able* to supply the information requested—the information must be within the respondent's accessibility, either by memory or otherwise. The respondent must be *willing* to supply the information—the request must not be unreasonable either in terms of the effort required or in terms of the confidential nature of the information.

Sequence of Questions

The order in which questions occur establishes the mental framework in which each successive question is answered. The order also influences the rapport achieved. A logical flow should be established. Shifting unnecessarily among topics may hinder the thought process and may also reduce rapport.

The opening questions pose a difficult problem. They should simultaneously arouse interest, be easy to answer, and not bias the answers that follow. A food shopping survey may use screening questions that qualify the respondent as one who does the food shopping within a particular geographic area. "When did you last take a vacation?" creates interest, is easily answered by most people, and does not arouse antagonism. "Precisely how far did you travel on your last vacation?" generates difficulties even though the subject of vacations has a high degree of natural interest.

The more difficult and personal questions should be placed toward the end of the questionnaire. The respondent must be at ease and involved in the project before his or her memory is taxed, complicated tasks are presented, or confidential inquiries are made. Classification questions should be placed toward the close for another reason as well: the respondent should not be thinking of age, family size, owner-renter status, income, and other socioeconomic characteristics as he or she responds to the basic research topic. The researcher who wishes responses to be consciously conditioned by such factors can introduce them at appropriate points. Otherwise, it is better to delay such inquiries until the final section of the questionnaire.

The actual sequence of subject matter questions depends on the specific project. Attitudes, purchases, exposure to media, consumption patterns—there is no correct sequence, but each possible sequence will probably change the mental set for succeeding sections.

Format for Responses

We discussed the format for responses under the subject of structure earlier in this chapter and also referred to its connection with the general rule to consider several alternatives before selecting one procedure. The precise format and procedure to employ in presenting a list of alternatives to the respondent is a pervasive source of potential bias. An item is more likely to be checked when it is the first item on the list than when it is in any other position. The bias against items not on the list is extremely strong.

The bias in favor of the first item on a list increases as the size of the list increases. The upward bias also extends beyond the first item when the size of the list is increased. With long lists, the items toward the center have a relative handicap in comparison with both the first items and the last items.

A further bias with respect to list questions is an overstatement bias. This is seen most clearly by positive responses to nonexistent items, regardless of whether use, familiarity, or other behavior is of concern. As discussed earlier, this is one relative advantage for unaided recall over aided recall although the bias is not removed entirely in the unaided approach. Listing of items in alphabetical order does not eliminate the bias, and it is unclear that it even reduces it. The use of several forms with rotated positions on the list can yield a balancing and remove the order bias. That procedure adds to costs and is not satisfactory when cross-classification of respondents is involved.

Consider the question, "From which of the following have you rented an auto during the past year?" If primary interest centered on Avis, Budget, Hertz, and National, 24 different sequences are possible. To achieve a perfect balance, all 24 sequences should be employed with 1/24 of the questionnaires using each sequence. A compromise would be to use only the four sequences presented below:

Hertz	Avis	Budget	National
Avis	National	Hertz	Budget
Budget	Hertz	National	Avis
National	Budget	Avis	Hertz

Each firm appears in each position once. Each firm also immediately precedes each other firm once and immediately follows each other firm once. More complex relationships are not completely balanced,[10] but these four may provide an acceptable compromise.

The list question requires specific instructions. Is a single alternative to be selected? If more than one, can each respondent name as many as he or she wishes or are all to name the same number? If more than one, are the items to be ranked or merely checked? If three (or any other number) are to be checked, what is done if fewer are named by some respondents?

Classification questions often pose problems in establishing the admissible responses. The researcher must set the precision required, the number of categories, and the class limits. Age might be requested in many different formats. Four are given below.

1. Date of birth: Year _____ Month _____ Day _____

2. Age: _____

3. Age: Under 18 _____, 18 or over _____

4. Age: 0–19 _____

    20–39 _____

    40–59 _____

    60–79 _____

    80 and over _____

Alternative 3 asks for the least detail. Two guiding principles should be checked before the simplest alternative is used: (1) does either the decision maker or researcher need more precise information and (2) is the question or format likely to introduce bias? The use of 18 as a point of demarcation suggests that the age of 18 is critical to the decision maker. If so, the question may secure sufficient detail. But will responses be biased by the format? The respondents are sensitized to 18 as potentially critical. Will they be led by some self-interest or some desired self-image to slip themselves into one category when the other is correct?

Alternative 1 asks for a precise date, probably greater precision than is required. The format may seem less threatening, however. Alternative 2 is an open-ended approach that runs the risk of differential rounding and unequal bias on the part of respondents. Some persons will respond to the nearest year; others will round to a multiple of five or ten—probably with some downward

---

[10]For example, Avis never follows Budget by two positions although it follows each of the others by two positions once.

bias. The researcher will have an uncertain mixture with no sure way of knowing the correct interpretation of the data.

Alternatives 1 and 2 both have analytic superiority over alternatives 3 and 4 if the researcher can have confidence in the data. The precision means that single numbers rather than ranges are associated with each respondent. This detail enables the researcher to do a more efficient job in the analysis.[11]

The general format of alternative 4 is probably used more often than the others. The researcher can vary the number of classes and the class limits according to the requirements of the particular research. Care should be exercised in the statement of the limits to prevent overlaps and gaps. The classes presented above suggest that the age of each individual is first thought of in terms of years and then the proper assignment is made. If this is not true, gaps appear in the classes—some individuals could not be assigned. Age categories of "0–20, 20–40, . . ." would overlap; the correct category for a person aged 20 would be ambiguous. Each unit should fall into no more than one category for characteristics such as age, education, and income. In general, class limits for the measurement of such characteristics should be *mutually exclusive* (no overlap) and *exhaustive* (no gaps).

If a given respondent can be placed into more than one category, the question then takes the form of a series of yes–no questions: "Is this category appropriate for you?" With a single alternative to be chosen from the list, the categories should be both mutually exclusive and exhaustive. The exhaustive property is often met by adding a final category of "Other."

"Don't Know" Answers

What does an answer of "Don't know" mean? Is it different from "No answer"? Consider the following question: "What brand of paper towels did you last purchase?" A blank gives no information. Answers of "I never buy paper towels" or "I don't remember" give specific information. Should three separate categories be established for classifying responses?

Another question in the same study might be concerned with expenditures for paper towels. Again possible confusion might develop among answers that do not provide the requested information. The desired information is numerical. Therefore caution must be employed that a blank or "I don't know" or "I don't remember" is not recorded as a zero—implying a price of zero. One or more separate categories must be established. This caution is particularly needed in punching information for computer input where the distinction between a zero and a blank will be critical. Care must also be exercised in the recording of answers such as "I can't remember" lest the processing interpret a numerical code as a dollars-and-cents figure.

---

[11]This is particularly true in the analysis of relationships among characteristics, a subject introduced in Part III together with a discussion of the appropriate techniques.

SCALES AND MEASUREMENT

Answers to any question presume a set of alternatives, and these alternatives exist on some type of measuring device or scale. "What brand do you prefer?" suggests the existence of several alternative answers. Are these alternatives merely different categories with no *a priori* order or is there a particular order? If there is an order, can the differences between alternatives be measured? The researcher must decide the kind of scale that is appropriate for each concept. Possible scales range from a simple two or three-category classification system to very precise numerical measurements.

Four-measure categories exist for the classification of scales: nominal, ordinal, interval, and ratio. Each has its own underlying assumptions, and each possesses its own mathematical properties. It should be stressed that the concept does not uniquely determine the scale to be employed. Most concepts can be measured on at least two of the scales. Usually the researcher must take the lead in considering what type scale to use since the decision maker may not even know there is an issue to settle.

A *nominal* scale consists of categories. If numbers are used to designate the various categories, they are for purposes of identification or labeling rather than any ordering or measurement—nonnumeric symbols would serve just as well. Units are classified according to their membership in the various categories. Units assigned to the same category are deemed equivalent with respect to property under investigation.

A typical textbook illustration for a nominal scale is football players' jersey numbers. The numbers serve as a basis for distinguishing among the players or their positions. The numbers are convenient labels. They neither order nor measure differences among players with respect to a particular characteristic. A preference test among five competing products might also employ a nominal scale. In this case the competing products would be numbered one through five and each respondent would be asked to designate which of the five he or she preferred. The only appropriate way of using the labels one through five would be to indicate the number of respondents who chose each one as his or her preference. Thus nominal scales permit only the most elementary mathematical operations: a counting of the number of units in each category, the calculation of the percentage of total units in a category, and certain tests based on one or the other of these two statistics. The nominal scale is usually the least precise of the four scales, giving the least detail in measurement but also imposing the smallest demands in the collection phase. Examples of characteristics frequently measured on nominal scales in marketing research are occupation, state of residence, store last visited, and newspaper read most frequently. As we continue to the other three types of scales, the reader should consider under what conditions and assumptions these characteristics might be measured on scales other than the nominal.

Sex is also a nominal scale. A coding of 0–1 (or 1–2 or any other two numbers) does not suggest that one sex is higher or lower than the other. Categories existing on a nominal scale can be transformed into a series of yes–no questions instead of a single question. "Which of the following sections of the newspaper do you usually read first?" is the equivalent of a series of questions asking whether a particular section is the one the respondent usually reads first.[12]

Ordinal scales are ranking scales. The use of numbers for an ordinal scale implies greater than or less than. It does not carry a connotation of how much more or how much less, but simply that an item ranked third has less of a given characteristic than an item ranked second. Use of an ordinal scale for a preference test comparing five different products would call for the ranking of the five different products.

An ordinal scale need not use numbers. Use of the three categories: "low," "average," and "high" would constitute an ordinal scale. Items assigned to the "average" category would possess less of the characteristic than items assigned to the "high" category. The same principle applies if the number of categories is considerably expanded. Any attempt by the researcher to assign numerical values to the word designations and to apply the arithmetic operation of addition to these numbers is technically not justified. Therefore, the researcher must be very careful in matching his or her problem definition and measurement scale with the analysis that is contemplated.[13] Many substantive marketing questions are often treated on ordinal scales in marketing research; some of those encountered quite often are attitudes, preferences, and various demographic data.

Attitudes or opinions are frequently studied by asking the respondent to react to a series of statements, indicating degree of agreement or disagreement. The respondent might be given the five alternatives of "Strongly agree," "Agree," "Not sure," "Disagree," and "Strongly disagree." A study of attitudes toward Israel included the following statements:

The United States should sell military weapons to Israel.

The recent rescue of hostages at Uganda by Israel was justified.

Many other statements were included. These two indicate favorable attitudes toward Israel. "Strongly agree" is more favorable than "Agree" which in turn is more favorable than "Not sure," etc. The five alternatives are "ordered." It is not clear, however, whether the difference in "favorableness–unfavorableness" between successive alternatives is equal. "Disagree" and "Strongly disagree" may be further apart than "Not sure" and "Disagree"; or the reverse

---

[12]This type of question gives rise to the "dummy variable" technique of multiple regression and discriminant analysis which will be discussed in Part III.

[13]Techniques do exist for transforming nominal, partial ordinal, and complete ordinal data into interval scales. We shall discuss these techniques in Part IV.

may be true. Thus conversion of the alternatives to 1, 2, 3, 4, and 5 and calculation of a mean is not justified.

The same situation exists if the respondent is asked to rate products or stores on various characteristics. For example, store patrons might be asked to rate the store's clerks on "helpfulness." The number of alternatives could be specified and descriptive phrases for each category specified. Alternatively, the number of categories might be specified with the dimension labeled as "helpful–not helpful." The categories at the two ends are, thus, the most extreme responses. This latter approach is called the *semantic differential*.[14] The respondent is given a set of bipolar adjectives similar to those in Table 4.1 and is asked to rate the subject store on each.[15]

An *interval* scale approaches our usual concept of "measure." Numerical values imply not only greater than or less than; they also imply constancy in the unit of measure. Consequently the difference between a "two" and a "three" is the same as the difference between a "seven" and an "eight." In the same way, a "five" is as much above a "four" as it is below a "six." The calculation of an "average" score by adding the values supplied by a group of respondents and dividing by the number of respondents assumes that the characteristic under study is measured on an interval scale. Calculation of an "average" score from a semantic differential assumes that respondents treat the categories as positions on an interval scale, not merely as positions on an ordinal scale.

The zero point of an interval scale is arbitrary. Temperature is probably the best known illustration, with both Fahrenheit and Celsius scales in com-

Table 4.1
Store Profile for Strawbridge & Clothier by a Semantic Differential

Modern	___	___	___	___	___	___	___ Old-fashioned
Deceptive advertising	___	___	___	___	___	___	___ Honest advertising
Friendly sales clerks	___	___	___	___	___	___	___ Unfriendly sales clerks
Convenient parking	___	___	___	___	___	___	___ Inconvenient parking
Sales clerks not helpful	___	___	___	___	___	___	___ Sales clerks helpful

[14]Charles E. Osgood, George J. Suci, and Percy H. Tannenbaum, 1957, *The Measurement of Meaning* (Urbana, Ill.: University of Illinois Press).

[15]The use of the semantic differential and other techniques in attitude measurement must deal with the number of categories employed and whether the alternatives should be symmetrical. Our purpose at this point is simply to illustrate the semantic differential as an ordinal scale.

mon use. It is not correct to say that a temperature of 80 °F. is twice as hot as a temperature of 40 °F. This can be seen by finding the corresponding Celsius temperatures (26 2/3° and 4 4/9°) which are in a ratio of about six to one.

If the scales given in Table 4.1 are assumed to be interval, the numbers assigned to the various categories are arbitrary. They must, however, correspond to equal "intervals." With seven categories, the numbers assigned could be 1 through 7; they could also be −3 to +3 with the midposition as 0.[16] The lack of descriptive phrases over each column is designed as an encouragement to impose an interval scale.

Consider the following question: "What is your overall rating of *The New Republic* magazine? Excellent____, Very good____, Good____, Fair____, Poor____, Very poor____." The categories do not form a symmetrical pattern. The words employed may not imply equal intervals. Consequently, the researcher would probably be remiss if he or she assumed the data represented more than an ordinal scale.

The *ratio* scale has a nonarbitrary zero point. Zero means the complete absence of the characteristic, and the ratio between scale values shows the ratio between observations with respect to the property being measured. For example, a price of six dollars is twice as much as a price of three dollars, a family of six is 50 percent larger than a family of four, and a store with 10,000 square feet of selling space has only 40 percent as much selling space as a store with 25,000 square feet.

The typical ultimate characteristic in business is the dollar, be it revenue, costs, or profit–loss. A value of zero has a unique meaning; it is not arbitrary. If the dollar is accepted as the principal characteristic of interest, decision criteria employ a ratio scale. This possesses a potential problem in research if characteristics are studied on scales that are of a lower order. If preference is measured on an interval or ordinal scale, the translation and comparison of results into a ratio scale of dollars may be impossible—or at best tenuous. Therefore, the decision maker must consider very carefully the relationship between the research results and the recommended action. What measure of preference warrants specific expenditures? How will preference convert into revenue?

Two-step Ordinal Scales

An interesting approach to determining a complete ranking may use two steps. At the first step, the respondent is asked to separate a group of objects into a limited number of categories. For example, the respondent may be asked to classify various product attributes as "Very important," "Important," or "Not important." These three categories are clearly on an ordinal scale, but all attributes within a particular category are deemed equivalent or tied.

---

[16]The assignment of the numbers 21, 27, 33, 39, 45, 51, and 57 would also conform to an interval scale. Any sequence with equal intervals meets the necessary condition.

The second step calls for a ranking or ordering of the attributes within each category. This step produces a complete ranking of all attributes. The two-step procedure has two distinct benefits. First, the respondent's assignment of generating a complete ranking is facilitated by breaking the task into steps. Second, the two-step process establishes critical points between categories.

Scale Properties and Subtleties

The distinctions among the four types of scales seem straightforward enough, but attempts to classify specific applications sometimes pose difficulties. Consider the following list of questions.

1. How many years of post high school education have you completed?

2. From what college did you graduate?

3. What was your income last year?

4. Rank the following five models from 1–5 according to which you would be most likely to purchase (1 for most likely, 2 for next, etc., to 5 for least likely).

5. If price per unit were decreased by ten cents, how many more or less units would you probably purchase per month?

6. Consider the following activities:
   a) Read a book, b) Play tennis, c) Make a cabinet. Which would you prefer?

The expected responses are that 2 and 6 are nominal, 4 is ordinal, and the others are ratio. The correct response is that none of the six can be classified until we know how the responses are to be interpreted and analyzed. The question form may suggest the nature of the scale, but it is not conclusive.

Number of years of post high school education would yield a nominal scale if all respondents with four or more were placed in one category and all others in a second category. A summary statistic could then present the percentage who have completed four or more years of post high school education. Retaining the question in its original form, is the zero an arbitrary point, or is it an absence of the characteristic studied? If the question had asked for years of formal education, the zero point would have been shifted. The ability to shift the zero point is associated with the interval scale rather than the ratio scale. One must be willing to defend the zero point as "correct" in order to claim one is working with a ratio scale. The reader should consider questions 3 and 5 from this same perspective. Are the zero points arbitrary for these characteristics?

College names would seem to be categories on a nominal scale, but suppose the decision maker is the director of admissions for a particular graduate school. He or she may have placed the various colleges in ordered categories in which case the scale employed is ordinal. He or she may have gone even further, and assumed that the scale possesses interval or even ratio properties. Once again it depends on how the response is treated in the analysis and interpretation. Question 6 can be revised from the apparent nominal scale in the same manner, again depending on the assumptions made.

Does the analyst or decision maker have any option in question 4 other than an ordinal scale? If only the first ranking model is worthwhile, the analysis may use the nominal approach of merely counting the number of first-place votes. If the ordinal scale is retained, could summary statistics be obtained by calculating the arithmetic mean rank? Only if two rankings in second place are equivalent to one rank in first and one rank in third. But that statement is appropriate for an interval scale—not for an ordinal scale.

Modal ranks or median ranks can be calculated with ordinal scales, but the arithmetic properties of these central tendencies are not usually very helpful in decision making. For this reason, the relevant characteristic for the decision maker is rarely on an ordinal scale. Research in which the ordinal scale is employed usually attempts to upgrade the scale to at least interval by various transformations and/or assumptions.

The two types of scales used in marketing research most frequently are nominal and ratio. With the nominal scale, a count of the number of sample units in each category is the basis for summary statistics. This figure is often expressed as a percentage and permits an estimate of the number of units in the total population that possess the given characteristic. The most useful summary statistic with a ratio scale is the arithmetic mean. This can be used for the sample as well as the population and provides a basis for estimating the total amount of the characteristic in the complete population. For example, the arithmetic mean per capita disposable income of $1,200 yields an estimate of $30 million for a community of 25,000 ($1,200 × 25,000).[17]

The interval scale permits the calculation of an arithmetic mean, but its interpretation is less certain because of the arbitrary nature of the zero point.[18] Use of the mean in estimating the total value in the universe rests on the assumption that the zero point is correct. The interval scale does permit comparisons between the means of different groups, showing how much larger or

---

[17]The reliability of percentages, means, and totals can be computed by appropriate formulas. These measures are discussed in Chapter 8.

[18]A "standard score" approach can be used in which responses are expressed in terms of number of standard deviations above or below the arithmetic mean. The scale is still interval in nature but adjusts for the degree of variability within the data. Standard scores may be calculated with respect to either aggregate measures across individuals or an individual's responses across a series of questions. The concept of standard score will occur within several of the analytic tools in later chapters.

smaller one group is than another—on the average. The interval scale thus permits only comparisons of differences while the ratio scale permits statements of absolute amounts.[19]

PRETESTS

The pretest is *not* designed to answer the decision maker's problem! It is not intended to yield substantive results! It *is* intended to determine whether the questionnaire—and associated field procedures—are satisfactory. Therefore, a representative sample is not required. But a sample in which the various subgroups of the population are represented is required. Males, females, young, old, rich, poor—whatever groups are in the universe—should be included in the pretest, but it is not necessary to include them in their correct proportions.

The pretest is designed to discover whether the questionnaire in its present form will generate data that are satisfactory estimates for the decision maker's problem. The interviewers must probe on all questions, attempting to determine whether the recorded answers conceal relevant material. Does a "Don't know" response arise from several factors? If so, should the factors be identified? Questionnaire layout and space for recording responses must also be evaluated in the pretest. All lists presented should be checked for omissions.

No questionnaire is ready for the field without a pretest. No researcher knows so much about the subject, the universe, and their interactions that the questionnaire cannot be improved by a field-test. The alternative wordings of various questions might each be included within the pretest. The consistent questions in the pretest are "What does the word (or question) say to you?" and "What do you mean by that answer?" The interviewer also keeps probing in order to discover whether vital factors are unrevealed in the present approach. The pretest also can yield an estimate of time requirements for interviewing.

Evaluation of Alternatives

How does the researcher judge which alternative wording, sequence, or response format is the best? No neat and simple answer is available. The evaluation of the various alternatives is highly subjective and fraught with problems. One sure way to go astray is to lose sight of the research objective. In most instances the researcher has the ultimate objective of understanding or predicting behavior. The approach in determining the best question or task should focus first on: "How does the respondent think about (or perform in)

---

[19]In later chapters we will discuss transformations in conjunction with estimating equations. Ratio scales, being more powerful, lend themselves to certain transformations that are not justified with interval scales. For example, a logarithmic transformation assumes a ratio scale. See Chapter 14 in particular.

the subject matter studied?'' Unless the question captures the respondents' mental set, it is probably on the wrong track.

A second overriding consideration must be the ease and cost of administering the various alternatives. Closely related to this consideration is the extent of "No answers." The ease and cost of *getting useful data* are the relevant considerations; incomplete questionnaires, no matter how many, do not answer research objectives.

A third approach to evaluation is test–retest reliability. If an individual provides inconsistent answers to the same question, the data and the instrument are suspect. An alternative approach that yields consistency would be preferable.

Finally, the performance records of specific approaches or specific questions can be used in the evaluation process. Those alternatives that have yielded accurate predictions of behavior or verified estimates are usually considered prime candidates for later use. Their use, of course, rests on the assumption that the new situation is "essentially similar" to the former situations. But there is no way of escaping that assumption in any undertaking: adoption of procedures that have been successful in the past assumes that the critical factors of the problems are similar.

DUMMY TABLES

A dummy table consists of the column and row descriptors of a table without the numerical data. The dummy tables of a research project should be envisioned by the researcher before the data have been collected. The pattern formed by the numbers within the various tables will determine what recommendations are passed on to the decision maker. Therefore, the dummy tables incorporate the essential objectives of the research.

The researcher should compose a few crucial dummy tables early in the problem formulation. The data collection instrument should then be judged according to whether it generates data that are relevant for those tables. Any questions that do not generate data for these tables are suspect: they are probably superfluous. If there are dummy tables without matching questions, the questionnaire has failed to address some critical area(s).

Table 4.2 presents a dummy table for an airline interested in determining its rating among different market segments. The segments are defined by income level of the respondent and the number of air trips taken during the past year. The table specifies the information that must be determined by the questionnaire.

Each respondent must be classified with respect to income. The three categories in their present phraseology are nonoperational. At least two options exist: (1) determine precise income values by the questionnaire and divide the respondents into a prespecified percentage distribution such as 25–50–25, or

Table 4.2
Dummy Table. Image Study. Airline X

Income level	Number of trips	Image		
		Below average	Average	Above average
High	4 or more			
	2–3			
	1			
	0			
Middle	4 or more			
	2–3			
	1			
	0			
Low	4 or more			
	2–3			
	1			
	0			

(2) establish arbitrary levels before the collection stage; for example, high is over $40,000, middle is $20,000 to $40,000, and low is under $20,000. The number of air trips taken by each respondent must be determined; no greater precision need be exercised than the four categories in the table. Finally, the image of Airline X must be determined. As stated, comparative images are required. Does each respondent place X in one of three categories, using his or her own subjective concept of average? Or does each respondent rate a number of airlines, selected by the researcher or the respondent? Following this option, how is the relative position of X determined in the analysis? How much deviation is permitted in order to have an "average" rating? Nothing has been said about the meaning of image. Is it some vague gestalt, or are its dimensions to be made more explicit?

Why does an airline decision maker want this kind of information? How would different patterns of actual data within the table lead him or her to different actions? At this point the researcher should do two things. First, he or she should fill in several copies of Table 4.2 with widely different numbers, hand them to the decision maker, and ask how the decision maker's actions would differ. Second, if the results of step one indicate the table is of operational value, the researcher should compose the specific questions needed to generate the required data.

If the percentage distribution is the same within each row of Table 4.2, X's image does not differ by these market segments. X might be most interested in its image among air travelers who made four or more trips last year. If image differs within this segment by income, special promotions might be undertaken through media most likely to reach the income groups that have the lowest image of X. The absolute number of persons in each of the 12 segments should be cited, lest undue effort be expended on too small a total market.

We have pursued this particular example in some detail in order to indicate the purpose of the dummy table. Every research endeavor can be couched in terms of dummy tables. Some are less complex than the airline case, but many are much more complex. The adequacy of every questionnaire rests on the utility of the data it will generate, and this utility is often best appraised by the dummy table plus two or three sets of hypothetical data.

The concept of a dummy table can be extended and generalized to the concept of projected output. What will be the output of the analysis—percentages, equations showing relationships, estimated totals, etc. The researcher should handle each of these in precisely the manner discussed for Table 4.2. Consider several potential results. Will they lead to different action recommendations? What questions are needed to obtain the input data?

The concept of a dummy table can be extended even further to the dummy report. What is the overriding research question and the three or four principal derivative questions? What tables will best permit analyses of these questions and lead to specific recommendations? What are the main sections of the report, and what is the best sequence? How should methodology be covered? Are summary tables showing the composition of the sample appropriate? The answer to each of these questions deserves a "why or why not?" The rationale must always focus on the decision maker's problem; otherwise the report may be useless.

SECONDARY DATA

There is no virtue in generating primary data if satisfactory secondary data are available. Primary data are costly. If governmental agencies, academic institutions, trade associations, or a wide variety of other sources provide data of acceptable quality at a lower cost, it is obviously proper to use those alternatives. Frequently, the data provided by such organizations is superior to the data a private firm could secure in its own research.

Two principal questions must always be asked of secondary data. In these two questions lie the hazards of using secondary data. First, how were the terms defined? Second, what quality controls were employed in collection and processing? The first asks whether the concepts are appropriate for your research objectives. The second asks whether you can trust the results.

The appraisal of secondary data in terms of bias is no different from that of primary data. All the issues raised in this chapter and the next are appropriate. The better sources provide detailed descriptions of their procedures and data collection instruments. If adequate descriptions are not supplied, it is best to use the data with extreme caution. Secondary data may be internal to the firm, or the source may be external. The same considerations in appraising its utility apply in each case. Strange as it may seem, internal sources are not always easier to appraise, and certainly are not always superior.

The principal external sources of secondary data are (1) the federal government, (2) state and local governments, (3) trade and professional associations, (4) educational institutions, (5) commercial services, and (6) periodicals. The United States Bureau of Census is perhaps the most comprehensive source of general statistics. The United States Superintendent of Documents issues a monthly catalog that indexes all federal publications. The card catalog of every library is also a fast source of bibliographic information. Finally, most organizations have a wealth of internal data that serve as secondary material.

Internal Secondary Data

Data that originate within the firm and are (or were) collected for some purpose other than the current research are internal secondary data. Sales and cost data from accounting reports are prime sources of valuable data. These figures are often available on a wide variety of bases; for example, geographic divisions, products, types of customers, departments, and channels of distribution. The availability of both sales and cost data enables the researcher to identify profitability if the records are kept on similar bases. The researcher should not accept these data at face value any more than he or she should accept other data without careful appraisal. The assumptions made in assigning costs to products, departments, and time periods must be critically evaluated before the data are accepted.

Internal secondary data have two major advantages: availability and low cost. Researchers should familiarize themselves with the kinds of data and reports available. These should be utilized before turning to external secondary sources or research involving primary data.

Published External Secondary Data

The amount of published external secondary data is overwhelming. Some of the publications are highly specialized, referring to particular products or geographic areas. Others are more general, one of the prime sources being the Bureau of the Census of the Department of Commerce. The task of finding the right source is frequently facilitated by using one of the many published guides to secondary data. The Bureau of Census has a comprehensive guide to its work plus a monthly publication covering its recent activities.[20] Gale Research

---

[20] *Census Bureau Programs and Publications: Area and Subject Guide,* 1968 (Washington, D.C.: United States Bureau of the Census) and *Catalog of Census Publications* (Washington, D.C.: United States Bureau of the Census).

Corporation also has two guides that include both governmental publications and private publications.[21]

The Bureau of the Census covers population, housing, business, manufacturers, agriculture, transportation, mineral industries, and government on a continuing basis at regular intervals, all in great detail. Their principal disadvantage concerns their currency. This stems from their periodic nature (every ten years for population) and the delay between collection and publication (frequently two years or more). The *Statistical Abstract of the United States* is published annually by the Bureau of the Census. It contains data from many different sources and also serves as a guide to the original sources that provide greater detail.

Other sources of general statistics are extremely diverse. The Office of Business Economics publishes the monthly *Survey of Current Business* dealing principally with current economic activity. The Internal Revenue Service provides various reports derived from tax reports. *Fortune* magazine lists the largest corporations by categories annually. *Sales Management* magazine publishes estimates of buying power for individual geographic areas—again with annual revisions. Standard & Poor and Moody's publish a wealth of financial information on various companies. These are only a few illustrations of the multitude of external secondary data sources, all available through general publications.

Commercial Data Services

Several firms collect data concerning various aspects of marketing and market behavior. This information is then sold on a subscription basis to clients. It is more expensive than the published data discussed above, but it is typically much less expensive than primary data. The firms offering these services can offer this saving by spreading the cost over a large number of clients. The data may not uniquely fit the specific needs of individual clients, although it may be possible for individual clients to "piggyback" specific questions on the general format at an additional fee. The types of services available can be divided into three categories: channel movement of goods, consumer data, and organizational information.

Channel movement of goods is useful to a manufacturer in knowing what happens to a product after it leaves the warehouse. Unless the firm is vertically integrated, the product may pass through several intermediaries. Without good data, the manufacturer does not know whether the product is moving at each stage or whether it is standing still at a particular point. Selling Area-Marketing, Inc. (SAMI) collects data on warehouse shipments. At the retail level, A. C. Nielsen and Audits and Surveys provide physical audits of merchandise

---

[21]*Encyclopedia of Business Information Sources,* 1970 (Detroit: Gale Research Corp.) and Paul Wasserman et al., 1971, *Statistics Sources* (3rd ed.) (Detroit: Gale Research Corp.).

in stores and estimate sales by the disappearance method: beginning inventory + purchases − ending inventory = sales.[22] They also supply a variety of related information on market share, out-of-stock conditions, prices, advertising support, and deals. Nielsen's service covers supermarkets, drug stores, and mass merchandisers. Audits and Surveys uses a product approach, requiring different store coverage for different products.

The principal *consumer data* services fall into three types: purchase data, TV viewing, and ad readership. *Purchase data* is typically collected through a consumer panel that supplies information on a continuing basis. Perhaps the best known is that conducted by the Market Research Corporation of America (MRCA).[23] Panel members record detailed data concerning purchases; for example, brand, quantity, price, store, and whether a special deal was involved. Additional demographic data about panel members can be compared to buying behavior in order to study particular market segments.

TV viewing is measured or monitored by several different firms. The Nielsen Television Index is probably the most familiar. The basic data are gathered through audimeters that are installed in the sets of the panel families. TV viewing is then automatically recorded. Demographics concerning panel members can be compared with viewing as an aid to advertisers as well as the networks in planning strategy.

Ad readership is measured by such firms as Starch and Simmons. Starch records three basic measures: (1)"noted"—the percentage of readers who remembered seeing a particular ad in the issue analyzed, (2) "seen associated"—the percentage who remembered reading the particular ad, and (3) "read most"—the percentage of readers who read 50 percent or more of the written material in the ad.[24] These various measures can also be related to ad cost. Simmons' data cross reference ad exposure and product usage.[25] Demographic variables are also tabulated, permitting the advertiser to study particular target groups and their response to various ads.

This discussion is illustrative of the type of secondary data available. Any person doing research in a particular field should become familiar with its literature, the activities of trade associations, and particular data services catering to the relevant economic activities. New services come into existence continually. Two of the more recent services specialize in organizational information.

---

[22]*Nielsen Retail Index Services,* 1971 (Northbrook, Ill.: A. C. Nielsen Co., Retail Index Division and Media Research Division.) Audits and Surveys is located at 1 Park Avenue, New York City.

[23]*An Introduction to the National Consumer Panel,* 1973 (Chicago: Market Research Corporation of America).

[24]*Starch: Scope, Method, and Use,* 1973 (Mamaroneck, N.Y.: Starch/INRA/Hooper).

[25]*The 1974–1975 Study of Selective Markets and the Media Reaching Them,* 1974 (New York: W. R. Simmons and Associates).

Dun & Bradstreet, historically a source of financial information, has expanded its service to provide marketing information through "Market Identifiers." This service identifies each industrial establishment according to Standard Industrial Classification Code—a numerical code that pinpoints the products manufactured, sales volume, number of employees, and other pertinent data. International Business Machines has also started a service in this general field by utilizing an input–output matrix to help identify potential customers and the size of their purchases by product.

SUMMARY

The instrument design phase of data collection involves the translation of the problem definition into the nitty-gritty of the wording of individual questions, the sequencing of the questions, and the establishment of the admissible responses for the individual questions. The existence of different parties in the research process establishes a crucial perspective for the instrument design phase because of the communication and cooperation necessary among them in their different roles. The four roles are decision maker, researcher, observer, and observed, with the latter three all vitally involved in data collection. The UAW test must be passed by all questions or the data are of dubious meaning: (1) the questions must be *understood* by all parties, (2) all parties must be *able* to provide that portion of the data required of them, and (3) all parties must be *willing* to supply the portion required of them.

The individual questions, the sequence of questions, and the admissible responses may be structured or unstructured and disguised or undisguised. Structured approaches assure uniform application and ease of interpretation. Unstructured approaches are particularly appropriate for exploratory research or situations with complex procedures requiring flexibility or conditional question sequences. Disguised questions are typically used when the respondent may be unwilling or unable to reveal his or her true feelings.

Projective techniques are frequently employed in disguised questionnaires. These include the third-person technique wherein the respondent is assumed to "project" his or her feelings onto others. Sentence completion, word association, storytelling, and the interpretation of pictures are other approaches commonly used.

Most of instrument design problems arise in conjunction with *bias*—defined as the difference between the true value in the universe and the average value that would be obtained by repeated applications of the research procedure. Instrument design is much more of an art than a science, but a few rules-of-thumb are worth constant application. Some of these are the avoidance of unnecessary questions, use of simple words, avoidance of "leading" questions, focusing on the desired issue, the consideration of alternative wordings, and constant application of the UAW test.

The sequence of questions is chosen to secure rapport, to facilitate a smooth transition, and to establish the proper mental set for the respondent. The establishment of admissible responses takes on all shades of possibilities. They can range from the completely free open-ended question to the highly constrained dichotomous situation. The enumeration of admissible responses may be presented to respondents, or their apparently "free" response may be placed into previously established categories by the interviewer.

The measurement of any characteristic requires the use of a scale. The nominal scale employs categories without a concept of "more than–less than" or "higher–lower." Categories are simply different. The ordinal scale employs a ranking but does not consider "how much" more or less. The concept is simply higher than or lower than. The interval scale adds the measurement of differences, the subtraction of scale positions showing which values are closer and which are further apart. The ratio scale differs from the interval scale by establishing a unique zero point that corresponds to absence of the characteristic.

The necessity of pretesting individual questions as well as the entire questionnaire cannot be stressed too strongly. The pretest plus the use of dummy tables are the insurance policies of sound research; they are omitted at the researcher's peril. Secondary data should be appraised by precisely the same standards as primary data, but one should not embark upon an original research design without checking existing literature and data.

EXERCISES AND PROBLEMS

1. Distinguish among the terms within each of the following sets.
   a) Instrument design and fieldwork
   b) Primary data and secondary data
   c) Data collection and problem definition
   d) Open-ended, multichotomous, and dichotomous
   e) Disguised question and unstructured question

2. Name and discuss the four different types of scales.

3. a) Explain the UAW test.
   b) Give original examples of questions that fail the different parts of this test.
   c) Propose an alternative procedure for each example—an alternative that would not fail the test. Explain the total procedure in detail.

4. Name and discuss the four different roles or parties involved in a research endeavor.

5. What is the "two-step ordinal scale"? What are its advantages and disadvantages?

6. Is there any advantage in setting up statistical tables in the planning stage of a project? Explain.

"Are you currently watching television?" (2) "If yes, what program (or channel) are you watching?" Are there any potential sources of bias with this procedure? Discuss. Include identification of the problem universe and the characteristic of interest.

11. Evaluate the following questions; each is proposed for inclusion in a survey of purchasing agents. Your evaluation should discuss any relevant instrument design considerations.

   a) How many reams of paper did you purchase last year?

   b) Do you think mandatory wage–price controls should be instituted?

   c) What is your prediction of the unemployment rate for the last quarter of the current year?

   d) How many employees report directly to you?

   e) What is the current inventory of "goods in process" for your company? How does this compare with the figure for last year?

12. A chemical company wishes to evaluate your local area as a possible location for a new plant. Enumerate and evaluate the major sources of secondary data that would be relevant in the initial stages of this investigation.

13. Kray Research is a manufacturer of peripheral equipment for computer installations. Its equipment is compatible with IBM equipment. Its president wants to secure a better understanding of Kray's image among larger retailers and financial institutions.

   a) Would you recommend open-ended, multichotomous, or dichotomous questions? Discuss.

   b) Design a questionnaire that would provide the desired information.

14. A large manufacturer of wood products is particularly concerned about the immediate outlook for the construction of new residential housing.

   a) What information, if any, could be obtained from secondary sources?

   b) What information, if any, could be obtained from primary sources?

   c) If any useful information can be obtained in (b), establish the proper wording for the principal questions.

15. Select an ad from a recent magazine.

   a) State what you believe to be the objective of the ad.

   b) Prepare a series of questions for the target audience that will best reveal whether the objective was realized.

   c) What are the relative merits of structured–disguised, structured–undisguised, unstructured–disguised, unstructured–undisguised questions for this problem?

16. Past behavior and future intentions have both been proposed as indicators of future behavior. Select two different problems, one in which past behavior would be a better indicator and one in which future intentions would be a better indicator. Explain your reasoning.

17. Analyze, criticize, and explain:

a) Bias can occur with or without prejudice, but prejudice cannot occur without introducing bias.

b) The disguised question is unnecessary as long as all parts of the UAW test are met. Therefore, the researcher would be well advised to use undisguised questions most of the time.

c) If the substantive results of a pretest reveal a strong consensus, it probably indicates that a biased sample has been employed.

d) The unstructured approach may pose greater editing and processing problems, but it also permits greater confidence that the data are comparable and consistent.

e) Multichotomous categories should be both mutually exclusive and exhaustive. This holds true whether the respondent is asked to select only one category or is permitted to select more than one.

f) Projective techniques fail to realize their true purpose when the respondent answers the question as presented.

g) The depth interview is most helpful as a follow-up to a structured questionnaire. This procedure permits the researcher to probe without biasing the quantitative results already obtained.

h) An arithmetic mean computed from an interval scale is of limited utility to most business firms. It is only when the firm can assume a ratio scale that the result takes on operational significance.

i) Bipolar adjectives with a series of intermediate but unlabeled categories is preferable to labeling all intermediate categories. The former is more likely to yield an interval scale and justify the calculation of an arithmetic mean.

j) Questions regarding one's own past behavior automatically are suspect since they rely on both memory and social acceptability. Since projective techniques are less threatening, they offer a preferable approach.

k) Rotation of list positions with several forms of the questionnaire permits elimination of order bias and facilitates cross-classification analyses.

CHAPTER 5

DATA COLLECTION—FIELDWORK

PLANS ARE USELESS WITHOUT EXECUTION

High-quality data collection instruments plus poor fieldwork equals a fiasco. The most vulnerable point in the typical research plan lies in the fieldwork. Adequate attention must be given to the selection, training, and supervision of the field staff; these are the individuals responsible for the actual data collection. The right question becomes an incorrect question when improperly administered. Proper field procedures involve the same kind of issues involved in instrument design; but the data collection setting is extremely variable, thus more difficult to predict and control.

Fieldwork encompasses the details by which the observer secures the desired information from the observed. It may entail questioning, observation, or a combination of the two. The information obtained is recorded on the instruments provided for the purpose. It sounds so simple; its simplicity is probably the reason its execution is so often neglected.

"I've been asking questions all my life. I guess that makes me a natural interviewer." "I've been selling all my life. I meet and talk with people easily. I shouldn't have much trouble interviewing." Both reactions raise issues that may disqualify rather than qualify the individuals concerned. An interviewer must collect unbiased information; it is not enough to ask questions and get "put off" with the easiest or most socially acceptable answer. The natural gossip may even encourage erroneous data. The natural sales person, on the other hand, must guard against his or her persuasiveness. Persuasiveness is fine when it leads to cooperation and participation in the survey. It is undesirable when it spills over into any type of "leading" with regard to the substantive nature of individual responses. Any natural gregariousness must remain substantively neutral—a most difficult task.

There are only three issues to settle in establishing the procedures for the fieldwork of research. (1) What medium of communication is to be employed in obtaining the desired data? (2) Who is to enter the research environment in order to collect the data? (3) What approach is to be used in requesting cooperation? Many other issues are influenced by field plans; for example, degree of intervention by the observer, precise wording of questions, and extent of structure employed. Such decisions are part of research design and instrument design. Fieldwork is merely charged with proper execution of those decisions although a good research plan should recognize the interdependence of the various phases.

The three principal media of communication are the personal interview, the telephone interview, and the mail questionnaire. A fourth medium used less often is the telegram. Personal distribution of questionnaires to be returned later by mail and in-product distribution, also with mail returns, are illustrative of the wide range of modifications possible. The alternatives available when observation is employed are more restricted although the possible use of mechanical aids such as the audimeter, camera, electric eye, and traffic counter opens a whole new dimension. The "who" of fieldwork concerns the characteristics of those collecting data, the method of selecting personnel, and the training/control procedures. The request for cooperation or participation is basically similar to a sales question. Potential respondents are being asked to invest their time and effort; the interviewer must convince them that participation is appropriate. The researcher must decide what, if any, incentives to offer and how to facilitate participation.

COMMUNICATION MEDIA FOR QUESTIONNAIRES

Questioning, as opposed to observation, relies exclusively on verbal communication with the units selected for the research project. Any medium through which the spoken or written work can be transmitted is a possible means of administering a questionnaire; two-way radio, television with telephone or mail response, bumper stickers, and skywriting are unlikely, but possible, candidates. The criteria for evaluating any procedure are basically two: cost (in both time and money) and degree of potential bias. A procedure should be rejected because some alternative procedure is superior with respect to those criteria. Our principal discussion will focus on the three most widely used questioning methods: the personal interview, the telephone interview, and the mail questionnaire.

Personal Interview

The personal interview involves a face-to-face situation. Therein lies both its strength and its weakness. The personal presence of the interviewer increases the probability of participation, permits clarification of ambiguities, and adds flexibility. His or her presence, however, introduces an additional factor that may bias the results obtained. The interviewer's task are four-fold: the interviewer must (1) locate the units within the assignment; (2) secure participation from those units; (3) administer the questionnaire according to instructions, providing clarification when appropriate without biasing the responses; and (4) record the responses completely and accurately.

A well-planned research project will have a specific statement to be used as an opening. The interviewer is to comply with instructions, gain cooperation, and not bias the results. "We're conducting a survey in order to secure lower utility rates" might gain participation, but it would hardly establish an unbiased mental set.

The interviewer's assignment, after gaining cooperation, is to ask the questions and record the answers. Such a statement is deceptively simple. The interviewer must follow the instructions given, both explicit instructions and implicit instructions. Structured questions must be asked in precisely the form specified. Not quite! *Neutral* rewordings are permitted if the meaning is ambiguous to a specific respondent. But the rewording must be neutral, and the interviewer must avoid the temptation to adopt a specific rewording for all future respondents. One question on a small survey of purchasing agents had to be discarded because one of two interviewers changed "reading material" to "magazines."

Recording of responses to unstructured questions is particularly troublesome. The interviewer must record responses as fully as possible, exercising care to avoid any distortion by changing or omitting words. An attempt "to catch the essence of the reply" by a concise rephrasing invites disaster. The task may be even more difficult with an unstructured question to the respondent and a structured set of admissible responses provided for the interviewer. Consider the question, "Why do you prefer brand X?" The interviewer has been provided with a list of several alternatives including both price and quality as well as a possible miscellaneous category. How should the interviewer classify, "They charge a fair price for an above average product"? This probably illustrates a case of inadequate planning or instructions, but the situation is not unusual.

The personal interview has several advantages over the telephone interview or the mail questionnaire. More information can normally be collected by the personal interview since it can be substantially greater in length than the others. The personal presence of the interviewer also permits clarification of ambiguities and inclusion of complex issues. Unstructured questionnaires and depth interviews are best handled by personal interviews. The nonresponse problem is easier to solve in the personal interview than it is in the other procedures.[1] A good interviewer can (1) locate and identify the units that are to be part of the research sample and (2) convert the sample units into respondents.

A slight modification of the nonresponse problem is the incomplete questionnaire problem. The presence of a personal interviewer facilitates the securing of answers to *all* questions. By establishing rapport with the respondent, the interviewer can return to questions that may have been skipped initially. The existence of missing data becomes particularly troublesome in the

---

[1] A detailed analysis of the nonresponse problem is given later in the chapter.

analysis phase when the researcher wants to compare answers on several questions.

The principal disadvantages of the personal interview relate to costs—primarily travel costs and time costs. A survey covering a wide geographic area, particularly if the same interviewers are employed in many locations, obviously incurs greater costs than one conducted in a highly compact area. The higher costs occur because of actual travel costs plus the personnel costs for idle time during travel. Use of different interviewers in different areas increases both training and supervision problems.

An added problem with the personal interview is the possible introduction of an interviewer bias or an interviewer–respondent interaction bias. The interviewer is an additional person in the setting. He or she has certain characteristics that are perceived by the respondent and many influence the mental set of the respondent. Black interviewers may receive responses that are quite diverse from those received by white interviewers, depending on the research subject.[2] The interviewer's mode of dress, age, sex, and general appearance all have a potential impact on the respondent. Most surveys attempt to match respondent characteristics with interviewers possessing similar characteristics. A study to determine business volume posed a problem when the interviewer was identified as an employee of a federal agency. Identification with the local business community generated much better rapport and openness. A number of studies have shown definite interviewer effects within the results by comparing answers obtained by different interviewers.[3]

It is one thing to demonstrate the existence of an interviewer effect; it is quite another to identify who are the better interviewers or which method of assignment is better. External criteria of "known true values" are rarely available. The usual approach of attempting to match interviewer and respondent characteristics is based on the rationale that rapport will be obtained more easily in such a situation. But will rapport reduce role playing and bias? Probably not if the respondent holds opinions or has behavior patterns that are at variance with the stereotype of his or her reference group. Matching of interviewer and respondent characteristics is probably the best procedure, but the reader should recognize that there is limited empirical evidence to substantiate that recommendation.[4]

---

[2] K. R. Athey, Joan Coleman, Audrey Reitman, and Jenny Tang, 1960, Two experiments showing the effect of the interviewer's racial background on responses to questionnaires concerning racial issues, *Journal of Applied Psychology* (August): 244–246.

[3] See for example, J. Allen Williams, Jr., 1964, Interviewer–respondent interaction: a study of bias in the information interview, *Sociometry* 27: 338–352; and Harper W. Boyd, Jr. and Ralph Westfall, 1964, Interviewer bias revisited, *Journal of Marketing Research* 2: (February): 58–63.

[4] See Robert L. Kahn and Charles L. Cannell, 1957, *The Dynamics of Interviewing* (New York: Wiley); and Robert H. Hanson and Eli S. Marks, 1958, Influence of the interviewer on the accuracy of survey results, *Journal of the American Statistical Association* (September): 635–655.

Finally, there is the problem of interviewer cheating. Blatant cheating occurs when the interviewer completes questionnaires without even contacting the supposed respondent. Less obvious cheating occurs when the harassed interviewer makes intelligent guesses concerning some portion of the questions. Cheating may also be said to occur when "Don't know," or "Refusal" is too readily accepted or when instructions to probe are ignored. A shopping survey conducted by the author contained classification questions on age and income. One interviewer recorded over 25 percent refusals on age, and another recorded over 20 percent refusals on income. No other interviewer had as many as 10 percent refusals on either question. Whether this should be classified as poor interviewing or cheating is a problem of semantics, but it illustrates the personal interaction dimension raised in interviewing.

The best way to cope with the cheating problem is through careful selection and training of interviewers rather than through its detection and correction. Close and visible supervision is also required. Follow-up validations, both with respect to whether the interview was made and with respect to the responses to specific questions, is another way of dealing with cheating. If the interviewers know such checks are to be made, the technique has added benefit. A check of individual questionnaires for internal consistency is yet another technique.

Telephone Interview

The telephone interview bears many similarities to the personal interview. Both rely on the spoken word with all its advantages. But both are also subject to the potential biases introduced by an additional person, the interviewer. The telephone interview of course lacks the face-to-face aspect of the personal interview. This brings both advantages and disadvantages. Potential bias from the interviewer's appearance and bearing are removed although voice clues remain. But the face-to-face advantage in gaining cooperation and establishing rapport are lost as well.

The telephone interview eliminates both the costs of travel and the costs of travel time. Call-backs do not require the retracing of steps necessary in the personal interview. Safety, which is becoming more and more a concern in personal interviews, is not a problem in telephone interviews. Closely related is the number of hours available for interviewing. Evening calls pose no problem by telephone; in fact evening calls offer several "pluses" for the telephone. The "nine-to-five" working group—a hard-to-reach group for the personal interview—can be reached conveniently by evening telephone calls. An additional advantage is that national surveys can gain additional interviewing hours by placing calls to the east in the early morning (before those in the west have arisen) and the west in the late evening (after those in the east have retired).

Wide Area Telephone Service (WATS) has also added a new dimension to telephone interviewing. This service provides unlimited telephone calls from a specific location to any telephone in a given geographic region for a fixed charge. This permits a small number of interviewers to make a large number of calls from a central location; thus a large number of interviews can be completed rapidly without incurring excessive costs. The WATS approach has the added psychological impact on the potential respondent of "a long-distance call just to get my opinion."

A WATS installation can exercise control and supervision not available in the personal interview. A supervisor is typically at a master phone that can be used to monitor the work of any interviewer at any time. A continuously operating WATS installation also permits the recruitment and training of highly competent personnel. Interviewers employed in personal interviewing are usually part-time employees working for relatively low pay. The better interviewers are used by commercial research houses on a repetitive basis, but their availability is restricted by geography. This is not the case with WATS telephone interviewing.

The principal disadvantage of the telephone interview compared with the personal interview is the missing physical presence and eye contact. Visual aids cannot be used—eliminating the possibility of presenting lists or diagrams. Despite the lack of face-to-face contact, good telephone interviewers have conducted 30–45 minute interviews. This illustrates that the potential is there, but the personal interview is still the preferred medium for long or complex questionnaires.

A final potential limitation of the telephone interview is an obvious one: only persons with telephones can be interviewed. This is much less critical than it once was, and the percentage of households with telephones is still increasing. The use of current directories poses a more serious problem; unlisted telephones are likely to be located in households that differ considerably from households with listed telephones. Persons who have recently moved and persons who have chosen to have unlisted numbers may have market-oriented characteristics that differ from those of the general population. This difficulty can be overcome by random[5] dialings within designated exchanges, but the opening statements must be carefully chosen.

Mail Questionnaire

The mail questionnaire eliminates travel costs and interviewer time costs. It also permits simultaneous collection of data without hiring a large staff. With the elimination of the interviewer, a potential source of bias is also removed. Geographic coverage poses even less of a problem with mail questionnaires than with telephone interviews although the time between initial mailing and receipt of questionnaires may rule out the mail questionnaire method when fast results are essential. The respondent to the mail questionnaire may choose

---

[5]The meaning and place of "random" will be discussed in Chapter 6.

his or her own time for completion of the questionnaire. This reduces the danger of inconvenient timing and the not-at-home problem.

The more serious problem in the mail questionnaire is nonresponse. This is particularly serious because those most interested in the subject matter are the most likely to respond. In some cases this results in a much more favorable (or unfavorable) rating than is warranted. In other cases, there is an overrepresentation of both highly favorable and highly unfavorable opinions. The average computed may be reasonably accurate, but the percentage of the universe in each category may be grossly inaccurate.

Another problem with the mail questionnaire involves the length of the questionnaire itself. Response rates decrease considerably as the length of the questionnaire increases. The practical effect of this is that lengthy studies cannot rely on a mail questionnaire approach. If complexity is added to length, understanding on the part of the respondents may be reduced and the utility of the total study becomes suspect. The use of telephone or telegram contact prior to the initial questionnaire mailing and the offering of incentives for cooperation may help overcome some of these problems.[6]

THE NONRESPONSE PROBLEM

The nonresponse problem in surveys is *not* a matter of sample size. It is a question of whether the group of respondents is different from the group of nonrespondents—with respect to the characteristics under study. The problem can best be illustrated by Fig. 5.1. The researcher wishes to estimate the percentage of the target population falling into each of four age groups: youth, 25–45, 46–65, and elderly. These percentages, unknown to the researcher, are 10, 30, 35, and 25 percent, respectively. Suppose the researcher follows proper sampling procedures, and selects a sample that coincides precisely with these percentages.

The next task is to locate the sample units and classify each unit with respect to age. Enter the nonresponse problem! According to Fig. 5.1, less than half (3/8) of the youth are converted into respondents; precisely half (1/2) in the 25–45 age group become respondents; slightly more than half (5/8) from the 46–65 age group respond; and well over half (3/4) of the elderly are in the respondent category. Using these figures, the age distribution of the respondents is 6 percent youth, 25 percent in the 25–45 age group, 37 percent in the 46–65 age group, and 32 percent elderly. Greater disparity in response rates would produce greater distortion in estimates of the population age distribution. But even these distortions result in a 40 percent (6 versus 10) understatement for the youth and a 28 percent (32 versus 25) overstatement for the elderly.

---

[6]A particular experiment, using incentives with mail questionnaires, is discussed later in the chapter.

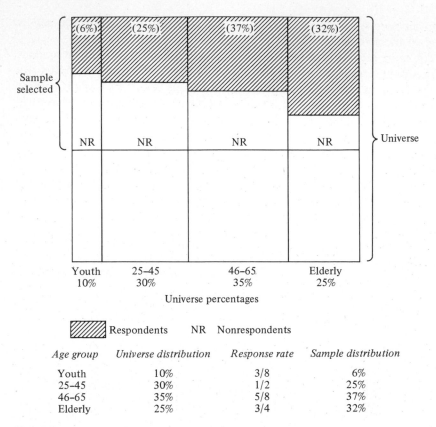

Age group	Universe distribution	Response rate	Sample distribution
Youth	10%	3/8	6%
25–45	30%	1/2	25%
46–65	35%	5/8	37%
Elderly	25%	3/4	32%

Fig. 5.1

Nonresponse bias. Age distribution of universe, sample, and respondents.

Any procedure that assumes the respondents are representative of the total sample selected and the sample selected is representative of the universe is likely to be misleading. As long as persons with certain characteristics are more likely to be in the respondent group than are persons with other characteristics, results based upon the respondent group will be misleading. This is referred to as a *nonresponse bias* because certain groups are not adequately represented. The personal interview copes with this problem by trying to keep the number of nonrespondents to a minimum. This does not solve the problem, but it does reduce the magnitude of its impact on population estimates. Differential effort devoted primarily to known hard-to-reach groups can be even more helpful.

Nonresponse bias remains a possibility even with high overall response rates, but its impact diminishes as the total response rate increases. With a 30 percent response rate, the nonresponse group comprises 70 percent of the total and could bring a large swing in overall statistics since its weight in calculations would be more than twice that of the response group. Suppose the consumption rate is 5 units per year for respondents and 2 units per year for nonrespondents. The correct rate for the total sample selected is 2.9 while the calculated rate (for the respondents only) is 5.0—an overstatement of over 70 percent. If the consumption rates of 5 and 2 still apply for respondents and nonrespondents but the total response rate is 90 percent, the distortion is much less since the appropriate weight for the nonrespondents is much less. The correct consumption rate would be 4.7 in this latter case. The calculated rate of 5.0 would still be a biased estimate, but the magnitude of the bias would be much smaller.

INCREASING RESPONSE RATES

The researcher is constantly looking for ways to increase response rates. First, higher response rates, as discussed in the preceding section, reduce the impact of nonresponse bias although they do not remove that bias. Second, higher response rates mean a larger absolute number of respondents. The larger the realized sample size, the more confident the researcher can be that the result approximates the result that would be obtained by applying the research procedure to the entire universe.[7]

The use of preliminary contacts by letter or telephone, various types of cover letters, monetary or gift incentives, and various types of postal arrangements have been attempted and experimented with in order to increase the response rates for mail questionnaires. Most of these experiments have yielded logically consistent results but they are hardly surprising. Basically, they demonstrate that persons are more likely to become respondents if they are given personal attention, if they receive some incentive, if they are convinced the survey is important, if response is made easy, and a broad range of somewhat similar propositions. What has not been well documented by most of these experiments is the extent to which the extra efforts eliminate differences between the characteristics of the response and nonresponse groups and whether some of these extra efforts might not bias the respondents' answers to some of the questions.

The first and most obvious way to increase response rates is by follow-ups or call-backs. In personal or telephone interviews, note should be made of the day and hour when attempts were unfruitful. Call-backs are more likely to succeed if they are made at other times. Covering the spectrum of morning, afternoon, evening, and weekend is a much more efficient procedure than six afternoon attempts. With personal interviews, inquiries at neighbors' homes may guide in the selection of an appropriate time to call again. With mail questionnaires, follow-up requests—including a second copy of the questionnaire

---

[7]The technical word is "reliability." We shall examine this property in detail throughout Part II.

—serve the same purpose as call-backs for telephone or personal interview projects.

Follow-ups and call-backs delay completion of the research, and their cost per completed questionnaire is greater than the initial phase. It is often suggested that a larger sample be drawn initially in order to compensate for the expected nonresponse rate. Hopefully the reader can see that such a procedure ignores the nonresponse bias.

Some of the standard techniques in attempting to increase response rates are the use of postage stamps instead of metered mail, personalized correspondence (or address by the interviewer), explanations of benefits accruing to the respondent because of the research, citation of well-respected sponsors, matching of interviewer characteristics with those of respondents, forms that are easy to read and complete, and various types of incentives. The reverse of these is of course detrimental. The worst procedure of all is the failure to supply return postage. A close second is poorly designed forms, including return envelopes that are too small to receive the completed questionnaire without excessively folding it.

A definite distinction should be made between refusals and "not at homes." The conversion of the former into respondents is an extremely difficult task. A survey requiring financial information was started with telephone interviews. After a high proportion of refusals was encountered, the research plan was changed to a personal interview approach. This approach was very successful—except with those who had already refused when contacted by telephone. Good documentation of both categories (refusals and "not at homes") should be maintained in order to plan follow-ups and in order to better cope with future surveys.

An Experiment with Various Incentives

Incentives and gifts are by their nature specific. Therefore, experiments with incentives do not lend themselves to generalizations. Not only are the incentives specific, but the subject and the universe are specific. Despite this specificity, experimental results of surveys made for the Atlantic City Press Bureau may be informative.[8]

Mail questionnaires were sent to five samples from the universe of telephone listings in two Philadelphia area telephone directories. The same questionnaire was sent to each group, and the cover letters were as similar as possible—modifications being necessary because different incentives were employed for the different groups.

---

[8]The three studies referred to were class projects done for the Atlantic City Press Bureau by three different marketing research classes at the Wharton School, University of Pennsylvania, in 1962, 1965, and 1970.

The experiment was first conducted in 1962. Five different incentives were employed: (1) A box of saltwater taffy accompanied the questionnaire. (2) A box of saltwater taffy was promised for completion and return of the questionnaire. (3) An unspecified small gift was promised for completion and return of the questionnaire. (4) The name of each person completing and returning the questionnaire was to be entered in a drawing for a free weekend for two, American Plan, at a beachfront hotel. (5) Respondents received a thank you. An interesting exercise for readers at this point is to make their own estimates of the results. The response rates achieved for the various groups are presented in Table 5.1.

The high response rate for the group receiving the taffy with the questionnaire is consistent with other studies. Receipt of a gift seems to create a sense of obligation. Repetition of the same experiment, with slight modifications, in 1965 and 1970 again yielded the highest response rate for the group receiving the taffy with the questionnaire. In 1970, another group was placed in the "obligation" category but with a plastic beach bag rather than a box of saltwater taffy. The monetary value of the two was markedly different. The beach bag obligation yielded no better results than the taffy *promise*. Thus response seems to be a joint function of receipt–promise and intrinsic value of the gift.

The failure of the raffle to generate any better response than a simple "thank you" was unexpected. It was repeated again in 1965 and 1970 but with information concerning the potential number who might be entered. With the low number involved in these experiments (maximum of 300 eligible for the

Table 5.1
Response Rates, Atlantic City Study with Different Incentives, 1962

Incentive†	Response rate (%)
1) Taffy sent with questionnaire	51
2) Taffy promised	39
3) Small gift promised	42
4) Raffle for weekend	26
5) Thank you	29

†1) A one-pound box of saltwater taffy accompanied the questionnaire.
  2) A one-pound box of saltwater taffy was promised for completion and return of the questionnaire.
  3) An unspecified "small gift" was promised for completion and return of the questionnaire.
  4) The name of each person completing and returning the questionnaire was entered in a drawing for a free weekend for two, American Plan, at a beachfront hotel.
  5) The respondent was thanked.

drawing), the response rates in 1965 and 1970 were aproximately equal to the response rates achieved with the promise of a gift.

The similarity of response rates with the promise of saltwater taffy and the promise of a small gift does not seem to lead to any general conclusions.[9] The surprise element and the intrinsic value of a specific known item seem to balance in this case. In another study, there was evidence of disappointment when a "small gift" turned out to be a copy of the Declaration of Independence.[10]

The use of incentives has the potential to inject bias in two ways: (1) by appealing to some groups more than others and (2) by changing the respondents' answers to specific questions in the questionnaire. There is some evidence that the group responding to the raffle incentive was more likely to be a two-person household. The nature of the offer in 1965 and 1970 was changed to a dollar figure instead of specifying a weekend for two. Whether this change or the knowledge of the odds increased the response rate cannot be inferred from the data at hand. The gift of saltwater taffy for some groups and not others had the potential to establish differential mental sets among groups. It was thought that this difference might appear in the question, "With what do you associate Atlantic City most closely?" No such result occurred as only one person in the entire study responded with "saltwater taffy" and that person was from group 3 which had been promised a "small gift." Despite this result, the researcher is inviting difficulty if he or she uses incentives that are closely related to the subject matter of the research.

Are Nonrespondents Different from Respondents?

How does the researcher know whether the respondents and nonrespondents are different? This is after all the critical concern. Two approaches may be used: (1) a comparison of the two groups on known characteristics and (2) a comparison of results by number of call-backs employed.

Suppose a study of voter preference reveals that 57 percent of the relevant universe are registered Democrats and only 46 percent of the respondents are registered Democrats. A suspicion of unrepresentativeness and potential bias is raised. Suppose, on the other hand, 57 percent of the respondents are Democrats. Less suspicion exists, but it does not give complete confidence. The greater the number of similar characteristics, the more the researcher thinks the nonresponse bias may be minimal. But it is always possible that differences may still exist on the characteristics under study.

---

[9]The differences between the response rates for groups 2 and 3 and between those of groups 4 and 5 are not "statistically" significant. This concept is explained in Chapter 9. The data from this experiment are further analyzed, using all three years, in Chapter 13.

[10]This, too, was a class project at the Wharton School, University of Pennsylvania. No alternative incentives were employed in this project. The "evidence of disappointment" was limited to a few isolated letters.

Suppose three waves of interviews are employed for a shopping study, the second and third waves as call-backs. If the results are identical for all three waves, less concern exists for the nonresponse bias. But again, the evidence is not conclusive. If the results for the three waves differ appreciably, the possibility of a nonresponse bias is greater. The best assumptions concerning those who are still nonrespondents is debatable, but most persons would argue that the results of the third wave are closer to the remaining nonrespondents than are the results of the first wave.

MODIFICATION AND COMPARISON OF QUESTIONING METHODS

Various organizations and various individuals stress the use of one data collection method over others. This is particularly true of commercial services that specialize in a single method, having assembled and trained a staff with expertise in "the best method." Each method, however, has its own advantages and disadvantages. The requirements of a particular project should be established, and then the appropriate data collection method should be selected. Techniques other than the three basic questioning methods are also possible. The following are illustrative and not meant to be exhaustive.

In-product distribution with mail return is a convenient way of reaching the correct universe. An incentive to respond may be coupons or a gift. The familiar warranty card with a new product is but a slight modification of this approach.

The *group interview* is but a modification of the personal interview. Even greater skill is required of the interviewer in this setting. An unstructured format is almost mandatory, and the interviewer must draw out the more reticent group members. Frequently, the group interview can be supplemented with before and/or after self-administered questionnaires.

A widely used version of the personal interview is the *fixed location* interviewer. This procedure samples units as they pass a specific location rather than going to units at "their locations." The universes to which the samples apply raise problems that require careful analysis, but the costs saved by reducing idle time are considerable. Origin and destination (O and D) studies of automobile traffic flow and store traffic analyses are but two of the more common marketing research applications of this approach.

One of the better lists of advantages and disadvantages of the personal interview, mail questionnaire, and telephone interview was prepared by Ferber and Verdoorn in 1962.[11] The WATS approach has modified some of their statements concerning the telephone interview, but it is still an excellent summary and is reproduced with slight modifications as Table 5.2.

---

[11]Robert Ferber and P. J. Verdoorn, 1962. *Research Methods in Economics and Business* (New York: Macmillan), p. 210.

Table 5.2
Relative Merits of Principal Methods of Data-collection†

Personal interview	Mail	Telephone
Advantages		
Most flexible means of obtaining data	Wider and more representative distribution of sample possible	Representative and wider distribution of sample possible
Identity of respondent known	No field staff	No field staff
Nonresponse generally very low	Cost per questionnaire relatively low	Cost per response relatively low
Distribution of sample more controllable	People may be franker on certain issues, e.g., sex	Control over interviewer bias easier; supervisor essentially present at interview
	No interviewer bias; answers are in respondent's own words	Quick way of obtaining information
	Respondent can answer at leisure, has time to "think things over"	Nonresponse generally very low
	Certain segments of population more easily approachable	Callbacks simple and economical
Disadvantages		
Likely to be most expensive of all	Bias due to nonresponse often indeterminate	Interview period not likely to exceed five minutes
Headaches of interviewer supervision and control	Control over questionnaire may be lost	Questions must be short and to the point; probes difficult to handle
Dangers of interviewer bias and cheating	Interpretation of omissions difficult	Certain types of questions cannot be used, e.g., thematic apperception
	Cost per return may be high if nonresponse is very large	Those who have no phones cannot be reached
	Certain questions, such as extensive probes, cannot be asked	
	Only those interested in subject may reply	
	Not always clear who replies	
	Certain segments of population not approachable, e.g., illiterates	
	Likely to be slowest of all	

†Source: Adapted from Robert Ferber and P. J. Verdoorn, 1962, *Research Methods in Economics and Business*. New York: Macmillan, p. 210.

PANELS

The term *panel* is used in two different senses within marketing research. The first refers to a group that serves as a jury to evaluate a new product or some other marketing act—usually as a pretest rather than as a test in the marketplace after the decision has been implemented commercially. This jury type of panel normally acts on a *one-time only* basis. The other use refers to a group from which information is obtained on a *continuing* basis.

The continuing panel approach permits the monitoring of widely different environments. Consumer purchase panels record actual expenditures on widely varied products in "diaries," submitting them periodically to the sponsor. The Market Research Corporation of America panel discussed in Chapter 4 is perhaps the outstanding example, maintaining a national panel of over 10,000 families. Dealer panels such as A. C. Nielsen and Audits and Surveys permit the monitoring of product movement at the retail level, allowing manufacturers to carry their analysis beyond their own sales data. Panels for determining radio, television, and print media audiences and advertising exposure comprise the third common use of the continuing panel.[12]

The continuing panel permits the use of both experimental and nonexperimental designs.[13] The sponsor can administer selected treatments to various subgroups while maintaining an "untreated" control group as the standard for comparison. The continuous monitoring yields time-series data that can be analyzed for growth patterns and more careful identification of history and maturation effects. Since the sponsor can spread costs over many clients and time periods, he or she can afford to collect comprehensive data concerning panel characteristics. This information then permits both the identification of particular segments of interest and the matching of groups on relevant variables.

The principal limitations of panel data stem from the selection and testing effects. No matter how carefully the sponsor selects the sample he or she desires, the actual panel members can be only those who agree to participate. This self-selection bias raises doubts on the representativeness of the panel, both on demographic and personality variables. This is further complicated with high dropout rates within the first few periods. Testing effects are evident in the results when panel members behave differently because they are keeping records (or being monitored). It is hoped that panel members revert to their natural behavior after a few periods.

Analytic techniques often measure effects as differentials against a control group. As long as the researcher's interest is satisfied by this type of measure, the self-selection bias of the panel may be of less significance. As an

---

[12]See the section "Secondary Data" (and the relevant references) in Chapter 4 for further discussion of specific sources.

[13]Hans Zeisel, 1957, *Say It with Figures* (New York: Harper & Row). Chapter 10 has an extended discussion of the advantages and uses of panel data.

example of this argument, the self-selection bias may generate a panel that consumes more (or less) of a specific product than the general population. Despite this bias, a researcher may accept the difference in consumption of urban and rural households within the panel as satisfactory approximations of the difference between urban and rural households in the general population. It is thus a lower order assumption although no confirmation of it is usually possible.

A manufacturer of a frequently purchased consumer nondurable subscribes to a consumer panel service. Per capita consumption of the manufacturer's product within the panel is 2.7 ounces per week. Per capita consumption for the total United States is 2.2 ounces per week, a significantly lower figure. If the rate of consumption within the panel is 3.1 for urban households and 2.1 for rural households, is the manufacturer justified in concluding that urban households have a higher consumption rate than that of rural households for the entire population? Does the existing upward bias for the total destroy its utility for comparisons among groups? Or is its usefulness for before-and-after experiments diminished? No definitive answer can be given, but many users of panel data rely on "after adjusting for selection bias, we can identify the effects of other variables."

OBSERVATION

Observation rather than questioning may be used to obtain information on both current and past behavior as well as physical states. Past behavior may be observed by means of current inventories; for example, store audits, a pantry inventory in a household, or a simple check of current equipment in a household or business establishment. Current behavior can be observed either in the marketplace or in a laboratory situation. The more common way of making such observations is by means of a human observer. Coincidental recording devices are an alternative. A traffic counter used on highways is a very familiar instrument to most of us. TV and radio recording devices have been used for a number of years in measuring audiences. Among the more esoteric instruments used to measure physical states and behavior are the eye camera and the psychogalvanometer. The former is used in recording eye movements, particularly as subjects are reading advertisements or examining packages. The latter measures perspiration rates and has been studied in conjunction with response to TV programming and TV advertising.

Observational studies may be classified on five bases:[14] (1) whether the setting is natural or contrived, (2) whether the respondent knows he or she is

---

[14]Much of this discussion is based on the excellent work of Eugene Webb, Donald Campbell, Richard Schwartz, and Lee Secrest, 1966, *Unobtrusive Measures: Nonreactive Research in the Social Sciences* (Chicago: Rand McNally).

being observed, (3) whether observations are made by human observers or by mechanical means, (4) whether the task is structured or unstructured, and (5) whether behavior is observed directly or inferred. A sixth related consideration is whether the reseach stops at behavior or whether it attempts to make inferences concerning the motives and reasons for the behavior. An alternative procedure is to supplement observation of behavior with questioning in order to determine motives.

Laboratory settings normally produce more definite results than the marketplace. However, the question answered may be less pertinent to the decision maker. Behavior in a 12 × 20 room when all factors except two are held constant may change considerably when 25 factors vary in the marketplace. This may be even more apparent if the respondent plays the role of a careful, analytic purchaser in the laboratory. The environment chosen for the observation is a part of research design, but the task of recording the necessary data is data collection fieldwork. Recording observations is usually easier in the laboratory, but the potential for nonrelevancy and role playing must be recognized.

The intervention to record observations is akin to, but distinct from, the natural–contrived dimension. Role playing is again the potential culprit, but it is now strictly a case of role playing for the benefit of the observer. Disguised objectives may be introduced in order to offset the respondent's potential modification of behavior. One strategy is to have the observer role play without divulging his or her observer status. For example, the observer may take the role of a customer within the store. In this guise, he or she may observe other customers or store employees as well as their interactions. Alternatively, his or her role as observer may be revealed, but the object of the research may be concealed. One project using this approach used clues that suggested the main interest was in advertising exposure. The true interest of the research concerned in-store traffic patterns and the extent of customer handling of merchandise.

Mechanical recording of observations is frequently more precise and less costly. This is particularly true if the mechanical devices can be used over a lengthy time interval. Mechanical devices also offer continuous monitoring around the clock, frequently impossible with human observers even at excessive costs.

Observation may be highly structured as in the case of traffic counts, or it may be highly unstructured as in the following study of magazine reading. Subjects entering a waiting room are observed with respect to whether they pick up any of the magazines available, what magazines they select, what articles or advertisements they read, how thoroughly individual pages are read, apparent reaction to specific portions, and degree of uninterrupted attention given each portion. Structure in the magazine reading study is completely lacking as far as the respondent is concerned. No tasks have been assigned and no questions have been posed. The amount of structure introduced in recording responses depends on the forms and instructions provided for the observer. Note this is the case no matter whether the observer is in the waiting room, observing from an adjoining location, or using mechanically recorded pictures.

Finally the observer may record the behavior as it takes place, or the observer may infer past behavior from observation of present conditions. Most audits infer sales and purchases by piecing together physical inventories and invoices. This procedure is much less costly than a monitoring of sales and purchase transactions; it is also more accurate despite the problem of shrinkage. On the other hand, information concerning selling techniques or time spent in various activities requires on-the-spot observation.

Interpretation of behavior is a common problem in observational studies whenever any attempt is made to "internalize" the observations. What behavior coincides with "consideration," "rejection," and "comparison?" Only the overt behavior can be observed. A customer may pick up a can of spaghetti sauce, look at it, and then replace it. If the customer then moves on to the ice cream, what is the proper classification of his or her behavior with respect to the spaghetti sauce? Does the absence of a recording of "purchased spaghetti sauce" tell all that should be told? If not, what did happen?

Some questionnaire procedures almost call for behavior by the respondent. The *sorting box* is one such device. The respondent is given a deck of cards, each card with a word printed on it; for example, delivery, quality, reputation, convenience in use, and honesty. The respondent is instructed to place each card in one of seven slots numbered from "1" to "7" according to his or her rating of specific suppliers on the different characteristics. A large number of ratings can be collected by this procedure before the respondent becomes bored or fatigued. The objective is to secure involvement on the part of the respondent; the technique does this well, almost resulting in behavior rather than in answering. In one study of department store image, respondents made nine sorts of 35 characteristics each with no apparent adverse effects. Even at the end respondents seemed to engage in internal debates concerning the proper assignment.

SELECTION AND TRAINING OF INTERVIEWERS

A good interviewer is a good listener with sufficient communication skills to draw out potential respondents. He or she must have sufficient intelligence to follow instructions, and sufficient humility to accept directions. A pleasant appearance and a pleasing personality are definite assets but are not sufficient alone. Beyond these general considerations, specific characteristics are required for individual research projects. These specific characteristics relate to (1) matching factors with respect to potential respondents that will facilitate the obtaining of participation and the establishment of rapport, (2) substantive expertise in the subject matter, and (3) perhaps interviewing experience of the type required by the specific assignment.

High-quality interviewers are a rare breed—largely because pay is low and employment is unstable. A research firm's best source of quality interviewers is usually its own past records. Each firm should maintain complete files on each interviewer: refusal rates, incomplete questionnaires, meeting of deadlines, satisfactory implementation of sampling plans, need of excessive editing, and results of verification checks. Each of these should be expressed in terms of the firm's experience with other interviewers working in similar areas or similar assignments.

Training and supervision are at least as important as selection. No interviewer should be sent into the field without a thorough understanding of the project and the data requirements. The pretest should alert the researcher to potential trouble spots. It is unforgivable not to inform the interviewers of these spots and not to give them specific instructions concerning how the trouble spots should be handled.

Ideally, interviewers should be given both oral and written instructions. A group meeting with interviewers is the best way to acquaint the field-workers with the entire project but, because of cost considerations, indoctrination is more often handled by mail alone. This procedure places an added burden on written instructions, and every possible precaution should be used to be sure every detail is adequately covered.

The best training session is one in which the interviewer is exposed to the most trying responses and respondents. This can be done with the supervisor playing the role of respondent, initially with a single interviewer while other interviewers observe. This can be repeated as often as necessary, followed by the interviewers working one on one.

The training session should also include appraisal of completed written questionnaires. What type of information is inadequate, and what is needed to correct it? This appraisal is best made by having the trainees turn in practice questionnaires based on their practice interviews. The accuracy of the completed form can be judged by detailed probing after the completed interview. The procedure suggested here is not at all common, but any shortcut of it introduces possible communication failure.

Every training program must include instructions in locating the respondents. A probability sample is a detailed technical matter. Each step must be enumerated; examples are most helpful, especially with sample maps. This step is crucial since well-conducted interviews with the wrong respondents are totally unacceptable.

The supervisor must review completed forms as they are received. Failure to perform this review at the earliest possible moment permits improper procedures to continue. The supervisor's final duty is to verify a sample of the questionnaires for accuracy of information and for blatant cheating.

A large-scale personal interview project was conducted in five United States cities. Training sessions of one-half day were conducted with the interviewers in three cities by the senior investigators. Training and interviewing in the fourth city was contracted to a commercial research house. In the fifth, neither senior investigator was involved in the training although a five-page set of written instructions was distributed. Refusal rates were 50 percent in the fifth city and less than 10 percent in each of the first three cities—reaching 20 percent in city four. Good interviewers know their questionnaire, their instructions, and are convinced they are asking questions that the potential respondents will answer. Good interviews are produced by good interviewers, and good interviewers are produced by adequate training and supervision.

SUMMARY

Fieldwork involves the accurate application and administration of data collection instruments. Data are collected by either questioning, observation, or a combination of the two. Fieldwork involves three different issues: (1) the medium of communication to be employed, (2) the persons who are to enter the research environment to collect the data, and (3) the approach to use in requesting cooperation.

The principal techniques used for fieldwork are the personal interview, the telephone interview, and the mail questionnaire. Each has its own advantages and disadvantages. Costs, complexity of the research questions, geographic coverage, need for flexibility, availability of a field staff, and specific bias sources for the particular research must all be evaluated. The potential nonresponse bias and the availability of incentives to stimulate higher response rates call for particular attention.

Selection, training, and supervision of the field staff is a greatly ignored aspect of research work. The critical considerations relate to general management techniques rather than specific research considerations. Good interviewers must be skillful in communication, intelligent enough to follow instructions, good listeners, and willing to accept directions. Their training should thoroughly familiarize them with the overall project, the forms and questions to be employed, and the data desired.

Observation refers to the recording of overt behavior. The various alternatives differentiate according to whether (1) the environment is natural or contrived, (2) the respondent knows he or she is being observed, (3) the observations are made by mechanical means or a human observer, (4) the task is structured or unstructured, and (5) behavior is observed directly or inferred.

EXERCISES AND PROBLEMS

1. Distinguish among the terms within each of the following sets.
   a) Increasing response rates and increasing sample size
   b) Refusals, not-at-homes, and "no answers"
   c) Random digit dialing and directory sampling
   d) Inferred behavior and inferred motivation

2. Briefly explain the meaning and importance of each of the following in marketing research:

   a) Interviewer bias
   b) Panel
   c) Incentives
   d) Follow-up
   e) Observer role playing
   f) Group interview

3. Compare the mail questionnaire, personal interview, and telephone interview with respect to each of the following:

   a) Nonresponse bias
   b) Costs
   c) Time required to completion
   d) Completeness of data

4. Questioning and observation are alternative ways of collecting information.

   a) Discuss the advantages and disadvantages of each.

   b) In view of your answer in (a), select a marketing research problem in which each would be the preferable method.

5. Hallmark Cards attempts to monitor movement of each individual seasonal card by obtaining ending inventory figures on each card from its customers at the close of the season. Assume all customers are independent retail stores.

   a) Would you advise that this information be collected by mail questionnaire, personal interview, telephone interview, or some other method? Why?

   b) What, if any, additional information beyond ending inventory would be necessary in order to estimate sales of each card?

   c) How should the company obtain the information in (b) and how would it be used in realizing the company's objective?

   d) Would you expect the results of this research to be biased? Why or why not? If you expect bias, in which direction would the results be biased?

   e) Would your answer in (d) apply to both estimates for the individual store and the aggregate for all stores? Discuss.

6. The J&P Research Company has exclusive rights to interview within the Ford Valley Shopping Mall. Its interviewers are all high school graduates who have been given one day's training in a seminar workshop environment by J. P. Getz, the president of J&P. Records concerning past work are available for each interviewer. A large department store within the mall wishes to determine the percentage of potential customers entering its store who leave without making a purchase. The store can use J&P interviewers and specify the sampling plan to be followed. It can also specify any "reasonable" characteristics that the interviewers must possess. Assume the store has established a satisfactory sampling plan. The principal instruction to the interviewer is that every tenth person leaving a designated exit (within a designated time period) is to be interviewed.

   a) Specify the principal items of information to be obtained from each respondent.

   b) Would you recommend that the department store contract with J&P for this research? Discuss.

   c) Assume the store employed J&P for the research. What, if any, "reasonable" characteristics of the interviewers should be specified? Why?

d) The store, at its own expense, can give additional training before the fieldwork starts. What, if any, additional training, would you recommend? Be precise.

e) What do you believe would be the principal sources of bias in this research?

7. Refer to Exercise 7 in Chapter 4.

   a) The planned approach is a series of "fixed location" interviews. What problem does this pose in identifying the population studied?

   b) Name an alternative procedure for which this problem is not as serious. Are any other problems introduced by the alternative that do not exist with the "fixed location" approach?

   c) Which of the two alternatives would you recommend? Defend your choice.

8. Choose an original marketing research problem that can be studied by the observational method—either in the laboratory or the marketplace.

   a) State the problem briefly but clearly.

   b) Prepare the data forms that must be completed, and specify the procedure by which the data will be obtained.

   c) Classify your research proposal on the five bases proposed by Webb, Campbell, Schwartz, and Secrest. (Refer to the text section on "Observation.")

9. The Chamber of Commerce of your hometown wishes to survey trade and professional associations concerning the bases upon which they select the cities and hotels for their conventions. The questionnaire will cover image of various localities, appraisal of facilities, decision process, identity of decision maker, and other related matters.

   a) Prepare a cover letter for the survey.

   b) Present your rationale for the features incorporated in your letter. Include a discussion of the advisability of offering an incentive.

10. A survey of newspaper readership reveals that the mean income for subscribers to the local paper, the *Colera Sun,* is $18,200. This figure is, of course, based on only the respondents. The response rate was 40 percent.

    a) If the mean income among nonrespondents is $20,000, how large is the bias in the study?

    b) Discuss how and why a larger response rate would reduce the bias.

    c) Would a larger initial sample also reduce the bias? Discuss.

11. Analyze, criticize, and explain:

    a) If the responses to a telephone survey are all truthful and accurate, the results are unbiased.

    b) The characteristics of the interviewer should coincide as closely as possible with those of the persons to be interviewed. This procedure produces rapport and also minimizes the probability of role playing.

    c) Focusing on the differences between the opinions of males and females within a panel overcomes the problem that the panel may not be representative of the target population.

d) One of the principal problems with inexperienced interviewers is their tendency to concentrate on obtaining participation rather than concentrating on obtaining good data.

e) The nonresponse problem is best handled in personal interview studies by substituting units with characteristics similar to the units that have been missed. With consumer surveys this is often accomplished by using a next-door neighbor.

f) The laboratory experiment usually provides higher quality data than the marketplace experiment. It is also less expensive and eliminates the risks associated with an error in the marketplace.

g) Persons with special interest in the subject matter of a study are more likely to respond than persons without that interest. Therefore, the researcher should adjust the data for this tendency.

h) Fieldwork plans should take the data collection instrument as given. To revise the instrument based on fieldwork considerations introduces the danger of gathering the wrong information.

CONCLUSIONS
FROM SAMPLES

Problem definition, research design, and data collection keep the bias as small as possible. The bias introduced by these phases of a research plan would exist whether they were applied to the entire universe or just to a part of that universe. In Part II we consider the particular problems raised when the research is based on a sample rather than the entire universe. Two fundamental questions are addressed: (1) how to select a sample without introducing an additional source of bias, and (2) how to select a sample that will yield reliable results. The discussion is divided into four parts: Chapter 6, a general consideration of sampling and various sampling plans; Chapter 7, the critical role of probability theory in measuring sampling reliability; Chapter 8, the determination of required sample size; and Chapter 9, the particular problem of comparing two sample results.

SAMPLING
HOW TO AVOID MISLEADING EVIDENCE

Any subgroup of a universe is a *sample* of that universe. A *census* is a complete enumeration of the universe. The sample size may vary from one up to but not including the size of the universe. Thus a sample cannot also be a census. The crucial question with sampling, as with every other phase of a research plan, is whether it will yield useful results for the decision maker.

Almost all decisions, both business and personal, are based upon samples: the choice of a package design, the selection of an employer, the decision to "go national" with a new product, the determination of a marketing mix, the purchase of a house, and even the selection of a spouse. These apparently unlike events have a central core of similarity. Each is made with incomplete evidence, and each possesses many potential sources of bias. The group appraising the package design—the marketing department executives—may differ substantially from the customers in the target market segment. The evidence presented by the potential employer may be unrepresentative of the behavior and conditions that will be encountered after employment. The sample of customers in Syracuse—a city frequently used as a test market—during the month of April may have needs and life-styles radically different from the total United States market. And certainly the sample evidence presented by a potential spouse during a whirlwind courtship is a far cry from the behavior pattern during marriage. All of these situations illustrate the prevalence and necessity for sampling in our lives, in our business, and in our marketing research. Our sampling task is *the selection of a sample that is representative of the universe*. Or conversely, the task is the avoidance of samples that are grossly misleading.

A critical question in sampling is the identification of the universe and the unit of analysis. Much marketing research is concerned with "customers" as the units; a sample of customers is then required. In other situations, the universe consists of one or a small number of persons. We may want to understand more about the behavior of a particular purchasing agent or corporation. A sample of "behaviors" is then required—a series of observations on the same entity. We wish to estimate the average behavior of *that individual*, not the average behavior of *individuals*.[1] A third situation occurs in the construction of an attitude battery or a proficiency test. A sample of items covering the concept is required. Sampling is here concerned with the construction of a proper measuring instrument rather than the determination of a relevant "state of nature" in some target universe. Sampling is involved, but the rationale and procedure has a focus different from the usual sample selection considered in this chapter.[2]

A census is not an acceptable alternative to sampling. It is too costly and too time consuming. Even apart from these considerations, it cannot possess the proper time coordinate for the marketing decision maker. Why secure such complete information for the past when the universe faced by the decision maker will almost certainly be different? A census for the wrong time coordinate is clearly a poor strategy. A sample with the hope that it is a fair representation of the correct time coordinate is a much better strategy.

The goal of a representative sample raises an obvious question: "When is a sample representative of its universe?" An answer to this question would be, "When the sample characteristics are approximately the same as those of the universe." This answer is not very helpful; what does "approximately the same" mean? Two concepts—bias and reliability—are helpful in determining whether a particular sample is satisfactory for the problem at hand.

Bias is measured by the difference between the true value in the universe and the average value obtained by repeated applications of the procedure adopted. It is convenient to separate bias into two components: that associated with the sampling design and that associated with nonsampling considerations. Part I was primarily addressed to bias caused by nonsampling considerations. Problem definition, research design, instrument design, and fieldwork are all aimed at establishing a research plan that if it were applied to the entire universe would yield results with as small a bias as possible. We now turn to potential bias introduced because the entire universe is not covered. Is a bias introduced because we settle for a sample rather than the entire universe? If yes, how large is that bias?

The second concept, *reliability*, is introduced because repeated applications of the same sampling procedures do not produce identical samples or identical answers. The magnitude of the differences among the various possible sample results is the measure of the reliability of a particular sample design.

It must be recognized at the outset that bias and reliability are two different properties. A sample design may be unbiased but unreliable. Another

---

[1] Fifty observations on a single laboratory mouse may tell us a lot about that mouse but very little about mice.

[2] "Sampling of variables" and related issues will be discussed in Chapter 19.

may be reliable but biased. The researcher should seek both reliability and freedom from bias.

Consider the case of a firm specializing in weight reduction under the supervision of medically trained doctors and nurses. The firm currently operates in a number of states but under two different names: Shape-Up Weight Control Centers and Weight Loss Medical Centers. It believes operations should be consolidated under a single name and will rely on research to choose between the two names. How might the sample selected be reliable but biased? unbiased but also unreliable?

The firm has a list of its current customers that could serve as a research universe to be sampled. A large sample from such a universe might be very reliable: repeated samples might show similar results. These results might be biased, however, since the opinions of current customers might differ from those of potential customers. The procedure for selecting the customers for the sample might be an additional source of bias, depending on the balance between those currently patronizing one or the other of the present operations. Bias results if this balance does not coincide with the views of potential customers.

A sample might be unbiased if a great deal of preliminary work is done in establishing the characteristics of the target market and clearly defining that universe. If the sample is then chosen from a single community allowing chance to determine which community, the method might be unbiased. On the average, repeated applications of the procedure would yield the true universe characteristic. The method might be highly unreliable, however. Different samples would yield different results, depending on the community selected. Even less reliability would be obtained if the actual sample contained a small number of respondents. At the extreme, one person selected at random would show preference for one name or the other. Another sample of one person might prefer the other name. The method could be unbiased, but its reliability would be extremely low.

We would like to express both reliability and bias quantitatively. If this can be achieved, we are in a much better position to appraise the utility of a particular sample design. The most convenient way to explain the measurement of these two concepts is through simple random sampling.

SIMPLE RANDOM SAMPLING

The simple random sample is the foundation for all probability sampling. In fact, every probability sample is either a simple random sample or a series of simple random samples. We cannot proceed to more complex designs without a thorough understanding and appreciation of the simple random sample. The simple random sample is, therefore, useful (1) as a distinct sampling plan and (2) as a basis for appraising the advantages and properties of more complex designs.

Table 6.1
Sales by E-Z Wipe Sales Agents,
June 1977

Sales agent	Sales
A	$ 9,500
B	8,200
C	11,100
D	10,300
E	9,800
F	9,300

A simple random sample is defined as a subset of size n selected from a universe size N ($n < N$) so that every subset of size n is equally likely to be chosen. Consider the six sales agents of the E-Z Wipe Company. Their sales in June 1977 are presented in Table 6.1. We wish to select a sample size two by using simple random sampling.

It is not sufficient to state that each unit has an equal probability of being included in the sample. This condition could be accomplished in the present problem by selecting either the sample composed of A and E or the one composed of B and C or the one composed of D and F. If the selection were made in such a way that each of these three had a 1/3 probability of being chosen, each sales agent would also have a probability of 1/3 of being chosen. This does not demonstrate that the plan is poor; it simply is not a simple random sample. A by-product of a true simple random sample is that each unit also has an equal probability of inclusion in the sample. But it is not a second condition; it is the result of the single condition which relates to the number of possible samples of size n.

There are 15 different possible samples of size two for this population. They are listed in Table 6.2 along with their respective arithmetic means and the deviation of each mean from the population mean of $9,700. In this particular example none of the sample means coincides precisely with the population mean. The sample composed of sales agents C and D yields a mean that exceeds the true value by $1,000; the sample mean from B and F is $950 lower than that of the population. Other samples (particularly AE and BC) have means much closer to the population figure.

If simple random sampling is employed, a single sample of size two will be selected in such a manner that each sample listed in Table 6.2 will have a probability of 1/15 of being the sample selected. By fulfilling that condition, it will be a simple random sample. But is that necessarily good? Will the procedure be biased? Will it be reliable? Table 6.2 provides the basic data for answering these questions.

Table 6.2
List of All Possible Samples, Size Two, for E-Z Wipe
Sales Agents

Sample	Arithmetic mean	Deviation from population mean
AB	$ 8,850	− 850
AC	10,300	+ 600
AD	9,900	+ 200
AE	9,650	− 50
AF	9,400	− 300
BC	9,650	− 50
BD	9,250	− 450
BE	9,000	− 700
BF	8,750	− 950
CD	10,700	+ 1000
CE	10,450	+ 750
CF	10,200	+ 500
DE	10,050	+ 350
DF	9,800	+ 100
EF	9,550	− 150

Presence or absence of bias is shown by comparing the arithmetic mean of Table 6.2 with that of Table 6.1 ($9,700). The required calculation shows the two to be equal; the sampling plan is unbiased! What if we had selected a simple random sample of size three?

There are 20 possible samples of size three. The samples, their arithmetic means, and the deviation of each mean from the population mean are presented in Table 6.3. Arithmetic calculations show that a simple random sample of size three also provides an unbiased estimate of the universe mean.

A *random sampling distribution* is an enumeration of all possible samples that could be obtained using a particular sampling plan. Tables 6.2 and 6.3 are, therefore, random sampling distributions. It is more common and more enlightening to present a random sampling distribution arrayed in order of magnitude, either in tabular or graph form. Figure 6.1 shows the random sampling distribution for E-Z Wipe sales agents, both for samples size two and size three. These graphs show both the extent of variability among the sample results and a general impression of the central tendencies. The reduction in dispersion as the sample size is increased from two to three is particularly evident. Further reductions, although not as pronounced, would occur if the sample size were increased to four and five ($n = 6$ would of course be a census).

Table 6.3
List of All Possible Samples, Size Three, for E-Z Wipe Sales Agents

Sample	Arithmetic mean	Deviation from population mean
ABC	$ 9,600	− 100
ABD	9,333	− 367
ABE	9,167	− 533
ABF	9,000	− 700
ACD	10,300	+ 600
ACE	10,133	+ 433
ACF	9,967	+ 267
ADE	9,867	+ 167
ADF	9,700	0
AEF	9,533	− 167
BCD	9,867	+ 167
BCE	9,700	0
BCF	9,533	− 167
BDE	9,433	− 267
BDF	9,267	− 433
BEF	9,100	− 600
CDE	10,400	+ 700
CDF	10,233	+ 533
CEF	10,067	+ 367
DEF	9,800	+ 100

The term *expected value* (E) is used for the arithmetic mean of a random sampling distribution. It is calculated for simple random sampling by weighting each possible sample result by the number of samples that would yield that result. A slightly different statement, which the reader should recognize as equivalent, is that the value associated with each sample should be weighted by the probability of selecting that sample. The latter statement shows that random sampling distributions and expected values are not restricted to simple random sampling but extend to all forms of probability sampling. The general definition for expected value (E) is incorporated in Eq. (6.1)

$$E(\hat{X}) = \Sigma X_i P_i \qquad (6.1)$$

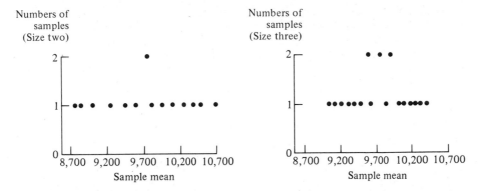

Fig. 6.1
Random sampling distribution. E-Z Wipe sales agents.

where

$$X_i = \text{result from sample } i.$$
$$P_i = \text{Probability of selecting sample } i.$$

Bias is then defined by Eq. (6.2).

$$\text{Bias} = E(\hat{X}) - X \qquad\qquad (6.2)$$

where

$$X = \text{universe parameter.}$$

It can be demonstrated that the arithmetic mean of a simple random sample is an unbiased estimate of the corresponding population arithmetic mean, regardless of the sample size.[3] Estimators of population proportions and totals are also unbiased estimators when based on simple random samples.[4]

The sample arithmetic mean yields an unbiased estimate of the population mean in a very limited sense. It is an unbiased estimate of the figure that would have been calculated had the same procedure been used for a complete census. Suppose there is something about the data collection procedure that leads to

[3]See any standard work on sampling: for example, Morris H. Hanson, William N. Hurwitz, and William G. Madow, 1953, *Sample Survey Methods and Theory* (New York: Wiley).

[4]We must be careful to ask whether sample designs other than simple random sampling yield unbiased estimators and whether statistics other than those mentioned will be unbiased estimators even with simple random sampling. We shall not pursue this subject at the moment, but it would be improper to assume that all sample designs for all sample statistics were unbiased. Most sampling texts discuss these matters in detail.

overstatement of sales by two of the E-Z Wipe sales agents. Specifically, let us assume that sales agent B would state his or her sales as $8,800 instead of the correct figure of $8,200 and that sales agent E would state his or her sales as $10,100 instead of $9,800. The arithmetic mean that would be obtained by complete enumeration is $9,850 (an error of $150). The expected value of the random sampling distribution would also be increased to $9,850. This expected value is unbiased with respect to the result from a complete enumeration but not with respect to the true population parameter. Sampling plans can be unbiased only in the limited sense of not introducing additional biases; we must not expect them to remove biases introduced by other phases of the research plan.

A procedure that would be correct on the average but usually wrong by a large amount is of little utility. Consider the sampling plan that generates two kinds of samples: those that overstate the universe mean income by $5,000 and those that understate the mean by $5,000. If 50 percent of the samples are in each category, the plan is unbiased. Knowledge concerning the magnitude of the differences between the various sample results and their average (the expected value) helps us appraise the utility of a sampling plan. This measurement requires knowledge of the expected value and the various sample results—precisely what we have in a random sampling distribution. We do not usually know the amount of error present for a particular sample, but an overall appraisal of the sampling plan can be determined from general knowledge of random sampling distributions.

Inspection of Table 6.2 shows that the total range of results is $1,950 with a low of $8,750 and a high of $10,700. It also shows that seven of the 15 samples are within $400 of the population mean ($9,300 to $10,100). Inspection of Table 6.3 shows that samples size three have a total range of only $1,400 ($9,000 to $10,400) and that 12 of the 20 samples are in the interval $9,300 to $10,100. The dispersion, not unexpectedly, is less in the distribution for samples size three than in the distribution for samples size two. A sample of size three is less likely to lead us astray than is a sample size two.

The standard deviation (σ) and the variance (σ^2) are the measures of sampling reliability with the greatest utility. Equations (6.3) and (6.4) provide the formulas for their calculations.

$$\sigma^2 = \Sigma\left(X_i P_i - \mathrm{E}(\hat{X})\right)^2 \div \Sigma P_i. \tag{6.3}$$

$$\sigma = \left(\sigma^2\right)^{1/2}. \tag{6.4}$$

These formulas should make it apparent that their utility is not in their interpretability. The variance is the average squared deviation from the expected value, and the standard deviation is the square root of the variance. Their utility is in their central role in probability models, most importantly the normal equation. For the moment, we merely calculate σ and σ^2 for the E-Z

Wipe random sampling distributions of Tables 6.2 and 6.3. The resulting values are: size two, $\sigma^2 = 318,667$ and $\sigma = 564$; size three, $\sigma^2 = 159,333$ and $\sigma = 399.$[5]

Random Numbers and Sample Selection

Any procedure that accomplishes the one condition of simple random sampling generates a simple random sample. The operational question is how to choose sample elements so that the condition is fulfilled. Theoretically, we could assign numbers to each element in the population, write the numbers on slips of paper, place the slips in a hat or bowl, and draw n slips from that bowl. This is too cumbersome a process for most practical problems. Even when it is not, the task of maintaining equal likelihood for all numbers is almost impossible to fulfill. A more efficient and theoretically sound procedure is to use a table of random numbers such as Table 6.4 or Table A.1 of the Appendix. Note that in Table 6.4 columns are grouped by twos.

Suppose we have a population consisting of 8,592 invoices. We wish to select 100 at random. First we must assign the numbers 0001 through 8592 to the population of invoices. Next we enter the table at a stated location, not chosen with regard to the numbers at that location. For example, let us choose the seventh row and eighth column of Table 6.4.[6] At row seven and column eight we find the digit 0. Reading to the right we find 0, 7, and 3. Since we are using four-digit numbers, the first number in our sample is 0073. The first unit in our sample is invoice number 73. The four-digit number immediately below is 0158, below which are 7047, 7317, and 3073. We have now identified the first five units of our sample: invoices 73; 158; 3,073; 7,047; and 7,317. We would proceed through the table until we have selected 100 different invoices.[7] Any four-digit sequence encountered in the table between 8593 and 9999 will be ignored because there is no invoice corresponding to those numbers (nor is there an invoice corresponding to the sequence 0000).

Suppose there were only 1,003 invoices. The same procedure could be followed as in the preceding case with any four-digit sequence between 1004 and 9999 ignored. Such a plan poses no theoretical problems, but the actual selection could be time consuming and tedious. Each unit could be assigned

---

[5] Sample reliability calculations, interpretations, and implications are developed in detail in a later section of this chapter.

[6] We could enter the table in the upper left-hand corner, working our way through the complete table over the selection of many different samples. Some problems would involve three digits, others two, others five, etc. We are also not restricted to reading from top to bottom or from left to right. Almost any procedure of choosing the numbers from the table is acceptable, so long as it is not dependent on the numbers at specific locations.

[7] With 100 *different* invoices, we are sampling without replacement. Once an element is selected, its number is eliminated from further selection. Sampling with replacement—the same invoice could appear more than once—could be employed but would decrease reliability with no offsetting advantages. Most marketing research problems will use sampling without replacement.

Table 6.4
Table of Random Digits

				Columns			
1, 2	3, 4	5, 6	7, 8	9, 10	11, 12	13, 14	15, 16
35	89	14	12	99	27	08	92
23	82	41	79	03	59	19	83
47	01	49	55	64	26	61	43
88	35	60	20	23	92	78	21
43	69	51	82	63	46	35	58
57	67	04	68	50	32	81	65
29	02	85	30	07	34	14	41
51	37	74	90	15	84	23	02
73	18	62	37	04	71	73	82
70	35	28	67	31	79	06	11
14	53	89	73	07	31	24	74
32	98	02	17	46	73	53	79
66	09	29	44	82	09	79	40
24	71	66	00	96	82	90	95
96	41	79	85	08	07	67	02
03	87	27	36	04	42	71	86
06	97	62	01	53	18	66	08
89	34	52	79	22	58	97	51
53	29	43	50	74	60	15	67
25	45	10	48	35	57	46	24

several four-digit sequences; for example, the first invoice could be assigned 0001, 1004, 2007, 3010, 4013, 5016, 6019, 7022, and 8025. The four-digit sequence 9028 would not be assigned to that invoice because 1003 numbers do not remain between 9028 and 9999. Equal probability must be maintained.

This description may seem to run counter to the earlier discussion that stressed equal probabilities for complete samples as opposed to equal probabilities for individual units. The crucial consideration is whether the selection of sample units is independent of the units that have already been drawn for the sample. Suppose a sample of public utility companies is to be selected. One company included is Dayton Power and Light. If that knowledge either increases or decreases the probability that Delmarva Power and Light is in the sample, it is not a simple random sample. Note that the independence concept leads to the idea that all combinations must be equally likely. Some combinations are not more likely and others less likely. If a sample of persons is selected in such a way that both husband and wife cannot appear in the sample, it cannot be a simple random sample of persons.

We shall discuss several very useful sampling methods other than simple random sampling in the next few sections. In many respects they are superior to simple random sampling, but the formulas for estimating universe parameters and their reliability are more complex. Since each method is a modification of the simple random sample, the required formulas also involve modifications.

Random dialings with WATS lines are greatly facilitated with tables of random digits. After the proper exchanges are identified, either through problem definition or a sampling of exchanges, four-digit random numbers are selected from a table of random digits in precisely the same manner discussed earlier in this section. If no numbers between 0000 and 9999 have been blocked out of use, the person dialing can proceed straight through the table of random numbers. What of disconnected telephones? Obviously numbers corresponding to disconnected numbers result in uncompleted calls. But they are not nonrespondents; they are not units in either the universe or the sample. Does this distort the sampling plan, resulting in unequal probabilities? Not if the numbers are chosen independently! It does cause a problem if 7236 is called because 7235 is a "disconnect." The probability for each number then varies, according to the number of "disconnects" immediately preceding it. Clearly this would violate simple random sampling. What, if any, biases would be introduced? None unless the characteristics of potential respondents vary according to the number of "disconnects" preceding their four-digit sequence.

The number of applications possible with random digits is endless. Selection of highway locations, corners of intersections, file drawers, pages in a directory—all are basically the same. The universe units are actually or conceptually listed, with each unit assigned a number. With N numbers assigned to the N units, the table of random numbers is entered at an arbitrary location and n numbers are selected. Units whose assigned numbers correspond to those n numbers comprise the sample.

MEASUREMENT OF SAMPLING RELIABILITY

Equations (6.3) and (6.4) are general formulas for a variance and a standard deviation, referring as they do to dispersion around the expected value of a distribution. When the distribution is a random sampling distribution, which by definition is based on a particular characteristic calculated from each possible sample of size n, the standard deviation is referred to as the *standard error* of the given characteristic. Since Tables 6.2 and 6.3 present sample arithmetic means, the standard deviations calculated from them are standard errors of arithmetic means.[8]

The points of reference for calculating these standard errors are the expected values of the tables. If we knew those values, there would be no need to select the sample in the first place. If we cannot estimate reliability without knowing the complete random sampling distribution, our discussion may have been theoretically interesting but utterly futile in terms of practical applications.

Fortunately, the variance of a random sampling distribution can be calculated without having the complete random sampling distribution. Its formula for the arithmetic mean is given by Eq. (6.5).

$$\sigma_{\bar{x}}^2 = \frac{\sigma^2}{N}(1 - f),\tag{6.5}$$

σ^2 = population variance among elements,

n = sample size

$f = \dfrac{n}{N}$ = proportion of universe included in sample.

The formula states that the reliability of a simple random sample (for estimating a mean) is dependent on two features of the sampling plan and one feature of the population.[9] The relevant sampling plan characteristics are the sample size (n) and the sampling fraction (f). The population characteristic of concern is the amount of dispersion, specifically as measured by the variance (σ^2).

First, the larger the absolute size of the sample, the more reliable the estimate. As seen in Eq. (6.5), the variance of the random sampling distribution varies inversely with the sample size (n). Second, the larger the sample is as a proportion of the universe, the more reliable the estimate. This appears in the equation through its complement ($1 - f$)—the proportion of the universe *not* included in the sample.

The term ($1 - f$) is often called the *finite multiplier*. If the entire universe is covered in the sample, f is equal to 1 and the finite multiplier is equal to 0. In this case, $\sigma_{\bar{x}}^2$ is also equal to 0 and the sampling plan has perfect reliability. It is "perfect" in the sense that every application of the sampling plan would give precisely the same answer because every application would be over the same units—namely the total population. If the sampling fraction is very small, the

---

[8] The present discussion is restricted to the sample arithmetic mean associated with simple random sampling. Other statistics and other sampling schemes have different formulas for their reliabilities. They will be presented in later discussions.

[9] To be technically correct, Eq. (6.5) should be multiplied by $N \div (N - 1)$. This value is so close to 1 for meaningful marketing research problems that we will not include the modification. A check against $\sigma_{\bar{x}}^2$ for Tables 6.2 and 6.3 will show substantial differences when N is only six.

finite multiplier is almost equal to 1 and $\sigma_{\bar{x}}^2$ is almost equal to σ^2/n. The frequent presentation of the formula for $\sigma_{\bar{x}}^2$ in this form is merely an approximation and is a satisfactory approximation only if the finite multiplier is almost equal to 1. The term "finite multiplier" is derived from the fact that it is appropriate only with finite populations. If the population truly is infinite, the sampling fraction (f) is equal to 0 and the finite multiplier vanishes from Eq. (6.5).

In Eq. (6.5), σ^2 is not dependent upon the sampling plan. It is the variance in the universe among the elements. If sample size and sampling fraction are held constant, the more variable the population is, the less reliable the sample estimate will be. If dispersion among the population units is very small, very reliable estimates of the population mean are obtained. We see this in Eq. (6.5) where the variance of the random sampling distribution varies directly with the variance of the population.

The sample size and the sampling fraction will be specified in a sampling plan; consequently their values may be "plugged into" Eq. (6.5) prior to any fieldwork associated with the research. The same statement cannot be made with respect to σ^2. In fact σ^2 usually is unknown even after the fieldwork is completed. Unbiased estimates for σ^2 may be made from the sample data and these values are normally employed in estimating the reliability of results. If one wishes to estimate the reliability of a given research plan before the work is actually done, it must be based upon estimates of σ^2 available at the time the plan is being made. If these estimates are good estimates, the reliability achieved in the research will be in accordance with the plan. If the estimates of σ^2 are poor, reliability will be either less than or greater than that expected prior to the research—depending on the nature of the error in estimating σ^2.

How is knowledge of reliability (as shown by $\sigma_{\bar{x}}^2$) useful in interpreting sample results? First, the smaller $\sigma_{\bar{x}}^2$ is, the more confidence the researcher can have that the sample result is fairly close to the corresponding universe parameter. Sampling plans with small standard errors, all other things constant, are better than sampling plans with large standard errors. Second, knowledge of $\sigma_{\bar{x}}^2$ plus knowledge of the form of the random sampling distribution permits precise statements with respect to the most likely values of the population parameter. We shall develop these concepts in conjunction with probabilistic statements in the next chapter.[10]

Equation (6.5) supplies a standard against which to compare the reliability of sampling plans other than simple random sampling. It also establishes a means for evaluating the effect of changes in sample size on sample reliability. Other sampling methods are discussed in the remainder of the present chapter. The determination of the required sample size is considered in Chapter 8.

---

[10]The type of statement possible is that the researcher is 99 percent confident that the universe per capita expenditure lies in the interval $5.63 to $5.78.

SYSTEMATIC SAMPLING

A company has 5,000 current accounts and wishes to determine additional information about the buying habits of these accounts. The company wishes to select a sample of 250 accounts. How might it proceed? The sampling fraction (f) has been established as 1/20 (250/5,000). One possible sampling procedure is to select a random number between 1 and 20 in order to locate the first account to be included in the sample and then to include every twentieth account thereafter. Each account will have a probability of 1/20 of being included in the sample, but will it be a simple random sample? No! Each possible sample of size 250 will not have an equal probability of becoming the sample selected. The sample design is a *systematic sample*.

A systematic sample uses a random starting point and every kth element thereafter. Adjacent units on the universe list cannot appear in the sample. One and only one unit in any sequential group of k elements will be included. There are only k samples possible with this plan. In our example of 250 accounts selected from a universe of 5,000 accounts, only 20 samples are possible. Each has a probability of 1/20 of being chosen. These 20 samples are: (1) accounts 1, 21, 41, 61, . . . , 4,981; (2) accounts 2, 22, 42, 62, . . . , 4,982, etc. until sample (20), which includes accounts 20, 40, 60, 80, . . . , 5,000.

A systematic sample requires only one random number in order to locate the first unit. The clerical job is therefore less tedious. That consideration, however, is trivial compared with an appraisal of the method for bias and reliability. The systematic sample yields unbiased estimates for the population mean and proportion. Estimates of population totals, using either a sample mean or proportion, are also unbiased. This freedom from bias derives from the fact that each universe element has an equal probability of inclusion in the sample. Samples selected with equal probability for all universe elements are "self-weighting" samples, and the term applies to many sampling methods other than systematic sampling and simple random sampling. Self-weighting designs are extremely helpful if the data are to be subjected to a variety of analyses since complex weighting schemes are typically required for other types of sampling designs.

The reliability of any sampling plan depends on the amount of variability in its random sampling distribution. This, in turn, depends on the degree of similarity among the various samples that could be selected. With systematic sampling, only k different samples are possible. The similarity among these samples depends on whether any systematic pattern exists in the arrangement of the list. Any periodicity within the list could cause difficulty, particularly if the periodicity were k. Consider an extreme case in which the universe is composed of persons in two-person households with the female listed first and the male second. A systematic sample with k equal to ten (or any other even number) would contain only persons of the same sex. Five of the possible samples would show a preponderance of female traits, and five would show a preponderance of male traits. The expected value would be unbiased, but none of the five samples would provide good approximations of the population characteristics.

The difficulty with systematic samples goes even further. It will be recalled that the reliability of a simple random sample can be estimated by using the variance among sample elements. This is true because the elements in the sample are selected independently. This is not true in systematic sampling.

The reliability of a systematic sample cannot be estimated in the usual case. Its reliability depends on how similar the various possible samples are to each other. Since only one of these samples is selected, the researcher has no theoretical basis for estimating the extent of similarity and thus no basis for estimating the sample's reliability.

One possible procedure is to assume that a systematic sample is an approximation of a simple random sample and to calculate standard errors on that assumption. This approach relies on subjective considerations of the forces that produced the order within the list. What would occur if a list of persons were arranged alphabetically? If the first n persons or last n were accepted as the appropriate sample, different ethnic characteristics might result. Would this balance out in a systematic sample? The systematic sample might be even better than a simple random sample since it would rule out samples composed primarily of persons with similar names.

Lists arranged in order of magnitude will not reveal the periodicity that raised our initial concern with systematic sampling. Here again the systematic sample may be more reliable than the simple random sample since the sample is spread over the range of values. The most unusual groupings of units are eliminated as possible samples.[11] Regardless of the subjective conclusion concerning the reliability of systematic sampling versus simple random sampling, it remains a subjective conclusion. Well-documented estimates of reliability are not ordinarily possible.[12]

If the population list is generated by a random process, a systematic sample will be equivalent to a simple random sample. The appropriate standard error formulas are those given by Eq. (6.5). If the list truly has been generated by a random process, the first or last n units of the list could also be used as a simple random sample—as can almost any other method of selection. Although the systematic sample is often used in practice, researchers must be aware of the assumptions they are making when they estimate its reliability.

STRATIFICATION

A particular simple random sample may be unrepresentative of the universe from which it was selected. For example, a simple random sample of 100 persons selected from the population of the United States could include only

---

[11]This gain is similar to that accomplished with stratification which is discussed in the next section.

[12]See William Edwards Deming, 1950, *Some Theory of Sampling* (New York: Wiley), pp. 352–355 for a systematic design yielding estimates of reliability.

females or only senior citizens. Such extremes are unlikely (but possible), but samples with disproportionate representation of some particular groups are to be expected: the sample contains 62 percent urban when 73 percent of the population is urban or the occupational category of 18 percent of the sample is "professional" although this is true of only 12 percent of the population. Through stratification we can guard against such unrepresentative samples and the erroneous estimates they may generate.

Suppose we wish to estimate the distribution of expenditures over five or six broad categories. Suppose further that we believe the expenditures pattern varies according to age, income, and owner–renter status. In order to ensure that the sample includes persons from each of these different groups, a stratified sample could be employed. In this particular case we might establish three categories with respect to age, two with respect to income, and two with respect to owner–renter status—yielding the 12 different subgroups or strata enumerated in Table 6.5. A simple random sample would be selected from each of the 12 strata, thus securing representation from each of the groups. Note how rapidly the number of strata increases with three bases of stratification. The addition of one more category with respect to income would increase the number of strata from 12 to 18; a further increase of one more age category would lead to 24 strata. The benefits of statification rapidly diminish either as the number of categories is increased or as additional bases of stratification are added.

Unbiased estimates for the population would be possible even if different sampling fractions were used for the different strata, but often the same sampling fraction would be employed for all strata. The "self-weighting" feature with equal sampling fractions means that the sample means and proportions may be used as estimates of the corresponding universe parameters. If differential sampling fractions are employed, each stratum must be weighted according to its number of units in the universe rather than its number of units in the sample. Consider a universe divided into two strata: firms with multiple locations and firms with a single location. If multilocation firms comprise 25

Table 6.5
Strata to Be Employed in Stratified Sample. Strata Based on Age, Income, and Owner–renter Status

	Income			
	Less than $15,000		$15,000 and over	
Age	Renter	Owner	Renter	Owner
Under 40	(1)	(2)	(3)	(4)
40–60	(5)	(6)	(7)	(8)
Over 60	(9)	(10)	(11)	(12)

percent of the sample but only 10 percent of the universe, an unweighted arithmetic mean number of employees per firm calculated from the sample would overstate the universe parameter. (See Table 6.6.) This results because the mean of 192 for multilocation firms is given more weight in the sample than it is given in the universe; the sampling fractions for the two strata in this problem are 1/20 for multilocation firms and 1/60 for single-location firms.

Stratification yields more reliable estimates than simple random sampling if the strata are relatively homogeneous with respect to the characteristics estimated. This increase in reliability occurs because the separate estimates for individual strata are made with high reliability. The separate estimates—each highly reliable—are then combined into an overall estimate for the population.

Consider the highly artificial situation in which a universe is subdivided into four strata, and all units within each stratum are identical with respect to the characteristic of interest. In such a case, a sample of size one from each stratum would yield a perfectly reliable estimate for each stratum. If each such estimate is weighted by the number of universe units in that stratum, an estimate with perfect reliability is obtained for the universe. This ultimate is not achieved in practice; but if the strata are formed in a manner that minimizes within-stratum variance and maximizes among-strata variance, great gains in reliability are achieved.[13]

Table 6.6
Weighting Implications of Stratification with Unequal Sampling Fractions

Stratum	Number of employees in sample	Number of firms	
		In sample	In universe
Single-location firms	4,950	150	9,000
Multilocation firms	9,600	50	1,000
Total	14,550	200	10,000

$$\text{Raw sample mean} = \frac{14550}{200} = 72.75$$

Stratum means: single-location (4950/150) = 33.0
multilocation (9600/50) = 192.0

$$\text{Estimated universe mean} = \frac{(33 \times 9000) + (192 \times 1000)}{10,000}$$

$$= 48.90$$

---

[13]In many marketing cases, we are more interested in estimating a total than an arithmetic mean. However, the arithmetic mean is a necessary intermediate step. Therefore, we can talk about estimating the mean with reliability even though the ultimate objective is to estimate a total.

The gain from stratification can be illustrated with the data in Table 6.6. Assume the true universe mean is 49.0 and the distribution is decidedly bi-modal. Single-location firms are concentrated around a lower figure of 25 to 30, with a few larger firms pulling the mean up to 33. The deviations of single-location firms from the overall mean (49.0) are thus often 20 or more units. The multilocation firms are typically much larger than the overall mean of 49.0, with a mean of 192. Deviations of most of these firms from the overall mean are in excess of 100 units and not uncommonly over 150 units.

Reliability of estimates based on a simple random sample would depend on an extremely large population standard deviation. With stratification, the magnitude of deviations within strata would be greatly reduced. The bulk of the single-location firms would be within ten units of the stratum mean, resulting in a highly reliable estimate for the mean of that stratum. Deviations of the multilocation firms from the mean of 192 would be larger than those of the single-location firms from their mean, but the observations would be closer to the stratum mean than to the overall mean. The larger sampling fraction for this stratum will also help obtain greater reliability.

The bases for stratification should be characteristics that the researcher believes are related to the characteristic under investigation. Income may be a relevant basis for stratification in a study of expenditures; age may be relevant for a study of leisure activities; education or occupation may be relevant for a study of reading habits; and sex may be relevant for a study of attitudes toward automobiles. Color of hair may be inappropriate for any of the foregoing studies but useful in a study of clothing preferences. The point to be underlined is that the basis for stratification is chosen for a particular project and purpose. The gain realized by stratification over simple random sampling depends on the insight exercised by the researcher in choosing the basis for stratification.

Let us review the essential characteristics of stratification. First, let us look at the mechanical operation without asking whether stratification is a good idea. Second, let us consider when stratification seems like a good idea.

Stratification first demands a division of the population into mutually exclusive subgroups (strata). A simple random sample is then selected from each stratum, not necessarily with the same sampling fractions. Unbiased estimates of population parameters are obtained by weighting each stratum result by its number of units in the population. The reliability of the estimate is also obtained by weighting the reliabilities of the individual stratum estimates.[14]

Stratification results in substantial gains over simple random sampling when the individual strata differ with respect to the characteristic under study but the units within each stratum are similar with regard to that characteristic. It must be possible to divide the population into these strata without excessive

---

[14]Reliability of stratified samples is developed in Chapter 8.

costs; thus the best bases for forming the strata are those that can be easily identified on the listing of the population. Obviously a trade-off may be necessary between ease of forming the strata and the within-stratum homogeneity that results.

The researcher must have more information to select a stratified sample than is needed to select a simple random sample. First, the researcher must have relevant substantive knowledge in order to know which characteristics will reduce within-stratum variance. Second, and often more difficult, the researcher must be able to place each unit in the proper stratum. Often those who have used a product have attitudes toward that product different from the attitudes of those who have not used the product. Thus product usage might seem an appropriate basis for stratification in an attitude survey. Unfortunately most lists of ultimate consumers do not contain product-use information. Unless the researcher can place the universe units in the appropriate strata, it is impossible to use stratification on the desired basis. An alternative—stratification after sampling—is a possibility, but this approach does not permit the allocation of resources to the various strata according to any predetermined plan.

CLUSTERING

A simple random sample of *n* elements or a stratified random sample of the same size may be very costly to administer. This is particularly true if personal interviews are used over a large geographic area. The greater the distance between interviews and the more time spent in travel, the higher the cost of a survey for a given size sample. Interviewing units in close promixity to one another reduces cost; and when this *clustering* is properly employed, the result is greater reliability for a given cost. It does not yield greater reliability for a given sample size—only greater reliability for a given cost.

The principles of simple random sampling are also employed in cluster sampling. However, they are applied in one or more stages to clusters of units rather than to individual units. Consider the advertising campaign by a large department store. The advertising manager wishes to know the current image of the store in the local metropolitan area. A simple random sample of 500 or 1,000 potential customers in the area would involve much travel time and run the risk of a costly call-back procedure. An alternative sampling plan would be to divide the metropolitan area into blocks or portions of blocks, and then select 25 or 30 such areas for complete enumeration. Administration difficulties, travel time, and overall cost would be considerably reduced by this second procedure. This is an example of one-stage cluster sampling, but the principle could be extended to several stages.

A national survey using clustering might use as a first stage the division of the country into counties or parishes. At each succeeding stage, smaller geographic divisions would be employed, for example, cities and townships, census tracts, blocks, dwelling units, and finally persons. The number of stages and the designation of the final sampling unit depend on the nature of the project and its magnitude. The principle involved is that at each stage a simple random sample is selected, using units smaller than those employed at the preceding stage.

Clustering, in contrast to simple random sampling or stratified sampling, does not require a complete list of the units in the universe. It requires only a complete list of the first-stage units in the population. In the department store illustration, a complete list would be needed of blocks or portions of blocks. In the national survey suggested, the complete list would be of counties or parishes. Complete lists of second-stage units are needed only for those first-stage units included in the sample; complete lists for third-stage units, only for those second-stage units in the sample; etc. In the national example, lists of persons would be needed only for those dwelling units included in the sample.

The disadvantage of the cluster sample comes from a practical fact: units in close proximity to one another normally are similar in the characteristics under study. The department store advertising manager may have reservations about sampling only 30 different spots in the metropolitan area; if the manager does not have reservations about 30, he or she certainly might about five. These reservations would not be based on the total size of the sample; that may be quite large. The manager's concern would be that potential customers in each of the spots sampled may have similar images of the store and potential customers in those spots not sampled may have different images from those in the sample. Therefore, the manager must balance the decrease in cost associated with fewer and larger clusters against the risk that fewer clusters may yield unrepresentative estimates.

All of our examples of clustering have referred to units that are in close geographic proximity: this is called *area sampling* and is only one form of cluster sampling. Other examples of clustering are filing cabinets or filing drawers, pages from a directory, and specific time intervals. Each would be appropriate if and only if adjacent or nearly adjacent units could be included in the study more economically or with less administrative difficulty than could nonadjacent units. Appropriate bases of clustering must be chosen according to each specific problem.

Suppose we wish to determine the radio-listening habits of the residents of St. Louis, Missouri. We wish coincidental measurements, fearing recall biases would be too great. Since it is a one-shot project, we also rule out mechanical recording devices. We settle on telephone interviews, satisfied that the individuals without telephones may be excluded from the universe of interest. Random dialings over all St. Louis exchanges seems an extremely cumbersome procedure. Therefore we think in terms of a two-stage sampling plan: first selecting a sample of exchanges and then selecting numbers within each exchange.

We first list all exchanges in St. Louis, assigning a number to each exchange. We then select a simple random sample of exchanges, having determined the number of exchanges desired. This first stage is definitely a cluster sample. The second-stage sampling plan may be any sampling method; it is not restricted to that employed at the first stage. It may be simple random sampling within exchanges; it may be stratification; or it may be clustering again.

The number of exchanges included in the sample depends on the researcher's subjective estimate of heterogeneity in the listening habits among exchanges. If he or she thinks each exchange is a miniature of the entire area, there is no need to select more than one. If he or she believes the exchanges are extremely dissimilar, many exchanges should be included. The total sampling plan will be self-weighting if the same sampling fractions are employed at the second stage, regardless of whether it is simple random sampling or a more complex plan.

The systematic sample is really a camouflaged cluster sample. The universe is divided into k different clusters, one of which is selected as the sample employed.

COMPARISON OF STRATIFICATION AND CLUSTERING

Both stratification and clustering are started by dividing the universe into subgroups. There the similarities cease. In stratification, a simple random sample is selected *from each* subgroup. In clustering, a simple random sample *of* subgroups is selected. Because of this basic difference in procedure, the two are at oppostite poles with respect to what is most desirable concerning the nature of the subgroups. Stratification is most useful when the units within each subgroup are homogeneous. Clustering is most useful when the units within each subgroup are heterogeneous.

The researcher cannot change the basic nature of the units in the population, but sometimes can alter the way in which the subgroups are formed. Instead of establishing division lines along main traffic arteries or natural boundaries, the lines may cut across these logical divisions—thus making the subgroups more heterogeneous. Barring this approach the researcher might combine stratification and clustering using stratification where the subgroups are homogeneous and clustering where they are heterogeneous. For example, a national sample could divide the country into counties. This seems to be clustering. However, the researcher could establish four or five different categories of counties based upon population size. Having done this, he or she may take a sample of counties from each of the five categories—thus making each category a stratum. Within each county included in the sample, the researcher may then use clustering. The basic approach is to visualize whether subgroups at the last sampling stage will be homogeneous or heterogeneous. If they are heterogeneous, the researcher should attempt stratification at an earlier stage in order to decrease the variance among the subgroups at the later stages. In the example given, the establishment of five strata would mean that the counties within each stratum would be relatively homogeneous although the list of all United States counties might be heterogeneous. This reasoning assumes that counties with similar population sizes are more likely to be similar in the characteristic under study. If this is not true, the plan would be ineffective.

The preceding discussion should alert the reader to the fact that postal zip codes may be used either in stratification or in clustering. Distribution of samples of a new product by direct mail may use zip codes. Random selection of 15 or 20 different zip codes would permit a type of market test. In this situation, zip codes form the basis for a cluster sample. Alternatively, postal zip codes may be grouped into four or five strata, established according to known demographic characteristics such as population density and income. Random selection of persons or households within these subgroups illustrates stratification. Random selection of specific zip codes within the strata illustrates the sequential combination of stratification and clustering.

NONPROBABILITY SAMPLING

A good sampling plan is one that will yield satisfactory estimates of universe parameters. This is best accomplished by samples that are representative of the universe. The goal is a representative sample, not a random sample. The simple random sample, or some modification, is chosen because its probability of "representativeness" can be objectively appraised. An alternative approach is to have a person thoroughly familiar with the problem exercise judgment in the selection of a representative sample. This is not necessarily a poor procedure, but its dangers must be recognized. If the person exercises good judgment, the results will be fine; if judgment is poor, the results will also be poor. Unfortunately, this is the only answer we can give. *Neither the bias nor the reliability of a nonprobability sample can be appraised objectively.*

Nonprobability samples have a place in marketing research despite the fact that objective appraisals of bias and reliability are lacking. Their place in pretesting instruments and exploratory research is firmly established. Probability samples for these tasks are usually not worth the extra cost. Nonprobability sampling is also appropriate for use in many problems in which the research design specifies the characteristics various units should possess—experimental design problems. Finally, nonprobability samples can be used in survey work, either by relying on expert judgment exclusively or by a quota sample in which the guides for selecting units are explicit.

The distinction between a probability sample and a nonprobability sample does not rest on the use or nonuse of expert knowledge; it rests on the point at which that knowledge is introduced in the sampling plan. Both stratification and clustering take advantage of expert knowledge. But that knowledge is introduced in the establishment of subgroups, not in the actual selection of the units to be included in the sample. In the nonprobability sample, judgment is used in the selection of the units themselves.

Pretesting of data collection instruments requires a broad coverage of the universe but not a representative sample. Therefore, nonprobability sampling is better than a representative approach. The principal precaution that must be exercised is that the test units cover the range of characteristics that are found in the universe. It is tempting to accomplish this with respect to obviously relevant factors such as age, income, sex, occupation, and whatever else might apply to the particular problem while ignoring factors such as personal acquaintance, ability to articulate, and geographic location. Any of these latter factors may complicate the administration of the instrument. Therefore, their influence should be tested. Note this does not suggest a probability sample but a well-conceived nonprobability sample.

Exploratory research is somewhat similar in concept to the pretest. The distinction is that exploratory research is searching for substantive hypotheses while the pretest is appraising a portion of the research plan. The researcher is not concerned about the reliability or bias of substantive results in either case. Reliability and reduction of bias both cost money; why pay for them when they are not needed?

Experimental designs specify the values of the relevant characteristics that are of particular concern. For example, consumer response to in-store promotions and prices might be the research problem. A series of probability samples of stores, selected from each cell of the research design table, would be desirable, but it is probably more than the research can obtain. This is especially true if we are asking for a sample of size one or two from each cell. The uncontrolled variables, such as store size and chain membership, might have even more impact than the test variables—resulting in data containing a lot of "noise."[15] A nonprobability sample in which the investigator attempts to hold these other variables constant is an alternative that might be more informative.

Another complicating factor in many experimental designs is the securing of cooperation. The investigator may be forced to use a sample consisting of stores willing to participate, either by trying the treatment variables as requested or by providing the required data. The nonprobability approach in these cases supplies data not available on a probability basis. While the theoretical justification for measures of bias and reliability is lacking, the data are the best available. The nonprobability aspect often means that the results should be classified as case studies that do not necessarily refer to the universe of interest. Replication of the design, involving several case studies, will increase the decision maker's confidence in the generality of the results.

---

[15]The term "noise" refers to the presence of high variability due to factors other than those being examined. This presence often complicates the identification of the effect of the treatment variables.

A superior alternative is to secure the participating nonprobability sample of units initially. A random assignment of these units to the various cells of the design eliminates the self-selection bias as far as the treatment variables are concerned. Of course, the potential for a self-selection bias of the entire sample remains.

The use of nonprobability samples in *survey* work is even more suspect than it is in experimental design work. The usual method of minimizing potential bias in nonprobability surveys is by the *quota* sample. The quota approach is the nonprobability counterpart of stratification in probability sampling. The subgroups are established in precisely the same way and with the same general criteria. The difference is in the selection of the units. The interviewer is charged with the responsibility of securing a prescribed number of interviews from each specified subgroup, usually a different number from each. The potential bias with the quota sample occurs because the interviewers tend to select units that can be reached most conveniently. The definition of subgroups imposes certain constraints, but within those constraints the interviewers tend to select acquaintances, other units that match the individual interviewer's general characteristics, and units that minimize travel. One procedure that partially offsets these biases is to employ a large number of interviewers and interviewers with diverse characteristics. Unfortunately this is not easily accomplished, given the desired areas of competence plus the part-time nature of interview work. The areas of competence narrow the range of acceptable interviewers, and the part-time nature of interviewing further restricts the list of those available.

The principal attractions of nonprobability sample designs are their cost and ease of administration. Probability samples specify the particular units to be included, and their selection is determined by chance. Nonprobability samples do not typically identify particular units to the interviewer. The interviewer is given general guidelines, but the selection of specific units is within his or her discretion. In practice this means that "not at homes" and "refusals" are replaced by somewhat similar and adjacent units. The cost saving is obvious and the need for close supervision is reduced. These advantages must be weighed against the possible increase in bias from two directions: (1) the interviewer's bias in selecting respondents and (2) a bias akin to the nonresponse bias. The latter develops in nonprobability sampling because the types of units that are more difficult to reach may differ from those that are more accessible. These two biases are the principal disadvantages of nonprobability samples. The third, a more technical consideration, is the inability to objectively determine the reliability of the results.

One of the more convincing arguments in favor of nonprobability sampling is that research results should be appraised in terms of total error. This total error is produced by nonsampling errors as well as sampling errors. Excessive costs directed toward the reduction of sampling errors might be better spent on the reduction of nonsampling errors, particularly when the latter may be very large.

SUMMARY

Sampling has the same purpose as any other phase of practical research—helping the decision maker reduce uncertainty while choosing among alternatives. More specifically, a sample should be an appropriate basis for estimating universe characteristics; this is achieved most simply if the sample is representative of the universe. Sampling is used rather than complete enumeration primarily because of the economics involved, although the ability to supervise and administer a small project may also bring gains of a nonsampling type. There are two main questions to be asked of a sample design: (1) Is any bias produced by the design? (2) How reliable are the estimates?

Bias is defined as the difference between the expected value of the sampling procedure and the true value of the universe. Simple random sampling has the great advantage that the most frequently used statistics (mean, proportion, and total) yield unbiased estimates of the corresponding universe parameters. Thus no bias is introduced by the sampling procedure although it cannot correct any biases introduced by the definition–collection–processing steps.

Reliability is associated with the fact that one of many possible samples is selected and that not all samples would yield identical results. We measure reliability by the dispersion among these various possible results. We desire unbiased estimators and high reliability from our sample design, but we must be careful not to demand more from our sample design than is needed for our decision—especially if we have to pay a lot to achieve it.

The basis for all probability sampling is the simple random sample. A *simple random sample* is a sample selected in such a way that every possible sample of size *n* is equally likely to be the sample that is actually selected. A systematic sample is not a simple random sample although it possesses certain superficial similarities. The systematic sample is selected with a random start, and the subsequent inclusion of every *k*th element in the universe.

More efficient sample designs can frequently be achieved by moving either into stratification or clustering. Stratification consists of subdividing the universe into subgroups (called strata) and selecting a simple random sample *from each subgroup*. Clustering consists of dividing the universe into subgroups and then taking a simple random sample *of subgroups*. Stratification is introduced in order to achieve greater reliability for a given sample size and is most efficient when the units within each subgroup are homogeneous. Clustering is introduced in order to achieve greater reliability per unit of cost and is most beneficial when costs can be reduced by selecting units that are in close proximity to one another.

The random sampling distribution is a complete enumeration of every possible sample that could have been selected along with the statistical results of each. The expected value and standard deviation of this distribution are the critical measures used in determining the bias and reliability of a particular sampling plan. In any practical problem, the random sampling distribution is a theoretical construct that is unknown to the researcher. Despite this, there are techniques by which unbiased estimates may be made of the amount of variability in the random sampling distribution. For a random sampling distribution of sample means (chosen by simple random sampling), reliability is measured by $\sigma_{\bar{x}}^2$ and is equal to $(\sigma^2/n) \times (1 - f)$. This formula identifies that reliability depends on sample size (n), sampling fraction (f), and variance in the universe (σ^2).

Nonprobability samples have the primary weakness that objective measures of bias and reliability cannot be computed for them. Offsetting this disadvantage are lower costs and simpler supervision tasks. Expert judgment and judicious avoidance of the natural tendency to interview friends, those of like characteristics, and the easily accessible are the keys to useful nonprobability samples.

EXERCISES AND PROBLEMS

1. Distinguish among the terms within each of the following sets.
    a) Bias and reliability
    b) Stratification and clustering
    c) Sampling error and nonsampling error
    d) Quota sampling and stratification
    e) Simple random sample and self-weighting sample
    f) Expected value and standard error
    g) Within-stratum variance and among-strata variance

2. Briefly explain the meaning and importance of each of the following in sampling.
    a) Random sampling distribution
    b) Probability sample
    c) Area sample
    d) Finite multiplier
    e) Cluster homogeneity

3. Present an original problem in which you would expect a stratified random sample would be no more reliable than a simple random sample. Assume the samples are of the same size. Explain why you expect this result.

4. The George Boene Advertising Agency added ten new accounts in 1978. Total billing (in $1,000) to these accounts in 1979 is given below.

Account	Billing	Account	Billing
801	5.2	806	7.7
802	21.3	807	8.3
803	0.5	808	11.0
804	9.6	809	9.8
805	10.1	810	8.5

a) Calculate the mean and standard deviation in billing for these ten accounts in 1979.

b) What is the mean of the random sampling distribution of sample means from simple random samples size two? of samples size five?

c) What is the standard deviation of each random sampling distribution referred to in (b)?

d) Are your two answers in (b) the same or different? Why?

e) Are your two answers in (c) the same or different? Why?

f) How did the standard deviations in (c) compare to the one in (a)? Why?

g) Select three random samples size five from the list above, using a table of random numbers. Calculate the mean and standard deviation of each.

h) Compare the results obtained in (g) with the results in (a). Should they be the same? Why?

5. The George Boene Advertising Agency referred to in Exercise 4 has a total of 47 active accounts, including the ten mentioned in that question.

a) How would you expect the mean and standard deviation (in 1979 billing) for all 47 accounts to compare with the figures calculated in 4(a)? Why?

b) How would your answer in (a) affect the mean and standard deviation of the random sampling distribution of sample means for simple random samples size five? Contrast the results expected from the 47-account universe versus the results from the ten-account universe. Explain any expected differences.

c) Would the finite multiplier be equally important to both calculations in (b)? Why?

6. A commercial research service has been employed to study employment within a certain state. The population of interest consists of all persons in the labor force, defined rather arbitrarily by state officials as all individuals registered with the state Department of Employment. The state can obtain a computer printout of all registrants, arranged either alphabetically or by date of first listing. The two most important characteristics to determine are the number of hours worked in a designated week and total earnings in the same week. Estimates of arithmetic means for the population, as defined, are to be made from sample evidence.

a) Would you be willing to use a systematic sample drawn from either computer list? Why?

b) Would a cluster sample be advisable? Discuss.

7. Discuss the similarities and differences between a stratified sample and a cluster sample. Be sure to include all of the following.

a) The mechanics of selecting the sample

b) The relationships among subgroups that are most beneficial

c) The type of information required to choose the sample

8. Discuss the effect of each of the following on the reliability and bias of a simple random sample.

    a) Sample size

    b) Problem universe different from research universe

    c) Variance in universe

    d) Ambiguous questions

    e) Sampling fraction

9. Obtain on an anonymous basis information from every class member on (i) total individual income—last year and (ii) age in months.

    a) Calculate the reliability of a simple random sample size four for each characteristic.

    b) Do you think a stratified sample would be more reliable for either characteristic? Discuss, indicating the bases you have considered for stratification.

    c) Suppose you employed a stratified sample with two strata and a sample of two from each stratum. How would you calculate your estimate of the universe mean(s)?

10. Analyze, criticize, and explain:

    a) One should always choose a probability sample rather than a nonprobability sample because the former is always more representative of the universe.

    b) A sample in which each population unit has an equal probability of inclusion is a necessary but not a sufficient condition for a simple random sample.

    c) The careful application of substantive knowledge is important in problem definition, research design, and data collection. But substantive knowledge has no place in sampling design or sample selection.

    d) Clusters should be selected in a way that will minimize cost rather than increase within-cluster variability. This is made abundantly clear by the statement that clustering is designed to yield greater reliability for a given cost rather than greater reliability for a given sample size.

    e) A census is perfectly reliable although it may still contain bias.

CHAPTER 7

REACHING CONCLUSIONS FROM SAMPLE RESULTS

HOW RELIABLE IS YOUR ANSWER?

The decision maker is interested in the universe value, not in a sample value! A sample is of interest only as it sheds light on the universe. If a sample shows that 55 percent of the persons studied prefers the new model of a product to the old, what should the product manager conclude is true for the universe? Is that value precisely 55 percent? If not, how large a difference might exist between the sample result and the universe value? Might the universe value be less than 50 percent? Can the product manager be certain that the universe value is no more than 75 percent?

The process of generalizing from the narrow to the broad is common to all aspects of life. Specific information is used as the basis for more general conclusions. This process of generalization is called *inference*. We infer that certain acts or decisions are appropriate on the basis of sample evidence—evidence that is incomplete and imperfect. Occupations and employers are selected with limited data, based on the assumption that the sample evidence is representative of the whole. The selection of politicians and products is also based on inference. Marketing management decisions are made in precisely the same way. Our task in marketing research is to formalize and follow defensible procedures in making inferences and to understand some of the assumptions embodied in the process. Only then will we know the appropriateness of the procedures, their strengths, and their limitations.

Statistical inference is generally discussed under three headings: point estimation, interval estimation, and hypothesis testing. Point estimation is addressed to the task of selecting a specific value as an estimate for a population characteristic; for example, we estimate that the percentage of housewives perferring brand X is 29 percent, or we estimate that the average income for purchasers of model Y is $19,250. Interval estimation is a closely associated task. Here we use the sample evidence to establish a range within which the population parameter is likely to lie. We estimate that the percentage of housewives preferring brand X is between 23 percent and 35 percent, or we estimate that the average income for purchasers of model Y is between $18,975 and $19,525. Hypothesis testing—in contrast—uses the sample evidence to determine whether particular statements about the population are likely to be true or false; for example, market potential for the new model exceeds $250,000. Hypothesis testing is designed either to accept or to reject such statements.

Statistical inference can also be discussed from the perspective of the number of different characteristics involved in the analysis. A convenient and quite logical division is (1) a single characteristic—also called *univariate analysis,* (2) two characteristics—*bivariate analysis,* and (3) more than two characteristics—*multivariate analysis.* Univariate analysis lays the foundation for the other two and will be developed in this chapter.

POINT ESTIMATION

The sales manager of the Kennedy Vacuum Company wishes to estimate the percentage of calls resulting in sales and the average dollar value of sales per call. The identification of the appropriate universe for this problem causes certain difficulties. The sales manager is interested in this estimate for the future and not for the past. Existing records obviously refer to the past, and a current survey will refer only to the present. Kennedy follows a policy of providing its salespeople with leads obtained from inquiries and referrals. The results of calls made from these leads are maintained in written form within company headquarters. The sales manager decides to take a simple random sample from these records and base the estimate of the two parameters upon this sample. (Would you concur with this decision? Why or why not?)

The sample shows that 10 percent of the leads resulted in sales and that the arithmetic mean sales per call was equal to $39.50. What are the best estimates for the corresponding population parameters? Most of us would state that the best estimates are given by the sample results. For many purposes, this is a correct statement; but we should recognize the assumptions implicit in the statement.

There are several criteria by which the "goodness" of a point estimate may be evaluated. An estimator cannot be considered "best" except with respect to some established criterion. The criterion of unbiasedness was defined in the last chapter: an unbiased estimator is one whose expected value is equal to the universe parameter. Only if this is accepted as the proper definition of "best" is an unbiased estimator the "best" one to use.[1] It is in this sense that the 10 percent and $39.50 are the appropriate estimates for the sales manager to use since the sample proportion and the sample mean are each unbiased estimators.

---

[1]Other criteria whereby statisticians evaluate the goodness of a point estimate are consistency, efficiency, and sufficiency. These are discussed in most advanced statistic texts; for example, John E. Freund, 1971, *Mathematical Statistics,* (Englewood Cliffs, N.J.: Prentice-Hall).

These two statistics are encountered repeatedly in marketing research problems. What percentage of last month's customers were first-time purchasers? What is per capita consumption of gasoline? of unleaded gasoline? What is the average price paid for aspirin? How much time a week does the average teenager spend watching TV? What proportion of major appliance purchases are joint decisions by husband and wife? How often does the average sales person change jobs? All of these refer to a percentage or an arithmetic mean. In each case the sample result is an unbiased estimate of the true universe value—if simple random sampling is employed.

A sample statistic is not always an unbiased estimator for the corresponding universe parameter. For example, the sample variance (s^2) is a biased estimator of the population variance (σ^2). The magnitude of this bias decreases as the sample size increases, but most practitioners prefer to use an alternative to the sample variance that is unbiased. This is accomplished by using $\overset{*}{\sigma}{}^2$ as defined by Eq. (7.2) instead of s^2 as defined by Eq. (7.1). It can readily be observed that these two equations differ by "n" compared to "$n - 1$," a difference that decreases as sample size increases.

$$s^2 = \frac{\sum (x_i - \bar{x})^2}{n},\tag{7.1}$$

$$\overset{*}{\sigma}{}^2 = \frac{\sum (x_i - \bar{x})^2}{n - 1} = \frac{ns^2}{n - 1}.\tag{7.2}$$

A fourth parameter of frequent interest in marketing research is the population total. One of the most commonly asked questions in new product development is the size of the potential market or the estimation of dollar sales. Both are illustrations of population totals. For some problems the market is defined in terms of the number of persons who will or might make a purchase; in others, the market is defined in terms of the volume of sales measured either by dollar value or number of units.

Suppose we wish to estimate the total income of a group of 1,500 persons. If we estimate that the arithmetic mean income is $15,000, it is obvious that our estimate of the total income for the entire group is $22,500,000. This simple calculation is given by Eq. (7.3).

$$x' = N\bar{x} = \frac{N}{n}\sum x_i = \frac{\sum x_i}{f}.\tag{7.3}$$

If the arithmetic mean is an unbiased estimator for the population mean, Eq. (7.3) is an unbiased estimator for the population total. Equation (7.3) also indicates that the population total may be estimated by "blowing up" the total found in the sample. The "blowup" factor is the reciprocal of the sampling fraction. If the sample contains 5 percent of the universe units, the blowup factor is 20. In a self-weighting sample, the proportion of units included in the sample is an unbiased estimate of the proportion of any particular characteristic in the sample.

How many companies would subscribe to an annual maintenance contract if it were available? The estimate follows the same logic as that of Eq. (7.3), substituting a proportion for the mean. The precise form is given by Eq. (7.4).

$$x' = N\bar{p}. \tag{7.4}$$

The equation highlights the fact that a proportion is a special type of arithmetic mean, special in the sense that only 0 and 1 are possible for the individual elements.

Consider the proportion of customers who prefer the deluxe model of Johnson and Jackson's Electric Frying Pan. The calculation is made by assigning a "1" to each person who prefers the deluxe model and a "0" to each person who does not. These values are summed, and the sum is divided by the total number of persons involved. The interpretation of a proportion then becomes very similar to the interpretation of an arithmetic mean. The arithmetic mean indicates the amount of a particular characteristic each unit would receive if the total possessed by all units were equally divided among the units. This calculation frequently results in a number that is physically impossible. An arithmetic mean number of persons per household equal to 4.7 is such a number. Fractional values of the characteristic under study are impossible. A proportion of necessity falls into this classification since only 0's and 1's are possible. Nevertheless the resulting proportion can be interpreted in a similar manner. A result that 43 percent of the purchasers prefers the deluxe model can be interpreted to mean that, on the average, 43/100 of each person prefers the deluxe model.

While the interpretation of a proportion as an average per unit seems somewhat contrived, the use of the proportion in estimating the number of persons in the universe who will be in a certain category is extremely useful. Given that 43 percent is an unbiased estimate of the proportion of the universe preferring the deluxe model, the estimate of the *number of persons* in the universe who prefer the deluxe model is given by multiplying .43 by the total number of customers in the universe. If the total number of customers is given as 150,000, the total number preferring the deluxe model is estimated to be 64,500 (.43 × 150,000). The determination of 150,000 as the total number of customers is a problem in estimation just as the one we are currently considering. Many times the innocent sounding statement "the total number of customers is . . ." should not be blindly accepted but should be subjected to further research.

We have identified four parameters for which we have unbiased estimators: an arithmetic mean, a proportion, a total, and a variance. The first two are estimated by sample statistics calculated by mathematical expressions completely analogous to the desired parameter. The third is estimated by applying an appropriate blowup factor—the number of units in the universe. The unbiased estimator for the universe variance is given by Eq. (7.2), almost analogous to the definition of the universe variance but differing by the factor $n/(n - 1)$. All four of these point estimates are unbiased, but we are practically certain that all four will be in error. The magnitude of the likely errors is incorporated in interval estimation.

INTERVAL ESTIMATION

Interval estimation is designed to cope with the problem that a point estimate cannot be expected to coincide precisely with the universe parameter. The interval estimate establishes a range within which the universe parameter probably falls. Reliability, as measured by the variance of the random sampling distribution, is the key to establishing appropriate intervals. A typical form used to establish such an interval for an arithmetic mean is

$$\bar{x} \pm 1.96 \, \overset{*}{\sigma}_{\bar{x}}.$$

The range is established by adding and subtracting appropriate values to the sample arithmetic mean. The crucial question of interval estimation is how to decide the appropriate values to add and subtract and whether equal amounts should be added and subtracted.

The amount to be added and subtracted must relate back to the dispersion in the random sampling distribution for the statistic under consideration. We have indicated that the standard deviation of a random sampling distribution is called the *standard error of the sample statistic*. The amount to add and subtract depends on the magnitude of this standard error, the symmetry of the random sampling distribution, the proportion of the distribution within various intervals (expressed in terms of the standard error), and the amount of confidence desired in presenting the interval estimation. The procedure presented above ($\bar{x} \pm 1.96 \, \overset{*}{\sigma}_{\bar{x}}$) incorporates answers to all these issues. Before adopting it as an appropriate procedure for any particular problem, we should be sure that we are satisfied with the answers contained therein.

Standard errors for most sample statistics have been mathematically derived. We are not concerned with mathematical derivations in this text, but it is obviously necessary that mathematically correct formulas for standard errors be employed. The addition and subtraction of equal values to the unbiased estimate assumes that the random sampling distribution is symmetric about that value and that we wish the smallest interval possible for a given degree of confidence. The value "1.96" corresponds to the z-value which establishes the central 95 percent of the unit normal distribution. Therefore, its use is based upon an assumption that the random sampling distribution follows the unit normal and that the researcher desires "95 percent confidence."

Coefficients corresponding to various confidence levels, when using the unit normal, can be determined from Appendix Table A.2. The table shows the percentage of the distribution between its expected value and a deviation of z standard deviations. For example, the table indicates a value of 47500 for a

z-value of 1.96, meaning that 47.5 percent of the unit normal distribution lies between the mean and a deviation of 1.96 standard deviations in either direction. Therefore 95 percent of the distribution falls within ± 1.96 standard deviations. What z-value would correspond to 98 percent confidence? Readers should review Table A.2 and its meaning if they would venture an answer other than 2.32 or 2.33. Figure 7.1 shows the unit normal distribution with the percentage included in selected intervals of one, two, and three standard deviations.

Why would or would not the random sampling distribution be normal? The Central Limit Theorem and the Student t-distribution come to our aid here. In nonformal terms, the *Central Limit Theorem* states that the sampling distribution of $\bar{x}$ (the sample mean) approaches normality as sample size increases *regardless of the form of the population distribution.* These last few words are particularly important in marketing research since many of the characteristics of interest depart significantly from normal. Thus the Central Limit Theorem can be employed as long as we deal with sufficiently large samples. But when is a sample large enough to justify the use of the normal curve? The answer depends on how much the population differs from normality; the greater the disparity, the larger the sample must be to justify use of the normal.[2] A rough rule of thumb is that the normality assumption is (1) dubious for samples of less than 30, (2) justified for samples over 100, and (3) dependent upon the particular characteristic and population for values between 30 and 100.

The Central Limit Theorem applies when the population standard deviation is known. In almost all practical problems, it is unknown and must be estimated from sample evidence. The Student t-distribution describes the random sampling distribution of sample means drawn from a normal population with the population standard deviation estimated from sample evidence. The t-distribution is not a single distribution but a family of distributions, the precise form depending on the *number of degrees of freedom.* The number of de-

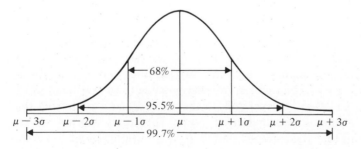

Fig. 7.1
The unit normal curve.

[2]If the population distribution is normal, the sampling distribution is normal regardless of sample size.

grees of freedom is one less than the sample size ($n - 1$) for the arithmetic mean. As the number of degrees of freedom increases, the t-distribution approaches the normal curve. Note in Appendix Table A.3 that a coefficient of 1.96 is indicated for .05 probability and ∞ degrees of freedom. The rate at which t approaches normality can be judged by observing the changes in the coefficients as the degrees of freedom increase.

We are thus in the position of being able to use (1) the normal curve if we know the population standard deviation and the sample is large ($n > 100$ and maybe $n > 30$) or (2) the t-distribution if the population distribution is normal and the population standard deviation is unknown. What of the situations which are more typical: population nonnormal and population standard deviation unknown? With sample sizes over 100, the normal curve is still a satisfactory approximation.

With samples smaller than 100, the marketing researcher has a serious problem. He or she is in a highly subjective area. The t-distribution coefficients are better to use than the normal, but their use rests upon the underlying assumption that the units of the population are distributed according to the normal curve. As a check, the researcher should compare the distribution of units within the sample to the normal curve. The greater the disparity, the more dubious the procedure. Unfortunately, this comparison is both more critical and more difficult with very small samples.[3] Since the typical marketing research problem does not permit the normality assumption, the safest procedure is to use samples larger than 100, and certainly larger than 30.

Let us illustrate the establishment of 95 percent confidence limits. The editor of *Purchasing Today* wishes to estimate the arithmetic mean amount of time spent reading a recent copy of the magazine by those on its mailing list. The relevant sample statistics are the following: $n = 100$, $\bar{x} = 23$ minutes, and $s = 9$ minutes. The necessary calculation (assuming the normal curve is appropriate) is given by

$$\bar{x} \pm 1.96 \, \overset{*}{\sigma}_{\bar{x}} = 23.0 \pm 1.96(9.0) \div (100 - 1)^{\frac{1}{2}}$$
$$23.0 \pm 1.8,$$
$$21.2 \text{ to } 24.8 \text{ min.}$$

The 95 percent confidence interval for the population mean in this problem is 21.2 to 24.8 minutes. Is there a 95 percent probability that the true mean falls in the interval established? Purists object violently to such a conclusion, asserting that there is no probability that the true mean is in that interval; it either is or is not. They assert that a probability statement applies to the method and not a particular application. The theoretically correct interpretation then is that intervals established by "$\bar{x} \pm 1.96 \overset{*}{\sigma}_{\bar{x}}$" will generate intervals that contain the population mean 95 percent of the time and will fail to include

---

[3] The actual comparison and test is by curve fitting. See Wilfrid J. Dixon and Frank J. Massey, Jr., 1957, *Introduction to Statistical Analysis* (New York: McGraw-Hill), p. 61. An alternative procedure is to use coefficients from the Tchebycheff inequality that states that the probability a sample will differ from the expected value by k standard errors does not exceed $1/k^2$.

the population mean 5 percent of the time. Any specific population mean, as the purist says, is not floating around between two limits. It has a specific location which either is or is not within the limits established.

A research worker who has generated a large number of interval estimates by this method can state that approximately 95 percent of the intervals have included the population mean of interest and about 5 percent of those intervals have not included the mean of interest. Any particular application then has a probability of being in the first category of .95 and a probability of .05 of being in the second category. Despite the purist's objection, the decision maker knows that there is a 5 percent chance that any particular application of the method will generate an interval that does not include the parameter of interest.

The choice of the particular coefficient to apply is determined by the risk the researcher and decision maker are willing to run. Suppose they opt for 99 percent instead of 95 percent; only 1 percent of the time will the method fail to include the population parameter. A price is paid for this increase in confidence: the width of the interval is increased. The appropriate coefficient is now 2.58 instead of 1.96, and the resulting interval is now 20.7 to 25.3. Confidence may be increased still further, but only by increasing the coefficient and the width of the interval. A 100 percent confidence would be achieved by using a coefficient of infinity—complete confidence but no information. Smaller intervals are generated in the reverse direction, smaller coefficients and lower levels of confidence.[4]

Figure 7.2 shows the effect of different confidence levels on the width of the confidence interval. Using the data for the readership survey, a 50 percent level of confidence would result in an interval of 22.4 to 23.6 minutes—a difference of only 1.2 minutes. The graph shows how the width of the interval increases as greater confidence is required, reaching a width of 5.0 minutes when a 99.5 percent confidence level is employed.

Precisely the same logic is involved in the establishment of a confidence interval for any other population parameter—but different formulas are required. The general form is given by Eq. (7.5).

$$x - k_1\sigma_x \text{ to } x + k_2\sigma_x, \tag{7.5}$$

where

k_1 = appropriate coefficient for lower
      tail of distribution,

k_2 = appropriate coefficient for upper
      tail of distribution.

Note that the standard error always refers to the sample statistic under consideration. The coefficients k_1 and k_2 are equal whenever a symmetric interval is

---

[4]We shall return to this concept and question in the next chapter as we deal with how large a sample is required for a given problem.

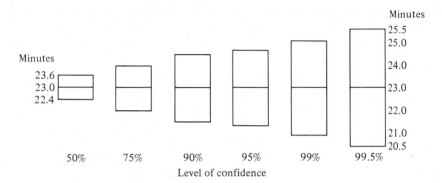

Fig. 7.2
Comparative widths of confidence intervals for selected levels of confidence.

established around the sample statistic. The *k*-values are selected in accordance with the confidence demanded, usually excluding half the appropriate percentage from each tail of the random sampling distribution.

The true variance of a random sampling distribution is determined by the sampling plan and certain population parameters but not by any sample statistics. Recall that the variance of a mean depended on the universe variance, not on the sample variance. This is also true of the variance of a sample proportion. Its formula, ignoring the finite multipler, is given by Eq. (7.6).

$$\sigma_{\bar{p}}^2 = \frac{pq}{n}, \tag{7.6}$$

where

$$p = \text{population proportion,}$$
$$q = 1 - p.$$

An unbiased estimator of $\sigma_{\bar{p}}^2$ is given by $\overset{*}{\sigma}_{\bar{p}}^2$ in Eq. (7.7) where the population proportion (p) and its complement (q) are replaced by the sample estimates ($\bar{p}$ and $\bar{q}$) and the sample size is replaced by ($n - 1$).

$$\overset{*}{\sigma}_{\bar{p}}^2 = \frac{\bar{p}\bar{q}}{n - 1}. \tag{7.7}$$

Consider again the sample result that 43 percent of the customers preferred the deluxe model. If this result is based upon a simple random sample size 600 and the researcher wishes a 99 percent confidence interval, the appropriate calculations are given below.

$$\bar{p} \pm 2.58\overset{*}{\sigma}_{\bar{p}} = .43 \pm 2.58 \, (.43 \times .57 \div 599)^{1/2}$$
$$.43 \pm .05,$$
$$.38 \text{ to } .48.$$

The 99 percent confidence interval for this estimate is given by the range 38 to 48 percent. The term $\bar{p}$ may be presented either as a percentage or a proportion. Once the calculations are started in one form, that form must be retained throughout the remainder of the calculations. Either one is correct but the mixing of them leads to chaos. The standard error in percentage form would be calculated as $(43 \times 57 \div 599)^{1/2} = 2.0$.

Interval estimation for population totals is merely an extension of interval estimation for means and proportions. Either of two procedures leads to arithmetically identical results: (1) intervals are estimated for the mean or the proportion and the endpoints of the interval established are multiplied by the number of elements in the population or (2) an unbiased estimate of the population total is made in the form of Eq. (7.3) or (7.4) and is used with the standard error of an estimated total. Since the second form is not usually presented in elementary statistics or marketing research texts, we shall illustrate that procedure.

Equation (7.8) gives the variance of an estimated total when that estimate is computed by multiplying the sample mean by the number of units in the population. The successive steps shown in the equation illustrate an important principle in determining variances for various estimators. The appropriate subscript for the variance is always the symbol for the estimator being employed, x' in this case. The next step is to ask how the estimator is calculated ($N\bar{x}$). When the estimator is calculated by taking a constant times a variable for which the variance is already known, the appropriate variance is given by the constant squared times the variance for the variable—$N^2\sigma_{\bar{x}}^2$ or its unbiased estimator $N^2\overset{*}{\sigma}_{\bar{x}}^2$. Given Eq. (7.8), we are now ready to establish a confidence interval for an estimated total.

$$\sigma_{x'}^2 = \sigma_{N\bar{x}}^2 = N^2\sigma_{\bar{x}}^2 = N^2\overset{*}{\sigma}_{\bar{x}}^2 = N^2\frac{s^2}{n-1}. \tag{7.8}$$

Suppose a supermarket chain wishes to estimate total annual consumption of meat in a local community. A simple random sample of 500 individuals is selected from the total population of 25,000. The sample arithmetic mean is 188.3 pounds and the sample standard deviation is 22.6 pounds. Using Eq. (7.8) the variance and standard error of the estimated total are given by:

$$\overset{*}{\sigma}_{x'}^2 = (25{,}000)^2 \frac{(22.6)^2}{499},$$

$$\overset{*}{\sigma}_{x'} = 25{,}293.$$

The 90 percent confidence interval for the amount of meat consumed by the population is given by:

$$N\bar{x} \pm 1.64(25{,}293)$$
$$25{,}000(188.3) \pm 1.64(25{,}293)$$
$$4{,}707{,}500 \pm 41{,}480$$
$$4{,}666{,}000 \text{ to } 4{,}749{,}000 \text{ lbs.}$$

Now compare this interval with the one that would result with a smaller sample size, assuming all other figures are the same. The variance and standard error with $n = 200$ (a decrease of 60 percent in size) are:

$$\overset{*}{\sigma}{}^{2}_{x'} = (25,000)^2 \frac{(22.6)^2}{199},$$

$$\overset{*}{\sigma}_{x'} = 40,052.$$

The 90 percent confidence interval is now:

$$4,707,500 \pm 65,685,$$
$$4,641,815 \text{ to } 4,773,185.$$

The interval with $n = 200$ is slightly more than 50 percent larger than with $n = 500$. Would a stratified sample—as opposed to a simple random sample—yield a smaller interval for the same size sample? The answer is almost certainly yes. As long as the strata are more homogeneous than the overall population, stratification will yield greater reliability. The amount of increase in reliability cannot be generalized since it depends on the relationship between the within-stratum variance and the overall variance.

HYPOTHESIS TESTING

Marketing decisions that involve a selection among alternatives fit neatly into a hypothesis testing framework. Do our salespeople spend more than three hours a day on nonselling activities? Is our market share less than 10 percent? Are more than 20 percent of our customers female? Does market potential exceed $100,000? Does less than 50 percent of our target market recognize our logo? Do elementary school children have more than $2.00 a week to spend? Does the average industrial sales person spend more than $50 a month on long-distance telephone calls? Hypothesis testing demands that the decision maker establish critical values.

Hypothesis testing has certain similarities to estimation, but it approaches the problem in a much different way. Estimation asks what the parameter is. Hypothesis testing asks whether the parameter is a stated value. Therefore estimation provides either a number as a point estimate or two numbers that establish an interval estimate. Hypothesis testing results either in the acceptance or in the rejection of the parameter hypothesized: the hypothesis is judged to be either true or false.

Hypothesis testing is decision-oriented. Each hypothesis being tested should correspond to a particular decision. If the test is constructed properly, the decision maker can select one and only one of the hypotheses as correct. This means that the decision maker and the researcher must decide in advance what values of the parameter under investigation are critical.

Problem definition and research design lead to the establishment of specific hypotheses to be tested. In the simplest situation, the decision maker wishes to choose between two statements, each uniquely paired to a possible action to be taken. Consider the advertising manager who must decide whether the proposed "Affluent Sophisticate" campaign is to be adopted. The decision is to be based on product choice in a laboratory environment after exposure to the campaign theme. The criterion for adoption is a score in excess of 65. Therefore the two hypotheses (or statements) under test are: (1) the test score is over 65 and (2) the test score is not over 65.

These are statements with respect to the universe; they do not refer to the sample result. The sample result will serve as the basis for choosing between them. One will be accepted, and one will be rejected. The critical sample score might be established as 65, but the usual statistical test uses a critical sample value other than the one specified in the hypotheses. The rationale for this procedure is based on the probabilities of different kinds of errors and is illustrated by the following example.

A common marketing research problem is the evaluation of new products. Let us simplify the problem into two possible decisions and construct two hypotheses. The product will either be marketed regionally, or it will be dropped from further consideration. Consumer acceptance as measured in a blind comparisons test is agreed upon as an appropriate basis for evaluation. It is agreed that regional marketing will be pursued only if the acceptance rate exceeds 30 percent.[5] As stated, this means that one action will be taken if the percentage is anything greater than 30 and the alternative action will be taken if the percentage is 30 or less.

Recall from elementary statistics that the "null" hypothesis is tested and that the testing takes place at the equality. The alternative hypotheses are then established as:

$$H_0: p \leq 30,$$
$$H_1: p > 30.$$

The sample evidence will be used to choose between H_0 and H_1. The null hypothesis will be accepted unless sufficient doubt is cast upon it by the evidence. In this particular problem, the manager has decided not to market the product unless the sample evidence shows that the population parameter is greater than 30 percent. The sample result must be "significantly" greater than 30 percent; otherwise the manager will conclude that the population parameter may be 30 percent and that it is not large enough to warrant regional marketing.

The problem could have been structured in a completely different manner. Here the hypotheses would be structured as:

---

[5]One of the most difficult tasks in marketing research is establishing the appropriate levels needed for various decisions. The "What if?" approach is frequently helpful. In this approach, the marketing manager is asked to specify the appropriate actions for a whole range of possible values of the pertinent parameter—before the research is done. This approach avoids the uncomfortable position of staring at research results and wondering what to do about them.

$$H_0' : p \geq 30,$$
$$H_1' : p < 30.$$

In this structure, the manager will initiate regional marketing if H_0' is accepted, and will drop the product if H_1' is accepted. Here the manager is saying that regional marketing is justified if the population parameter is 30 percent or more and that he or she will conclude this to be the case unless the sample evidence convinces him or her to the contrary.

The selection between these two ways of structuring the problem depends on the cost of different errors and the manager's willingness to run different kinds of risks. If the sample evidence differs greatly from the value specified in the null hypothesis (30 percent), the two structurings will yield the same recommendation. If the sample results are close to the number specified for the parameter, the two structurings will yield contrary recommendations. It should also be noted that the two structurings are more likely to yield contradictory recommendations with small samples than they are with large samples.

Suppose we take a simple random sample of 200 potential customers and use the first structuring of the hypotheses. Our first task is to determine what sample values will lead to regional marketing for the new product and what sample values will not. In order to find the appropriate values for the sample statistic, we must specify the risk we are willing to run of rejecting H_0 when it is true. In terms of this problem, we are asking how large a risk we are willing to run (α) of going to regional marketing when the percentage acceptance of the product is *precisely* 30 percent—a value that we have stated is not large enough to warrant regional marketing.[6] The manager may say this is not a very serious error and be willing to run a 10 percent risk. (The rejection of the null hypothesis when it is true is a Type I error. In this problem, the manager places a maximum value of $\alpha = .10$ for that error.)

The appropriate standard error to be used in analyzing this problem is the standard error associated with the random sampling distribution when p is precisely equal to 30. (Should it be called .30? Does it matter?) The necessary calculation shows that

$$\sigma_{\bar{p}}^2 = \frac{30 \times 70}{200},$$

$$\sigma_{\bar{p}} = 3.24.$$

Because the manager has stated a willingness to reject H_0 when it is true 10 percent of the time, it becomes necessary to divide the random sampling distribution so that 10 percent is in the upper tail. Since the distribution is approxi-

---

[6]Alpha, α, is not the risk of going regional when the company should not. The risk reaches the maximum value of α when H_0 is true at the equality figure of 30 percent. For values less than 30 percent—H_0 still being true—the risk of concluding H_1 will be less than α.

mately normal, we refer to Appendix Table A.2 and find that a z-value of 1.28 will accomplish such a division. The critical value is then established by

$$p + 1.28\sigma_{\bar{p}},$$
$$30 + 1.28(3.24) = 30 + 4.1 = 34.1.$$

If the sample result is anything greater than 34.1 percent, H_0 should be rejected and the product should be introduced with regional marketing. Any sample value less than 34.1 percent would result in a recommendation to drop the product from further consideration.

The second way of structuring this problem yields the same value for $\sigma_{\bar{p}}$. A Type I error now has the completely opposite meaning: the product will be dropped when it should have gone to regional marketing. Again the manager must decide how serious this error is. If again the manager is willing to run a 10 percent risk, the random sampling distribution will again be divided 10 percent versus 90 percent; but this time the 10 percent will be in the lower tail. The resulting critical value for this formulation will be $30 - 4.1$ or 25.9. Any sample result less than 25.9 percent will lead to discontinuance of the product.

We can now compare the two formulations and determine when they lead to different recommendations. Both lead to a recommendation to discontinue whenever the sample result is less than 25.9 percent; both lead to a recommendation for regional marketing whenever the sample result is greater than 34.1 percent. However, for sample results between 25.9 percent and 34.1 percent, the formulations lead to conflicting recommendations. If the sample size is increased to 500, the region in which conflicting recommendations would result is narrowed to between 27.4 and 32.6 percent.

The market researcher should be conscious of the magnitude of Type II errors as well as the magnitude of the Type I error. The Type II error consists of accepting the null hypothesis when it is false. Returning to the first structuring of our problem, use of a critical value of 34.1 percent obviously means that H_1 will often be rejected (the converse of accepting H_0) if the population parameter is 31 or 32 percent. The manager has already expressed a desire to go regional if p is over 30 percent. The manager wants to know how often H_1 will be rejected when it should be accepted: the manager wants to know how *discriminating* the test is. This is shown by the *power curve*. The "power" of a test is measured by the probability of accepting H_1 when it is true. H_1 is true at many different values; for example, 30.2, 31.5, 32.8 percent, and all values running between 30 and 100 percent. The graph of the power curve (Fig. 7.3) shows each of these points and the probability of accepting H_1 for each.

The calculation of the power curve is extremely cumbersome when dealing with a proportion because the standard error of a proportion is dependent on the true universe value. A different numerical value for $\sigma_{\bar{p}}$ applies at each point of the x-axis. The power curve, using a sample size of 200, is shown in Fig. 7.3. This figure shows that the population percentage finding the product acceptable must reach about 39 or 40 percent before there is a 90 percent probability

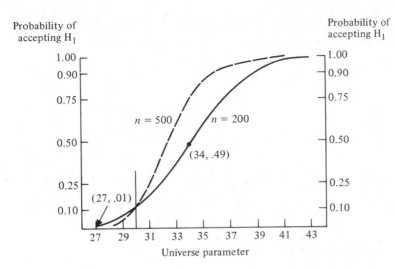

Fig. 7.3
Power curve for H_0: $p \le 30$ versus H_1: $p > 30$. Sample sizes 200 and 500.

of introducing the product in regional marketing. The probability is only about .5 when the population proportion is 34 percent. The curve does show that there is very little chance (.01) of introducing the product regionally when the population proportion is only 27 percent.

The broken line in Fig. 7.3 shows the improvement in the design when the sample size is increased to 500. For every universe parameter over 30 percent, the probability of accepting H_1 is greater with a sample of 500 than with a sample of 200. For every universe parameter less than 30 percent, the probability of accepting H_1 is less. Only at the universe parameter of 30 percent does the probability remain the same: .10 which has arbitrarily been chosen as the maximum probability of a Type I error. The entire power curve could be raised on the graph by increasing the probability of a Type I error, or it could be lowered by making the probability of a Type I error less than 10 percent. Thus the choice of α plays a critical role in hypothesis testing. Fortunately, the impact of α diminishes for universe values removed from the number specified in H_0—particularly as sample size is increased.

Suppose the manager had used a sample result of 30 percent as the critical value for choosing between H_0 and H_1. With this structure for the test, the manager would conclude that H_0 was true one half of the time when the universe value was precisely 30 percent and would conclude that H_1 was true the other half. The probability of a Type I error (at the 30 percent mark) would equal .5, and the maximum probability of a Type II error would approach .5 as the value approached 30 percent. This test structure is not incorrect, but it is contrary to the classical procedure that sets the Type I probability at much lower levels.

Hypothesis testing with respect to an arithmetic mean follows precisely the same format as that for a population proportion. (1) The characteristic upon which the decision is to be based is chosen. (2) Possible values of this characteristic are partitioned in ways corresponding to different alternative actions with respect to the problem under investigation. (3) Hypotheses corresponding to this partitioning are constructed with due care to the identification of a Type I error and the resulting power curve.

The marketing research manager of a large chain restaurant has been asked to conduct a survey of its customers in a particular community. The president is interested in the mean income of the chain's customers, with special reference to a comparison against the mean income of the community established in a recent government census. The mean income figure published was $14,275. The president wishes to reach one of three conclusions: (1) mean income of the firms's customers is the same as that of the community, (2) mean income of the firm's customers is greater than that of the community, or (3) mean income of the firm's customers is less than that of the community. The marketing research manager suggests that three hypotheses be established, corresponding to these three different conclusions:

$$H_0 : \mu = 14,275,$$
$$H_1 : \mu > 14,275,$$
$$H_2 : \mu < 14,275.$$

This situation is slightly more complex than the previous example because we have two alternatives to the null hypothesis. The test to be constructed must specify (1) the Type I risk to be associated with rejecting a true H_0 by accepting H_1 and (2) the Type I risk to be associated with rejecting a true H_0 by accepting H_2. Suppose the manager decides to run a combined Type I risk of 5 percent, with 2.5 percent associated with each alternative. The random sampling distribution that coincides with H_0 when it is true will be divided with 2.5 percent in each tail and two critical values: one specifying the sample value above which H_1 will be accepted and the other specifying the sample value below which H_2 will be accepted.

The population standard deviation is unknown. Therefore, an unbiased estimate of that value will be made from the sample evidence. This being the case, we cannot specify before the survey is taken what the critical values will be—a situation different from that encountered when dealing with proportions. Assume a simple random sample of 300 customers is selected, yielding an arithmetic mean income of $13,319 and a standard deviation of $2,869. The observed sample result is $956 lower than the community mean. However, the absolute size of this difference is not a sufficient basis for reaching a decision; the difference must be expressed in terms of the standard error of the arithmetic mean. The appropriate calculations reveal that $\overset{*}{\sigma}_{\bar{x}}$ is $166.

The observed difference between the sample mean and the hypothesized parameter is much larger than we would typically observe if H_0 were true, more than five times the estimated standard error. The probability of observing such a difference (if H_0 is true) is less than the 2.5 percent which we established; in fact the probability is less than .00002 (the lowest value shown in Appendix Table A.2). Therefore we conclude that the mean income of the chain's customers is less than the mean income for the community as a whole. The president now must adopt appropriate policies in the face of such a decision—it is hoped the president had these in mind before the survey results were obtained.

A better structure for the problem might be the establishment of *population* mean income figures that would identify substantively significant departures from the community mean. The president would then ask for tests against these figures instead of tests against the community mean. It is almost always possible to reject a single-valued null hypothesis by taking extremely large samples, thus demonstrating a statistically significant difference that is of no practical import. With a sample of 3,000 (assuming the same sample standard deviation), a difference of only $125 would be statistically significant.

The three hypotheses conforming to the restructuring could be the following:

$$H_0' : 13,775 < \mu < 14,775,$$

$$H_1' : \mu > 14,775,$$

$$H_2' : \mu < 13,775.$$

According to this structure, a mean income for chain customers that is within $500 of the community mean calls for no action. In this alternative, the observed sample mean of $13,319 would be compared to $13,775 instead of the community mean of $14,275. Sample results above the community mean would be compared with $14,775.

The first example cited in hypothesis testing is referred to as a one-tailed test. The second is identified as two one-tailed tests. The remaining possibility is the two-tailed test; in this situation H_0 states a specific universe parameter while H_1 is simply an inequality.[7] Although it is easy enough to establish such a pair of hypotheses, it is rare to find instances in which the action to be taken is independent of whether the parameter is higher or lower than the specified value.

Consider the case of the sales manager who was considering a new door-to-door sales approach. The new manager knows that the current approach produces a sale 6 percent of the time.[8] The pair of hypotheses established for this problem is given by:

---

[7] If H_0 is an interval, H_1 contains all values except those within the interval of H_0.

[8] "The manager knows" makes the manager sound omniscient. A more reasonable approach might be to compare the two methods, assuming that each result is based upon sample evidence. We shall use this approach in the next chapter, but for the present we shall assume that the stated value truly is known.

$$H_0 : p = 6\%,$$
$$H_1 : p \neq 6\%.$$

The random sampling distribution associated with H_0 is established and the appropriate standard error is calculated. H_0 will be rejected if the sample proportion is either too high or too low. Therefore the probability chosen for a Type I error is distributed between both tails of the distribution. The difficulty with this approach is that the manager hardly knows what to do if H_1 is accepted. The manager wants to know whether the new method is better than or worse than the existing method. Most practical problems are of this nature and are much more logically treated as two one-tailed tests instead of a single two-tailed test.

SUMMARY

In this chapter we have reviewed statistical inference under the topics of point estimation, interval estimation, and hypothesis testing. Unbiasedness is only one of several possible criteria to use for point estimation, but it is used for much marketing research. Using simple random sampling, the sample arithmetic mean and the sample proportion are unbiased estimators for the corresponding universe parameters. The sample variance is a slightly biased estimator for the universe variance; $\overset{*}{\sigma}{}^2$, in which $n - 1$ replaced n in the denominator, is an unbiased estimator of the universe variance and is usually used instead of s^2. The sample mean and the sample proportion, when multiplied by the number of units in the universe, yield unbiased estimators for universe totals.

Interval estimation is introduced so that the decision maker has a better idea of the reliability of the sample results and estimators. The standard error of the random sampling distribution is the key to establishing interval estimations. This standard error is the measure of dispersion in the random sampling distribution, and it shows how closely the sample results are clustered. Through use of the t-distribution and the Central Limit Theorem, we can generate intervals for the mean, proportion, and universe total with known confidence in most marketing research problems. The researcher must establish the confidence wished for the interval presented, balancing a desire for more confidence against a desire for a more narrow interval.

Hypothesis testing, in contrast to estimation, chooses among alternative statements with respect to the value of parameters in the universe. These alternative statements, to be of practical utility, must coincide with alternative actions the decision maker has available. Each time the researcher accepts one hypothesis, he or she rejects the other. Hypothesis testing identifies and permits the measurement of the risks associated with any particular test design. Both the choice of the appropriate null hypothesis and the evaluation of the power curve must relate back to the decision maker's problem in view of the risks involved.

EXERCISES AND PROBLEMS

1. Distinguish among the terms within each of the following sets.
    a) Point estimation, interval estimation, and hypothesis testing
    b) $\overset{*}{\sigma}^2$ and s^2
    c) Type I error and Type II error
    d) One-tailed test, two-tailed test, and two one-tailed tests
    e) Power curve and random sampling distribution

2. Briefly explain what effect each of the following would have on the power curve for a particular one-tailed test.
    a) Increasing the sample size
    b) Decreasing α
    c) Transferring the equality portion of the null hypothesis (H_0) to the alternative hypothesis (H_1)

3. Discuss when and how each of the following is involved in marketing research.
    a) Central Limit Theorem
    b) t-distribution

4. A product manager wishes to estimate the mean per capita consumption of a product. A simple random sample of 500 "users" of the product is selected from a national panel.
    a) Do you think the sample should be employed in making the desired estimate? Discuss.
    b) Assuming the sample is appropriate, will the sample mean be an unbiased estimate for the population mean? Why?
    c) Will the normal curve be appropriate to use in constructing an interval estimate? Discuss.

5. Assume the sample in Exercise 4 is used and is appropriate. The sample mean and standard deviation are 22.4 ounces per week and 5.3 ounces per week, respectively. Construct a 95 percent confidence interval for the population mean.

6. A simple random sample of 200 "active accounts" for a furniture manufacturer reveals that 79 percent of the "contact persons" are owners of the buying firm.
    a) Would you be willing to conclude that over 60 percent of the population "contact persons" are owners?
    b) With your decision rule, what is the probability of a Type II error if the population percentage is 70 percent? if the population percentage is 50 percent?

7. The sample in Exercise 6 also yields a mean age of 43.6 years for "contact persons" ($s = 12.5$ years).
    a) Would you be willing to conclude that the population mean age of "contact persons" was under 50? over 40?

b) Do your answers in (a) employ the same data and random sampling distributions? Discuss.

8. The First National Bank of Locala wants to determine how many of its checking account customers also have saving accounts.

   a) What would be some of the practical problems involved in selecting a simple random sample of checking account customers?

   b) Assume a simple random sample of 600 checking account customers has been selected. The sample reveals that 180 of the customers in the sample have savings accounts with the bank. Construct a 92 percent confidence interval for the population estimate.

9. A research firm wishes to estimate the market shares held by the major companies in the headache remedy field. The largest of the companies probably has about 30 percent of the relevant market.

   a) State and defend your choice of a definition for "market share."

   b) What unit of analysis for the universe is implicit in (a)?

   c) A random sample of 1,000 drug store patrons who purchased at least one headache remedy on their last visit is available. Of the patrons sampled, 180 purchased brand A. Do you believe 18 percent is a good point estimate of brand A's market share? Discuss.

   d) Disregard, if necessary, your answer in (c) and any reservations you have concerning the data. Construct a 95 percent confidence interval for brand A's market share.

10. A random sample of 50 delinquent charge accounts at the A. C. Anderson Department Store shows a mean of $78 and a standard deviation of $20.

    a) Estimate the arithmetic mean size of the store's delinquent accounts.

    b) The sample above is equal to 2 percent of the store's delinquent accounts. Construct a 90 percent confidence interval for the total amount outstanding in delinquent accounts.

11. A manufacturer received a shipment of 20,000 fuses from Supplier M. The manufacturer did not wish to accept any shipment that contained over 4 percent defectives. A simple random sample of 200 fuses was selected.

    a) Construct the power curve associated with this problem.

    b) What is the minimum *number* of defectives (from the sample of 200) that would lead you to recommend that the whole shipment of 20,000 be rejected?

12. A consumer activist questions the effectiveness of a new drug made by your firm for the treatment of arthritis. Assume that an "effectiveness" of 70 percent is accepted by both the consumer activist and the company as a satisfactory level. Is it possible that there may be disagreement with respect to the appropriate null hypothesis to be tested? Discuss.

13. A manufacturer of business forms and envelopes is considering the addition of a line of products for a relatively new industry thought to offer an excellent growth

potential. The general manager is willing to add the new line if gross purchases by the industry for business forms exceeds $1 million. A sample of 25 firms within the industry shows mean purchases of $7,500.

a) Assuming the sample to be the equivalent of a simple random sample, how many firms must be in the industry if the unbiased estimate for the industry is to reach at least $1 million?

b) The general manager has heard talk of Type I and Type II errors and wishes to minimize the probability of adding the new line when that would be an error. How many firms must there be in the industry if the manager wishes the risk of that error to be no more than 5 percent? Assume and identify any additional data needed to answer the question.

14. Analyze, criticize, and explain:

a) A point estimate that is unbiased has less than a 50 percent chance of error.

b) If an interval estimate is constructed by adding and subtracting equal amounts to the sample statistic, the researcher is assuming that the population distribution is symmetric.

c) The Central Limit Theorem is theoretically applicable only if the sample size is over 100 and the standard deviation of the population is known.

d) The term "95 percent confidence" in a 95 percent confidence interval means that the probability that the population parameter will not be in the interval established is 5 percent or less.

e) If the sample size is increased and α is held constant, the probability of a Type II error will be lower for all values except the one specified in the null hypothesis.

f) The relevant standard error of the sample statistic will almost always be estimated rather than known. This is true for both interval estimation and hypothesis testing and for both means and percentages.

g) A two-tailed test usually is a poor structure for the decision maker's problem.

CHAPTER 8

SAMPLE RELIABILITY AND SAMPLE SIZE
WHEN IS A SAMPLE BIG ENOUGH?

A sample result is subject to error. It may mislead rather than lead. When is a sample large enough to ensure that the decision maker is not being misled? Never! Sampling never yields certainty. It yields degrees of confidence and measures of reliability.

The often-asked question, "How large a sample should I select?" cannot be answered until the *decision maker* states the precision required. The researcher must ask the right questions, but the decision maker's answers determine the sample size. The right questions are implicit in our previous discussion of interval estimates. We shall first consider the determination of sample size with random sampling and later turn to stratification and clustering.

CONFIDENCE LEVEL AND REQUIRED PRECISION

A confidence interval estimate for a proportion is established by $\bar{p} \pm t \overset{*}{\sigma}_{\bar{p}}$ where $\bar{p}$ is the sample proportion, $\overset{*}{\sigma}_{\bar{p}}$ is the estimated standard error of the random sampling distribution of the sample proportion, and t is the coefficient corresponding to the desired confidence level. The determination of the proper sample size starts with the result of such a confidence interval and works backward. How large an interval will the decision maker tolerate? Or alternatively, how small an interval does the decision maker demand? The answer to either one of these questions establishes the numerical value of $\pm t \overset{*}{\sigma}_{\bar{p}}$. Assuming we are working with large samples, t can be replaced by z of the normal curve.

The Jefferson Soap Company is considering the distribution of samples as its next promotion campaign. The president wants to know the percentage of households receiving a sample that will purchase Jefferson Soap at least once in the following two-month period. (Should the president be satisfied with this as the proper variable of interest?) The research director assures the president that a relatively small test will give a good approximation of that percentage.

The president asks how small the test can be. The research director in turn asks how close to the true percentage the president desires the sample result to be. After initially responding the "true percentage," the president agrees to an interval of 8 percentage points. This figure was generated by the president's statement, "I want the test result to be within 4 percentage points of the true value." Since the test result may be either higher than or lower than the universe parameter, the total interval permitted is 8 and $z\overset{*}{\sigma}_{\bar{p}}$ is 4.

But $z\overset{*}{\sigma}_{\bar{p}} = 4$ cannot be solved. The president must answer at least one more question: "How much confidence do you want to have that the true percentage is in the interval established?" The president's immediate reaction was, "I have given in enough by settling for an approximation. Less than complete confidence after that concession is unacceptable." Finally, the president instructed that a 99 percent confidence interval be established. This instruction led to the following calculation.

$$2.58\overset{*}{\sigma}_{\bar{p}} = 4,$$
$$\overset{*}{\sigma}_{\bar{p}} = 1.55.$$

Substituting the formula for $\overset{*}{\sigma}_{\bar{p}}^2$ we have

$$\frac{\bar{p}\bar{q}}{n-1}(1-f) = (1.55)^2.$$

We wish to solve for n, but no solution is possible without substituting numerical values for $\bar{p}, \bar{q}$, and f. We dispose of f by assuming the sample is small relative to the universe. The remaining terms, $\bar{p}$ and $\bar{q}$, are not disposed of so easily.

Table 8.1 gives the required value of n, depending on the values of $\bar{p}$ and $\bar{q}$. If $\bar{p}$ is only 10 percent, a sample of 376 will meet the president's specifications. Larger $\bar{p}$ values seem to require larger samples. The largest sample size shown on the table is 1,042. What would happen with $\bar{p}$ values larger than 50 percent? The crucial factor is not the value of $\bar{p}$, but the value of $\bar{p}\bar{q}$. This value is a maximum when both $\bar{p}$ and $\bar{q}$ are 50 percent. The required sample size decreases as $\bar{p}$ increases beyond 50 percent, taking on the same value when $\bar{p}$ is 60 percent as when it is 40 percent, etc.

What sample size would the research director recommend to the president? A sample of 1,042 will meet the president's requirements, but it might be larger than necessary. Unless the president or some other knowledgeable person can supply boundary points for $\bar{p}$, the director should recommend 1,042. If the president thinks the percentage will not exceed 20 percent, a sample of 667 will be sufficient. If the president thinks the percentage will certainly be over 60 percent and perhaps as high as 90 percent, a sample of 1,000 will be needed. This is calculated from the figure nearest 50 percent: 60 percent, not 90 percent. Suppose the president expects the percentage to be somewhere between 25 and 60 percent? The correct sample size is again 1,042 because $\bar{p}$ may be 50 percent.

Table 8.1
Required Sample Size for Various $\bar{p}$ and $\bar{q}$ Values. Jefferson Soap Company Problem†

$\bar{p}$	$\bar{q}$	n
10	90	376
20	80	667
30	70	875
40	60	1,000
50	50	1,042

†Based on specification that $\overset{*}{\sigma}_{\bar{p}} = 1.55$.

The determination of the proper sample size is based on estimates of what the sample result will be. What if those estimates are incorrect? For example, suppose a sample of 1,042 is selected for the Jefferson Soap Company problem and 396 of the sample purchase Jefferson soap in the following two months. The sample proportion is 38 percent, not 50 percent. The sample will possess greater reliability than the president required. The resulting $\overset{*}{\sigma}_{\bar{p}}$ will be 1.50 rather than 1.55, and the 99 percent confidence interval will have a width of 7.74 percentage points rather than 8 percentage points.

An error could be made in the opposite direction. The sample result could be closer to a 50–50 split than expected. In this case, the required reliability would not be achieved. In order to guard against this possibility, the $\bar{p}\bar{q}$ employed in sample size determination is usually chosen as an "outside" possibility. This approach will yield a higher degree of reliability than that specified by the decision maker. This "bonus" is more reliability than the decision requires—not a disadvantage in itself. But this "bonus" is achieved at a higher cost than necessary because larger samples cost more than smaller samples.

The general question of the required sample size, thus, requires two answers from the decision maker: (1) the specification of a maximum acceptable difference between the universe parameter and the sample statistic and (2) the specification of the confidence level desired. The formula for determining sample size when dealing with a proportion is given by Eq. (8.1).[1]

---

[1]A dilemma exists for the purist in discussing required sample size. The true standard errors depend on population values. If possible values for the population are used in calculating n^*, the denominator of the standard error is n^*, not $n^* - 1$. When the actual sample is selected, the standard error will be based on sample values and $n^* - 1$ should be used in the calculations rather than n^*. Since specifications should be set in terms of the results demanded, this argument suggests that the formulas be based on $n^* - 1$. We shall use the value n^* since the formulas are more tractable and the differences are so slight. Arithmetic results, of course, depend on the sequence of operations and rounding.

$$n^* = \frac{z^2 p^* (100 - p^*)}{D^2} \tag{8.1}$$

where

n^* = required sample size,

z = normal curve coefficient for desired confidence level,

p^* = estimate of sample results which will yield maximum possible value for p^* $(100 - p^*)$, and p^* = 50 if no estimate is made,

D = maximum acceptable difference between universe parameter and sample statistic.

In order to review this procedure, let us consider the problem faced by the Whyte Appliance Company. The marketing vice-president wishes an estimate of the percentage of persons willing to pay $75 for an ice-maker attachment to their present refrigerators and specifies that the total 95 percent confidence interval should not exceed 4 percentage points. The vice-president does not think the population parameter will be as large as 20 percent. What size sample is required? Is the vice-president realistic in requiring that the interval be so small?

First, what size sample is required? Substituting in Eq. (8.1) we have

$$n^* = \frac{(1.96)^2 (20) (80)}{(2)^2} = 1537.$$

Suppose the vice-president is willing to increase the width of the interval to 5 percentage points. The required sample is now only 983, a rather substantial reduction. If the sample proportion is 20 percent, the confidence interval will be 18 to 22 percent with a sample of 1,537 but 17.5 to 22.5 percent with a sample of 983.

If the sample proportion is smaller, the interval will not be as wide. Suppose the sample proportion is only 10 percent. What would be the 95 percent confidence interval? With a sample 1,537, $\hat{\sigma}_p$ would be .765 percentage points and the interval would be from 8.5 to 11.5 percent. The total width would be 3 rather than the required 4 percentage points. The specified maximum interval will always result at the value of p^*; if $\bar{p}\bar{q}$ is less than p^*q^*, a smaller interval will result. How wide would the interval be if the sample size 983 yielded a proportion of 10 percent?

Table 8.2 presents the required sample size for selected problems. Note how rapidly the required size increases as the maximum deviation is reduced. Reliability within 1 percentage point demands a sample 100 times as large as reliability within 10 percentage points. Also note how much larger the sample must be when the expected percentage division approaches the 50–50 figure.

Table 8.2
Illustrative Sample Sizes for Specified Reliability and Confidence.
Sample Percentage Problems

95% confidence

Expected percentage division	Maximum deviation permitted			
	1	2	5	10
50–50	9,603	2,400	383	95
40–60	9,219	2,304	368	91
30–70	8,066	2,016	322	80
20–80	6,146	1,536	245	60
10–90	3,456	863	137	—†
5–95	1,824	455	—†	—†

99% confidence

Expected percentage division	Maximum deviation permitted			
	1	2	5	10
50–50	16,640	4,159	665	165
40–60	15,974	3,993	638	159
30–70	13,977	3,494	558	139
20–80	10,649	2,662	425	106
10–90	5,990	1,497	239	—†
5–95	3,161	789	—†	—†

†Specifications concerning the maximum deviation permitted and the expected percentage division make these problems unlikely at the practical level, and the resulting random sampling distribution is nonsymmetric as well.

The same maximum deviation is achieved at a 20–80 division with a sample that is less than two-thirds as large, and a 10–90 division requires only one-third the sample size.

Finally, the effect of the confidence level is obvious. An increase from a 95 percent confidence level to a 99 percent confidence level increases the required sample size by over 70 percent.

Required Sample Size from Finite Population

Our considerations thus far have ignored the finite multiplier $(1 - f)$. What effect would its inclusion have on the determination of sample size? In order to even consider the question, the universe must be defined so that its size (N) is known or can be determined. Suppose in the Jefferson Soap Company problem, the president is considering the distribution of samples to five million United States households. N is then 5,000,000, and n^* should be calculated from

$$\frac{p^* q^*}{n^*}\left(1 - \frac{n^*}{5,000,000}\right) = (1.55)^2.$$

If the president refuses to choose a value of p^* other than 50, the calculation is

$$\frac{2500}{n^*}\left(1 - \frac{n^*}{5,000,000}\right) = (1.55)^2.$$

Solving the equation above, n^* is 1,040—the introduction of the finite multiplier has complicated the calculation and decreased the required sample size by only two. Table 8.3 shows the required sample size for different size

Table 8.3
Reduction in Required Sample Size for Finite Populations. Jefferson Soap Company Problem

Population size	Required sample size†
5,000,000	1,040
1,000,000	1,039
200,000	1,035
100,000	1,029
50,000	1,019
25,000	999
12,500	960
7,500	913
6,250	892
5,000	861
4,000	825
3,000	772
2,500	734
1,500	614
1,000	510

†Calculated sample size is based upon a 99 percent confidence interval with a maximum width of 8 percentage points ($2.58\hat{\sigma}_{\bar{p}} = 4$) and assuming the sample proportion might be 50 percent. These figures are calculated from Eq. (8.2) which uses n^* rather than $n^* - 1$ in the denominator of $\hat{\sigma}_{\bar{p}}$.

populations while retaining the same specifications throughout. Even when the population is only 25,000, the required sample size is still 999—a decrease of only 43 from the size required with an infinite population. The required sample size decreases much more rapidly as the population size falls below 25,000 and particularly below 10,000. The controlling factor in this decrease is the sampling fraction (f) rather than the absolute size of the population (N). Until f exceeds .05 or .1, the finite multiplier may be ignored without appreciable effect. The general formula for determining sample size, including the finite multiplier adjustment, is given by Eq. (8.2).

$$n^* = \frac{z^2 N p^* q^*}{N D^2 + z^2 p^* q^*}.$$
(8.2)

SAMPLE SIZE: MEANS VERSUS PROPORTIONS

The logic involved in determining the appropriate sample size is the same, regardless of whether a mean or a proportion is being estimated. The formulas are different because different standard errors are involved. In each case, the starting point is the decision maker's requirements with respect to the confidence interval to be generated. Two values must be specified: (1) the confidence level required and (2) the magnitude of an acceptable difference between the sample and universe values. Both must be chosen with care. They detemine the sample size and its cost. The decision maker should not pay for greater reliability than is required.

With a sample proportion, the critical question is the acceptable numerical value of $z\hat{\sigma}_{p}^*$; the corresponding consideration with a sample mean is $z\hat{\sigma}_{\bar{x}}^*$. This is the amount to be added to and subtracted from the sample mean. The decision maker wants to have a stated level of confidence that the sample mean is at least within $z\hat{\sigma}_{\bar{x}}^*$ of the universe mean.

The owner of Walton's, a popular center city restaurant, is considering opening a second restaurant in an adjacent suburban community. The owner is concerned about the frequency of "eating out" in this suburban community and wishes an estimate of this characteristic. After considerable discussion of seasonal differences and the appropriate time period to cover, the owner instructs the marketing consultant to select an appropriate sample and determine the average figure for a one-month period, beginning March 1. The owner is willing to adjust this figure for seasonal factors by experience at the center city restaurant. Would you concur with this procedure?

The owner wishes to estimate the per household monthly mean within .1 with 98 percent confidence. How large a simple random sample is required? Here $2.33\hat{\sigma}_{\bar{x}} = .1$, and $\hat{\sigma}_{\bar{x}} = .043$. We need only solve for n^* by substituting in the appropriate formula. This substitution, ignoring the finite multiplier, yields

$$(.043)^2 = \frac{s^2}{n^*}.$$

As was the case with proportions, we need to know something about the sample result before we can determine the proper sample size. But contrary to the case with proportions, we cannot take the most conservative position when dealing with means. The value $\bar{p}\bar{q}$ reaches a maximum at 50–50, but there is no maximum value for s^2. We must substitue a numerical value for s^2 in order to determine n^*.

We must know s^2, the variance among elements in the sample. How great will the dispersion be among households in monthly frequency of "eating out"? Might $s^2 = 100$? Quite unlikely! This would mean that $s = 10$. Although we would not expect the distribution of households to follow the normal curve, $6s$ is often used as a rough estimate for 99 + percent of the total range. The upper and lower limits for the characteristic of interest in this problem are 0 and 31, much less than the 60 implicit in $s = 10$. The theoretical upper limit of 31 is probably much too high to use in estimating s^2 through this approach. Would you concur that 31 is the upper limit? Why or why not?

A better procedure for estimating s^2 might be research in comparable communities or earlier data for the same community. Somehow the researcher or the owner must establish a realistic estimate of s^2. If no basis is available, a small pilot test can provide an estimate—at least giving an order of magnitude.

The owner believes very few households in this community "eat out" more than once a week, suggesting that s is less than 1. Using $s = 1$ as a conservative estimate, we can now solve for n^* in Eq. (8.3).

$$n^* = \frac{z^2 s^2}{D^2}. \tag{8.3}$$

Appropriate substitution yields

$$n^* = \frac{(2.33)^2 (1)^2}{(.1)^2} \quad \text{or} \quad \frac{(1)^2}{(.043)^2} = 541.$$

If s^2 as determined from the sample is less than one, the estimate of the population mean will have greater reliability than the owner required.

Table 8.4 presents a worksheet for determining the required sample size. The decision maker and researcher must supply four pieces of information: the size deviation between the sample and universe that is acceptable, the confidence required, an order of magnitude estimate of the sample result (either the percentage or the standard deviation) and finally the size of the universe. Each piece of information fits into the calculation; together they permit the determination of the required sample size. Equation (8.4) gives the appropriate formula for determining sample size in estimating a mean when the finite multiplier is included.

$$n^* = \frac{z^2 N s^2}{ND^2 + z^2 s^2}. \tag{8.4}$$

Table 8.4
Worksheet for Determining Required Sample Size. Simple Random Sampling

Information to be supplied by decision maker

1. How large a deviation between sample result and universe value is acceptable?
2. How much confidence is required?
3. What order of magnitude is expected as the (1) sample percentage or (2) sample standard deviation?
4. How large is the universe?

How information from decision maker is used

1. Limit on deviation sets value for z times standard error.
2. Confidence required establishes z—based on normal curve.
3. Order of magnitude expected is substituted in the appropriate standard error formula.
4. Size of universe determines whether finite multiplier should be used in standard error formula.†

Example (using percentages)

1. Sample result must be within 3 percentage points of universe value: $z\overset{*}{\sigma}_{\bar{p}} = 3.$
2. A 95% confidence is required: $1.96\overset{*}{\sigma}_{\bar{p}} = 3;$ $\overset{*}{\sigma}_{\bar{p}} = 1.53.$
3. Expected sample percentage is between 10 and
   35%: $\overset{*}{\sigma}_{\bar{p}}^{2} = \dfrac{35 \times 65}{n^{*}} (1 - f).$
4. Universe is 100,000:   ignore $(1 - f)$.

Solution: $\overset{*}{\sigma}_{\bar{p}}^{2} = (1.53)^{2} = \dfrac{35 \times 65}{n^{*}};$ $n^{*} = 972.$

Example (using means)

1. Sample result must be within \$50 of universe value: $z\overset{*}{\sigma}_{\bar{x}} = 50.$
2. A 98% confidence is required: $2.33\overset{*}{\sigma}_{\bar{x}} = 50;$ $\overset{*}{\sigma}_{\bar{x}} = 21.46.$
3. Expected sample standard deviation is between \$750 and \$1,000: $\overset{*}{\sigma}_{\bar{x}}^{2} = \dfrac{(1,000)^{2}}{n^{*}}$
4. Universe is 1,500:   cannot ignore $(1 - f)$.

Solution: $\overset{*}{\sigma}_{\bar{x}}^{2} = (21.46)^{2} = \dfrac{(1,000)^{2}}{n^{*}}\left(1 - \dfrac{n^{*}}{1,500}\right);$ $n^{*} = 887.$

Direct solution from Eq. (8.4)

$$n^{*} = \frac{z^{2}Ns^{2}}{ND^{2} + z^{2}s^{2}} = \frac{(2.33)^{2}(1,500)(1,000)^{2}}{1,500(50)^{2} + (2.33)^{2}(1,000)^{2}} = 887.$$

---

†If the finite multiplier is ignored and should have been included, this will be apparent in the fact that the calculated sample size is more than 10 percent of the universe.

SEQUENTIAL SAMPLING

An alternative to determining sample size at the outset is to use sequential sampling with periodic recalculations of $\overset{*}{\sigma}_{\bar{x}}$. The sample size is then dependent on the sample evidence itself. This approach requires careful supervision or bias may be introduced. The sample must be a simple random sample of the appropriate universe at every stage of the sampling process.

The temptation to contact the most accessible in the early stages and the least accessible later must be avoided. This approach not only yields a biased sample but it usually understates s because the group included is more homogeneous than the total universe. Thus improper use of the sequential approach results in both a biased estimate and a claim of greater reliability than is warranted. Correct use of the sequential approach avoids the selection of an unnecessarily large sample and the costs associated with it. Of course sequential sampling is possible only when the collection stage is to be spread over a period of time.

Sequential sampling can also be used with proportions in precisely the same way as for means. The acceptable value for one standard error is determined from the decision maker's requirements. As the sample evidence is collected, the resulting standard error is calculated at administratively appropriate stages—each successive calculation is based on a larger sample size with the then current $\bar{p}\bar{q}$. Sampling continues to the next stage as long as the standard error exceeds the acceptable value.

A large utility wishes to determine the percentage of shareholders who are concerned with the energy conservation measures taken by the company. It wants to estimate the true percentage within 5 percentage points (95 percent confidence) and has no idea what the true percentage is. It decides to use sequential sampling with telephone interviewing in blocks of 50 interviews. The first block of 50 reveals that 12 persons are "concerned about energy conservation measures taken by the company." The calculated standard error is

$$\overset{*}{\sigma}_{\bar{p}} = \left(\frac{24 \times 76}{49}\right)^{1/2} = 6.10.$$

Clearly, the specified reliability has not been attained. Table 8.5 shows the results obtained in increments of 50 with the sampling error gradually diminishing until the reliability required is reached with a sample of 300.

What size sample would have been required had the firm started with a single sample? Since the percentage is unknown, sample size is determined by Eq. (8.1) with p^* equal to 50 percent. The necessary calculations reveal that a sample of 385 would be required. Sequential sampling results in a reduction of 85, and the reduction would be even greater if the sample percentage were very small or very large.

Table 8.5
Sampling Error Reduction with Sequential Sampling. Utility Shareholder Survey

Sample size	Sample proportion†	Standard error	1.96 Standard error
50	24.0	6.10	11.96
100	26.0	4.41	8.64
150	24.7	3.53	6.92
200	25.0	3.07	6.02
250	24.8	2.74	5.37
300	25.7	2.53	4.96

†Sample proportion refers to the percentage of shareholders who are "concerned about energy conservation measures taken by the company."

ESTIMATION OF TOTALS

Specifications set for the required reliability in estimating proportions or means have frequently been less demanding than were necessary. This surprising twist occurs because a seemingly small difference in an average generates a large difference in a total. Estimation of the average number of times a household eats out per month within .1 sounds like a high degree of reliability. When applied to a community of 15,000 households, this leads to a difference of 1,500 "outings." If the community has 25,000 households, the difference is 2,500 outings.

The determination of sample size for estimating a universe total follows precisely the same format as that for proportions or means. The decision maker must set the acceptable level for $z\overset{*}{\sigma}_{x'}$. In marketing problems this is often a total sales figure, either in total revenue or in number of units. The size of the universe (N) is a critical value in generating a total, and this value appears when we set $z\overset{*}{\sigma}_{x'} = zN\overset{*}{\sigma}_{\bar{x}}$ (or $zN\overset{*}{\sigma}_{\bar{p}}$). The acceptable level for the standard error of the mean is thus equal to the number specified by the decision maker divided by zN.

$$z\overset{*}{\sigma}_{x'} = zN\overset{*}{\sigma}_{\bar{x}}; \qquad \overset{*}{\sigma}_{\bar{x}} = \frac{z\overset{*}{\sigma}_{x'}}{zN}.$$

If the decision maker wishes to estimate a total within $10,000 (with 95.5 percent confidence: $z = 2$), the standard error of the mean must be only $.20 if N is 25,000 and only $.05 if N is 100,000.

Suppose the owner of Walton's wishes to estimate the number of meals eaten out a month by the households within the community. The mean number of times the households eat out is not the relevant mean to consider. The mean number of *meals* is the appropriate characteristic. Given this frame of reference, the owner desires 98 percent confidence that the estimated total is within 2,000 meals of the true monthly total. If there are 15,000 households in the community, $\overset{*}{\sigma}{}^2_{\bar{x}}$ is set equal to

$$\overset{*}{\sigma}{}^2_{\bar{x}} = \frac{(2,000)^2}{(2.33)^2 \, (15,000)^2} = .003275.$$

This expression in turn is set equal to

$$\frac{s^2}{\overset{*}{n}} = .003275.$$

Our previous discussion suggested that s^2 for number of outings per month would probably be less than 1. Dispersion with respect to number of meals does not have the upper limit of 31. Estimation of s^2 with respect to number of meals per household is a more substantive issue. Knowledge of the subject and the geographic area is required. If that knowledge is available and s^2 is estimated at 2.25, $\overset{*}{n}$ is calculated to be 687.

Suppose the owner wishes to use the same survey to estimate the number of households in the suburban community who have visited Walton's center city restaurant. The owner wishes to estimate this number within 500 with 95 percent confidence but has no idea what the percentage is. Will the sample of 687 meet these additional requirements?

Several steps are required. First, $1.96\sigma_{x'} = 500$ or $\sigma_{x'} = 255.10$. What units are applied to this measure? Households, the same as the 500! Second, $\sigma_{x'} = N\overset{*}{\sigma}_{\bar{p}}$ or $\overset{*}{\sigma}_{\bar{p}} = (255.10)/(15,000) = .0170$. This result is expressed as a proportion, not as a percentage. Therefore, the standard error is 1.70 percent. Now we are ready to solve for the required sample size.

$$\overset{*}{\sigma}{}^2_{\bar{p}} = \frac{50 \times 50}{\overset{*}{n}} = (1.70)^2; \qquad \overset{*}{n} = 865.$$

A sample of 687 would not be large enough to accomplish both objectives. A larger sample would be needed for the second objective than for the first, despite the lower confidence level.

Should this calculation have been made without the finite multiplier? The calculated sampling fraction is over 5 percent. Substituting

$$\overset{*}{\sigma}{}^2_{\bar{p}} = (1.70)^2 = \frac{2,500}{\overset{*}{n}} \left(1 - \frac{\overset{*}{n}}{15,000}\right)$$

and solving for $\overset{*}{n}$ yields a result of 818, a reduction of 47 in the required sample size.

The restaurant owner must now decide whether the second objective is important enough to justify increasing the sample from 687 to 818, roughly a 20 percent increase in size. Given this type of information, many decision makers revert to the sample size necessary for their announced number-one priority, settling for whatever reliability that sample size yields on the second objective. What reliability will be obtained for the second objective with a sample size 687?

ESTIMATES FOR SUBGROUPS

Marketing managers, encouraged by marketing researchers, often expand their requests for data. Estimates for the total United States are fine, but wouldn't estimates for individual states or standard metropolitan statistical areas (SMSA's) be even better? If one is not careful, one slips into thinking that the reliability associated with the estimate for the total universe applies to estimates for the subgroups as well. This just is not true as a little reflection shows.

A national sample of 10,000 households is employed for an expenditure study. Expenditures per household for a particular product category are estimated at $420.84 with $\overset{*}{\sigma}_{\bar{x}}^2 = \$1.57$. How reliable is the corresponding expenditure estimate for Missouri households? An argument that focuses on a sample of 10,000 is no longer relevant. We must now ask what the sample size is for Missouri. If only 100 or 200 households were sampled within that state, we must not be surprised if the standard error is $15 or $25. If the subgroups are further refined (for example, rural households in Missouri), the sample size may be only 30 or 40. With that size sample, the resulting standard error may be so large that the confidence interval is useless to any decision maker.

Each estimate for a subgroup is a different problem in estimation and is attacked in precisely the same way as are problems already considered. That portion of the sample drawn from the relevant subgroup must be considered independently. How large is the sample from that subgroup? What is the sample variance or proportion within that subgroup? And if appropriate, how large is the subpopulation of that group? These questions determine the standard error that in conjunction with the sample statistic establishes the confidence interval. The procedure must be repeated for each subgroup considered.

This approach to estimations for subgroups assumes that the sample from each subgroup is a simple random sample of that subgroup. But what if only the total sample is selected as a simple random sample? If the initial sample of 10,000 was selected as a simple random sample of United States households, the sample of 146 households in Missouri has not been selected as a separate sample. It was simply a part of a larger simple random sample. As long as the total sample is selected by simple random sampling, every subsample is a simple random sample of its corresponding subgroup. Therefore, the 146 sample households in Missouri would be a simple random sample of Missouri households.

If the decision maker is interested in subgroup estimates, that objective should be recognized early in the planning stage. If it is not, we must expect that the reliability of some subgroup estimates will be unnecessarily low. The only way to accomplish the objective of subgroup reliability is to determine the sample size required in each subgroup. This is precisely the problem we have been considering. The introduction of various subgroups merely changes a single problem into a series of problems, one for each subgroup. The researcher who does not choose to design the sample as a series of separate samples must risk the possibility of low reliability for some of the subgroup estimates.

Consider the following problem. A manufacturer of cleaning products for building maintenance wants to determine customer reaction to a proposed new product. The firm sells to three different markets: (1) large national building maintenance firms, (2) firms responsible for the maintenance of the buildings within a single shopping center, and (3) specialized departments or persons charged with maintenance of a single building. The categories pose minor problems in the classification of some customers, but the manufacturer has found the system useful and operational. It desires separate estimates for each of three categories, with roughly equal reliability for each estimate.

The manufacturer, upon examining its files, discovers that 10 percent of its accounts are national building maintenance firms, 30 percent come from single shopping center operators, and the remaining 60 percent come from single-building operations. A simple random sample of accounts—or a proportionate stratified sample—will result in relatively small samples from the first two categories. Such a sample design may be appropriate for overall population estimates, but it is undoubtedly a poor design for estimates of the individual subgroups.[2] Taking equal size samples from each subgroup will yield a much better first approximation when subgroup estimates are the major interest.[3]

If the subgroups of interest are formed on two variables (for example, response both to price differences and package design), the number of subgroups increases rapidly. With three alternatives for each variable, estimates may be desired for all nine subgroups. The sample size of each cell or subgroup determines the reliability achieved for the separate estimates. Unless the issue is considered in the planning stage, the sample results may lack the required reliability for subgroup estimates.

THE COEFFICIENT OF VARIATION

"I don't want the sample statistic to differ from the correct answer by more than 5 percent." This is not an *absolute* difference specification but a *relative* difference specification. A coefficient of variation (V) is defined as a standard

---

[2]The merits and proper use of proportional and disproportional stratified samples are discussed later in this chapter.

[3]A better procedure is to solve for the proper sample size for each subgroup. The equal size rule-of-thumb assumes large population subgroups, equal subgroup variances, and interest in means or proportions rather than totals.

deviation divided by the corresponding expected value. In its most elementary form it is given by Eq. (8.5),

$$V = \frac{\sigma}{\mu},\qquad(8.5)$$

the standard deviation of the population distribution divided by the mean of the population. Somewhat analogous measures can be used in determining the necessary sample size when specifications express standard errors as percentages of the values estimated.

Suppose a product manager wishes to estimate the mean income of a particular market segment. The specifications are 99.7 percent confidence with a maximum error of 6 percent. These specifications mean that the standard error of the mean may be no more than 2 percent of the population mean.

$$\frac{3\overset{*}{\sigma}_{\bar{x}}}{\mu} = .06; \qquad \frac{\overset{*}{\sigma}_{\bar{x}}}{\mu} = .02.$$

The usual way of expressing such a specification is simply $V_{\bar{x}} = .02$.

The sample size required when the decision maker's specifications are stated in relative terms can be solved by using V instead of σ (or s) in formulas for n^* as shown in Eq. (8.6) for sample means

$$n^* = \frac{z^2 V^2}{D^2}\qquad(8.6)$$

and in Eq. (8.7) for proportions.[4]

$$n^* = \frac{z^2 p^* q^*}{D^2 p^{*2}} = \frac{z^2 q^*}{D^2 p^*}.\qquad(8.7)$$

The z-values again refer to the normal curve. The D-values are the decision maker's specifications expressed as a decimal fraction: .04 for 4 percent, etc. The coefficient of variation V is as defined by Eq. (8.5), and V is also expressed as a decimal fraction. The population coefficient of variation is pq/p when dealing with a proportion. Conservative estimates of these values (p^* and q^*) are substituted in Eq. (8.7). Let us illustrate the use of these equations with specific problems.

The product manager who wishes to estimate the mean income of a particular market segment has set $z = 3$ and $D = .06$. All that remains is to estimate V. We need not estimate the absolute value of σ (or s), but only its value as a proportion of the mean. An estimate of $s = \$3,000$ and $\bar{x} = \$15,000$ would yield the same coefficient of variation as $s = \$4,000$ and $\bar{x} = \$20,000$; both have $V = .2$. Many other combinations also yield $V = .2$, and we need

---

[4]Equations (8.6) and (8.7) ignore the finite multiplier and are based on n rather than on $(n - 1)$. More precise formulas and their derivation are given in Morris H. Hansen, William N. Hurwitz, and William G. Madow, 1953, *Sample Survey Methods and Theory*, Vols. I and II (New York: Wiley).

not stipulate which one we believe to be most likely. Using $V = .2$ along with the product manager's specifications, we see that a sample of 100 is required.

$$n^* = \frac{9(.2)^2}{(.06)^2} = 100.$$

Problems involving the estimation of percentages or proportions present certain subtleties when specifications are stated in relative terms. It will be recalled that a most conservative position ($p^* = q^* = 50$) was possible when the specification was stated in *percentage points*. Substitution of these values leads to an n^* that assures the realization of the specifications. There is no corresponding approach when the specification is expressed as a *percentage*. This is shown by the expression q^*/p^* of Eq. (8.7) that has no upper limit.

The smaller p^* is relative to q^*, the larger the sample must be in order to realize any given specification. This is not surprising when we reflect on the meaning of estimating a proportion with a maximum tolerance of 10 percent. If the sample result is 90 percent, a deviation of 9 percentage points is acceptable. But if the sample result is 40 percent, the deviation must be no more than 4 percentage points. The lower the sample result, the smaller the acceptable deviation. The expression q^*/p^* incorporates this concept.

Consider the marketing director who wishes an estimate of the percentage of customers in the target market who have "tried" the product. The director wishes to be 90 percent confident, and the acceptable difference is 8 percent. (Be sure you understand the meaning of each of these percentages and the difference between them.) The director must first choose q^*/p^*. A conservative approach is to estimate a value for the ratio that is not likely to be exceeded. Suppose the marketing director believes that 20 to 25 percent of the target market have tried the product. By these figures the director estimates that the ratio of q/p is between 4.0 and 3.0, but that is not the most conservative position. If the director believes that p is at least 15 percent, the most conservative value for q^*/p^* would be $.85/.15 = 5.67$. Substituting in Eq. (8.7), the required sample size is 2,383.[5]

$$n^* = \frac{(1.64)^2}{(.08)^2} (5.67) = 2,383.$$

If the marketing director had been able to assert that at least 50 percent of the target market had tried the product, the same relative reliability ($1.64V_{\bar{p}} = .08$) could be achieved with a sample of only 420.

The determination of the proper sample size for estimating totals does not require separate formulas when specifications are stated in relative terms. This is much different from our conclusion when specifications were stated in abso-

---

[5]A nomogram for determining the required sample size, given the required precision and the population coefficient of variation is presented in Irving Roshwalb, 1969, *Nomograms for Marketing Research* (New York: Audits and Surveys, Inc.), p. 15. Similar graphs can be devised for specifications given in absolute values, using as a guide the worksheet of Table 8.4.

lute terms. When using relative specifications, the formulas for means and proportions also yield the correct sample sizes for estimates of totals. This somewhat surprising result occurs because both numerator and denominator of V are "blown up" by N. Therefore reliability of X percent in estimating a mean or a proportion also yields reliability of X percent in estimating a total derived from them.

PROPORTIONAL STRATIFICATION

Since a stratified sample normally yields greater reliability than a simple random sample of the same size, a given level of reliability should be obtainable from stratification with a smaller sample. We wish to apply that logic, but we also wish a specific answer to the question, "How large a sample must be selected, using stratification, to secure a stated level of reliability?" First, we shall consider the question using the same sampling fraction within each stratum—proportional stratified sampling.

The gain in reliability from stratification depends on the dispersion of units within strata s_w^2 relative to the dispersion among units without regard to strata (s^2). The complement of the ratio of these two variances $(1 - s_w^2/s^2)$ indicates the possible reduction in sample size by switching to a proportional stratified sample without loss of reliability.[6]

Table 8.6 illustrates the type of gain possible from stratification where the strata differ appreciably in the characteristic of interest. The company under question had much better distribution in the west than in the east or central regions. The variance in unit sales is not known but estimated. Note that the estimated overall variance is thought to be much higher than any of the three within stratum variances (7,500 compared to 3,000, 2,500, and 4,000). The higher figure of 4,000 for the west is partially explained by a higher average level of operation for these outlets than for outlets in the other two strata. The pooled within stratum variance is 52 percent less than the total variance, indicating that the same reliability could be obtained from a simple random sample of 1,000 or a proportional stratified sample of 480.

The simplest procedure to follow in determining the required sample size is to first solve for n^*, assuming a simple random sample is to be selected. This sample size is then reduced by the ratio of s_w^2/s^2. Note that s_w^2 must be computed as a weighted figure with the number of units in each stratum serving as the weighting factor.[7] The estimation of the individual stratum variances is the

---

[6]See Hansen, Hurwitz, and Madow, *op. cit.*, Vol. I for detailed discussion, and Vol. II for proofs. The relationship becomes more complex if the finite multiplier is needed.

[7]The proportion of units in each stratum would serve equally well as weights. It is also possible to use the relationships between the stratum variances and the total variance instead of their absolute magnitudes. If specifications are set in relative terms, it is thus possible to solve for the required sample size for either a simple random sample or a proportional stratified sample without using any absolute values.

Table 8.6
Basic Data for Stratification. Number of Outlets and Variance in Unit Sales by Region

Stratum (h)	Number of outlets (N_h)	Variance in unit sales (S_h^2)
East	10,000	3,000
Central	20,000	2,500
West	70,000	4,000
Total	100,000	7,500

Pooled within-stratum variance:
$$\frac{10,000(3,000) + 20,000(2,500) + 70,000(4,000)}{100,000} = 3,600$$

Possible sample size reduction:†
$$1 - \frac{3,600}{7,500} = 1 - .48 = .52(52\%).$$

†Achieved by proportional stratified sampling compared with simple random sampling, both yielding the same reliability.

same problem encountered in determining sample size for a simple random sample. It should not be brushed lightly aside; some justification is needed for the figures employed. But the typical gain from stratification is enough to warrant the incurring of some costs at the planning stage in order to realize greater savings in the cost of sampling.

Stratification versus Subgroup Estimation

Stratification is introduced in order to secure more reliable estimates for the universe under study. It is not a procedure designed to yield estimates for subgroups. Since the reliability of subgroup estimates is not incorporated in the sample design, it should not be surprising to find low reliability for individual subgroup estimates.

Stratification attempts to place together elements that are homogeneous with respect to the characteristic to be estimated. Homogeneity is also the focus in market segmentation, but the unifying characteristic is response to the firm's product or communications. The subgroups that result from the two approaches may or may not be similar. Strata are often based on easily identified socioeconomic characteristics that have limited utility in segmentation. Interest in particular subgroups should be specified so that strata can be established in ways that have double utility—good overall reliability and appropriate subgroup definitions.

The principal objective of stratification is the realization of an overall reliable estimate. This is often achieved by allocating the same sampling fraction to each stratum. Consequently, the sample may contain only a few elements from the smaller subgroups. Estimates for these subgroups may not possess the high degree of reliability desired in their separate consideration.

The marketing executive must articulate research objectives early in the planning stage of the research and not expect that a well-designed stratified sample will also provide the best market segment information. Often the desire for greater overall reliability and subgroup reliability are conflicting objectives. Only by recognizing the existence of both objectives is compromise possible in order to achieve a stated level of reliability for each.

Stratification for Estimates of Proportions

The gains realized with stratification are not typically as large for estimating proportions as they are for estimating means. Consequently, the reduction in the required sample size is typically much less when the characteristic to be estimated is a proportion. This limited reduction results from the determinants of within strata variance (s_w^2) and total variance (s^2), $\bar{p}$ and $\bar{q}$. The calculations of the two variances are shown by Eqs. (8.8) and (8.9).

$$s^2 \doteq \bar{p}\bar{q} \tag{8.8}$$

$$s_w^2 \doteq \frac{\sum\limits^{L} N_h \bar{p}_h \bar{q}_h}{N} \tag{8.9}$$

where

$\quad h =$ stratum designation,

$\quad L =$ number of strata.

According to these two equations, the gain from stratification depends on the product of $\bar{p}\bar{q}$ in contrast to the average product of the same calculation across all strata. If $\bar{p}$ and $\bar{q}$ are both 50 and the strata can be formed so that $\bar{p}_h$ is either very large or very small, large gains can be achieved through stratification. Such situations are rarely encountered in practice. Nevertheless, knowledge of the factors which generate the amount of gain should aid the researcher in choosing the basis for stratification.

An illustration of the gains realized by stratification is given by the proportion of industrial firms using supplementary maintenance contracts. Suppose there are 5,000 such firms within a certain SMSA, and unknown to the investigator 2,000 have current contracts (40 percent). The gain from stratification depends on the potential bases for stratification and the percentage figures within the various strata. Table 8.7 gives three alternative bases for forming strata and the resulting values of s_w^2. The most efficient (Alternative III) would permit a reduction of 18.8 percent in the sample size while maintaining the reliability available with a simple random sample. Alternative I results in a potential reduction of only 2 percent.

Table 8.7
Estimation of the Percentage of Industrial Firms with Supplementary Maintenance Contracts. Alternative Bases of Stratification

Alternative	Stratum	Number of firms	Percentage of firms with contracts	$N_h \bar{p}_h \bar{q}_h$ (in thousands)
I	A	2,500	40	6,000
	B	2,000	35	4,550
	C	500	60	1,200
		5,000		11,750
II	A'	2,500	32	5,440
	B'	2,000	40	4,800
	C'	500	80	800
		5,000		11,040
III	A"	2,500	22	4,290
	B"	2,000	50	5,000
	C"	500	90	450
		5,000		9,740

$s^2 = (40)(60) = 2,400.$

$$s_w^2 = \frac{\overset{L}{\Sigma} N_h \bar{p}_h \bar{q}_h}{N}.$$

	s_w^2	Potential percentage gain
Alternative I : 2,350		2.1
Alternative II : 2,208		8.0
Alternative III: 1,948		18.8

The small gain from Alternative I results because the individual $\bar{p}_h \bar{q}_h$ values are so similar to the overall value—2,400, 2,275, and 2,400 compared with the overall figure of 2,400. The gain from Alternative III is realized because two of the strata (A'' and C'') generate small values for $\bar{p}_h \bar{q}_h$—1,716 and 900—even though the value for B'' is 2,500; the deviations below 2,400 more than offset the slight deviation above 2,400 by B''.[8]

DISPROPORTIONAL STRATIFICATION

A stratified sample need not be selected with a constant sampling fraction across all strata. If greater reliability could be realized by employing a variable sampling fraction, then a disproportional stratified sample is worth consideration. Disproportional stratification is a more efficient design when one or a

[8]The determination of the amount of gain in reliability, of course, requires that the $\bar{p}_h \bar{q}_h$ values be weighted by N_h.

few strata produce a large portion of the overall standard error that would be obtained with proportional sampling. A change in the sample design by shifting more resources to these strata will yield more reliable estimates within these strata without undue sacrifice of reliability in the remaining strata.

The situation is much like marginal analysis in economics. Sampling within each stratum is continued until the contribution of the last sample unit from each stratum is equal to the contribution of the last sample unit from every other stratum. "Contribution" in the sampling context is measured in terms of the reduction in the standard error.

Optimum allocation of a sample size n^* to the various strata is achieved by Eq. (8.10).

$$n_h^* = \frac{N_h S_h}{\sum N_h S_h} \, n^*. \tag{8.10}$$

Let us illustrate with the data of Table 8.6, assuming a sample of size 500 has been determined. The individual $N_h S_h$ calculations are

$$N_1 S_1 = 547{,}723, \qquad N_2 S_2 = 1{,}000{,}000, \qquad N_3 S_3 = 4{,}427{,}189.$$

$$\sum N_h S_h = 5{,}974{,}912. [9]$$

The resulting calculations, using Eq. (8.10), yield optimum sample sizes of 46 in the east, 84 in the central region, and 370 in the west. This contrasts to samples of 50, 100, and 350 according to proportional allocation. Would this reallocation be worth the effort? This is best determined by a comparison of the standard errors. The resulting $\sigma_{\bar{x}}^{*2}$ with proportional allocation is 7.20; with disproportional allocation $\sigma_{\bar{x}}^{*2}$ is 7.14. In terms of standard errors, the reduction is only from 2.68 to 2.67. A disproportional stratified sample of 496 with allocation of 45, 83, and 368 would yield approximately the same reliability as a proportional stratified sample of 500. In this case, the departure from proportional allocation would cause more problems than it would be worth.

Very large variations in the standard deviation of the strata will warrant the use of disproportional sampling. With small variations such as those in the present illustration (standard deviations of 50, 54.8, and 63.2), proportional allocation should be used. When in doubt, use proportional sampling! This recommendation is dictated by two considerations. (1) A proportional stratified sample is self-weighting, thus facilitating both the calculation of unbiased estimates and the use of more sophisticated analyses. (2) Disproportional sampling may lead to *lower* reliability than a proportional design if the estimates of the S_h values are incorrect. This possibility of lower reliability is most obvious if the ranking of the S_h values is reversed; for example, if the standard deviation within the west were estimated as lower than that of the east or central (Table 8.6). Lower reliability could also occur if the disproportional

---

[9]Note optimal allocation involves the use of S_h, not S_h^2. Variations among the S_h values will be less than variations among S_h^2 values.

allocation were pushed too far; for example, a sample of 410 from the west, 60 from the central, and 30 from the east.

A desire to make reliable estimates for subgroups as well as an overall estimate for the total universe will often lead to disproportional sampling. In this situation sample size and its allocation among strata may be the result of a series of subgroup decisions rather than a conscious decision to use disproportional sampling. At the very least, the researcher should estimate the overall standard error before implementing the design. Concern for a particular subgroup as a separate estimate must not be permitted to destroy the reliability of the overall estimate.

CLUSTERING[10]

Cluster sampling and required sample size can best be understood by comparing the reliability of a cluster sample of a given size with that of a simple random sample of the same size. Except in the most unusual cases, the reliability of the cluster sample will be less than that of the simple random sample. The difference in reliability is best seen in Eq. (8.11) that expresses the relative reliability of the sample mean in two parts: (1) the portion that reflects the reliability of a simple random sample of size n and (2) the portion that shows how the first part is modified because a cluster sample is involved rather than a simple random sample.[11]

$$V_{\bar{x}}^2 = (1 - f) \, \frac{V^2}{n} \left[1 + \delta(\bar{n} - 1) \right] . \tag{8.11}$$

Our present concern is with the second portion, that within the brackets, since it shows the effect of cluster sampling. The term $\bar{n}$ is the average number of units per cluster in the sample. According to the equation, clustering leads to rapid loss in reliability as $\bar{n}$ increases unless δ is very small or negative. The term δ is the intraclass correlation. It measures the similarity of units within a cluster. If all units within a cluster are alike, $\delta = 1$. If the means of all clusters are identical, $\delta = -1/(\bar{N} - 1)$ where $\bar{N}$ is the average number of population units per cluster. The specific value of δ must be determined or estimated for each problem. Its value is positive in almost all practical problems and will decrease as the size of the cluster increases; small groups are usually more homogeneous than large groups. If two-stage cluster sampling is employed with simple random sampling at the second stage, it is unusual for δ to be as large as .10.

---

[10]The discussion of cluster sampling is on a general and pragmatic level designed to give the reader an overview. Technical problems of estimation, the components of reliability, and multistage designs are beyond the scope of a basic marketing research text. The interested reader is referred to any standard work on sampling theory.

[11]See Hansen, Hurwitz, and Madow, Vol. I, *op. cit.,* Chapter 6 for derivation, technical considerations, and an extended discussion.

Table 8.8
Loss in Reliability with Cluster Sampling Compared
with Simple Random Sampling. Selected Values of
δ and $\bar{n}$

δ	Increase in variance†				
	$\bar{n} = 2$	$\bar{n} = 5$	$\bar{n} = 10$	$\bar{n} = 25$	$\bar{n} = 50$
.10	10%	40%	90%	240%	490%
.07	7	28	63	168	343
.04	4	16	36	96	196
.01	1	4	9	24	49

†The indicated increase in variance can be offset by increasing
the total sample by the same percentage. The increase must be
an increase in the number of first-stage sampling units, not an
increase in the number of units sampled within each cluster.

Table 8.8 shows the percentage increase in variance associated with cluster
sampling for selected values of δ and $\bar{n}$. The base for the calculation is a simple
random sample of the same size. For example, the variance derived from a
cluster sample with $\bar{n} = 25$ and $\delta = .07$ would be 168 percent more than the
variance derived from a simple random sample of the same size. If δ were .01,
the variance would be only 24 percent greater for the cluster sample. The increase in variance can be offset by increasing the total sample size by the
percentage shown within the table. This increase must be achieved by selecting
more clusters, not more units per cluster. An increase of the number of units
per cluster would change the value of $\bar{n}$.

COSTS

The critical factor involved in choosing between alternative sample designs is
the relative cost associated with the different stages of the sampling plan. Let
us compare three different sample designs each of which has the same reliability: (1) a simple random sample of 600, (2) a cluster sample (with $\delta = .10$)
using $\bar{n} = 5$ and total sample of 840, and (3) a cluster sample (still with
$\delta = .10$) using $\bar{n} = 10$ and a total sample of 1,140. The choice between the
two cluster designs depends on the cost of including more clusters compared
with the cost of reaching units within a cluster. Design (2) requires the inclusion of more clusters, a total of 168, while design (3) requires only 114.

Assume that the cost of including each cluster is $100 ($C_1$). This cost is
incremental. It is generated by the necessity of going into the specific area in
order to draw the sample and oversee the operation. It includes all travel and
administrative expenses associated with each additional cluster. Further
assume that the cost of including each additional unit is $10 ($C_2$); this figure

represents interviewing costs, including travel within the cluster. Using these figures, design (3) is slightly less expensive than (2)—$22,800 versus $25,200.

A general formula for the optimum $\bar{n}$ is given by Eq. (8.12).[12] Note that application of this formula to the present problem indicates a value for $\bar{n}$ between nine and ten. If δ were only .04, $\bar{n}^*$ would increase to approximately 15. How small would δ have to be to dictate $\bar{n}^* = 50$?

$$\bar{n}^* = \left(\frac{C_1}{C_2} \times \frac{1 - \delta}{\delta} \right)^{1/2}. \tag{8.12}$$

Would design (3) be superior to a simple random sample of 600? That is, which would cost less? The answer depends on the geographic area involved. A $C_1 = \$100$ suggests that the cost of reaching each individual unit might be over $50 and might approach the $100 figure. If that is true, design (3) is superior. Design (2) would also be superior to simple random sampling. C_1 is generated by travel costs to reach the general location plus general supervisory and administrative costs at each cluster. Some of these costs would be eliminated in the simple random sample, but large travel costs (and interviewer time costs) would still be incurred if the total area of the survey were large. Even if we reduce the cost per unit to $40 with simple random sampling, design (3) is still slightly superior.

Might a stratified sample be better than the cluster approach? It depends on the effectiveness of the stratification. Assuming the cost per unit would be slightly higher with stratification than with simple random sampling (perhaps $60), stratification would be superior to design (3) if it achieved the same reliability with a sample of 380 or less—determined by dividing the cost of design (3) by per unit cost with stratification.

$$\frac{22,800}{60} = 380.$$

A proportional stratified sample of 380 would possess greater reliability than design (3) only if within-stratum variance (s_w^2) were considerably less than total variance, (s^2). Since design (3) and a simple random sample of 600 have the same reliability, we may use the simple random sample as a point of reference. If s_w^2 is more than 36.7 percent less than s^2, the proportional stratified sample will be superior to the cluster sample of design (3).[13]

$$1 - \frac{s_w^2}{s^2} = 1 - \frac{n^* \text{ (stratified)}}{n^* \text{ (simple random)}} = 1 - \frac{380}{600} = .367.$$

[12]*Ibid.,* Vol. I, p. 286.

[13]Recall that the required sample size with proportional stratified sampling is equal to the required sample size with simple random sampling reduced by the ratio s_w^2/s^2.

Assuming s_w^2 is not that small relative to s^2, design (3) should be accepted and implemented.

The proper sample design can be determined for any particular problem only by introducing the specific costs, variances, and intraclass correlations of that problem. The approach is to first determine the required sample size with a simple random sample. This serves as the base against which alternative cluster designs and stratification schemes can be compared.

Table 8.9 provides a general worksheet for determining sample sizes when stratification or clustering is used as an alternative to simple random sampling. This worksheet is much different from Table 8.4 that provides a guide for determining the necessary size for a simple random sample. That determination starts with the decision maker's substantive demands. The worksheet of Table 8.9 is more technical in nature. What are the expected variances when strata are established on a particular basis? What are expected costs in the successive steps of clustering? What is intraclass correlation? The two worksheets are supplementary and should be used together and sequentially.

Table 8.9
Worksheet for Determining Required Sample Size. Alternatives to Simple Random Sampling

Information required

Stratification

1. Estimates of variances in each stratum.

2. Number of units in each stratum.

3. Estimate of overall variance.

Clustering

1. Estimate of intraclass correlation.

2. Cost at each stage of sample selection.

How information is used

Proportional stratification

1. Stratum variances and number of units are used to calculate within-stratum variance.

2. Within-stratum variance divided by overall variance indicates relationship between required sample size with proportional stratified sample compared with required size with simple random sampling.

Disproportional stratification

The product of each stratum standard deviation times the number of units determines the relative proportion of the sample to be allocated to each stratum.

(continued)

Table 8.9
(continued)

Clustering

1. Intraclass correlation and ratio between costs are used to calculate the optimum average number of sampled units per cluster.
2. Derived optimum from preceding step and intraclass correlation are used to calculate the decrease in reliability of clustering versus simple random sampling for samples of the same size.

Example (proportional stratification)

1. Stratum variances are 3, 4, and 6 while number of units are 100, 150, and 200, respectively, for three strata: within-stratum variance = 2,100/450 = 4.67.
2. Overall variance = 8.
3. Within-stratum variance/overall variance = 4.67/8 = .58. Proportional stratified sample need be only 58 percent as large as the simple random sample in order to yield equal reliability.

Example (disproportional stratification)
(Same data as preceding example)

1. Stratum standard deviations are 1.73, 2.00, and 2.45.
2. Overall aggregate for stratum standard deviation times number of units is 963.
3. Respective contributions of the individual strata to the aggregate in the preceding step determine proportion of sample: 18, 31, and 51 percent.

Example (clustering)

1. Intraclass correlation is estimated to be .08: $\delta = .08$.
2. Costs are estimated as $75 at the first stage and $15 at the second stage: $C_1 = \$75$ and $C_2 = \$15$.
3. Optimum sample units per cluster:

$$\bar{n}^* = \left(\frac{75}{15} \times \frac{.92}{.08} \right)^{\frac{1}{2}} = 7.6.$$

4. Decrease in reliability due to clustering: $1 + .08(7.6 - 1) = 1.53$. Cluster sample must be 153 percent of simple random sample size in order to have the same reliability.

AN EXAMPLE: COMPARISON OF
THREE ALTERNATIVE SAMPLE DESIGNS

Lincoln Office Supply, a manufacturer and distributor of business forms, is concerned about a recent sales decline in the Philadelphia SMSA. After much discussion, the company decided a survey of users in the SMSA is appropriate. The principal goal is to measure average use of the type of forms produced by

Lincoln. The marketing research consultant is weighing the relative merits of simple random sampling, stratification, and clustering. The first step is to determine the reliability required by Lincoln in its estimate.

The universe of interest is defined by Lincoln as all business establishments in the eight-county area with 1980 sales in excess of $500,000. The marketing manager agrees to a reliability specification of a sample mean within 30 reams of the true mean with 95 percent confidence. Substituting:

$$1.96 \overset{*}{\sigma}_{\bar{x}} = 30 \quad \text{or} \quad \overset{*}{\sigma}_{\bar{x}} = 15.31.$$

With the varied size of businesses and their diverse usage of business forms, Lincoln's marketing manager thinks the standard deviation may be as large as 350 reams. Substituting these values and solving for the necessary sample size with simple random sampling, we have

$$n^* = \frac{(350)^2}{(15.31)^2} = 523.$$

A cluster sample might employ the Business Enumeration Districts (BED's) of the Bureau of Census as the basis for establishing subgroups. These BED's are composed of contiguous areas containing a number of businesses that requires one worker-day for an enumerator in the Census of Business. Since the BED's are composed of contiguous areas, the consultant believes the type of businesses and need for business forms will be similar within clusters but diverse among clusters. The consultant, therefore, estimates that $\delta = .15$, a rather high intraclass correlation.

The research consultant must also estimate C_1 and C_2. C_1 (the cost of sending a supervisor into a BED for preliminary work and the necessary overseeing and administration) is estimated at $30. C_2 (the incremental cost per interview within each selected cluster) is estimated at $8.

We can now determine the optimal number of units per cluster by Eq. (8.12).

$$\bar{n}^* = \left(\frac{30}{8} \times \frac{.85}{.15} \right)^{1/2} = 4.61.$$

The expression $1 + \delta(\bar{n} - 1)$ from Eq. (8.11) shows the loss in reliability by using a cluster sample rather than a simple random sample. Substituting, we have

$$1 + .15(4.61 - 1) = 1.54.$$

The loss in reliability is 54 percent; consequently, a cluster sample of 805 (523 × 1.54) would be needed to give the same reliability as a simple random sample of 523. The cluster sample would consist of 175 BED's with an average of 4.61 businesses selected from each. This would result in a total cost of $11,690, derived from $30(175) + $8(805). The cost per interview for the simple random sample was estimated at $17.50, much higher than C_2 because the interviews would not be "clustered" together. Despite the higher cost per interview and the lower sample size, the simple random sample is superior to the cluster sample in the Lincoln case. Total cost for the simple random sample is $9,153 for the same reliability.

Simple random sampling is superior in the Lincoln problem for two principal reasons. (1) Clusters are quite dissimilar in the characteristic to be studied. Therefore, many clusters must be included in the sample with a small number of units included from each sampled cluster. (2) The area to be surveyed is relatively compact. The cost of reaching and interviewing units spread throughout the area is not excessive in comparison with the cost of reaching and interviewing units that are in close proximity.

Would a stratified sample be an improvement over a simple random sample? The answer depends on the degree of within-stratum homogeneity. Lincoln found that the available list of businesses was classified by type of business and by number of employees. The marketing manager indicated that both characteristics influenced the need for business forms of the type Lincoln produced. Four strata were suggested based on two characteristics: (1) retailers versus other businesses and (2) 25 employees or more versus under 25 employees. The estimated standard deviations and percentage distribution among the four strata are shown in Table 8.10. The gain from stratification is striking. The sample size can be reduced to 100—(523)(23,232.5/122,500)—with stratified sampling while still retaining the required reliability. Interviewing costs were estimated as the same, regardless of whether simple random sampling or stratification were employed. The net result is an estimated cost of $1,750(100 × $17.50) plus a small expenditure in preliminary work on the list.

If no list had been available, the survey would have moved by default to the cluster approach although it might have been preceded by grouping the BED's into strata in order to reduce δ. The data within Table 8.10 also suggest

Table 8.10
Estimated Standard Deviation and Percentage Distribution among Strata. Lincoln Office Supply Problem

Strata	Estimated standard deviation	Percentage of firms
Small retailers	70	50
Large retailers	275	10
Small nonretailers	60	20
Large nonretailers	250	20

Pooled within-stratum variance:
$.5(70)^2 + .1(275)^2 + .2(60)^2 + .2(250)^2 = 23,232.5.$
Population variance: 122,500.

that disproportional stratification would be even better than proportional stratification since the estimated standard deviations are much larger for the strata of large firms than are the standard deviations for the strata of small firms.

SUMMARY

The necessary sample size for a marketing research project cannot be determined without specifications from the decision maker. These specifications must indicate (1) how large a deviation between the true universe value and the sample result is acceptable and (2) the confidence level required by the decision maker. Given these values, the determination of sample size uses the confidence interval rationale. The same rationale is used for each determination of sample size, different formulas being required for different statistics. In each case the decision maker's specifications determine the acceptable value for the standard error. The required sample size (n^*) may then be calculated by the appropriate formula. The paradox that some estimates of the anticipated sample results are needed before n^* can be determined is sometimes troublesome, but it is a necessity that must be recognized. The better the initial estimates, the more likely the sample results will be neither more or less reliable than the problem requires.

The decision maker must make several choices with respect to reliability specifications. The decision maker must decide (1) whether he or she is more concerned with the reliability of overall estimates or the reliability of separate subgroup estimates, and (2) whether it is better to set specifications in terms of absolute reliability (within X, Y households, etc.) or in terms of relative reliability (within Z percent of the universe value). The decision maker must also decide on the required reliability for various estimates to be made—including means and proportions as well as totals. Sample designs and determination of the required sample size are flexible, but the time to make choices is before the design has gone into the field.

The alternatives to simple random sampling are (1) proportional stratified sampling, (2) disproportional stratified sampling, and (3) cluster sampling. The selection of which to use for any particular question requires knowledge of (1) the substantive nature of the specific universe involved, (2) the relationships among the units of that universe when it is divided into strata or clusters, and (3) the cost structure of various sampling plans.

The specifications of the decision maker enable the determination of the required sample size if simple random sampling is employed. This provides the base against which both stratification and cluster designs can be compared. The relative efficiency or inefficiency of various designs can be used to determine the required sample sizes associated with each alternative. The costs involved in each design can then be introduced in order to ascertain which sampling plan will yield the desired reliability at the lowest cost.

EXERCISES AND PROBLEMS

1. Distinguish among the terms within each of the following sets.

    a) C_1 and C_2

    b) Stratified sample reliability and subgroup reliability

    c) Within-stratum variance, total variance, and among strata variance

    d) $\bar{n}^*$, $\bar{n}_h^*$, and n^*

    e) V_p, $\overset{*}{\sigma}_p$, $V_{x'}$, and $\overset{*}{\sigma}_{x'}$

    f) D, p^*, z, and s

2. Briefly explain the meaning and importance of each of the following in sample design decisions.

    a) Finite multiplier

    b) Required confidence

    c) Acceptable interval width

    d) Intraclass correlation

    e) Two-stage cluster sample

    f) Disproportionate stratified sampling

    g) Self-weighting

3. A research director who wishes to study the "reach" of a particular ad campaign is particularly concerned about the percentage of the target market that have seen at least a portion of the campaign. The director does not think the figure will exceed 25 percent. (Make any additional assumptions necessary for the following questions, but be sure to state them in your answer.)

    a) What size simple random sample should be employed if the director wishes the estimate to be within 3 percentage points of the true value and 90 percent confidence is specified?

    b) Is the specification above the same as a desire that the sample statistic be within 3 percent of the universe parameter? Discuss, indicating the sample size required for this request if the answer would be different.

4. Your immediate supervisor has asked what size sample should be employed in a study of the firm's 10,000 accounts. The number of annual transactions is expected to range from zero to over 50, but the typical active account has one transaction per month. Your supervisor wishes to estimate the mean number of transactions per year and the percentage of accounts that have fewer than two transactions per year. What size sample would you recommend? Why? Explicitly state any assumptions you are making, including the values of any data that you used in your calculations.

5. An opinion research organization wishes to forecast what is expected to be a close election. It wishes to be practically certain that the sample estimate of the percentage of votes received by the winner will not differ from the election result by more than 2 percentage points. The firm wishes to spend no more than $5,000 on interviewing costs. (Cost per interview is estimated at $2.00.)

a) Can the objective be realized with the resources available?

b) Did you have to make any additional assumptions in order to answer part (a)? Discuss.

6. A universe of firms within a particular industry has been tentatively divided into three groups, established on the basis of estimated annual sales. This division yields 500 large firms, 1,000 medium-sized firms, and 2,000 small firms. Your immediate superior wishes an estimate of the mean number of employees per firm for the entire industry. The estimated standard deviations for the total population and the three groups are: total population—2,000, large—1,000, medium—200, and small—5.

a) Would it be advisable to use a stratified proportional sample rather than a simple random sample? Justify your answer in terms of the reliability associated with each.

b) How large a sample would you recommend?

c) Should a disproportional stratified sample be considered? Why?

d) Would your answers in (b) and (c) be appropriate if your superior desires estimates for the means of each size group? Explain.

e) Suppose your superior also wishes an estimate of the mean years in the industry for purchasing agents. Would the results of the preceding considerations be relevant in the sample design for this characteristic? Might sampling decisions based on mean number of employees reduce the reliability of estimates for "mean years in the industry for purchasing agents"? Discuss.

7. A fast-food chain wishes to estimate the total annual expenditures in fast-food operations by residents of Iron City. There are 5,000 dwelling units in Iron City. The estimated standard deviation in annual expenditures, based on knowledge of "similar" communities, is $40. The marketing manager insists that the estimate be within $25,000 with 95 percent confidence.

a) How large a sample would you recommend?

b) The city has been divided and mapped into blocks. A colleague suggests that you use a cluster (area) sample, taking an average of ten dwelling units from each sampled block. If $\delta = .04$, how much larger must the cluster sample be than the simple random sample if the two samples are to have the same reliability?

c) You estimate that the cost of including each sample block will be small—only $5—while the cost of obtaining the required information from each dwelling unit within each sampled block will be $1.75. The cost for each dwelling unit in a simple random sample will be $2.50. Clerical work with the simple random sample, over and above that required in the cluster sample, is estimated at $30. What sampling plan do you recommend?

8. You have been asked to estimate mean summer earnings for students within your school. Specified reliability is "within $25 with 99 percent confidence."

a) What size simple random sample would be needed?

b) What would be a good basis of stratification? Would it increase reliability enough to warrant its use? Discuss.

    c) Would a cluster sample be a feasible alternative? Discuss possible bases for clustering, their advantages, and their disadvantages.

9. Analyze, criticize, and explain:

    a) It is impossible to calculate the required sample size without knowing the universe values. Since the universe values are never known, any attempt to solve for the proper sample size is at best an approximation and at worst grossly incorrect.

    b) If one wishes to increase the reliability of a sample statistic, two alternatives are available. Either the sample size can be increased or the sampling plan can be changed. For example, the relevant standard error could be reduced 50 percent by either doubling the sample size or substituting a stratified sample with two strata in place of a simple random sample.

    c) Cluster sampling is really a specific type of stratified sampling. The clusters are the strata, and one should endeavor to make the clusters as homogeneous as possible.

    d) In solving for sample size, one should set $p^* = q^* = 50$. Nothing is lost by this procedure since it will always yield the specified reliability. Any other procedure runs the risk that the specified reliability will not be achieved.

    e) If the desired reliability is stated as a percentage, the usual standard error formulas are not relevant. Both the logical process and the mathematical derivations require a completely different orientation.

    f) Stratification is less likely to be beneficial in estimating proportions than it is in estimating means. This results because within-stratum variance is weighted for means but is unweighted for proportions.

    g) The average number of units per cluster ($\bar{n}$) should be small if δ is small, but it can be increased if δ is large. The increase in $\bar{n}$ will result in a larger standard error, but it will be beneficial because the cost will be lower.

CHAPTER 9

COMPARISON BETWEEN TWO SAMPLE RESULTS
MY GROUP'S BETTER THAN YOUR GROUP

Many marketing research problems involve a comparison between alternative actions. Which product formulation is preferrred by potential customers? Which advertising copy has the greatest "pull"? Which channel of distribution is the most efficient? Which price will result in the greatest revenue? the greatest profit? Which market segment has the larger mean discretionary income? These and a host of similar types of problems are decided from sample evidence; universe parameters are rarely known.

In the preceding chapters, we have considered problems involving only one universe. We tested hypotheses for a single universe, asking whether it was proper to conclude that the relevant parameter of that universe was a stated value. We also made estimates of universe parameters, considering both point estimates and interval estimates. When more than one universe is involved, comparisons are often of greater interest than are estimates for the individual universes. These comparisons may be couched as estimates or as hypotheses—just as is true for a single parameter.

A marketing manager may wish to estimate the difference between men and women in per capita consumption of a product, or may wish to test the hypothesis that their per capita consumptions are equal. The two approaches are merely different structurings of related problems. Both approaches will be considered, first hypothesis testing and then estimation.

The number of universes to be compared is limited only by the number specified in the marketing manager's problem. In one problem the manager may wish to compare five different market segments; in another, only two. The marketing manager's problem is the same in each: (1) should one conclude that the different segments have equal parameters and (2) if not, how large are the differences among them. We shall limit the discussion in this chapter to problems comparing only two parameters, extending the discussion to more than two in later chapters.

CONSTRUCTION OF HYPOTHESES: TWO-SAMPLE PROBLEM

Our first consideration in attacking two-sample problems is the statement of the appropriate hypotheses. Consider the case of Bates Manufacturing that has experienced great success with a new promotion in Zenox, a midwest city. The president thinks the wisdom of using the same campaign in Malone, another midwest city, depends on whether the two cities have the same mean income. Therefore, the president wishes to classify Malone in one of three categories: (1) it has the same mean income as Zenox, (2) it has a larger mean income than Zenox, or (3) it has a smaller mean income than Zenox.

The research director of Bates informs the president that the mean income of Zenox is $14,475 and advises that a sample be taken in Malone. If the Zenox figure is a known parameter, this problem is no different from the problems discussed in Chapter 7. The research director should establish the following set of hypotheses concerning the Malone mean income.

$$H_0 : \mu = \$14,475,$$
$$H_1 : \mu < \$14,475,$$
$$H_2 : \mu > \$14,475.$$

But suppose the Zenox figure is a sample result. The logic is now different! The president does not want to know how the Malone mean compares to $14,475 but how it compares to the true Zenox mean that is unknown. In each case the comparison is with the true Zenox mean. But in one case that number is known, and in the other case it is not. The basic question is, "Does the Malone mean equal the Zenox mean?" Using that approach and designating Zenox as City 1 and Malone as City 2, the set of three hypotheses may be expressed symbolically as

$$H_0 : \mu_1 = \mu_2,$$
$$H_1 : \mu_1 > \mu_2,$$
$$H_2 : \mu_1 < \mu_2.$$

The problem is more easily manipulated if the hypotheses are restated in terms of differences.

$$H_0 : \mu_1 - \mu_2 = 0,$$
$$H_1 : \mu_1 - \mu_2 > 0,$$
$$H_2 : \mu_1 - \mu_2 < 0.$$

The parameter identified in the hypotheses is the difference between universe means. The statistic to be employed in testing the null hypothesis is the difference between sample means $(\bar{x}_1 - \bar{x}_2)$. Therefore we have an entirely new type of random sampling distribution: a random sampling distribution of differences between sample means. The standard error associated with this distribution is the standard error of the difference between sample means $(\sigma_{\bar{x}_1 - \bar{x}_2})$.

The variance for the difference between sample means is given by Eq. (9.1).[1]

$$\sigma_{\bar{x}_1 - \bar{x}_2}^2 = \sigma_{\bar{x}_1}^2 + \sigma_{\bar{x}_2}^2. \tag{9.1}$$

Each mean has been estimated and is subject to error. Therefore the reliability of each estimate must be included in the measure of overall reliability. This is shown in Eq. (9.1) by the fact that the variance of the difference is given by the sum of the variances associated with each estimate. The right-hand side of Eq. (9.1) is composed of true variances that depend on knowledge of dispersion in the universes. We do not have this kind of information in the typical problem. Therefore we must substitute estimates of these variances. The typical problem will be approached in terms of Eq. (9.2)

$$\overset{*}{\sigma}_{\bar{x}_1 - \bar{x}_2}^2 = \overset{*}{\sigma}_{\bar{x}_1}^2 + \overset{*}{\sigma}_{\bar{x}_2}^2. \tag{9.2}$$

Now let us set up the solution of the Bates problem, assuming both the Zenox mean and the Malone mean are based upon sample evidence. The sample results for Malone show $\bar{x} = \$13{,}621$ and $s = \$2{,}952$ from a simple random sample of 300. We must also know s and n for the Zenox sample. The fact that $\bar{x} = \$14{,}475$ is not sufficient; we must know how reliable that figure is. Given that $s = \$3{,}262$ and $n = 500$ for the Zenox sample, we can substitute in Eq. (9.2) and estimate the required standard error.

$$\sigma_{\bar{x}_1 - \bar{x}_2}^2 = \frac{(3{,}262)^2}{499} + \frac{(2{,}952)^2}{299} = 50{,}469,$$

$$\overset{*}{\sigma}_{\bar{x}_1 - \bar{x}_2} = 225.$$

Now let us follow step by step how this standard error of $225 can help solve the president's problem. First, we know that the difference between the sample mean of Zenox and the sample mean of Malone is $854 ($14,475 − $13,621) with the mean for Zenox larger. Second, this difference must be expressed in terms of standard errors before it can be properly appraised.

$$\frac{\bar{x}_1 - \bar{x}_2}{\overset{*}{\sigma}_{\bar{x}_1 - \bar{x}_2}} = \frac{854}{225} = 3.80.$$

The observed difference is equal to 3.80 standard errors. Third, the probability of obtaining such a difference if the null hypothesis is true must be determined. The normal curve is appropriate since the samples are "large" and we are working with means. According to Appendix Table A.2 the probability of a difference this large is less than .0002. Finally, we must accept or reject H_0 based upon this probability. Using an α of .05 (or even .01), we should recommend the rejection of H_0. The president should conclude that the mean income of Malone is less than the mean income of Zenox. The president's reasoning

---

[1]Equations (9.1) and (9.2) are correct as presented only if the sample selections are independent of each other. The more general form has a third term that involves covariance or correlation. Equation (9.12), which is discussed later, incorporates this third term.

would then indicate that the promotion used in Zenox should not be used in Malone. Would you concur in this last step?

Two-sample Power Curve

Shifting from a single sample to the comparison of two samples has a great effect on the ability to discriminate against the null hypothesis, that is, on the power of the test. This is most readily observed through comparison of the critical values established—those values that state the sample result required in order to reject H_0. These critical values depend on the standard error of the random sampling distribution. If the standard error is large, the difference between the sample result and the hypothesized parameter must be large in order to reject H_0. Since the standard error of a difference between sample means will be larger than the standard error of either one of those arithmetic means, the two-sample test is not as powerful in discriminating as is the one-sample test.

The lower discriminatory power of the two-sample case is illustrated in Table 9.1 and Fig. 9.1 for the Bates Manufacturing problem. The comparison is between a one-sample case in which the Zenox mean is treated as a known universe parameter (only the Malone data coming from a sample) and a two-sample case in which the data from both cities are treated as sample figures. The crucial difference between the two stems from their respective standard errors: $\overset{*}{\sigma}_{\bar{x}} = 171$ for the one-sample case and $\overset{*}{\sigma}_{\bar{x}_1 - \bar{x}_2} = 225$ for the two-sample case.

The critical values (using $\alpha = .05$ and a two-tailed test) in the one-sample case are \$14,140 and \$14,810. As long as the Malone sample mean is within

Table 9.1

Comparison of Two Universe Means. Discriminatory Power of Two-sample Test versus One-sample Test. Bates Manufacturing Problem†

Difference between universe means	Power of test‡	
	One-sample test	Two-sample test
150	.14	.10
300	.42	.26
450	.75	.52
600	.94	.76
750	.99	.91

†The figures within this table are based on hypotheses structured as two one-tailed tests with a total $\alpha = .05$.

‡The test constructed runs a slight risk of concluding H_1 when H_2 is true (or of concluding H_2 when H_1 is true).

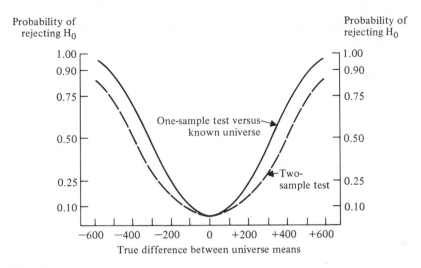

Fig. 9.1
Comparison of two universe means. Two-sample test versus one-sample test.
Bates Manufacturing problem.

this range, H_0 should be accepted—the two cities should be judged as having the same mean. The critical values in the two-sample case are expressed as differences between the sample means rather than as specific mean values. The critical difference is $441 (again using $\alpha = .05$ and a two-tailed test). The larger range between critical values in the two-sample case (2 × 441 = $882 versus $670) leads to its lower discriminatory power.

Table 9.1 shows that the probability of detecting a difference between the universe means is less in the two-sample case than in the one-sample case regardless of the size of the difference. (In order to facilitate the comparisons, the one-sample figures have been expressed as deviations from $14,475 instead of the absolute value of the mean.) The true difference between the universe means must be almost $450 before the two-sample test has a 50–50 chance of identifying it and the difference must be over $700 before it has a 90 percent probability of discerning that a difference exists. The one-sample test reaches a 50 percent probability at $335 and 90 percent probability at about $550.

COMPARISON OF TWO SAMPLE PERCENTAGES

A direct-mail insurance company wishes to compare the pulling power of two different campaigns. It selects two simple random samples from the target universe for market tests. Each sample contains 250 persons. The null hypothesis to be tested is that the universe proportion who will respond favorably is the same for each mailing piece. Again there are two alternatives to the null hypothesis: one for the superiority of each alternative mailing piece. Symbolically the three hypotheses are

$$H_0 : p_1 - p_2 = 0,$$
$$H_1 : p_1 - p_2 < 0,$$
$$H_2 : p_1 - p_2 > 0.$$

The general form for the variance of the difference between two proportions is analogous to Eq. (9.1) and is given by Eq. (9.3).

$$\sigma^2_{\bar{p}_1 - \bar{p}_2} = \sigma^2_{\bar{p}_1} + \sigma^2_{\bar{p}_2} = \frac{p_1 q_1}{n_1} + \frac{p_2 q_2}{n_2}. \tag{9.3}$$

Equation (9.3) contains universe proportions and their complements, but the marketing researcher is forced to estimate the variance of the random sampling distribution from the sample evidence as shown in Eq. (9.4).

$$\overset{*}{\sigma}{}^2_{\bar{p}_1 - \bar{p}_2} = \frac{\bar{p}_1 \bar{q}_1}{n_1 - 1} + \frac{\bar{p}_2 \bar{q}_2}{n_2 - 1}. \tag{9.4}$$

In a null hypothesis of equality between universe proportions $p_1 = p_2$ and $q_1 = q_2$. These values are not known, and their unique numerical values are not a part of the null hypothesis. Unbiased estimates can be obtained from the sample evidence, weighting each sample statistic by the sample size. This estimate is given by Eq. (9.5) that is a weighted average of the two samples.

$$p' = \frac{n_1 \bar{p}_1 + n_2 \bar{p}_2}{n_1 + n_2}; \qquad q' = 1 - p'. \tag{9.5}$$

The two samples are thus "pooled" into a single sample in order to secure a single estimate of the shared value of p_1 and p_2 under the null hypothesis. The denominator is the total number of units in the two samples combined, and the numerator is the total number of sample units that possess the specified characteristic. The value q' is merely the complement of p'. The best estimate of $\sigma^2_{\bar{p}_1 - \bar{p}_2}$ for the null hypothesis of equality between universe proportions is given by Eq. (9.6) in which p' and q' are substituted in Eq. (9.4).

$$\overset{*}{\sigma}{}^2_{\bar{p}_1 - \bar{p}_2} = \frac{p' q'}{n_1 - 1} + \frac{p' q'}{n_2 - 1} \tag{9.6}$$

$$= p' q' \left[\frac{1}{n_1 - 1} + \frac{1}{n_2 - 1} \right].$$

The structure of the problem has now been completed. Two samples, each of size 250, are selected; one group will receive mailing piece A and the other mailing piece B. The results show 25 favorable results with A and 35 favorable results with B. Are these results sufficient to conclude that mailing piece B is superior to mailing piece A? One additional point in the structure of the problem is necessary before we can answer this question: the company must specify the probability it is willing to run with respect to a Type I error. Assume this value is specified as .06 with 3 percent in each tail. The pooled estimate for p' is 12 percent (25 + 35 divided by 500). The value $\overset{*}{\sigma}{}^2_{\bar{p}_1 - \bar{p}_2}$ is given by

$$\overset{*}{\sigma}{}^2_{\bar{p}_1 - \bar{p}_2} = (12)(88)\left[\frac{1}{249} + \frac{1}{249}\right] = \frac{(12)(88)(2)}{249},$$

$$\overset{*}{\sigma}_{\bar{p}_1 - \bar{p}_2} = 2.9.$$

The two-sample results differ by 4 percentage points or 1.4 standard errors. The probability of such a difference, if H_0 were true, is over 16 percent—more likely than the level established for a Type I error. Therefore the company should conclude that the two promotion pieces possess equal pulling power.

What Level of Significance?

Suppose the president of the direct-mail insurance company decides that the difference between the two mailing pieces is large enough to conclude that the pulling power of B is superior to A. The president might justify this position by increasing α to .2—or by simply saying that the observed difference was more than one standard error. What α is implicit in a criterion of one standard error?

What level of significance should the president use? Why is .06 better than .2? The use of a .2 level of significance can be justified only by a willingness to reject the null hypothesis when it is true 20 percent of the time or with a probability of .2. Suppose α were set at the more typical values of .05 or .01? The null hypothesis of "no universe difference" would be accepted at each of these levels. There is no "proper" level to employ for α; the president must make this decision.

Although there is no "proper" level for α, the decision maker must avoid the "shifty alpha" approach. This approach chooses an α-value after examining the data and chooses so that the null hypothesis is rejected. If the president uses this approach, $\alpha = .2$ could be chosen (or perhaps $\alpha = .17$ if the president really wants to be sneaky); thereby allowing the president to conclude that program B is superior.

ESTIMATION OF DIFFERENCE BETWEEN UNIVERSE PARAMETERS

Marketing managers are often not satisfied merely to know that one alternative is superior to the other; they wish to know how much better it is. This is a problem in estimation rather than a problem in hypothesis testing.

An unbiased estimate of the difference between universe means or between universe proportions is given by the difference between the corresponding sample statistics. Thus an unbiased estimate of the difference between the mean income of Zenox and Malone is $854 ($14,475 − $13,621) with the Zenox mean larger. The same procedure applies for estimating the difference between universe percentages. The basis for this procedure is that the expected value (E) of the difference between the sample statistics is equal to the difference between the universe parameters. $E(\bar{x}_1 - \bar{x}_2) = \mu_1 - \mu_2$ and $E(\bar{p}_1 - \bar{p}_2) = p_1 - p_2$.

The establishment of a confidence interval for the difference between universe parameters is simply an extension of interval estimation as covered in Chapter 7. We merely keep in mind that the parameter estimated is a difference and that the standard error refers to the difference between sample statistics. The appropriate procedure for means is given by

$$(\bar{x}_1 - \bar{x}_2) \pm z \overset{*}{\sigma}_{\bar{x}_1 - \bar{x}_2}$$

where z comes from the normal curve and depends on the confidence desired for the estimation.[2]

A tire manufacturer wishes to estimate the improvement in gasoline mileage achieved by using a new type of tire. Two samples, each of size 100, are selected. One sample is equipped with the company's Road Master tires, its current best seller; the other sample is equipped with Road King tires, the proposed new tire. The Road Master sample has a mean of 16.5 miles per gallon and a standard deviation of 1.9. The Road King sample has a mean of 21.2 miles per gallon and a standard deviation of 2.1.

The marketing manager understands that the best single estimate of the difference in mileage between the two is 4.7 miles per gallon (21.2 − 16.5), but wishes the research director to establish a range within which this difference is likely to fall. After considerable debate and explanation, the manager agrees to be satisfied with a 90 percent confidence interval. The appropriate interval is calculated with a z of 1.64 applied to the estimated standard error of the difference between means ($\overset{*}{\sigma}_{\bar{x}_1 - \bar{x}_2}$) and is centered about the unbiased estimate of 4.7.

$$(21.2 - 16.5) \pm 1.64 \left[\frac{(2.1)^2}{99} + \frac{(1.9)^2}{99} \right]^{1/2},$$

$$4.7 \pm 1.64(.28),$$

$$4.7 \pm .5,$$

4.2 to 5.2 miles per gallon.

The marketing manager can be 90 percent confident that gasoline mileage with the Road King tire will be between 4.2 and 5.2 miles per gallon better than the gasoline mileage with the Road Master tire.

Now let us consider a problem dealing with proportions. A prospective advertiser was considering two television programs for sponsorship and

---

[2]As was the case in our earlier discussion of confidence interval estimation, the use of the normal curve relies upon the Central Limit Theorem and large samples.

wanted to test the recall of the ad message when it was presented with the two different programs. Independent tests were run: Program A with a sample of 150 and Program B with a sample of 200. Recall rates were 40 percent with Program A and 30 percent with Program B. We must not pool the two samples in determining the standard error because we are not assuming the two universe proportions are equal. Equation (9.6) is appropriate only for a test of the null hypothesis.

The appropriate variance formula to use is the sum of two estimated variances, one associated with each sample, as shown in Eq. (9.4). The relevant calculation with 90 percent confidence is given by

$$(40 - 30) \pm 1.64 \left[\frac{40 \times 60}{149} + \frac{30 \times 70}{199} \right]^{1/2},$$

$$10 \pm 1.64(5.16),$$

$$10 \pm 8.5,$$

$$1.5 \text{ to } 18.5 \text{ percentage points.}$$

On seeing the results, the advertiser was dismayed at the wide interval. The advertiser was told that the interval could be decreased either by reducing the confidence demanded or by increasing the size of the samples employed.

First, suppose the advertiser decreases the confidence level, using 80 percent confidence rather than 90 percent. The z-value is 1.28 instead of 1.64. Performing the necessary arithmetic, the resulting interval is 3.4 to 16.6 percentage points. This is still a wide interval. Even reduction to 68 percent confidence ($z = 1.0$) would yield an interval of 4.8 to 15.2 percentage points. An interval that is wider than desired should be corrected before the sample is selected, not after the fact. We now turn to the second alternative: selection of a larger sample.

DETERMINATION OF SAMPLE SIZE

The determination of the proper sample sizes in the two-sample case is not conceptually different from the determination of sample size in the one-sample case. The decision maker must specify (1) the maximum width of the resulting confidence interval and (2) the degree of confidence required. These two specifications must then be supplemented by substantive estimates of "outside" limits concerning the characteristics of interest.

Proportions

Consider the advertiser who wished to compare recall rates of an ad message when presented with two different TV programs. The advertiser was dissatisfied with an interval of 17 percentage points, but a reduction to 8 percentage points might be acceptable. Using this value and retaining the 90 percentage confidence level, we have established

$$1.64 \overset{*}{\sigma}_{\bar{p}_1 - \bar{p}_2} = 4,$$

$$\overset{*}{\sigma}_{\bar{p}_1 - \bar{p}_2} = 2.44.$$

We can substitute Eq. (9.4), but we encounter the same type of problem as we did for the one-sample case. The sample results ($\bar{p}_1$ and $\bar{p}_2$) or "outside" estimates (p_1^* and p_2^*) are needed. The two-sample case is further complicated by the presence of two sample sizes rather than one. The appropriate substitution in the present problem yields

$$(2.44)^2 = \frac{p_1^* q_1^*}{n_1 - 1} + \frac{p_2^* q_2^*}{n_2 - 1}.$$

Using $p_1^* = p_2^* = 50$ and equal values of n_1 and n_2 permits the determination of n^* (the size of each sample).

$$(2.44)^2 = \frac{(2)(2,500)}{n^* - 1},$$

$$n^* = 841.$$

Each sample should be of size 841. The use of the 50 percent values provides, as it did for the one-sample case, a most conservative position. If the decision maker can provide "outside" limits for either p_1^* or p_2^* that will decrease the required sample size, those values should certainly be used. The advertiser who has past data showing recall rates with one of the programs (A) that vary within a range of 15 to 35 percent can use p^* of 35 percent for that program. If the advertiser has no idea of the value for the other program, p^* of 50 percent should be used. The calculated sample sizes would then be 803 for each program.[3]

The selection of samples of equal size from each group is the preferred approach unless the decision maker is confident that (1) the two $\bar{p}$ values differ appreciably and (2) the two $\bar{p}$ values can be estimated accurately. Assuming equal samples are to be selected, the required sample size for each is given by Eq. (9.7).[4]

$$n^* = \frac{z^2 (p_1^* q_1^* + p_2^* q_2^*)}{D^2}. \tag{9.7}$$

Equation (9.8) might be used if the decision maker is unable to make separate estimates of p^* for the two groups. However, the researcher must recognize that Eq. (9.8) may produce a larger interval than stipulated if there is a signifi-

---

[3]As we saw earlier, sample size with proportions is most sensitive to p^* when it is very large or very small. As long as its value is between 30 and 70, the resulting change in required sample size is slight.

[4]The calculated values of 841 and 803 for n^* are based on formulas using $n - 1$ while Eq. (9.7) is derived using n. The finite multiplier has been ignored in both approaches.

cant difference between the resulting $\bar{p}_1$ and $\bar{p}_2$.

$$n^* = \frac{2z^2p^*q^*}{D^2}.$$ (9.8)

The selection of two samples of 803 for the advertiser's problem will assure a 90 percent confidence interval that is no wider than 8 percentage points—but only if the use of a p^* value of 35 percent for Program A is correct. (Why doesn't the use of 50 percent for the other program introduce a similar risk?) If the samples reveal recall rates of 40 percent for Program A and 30 percent for Program B, the 90 percent confidence interval would be given by

$$(40 - 30) \pm 1.64 \left[\frac{40 \times 60}{802} + \frac{30 \times 70}{802} \right]^{1/2},$$

$$10 \pm 1.64(2.37),$$

$$10 \pm 3.89,$$

$$6.1 \text{ to } 13.9.$$

The advertiser can be 90 percent confident that the recall rate with Program A is superior to that with Program B by between 6.1 and 13.9 percentage points.

The advertiser's estimate that the recall rate with A would be no more than 35 percent was wrong, and this error could have led to lower reliability than was required. It did not lead to this result because the recall rate with B was considerably lower than the 50 percent that was allowed for in determining sample size. An initial attempt to take a smaller sample from A because p^* was only 35 percent and a larger sample from B where p^* was 50 percent would have worked in just the wrong direction. Selecting samples of equal size is the best procedure unless there is ample evidence for samples of unequal sizes.[5]

Means

The determination of sample size when estimating the difference between two universe means follows the same logic as that used when estimating the difference between two universe proportions. The only difference is that $\overset{*}{\sigma}_{\bar{x}_1 - \bar{x}_2}$ is involved instead of $\overset{*}{\sigma}_{\bar{p}_1 - \bar{p}_2}$. Once more it is best to select samples of the same size from each group unless the evidence is conclusive that one group is more variable than the other. Using this approach, the proper sample size to select from *each group* is given by Eq. (9.9).

$$n^* = \frac{z^2(s_1^2 + s_2^2)}{D^2}.$$ (9.9)

How large a sample should be selected if a manufacturer wishes to estimate the difference between shelf life using a new package and shelf life using

---

[5]This advice is somewhat similar to the recommendation to use proportional stratified sampling unless the evidence in favor of disproportional allocation is strong.

the present package? Once more the decision maker must stipulate requirements. Suppose the decision maker wishes to have 95 percent confidence and sets the maximum size of the interval at one week.

The manufacturer must also establish "outside" limits for the variance of each package (in shelf life of course). The manufacturer believes the variance will be greater for the present package but does not have sufficient confidence in that belief to depart from equal sample sizes. The "outside" limits on the two variances are 3 for the new package and 5 for the present one. Substituting in Eq. (9.9), a sample of size 492 should be selected for each package (setting one week equal to .25 month because the units for the two variances are months squared).[6] The calculations are

$$n^* = \frac{(1.96)^2(3 + 5)}{(.25)^2} = \frac{3.8416(8)}{.0625}$$

$$= 492.$$

Equations (9.7), (9.8), and (9.9) are technically correct only for infinite populations since they ignore the finite multiplier. For problems involving such things as package design and ad recall, a working assumption that the population is infinite is probably valid.[7] For other problems—such as customers of two small neighborhood stores or members of two professional associations—the population sizes may be small enough to have significant impact on the required sample sizes. Equations (9.10) and (9.11) present the appropriate formulas for determining sample sizes when the finite multiplier is included.[8]

$$n^* = \frac{Nz^2(p_1^* q_1^* + p_2^* q_2^*)}{ND^2 + z^2(p_1^* q_1^* + p_2^* q_2^*)}. \tag{9.10}$$

$$n^* = \frac{Nz^2(s_1^2 + s_2^2)}{ND^2 + z^2(s_1^2 + s_2^2)}. \tag{9.11}$$

Table 9.2 presents a general worksheet and guide for determining the required sample sizes when two sample results are to be compared. The general approach is analogous to that involved for a single sample and follows the format of the worksheet of Table 8.4. Additional care must be exercised in the two-sample case because two universes are involved as well as two samples.

---

[6]If one week is set equal to .233 (7 days divided by 30 days), the required sample is 566.

[7]The task of selecting simple random samples from infinite populations poses difficult problems. A list is obviously not available. If a finite research universe is substituted for the infinite problem universe, the researchers must decide whether they wish to claim their estimates apply to the research universe or to the problem universe. This decision determines whether the finite multiplier is appropriate. The issue of whether the samples are appropriate for the decision maker's problem is usually much more critical than whether the finite multiplier should be employed.

[8]Equations (9.10) and (9.11) assume both universes are of the same size. The formulas are more complicated when the universes differ in size, and the formulas lead to unequal sample sizes from the two universes.

Table 9.2
Worksheet for Determining Required Sample Sizes. Comparison of Two Samples

Information to be supplied by decision maker

1. How large a deviation between the result of the sample comparison and the true universe comparison is acceptable?

2. How much confidence is required?

3. What order of magnitude is expected for (1) the sample percentages or (2) the sample standard deviations?

4. How large is the universe?

How information from decision maker is used

1. Limit on deviation sets value for z times standard error.

2. Confidence required establishes z—based on normal curve.

3. Order of magnitude expected is substituted in the appropriate standard error formula.

4. Size of universe determines whether finite multiplier should be used in standard error formula.†

Example (using percentages)

1. Difference between samples must be within 4 percentage points of universe difference: $z\overset{*}{\sigma}_{\bar{p}_1 - \bar{p}_2} = 4$.

2. A 95.5% confidence is required: $2\overset{*}{\sigma}_{\bar{p}_1 - \bar{p}_2} = 4$; $\qquad \overset{*}{\sigma}_{\bar{p}_1 - \bar{p}_2} = 2$.

3. Expected sample percentages are between 60 and 90 percent for one sample and between 75 and 95 percent for the other:

$$\overset{*}{\sigma}^2_{\bar{p}_1 - \bar{p}_2} = \left[\frac{60 \times 40}{n^*} + \frac{75 \times 25}{n^*} \right] (1 - f).$$

4. Universes are 50,000 and 75,000: $\qquad$ ignore $(1 - f)$.

Solution: $\overset{*}{\sigma}^2_{\bar{p}_1 - \bar{p}_2} = (2)^2 = \dfrac{2400}{n^*} + \dfrac{1875}{n^*}$;

$\qquad n^*$ (size of each sample) $= 1069$.

Example (using means)

1. Difference between sample means must be within $25 of universe difference:

$$z\overset{*}{\sigma}_{\bar{x}_1 - \bar{x}_2} = 25.$$

2. A 95% confidence is required: $1.96\overset{*}{\sigma}_{\bar{x}_1 - \bar{x}_2} = 25$; $\qquad \overset{*}{\sigma}_{\bar{x}_1 - \bar{x}_2} = 12.76$.

3. Expected sample standard deviations are between $250 and $300:

$$\overset{*}{\sigma}^2_{\bar{x}_1 - \bar{x}_2} = \left[\frac{(300)^2}{n^*} + \frac{(300)^2}{n^*} \right] (1 - f).$$

4. Universes are both approximately 2000: $\qquad$ cannot ignore $(1 - f)$.

Solution: $\overset{*}{\sigma}^2_{\bar{x}_1 - \bar{x}_2} = (12.76)^2 = \dfrac{2(300)^2}{n^*} \left(1 - \dfrac{n^*}{2,000}\right)$; $\qquad n^* = 712$.

Direct solution from Eq. (9.11):

$$n^* = \frac{2,000(1.96)^2(300)^2(2)}{2,000(25)^2 + (1.96)^2(300)^2(2)} = 712.$$

---

†If the finite multiplier is ignored and should have been included, this will be apparent in the fact that the calculated sample size is more than 10 percent of the universe.

TWO SAMPLES: FROM ONE UNIVERSE OR TWO?

Comparisons between two sample results may involve two different universes or they may involve a single universe "treated" in two different ways. We have used both types of problems within this chapter. The Zenox and Malone comparison involved two universes, asking whether the parameters (means, in this case) were identical. The two direct mail campaigns were appraised within a single universe. The tire manufacturer wished the same type of analysis—the gasoline mileage each of two tires would yield if used by the same universe. The comparison of two TV programs as the vehicles for an advertiser's message and the comparison of two packages for shelf life are similar, a single universe but treated in two different ways.

Our present concern is whether these two types of problems require any differences in terms of sample design or analysis. The sample designs involved have been a pair of simple random samples, each drawn independently and each drawn from the universe that is relevant according to the problem definition. The analysis in each case has employed the standard error of a difference between two sample statistics, this standard error interpreted in a probability context according to the normal curve.

Whether one universe or two universes are appropriate depends on the problem definition. As long as simple random samples are selected from the correct universe(s), no complications arise.[9] A major practical difficulty is often encountered in the one-universe type of problem because the samples are not selected from the same universe. Package A is presented to one group, and package B is presented to a second group; or statistics for the new product are collected from one time period, and statistics for the old product are collected from a different time period. These are important practical questions, but the same care must be exercised in sampling from two universes. The general conclusion is that both the one-universe and the two-universe situations are approached in the same manner with respect to sample design. Each sample must be selected (1) from the appropriate universe, (2) according to a specific sampling method (simple random sampling in all of our illustrations), and (3) independent of the other sample.

Samples are not selected independently when the specific units to be included in one sample are determined by the specific units selected for the other sample. When this "dependence" exists, the total sample results are also dependent on each other and more complex formulas are needed for the standard errors. The specific form of $\overset{*}{\sigma}{}^2_{\bar{x}_1 - \bar{x}_2}$, for example, is approximately equal to Eq. (9.12), where ρ is the coefficient of correlation.[10]

---

[9] Other probability sample designs could also be employed without introducing complications. We restrict our discussion to simple random samples because the formulas used stem from simple random sampling.

[10] The precise meaning and measurement of ρ is developed in Part III, particularly in Chapter 12.

$$\overset{*}{\sigma}{}^2_{\bar{x}_1 - \bar{x}_2} = \frac{s^2_1}{n_1 - 1} + \frac{s^2_2}{n_2 - 1} - \frac{2\rho s_1 s_2}{(n_1 - 1)^{1/2}(n_2 - 1)^{1/2}} \,. \qquad (9.12)$$

If both samples are the same size, Eq. (9.12) reduces to Eq. (9.13).

$$\overset{*}{\sigma}{}^2_{\bar{x}_1 - \bar{x}_2} = \frac{s^2_1 + s^2_2 - 2\rho s_1 s_2}{n - 1} \,. \qquad (9.13)$$

The test of hypotheses concerning differences between universe parameters or the estimation of such differences rests on the standard errors involved and their correct probability interpretation. The appropriateness of the normal curve does not depend on whether one or two universes are employed but on the nature of the population distributions and the sampling distributions. These considerations are the same as they were in the one-sample case; no new issues are involved. But the appropriateness of the normal should always be evaluated; it should not be employed automatically. Once more the conclusion is that the procedure is precisely the same regardless of whether the two samples come from one universe or two universes. The only distinctions between the two types of problems occur in problem definition and details with respect to research design, data collection, and interpretation of results.

Both problems can best be viewed as comparisons of two-universe parameters that may refer to either two different universes or a single universe. The one-universe problem typically asks whether the parameter of that universe is (or will be) different, depending on which of two "treatments" is applied. The two-universe problem asks whether the parameters of the two universes, as defined and treated, are different.

THE 2 × 2 TABLE

Null hypotheses concerning the equality of two-universe proportions can be tested by use of the Chi Square (χ^2) statistic in a 2 × 2 table or by $(\bar{p}_1 - \bar{p}_2)/\overset{*}{\sigma}_{\bar{p}_1 - \bar{p}_2}$ as shown earlier in the chapter. The 2 × 2 table often gives the decision maker additional understanding and insight into the test process. Table 9.3 presents in a slightly recast form the data concerning ad message recall when presented with two different television programs.

The null hypothesis asserts that the two-universe proportions are equal. The data in Table 9.3 indicate an unbiased estimate of that proportion in the total column: 120/350 or 34.3 percent. Using Eq. (9.6), $\overset{*}{\sigma}_{\bar{p}_1 - \bar{p}_2}$ is equal to 5.14. The comparison $(\bar{p}_1 - \bar{p}_2)/\overset{*}{\sigma}_{\bar{p}_1 - \bar{p}_2} = 10/5.14$ reveals that the observed difference between the two-sample statistics is equal to 1.95 standard errors. (The null hypothesis would be accepted at $\alpha = .05$ but rejected at .06.)

Chi Square provides an alternative approach to the same problem. This approach compares the sample results of Table 9.3 with the results that would be expected if the null hypothesis is true. The greater the discrepancies, the

Table 9.3
Message Recall When Presented with Two Different Television Programs

| | Television program | | |
Result	A	B	Total
Message recalled	60	60	120
Message not recalled	90	140	230
Total	150	200	350

more doubt is cast on the null hypothesis; the smaller the discrepancies, the less doubt is cast on it.

If the null hypothesis is true, the "expected" results in Table 9.3 are that 34.3 percent of those viewing each program would recall the advertiser's message. Applying this percentage, the expected number to recall the message from the group viewing Program A would be 51.4 and the expected number recalling the message of those viewing Program B would be 68.6. Obviously the remaining number from each group would be in the category "message not recalled." The calculated Chi Square value depends on the discrepancies between these theoretical values and the values that were obtained in the experiment.

Chi Square for a contingency table such as Table 9.3 is calculated according to Eq. (9.14).[11]

$$\chi^2 = \sum \frac{(f_o - f_e)^2}{f_e},\tag{9.14}$$

where

$$f_o = \text{observed frequency},$$
$$f_e = \text{expected frequency}.$$

If every observed frequency coincided with the expected frequency, the calculated value for Chi Square would be 0. The larger the discrepancy, the larger the value of Chi Square. The calculated value for the data of Table 9.3 is

$$\chi^2 = \frac{(60 - 51.4)^2}{51.4} + \frac{(60 - 68.6)^2}{68.6} +$$

$$\frac{(90 - 98.6)^2}{98.6} + \frac{(140 - 131.4)^2}{131.4} = 3.83.$$

---

[11]The χ^2 distribution applies to many statistical problems; its application to a 2 × 2 table is merely one of many applications. We shall illustrate its use in other contingency tables and curve fitting problems, but it is even more general than those that we shall consider. The mathematics of χ^2 is beyond the scope of this text. The interested reader is referred to Marek Fisz, 1963, *Probability Theory and Mathematical Statistics* (New York: Wiley), pp. 339–343.

Chi Square, unlike the normal but like "t," is a family of distributions, the precise form depending on the number of degrees of freedom. (See Appendix Table A.4.) The significance of any particular numerical value of Chi Square depends on the number of degrees of freedom in the analysis. A 2 × 2 table has only one degree of freedom; therefore we are at present concerned only with the first row of Table A.4.[12] Referring to the table we see that the result of this analysis is consistent with the former approach. The critical level for Chi Square is 2.706 for α = .1 and 3.841 for α = .05. The calculated Chi Square value (3.83) is large enough to reject H_0 at the first level and not quite large enough to reject it at the 5 percent level.[13]

The consideration of two additional examples in Table 9.4 provides further insight into the use of Chi Square with the 2 × 2 table. First, consider the first example in which the observed values are all doubled; percentage distributions remain the same for the samples but the resulting Chi Square is 7.66,

Table 9.4
Effect of Sample Size Change on Chi Square.
Message Recall Data

Sample size doubled

| Result | Television program | | |
	A	B	Total
Message recalled	120	120	240
Message not recalled	180	280	460
Total	300	400	700

$$\chi^2 = 7.66; \quad P(\chi^2 > 7.66) < .01.$$

Sample size halved

| Result | Television program | | |
	A	B	Total
Message recalled	30	30	60
Message not recalled	45	70	115
Total	75	100	175

$$\chi^2 = 1.92; \quad P(\chi^2 > 1.92) < .20.$$

[12]We shall consider the determination of the number of degrees of freedom in Part III. Here we merely assert that there is one degree of freedom for a 2 × 2 table. Another unique property of Chi Square associated with a 2 × 2 table is that the numerical value of the numerator of each term is precisely the same: for our example this value is $(8.6)^2$ or 73.96.

[13]Appendix Table A.4 gives the probability that the calculated χ^2 value will reach the level stated within the table if the null hypothesis is true. For example, with six degrees of freedom the probability that the calculated χ^2 value will be 12.592 or more is equal to .05 and the probability that it will be equal to 15.033 or more is equal to .02. Large values of χ^2 cast doubt on the validity of the null hypothesis; small values of χ^2 fail to cast doubt on the validity of the null hypothesis.

larger than the critical value for an α of .01. Then, consider the second example in which the percentage results of the two samples are retained but the sample sizes are cut in half, the resulting Chi Square value is 1.92—significant at the .20 level but not at the .10 level.

The comparison of these three results with samples size 175, 350, and 700 indicates that sample size is of significance in a Chi Square test even though there is only one degree of freedom in each test. The change in Chi Square value occurs because the overall percentage distributions are applied to different absolute values. Small percentage discrepancies yield large absolute discrepancies when applied to large samples. Both the numerators and denominators of the individual terms are affected by the change in sample size, but the impact is greater in the numerator because of the squaring process. In the two examples in Table 9.4 it can be seen that the resulting χ^2 value is obtained by multiplying the χ^2 of Table 9.3 by the sample size relationship: $7.66 = 2(3.83)$ and $1.92 = .5(3.83)$. If sample size were increased by 50 percent, χ^2 would be 50 percent greater than 3.83—5.74 provided of course the percentage distributions remained constant.

USE OF CHI SQUARE IN A ONE-SAMPLE PROBLEM

Chi Square can also be used for testing a hypothesis with respect to a single universe proportion. A frequent problem in consumer marketing is the choice of the appropriate package design. With two potential package designs, the company can select a single sample and determine the percentage of respondents who prefer each package. If the two package designs are equally good, the expected result will be 50 percent selection of each package. Table 9.5 presents the results of such a test along with the expected values.

Tables similar to Table 9.5 are often referred to as one-way tables because a single characteristic is considered for a single universe. The resulting Chi Square for Table 9.5 is 4.51.

$$\chi^2 = \frac{(88 - 75)^2}{75} + \frac{(62 - 75)^2}{75} = 4.51.$$

For a one-way table, the number of degrees of freedom is equal to one less than the number of categories involved in the classification scheme; therefore

Table 9.5
Observed versus Expected Results of a Package Design
Preference Test. Two Packages

Package preferred	Sample results	Expected results
X	88	75
Y	62	75
	150	150

only one degree of freedom is present for testing the data of Table 9.5. If the null hypothesis of equality in preference is tested at a significance level of .05, the observed difference is greater than we are willing to attribute to chance. Therefore H_0 would be rejected and package X would be deemed preferable to package Y. Note that the resulting Chi Square value would be precisely the same if 88 preferred Y and 62 preferred X; again H_0 would be rejected but in this case package Y would be deemed preferable. The test is thus a two-tailed test, or more properly two one-tailed tests.

If the hypothesis under consideration is a single one-tailed test, the probabilities of Appendix Table A.4 must be cut in half in order to coincide with the stated probability for Type I errors. For example, suppose the null hypothesis tested with the data in Table 9.5 were $p_Y \geq p_X$ against $p_Y < p_X$. Chance would produce a Chi Square value of 1.642 or greater with X preferred over Y only 10 percent of the time. Thus the numerical value required to reject the null hypothesis is smaller in a one-tailed test than in a two-tailed test because the decision maker has specified in advance the direction in which the superiority must occur. That specified direction is responsible for only one-half of the large deviations that will result when equality exists in the universe. The superiority must of course occur in the direction specified in the alternative hypothesis in order to reject the null hypothesis.

The one-way table can be expanded to include several categories rather than just two. Assume that the manufacturer wished to compare five different package designs. If all five are equally acceptable, the expected result would be that 20 percent of the sample preferred each package design. Chi Square is then computed to determine whether the discrepancies from an equal division are large enough that we do not believe they were produced by chance forces. If we conclude that they were not produced by chance forces, we simultaneously conclude that they were produced because the packages differ in consumer preference.

Table 9.6 presents the results of such a package preference test using five different packages. Since we have five different categories, there are four

Table 9.6
Observed versus Expected Results of a Package Design
Preference Test. Five Packages

Package preferred	Sample results	Expected results
V	34	40
W	50	40
X	42	40
Y	33	40
Z	41	40
	200	200

degrees of freedom. The resulting Chi Square value is 4.75, not large enough to reject the null hypothesis that the five are equally preferred ($\alpha = .05$). The calculation is shown below.[14]

$$\chi^2 = \frac{(34 - 40)^2}{40} + \frac{(50 - 40)^2}{40} + \frac{(42 - 40)^2}{40} + \frac{(33 - 40)^2}{40}$$

$$+ \frac{(41 - 40)^2}{40} = \frac{36 + 100 + 4 + 49 + 1}{40} = \frac{190}{40} = 4.75$$

SUMMARY

Much of marketing research involves comparisons. These comparisons may take many different forms: one business entity versus another, the same organization at different points in time, results with one action versus results if alternative actions are taken, etc. In all of these situations, our hypotheses or our estimations refer not to a single parameter but to the comparison of two or more parameters. In this chapter, we restricted ourselves to a comparison of two parameters although we shall expand this to more than two in later chapters.

The typical null hypothesis for two parameters is that the universe means (or percentages) are equal, usually stated in the form that the difference between the two parameters is 0. The appropriate standard error used in testing this hypothesis is either $\sigma_{\bar{x}_1 - \bar{x}_2}$ or $\sigma_{\bar{p}_1 - \bar{p}_2}$, with the variance equal to the sum of the variances for the two independent sample statistics to be compared. As was the case in estimation and hypothesis testing for a single parameter, the relevant standard errors are usually estimated from sample evidence. In the case of testing the null hypothesis that universe proportions are equal, the standard error is best estimated by pooling the results of the two samples into a single estimate of the universe proportion.

Point estimation and interval estimation for the difference between universe parameters follows precisely the same procedure as that involved for a single characteristic. The estimates of differences between universe percentages are based on the fact that the difference between the relevant sample statistics is an unbiased estimate of the difference between the corresponding universe parameters. Since two samples are involved and since each has a standard error, the width of the resulting interval estimate is of necessity wider than that of an estimate for either parameter alone (assuming the same degree of confidence is desired). Only by recognizing this fact in the planning stage can unsatisfactorily wide intervals be avoided.

---

[14]Note that the calculated χ^2 for Table 9.6 is larger than the calculated χ^2 was for Table 9.5 (4.75 versus 4.51). The increase in number of degrees of freedom more than offsets the increase in χ^2 with the result that the null hypothesis is accepted in Table 9.6 whereas it was rejected in Table 9.5. Also note that the numerators for the various terms of χ^2 differ for the Table 9.6 calculation. This is the more general situation and will prevail in most of our later work.

The determination of the proper sample sizes for the two-sample case involves the same rationale as that for the one-sample case. The decision maker must specify the acceptable width of the confidence interval and the confidence level required. These two values plus estimates of the "outside" limits for the characteristics of interest permit the calculation of minimum required sample sizes.

The distinction between two samples from the same universe and two samples from different universes is extremely significant in the problem definition and research design stages. Once the relevant problem and design are determined, the sampling plan and analytic techniques are similar.

The null hypothesis of equality between universe proportions can also be tested through the 2 × 2 table, using the Chi Square distribution. This approach was introduced in the chapter and will be employed for more complicated comparisons in later chapters. The one-way table using Chi Square was also shown to be an alternative approach to testing hypotheses with respect to a single universe proportion. This was also expanded to include testing hypotheses for several classifications on a single characteristic.

EXERCISES AND PROBLEMS

1. Distinguish between the terms within each of the following pairs.

   a) Comparison between two sample results and comparison of a single sample against a known universe

   b) One-tailed and two-tailed tests—both with two samples

   c) 2 × 2 table and one-way table

   d) Level of significance and "shifty alpha"

   e) $\sigma_{\bar{x}_1 - \bar{x}_2}$ and $\sigma_{\bar{x}}$

2. Briefly explain the meaning and importance of each of the following in marketing research.

   a) Random sampling distribution of sample differences

   b) One-way table with more than two categories

   c) Pooled estimate—two samples

   d) Two-sample power curve

3. The Colonial Gift Shop attempts to monitor its traffic with respect to the proportion of patrons who are "just looking." The manager made a count of the number of persons who left the store without making a purchase during preselected time periods in both March and April. The results were 12 percent (total sample = 100) in March and 20 percent (total sample = 150) in April.

   a) Would you be willing to assume these figures correspond to
      i) "just looking"?
      ii) simple random samples?

b) Would you be willing to conclude that the proportion of patrons who are "just looking" was higher in April than in March? (Assume the data are appropriate for the question posed.)

c) Would equal size samples from the two months have provided a better research design? Why?

d) What would be the minimum sample size (assuming each sample is the same size) necessary in order for you to classify the observed difference—12 versus 20 percent—as "statistically significant"?

4. The J&K Co. uses its own salespeople in some areas and manufacturers' agents in others. Table E9.4 shows the number of calls made by each group in a test period and the number of calls that resulted in the placement of an order.

Table E9.4

	Order placed	No order placed	Total calls
Manufacturers' agents	50	250	300
Company salespeople	50	150	200
	100	400	500

a) Based on the evidence above (assuming each group called on prospects with equal potential) do you think the company salespeople are more effective? Test a hypothesis and state your conclusion specifically.

b) Assuming company salespeople are more effective, establish a 95 percent confidence interval for their superiority. (Disregard your answer to part (a) if necessary.)

5. A quasi-laboratory experiment was employed to test a geometric pattern package against a floral package for a particular product. Two matched groups were selected. Within each group, six premiums were offered. Five premiums were identical while the sixth was the test package, the geometric design for group A, and the floral design for group B. Group A was size 200, and group B was size 300. Eighty from A chose the geometric pattern, and 90 from B chose the floral pattern.

a) Would you be willing to conclude that the two designs generated different preference rates?

b) What is your best estimate of the "power" of this experiment in discerning a difference of 15 percentage points? Are there any complications or assumptions in calculating this figure? Explain.

6. A nonprofit organization received completed questionnaires from 500 subscribers to its monthly magazine. One hundred had made contributions to the organization within the most recent 12 months and 400 had not. The questionnaire covered expenditure data by product category and various items on mass communication. Data on purchases of small appliances was of particular interest to the organiza-

tion since it had done extensive research on safety, warranties, and "values" for such items. The means and standard deviations for expenditures on small appliances were: contributors—mean = $86.50, standard deviation = $21.04; noncontributors—mean = $79.12, standard deviation = $29.72.

a) Assuming the two samples can be treated as simple random samples, draw a graph of the power curve associated with the null hypothesis ($\alpha = .05$).

b) Would you be willing to conclude that contributors spent more for small appliances than noncontributors—on the average?

7. A survey of coffee-drinking habits was conducted in various sections of the country, with simple random samples of size 200 from each section. The marketing manager of a large coffee company is particularly concerned about the company's sales in the southeast and wants to ascertain whether its poor performance is unique to the company or whether low sales are common to the industry. The manager asks the research director for an estimate of the difference between per capita consumption in the southeast and per capita consumption for the rest of the country which consists of four of the five sections in the survey. The following figures were obtained:

Southeast: 19.8 pounds per adult per annum with a standard deviation of 9.3.

Remainder of the United States: 24.2 pounds per adult per annum with a standard deviation of 10.8.

a) Do you think the per adult figures are preferable to per capita figures? Why?

b) Estimate the difference between southeast mean annual consumption and the corresponding figure for the remainder of the United States. Use a 98 percent confidence interval. (Disregard your answer to (a) if necessary.)

8. A blind taste preference test between two leading cola drinks showed that 58 out of 100 chose brand C over brand P.

a) Based on this evidence would you be willing to conclude that brand C was preferred by a majority in the total population from which this sample was drawn? Use a one-way table with a Chi Square statistic.

b) Analyze the same data, using the standard error of the sample proportion. Compare your answers.

9. A simple random sample of 500 housewives was asked to rate four different laundry detergents in "cleaning power." The test was a blind test. Part of the test asked respondents to identify their top preference among the four. The results indicated that 136 preferred J, 118 preferred K, 124 preferred R, and 122 preferred T.

a) Would you accept the null hypothesis that J, K, R, and T are rated as the "top preference" with the same frequency?

b) Is the hypothesis tested in (a) the same as the hypothesis that 25 percent prefer J? Why or why not?

c) Would it be possible to accept the hypothesis in (a) but reject the one in (b)? Why?

10. Analyze, criticize, and explain:

   a) The expected value of the difference between two sample means is equal to zero regardless of the form of the parent populations, provided the samples are sufficiently large.

   b) The standard error of the difference between two proportions will be different, depending on whether a null hypothesis of no difference is tested or a confidence interval for the difference between proportions is estimated. This is true even if the same original data are employed.

   c) If two sample statistics are to be compared, the analysis will be more powerful if both samples are equal in size.

   d) The mathematical calculations involved in testing the difference between two sample statistics are the same regardless of whether the samples come from the same universe or from different universes.

RELATIONSHIPS AND ASSOCIATIONS

Highly refined data collection techniques, complex experimental designs, sophisticated sampling plans, and large samples are employed so that marketing managers can base their decisions on accurate and reliable estimates. These approaches have been discussed in Parts I and II. We now consider an alternative approach to obtaining greater accuracy and reliability: the basing of estimates on information about related variables. If variables are associated with each other, knowledge of one is helpful in estimating the other. Part III addresses the general problem of determining relationships among two or more variables and the measurement of those relationships.

Chapter 10 provides an introduction and overview of the issues involved, laying the framework within which the various techniques may be examined. Chapters 11 and 12 develop four basic techniques of analysis for bivariate problems, covering contingency tables and analysis of variance in Chapter 11 and regression and discriminant analysis in Chapter 12. All four techniques are extended to multivariate problems in Chapter 13, and modifications of the basic techniques are discussed in Chapter 14.

Chapters 15 and 16 extend the discussion of association to two special issues. Chapter 15 considers search techniques in contrast to hypothesis testing. These techniques involve semistructured exploratory research. They use trial and error, "searching" for hypotheses rather than formally testing them. Chapter 16 addresses the particular problems encountered with time-series data, both for a single series and for relationships among several series.

CHAPTER 10

ASSOCIATION–
THE GENERAL PROBLEM
HOW TO MAKE BETTER ESTIMATES

What characteristics differentiate between Plymouth and Chrysler buyers? How many cartons should we have on hand for a special on Ideal frozen peas at three for a dollar? Does a sales person's performance depend on the amount of his or her formal education? Is the answer different, depending on the product or customer involved? How, if at all, is our market share related to our price relative to competitors' prices? Is the relationship between per capita income and demand deposits constant among our branch banks? What variables explain the differences? All of these questions call for the introduction of additional variables as potential aids in estimating a characteristic of concern to management. The gain from introducing other variables depends on how close the relationship is—close relationship = big gain; no relationship = no gain.

The study of association may be motivated by any of three different reasons. The first and most obvious is the estimation of a particular variable of interest to management. The second and third relate to the identification of common patterns, either among the *variables* studied or among the *units* studied. The first approach partitions the variables into two sets: one to be predicted and the other the basis for the prediction. This is our principal concern in Part III. The second and third approaches involve nonpartitioned data, focusing either on an analysis of relationships among variables or among units. These topics will be considered in Part IV.

Techniques used for the prediction problem are the structured equivalents of detective novels or parlor games such as "Twenty Questions." Clues or additional information is utilized in order to make a better estimate. The objective of association studies is a model that is useful for generating many estimates. The particular numerical estimate or estimates are then appropriate input to managerial decision.

Three related but distinct objectives exist in attempting to improve prediction through the study of associations. These three objectives are: (1) an estimate for a particular variable of interest, e.g., sales are estimated at $131,000, (2) an estimate of how the variables are related, e.g., sales are expected to increase by $3,000 per week for every additional hour the store is open, and (3) an estimate of the degree of association on a percentage scale, e.g., sales and number of hours open show a 45 percent association. Related objectives are concerned with interval estimates or hypothesis tests that parallel these three point estimates.

The study of associations may lead to better estimates by incorporating the fact that low values of one variable tend to occur with low values of a second variable while high values of the two variables also tend to occur together. Alternatively, low values of one may occur with high values of the other. In either case, a known value of one variable enables us to make better estimates of the second variable. If we can quantify the nature of the relationship, we can quantify our point estimates and also establish a confidence interval.

The current chapter provides an overview of the general nature of association, establishing the framework for the study of the individual techniques. The chapter also identifies the most widely used techniques and the type of data required by each. It should be recognized at the outset that the four principal techniques considered all address the three objectives enumerated above. From this perspective, different techniques exist because the input data are measured on different scales—the same objectives are realized with all four techniques.

Our progress from a hypothesis concerning a single variable to the comparison of two groups to the general association problem can be summarized in three steps. We started by asking whether the characteristic of interest was a specific value. (Is brand awareness for our product equal to 60 percent?) In the last chapter we asked whether the value of a particular variable was the same in each of two groups. (Is brand awareness for our product the same among suburban households as among urban households?) Finally, in the study of association, we ask the general question of whether the value of a particular variable is the same for several different groups. (Is brand awareness the same, regardless of age?) Symbolically, the three questions are

(1) $E(x) \stackrel{?}{=} K,$

(2) $E(x|A) \stackrel{?}{=} E(x|B),$

(3) $E(x|A) \stackrel{?}{=} E(x|B) \stackrel{?}{=} \cdots \stackrel{?}{=} E(x|N).$

The symbol $E(x)$ has already been encountered and means "the expected value of x." It is simply the arithmetic mean of the population under study. The symbol $E(x|A)$ is also an expected value, but it refers to a particular subgroup—the subgroup being designated by "A." This mean (or expected value) is called a *conditional mean* because it refers to only a specific portion of the population. Its numerical value is "conditional" on membership in the specific group.

Step (3) extends the comparison to more than two groups, but again asks whether the groups differ with respect to the variable under study. Groups can be formed in any way the decision maker and researcher wish; for example, people exposed to different magazines, those offered a particular product at different prices, individuals who have purchased from various competitors, etc. There is no limit to the possibilities. We are interested in determining whether the characteristic of interest (for example, brand awareness) varies among subgroups or treatments. If differences exist, we are then interested in describing the nature of those differences. The conditional distribution is the focus of both inquiries: (1) Are they the same? (2) How can they be described?

CONDITIONAL DISTRIBUTIONS

The first two objectives in studies of association are realized in the conditional distribution. (1) Estimates of the characteristic of interest come directly from use of the conditional distribution. (2) The conditional distribution summarizes the relationship between the variables.

Consider a person currently standing at a designated spot on the corner of 42nd and Broadway. How much do you believe that person weighs? Most people are hesitant about making such an estimate, stating that the answer depends on many additional characteristics. Sex, height, and age are the variables mentioned most often as relevant. This perspective uses the existence of associations and conditional distributions as a basis for making different estimates depending on the precise values for sex, height, and age. A simple approach is to use only one of those variables as the basis for the estimate. A more refined and complicated approach is to use all three and perhaps a few more.

An estimate of the person's weight as 145 pounds because that is the mean of the population is based on an *unconditional* distribution—the estimate is not "conditioned" or dependent on the value of any other variable. An estimate of 128 pounds, given the person is female, uses a conditional distribution, namely, the mean of the distribution of weights of females.

If we are also told that she is 5′10″, we revise our estimate upward. If her height is 5′1″, we revise our estimate downward. But in each instance, the estimate is lower than it would be for a male of the same height. Knowledge of age would permit further refinement of our estimate.

Not only are our estimates conditional on knowledge of other variables but our confidence is also conditional on that knowledge. We believe the dispersion in weight for individuals of the same height and sex is less than the dispersion for all individuals regardless of height and sex.

Both accuracy and reliability have entered our discussion. An estimate of 128 pounds for a 5′10″ female would be an inaccurate estimate, much too low on the average. A more accurate estimate (149 pounds) is possible by using knowledge of height because height is *associated with* weight. Reliability is improved in the estimate because a confidence interval estimate around 149 pounds would be more narrow than a confidence interval around the mean of 128 pounds that is calculated without regard to height (assuming the same confidence level).

Suppose the questioner supplies the person's last name instead of information with respect to sex. Most people view the person's last name as irrelevant. A person's weight and last name are not thought of as being associated with each other. Different estimates of weight are not made for the names of Akers, Collins, and Walker. The expected value is the same regardless of last name. The conditional distribution is invariant in the estimate supplied because the two variables are not associated with each other.

A Marketing Conditional Distribution

The rationale and use of conditional distributions is precisely the same when marketing variables are involved. Advertising, awareness, product sales, and profit per unit are some of the marketing variables an executive may wish to predict—variables that are either intermediary or ultimate goals of the company. The executive may pose a series of other variables that are to be tested for their degree of association with these "goal" variables. The task is to determine which, if any, of the variables suggested by the executive yield accurate and reliable estimates of a particular "goal" variable.

The variables to be tested for their predictive efficiency usually fall into three categories: consumer characteristics, external environmental conditions, and a firm's discretionary actions. Consumer characteristics may be used to determine whether there are market segments that differ significantly in product purchases (the other side of sales). Such characteristics as life-style, income, and family composition are examples.[1] External environmental conditions may be used to investigate the impact of a competitor's marketing mix activities as well as more general political or social developments. The firm's own discretionary acts are of prime concern because they represent variables within its control (endogenous as opposed to exogenous); knowledge of their impact on product sales can guide in the proper selection of the marketing mix. A particular research endeavor may be limited to variables of one type, or it may contain a mixture.

A conditional distribution relating product sales to advertising expenditures and price per unit could be used by an executive in either of two ways, provided of course an association was demonstrated. First, it could be used as a basis of estimating sales, given advertising expenditures and price per unit. Second, it could be used to select appropriate advertising expenditures and price in order to realize a particular sales target.

Consider the case of Eternal Youth Beauty Cream as shown in Table 10.1. The characteristic of interest is unit sales, and the unit of analysis is the

---

[1] See Table 2.1 for a classification scheme of consumer characteristics used by Frank, Massy, and Wind.

Table 10.1
Unit Sales, Advertising Expenditures, and Unit Prices. Eternal Youth Beauty Cream

| Unit price | Advertising expenditures | | | |
	$ 50	$100	$200	*Average*
$1.98	615	726	843	728.0
2.19	552	659	780	663.7
2.29	533	626	751	636.7
Average	566.7	670.3	791.3	676.1

individual drug store. How might this information be useful for estimates or decisions? The unconditional mean is 676.1 units. This is the overall average, computed without regard to either price or advertising expenditures. Three different conditional distributions are available: one based on price, one based on advertising expenditures, and a third based on both price and advertising expenditures.

The column to the far right shows the conditional distribution of unit sales given price: average unit sales of 728.0, 663.7, and 636.7 for the three prices of $1.98, $2.19, and $2.29, respectively. The bottom row shows the conditional distribution for the three different levels of advertising expenditures: 566.7 units with expenditures of $50, 670.3 units with expenditures of $100, and 791.3 units with expenditures of $200. The nine cell values within the body of the table show the conditional distribution when both price and advertising expenditures are given. For example, expected unit sales with a $2.19 price and $100 advertising expenditure are 659. These various conditional distributions serve the basis for estimating sales, given knowledge of either price, advertising expenditures, or both.

The conditional distributions could also be used by the marketing manager of Eternal Youth in selecting a particular price level and advertising budget. If the objective is the maximization of unit sales, a price of $1.98 and advertising expenditures of $200 would be indicated. If a more defensible objective such as profitability is adopted, unit sales figures must be translated into dollar sales and then adjusted for costs before the appropriate action can be identified.

A conditional distribution relating product purchases to family composition and life-style would have the same two potential uses. First, sales levels by particular market segments could be predicted. Second, market segments could be identified for different market actions. The executive could take steps designed to strengthen weak segments, or could direct efforts to improving still further those segments in which the company is already strong.

The conditional distribution is the basis for prediction or action in each case. Known or assumed values for one set of variables are "plugged into" a conditional distribution in order to estimate the "goal" variable. The executive in each case wants an estimate that is as reliable and accurate as possible—thus increasing the executive's confidence in its use for decision making. The conditional distribution may be similar in form to that of Table 10.1 where the appropriate expected values must be located within the table or the distribution may be summarized as a mathematical equation.

Summarizing the Conditional Distribution

The conditional distribution is designed to answer a particular type of question: "Given knowledge of variables $x_1, x_2, \ldots, x_n$, what is the best estimate of variable y?" We are attempting to find a convenient way of summarizing the overall relationship between the variable the marketing manager wishes to predict or influence and one or more other variables.

The variable to be estimated is called the *dependent* variable, deriving its name from the fact that it is hypothesized as dependent on the other variable or variables. The candidate variables to be tested as predictors of the dependent variable are called the *independent* variables.[2]

A mathematical equation is a compact way of presenting this summary and is a useful aid in calculating expected results. The relationship between unit sales and price for Eternal Youth Beauty Cream might be expressed by an equation such as

$$(y|x) = 1348 - 3.12x$$

where

$$x = \text{price in cents,}$$
$$y = \text{unit sales.}$$

This equation yields an estimate for unit sales (y), given price expressed in cents (x). The equation will not yield precisely the same results as Table 10.1, but it represents an attempt to summarize the relationship. If the summary is valid, it also permits estimates of sales, given prices that are not included in the original data. The equation format of course can also be employed for conditional distributions involving several independent variables.[3]

The conditional distribution replaces a single-point estimate by a series of point estimates that vary according to the value(s) of the independent variable(s). In the illustration above, the overall mean of 676.1 unit sales that would serve as the single-point estimate is replaced by a series of calculated values for various prices.

---

[2]Another frequently used terminology is *criterion* (dependent) and *predictor* (independent) variables. The criterion variable is the measure or criterion for judging the utility of the independent (predictor) variables. The predictor variables are the ones to be employed in predicting the value of the dependent (criterion) variable.

[3]The method for determining the form of the equation, the numerical values, and their interpretation will be discussed later in this chapter and in the subsequent chapters of Part III.

Another equation, summarizing the relationship between the number of calls made by the salespeople of Young Foil Company and the number of orders received, is given by

$$E(y|x) = 5 + 3x$$

where

$$x = \text{number of calls,}$$
$$y = \text{number of orders.}$$

This relationship is presented as a graph in Fig. 10.1. The choice among the various methods of presentation (table, equation, or graph) depends on what the researcher believes will be most readily understood by his or her audience, the complexity of the distribution, and the use to be made by the audience.

A store manager who wishes to estimate total dollar sales for specific days illustrates another type of conditional distribution. The overall mean per day is $75,000. The manager believes that store volume may vary with day of week. A little research reveals this belief to be correct. The results are shown in Table 10.2. The data within the table describe a conditional distribution. Additional variables might improve the predictions, but a gain in accuracy can be realized by using these figures in place of a constant $75,000. Any attempt to place the data of Table 10.2 into a mathematical equation would probably obscure the results more than it would help.[4]

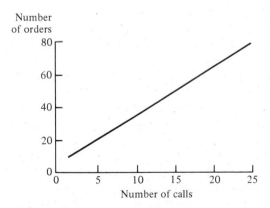

Fig. 10.1
Number of calls and number of orders received
by Young Foil Company salespeople.

---

[4]For example, an equation of $E(y|x) = 45,000 + 5,000x$; $x = 0$ (Tuesday), 1 (Monday), 3 (Thursday), 8 (Wednesday), 11 (Saturday), 13 (Friday) gives precisely that same information but would hardly be an improvement.

Table 10.2
Mean Store Volume
by Day of Week

Day	Mean
Monday	$ 50,000
Tuesday	45,000
Wednesday	85,000
Thursday	60,000
Friday	110,000
Saturday	100,000

A mathematical form might be superior as a summary description of the store's sales when related to other independent variables. Suppose the manager decides to investigate the relationship between sales and advertising expenditures. The manager might find that higher values of the two variables seem to coincide in timing as do lower values. This relationship—with both sales and advertising expenditures in dollars—might be summarized by

$$E(y|x) = 20,000 + 30x.$$

This equation allows the manager to predict sales for any level of advertising. If advertising expenditures are $2,500, predicted sales are $95,000. A slightly more complex mathematical form would be

$$E(y|x) = 25,000 + 50x - .007x^2.$$

The estimate of sales using this equation would be $106, 250 for an advertising espenditure of $2,500. The distinction between the two equations is shown in Fig. 10.2. Both are conditional distributions, but one assumes constant returns to advertising (using a straight line) while the other assumes decreasing returns (using a curved line).

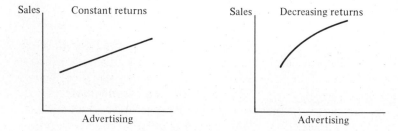

Fig. 10.2
Two alternative equations showing the relationship between sales and advertising.

Our purpose at this point is not to defend any particular form or equation, or even to interpret its various parts. The purpose is to consider various ways in which a conditional distribution can be presented. The store manager might think weather is another determinant of sales. Figure 10.3 shows the mean sales for rainy days against clear days. In this situation the independent variable is nominally scaled and the dependent variable is intervally scaled. This is in contrast to the graphs of Fig. 10.2 in which both variables were intervally scaled.

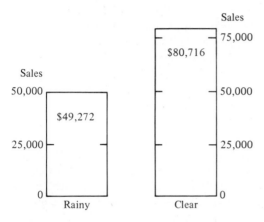

Fig. 10.3
Mean store volume on rainy days versus mean store volume on clear days.

SELECTION OF THE FUNCTIONAL RELATIONSHIP

A relationship between two variables can take many different forms. The final presentation of a conditional distribution with its mathematical precision has a tendency to obscure the decisions that precede that result. Most of these are highly subjective and may be arbitrary. Often the decisions are incorporated in computer routines with the result that other options are never consciously evaluated.

Four critical decisions are involved in any conditional distribution: (1) the scaling of the variables—nominal, ordinal, interval, or ratio; (2) the extent to which the mathematical nature of the relationship is specified beforehand—linear, linear transformation, nonlinear, or even nonmonotonic; (3) the allowance or nonallowance for interactions among the independent variables; and (4) the criterion for selecting among the many possible equations that incorporate the responses to the first three decisions. All of these issues are loaded with technical-sounding jargon. The immediate inclination is often to ignore these issues in one of three ways: (1) study one variable at a time—thus forget about the study of association, (2) use the simplest technique—or the one for which a canned program is available, or (3) leave these matters to someone else. The first approach robs the research of many powerful and useful techniques. The second stumbles through the analysis with no assurance that it is appropriate for the question at hand. The third is somewhat similar to the second but differs because the "expert" may have faulty or incomplete understanding of the substantive nature of the inquiry. All three reactions are unfortunate because the issues are not that difficult.

The first issue, the kinds of scales used for measuring the variables, was discussed and illustrated in Chapter 2. We shall not repeat that discussion, but the researcher must be satisfied that the scale stipulated is appropriate for each variable in the analysis. The other three issues will be discussed in greater detail as we consider specific techniques and the options available, but examples are appropriate as a part of the overview at this point.

Prior Specification of Functional Form

What restrictions, if any, should be placed upon the functional form of the conditional distribution? A linear form, perhaps the most common restriction, asserts that the change in the dependent variable should be constant for equal changes in the independent variable. A "finding" of constant returns is no finding at all if a linear function is specified in advance; it was a predetermined result.

What less stringent restrictions are possible? Should the relationship be nonreversible (monotonic)? If reversals are possible, should there be a limit on the number of reversals? The researcher and the decision maker must specify the general form of the functional relationships; the data then determine the precise numerical values within the general form.

A linear restriction states that the conditional distribution will be of the form

$$E(y|x) = a + bx.$$

A parabola of the form

$$E(y|x) = a + bx + cx^2$$

cannot result. Figure 10.2 illustrates the distinction between the two equations. The parabola may reveal either decreasing returns or increasing returns. The data determine which result occurs. The parabola also permits one reversal; either a maximum or a minimum may be established but not both.

Any mathematical form for the conditional distribution can be specified. Some of course are more tractable than others. But the important fact is that many of the mathematical properties are *imposed on* the data rather than *determined by* the data.

Does each exposure to an ad have the same incremental effect on product awareness? Or do the first few exposures yield increasing returns with decreasing returns setting in after four to six exposures? Neither a linear form nor a parabola can yield such a result. If either a linear or a parabolic function is used, the results will not justify rejection of the "increasing followed by decreasing returns" model. Only a more complex equation would permit such a finding, and that equation might force the hypothesized result rather than test for it.[5]

What is the best way to examine the relationship between housing starts and sales of a plumbing supply company? Should it be in terms of percentages or absolute amounts? Or should one variable be in terms of percentage differences and the other in terms of absolute amounts? Four different functional forms are available (when the analysis is restricted to linear relationships). Use of one of the four will not establish that the particular view is the "best"; its use imposes that view.[6]

Some techniques do not specify any particular mathematical function for the conditional distribution. These techniques let the data determine whether reversals and different response rates exist. The principal difficulties with these techniques is the absence of compact summaries for the conditional distributions and the accompanying lack of a general conceptual model.

Allowance for Interactions

Most techniques permit the inclusion of interactions in their functional form, but that possibility is often deleted in the most common applications. An interaction results if two or more variables have a synergistic or detrimental effect when combined. Their combined effect is thus more or less than the sum of their separate contributions. If the functional form specified is

$$E(y|x_1, x_2) = a + bx_1 + cx_2,$$

the research results cannot identify an interaction effect.

Most marketing executives believe the separate elements of a marketing mix should be integrated together so as to produce a consistent mix. They believe the various elements do interact, positively if chosen well and negatively if chosen poorly. Conditional distributions must test for interactions if they are to be identified; interaction terms must appear in the possible model. Exclusion of interaction terms from the tentative model eliminates the possibility of "finding" them in the research.

---

[5]The logistic curve which is a modified exponential equation increases by larger absolute amounts up to a point and then increases by smaller absolute amounts. See Frederick E. Croxton and Dudley J. Cowden, 1960, *Practical Business Statistics* (Englewood Cliffs, N.J.: Prentice-Hall), pp. 595–596.

[6]Focus and analysis in terms of percentage differences may be accomplished by using logarithms instead of the original data.

Interaction terms may be imposed upon the relationship in specific mathematical form or the type of interaction may be unspecified. An example of the former is

$$E(y|x_1, x_2) = a + bx_1 + cx_2 + d(x_1x_2)^{1/2}.$$

The interaction term is specified as a third independent variable—in this case the geometric mean of the two original independent variables. Alternatively, the interaction might be specified as their arithmetic mean or their product. Whenever the precise form is stipulated, the researcher must recognize that the form is not a "finding" of the research.

Other techniques test for interaction without specifying its form. In this case the interaction terms of the conditional distribution are determined by the data. This is the typical case when the independent variables are nominally scaled. Succinct summaries of the interactions are usually difficult to obtain in this situation; they are usually determined by detailed examination of the relevant tables.

Criterion for Selection of "Best" Equation

The criterion for selecting the equation that "best" describes the data usually involves a "minimization of discrepancies" between the sample values of the dependent variable and predictions of the dependent variable according to the conditional distribution. But the definition of "minimizing discrepancies" is not always the same. The most common definition when dealing with an intervally scaled dependent variable is a minimization of squared discrepancies. A minimization of differences—as opposed to squared differences—would yield a different "best" equation. A different definition of "discrepancies" is usually employed when the dependent variable is nominally scaled. In this case, a discrepancy is defined as a failure to predict the proper nominal category.[7]

The "sum of squared differences" was encountered earlier in our use of variance as a measure of dispersion for a single characteristic. The minimization of squared differences as a criterion in establishing the conditional distribution of "best" fit also leads to the use of squared differences in measuring how good the fit is. Thus the measure of dispersion in the conditional distribution is analogous to the measure of dispersion in the unconditional distribution, and the two measures can be compared.

The criterion of minimizing the sum of the squared differences can be applied at two different stages. First, it can be applied to select the numerical values to use for any particular functional form. For example, the numbers "5" and "3" might be inserted into the general equation $E(y/x) = a + bx$ because the sum of the squared differences is less with those two numbers than with any other pair of numbers. Second, the criterion can be applied in selecting which functional form gives the best fit to the data.

---

[7] With this approach, the conditional distribution must provide a rule for predicting a particular category. This idea is developed in Chapter 12 in conjunction with discriminant analysis.

DEGREE OF ASSOCIATION

The first two objectives in studies of association—prediction and a summary of relationships—are realized directly from the conditional distribution. The third objective—a measure of the degree of association—uses the concept of "improvement" or "reduction in uncertainty." The measure employed asks how much improvement the conditional distribution yields in contrast to the unconditional distribution.

The conditional distribution, if it is an improvement over the unconditional distribution, yields more reliable estimates. This increase in reliability is shown by the decrease in dispersion around the conditional distribution in contrast to the dispersion around the unconditional distribution. The comparison can be readily made by comparing the variances around the two distributions. If the two measures are identical, the variables are not associated. If there is no dispersion around the conditional distribution, the association is complete.

The coefficient of determination (r^2) is based on the preceding argument. It shows the percentage reduction in variance when dispersion is measured around the conditional distribution instead of around the unconditional distribution. It has a lower limit of 0 (no association) and an upper limit of 1 (perfect association). If $r^2 = .75$ (75 percent), the conditional variance is 75 percent less than the unconditional variance. Not all measures of association are derived from variance measures, nor do all of them have upper and lower limits of 1 and 0, respectively. Particular care must be employed in the interpretation of these measures lest misleading impressions be conveyed. We shall use percentage reduction in variance as our principal measure of association, comparing other association measures to this basic concept when they stem from other concepts.

A word of caution is in order concerning measures of association. They indicate whether the variables tend to vary together, not whether they tend to move in the same direction. If the number of units sold varies with price changes but in the opposite direction, the two variables are still associated with each other. A perfect inverse relationship is a perfect predictor and much more valuable than a weak direct relationship.[8]

CONFIDENCE INTERVALS

The conditional distribution provides the basis for point estimates of the dependent variable. But as was true with unconditional point estimates, no indication of reliability is contained in these estimates. A measure of dispersion is needed, and that measure can be used in generating confidence intervals. The standard error—determined from the sample standard deviation, the sample size, and the sampling fraction—provided the necessary measure of dispersion when dealing with the unconditional distribution. Analogous inputs

---

[8]Consider the man who is always *wrong*. Knowledge of his views would be extremely helpful. The position directly opposite to his would always be right.

are required for constructing a confidence interval for a conditional mean. But we may encounter a type of problem in association that was not discussed in the univariate situation—constructing a confidence interval for the value of a single unit as well as constructing an interval for the mean value.

A marketing manager choosing a specific marketing mix wishes an estimate of its unique result. The manager is not interested in a statement about the average result with repeated applications. Rather the manager wants to establish a confidence interval for this particular situation. We have not considered this type of problem in conjunction with unconditional distributions, primarily because we did not know the form of the population distribution. With conditional distributions, confidence intervals for single units are usually possible. The second type of estimate, for the mean result, is completely analogous in concept to the unconditional estimate although the appropriate variances to use are different.

The following problems, from a nonmarketing setting, illustrate the distinction between the two types of questions. (1) What is the best estimate of the weight of a male who is 5'10"? (2) What is the best estimate of the mean weight of 25 males who are 5'10"? The 95 percent confidence interval for the second question will be much smaller than for the first. It is important that the researcher and decision maker recognize the distinction between the two questions. Only then will they (1) ask the proper question and (2) use the proper standard deviations and standard errors.

A study of the relationship between sales performance and age encounters the same pair of questions. At the first stage, there is the desire to estimate performance by a particular sales person of age 34. At the second stage, there is the desire to estimate mean performance for a group of salespeople, age 34. Different reliability measures apply to each question.

Several other confidence intervals are often desired in association problems. They must not be confused with the two already discussed. The summary measure of association presented with most research results is a point estimate; confidence intervals can also be established for this measure. When a conditional distribution is expressed as an equation, there are often several different numbers. Each is a point estimate describing some part of the relationship. Confidence intervals can also be established for these estimates.

The study of the relationship between sales performance and age can illustrate these confidence intervals. How close is the association? The answer for a particular company might show a confidence interval of 12 percent to 19 percent (for a particular level of confidence). The conditional distribution would contain a number that summarized the expected change in performance with increasing age. This number might indicate that expected performance increased by .15 unit for every five years of age. The 95 percent confidence interval might be .08 to .22.

In summary, there are many different point estimates involved in the study of associations. The reliability of each can be indicated and quantified through the construction of appropriate confidence intervals. The researcher should at least weigh the possibility of investigating their inclusion in the analysis.

FOUR TECHNIQUES FOR TWO-VARIABLE ASSOCIATIONS

The most widely used techniques for examining associations employ either nominal or interval scales both for the dependent and the independent variables. With two types of scales and two variables, four different situations emerge. A different technique is appropriate for each situation and is designated in Table 10.3.[9]

It is convenient to limit our initial discussion to just two variables,[10] one dependent and one independent. In this way we avoid the mixed situations in which there are several independent (or dependent) variables, some measured nominally and some intervally. The two techniques in which the independent variable is nominally scaled are the contingency table and the analysis of variance. The techniques dealing with intervally scaled independent variables are discriminant analysis and regression/correlation.

We began our discussion of contingency tables in Chapter 9 with the 2×2 table. This is a highly restrictive case in which each variable has only two categories. The expansion to any number of categories follows the same rationale, recognizing that categories are not assumed to be in logical sequence nor are they assumed to have any numerical equivalents on an interval scale.

The contingency table would be used in a problem comparing a person's favorite magazine with furniture style preference. The number of categories on either variable is limited only by the interest of the decision maker. The categories are nominal in scale, assuming that the decision maker has not established a basis for placing them in a prespecified rank order. The analysis asks whether the percentage distribution of furniture style preference differs according to favorite magazine.

Table 10.3
Techniques for Analyzing Bivariate Relationships,
Classified by Type of Scale Employed

Dependent variable	Independent variable	
	Nominal scale	Interval scale
Nominal scale	Contingency table	Discriminant analysis
Interval scale	Analysis of variance	Regression/correlation

[9]Other techniques for these situations do exist. The four presented are the most widely used and provide a good foundation upon which to build our discussion.

[10]The discussion is limited to the bivariate case through Chapter 12. The multivariate case is introduced in Chapter 13.

The comparison of two-sample means provided an introduction to the case in which the independent variable is nominally scaled and the dependent variable is intervally scaled. The analysis of variance extends the comparison to any number of groups. Again there is no logical ordering of the groups specified in the independent variable. Del Monte, Ideal, Hunt's, and Ann Page may have a perceived ordering on specific characteristics; but the names, themselves, do not imply any numerical or rank relationships. The dependent variable might be the price of a particular sized can of pears, data collected from a number of stores. The analysis of variance would be an appropriate technique for testing whether the four brands differ in mean price.

Much of our discussion in the present chapter has been on a regression or correlation format. Here both variables are intervally scaled: height and weight, advertising expenditures and sales volume, and product usage and advertising recall. This technique is probably the most used—and most abused—technique for the study of relationships and associations. Regression determines the mathematical relationship between the two variables, according to the functional form specified by the analyst. Thus the conditional distribution obtained through a regression analysis would provide a compact mathematical summary of the relationship between number of salespeople and market penetration.

Finally, the fourth technique is discriminant analysis. The independent variable is intervally scaled, and the dependent variable is nominally scaled. This technique is rarely employed in bivariate problems. More than one independent variable is almost always involved. An illustration of its use in a bivariate situation would be an attempt to predict brand preference based on age.

ASSOCIATION VERSUS CAUSATION

If an association is established between product preference and product usage with the latter as the dependent variable, does product preference cause product usage? Must the marketing manager establish "cause and effect" before using the relationship for predictive purposes? Association exists when the two variables tend to vary together. The techniques used in studies of association establish (or fail to establish) covariation—a tendency to vary together. The techniques do not and cannot establish the existence of cause and effect relationships. Conclusions with respect to causation come from the human mind and its postulates. Philosophers have debated the meaning and verification of causal relationships for centuries. We cannot hope to settle the debate here, but we should recognize the possible interpretations that can be placed upon associative studies.

"Cause and effect" is usually construed as requiring that X must be both a necessary and a sufficient condition of Y before X can be identified as "the cause" of Y. In order to establish this relationship, one must demonstrate, "If X, then Y; if no X, then no Y." The mere existence of association can never establish causation. All possible environments must be included before true causation can be demonstrated—an impossible task.

A somewhat less demanding position is a "producer–product" relationship. The condition X is accepted as the producer of Y if X is a necessary condition: without X, Y does not occur.[11] Association may result from any one of four different producer–product situations. (1) Changes in the independent variable may produce changes in the dependent variable. (2) Changes in the dependent variable may produce changes in the independent variable. (3) Changes in a third variable may produce changes in both the dependent and independent variable. (4) Random factors may produce the association obvserved.

The fourth possibility can be addressed in a highly structured manner by the testing of a null hypothesis. The null hypothesis states that no association exists in the universe from which the sample is drawn. The random sampling distribution describes the kind of sample evidence that would result from random forces (chance) if the null hypothesis were true. The testing of the hypothesis, at a predetermined level of significance, then provides the basis upon which the fourth explanation is accepted or rejected.

If the fourth explanation for the observed association is rejected, one of the remaining three must be accepted. Either X produces Y, Y produces X, or a third variable (Z) produces both X and Y. The direction of flow from X to Y or from Y to X is often thought of according to priority in time. The one which occurs first may produce the second but not the reverse. This is not a bad first approximation, but it is not definitive because it rules out anticipatory acts. A forecast of X may generate act Y which actually precedes X. The data reveal that Y preceded X suggesting that Y produced X. The actual chain would be that the forecast of X produced Y which may or may not then be a producer of the actual event X.

Consider the relationship between sales and advertising. If next year's advertising budget is based on this year's sales, sales produce advertising. The usual model has advertising as a producer of sales. Are sales both the product of and the producer of advertising but for different points in time? Can either sequence be convincingly established as "necessary"? Without the so-called producer, would the product not occur?

Even if the relevant events and their timing could be obtained, the possibility that both X and Y are produced by Z should not be ignored. Changes in economic conditions (Z) may be responsible for both consumer behavior (Y) and a competitor's marketing mix fluctuations (X). Or changes in economic conditions (Z) may be responsible for both sales (Y) and advertising (X). If this be true, a prediction of consumer behavior from competitor's acts—or sales from advertising—may be misleading.

---

[11]See C. West Churchman, 1961, *Prediction and Optimal Decision: Philosophical Issues of a Science of Values* (Englewood Cliffs, N.J.: Prentice-Hall), pp. 214–218.

The choice of X as the producer of Y, Y as the producer of X, or Z as the producer of both X and Y rests on the logical chain management builds from its substantive knowledge and its subjective evaluations. The various techniques for studying associations can merely demonstrate covariation. But a good logical chain and theoretical construct should precede the collection and analysis of data. If this has been done, the researcher has submitted the model to an empirical test. The test cannot prove the model is correct, but it can show the results are consistent with the model.

A "black box" model in which no theoretical model precedes the analysis is fraught with danger. Predictions from such a model assume the associations discovered are not the result of chance forces; but without a specification of the model in advance, probability statements have dubious validity.[12] Secondly, the "black box" approach assumes that the covariation of the past will prevail in the future although the nature of the links has not been rationalized.

PARTITIONED VERSUS NONPARTITIONED DATA

Some association problems are *not* concerned with prediction of one variable, given information about other variables. Rather they are concerned with whether the variables display similar patterns of variation. The variables are not partitioned into two sets. They are placed into a single nonpartitioned set.

The analysis of associations within a single set of nonpartitioned variables may focus either on the relationships among the variables, the relationships among the units (subjects) on which the variables are measured, or on both the variables and units simultaneously. The first approach may have as its purpose the reduction of the number of variables to a few underlying factors. If successful, the summary may yield a more parsimonious picture. The second approach is appropriate for market segmentation studies or product positioning studies. The third approach examines variations (or similarities) across both the variables and subjects in order to discern interrelations in both directions, with possible interactions.

The analysis of nonpartitioned data is primarily a continuation of the age-old search for simplicity and essence. Factor analysis and cluster analysis seek to reduce the number of variables or subgroups. Multiple dimensional scaling seeks to reduce a large number of comparisons to a limited number of critical dimensions. These techniques will be considered in Part IV.

BIVARIATE AND MULTIVARIATE RELATIONS

Associations may be analyzed among any number of variables. The simplest case involves only two, one dependent and one independent. The next step is the addition of other independent variables in order to improve estimates of a

---

[12]The split-half technique can be attempted when no prior model exists. Half the data are used to generate the model, and the model is then tested with the other half of the data.

single dependent variable. As long as the several independent variables are measured on the same type of scale, the four basic techniques are easily extended. These extensions are covered in Chapter 13.

Complications arise when the scales of the independent variables are mixed between nominal and interval or when ordinal scales are used. The mixed scales are considered in Chapter 14 while the ordinal scales are postponed until Part IV along with the more general topic of nonparametric tests. The incorporation of multiple dependent variables along with multiple independent variables examines the relationships between two sets of variables, each of which might be viewed as a set of nonpartitioned data. This problem is handled in Part IV by canonical correlation.

SUMMARY

Marketing results can often be predicted from knowledge of other variables, for example, consumer characteristics, external environmental conditions, and a firm's discretionary actions. Predictions based upon this approach fall under the general topic of studies of associations. Each technique in this category substitutes a conditional distribution in place of an unconditional distribution as the basis for its predictions.

Within the study of association, there are three main objectives: (1) the estimation of a characteristic of interest, given knowledge of another variable(s), (2) a summary of how the variables are related to each other, and (3) the measurement of the degree of association. The first two are accomplished directly by the conditional distribution. The third is accomplished by comparing the conditional variance to the unconditional variance and expressing the reduction as a percentage.

Four widely used techniques exist for the study of association; each can be examined in terms of the scales used to measure the variables. These four techniques employ either nominal scales or interval scales and differentiate between the dependent variables (the variables to be predicted) and the independent variables (the variables serving as the basis for making the prediction). The four techniques are (1) contingency tables: both variables nominally scaled, (2) analysis of variance: a nominally scaled independent variable and an intervally scaled dependent variable, (3) regression/correlation: both variables intervally scaled, and (4) discriminant analysis: an intervally scaled independent variable and a nominally scaled dependent variable.

The form of the conditional distribution is critical in all studies of association. The researcher must specify the appropriate scales for measuring each variable, the restrictions to be imposed on the functional form, whether interaction terms are to be included, and the criterion for selecting the particular conditional equation. The restrictions incorporated in the functional form are not "findings" from the research. They represent prior opinions by the researcher and decision maker. Consequently, care must be exercised both in the selection of the equation and the presentation of the result. The same caveats apply to interaction terms or their absence.

Association demonstrates similarities within the data, not cause and effect. Substantive considerations and logical thought processes must be added to association in order to yield even a producer–product relationship. That finding then is subjective and not demonstrable by quantitative techniques.

The study of association may be pursued on either a partitioned or a non-partitioned basis and may involve a simple bivariate problem or multivariate relationships. Partitioned analyses focus on the estimation of one variable, given information about one or more other variables. This type of problem requires that management uniquely identify one or more specific characteristics of interest. Nonpartitioned analyses seek to discover the nature of the relationships among either the variables or the units of analysis; a particular variable is not selected as the one to be predicted. Multivariate analysis represents the extension of a simple two-variable analysis with one dependent and one independent variable to more complex functions with additional variables, most commonly additional independent variables but not restricted to that situation.

EXERCISES AND PROBLEMS

1. Distinguish among the terms within each of the following sets.
   a) Conditional distributions and unconditional distributions
   b) Dependent variables and independent variables
   c) Cause–effect, producer–product, and association
   d) Partitioned data and nonpartitioned data
   e) Degree of association and functional form of relationship

2. Name and briefly describe the three objectives in studying association.

3. Conditional distributions can be presented in three different forms. Name them and discuss their relative advantages and disadvantages.

4. Explain briefly the four decisions required in selecting the functional form for a conditional distribution.

5. Consider each of the following research endeavors. Using the 2 × 2 matrix of Table 10.3, which technique would be appropriate? Specify clearly how each variable would be measured.
   a) Predict brand usage, given size of family
   b) Predict expenditures, given marital status
   c) Predict sales performance, given education
   d) Predict product sales, given price
   e) Predict unemployment level, given volume of government contracts
   f) Predict market share, given legal structure of firm

6. Redefine one or both variables for the research endeavors in Exercise 5 so that a different analytic technique would be appropriate.

7. Briefly explain the meaning and importance of each of the following in studies of association.

    a) Interaction

    b) Reduction of variance

    c) Nonlinear functions

    d) Minimization of squared discrepancies

8. Using the data of Table 10.1, which of the nine alternatives would appear to yield the most profit? Assume unit cost is constant at $1.00.

9. Analyze, criticize, and explain:

    a) A linear equation is not a perfect approach to discovering whether decreasing returns are at work, but it is a good first approximation.

    b) Estimates based on conditional distributions will usually be superior to those based on unconditional distributions. This results because the individual estimates are based on the respective values of the independent variable. The principal difficulty is that the width of the confidence interval is usually greater when the conditional distribution is used.

    c) Although some results of an association study are imposed on the data rather than determined by the data, point estimates are not dependent on such impositions.

    d) The coefficient of determination (r^2) indicates the degree of association and the direction of the relationship.

    e) A conditional distribution is a much better tool for making predictions than it is for helping in management decisions. This stems principally from the fact that the independent variables are limited to consumer characteristics and/or external environmental conditions.

CHAPTER 11

CONTINGENCY TABLES AND ANALYSIS OF VARIANCE
SO YOU WANT TO COMPARE LOTS OF GROUPS?

Which brand is preferred in a blind taste test? Which location has the greatest market potential? Which college supplies the best qualified middle-management candidates? These and a host of other marketing questions fall into the format of "compare several groups." The decision maker defines the groups to be compared and the characteristic on which the comparison is to be made.

A multinational company comparing preferred shopping modes of the citizens of various countries and a campaign manager comparing voter intentions in a primary election have very similar analytic problems. A comparison of the sales levels achieved with four different point-of-purchase displays falls into the same format.

All of these problems address situations in which the independent variable—the basis on which the groups are established—is nominally scaled. Two different techniques exist, the selection depending on the scale employed for the dependent variable. If the dependent variable is also nominally scaled (color, previous brand, language, etc.), the appropriate technique is the contingency table. If the dependent variable is intervally scaled (dollar sales, mean income, package weight, etc.), the appropriate technique is the analysis of variance. Both techniques are considered in this chapter.

CONTINGENCY TABLES

We encountered contingency tables in Chapter 9 when we compared two percentages. We wanted to know how large the sample difference had to be in order to conclude that population percentages were different. The technique is much more general than that; any number of groups may be compared. The 2×2 table can be expanded to a $2 \times c$ table in order to compare c groups. Then the number of categories for the second variable can also be increased, yielding the general $r \times c$ table. We shall start our discussion in this chapter with the $2 \times c$ table since the 2×2 was covered in Chapter 9.[1]

---

[1]See "The 2×2 Table" in Chapter 9.

The 2 × c Table

Consider the dilemma of Joe Miller, a fledgling political candidate. He is battling Bill Palmer, a veteran campaigner, for his party's nomination in the primary election. His campaign manager advises that a small survey be made in order to determine whether voter preference seems to vary with age. They must first determine the appropriate way to partition the universe with respect to age. Table 11.1 indicates a partitioning into three groups: under 35, 35 to 55, and over 55. The table also contains the results of the survey.

The total figures indicate 50 percent for each candidate. Miller and his campaign manager decide that the null hypothesis[2] should be tested at the .05 level of significance. The necessary calculations, according to Eq. (9.14), show Chi Square equal to 7.74.

$$\chi^2 = \sum \frac{(f_e - f_0)^2}{f_e}$$

$$= \frac{(115 - 100)^2}{100} + \frac{(92 - 100)^2}{100} + \frac{(43 - 50)^2}{50} + \frac{(85 - 100)^2}{100} +$$

$$\frac{(108 - 100)^2}{100} + \frac{(57 - 50)^2}{50}$$

$$= 2.25 + .64 + .98 + 2.25 + .64 + .98$$

$$= 7.74$$

The test of the null hypothesis cannot be made until the number of degrees of freedom is determined. The number of degrees of freedom for a two-way classification table is given by $(r - 1)(c - 1)$ where r is the number of rows and c is the number of columns. Thus the number of degrees of freedom for this problem is equal to 2.[3]

Table 11.1
Voter Preference between Two Candidates by Age Group

Candidate	Age group			Total
	Under 35	35–55	Over 55	
Miller	115	92	43	250
Palmer	85	108	57	250
Total	200	200	100	500

[2]The null hypothesis may be verbalized in any of three forms: (1) there is no association between the variables, (2) the groups have equal population parameters, or (3) the variables are independent of each other. The three expressions are equivalent and will be used interchangeably.

[3]This calculation assumes a single sample of size n has been selected. If a separate sample were selected from each age group, there would be a total of three degrees of freedom, one for each column. See "One Sample or Several Samples" later in this chapter.

The critical value of Chi Square, referring to Appendix Table A.4 is 5.991. Therefore the null hypothesis should be rejected, and Miller should conclude that voter preference between the two candidates differs by age groups. He can see by the table that he is more popular with the younger age group which has a point estimate of 57.5 percent while only 46 percent of the middle group and 43 percent of the older group support his candidacy.

The prediction problem for the various subgroups should not be considered by Miller until the null hypothesis has been rejected. This follows because acceptance of the null hypothesis implies that the estimate of Miller's support should be the same for each age group. Once the null hypothesis has been rejected, both the point estimate and the interval estimate follow along the lines discussed in Chapter 7. The 95 percent confidence interval for the under 35 age group is given by

$$\bar{p} \pm 1.96\overset{*}{\sigma}_{\bar{p}} = 57.5 \pm 1.96 \,(57.5 \times 42.5 \div 199)^{1/2}$$

$$57.5 \pm 1.96 \,(3.50)$$

$$57.5 \pm 6.9$$

$$50.6 \text{ to } 64.4 \text{ percent.}$$

Precisely the same procedure is employed for making interval estimates for the other percentages of Table 11.1.

The $r \times c$ Table

Suppose there are more than two candidates. Table 11.2 gives voter preference when the name of Joseph Pizzo was added to the list. The resulting Chi Square

Table 11.2
Voter Preference among Three Candidates by Age Group

Candidate	Age group			Total
	Under 35	35–55	Over 55	
Miller	83	64	28	175
Palmer	55	79	41	175
Pizzo	62	57	31	150
Total	200	200	100	500

$$\chi^2 = \frac{(83 - 70)^2}{70} + \frac{(64 - 70)^2}{70} + \frac{(28 - 35)^2}{35} + \frac{(55 - 70)^2}{70} + \frac{(79 - 70)^2}{70} +$$

$$\frac{(41 - 35)^2}{35} + \frac{(62 - 60)^2}{60} + \frac{(57 - 60)^2}{60} + \frac{(31 - 30)^2}{30}$$

$$= 9.98.$$

is equal to 9.98. With four degrees of freedom, the result is again significant at the .05 level. And again Miller should conclude that voter preference—in this selection—differs with age. The specific null hypothesis refers to all three candidates, not just to Miller or to Miller versus Palmer. The specific hypothesis rejected is that voter preference among Miller, Palmer, and Pizzo is independent of age.

The general case in which both variables have more than two categories should not be confused with the case of more than two variables. We are still in the bivariate situation; we have merely increased the number of categories.

Table 11.3 presents an r by c contingency table for a sample of shoppers, each classified by her principal source of shopping information and type dwelling unit. The total column indicates that newspapers are the principal source of shopping information for 66.7 percent (400/600) of the respondents. Friends are the principal source for 25 percent, and radio/TV are the principal source for 8.3 percent. The null hypothesis, without specifying these precise figures, asserts that the percentage distribution among these three sources is the same for the four types of dwelling units: apartment, row house, semi-detached, and single.

The percentage of respondents citing newspapers as the principal source of shopping information varies from 53 percent for those living in row houses to 78 percent for apartment dwellers. The percentage citing friends varies from 12 to 38 percent—again with the row houses and apartments providing the extremes. The radio/TV percentages range between 6 and 10 percent. Our basic question is whether this amount of variation is a reflection of random fluctuations (with the null hypothesis true) or whether it is a reflection of real differences by type of dwelling unit.

The Chi Square statistic provides the criterion for this test. Again using Eq. (9.14), we have the following calculation.

$$\chi^2 = \frac{(12 - 25)^2}{25} + \frac{(38 - 25)^2}{25} + \frac{(42 - 37.5)^2}{37.5} + \frac{(58 - 62.5)^2}{62.5} + \cdots$$

$$= 20.6.$$

Since we have a 3 × 4 table, the number of degrees of freedom is 2 × 3 or 6. Referring to Appendix Table A.4 and using a .05 level of significance, we see that the critical value is 12.592. The null hypothesis should be rejected. Shoppers living in different types of dwelling units differ in their principal sources of shopping information.

The data of Table 11.3 illustrate a paradox that occurs with some frequency in marketing problems. The null hypothesis of equal percentage distributions should be rejected, but newspapers are the principal source of information for shoppers from all four types of dwelling units. It is paradoxical but valid to state (1) shoppers from row houses are less likely to have newspapers as their principal source of information than are shoppers from other types of dwelling units but at the same time to state (2) shoppers from row houses are

Table 11.3
Principal Source of Shopping Information by Type of Dwelling Unit

Principal source	Apartment	Row house	Semidetached	Single	Total
	Type of dwelling unit†				
Friends	12 (12.0)	38 (38.0)	42 (28.0)	58 (23.2)	150 (25.0)
Newspapers	78 (78.0)	53 (53.0)	99 (66.0)	170 (68.0)	400 (66.7)
Radio/TV	10 (10.0)	9 (9.0)	9 (6.0)	22 (8.8)	50 (8.3)
Total	100	100	150	250	600

†Percentage distributions by type of dwelling are given in parentheses.

more likely to have newspapers as their principal source of information than they are to have any other source as their principal source of information. The decision maker must recognize the difference between these statements and govern his or her actions accordingly. Rejection of the null hypothesis does not *necessarily* mean the groups differ in their modal values.

Rejection of the null hypothesis does not identify the precise nature of the differences. This identification comes from the comparison of the point estimates (or interval estimates) for the various percentages. The sample cell percentages are each unbiased point estimates for the corresponding universe values; for example, friends are the principal source of shopping information for 12 percent of the shoppers dwelling in apartments. This estimate would not be appropriate if the null hypothesis had been accepted; the estimate in that case would be 25 percent regardless of type of dwelling unit. The principal departures from the unconditional values (shown by the total percentages) occur in four cells: "Friends/Apartment," "Friends/Row house," "Newspapers/Apartment," and "Newspapers/Row house."

Interval estimates would be determined in precisely the same manner as discussed earlier. A 95 percent confidence interval for the percentage of apartment dwellers whose principal source of information is newspapers is

$$78 \pm 1.96 \left(\frac{78 \times 22}{99}\right)^{1/2}$$

$$78 \pm 1.96 \, (17.33)^{1/2},$$

$$78 \pm 1.96 \, (4.16),$$

$$78 \pm 8.2,$$

$$69.8 \text{ to } 86.2\%.$$

Measure of Association

How strong is the association between type of dwelling unit and principal source of information? or between age and preference for Miller or Palmer? We have reached the conclusion in each case that the two variables are associated, and we have determined point and interval estimates for various percentages. We now wish a summary measure, showing the strength of that association. Unfortunately, the measures of association derived from contingency table analysis are limited in their interpretability. The desire for a common concept—percentage reduction in variance—can be met only for the 2×2 table. For all other tables, variance as a measure of squared distance is completely lacking because a nominal scale does not even incorporate order let alone distance between categories.

The *Phi coefficient (ϕ)* is restricted to the 2×2 table, but it may be directly compared with other commonly used measures of association. It has a lower limit of -1 and an upper limit of $+1$. Its value is zero (0) if the two variables are independent. Finally, its square shows the percentage reduction in variance.

Table 11.4 presents data on brand preference and life-style. A shortcut to the calculation of Phi is given by Eq. (11.1), the location of the letters being shown in Table 11.4.[4]

$$\phi = \frac{ad - bc}{\left[(a + b)(c + d)(a + c)(b + d)\right]^{1/2}}. \tag{11.1}$$

The numerator of Eq. (11.1) will be small if the distributions of the two columns are similar. The greater the discrepancies between the two distributions, the larger the absolute value of the numerator—and thus the larger the Phi. The denominator is the standardizing factor, permitting comparisons regardless of sample size; it is simply the square root of the product of the four marginal totals.

Phi for the data in Table 11.4 is equal to

$$\phi = \frac{100(55) - 20(25)}{\left[(120)(80)(125)(75)\right]^{1/2}} = .527.$$

Table 11.4
Brand Preference versus Life-style

Brand preference	Life-style		Total
	Liberal	Conservative	
Horizons Unlimited	100 (a)	20 (b)	120 (a + b)
Econo Mate	25 (c)	55 (d)	80 (c + d)
Total	125 (a + c)	75 (b + d)	200

---

[4]The same result would be obtained by the following tedious calculation: (1) compute both the conditional and unconditional variances, (2) determine the percentage reduction, and (3) extract the square root. As we shall see by Eq. (11.4), this makes ϕ the precise equivalent of the correlation ratio (η).

The sign is positive because the cells with the greatest concentration are the upper left and lower right cells. If the lower left and upper right cells had the greatest concentration, the sign would be negative. For most 2×2 tables the order for the rows and columns is arbitrary; consequently, the significance of Phi comes from its magnitude, not its sign.[5]

The *contingency coefficient (C)* is a more general measure of association. It can be calculated for any size contingency table. It has a minimum value of zero, resulting when the percentage distributions are precisely identical for all columns—and for all rows as well if attention is focused in that direction. Unfortunately, its maximum value depends on the number of cells in the table and is always less than unity. Therefore direct comparison of contingency coefficients is appropriate only if the tables are of the same dimensions.

C is defined by Eq. (11.2)

$$C = \left(\frac{\chi^2}{\chi^2 + n}\right)^{1/2}. \tag{11.2}$$

It can be easily calculated and can be made for a table of any size. The values of C as calculated for Tables 11.1 through 11.4 are

Table 11.1;	$C = .12$ (2×3 table),
Table 11.2;	$C = .14$ (3×3 table),
Table 11.3;	$C = .18$ (3×4 table),
Table 11.4;	$C = .47$ (2×2 table).

Since each result is based on a table of a different size, the magnitudes of the C values cannot be directly compared.

The maximum value for C increases as the size of the table increases and is given by Eq. (11.3) where there are k categories for each variable. Interpolation is necessary for nonsymmetrical tables.[6]

$$C_{\text{Max}} = \left(\frac{k - 1}{k}\right)^{1/2}. \tag{11.3}$$

C divided by its maximum value then yields an adjusted contingency coefficient (C_{Adj}).

Neither the raw contingency coefficient nor the adjusted value coincides with Phi. Using the data from Table 11.4, the C is .466 while C_{Adj} is .659. Phi falls between them at .527. Phi and C_{Adj} will coincide only at 1.0 for perfect association and 0.0 for no association. Phi and C (unadjusted) will coincide only at 0.0 for no association.

---

[5] Phi is equal to the coefficient of correlation (r) if the categories of the two variables are assigned numerical values, typically visualized as 0 and 1 although the same result occurs with any two numbers.

[6] See Palmer O. Johnson and Robert W. B. Jackson, 1959, *Modern Statistical Methods: Descriptive and Inductive* (Chicago: Rand McNally), pp. 358–361; and Sidney Siegal, 1956, *Nonparametric Statistics for the Sciences* (New York: McGraw-Hill), pp. 196–202 for more extended discussions.

The Conditional Distribution

No *a priori* specification concerning the form of the conditional distribution is employed with contingency table analysis. The percentage in favor of Miller for the middle age group could have been higher than both the other age groups or lower than both of them or—as is the actual case in Table 11.1—between them. No systematic pattern is imposed on the data. Likewise, no numerical relationship concerning the magnitude of the differences between the groups is specified. With three groups, there is no requirement that the middle group be equally distant (or any other specified distance relationship) from the other two.

Referring to Tables 11.2 and 11.3, again no constraints are imposed on the permissible results. All three candidates in Table 11.2 could have shown diverse popularity figures by age groups. However, with the existing data we see that Pizzo received approximately equal support among all ages while the other two had differential support among the age categories. In Table 11.3, three of the four types of dwelling units could have been very similar in their conditional distributions concerning sources of information with the fourth dissimilar. Or, as is the case, two groups could be similar with the other two showing deviations in opposite directions. The number of possible relationships is unlimited.

The magnitude of the point estimates for the dependent variable is constrained in only one respect: the total over all categories must equal 100 percent. Individual point estimates and relationships among the point estimates of different categories are determined by the sample data alone.[7]

Dependent versus Independent Variables

Our examples have identified the dependent and independent variables in the context of the problems. Joe Miller wanted to compare age groups with respect to their voting preference. A marketing manager wished to determine whether shoppers living in different type dwelling units received their principal shopping information from the same sources. Could the variables have been reversed? Could principal source of information have been the independent variable and type of dwelling unit have been the dependent variable?

The sample of 600 shoppers was selected without regard to the variables to be analyzed. So this stage does not determine which variable is independent and which is dependent. In a mechanical way, it poses no difficulty to frame the null hypothesis in terms of the percentage distribution of dwelling types reached by each information source. Is the percentage division among dwelling type the same, regardless of whether the principal source of information is friends, newspapers, or radio/TV? The unconditional sample distribution is

---

[7]When more than two categories are involved, the appropriate distribution is the multinomial rather than the binomial. With several variables, the appropriate distribution is the joint multinomial. For the mathematical justification and development, see any standard probability text.

16.7 percent apartment, 16.7 percent row house, 25 percent semidetached, and 41.7 percent single. Are the row distributions different enough from this distribution to cast doubt on the null hypothesis?

The percentage distribution from row 1 (friends) is 8.0 percent apartment, 25.3 percent row house, 28.0 percent semidetached, and 38.7 percent single. Analogous percentage distributions can be calculated for the other two rows, but the test of the null hypothesis requires the calculation of Chi Square. The calculation yields a result of 20.6—precisely the same as before when the variables were reversed. In fact, the theoretical expected values for each cell are precisely the same regardless of which variable is considered the independent variable. The test for association does not specify which variable is dependent and which is independent. The two variables either are or are not associated with each other. The contingency coefficient and Phi coefficient are also computed without regard to which variable is dependent and which is independent.

The prediction question and the specification of the conditional distribution does require the identification of which variable is the dependent variable and which is the independent variable. However, this identification will be self-evident in the statement of the prediction problem. For example, concern for whether people living in apartments rely on newspapers as their principal source of information requires that dwelling place be independent and source of information be dependent. Concern for whether people relying on newspapers live in apartments requires the reverse. The respective point estimates for the two questions are 78 percent (78/100) and 19.5 percent (78/400).

One Sample or Several Samples

Referring to Table 11.1 and Joe Miller's problem, we recall that a sample of 500 voters was selected. Suppose instead of selecting a single sample of 500, three separate samples had been selected—one from each age group. Does this change anything?

We now have a sample size 200 from the under-35 age group, a sample size 200 from the 35–55 age group, and a sample size 100 from the over-55 age group. But isn't that precisely what we had before when it was a single sample? Yes and no! First, it changes the number of degrees of freedom. There is one degree of freedom within each of the three samples. Thus there is a total of three for the analysis instead of two as in the previous case. Chi Square is calculated in the same way, but its critical value is larger. The discrepancies observed must be greater in order to reject the null hypothesis. The critical value is now 7.815, larger than the calculated Chi Square (7.74). The null hypothesis should now be accepted; Miller and his co-workers are not justified in concluding that voters in the three different age groups differ in preference (Miller versus Palmer).

A further difference exists in the case of three samples versus a single sample. The total of 500 individuals may not be representative of the total universe. Estimates should be made for the total universe only if either of two situations can be substantiated. (1) The separate groups have been included in their correct proportions, that is, the sample is a proportional stratified sample.[8] (2) The null hypothesis of similar distributions should be accepted.

The second situation casts some interesting light on the nature of the contingency table and the test of no association between the variables. If the three age groups are similar in their voter preference, the weights applied to them are immaterial. Each sample comes from a universe in which the percentage is the same. Pooling of them together will simply yield a more reliable estimate of the values to be estimated. If the null hypothesis is rejected, we conclude the three groups differ in their percentage figures. They can be combined only if we know the proper weight to apply to each group. Without that knowledge, we have no basis upon which to estimate figures for the total universe.

The problem of several separate samples is common in marketing research. The marketing manager is interested in identifying separate market segments if they exist. If the manager selects separate samples of each potential segment and concludes they differ in the characteristic of interest, he or she cannot use the basic data to estimate total market figures. That estimate requires that the manager know the sizes of the separate segments.

The type sample is also a limiting factor in the interpretation of Phi and the contingency coefficient. Both measures summarize the degree of relationship found in the sample employed. If this sample is not representative of the total universe, it is obvious that the degree of association found in the sample may be misleading. For this reason, neither coefficient should be calculated unless the sample can be accepted as representative of the relevant universe.

Tests of Association—General or Specific?

The contingency table does not truly test the hypothesis that the two characteristics are independent of each other! If this be true, why have we wasted so much time? The situation is not as bad as the initial statement sounds. The analysis asks whether the variables are independent of each other *when a specific basis for partitioning is employed.* The analysis tests, of necessity, a specific hypothesis framed in terms of the variables as defined and categorized. It cannot test a completely general hypothesis that captures the essence of the variables apart from particular definitions. For example, the voter preference problem tests whether preference between Miller and Palmer is the same for each of three age groups, the three age groups being those specified in Table 11.1. A different basis for classifying age might yield a different conclusion with respect to the independence hypothesis.

The partitioning of the universe has two components—the number of subgroups and the specific lines of demarcation between the subgroups. For decision-making purposes, both must be generated by alternative actions available. This means that the decision maker must be able to distinguish between

---

[8]See Chapters 6 and 8.

the groups as specified, choosing different actions for each subgroup if the analysis leads to the rejection of the null hypothesis. This is basic to all market segmentation: segments must be identifiable, accessible, and of sufficient magnitude. Otherwise segmentation is not useful in decision making.

Is an Order Implicit?

The contingency table analysis is based upon nominal scales only. This means that the order established among the subpopulations is immaterial in the test of the null hypothesis. For example, if the voter preferences of Table 11.1 were transformed so that the data for the under-35 age group and the data for the 35–55 age group were interchanged, the conclusion would still be that voter preference and age were associated. In such a situation, both the younger group and the older group would be in favor of Palmer. Not only must the decision maker visualize that potential market segments may be treated differently but he or she must also visualize acceptable patterns of deviations among the groups. Nominal scales truly mean that no order is implied by the sequence in which the various subgroups are presented.

Consider the structure planned for the analysis in Table 11.5. In Part A (region versus color preference) the analyst is willing to accept any pattern of

Table 11.5
Nominal or Ordinal Scales for Contingency Tables

A. Region versus color preference

	Region			
Color preference	East	North	South	West
Blue			x	
Red				
Green	x			
Yellow		x		
White				x

B. Education level versus product usage

	Education level			
Product usage	Low	Low-average	Average-high	High
Low		x		
Low-medium				x
Medium	x			
High-medium				
High			x	

relationships; the pattern marked by x's is no more or no less reasonable than any other pattern. The concepts of direct, inverse, and curvilinear relationships do not apply to these characteristics. The same statements cannot be made with respect to Part B (education level versus product usage) of Table 11.5, although both are four by five tables. The x's indicated in Part B would suggest a somewhat erratic relationship between educational level and product usage with reversals in the general pattern. Before collecting any data, the researcher should (1) establish the tables for analysis, (2) visualize the different patterns the actual data may take, and (3) decide what conclusions and action implications should be drawn from each possible result.

After the data are in, most analysts can create rational explanations for any pattern observed. This is a dangerous procedure since the number of tables that can be generated from the typical research project is unlimited. Some of them will seem to indicate relationships where none exist in the universe of interest. This is precisely the meaning of a level of significance: where no relationship exists in the universe, the stated percentage of tables will indicate "significant" differences. If a researcher constructs 400 bivariate contingency tables from the data collected, the expected number of *true* null hypotheses rejected, using a 5 percent level of significance, would be 20. Since there is always the possibility that random forces may produce apparent relationships, the analyst should exercise restraint in requesting reams of computer printout results. When a few "statistically significant" relationships appear, it is always tempting to ignore the huge number of "nonsignificant" differences.

Overview of Contingency Table Analysis

Table 11.6 summarizes the key aspects of contingency table analysis. The basic questions are common to all of the techniques dealing with studies of association, with the same recurrent three key issues. First, should we use a conditional distribution as a basis for making estimates or predictions? Second, what is the best way to summarize the relationship? Third, how strong is the association? A common null hypothesis runs through all studies of association: the variables are *not* associated. This is the starting point; unless that hypothesis can be rejected, marketing decisions cannot rely on any conditional distribution derived.

Contingency table analysis tests the null hypothesis by means of the Chi Square statistic. If this hypothesis is rejected, point estimates may be read directly from the table. Since the dependent variable is nominally scaled, the appropriate point estimate is a percentage. This estimate is given by the cell entry divided by a row (or column) total. The relationship derived is not presented in a succinct mathematical equation; but it, too, comes directly from the table. As a result, a neat summary does not usually follow. The relationship observed will normally be erratic rather than smooth and regular.

There are two commonly employed measures of association. The Phi coefficient (ϕ) is restricted to the 2×2 table, and it does conform to a per-

Table 11.6
Contingency Table Analysis Summary

1. Test statistic: Chi Square (χ^2)

2. Estimate based on:
   a) Column or row *totals* if H_0 is accepted
   b) Cell value and relevant total if H_0 is rejected

3. Summary of relationship, if any:
   a) Read directly from table
   b) May be irregular jumps

4. Measure of association:
   a) Phi coefficient (ϕ) for 2 × 2 table (square root of percentage reduction in variance)
   b) Contingency coefficient (C) for others (not related to percentage reduction in variance)

5. Form of conditional distribution:
   a) No prior specification
   b) No constraints

centage reduction in variance concept—although (ϕ) is expressed as its square root. The contingency coefficient (C) can be computed for any contingency table, but it is neither a percentage reduction in variance nor is it a measure that has a clear interpretation.

ANALYSIS OF VARIANCE

We considered differences between the means of two groups in Chapter 9. A more general question is the comparison of the means of any number of groups. This type of problem may be analyzed by the analysis of variance (ANOVA).

The groups to be compared constitute the independent variable, nominally scaled. The characteristic upon which they are to be compared is the dependent variable, intervally scaled. The variables cannot be interchanged in ANOVA as they can be in a contingency table analysis.

The basic question posed is whether the observed differences among the sample means reflect differences among the group means or whether they merely reflect random fluctuations about a common mean. The term *analysis of variance* breaks down dispersion (as measured by variance) into component parts—that produced by random forces and that attributed to other factors.

The technique is illustrated by the following problem. A consumer-advocate group wished to determine whether supermarket chains operating in the area differed in their "out-of-stock" levels for advertised specials. After considerable discussion, the group determined that the relevant dependent variable was the percentage of advertised items not in stock.[9] The data of Table 11.7 represent only a portion of the data collected but are illustrative of the general pattern.

The basic question is whether, with a sample of size five from each chain, the observed differences are large enough for us to reject the null hypothesis that all three chains have the same mean percentage "out of stock". ANOVA approaches this by comparing the differences among the three means with an estimate of random fluctuations, using an F-test (Appendix Table A.5). The numerator of the F-ratio is a measure of dispersion among the three chain means, and the denominator is an estimate of the underlying variability among stores of the same chain.

The grand mean of all 15 observations is 13.2. ANOVA first calculates the dispersion of the 15 observations around this grand mean and then divides that total dispersion into the components required for the F-ratio. The total dispersion is shown in Table 11.8 as the total "sum of squares," calculated by summing the squared deviations of the 15 individual observations from the grand mean; the resulting sum is 144.640.

The analysis next separates this sum of squares into its two component parts: that which is produced by within-chain dispersion and that which is produced by dispersion among chain means. Within-chain (within-column) sum of squares is calculated by comparing each observation with the mean of its own chain. The individual observations within Chain L are compared with 15.78; those within Chain M, with 10.40; and those within Chain N, with 13.42. The resulting within-chain sum of squares is 71.916.

Table 11.7
Percentage "Out of Stock" on Advertised Specials
for Three Supermarket Chains

	Chain			
	L	M	N	Total
	15.3	9.7	16.4	
	13.7	13.6	10.4	
	19.8	8.0	13.9	
	14.3	8.3	11.5	
	15.8	12.4	14.9	
$Total \left(\sum\limits^{m} y_{ik} \right)$	78.9	52.0	67.1	198.0
$Mean\ (\bar{y}_k)$	15.78	10.40	13.42	13.2

[9]The initial formulation of the problem focused on the number of items not in stock. Use of this definition led to the amazing conclusion that the larger stores and those that advertised more items had higher "out-of-stock" levels than did smaller stores that advertised fewer items.

Table 11.8
Analysis of Variance for "Out-of-Stock" Data

Source of variation	Sum of squares	Degrees of freedom	Mean square	F-ratio
Among-chain	72.724	2	36.362	6.07($P < .05$)
Within-chain	71.916	12	5.993	
Total	144.640	14		

Total sum of squares $= \sum^{k}\sum^{m}\left(y_{ik} - \bar{\bar{y}}_k\right)^2$

$= (15.3 - 13.2)^2 + (13.7 - 13.2)^2 + \cdots + (14.9 - 13.2)^2$

$= 144.640.$

Within-chain sum of squares $= \sum^{k}\sum^{m}\left(y_{ik} - \bar{y}_k\right)^2$

$= (15.3 - 15.78)^2 + \cdots + (9.7 - 10.40)^2$

$\quad + \cdots + (16.4 - 13.42)^2 + \cdots$

$= 71.916.$

Among-chain sum of squares $= \sum^{k}m\left(\bar{y}_k - \bar{\bar{y}}\right)^2 = m\sum^{k}\left(\bar{y}_k - \bar{\bar{y}}\right)^2$

$= 5\left[(15.78 - 13.2)^2 + (10.40 - 13.2)^2 + (13.42 - 13.2)^2\right]$

$= 72.724.$

The among-chain (among-column) sum of squares can be obtained either by subtracting the within-chain figure (71.916) from the total (144.640) or by the calculation shown in Table 11.8. The latter procedure determines the squared deviation of each chain mean from the grand mean; for example, $(15.78 - 13.2)^2$. Each squared deviation is then weighted by the number of observations in the individual means, five in this instance.[10]

The F-ratio is defined in terms of variances; thus far we have only the sum of squared deviations. A variance is a mean squared deviation, but unbiased estimates of variances are obtained by dividing by the number of degrees of freedom rather than by the number of observations. The number of degrees of freedom for the among chain variance is one less than the number of means compared; for Table 11.8 this is (3 − 1) or 2. The number of degrees of freedom associated with the sum of squares for each chain is 4; since there are three chains, there is a total of 12 degrees of freedom for the within-chain variance. The sum of these two must equal the total number of degrees of free-

---

[10]The mathematical justification for partitioning the total sum of squares into these two component parts is given by the following algebra.

$$\sum(y_i - \bar{\bar{y}})^2 = \sum(y_i - \bar{y} + \bar{y} - \bar{\bar{y}})^2$$
$$= \sum\left[(y_i - \bar{y})^2 + 2(y_i - \bar{y})(\bar{y} - \bar{\bar{y}}) + (\bar{y} - \bar{\bar{y}})^2\right]$$
$$= \sum(y_i - \bar{y})^2 + \sum(\bar{y} - \bar{\bar{y}})^2 \text{ since the middle term} = 0.$$

dom (14 with 15 observations). The two desired variances are shown in Table 11.8 in the column labeled "Mean square."

The F-ratio asks whether the among-column variance is simply a reflection of inherent random deviations or whether it is so large that it reflects basic differences in the column means. Thus large values of F cast doubt on the null hypothesis, and small values of F do not cast doubt on the null hypothesis. The definitions of "large" and "small" depend on the number of degrees of freedom associated with each variance. As shown in Appendix Table A.5, the critical F-ratios for the present problems are 3.89 (for $\alpha = .05$) and 6.93 (for $\alpha = .01$).[11]

What conclusion should we reach, and what statements are warranted? At a 5 percent level of significance—hopefully chosen before examining the results—only one conclusion emerges at this stage: the universe percentage out of stock is not the same for all three chains. Can't we say more? Point estimates, and possibly interval estimates, for each of the chains are desired. That is our next task.[12]

Point Estimates

Point estimates for the means of the three individual chains are made in precisely the same manner as in our earlier work. The point estimate for each chain is given by its mean in Table 11.7. All three point estimates are contained in the following equation:

$$E(y_k) = 13.20 + 2.58x_L - 2.80x_M + 0.22x_N; \qquad x_i = 0, 1.$$

The only permissible values for the x-values are 0 and 1, 1 being substituted where the subscript identifies a chain for which an estimate is desired and 0 being substituted for the other two x-variables.

The equation reveals in compact form the grand mean and the deviation of each chain from that mean. No calculations are necessary to derive the equation; it comes from inspection of Table 11.7. The constant term (13.20) is equal to the grand mean. The coefficients for the x_i values are determined by subtracting the grand mean from the appropriate chain mean.

Given the equation, point estimates for the individual chain means follow directly. An estimate for Chain N would be given by

$$E(y_N) = 13.20 + 2.58(0) - 2.80(0) + 0.22(1) = 13.42.$$

---

[11]As is true for all such tests in statistics, these critical values are obtained from the random sampling distribution associated with a true null hypothesis. For the data in Tables 11.7 and 11.8 (with 2 degrees of freedom for the numerator and 12 degrees of freedom for the denominator), an F-ratio of 3.89 or greater will be obtained 5 percent of the time when the null hypothesis is true. The interpretation of other entries in Appendix Table A.5 is precisely analogous.

[12]If the null hypothesis had been accepted, it would be inappropriate to make separate estimates for each chain. For this reason, the null hypothesis should be tested before making estimates for the individual groups.

Interval Estimates

Interval estimation introduces a dilemma. If we were to follow the procedure established in Chapter 7, our interval estimate for Chain N would be based on the five observations from that chain, using its sample mean, sample variance, and estimating the standard error of the mean. ANOVA, in testing the null hypothesis concerning means, assumes the within-chain variance is the same for all three chains. If we make this assumption in testing the null hypothesis, should we not maintain that assumption in making interval estimates for the three chains?[13]

The within-chain variance is given in Table 11.8 as 5.993; this is an unbiased estimate since it has been calculated by using the number of degrees of freedom rather than the number of observations. The estimate of the within-chain standard deviation is 2.45 (the square root of 5.993). Separate calculations for each of the three chains yield figures of 2.39, 2.49, and 2.45—on a subjective level, all fairly close to 2.45.[14]

The confidence interval for the mean of any chain is established by using the following general format

$$E(y_k) + t \overset{*}{\sigma}_{\bar{y}}.$$

Here $\overset{*}{\sigma}_{\bar{y}}$ is calculated with $n = 5$; the sample size for the mean in question is used, not the sample size for the entire study. The estimated standard error of the mean will be the same for all three chains since each is based on the same size sample; $\overset{*}{\sigma}_{\bar{y}} = 1.10$. The coefficient should come from the t-distribution because the standard deviation has been estimated from sample evidence. (The sample size is too small to ignore the difference between t and z.) For a 95 percent confidence interval and four degrees of freedom, $t = 2.78$. (See Appendix Table A.3.)[15]

We are now ready to establish a confidence interval for the mean. For Chain N it would be equal to

$$13.42 \pm 2.78(1.10),$$
$$10.36 \text{ to } 16.48.$$

Effect of Sample Size

Suppose the sample size for the "out-of-stock" problem has been doubled with approximately the same distribution as shown in Table 11.7. How would this affect ANOVA, particularly the F-ratio? To simplify our arithmetic, let us

---

[13]The technical term meaning equality of variances is homoscedasticity. Thus ANOVA assumes homoscedasticity.

[14]See Johnson and Jackson, *op. cit.*, pp. 184–187 for tests of homoscedasticity. The null hypothesis is accepted for the data in question.

[15]The use of the t-distribution assumes, as it did in Chapter 7, that the population is normally distributed.

Table 11.9
Revised ANOVA for "Out-of-Stock" Problem with Doubled Sample Size

Source of variation	Sum of squares	Degrees of freedom	Mean square	F-ratio
Among-chain	145.448	2	72.724	13.65($P < .01$)
Within-chain	143.832	27	5.327	
Total	289.280	29		

suppose that each of the 15 original observations is repeated. The three means would be precisely the same: 15.78, 10.40, and 13.42 with the grand mean equal to 13.2.

Each of the three sums of squares would be doubled. The total and the within-chain figures are generated by adding the new observations to the calculations. The among-chain figure is generated by weighting each squared deviation by ten instead of five since each mean is based on ten observations. However, we must be careful when considering degrees of freedom. The total number is now 29, one less than the number of observations. The within-chain degrees of freedom are nine for each chain or 27 for all three combined. The among-chain degrees of freedom remain at two because there are still only three means to be compared. The summary ANOVA figures are presented in Table 11.9.

The effect of the sample size increase appears in the mean square and the *F*-ratio. The among-chain mean square is doubled while the within-chain mean square remains at about the same magnitude. The latter is the estimate of inherent variation among stores within a single chain. It is what it is; a larger sample does not change it. It may be estimated better, but no great change in its magnitude should be expected. The numerator of the *F*-ratio, among-chain mean square, is a different matter.

If the null hypothesis of equal means is true, the differences among the sample means should be small with larger sample sizes. Our data in Table 11.9 indicate just the reverse. The sample size has increased, but the sample means still show large differences. The among-chain mean square is much larger as a result. We now have more confidence in the estimates of the separate means. The resulting *F*-ratio (13.65) is significant at the .01 level. We are confident that the means for the three chains are *not* the same. Interval estimates for the means would reflect this same confidence since the resulting $\overset{*}{\sigma}_{\bar{y}}$ would be smaller.

Measure of Association

The degree of association shows the tendency of variables to vary together. In order to estimate this tendency, we desire an initial estimate of the inherent variableness in the dependent variable. Considering the data in Tables 11.7 and 11.8, the sample variance (in "percentage out of stock") can be computed by dividing the total sum of squares (144.640) by the sample size (15), yielding $s^2 = 9.643$. An unbiased estimate of σ^2 is $\overset{*}{\sigma}{}^2$ obtained by dividing by $n - 1$, yielding $\overset{*}{\sigma}{}^2 = 10.331$. Is this really a good estimate of σ^2? Only if the sample size 15 is a representative sample of the universe.

Several potential difficulties are often present in marketing experiments of this type. Only three chains are involved; these three are unlikely to be representative of the universe of all stores. Therefore, the figure of 10.331 may be biased; and we have no basis for adjusting it. This problem will disappear only if (1) we define the problem as limited to these three chains, or (2) we assume the three chains are representative of all stores.

The sample of 15 may even be unrepresentative of a universe consisting of the three chains. Chain L may be overrepresented while the other two are underrepresented. Only if the researcher is satisfied that $\overset{*}{\sigma}{}^2$ is an appropriate estimate for the correct universe should any summary measure of association be made. The null hypothesis of independence can still be tested, but no measure of association should be presented.

The *correlation ratio* (η) is a general measure of association appropriate for several different techniques. It is based on the initial variance in the dependent variable (calculated from the unconditional distribution) compared with the variance of the conditional distribution. Here η^2 is defined by Eq. (11.4) that is expressed in terms of universe values.

$$\eta^2 = 1 - \frac{\sigma^2(y|x)}{\sigma_y^2} \qquad (11.4)$$

The correlation ratio is the positive square root of this value, and has a lower limit of zero.[16] When only sample values are available, the correlation ratio can be computed using either the corresponding sample variances or unbiased estimates of the population variances.

Using the sample results of Tables 11.7 and 11.8, we have $s^2 = 9.643$ and $s^2(y|x) = 4.794$. Therefore, the sample η is equal to .71.[17]

$$\eta^2 = 1 - \frac{4.794}{9.643} = .5028,$$

$$\eta = .71.$$

The sample η^2 can be interpreted as the percentage reduction in variance by using the conditional distribution instead of the unconditional distribution. Both η and η^2 have a lower limit of zero and an upper limit of unity.[18]

---

[16]Since the independent variable is nominally scaled, the concept of direct or inverse relationship cannot be applied. Therefore, the sign of η is purely arbitrary.

[17]Using unbiased estimates of the population variances, the results are $\eta^2 = 1 - 5.993/10.331 = 1 - .580 = .420$ and $\eta = .65$.

[18]The correlation ratio, η, is analogous to the Phi coefficient. It also serves as a basis for evaluating the linearity assumption in linear regression. See Chapter 12.

The Conditional Distribution

ANOVA imposes no constraints on the general form of the conditional distribution. In this respect, it is similar to contingency table analysis. Since the researcher views the independent variable as nominally scaled, the sequence in which the categories are placed is arbitrary and of no significance. Therefore, the researcher should not construe any particular pattern of the related dependent variables as either appropriate or inappropriate. The calculated values need not conform to any regular sequence or progression. ANOVA allows this freedom in its approach. If some patterns of relationship are acceptable and others are not, the decision maker should specify these conditions in advance.[19]

Point estimates with the conditional distributions introduce no complications, but interval estimates are a potential problem. ANOVA assumes (1) equal variances for all groups and (2) the distribution within each group follows the normal curve. The test of the null hypothesis of independence is not sensitive to departures from these conditions, but the establishment of confidence intervals may be extremely sensitive to departures from them.[20]

As is true in all studies of association, ANOVA tests for association according to the specific definitions employed in the research. The test applies to the enumerated set of categories for the independent variable and to the specific definition employed for the dependent variable. Other definitions or classification schemes might yield different results. And clearly the conditional distribution established has dubious utility in an alternative structuring of the relevant variables.

Care should be exercised in both ANOVA and contingency table analysis to recognize the kinds of statements that have not been subjected to statistical analysis. Neither technique has asked whether the group with the highest (lowest) statistic is significantly higher (lower) than the next ranking group. This is a different, although related, question. Pairwise comparisons of several groups are handled most simply by specifying the pairs to be compared in advance and using the methods developed in Chapter 9.[21]

Groups of Unequal Sizes

The data in Table 11.7 consist of five observations from each of three groups. This design has much to recommend it, but it is rarely obtained if a single simple random sample is selected from the total universe. The data in Table 11.10 represent the more typical case: groups of unequal size.

---

[19]See the section, "Is an Order Implicit?" earlier in this chapter.

[20]See B. J. Winer, 1962, *Statistical Principles in Experimental Design* (New York: McGraw-Hill), pp. 220–222.

[21]For a discussion of other approaches, see Wilfrid J. Dixon and Frank J. Massey, Jr., 1957, *Introduction to Statistical Analysis* (New York: McGraw-Hill), pp. 152–155.

Table 11.10
Salespeople's Earnings† by College Major

	College major			
	Engineering	Business	Other	Total
	26.7	19.6	16.4	
	15.4	24.3	12.5	
	21.3	12.4	19.1	
	28.6	21.4	—	
	—	22.3	—	
Total $\left(\sum\limits^{m} y_{ik}\right)$	92.0	100.0	48.0	240.0
Mean $(\bar{y}_k)$	23.0	20.0	16.0	20.0

†Annual earnings in $1,000

The 12 salespeople of Table 11.10 are classified according to college major: four from engineering, five from business, and three from other fields that are all combined. The sample mean earnings of the three groups are $23,000 for engineers, $20,000 for the business majors, and $16,000 for the "other" category. The grand mean is $20,000. ANOVA calculations are shown in Table 11.11. The only difference between these calculations and those of the previous problem is the unequal weighting applied in determining the among-column (major) sum of squares. Each squared deviation is weighted by the number of observations making up the column mean.

The F-ratio for this problem is 1.79, less than the critical level of 4.26 (with 2 and 9 degrees of freedom and $\alpha = .05$). Therefore the hypothesis that

Table 11.11
Analysis of Variance for Salespeople's Earnings by College Major

Source of variation	Sum of squares	Degrees of freedom	Mean square	F-ratio
Among-major	84.00	2	42.0	1.79 ($P > .05$)
Within-major	211.38	9	23.49	
Total	295.38	11		

Total sum of squares $= (26.7 - 20.0)^2 + \cdots$
$$= 295.38.$$

Within-major sum of squares $= (26.7 - 23.0)^2 + \cdots$
$$= 211.38.$$

Among-major sum of squares $= 4(23.0 - 20.0)^2 + 5(20.0 - 20.0)^2 + 3(16.0 - 20.0)^2$
$$= 84.00.$$

the means are equal should be accepted; the observed sample differences are considered a reflection of natural differences among salespeople rather than a difference associated with college major. Since the hypothesis is accepted, point estimates for the various majors would be inappropriate. An estimate of the degree of association would also be inappropriate since the accepted null hypothesis states that the two variables are not associated.

Overview of ANOVA

Table 11.12 summarizes the key aspects of ANOVA. Similarities and differences between ANOVA and contingency table analysis are highlighted by a comparison with Table 11.6. The similarities are indeed striking. Point estimates may be read from the data table itself, requiring only the calculation of a percentage or a mean. Neither technique imposes any constraints on the form of the conditional distribution. The principal differences are the direct result of the scale employed for the dependent variable. These differences are most apparent in the need for a different test statistic in testing the null hypothesis and a different measure of association. ANOVA requires an F-ratio for the test and uses the correlation ratio (η) for the measure of association.

Table 11.12
Analysis of Variance Summary

1. Test statistic: F-ratio
2. Estimate based on:
   a) Grand mean if H_0 is accepted
   b) Conditional mean if H_0 is rejected
3. Summary of relationship, if any:
   a) Read directly from table
   b) May be irregular jumps
4. Measure of association: Correlation ratio (η)
5. Form of conditional distribution:
   a) No prior specification
   b) No constraints

SUMMARY

Contingency table analysis and the analysis of variance (ANOVA) consider problems in which the independent variable is nominally scaled. Contingency tables are addressed to those situations in which the dependent variable is also nominally scaled, and ANOVA is addressed to those in which the dependent variable is intervally scaled. The first step in each technique is a test of the null hypothesis that there is no association between the two variables. If that null hypothesis is rejected, three additional questions may be considered: (1) point and interval estimates using the conditional distributions, (2) a method of summarizing the relationship between the variables, and (3) a measure of the degree of association.

Contingency table analysis tests the null hypothesis by the Chi Square statistic. ANOVA tests it with an F-ratio. Unique critical levels for both tests depend on the number of degrees of freedom as well as the level of significance. The particular problem, the research design, the sample size, and the decision maker's specifications determine these values in any specific situation.

The most widely used measure of association for contingency tables is the *contingency coefficient* (C). It has a lower limit of zero but a variable upper limit, increasing as the number of cells increases but always less than unity. Consequently, strict comparability of C values is restricted to tables with the same dimensions. C divided by its upper limit permits comparability when the tables are of different dimensions, The Phi coefficient (ϕ) is more similar to other measures of association having a lower limit of -1, and an upper limit of $+1$. It is derived from the percentage reduction in variance approach. However it is restricted to 2×2 tables.

The correlation ratio (η) can be used as a measure of association in ANOVA. Its chief advantage is its comparability with other measures of association. It has a lower limit of zero, an upper limit of unity, and is analogous to the absolute value of (ϕ) or the correlation coefficient (r).

Point estimates for the conditional distributions can be observed directly from the data for both contingency table analysis and ANOVA, in each case corresponding to the sample statistic for each group. Confidence intervals can be established in the same manner as developed in Chapter 7 with one modification. ANOVA assumes that the variances are equal for all groups; having used this assumption in the test of H_0, it is probably better to use a common within-group variance in establishing confidence intervals.

No *a priori* limitations on the form of the conditional distributions are specified in either contingency table analysis or ANOVA. The conditional expected value of the dependent variable is determined by the data; the relationships among the various categories are free to take any form.

The various measures of association rest on the assumption that the sample is representative of the total universe. If this is not true, an unbiased estimate of the degree of association is impossible, although the null hypothesis of no association can be tested. Many marketing problems, particularly with ANOVA, violate this condition. Therefore, the researcher must guard against improper inclusion of these summary measures in reporting results. The researcher must also be conscious that even the null hypothesis is tested according to specific definitions and classification schemes. The results refer to those specifications, not to an association (or lack of association) between the general concepts involved.

EXERCISES AND PROBLEMS

1. Distinguish among the terms within each of the following sets.

   a) The symbols ϕ, C, and η

   b) Degree of association and test of no association

   c) No association and independent

   d) Conditional distribution and unconditional distribution

   e) Variance due to random forces and variance due to other factors

   f) Sum of squares and mean square

2. When is it appropriate to compute the degree of association between the dependent variable and the independent variable

   a) in ANOVA?

   b) in contingency table analysis?

3. What is the difference between the form of the null hypothesis tested in ANOVA and that tested in contingency table analysis?

4. What is meant by "ANOVA does not test for association between the generalized variables but for association between the variables in a specific structure"?

5. A group of 500 women purchasers of Softweave Paper Towels was asked for perceptions of a new product and for certain socioeconomic data. Table E11.5 shows which of three classifications respondents chose as most appropriate for the new product and the marital status of each respondent.

Table E.11.5

Marital status	Classification selected			Total
	Attractive	Absorbent	Rough	
Single	30	40	30	100
Married	45	155	50	250
Widowed	15	35	10	60
Divorced/separated	60	20	10	90
Total	150	250	100	500

   a) Should the table in its present form be analyzed by Chi Square? Why?

   b) Could the data be analyzed by ANOVA? Why?

   c) Would you conclude that there is a relationship between marital status and the classification selected? What, if any, is the nature of the relationship?

   d) What null hypothesis did you test in part (c)?

   e) Would you be justified in estimating the degree of relationship between the two variables? Why?

   f) Compute the degree of association shown by the data within the table. Disregard your answer to part (e) if necessary.

g) State in words the meaning of the value calculated in part (f).

h) Which variable did you select as the independent variable? Why?

6. Fifteen of the women in the study referred to in Exercise 5 played a simulation game. Equal samples were chosen of participants who placed the new product in each of the three classifications. The simulation involved the prices at which they would purchase the new product. The prices are listed in Table E11.6 according to the classification chosen.

Table E.11.6

Attractive	Absorbent	Rough
73	66	64
69	71	69
77	65	63
65	73	66
76	75	63

a) Would you conclude that the participants' opinion of the product influenced the price the participants were willing to pay?

b) Would data of this type ever truly warrant a conclusion that opinion "influenced" another variable? Discuss.

c) A co-worker observed that two classifications were favorable and the third was unfavorable. She suggested that a better question to pose would be whether those with favorable opinions were willing to pay more than those with unfavorable opinions. Would you concur? Why?

d) If it is possible to use the data to answer her question, make that analysis. If it is not possible, explain why it is impossible.

7. A simple random sample of 416 customers of the Accurate Computer Service Bureau were asked to rate the quality and promptness of service received. The customers were served by three different offices. An overall rating was included, and the results are presented in Table E11.7. The offices are identified by the manager's name.

Table E.11.7

Overall rating	Manager			Total
	Davis	Lachman	Peters	
Very good	50	41	35	126
Good	75	73	81	229
Fair or lower	15	18	28	61
Total	140	132	144	416

a) The analyst combined all answers of fair or lower together because "fewer than 20 assigned a rating below fair." Do you think that was wise? Discuss.

b) Using the data within Table E11.7, would you conclude that the three offices received equivalent ratings?

c) Would it be appropriate to assign numerical values of Very good = 1, Good = 2, Fair = 3, Poor = 4, and Very Poor = 5 to the responses and then use ANOVA? Why?

8. A consumer-testing bureau wished to test whether five makes of automobiles averaged the same number of miles per gallon. All five are advertised as "economy" automobiles. A random sample of two cars of each make was selected from each of three different cities. Table E11.8 shows the results of the test.

Table E.11.8

| City | Auto | | | | |
	A	B	C	D	E
Boston	25.3	24.5	27.1	22.6	28.6
	24.8	23.6	28.0	23.3	29.5
Nashville	26.6	25.1	26.0	24.2	22.6
	27.4	24.9	25.1	24.5	23.3
Phoenix	26.0	23.4	28.5	24.1	27.5
	25.4	22.1	27.0	23.5	28.1

a) Is there any good reason to use three cities instead of just one? Discuss.

b) What do you think would be an appropriate way of obtaining a random sample of two cars of a particular make from a specific city?

c) Do the data above indicate that the five makes have the same average?

d) Calculate a 95 percent confidence interval for the mean of automobile C.

e) What assumptions would be necessary in order to use the data in Table E11.8 for estimating the degree of association between gasoline mileage and make of automobile? Do you think these assumptions would be justified? Discuss.

9. A random sample of 175 engineers employed in the computer field was asked to select which of two publications was preferred. Seventy-two of the sample were currently involved in sales while the remainder were not. Of those involved in sales, 40 preferred publication A. Of those not involved in sales, 63 preferred B while the rest preferred A.

a) Would you conclude that preference between publications A and B differed for these two groups?

b) Establish a 90 percent confidence interval for the percentage of nonsales engineers who prefer publication B.

c) Calculate the degree of association between these two variables.

d) Explain in words the meaning of the value calculated in part (c).

10. The sample used in Exercise 9 supplied information concerning the market value of owned residences. One hundred and twelve owned their residence. Of these 112 persons, 45 were engaged in sales and 67 were not. The mean values for the two groups were $79,200 for those engaged in sales and $71,500 for the others.

   a) Supply what you believe to be reasonable estimates of the variances needed for ANOVA.

   b) Test the hypothesis that the mean value of owned residence is equal for the two groups.

   c) Can the sample of 112 be considered a simple random sample of "engineers employed in the computer field who own their residences"? Why?

   d) Assuming the data are valid to use, make an unbiased estimate of the degree of association between sales–nonsales involvement and value of owned residence.

11. A candy-vending machine owner wants to add a new candy bar to the offerings in place of the least popular of the current offerings. Weekly sales figures are given in Table E11.11 for each of the five candy bars currently offered.

Table E11.11

		Candy bar		
B	H	M	R	T
22	37	17	42	25
19	28	20	39	27
26	33	16	45	22
20	30	15	41	24

   a) Should the owner conclude that the five candy bars differ in mean weekly sales?

   b) Express the conditional distribution as an equation.

   c) How would the equation have been different if you had reached the alternative conclusion in part (a)?

   d) Has the analysis provided the answer the owner desired? Discuss.

12. Purchasers of a refrigerator made by a leading manufacturer were offered either the regular warranty at no additional cost or an extended warranty (all parts and labor for five years) at a cost of $75.00. Table E11.12(a) and (b) show the number who selected each alternative, cross-classified with respect to prior refrigerator purchases. Table E11.12(a) simply classifies purchasers according to whether the purchase was an initial purchase. Table E11.12(b) groups those who had purchased refrigerators according to the number of prior purchases (0, 1–2 and 3 or more).

Table E11.12

	Initial purchase	
Type of warranty	Yes	No
Regular	85	65
Extended	15	35

(a)

	Number of prior purchases		
Type of warranty	0	1–2	3 or more
Regular	85	45	20
Extended	15	15	20

(b)

a) Test, using both sets of data, whether type of warranty and prior experience in purchasing refrigerators are associated.

b) Did you arrive at the same conclusion with both sets of data? What would be (are) the implications if you did not? Discuss.

c) Establish a 95 percent confidence interval for the percentage of inital purchasers who select the extended warranty. Is this estimate the same regardless of the table employed? Discuss.

13. The effect of various incentives on mail questionnaire response rates was referred to in Chapter 5. The 1962 phase of the experiment cited in the section entitled "An Experiment with Various Incentives" yielded the data in Table E11.13.

a) Is there sufficient evidence to conclude that there is association between incentive and response rate?

b) Present the conditional distribution for estimating response rate, given incentive.

c) Establish a 95 percent confidence interval for the response rate if a box of taffy were sent with the questionnaire.

d) For what universe would the answer in part (b) be valid? Discuss.

Table E11.13

Incentive	Respondents	Nonrespondents
Taffy sent with questionnaire	77	73
Taffy promised	58	92
Small gift promised	63	87
Raffle	39	111
Thank you	43	107

14. Analyze, criticize, and explain:

a) Neither contingency table analysis nor ANOVA imposes constraints on the form of the conditional distribution. Consequently it is almost impossible to present the distribution by either a graph or an equation.

b) The contingency coefficient (C), like ϕ, has an upper limit of $+1.0$ and a lower limit of -1.0. Its advantage over ϕ is that it can be computed from a table of any size.

c) The degree of association computed from ANOVA is a valid estimate for the population as long as the sample from each subgroup can be considered a simple random sample.

d) Rejection of the null hypothesis tested by a contingency table analysis does not necessarily mean that the modal groups differ for all categories of the independent variables but at least one must be different.

e) The analysis of variance (ANOVA) breaks down total variance into two parts: within treatment and among treatment. If the within-treatment component is large relative to the among-treatment component, one should conclude that the treatments produce different effects. This logic follows because the result shows that the column means are equal. Therefore some other factor, namely differences in treatment effects, must have produced the observed "statistically significant" F-ratio.

f) The correlation ratio (η) is easily computed from the usual summary ANOVA table. The actual calculation requires that square roots of the relevant mean squares be compared. The resulting η must then be squared in order to express the degree of association in terms of percentage reduction in variance.

g) The pattern of differences revealed when either ANOVA or contingency table analysis rejects the null hypothesis must be examined subjectively from a substantive perspective in order for a decision maker to decide whether the results are helpful or merely interesting.

h) The cell values of a contingency table are unbiased estimates of conditional percentages only if the null hypothesis is rejected. If the null hypothesis is accepted, the marginal totals should be employed for all estimates.

CHAPTER 12

REGRESSION AND DISCRIMINANT ANALYSIS
FINER TUNING OF PREDICTIONS

Contingency table analysis and ANOVA are addressed to problems in which the independent variable is nominally scaled, often problems in which the object is to compare specified groups. Many marketing problems, however, are concerned with the effects of independent variables that are intervally scaled. Traffic count has typically been used in evaluating market potential for fast-food operations and gasoline stations. Per capita income and total population have been viewed as key variables in establishing branch department stores. Age has been thought critical in sales of fashion items. Intervally scaled independent variables are involved in all these problems. The same is true if a sales manager wishes to compare sales performance against age, years of experience, or score in a standardized personality test.

A similar situation exists when the groups formed for contingency table analysis or ANOVA conceal large deviations among the units of each group. Age groupings of "Under 30," "30 to 50," and "Over 50" may be treated as nominal, but more precise measurement on an interval scale may permit more detailed analysis. Regression/correlation and discriminant analysis are techniques addressed to these situations, intervally scaled independent variables.

Regression considers problems in which both the independent variable and the dependent variable are intervally scaled. Discriminant analysis considers those situations in which the independent variable is intervally scaled and the dependent variable is nominally scaled. The special case in which the dependent variable is dichotomous can use either technique. While the techniques permit greater precision in the analysis of association, they also require greater specification concerning the form of the relationship envisioned. This trade-off should be carefully considered as the marketing manager defines the problem.

White Paper Company wishes to determine the relationship, if any, between its price and its sales—both measured relative to competition. A series of analyses are desired, one for each of ten products. Price is measured by

White's price per hundred pounds divided by the industry average. Clearly, this variable is at least intervally scaled and probably ratio scaled. Sales are expressed in physical units as a percentage of industry sales. Again, this variable is intervally scaled.[1] Regression analysis is appropriate for the problem as defined. If sales are defined as "Good" or "Poor," the dependent variable is now nominal. With just two categories either a regression or a discriminant approach would be possible. If more than two nominal categories are established (for example, "good," "average," and "poor"), discriminant analysis is the proper approach.[2] We shall consider each of these techniques in this chapter, starting with regression—probably the most widely used of all analytic models of association.

REGRESSION

Most students have been exposed to simple two variable linear regression at some point in their careers. We will assume some familiarity with the basic concepts and stress its use and interpretation in the present chapter: improving decision making by the introduction of associations between variables.[3] The general problem is illustrated in Table 12.1 and Fig. 12.1 that refer to the same

Table 12.1
Sales of Mills & Jones Company and Published Buying Index for Each of Eight Areas

Area	(y) Unit sales (1,000's)	(x) Buying index
1	22	45
2	48	62
3	25	38
4	31	51
5	58	72
6	36	43
7	41	59
8	43	65
Total	304	435

[1]Data were gathered for each of 27 geographic regions. Thus the units of analysis were the regions.

[2]If the researcher is willing to consider "good," "average," and "poor" as the equivalent of three equally spaced positions on an interval scale, regression would be appropriate.

[3]The student who has not been exposed to regression techniques in another course is referred to any standard statistical text. For example, Morris Hamburg, 1970, *Statistical Analysis for Decision Making* (New York: Harcourt, Brace and World); or Richard C. Clelland, John S. deCani, and Francis E. Brown, 1973, *Basic Statistics with Business Applications* (New York: Wiley).

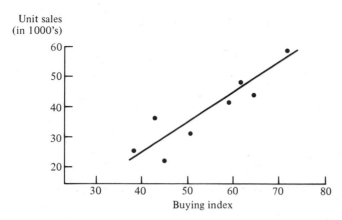

Fig. 12.1
Sales of Mills & Jones Company and published buying index
for each of eight areas.

data: Mills & Jones Company sales and a published "buying index" for each
of eight metropolitan areas.

   Figure 12.1 is called a *scatter diagram* since it shows the way in which the
observations are "scattered." The task of regression is to place a line on Fig.
12.1—a line that will summarize the relationship between company sales and
the buying index. Inspection of the chart reveals that the two variables seem to
vary together; high (low) values of one variable seem to be associated with high
(low) values of the other. This suggests a line starting in the lower left corner
and rising to the upper right corner. Such a line has been placed on the chart,
but why this line? Is it "better" than other possible lines? If yes, "better" in
what sense? Is there a "best" line?

   The line we are searching for is a line that states the conditional distribution of company sales, given the buying index. The buying index is the independent variable because the company wants to know whether it is a good
basis for (1) predicting probable sales levels in various metropolitan areas and
(2) evaluating the sales levels achieved in selected areas. If there is no relationship, there is no reason to make different estimates for different buying
indices. The mean of 38,000 (304,000/8) should be used for all estimates.

The Regression Equation

The line of Fig. 12.1 is of the general form of Eq. (12.1).

$$E(y_i) = a + bx_i; \qquad \text{both } x_i \text{ and } y_i \text{ intervally scaled.} \qquad (12.1)$$

In the same way that the analysis of variance gives different estimates for the
dependent variable depending on the values of the independent variable,
regression yields different estimates of the dependent variable, again depend-

ing on the values of the independent variable. The only difference is that in one case the independent variable is nominally scaled and in the other case the independent variable is intervally scaled.

Simple two variable linear regression, as the name implies, assumes that a straight line is a satisfactory way of summarizing the relationship between the two variables. If it is not, some other form should be employed. For the present we shall limit our consideration to linear relations.

The concept of a "best" line suggests a line that "fits" the data in the scatter diagram: one that is "close to" the observations. The distance between the points in the scatter diagram and the line should be as small as possible. Regression applies the criterion of least squares; that is, the line is drawn so that the sum of the squared deviations is a minimum. The line satisfying this condition is found by solving the system shown by Eq. (12.2) for the two constants a and b.[4]

$$\Sigma y = na + b\Sigma x,$$
$$\Sigma xy = a\Sigma x + b\Sigma x^2. \tag{12.2}$$

The procedure can be illustrated with the data in Table 12.1 that is reproduced along with the necessary calculations as Table 12.2. The constants of the regression equation may be obtained by solving Eq. (12.2) or Eq. (12.3) and (12.4) which have been derived from Eq. (12.2).

$$b = (\Sigma xy - n\bar{x}\bar{y})/(\Sigma x^2 - n\bar{x}^2), \tag{12.3}$$
$$a = \bar{y} - b\bar{x}. \tag{12.4}$$

Both calculations are shown in Table 12.2 and result in the following equation:

$$E(y|x) = -11.2148 + .9051x.$$

The Regression Coefficient

We should test the null hypothesis of no association before using this equation to make estimates. We should make different estimates of sales for different buying indices only if the two variables are associated. Otherwise the mean value, (38,000 units), should be used for all estimates. In the absence of association, the appropriate equation would be a horizontal line given by

$$E(y|x) = 38.0.$$

In this equation, $b = 0$.

What is the meaning of b? The term b is known as the *regression coefficient;* it determines the slope or incline of the line. The larger its value, the

---

[4]These equations are established by defining the deviation of an observation from the regression line as $y - (a + bx)$, squaring this value, and adding all similarly defined squared deviations for all observations. Two partial derivatives are taken, one with respect to a and one with respect to b. These partial derivatives are set equal to 0 and solved.

Table 12.2
Linear Regression Analysis for Mills & Jones Sales and Published Buying Index

Area	(y) Unit sales (1,000's)	(x) Buying index	(xy)	(y^2)	(x^2)
1	22	45	990	484	2025
2	48	62	2976	2304	3844
3	25	38	950	625	1444
4	31	51	1581	961	2601
5	58	72	4176	3364	5184
6	36	43	1548	1296	1849
7	41	59	2419	1681	3481
8	43	65	2795	1849	4225
Total	304	435	17435	12564	24653

Solution by Eq. (12.2):

$$304 = 8a + 435b,$$
$$17435 = 435a + 24653b,$$
$$304(435) = 8(435)a + (435)^2 b,$$
$$17435(8) = 435(8)a + 24653(8)b,$$
$$304(435) - 17435(8) = (435)^2 b - 24653(8)b,$$
$$132240 - 139480 = 189225b - 197224b.$$
$$b = \frac{-7240}{-7999}$$
$$= .9051,$$
$$a = -11.2148.$$

Solution by Eqs. (12.3) and (12.4):

$$b = \frac{17435 - 8(54.375)(38)}{24653 - 8(54.375)^2}$$
$$= .9051.$$
$$a = 38 - .9051(54.375)$$
$$= -11.2148.$$

$E(y|x) = -11.2148 + .9051x.$

greater the slope. It tells the rate of change in sales per unit change in the buying index. If the result of .9051 should be used, what would it mean?

Consider two estimates, one for a buying index of 50 and one for a buying index of 51. The sales estimates are

$$E(y|x = 50) = -11.2148 + .9051(50) = 34.0402.$$
$$E(y|x = 51) = -11.2148 + .9051(51) = 34.9453.$$

They differ by the regression coefficient (.9051). The estimate of sales is increased by 905.1 units (since y is in 1,000's of units) for each increase of one point in the buying index. The regression coefficient also establishes the *average* relationship observed within the sample. It does not mean that two areas have buying indices that differ by one point will differ in unit sales by 905.1 units; it means that the average difference between two such areas is 905.1 in unit sales. In fact, there are instances in which an area with a higher buying index will have lower sales; compare Area 1 and Area 3.

The null hypothesis (no association) is the equivalent of

$$H_0 : \beta = 0$$

where β is the universe regression coefficient. This hypothesis is tested in precisely the same manner as other hypotheses we have considered. The discrepancy between the hypothesized value and the sample value is compared to the standard error of the random sampling distribution where the null hypothesis is true. We are thus asking how much dispersion exists among sample regression coefficients when $\beta = 0$. The required standard error is designated as σ_b, and an unbiased estimate of it is given by Eq. (12.5).

$$\overset{*}{\sigma}_b = \frac{\overset{*}{\sigma}(y|x)}{(\overset{*}{\sigma}_x)(n - 1)^{\frac{1}{2}}}. \tag{12.5}$$

The numerator of Eq. (12.5) is an unbiased estimate of the universe conditional standard deviation. The denominator consists of two terms: an unbiased estimate of the standard deviation of the independent variable and $(n - 1)^{\frac{1}{2}}$ where n is the sample size. Before we can test $\beta = 0$, numerical values for (12.5) must be obtained.

The Conditional Standard Deviation

The conditional standard deviation is the measure of dispersion around the regression line. It is calculated by comparing actual unit sales of the various areas with predicted sales for an area with the same buying index. For example, unit sales of Area 1 are compared with predicted sales for an area with a buying index of 45. In general terms, y_i is compared with $E(y|x_i)$. For Area 1, sales of 22 are compared with predicted sales of 29.5—a difference of 7.5. Since we are interested in a standard deviation, the deviation must be squared (56.25).

Similar calculations are made for each of the eight observations, with the conditional variance defined by Eq. (12.6).[5]

$$s^2(y|x) = \overset{n}{\underset{}{\Sigma}}\left(y_i - E(y|x_i)\right)^2/n. \tag{12.6}$$

The calculations are shown in Table 12.3. The term $\overset{*}{\sigma}^2(y|x)$ is similar in concept but divided by the number of degrees of freedom in order to achieve an

---

[5]An alternative formula for the calculation of $s^2(y|x)$ is given by $(\Sigma y^2 - a\Sigma y - b\Sigma xy)/n$. This formula is derived from Eq. (12.6) but avoids the cumbersome decimal calculations and the potential rounding problems. The result, using the alternative formula, is 5.67 for the Mills & Jones problem while Eq. (12.6) yields 5.65 as calculated in Table 12.3.

Table 12.3
Deviation of Mills & Jones Sales from Predicted Sales

Area	(y) Unit sales (1,000's)	(x) Buying index	Predicted sales	Deviation	(Deviation)^2
1	22	45	29.5	−7.5	56.25
2	48	62	44.9	3.1	9.61
3	25	38	23.2	1.8	3.24
4	31	51	34.9	−3.9	15.21
5	58	72	54.0	4.0	16.00
6	36	43	27.7	8.3	68.89
7	41	59	42.2	−1.2	1.44
8	43	65	47.6	−4.6	21.16
				0.0	191.80

$s^2(y|x) = \Sigma(\text{Deviation})^2 \div n = 191.80 \div 8 = 23.975,$

$s(y|x) = 4.90,$

$\overset{*}{\sigma}{}^2(y|x) = 191.80 \div 6 = 31.9667,$

$\overset{*}{\sigma}(y|x) = 5.65.$

unbiased estimate of the universe conditional variance.[6] The formula for bivariate linear regression is given by Eq. (12.7).

$$\overset{*}{\sigma}{}^2(y|x) = \overset{n}{\Sigma}\left(y_i - E(y|x)\right)^2/(n - 2). \qquad (12.7)$$

As shown in Table 12.3, $\overset{*}{\sigma}{}^2(y|x)$ equals 31.9667, and $\overset{*}{\sigma}(y|x)$ equals 5.65. In what units are they expressed? The term $\overset{*}{\sigma}(y|x)$ is always in the same units as the dependent variable; this follows because it measures the dispersion between actual and predicted values of the dependent variable. For the present data, 5.65 is sales in 1,000's of units. Therefore, the estimated conditional standard deviation is 5,650 units. The conditional variance does not convey as much meaning to our understanding; it is approximately 32 million units squared, hardly a concept that would be helpful to a marketing manager.[7]

The term "standard error of estimate" is often applied to the conditional standard deviation. This terminology is unfortunate because it is not a stan-

---

[6]The number of degrees of freedom in regression is equal to the number of observations minus the number of constants in the regression equation: $n - 2$ in the present case.

[7]The interpretations of $s^2(y|x)$ and $s(y|x)$ are similar to $\overset{*}{\sigma}{}^2(y|x)$ and $\overset{*}{\sigma}(y|x)$ with the exception that they measure the dispersion within the sample instead of providing unbiased estimates of the dispersion in the universe.

dard error in the usual sense. It is not a measure of the dispersion in a random sampling distribution; it is a measure of dispersion among individual units.

We shall return to the conditional standard deviation for several aspects of our study of regression; for example, confidence interval estimation and determination of the degree of association. Before continuing with those matters, let us return to the null hypothesis of $\beta = 0$.

The Test of No Association

Equation (12.5) can now be solved for $\overset{*}{\sigma}_b$. Substituting the appropriate estimates of $\overset{*}{\sigma}(y|x)$ and $\overset{*}{\sigma}_x$, we have

$$\overset{*}{\sigma}_b = \frac{5.65}{(11.95)\,(7)^{1/2}} = .179.$$

The observed b-value is .905. The test is performed by $|b - \beta| \div \overset{*}{\sigma}_b$ using the t-distribution. Since β has been specified as 0 in the null hypothesis, the test reduces to $|b| \div \overset{*}{\sigma}_b$.

$$\frac{.905}{.179} = 5.06.$$

The observed regression coefficient is over five times its own standard error, more than enough to reject the null hypothesis. Sales and buying index vary together; in this problem we conclude the two variables are positively related because the regression coefficient has a positive sign. Having concluded that the variables are associated, we may now use the regression equation as a basis for estimating sales in areas other than the eight in the sample.

Estimation with Regression

Point estimates of sales come directly from the regression equation. The predicted sales values given in Table 12.3 were each determined from the equation by substituting the appropriate buying index. Interval estimates are based on the equation plus the conditional standard deviation. We wish to consider two different types of interval estimates: (1) a particular metropolitan area with a known buying index and (2) the arithmetic mean sales for areas with the same buying index.

What is the best estimate of sales for an area with a buying index of 40?

$$E(y|x) = -11.2148 + .9051(40)$$
$$= 24.99.$$

The best estimate is 25,000 units. What is the best estimate of the mean sales for all areas with buying indices of 40? This is an estimate of a population mean. The answer is the same: 25,000 units. We have accepted the regression line as the best estimate of the average relationship between units sales and the buying index.

The manager of Mills & Jones is suspicious of the omniscient ring of a single number and asks for an interval, first for a particular area that has a buying index of 40. The procedure depends on a few assumptions. Unless we know the form of the distribution around the regression line and the amount of dispersion in that distribution, we cannot provide the requested estimate. Linear regression assumes (1) the distribution of observations around the regression line follows the normal curve and (2) the standard deviation around the regression line is constant, not varying with different values of the independent variable.

The first assumption—a normal distribution—leads to the use of a t-distribution. Recall that a t-distribution is appropriate when the population distribution is normal and the standard deviation is estimated from sample evidence. The second assumption says that the same conditional standard deviation may be used for all estimates; the proper one to use does not depend on the value of the independent variable. Thus regression assumes homoscedasticity, as did ANOVA.

Putting this all together we may now estimate a 95 percent confidence interval for sales in an area with a buying index of 40. It follows the general form of Eq. (12.8).

$$E(y|x) + t\overset{*}{\sigma}(y|x). \tag{12.8}$$

Our problem has six degrees of freedom; therefore $t = 2.45$ (at 95 percent confidence). The resulting interval is

$$24.99 \pm 2.45(5.65),$$
$$24.99 \pm 13.84,$$
$$11.15 \text{ to } 38.83.$$

The 95 percent confidence interval for an area with a buying index of 40 is 11,150 to 38,830 units. This is a rather wide range; what can be done to narrow it?

Let us examine the separate components. Perhaps they can indicate a way to reduce the size of the interval. $E(y|x)$, the point estimate, does not influence the size of the interval. Therefore, we must examine $t\overset{*}{\sigma}(y|x)$. The t-coefficient is generated by the confidence level and the number of degrees of freedom. The confidence level is set by the decision maker and the researcher. A lower level of confidence will produce a smaller interval, but it hardly accomplishes the desired objective. More degrees of freedom would have some impact on the value of t, and more degrees of freedom would be achieved with a larger sample. Depending on how much larger the sample was, an increase in sample size might decrease the width of the interval by 10 to 20 percent. The resulting decrease would be welcome, but it would still leave much uncertainty. What of $\overset{*}{\sigma}(y|x)$? It is an unbiased estimate of the true amount of dispersion. A larger sample would yield a different $\overset{*}{\sigma}(y|x)$, but there is no *a priori* reason to expect the new $\overset{*}{\sigma}(y|x)$ is any more likely to be smaller than to be larger. The resulting interval for the most part reflects how "good" our estimates are when we predict Mills & Jones sales from the buying index. Very little can be done to reduce its size. Only a larger sample is likely to reduce the size of the interval, and the effectiveness of that strategy quickly diminishes.

Does the arithmetic result above also apply to a 95 percent confidence estimate for the *mean* of areas with a buying index of 40? Most certainly not! There is less dispersion in a random sampling distribution of means than there is in the population distribution of elements. Our question now takes the form of Eq. (12.9).

$$E(\bar{y}|x) \pm t\overset{*}{\sigma}_{(\bar{y}|x)}. \tag{12.9}$$

The symbols may look different, but the concepts are familiar. A conditional mean and the standard error of a conditional mean have replaced a simple unconditional mean and its standard error.

We have already determined the conditional mean when the buying index is 40. This value is 24.99. The conditional standard error of the mean is given by Eq. (12.10).

$$\overset{*}{\sigma}_{(\bar{y}|x)} = \frac{\overset{*}{\sigma}(y|x)}{n^{\frac{1}{2}}}. \tag{12.10}$$

Since the sample size is eight,

$$\overset{*}{\sigma}_{(\bar{y}|x)} = \frac{5.65}{(8)^{\frac{1}{2}}} = 2.00.$$

The 95 percent confidence interval for the mean, given a buying index of 40, is

$$24.99 \pm 2.45(2.00),$$

$$24.99 \pm 4.9,$$

$$20.09 \text{ to } 29.89.$$

The range in units is 20,090 to 29,890. This is a much smaller interval than we found for estimating sales for a particular area—not an unexpected result.

Another difference should be noted between the confidence interval for a conditional mean and the confidence interval for the estimate of a particular area. The confidence interval established for the mean varies with the sample size. If the sample size increases, the width of the interval will decrease. This principle is equally true regardless of whether unconditional or conditional means are involved. The confidence interval for individual units varies little as sample size increases beyond ten or twenty.[8]

The *Y*-intercept

What interpretation can we place on the *a*-value of the regression equation? If we rely blindly on the arithmetic implicit in the equation, we come up with a

---

[8] The small gain is evident by inspection of the coefficients given in Appendix Table A.3.

rather strange statement: "A metropolitan area with a buying index of 0 would be expected to sell minus 11,200 units." We trust that this statement illustrates that caution must be employed in attempting to interpret the a-coefficient. This value is simply what geometry identifies as the Y-intercept. For most regression problems, the Y-intercept will be an extrapolated value, that is, a calculation generated by a value for the independent variable that is not within the range of the sample data. Prediction is hazardous enough when limited to the range of the data. In our data, the buying index has a high of 72 and a low of 38. Use of the equation beyond that range assumes that the regression line embodies the true functional relationship. In many practical applications, the line describes the data and no more. In that situation, predictions should be limited to the range within the sample; extrapolation is not warranted. This is true whether the extrapolated result seems reasonable or not.

Suppose a linear regression is established between total costs and volume of production, resulting in the following equation.

$$E(y|x) = 22 + .035x,$$

x is a number of units produced,

y is total cost in $100.

What does $a = 22$ tell us? If we rely on a straight arithmetic approach, we might be tempted to estimate that fixed costs at zero production would be $2,200. That approach assumes that variable costs are constant per unit, regardless of the level of operation. Typically the level of operation covered in such a study would have a rather limited range. A linear relationship might be appropriate within the range covered but dubious outside of that range. A better procedure is to refrain from extrapolation. Fixed costs might be much higher with small incremental cost between zero and some minimum level of production. Alternatively, fixed costs might be much lower; almost all costs might disappear at zero production. Since we don't know, it is better not to place a managerial interpretation on the Y-intercept.

Standardized Regression Coefficients

The regression coefficient of .9051 is uniquely dependent on the units chosen for the independent and dependent variables. A switch in the unit of measure for either one or both of the variables would lead to a different numerical result. As long as the researcher and decision maker are careful in the interpretation of the result and in presenting it to others, no harm is likely to occur. However, the "gee whiz" reaction to very large or very small coefficients is sometimes tempting. Alternatively, it is sometimes tempting to compare regression coefficients derived from several different independent variables.[9]

[9]These regression coefficients may be derived from separate bivariate regressions or from a single multivariate regression. The problem is similar regardless of which analysis gives rise to it. We shall give particular attention to the multivariate case in Chapter 13.

As long as the selection of the units is arbitrary, a comparison of coefficients may mislead since the result is likewise arbitrary.

The standardized regression coefficient is an attempt to overcome the influence of arbitrary units. In this approach variables are expressed in terms of standard scores. Sales of 22,000 units for Area 1 are recalculated to a value of -1.42. This value is obtained by dividing: $(22 - 38)/11.25$ since $s_y = 11.25$. Area 1 is 1.42 standard deviations below the mean in sales. A similar calculation with regard to the buying index variable shows that Area 1 has a standard score of $-.73$ on that variable. If a new regression equation is determined using standard scores instead of the original variables, a new regression coefficient will be determined. This coefficient is not dependent on the arbitrary units employed for the initial measurement of the variables. It has been "freed" from the initial units by standardization, and the resulting regression coefficient is a *standardized regression coefficient*. The use of standard scores also removes the temptation to interpret an extrapolated Y-intercept since the Y-intercept is always equal to zero.

Applying the standardization technique to the Mills & Jones data yields $E(y_s|x_s) = .9x_s$ where y_s and x_s represent the initial variables transformed into standard scores. The interpretation of the .9 coefficient is that, on the average, two areas that differ by one standard deviation in buying index differ by .9 standard deviation in unit sales. The difference is in the same direction since the sign of the coefficient is positive. The Y-intercept of zero means that an area with a mean buying index is expected to have mean unit sales.

This numerical result also permits comparison with standardized regression coefficients from other studies. For example, a standardized regression coefficient of $+.7$ between unit sales and population would indicate a smaller impact for population than for the buying index. Comparison of the $+.9051$ with an unstandardized $+27.62$ would be meaningless without a lot of mental manipulations that tried to "equate" the units of the buying index and population. (The comparison of regression coefficients is even more important in multiple regression, which is covered in Chapter 13.)

The Coefficient of Determination

The most common way of measuring association between two intervally scaled variables is with the coefficient of determination (r^2).[10] This coefficient measures the percentage reduction accomplished by measuring variance around the regression line instead of measuring it around the mean of the dependent variable.

The concept is illustrated by Fig. 12.2. Part (a) of the figure shows dispersion of the observations from the mean of the dependent variable. Part (b) shows the regression line and the dispersion from this line. In general the

---

[10]As will be explained later in this chapter, the calculation of r^2 is justified only when a simple random sample has been selected from the universe.

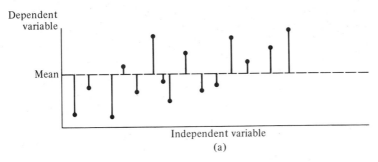

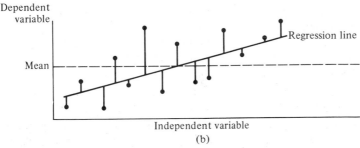

Fig. 12.2
Graphic representation of variance about mean and variance about regression line; (a) deviations from mean, (b) deviations from regression line.

deviations are smaller in Part (b) than they are in Part (a) although there are specific instances in which this is not true. The term, r^2, expresses the percentage reduction in variance in the sample rather than estimating that reduction in the universe. Both variances are computed as the average squared deviation for the sample elements—using n as the denominator rather than the number of degrees of freedom. These concepts are incorporated in Eq. (12.11).[11]

$$r^2 = \frac{s_y^2 - s^2(y|x)}{s_y^2}. \tag{12.11}$$

The calculation of r^2 for the Mills & Jones problem is shown in Table 12.4. Variance in the unconditional distribution of unit sales (in 1,000's) establishes the base from which r^2 is computed. This total variance is 126.5. The coefficient of determination breaks this total into two components that have been identified as the "explained variance" and the "unexplained variance." The unexplained variance is that portion that the regression line has failed to

---

[11]The universe coefficient of determination is designated by the symbol ρ^2 and its unbiased estimate is designated by $\overset{*}{\rho}{}^2$. The expressions σ_y^2 and $\sigma^2(y|x)$ are used in calculating ρ^2; $\overset{*}{\sigma}_y^2$ and $\overset{*}{\sigma}{}^2(y|x)$ are used in calculating $\overset{*}{\rho}{}^2$.

Table 12.4
Calculation of the Coefficient of Determination. Mills & Jones Sales and Published Buying Index

Area	(y) Unit sales (1,000's)	$(y - \bar{y})^2$	$E(y\|x)$ Predicted sales	$y - E(y\|x)$	$(y - E(y\|x))^2$
1	22	256.0	29.5	-7.5	56.25
2	48	100.0	44.9	3.1	9.61
3	25	169.0	23.2	1.8	3.24
4	31	49.0	34.9	-3.9	15.21
5	58	400.0	54.0	4.0	16.00
6	36	4.0	27.7	8.3	68.89
7	41	9.0	42.2	-1.2	1.44
8	43	25.0	47.6	-4.6	21.16
		1012.0		0.0	191.80

$$s_y^2 = \frac{1012.0}{8} = 126.5 \qquad \text{(Total variance).}$$

$$s^2(y|x) = \frac{191.80}{8} = 23.975 \qquad \text{(Unexplained variance).}$$

$$102.525 \qquad \text{(Explained variance).}$$

$$r^2 = \frac{126.5 - 23.975}{126.5} = .81.$$

remove. Perfect predictions have not been achieved; a portion of the variance remains "unexplained." The explained variance is the portion that has been removed or "explained" by computing variance from the regression line instead of the mean line. With this terminology, r^2 is equal to the explained variance divided by the total variance. It has an upper limit of 1.0 (100 percent) and a lower limit of 0.0 (0 percent). The data in Table 12.4 yield an r^2 value of .81 or 81 percent, reflecting a substantial degree of correlation.[12]

The coefficient of correlation (r) is calculated by the following rather complicated equation.

$$r = \left(r^2\right)^{\frac{1}{2}}. \tag{12.12}$$

Since r takes the sign of the regression coefficient, r for the present problem is equal to $+.90$. There are other forms for the calculation of r, but Eq. (12.12) is presented in order to stress its interpretation—it is simply the square root of a percentage. The result of $+.90$ for the present problem means that the square root of the reduction in variance is equal to $.90$.[13]

---

[12]The unbiased estimate of the universe coefficient of determination $\hat{\rho}^2$ is .78.

[13]Note that r is also equal to the regression coefficient obtained if both variables are transformed into standard scores.

Finally, marketing researchers often wish to test the hypothesis that r and r^2 are equal to 0. The actual test is made in terms of r, and follows the familiar procedure of comparing a sample statistic with the standard error of that statistic. In this case, the sample r-value is compared to its standard error. The formula for the standard error is given by Eq. (12.13).

$$\overset{*}{\sigma}_r = (1 - r^2)^{1/2} \div (n - 2)^{1/2}. \tag{12.13}$$

The calculations for testing our null hypothesis are the following:

$$t = \frac{r}{\overset{*}{\sigma}_r} = \frac{.90}{(.19 \div 6)^{1/2}} = \frac{.90}{(.0317)^{1/2}} = \frac{.90}{.18} = 5.0.$$

The observed sample correlation is significantly different from 0, and we may conclude that the two variables are correlated in the universe.[14] The tests of $\rho = 0$ and $\beta = 0$ are equivalent tests. Any differences in the test ratios are purely the result of rounding.[15]

Yet another equivalent test uses an F-ratio based on the comparison between unbiased estimates of "explained" and "unexplained" variance. As we have already discussed, the "unexplained" variance is the measure of dispersion around the regression line. The unbiased estimate of unexplained variance is obtained by dividing the sum of squared deviations by the number of degrees of freedom ($n - 2$ for linear bivariate regression). The "explained" variance is the difference between the total and "unexplained" dispersion, again computed by dividing by the number of degrees of freedom (1 for linear bivariate regression). For the data in Table 12.4 the calculation is made as follows:

$$F = \frac{102.525}{1} \div \frac{23.975}{6}$$

$$= \frac{102.525}{3.996}$$

$$= 25.66.$$

This result again demonstrates that the null hypothesis should be rejected.

The Linearity Assumption

True relationships between variables need not be linear. The determination of a regression line by Eqs. (12.2) to (12.4) forces a linear relationship on the data. Nonlinear relationships may be handled in any of three ways. (1) A linear

---

[14]The test as performed in this example is appropriate only for the hypothesis that the universe coefficient of correlation is equal to 0. For other values more complex tests with transformations are required. See Wilfrid J. Dixon and Frank J. Massey, Jr., 1957, *Introduction to Statistical Analysis* (New York: McGraw-Hill), pp. 200–201.

[15]Although the two tests are redundant in bivariate problems, each plays a distinct role in multivariate problems. See Chapter 13.

relationship may be employed as an "acceptable" approximation to the true relationship. (2) The data may be transformed so that the relationship after transformation is linear. For example, if one believes there is a constant relationship between the percentage change of the independent variable and the percentage change of the dependent variable, logarithmic transformations on both variables will permit the use of a linear function. Demand curves between selling price and quantity sold often employ this type of transformation. (3) The specified functional form employed may be nonlinear; for example, a parabola or an S-type growth curve.

The possibility of nonlinear relationships introduces an important qualification to the null hypothesis tested in linear regression. It is a test of "no linear association." Here $\beta = 0$ (or $\rho = 0$) could be accepted when a nonlinear relationship exists. Even when the null hypothesis is rejected, there is no assurance that a nonlinear relationship may not yield a better description of the relationship and better predictions.

Three approaches for checking the linearity assumption are possible: (1) a logical/theoretical approach in specifying the functional form, (2) inspection of the scatter diagram, and (3) a test against the correlation ratio (η). The first approach requires specification by the decision maker and researcher before the fact. Unlike the conditional distributions of ANOVA and contingency tables in which both the form and the parameter estimates are determined by the data, only the parameter estimates are determined by the data in regression. Nonlinear forms are possible with regression, but they must be specified by the analyst. These specifications are incorporated in the equations employed; use of Eq. (12.2) or (12.3) and (12.4) cannot yield a nonlinear conditional distribution.[16]

Inspection of the scatter diagram is a highly subjective approach and may undermine some of the probability statements possible. This approach has certain similarities to "letting the data decide" the functional form. The difficulty is that any number of reversals, accelerations, and decelerations become possible. The split-half method—determining the form with half the data and testing it on the other half—introduces safeguards against rationalizing whatever pattern appears.

The correlation ratio (η) offers a more explicit test of linearity. This approach compares r of a linear expression with η calculated by establishing several subgroups within the sample. The subgroups are established by subdividing the independent variable into classes—thus it is similar to ANOVA. The correlation ratio, η, cannot be less than r; their comparison serves as a test of linearity.[17]

---

[16]Specific nonlinear forms will be considered in Chapter 14.

[17]See Palmer O. Johnson and Robert W. B. Jackson, 1959, *Modern Statistical Methods: Descriptive and Inductive* (Chicago: Rand McNally), pp. 339–348 for the specific test. The statement "η cannot be less than r" is of practical significance only with grouped data and assumes that the same class intervals are used in both calculations.

Our earlier cautions concerning extrapolation stem from the fear that a linear equation is a satisfactory *approximation* of the true relationship, but only within a limited range. As the values of the independent variable deviate farther from the sample values, the analyst may think that the linearity assumption is no longer a satisfactory approximation.

Residuals

Column 5 of Table 12.4 shows the error in prediction for each area. The pattern displayed by these errors or "residuals" can sometimes be informative. Regression assumes that the residuals are distributed normally for both (1) any particular value of the independent variable and (2) the total distribution around the regression line. Since the least-squares criterion forces a balancing of positive and negative deviations, the fact that the column sums to zero does not convey any extra information.

Examination of the residuals often suggests additional variables that might improve the manager's understanding of the forces at work. Area 1 has the largest negative residual, and Area 6 has the largest positive residual. They have very similar buying indices but dissimilar sales. Area 6 has a high proportion of light industry while Area 1 contains a number of large manufacturers of industrial equipment. Study of the residuals for the remaining six areas does not seem to fit a light/heavy pattern, but the sample size is rather small to expect any firm indications.

Area-by-area comparison of the characteristics of the regional managers and the residuals is another possibility. This approach implies that the regression equation might be used as a standard in judging performance. This might be extended even further by establishing a band around the regression line —perhaps ± 1.5 conditional standard deviations or some other preselected figure. Observations falling outside of the band established could then be identified as unusually high or unusually low.

Finally the residuals might be examined sequentially. This is particularly appropriate with time-series data but can be considered in any analysis. The underlying motivation for examining the data from this perspective is to check whether the timing of observations contributes a separate force of its own.

Regression versus Correlation

The terms regression and correlation are often used interchangeably, but to do this is technically incorrect. The distinction arises in how the sample units are selected. In correlation, a simple random sample of the universe of interest is selected; thus the sample could be used as a basis for making inferences about either the independent variable or the dependent variable. In regression, the appropriate values for the independent variable are selected by the researcher.

The values chosen in regression may be designed to cover a broad range, for example, cities that differ greatly in per capita income. Such a sample would not permit valid inferences of either variable. The sample is selected in order to study relationships and is inappropriate for the study of either variable separately. The focus of interest is the conditional distribution. The sample unconditional distributions should not be accepted as valid estimates of the universe.

Marketing experiments are more likely to be regression problems than to be correlation problems. The marketing manager selects a few different values for some element of the marketing mix within his or her control in order to examine how sales or profits vary as he or she makes the specified changes in these elements. Even historical studies of the "effects" of various elements in the marketing mix contain the regression concept. The values of the independent variable represent conscious decisions by the marketing manager, not a random selection from some existing universe.

The distinction between regression and correlation is not just for status in precision of terminology. The coefficient of determination (r^2) and the coefficient of correlation (r) should not be calculated in a regression problem, but they are perfectly appropriate in a correlation problem. The reason for this is that the denominator of r^2 is the variance in the dependent variable, a value that cannot be determined in regression because we do not have a random sample from the universe with respect to that variable. If the variance with respect to the dependent variable is calculated in a regression problem, it may be a gross understatement or overstatement of the corresponding universe value depending on the values of the independent variable specified for the experiment.

Overview of Linear Regression/Correlation

Table 12.5 gives a summary of regression/correlation analysis. The test of the "no association" hypothesis may be made either with a t-statistic against the sample regression coefficient or with an F-ratio in terms of variance reduction.

Table 12.5
Linear Bivariate Regression/Correlation Analysis Summary

1. Test statistic: $t = b/\overset{*}{\sigma}_b$ or F-ratio
2. Estimate based on:
   a) Grand mean if H_0 is accepted
   b) Mathematical linear equation if H_0 is rejected
3. Summary of relationship, if any:
   a) Regression equation for total relationship—extrapolation dilemma
   b) Regression coefficient for incremental relationship
4. Measure of association: Coefficient of determination (r^2)
5. Form of conditional distribution:
   a) Prior specification
   b) Linear: $y = a + bx$
6. Criterion for "best" equation: minimization of squared deviations

If the null hypothesis is rejected, estimates of the dependent variable and the summary of the relationship are based on a mathematically derived linear equation of the form $y = a + bx$. This form is imposed on the data and not determined by it. The minimization of squared deviations—the least-squares criterion—is employed in choosing the line of best fit. The degree of association is measured by the coefficient of determination (r^2)—a measure of the percentage reduction in variance.

DISCRIMINANT ANALYSIS

Do "heavy" users and "light" users of our product differ in some other characteristics? Is income a good predictor of this user status? TV viewing can be analyzed in a similar manner. Does amount of formal education discriminate between viewers and nonviewers of educational TV? Favorite brand or preferred supplier can be approached by the same technique. Is size of operation a valid basis for classifying the supply source used most often? All of these questions fall into the category of "intervally scaled independent variable and nominally scaled dependent variable." Discriminant analysis is the appropriate technique for analyzing such problems.

A nominally scaled variable that has only two categories—high versus low, yes versus no, young versus old, A versus B, etc.—is a special case that differs in an important way from the situation in which there are more than two categories. In the case of two categories, a scale with two endpoints can be employed without violating the nominal scale concept. This can be seen in Fig. 12.3. The two possible answers of yes and no can be coded in any arbitrary way without distorting the results. As long as the decoding process is consis-

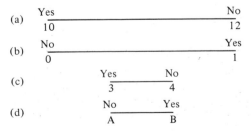

Fig. 12.3
Graphic representation of two-category nominal scale. (Scale values and distance between the two points are completely arbitrary, but they have no practical impact upon the analytic results.)

tent with the coding, the analysis can be done. This is true, provided the analytic technique assumes only an interval scale and not a ratio scale.[18] Since regression assumes only interval scales, we shall first consider the two-group discriminant problem as a regression problem. With this as the starting point, we shall consider the discriminant type of problem in three steps: (1) applying regression to a two-category nominal dependent variable, (2) using discriminant analysis for the same problem, and (3) moving to discriminant analysis for a nominal dependent variable with more than two categories.

Discriminant analysis with only one independent variable is rarely encountered in marketing research. However, in order to lay the foundation for the multiple case, it is useful to clarify concepts in the simple bivariate problem. This approach also should clarify the distinction between the case of multiple categories within a single variable and the case of several variables.

Regression Approach to Two-group Discriminant Analysis

A group of office managers of small-business establishments were the subjects of depth interviews concerning computer use. As a result of these interviews, they were classified as "Favorable," "Neutral," or "Unfavorable." For the present, we consider only the two extremes: favorable and unfavorable. These managers were also classified with respect to age. The data for the 16 managers who were favorable or unfavorable are presented in Table 12.6, and the scatter diagram is given in Fig. 12.4. We first approach the problem as a regression problem, coding "Favorable" as 1 and "Unfavorable" as 0.

A discriminant analysis seeks to determine a critical value that will partition the independent variable (age in this case) in such a way that one category of the dependent variable is more likely for one subgroup and the other category is more likely for the other subgroup. For our illustration, we seek to

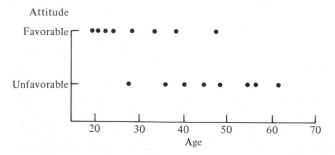

Fig. 12.4
Scatter diagram. Attitude of office managers toward computer by age of manager. Two groups.

---

[18]While any numerical assignment is possible, a 0/1 coding system facilitates both calculations and interpretations.

Table 12.6
Attitude of Office Managers toward Computer by Age of Manager. Two Groups

Respondent	Age	Attitude	Predicted by regression equation
1	19	Favorable (1)	Favorable
2	45	Unfavorable (0)	Unfavorable
3	38	Favorable (1)	Unfavorable
4	20	Favorable (1)	Favorable
5	47	Favorable (1)	Unfavorable
6	61	Unfavorable (0)	Unfavorable
7	28	Favorable (1)	Favorable
8	54	Unfavorable (0)	Unfavorable
9	22	Favorable (1)	Favorable
10	56	Unfavorable (0)	Unfavorable
11	40	Unfavorable (0)	Unfavorable
12	27	Unfavorable (0)	Favorable
13	36	Unfavorable (0)	Favorable
14	49	Unfavorable (0)	Unfavorable
15	24	Favorable (1)	Favorable
16	33	Favorable (1)	Favorable

determine the critical value for age below which a favorable attitude is more likely and above which an unfavorable attitude is more likely. (The data indicate the younger managers are more likely to be be favorable; this tendency was not specified before the research.)

Using a linear regression and letting 1 represent a favorable attitude and 0 represent an unfavorable attitude, we want to determine an equation that will allow us to predict attitude from age. A regression equation will yield decimal estimates for attitude, not 0/1 values. Intuition suggests that .5 might be an appropriate cutoff point: above .5 predict "favorable," below .5 predict "unfavorable."[19] Using this approach, the regression determined is

$$E(y|x) = 1.4322 - .0249x.$$

According to this equation, the age at which the two categories are equally likely is approximately 37.4 years. Using this as a critical point in our predictions, the predictions for the 16 office managers are given in column four of Table 12.6. We are interested in the number of "hits" and "misses"—correct

---

[19]This approach is valid, assuming a 50–50 division between the two groups and equal costs for the two possible classification errors. See Chapter 13 for further discussion.

and incorrect classifications. We have "missed" for four respondents: numbers 3, 5, 12, and 13. The other 12 are "hits" and have been properly classified. This information is summarized in Table 12.7 that shows where correct classifications were made and where incorrect classifications were made. Such a table is called a "confusion matrix" because it identifies where the predictive device is accurate and where it is "confused." The regression equation is not determined, however, in accordance with proper classification on a nominal scale; it is based on the minimization of the squared deviations of the observed dependent variable (coded 0 or 1) from a calculated decimal value. If we use regression, we must calculate the conditional variance in these decimal units.

As yet we have not tested a null hypothesis. Since we are using regression, we may use any of three equivalent test: $\beta = 0$, $\rho = 0$, or an F-test using the appropriate variances. The sample r^2 is equal to .43 ($r = -.65$). Using Eq. (12.13) and calculating the t-statistic for a test of $\rho = 0$, we have

$$t = \frac{|-.65|}{(.57/14)^{1/2}} = \frac{.65}{.20} = 3.25.$$

This value is large enough to reject the null hypothesis ($\alpha = .01$). We should conclude that age and attitude are related; younger office managers have more favorable attitudes toward computers than older office managers.

Table 12.7
Confusion Matrix for Attitude–Age Study. Two Groups

| Predicted attitude | Attitude | | Total |
	Favorable	Unfavorable	
Favorable	6	2	8
Unfavorable	2	6	8
Total	8	8	16

Discriminant Analysis—Two Groups

Discriminant analysis yields results that are equivalent to regression, but the results and approach have a different focus. Using the same data as in Table 12.6, we first focus on the mean ages for the two groups. If these means differ significantly, the next task is to determine an equation that will assign units to an attitude category based on age of the office manager.

Mean age for "favorable" managers is 28.875 years, and mean age for "unfavorable" managers is 46.0 years. Is the difference of 17.1 years large enough to reject the hypothesis of "no universe difference"? The test follows the precise format of ANOVA. Table 12.8 shows the required calculations.

Table 12.8
_F_-Test for Age Differences of Office Managers by Attitude. Two Groups

Source	Sum of squares	Degrees of freedom	Mean square	F-ratio
Between-groups	1173.06	1	1173.06	10.44 $(P < .01)$
Within-group	1572.88	14	112.35	
Total	2745.94	15		

The resulting F-ratio indicates that the null hypothesis should be rejected: attitude and age are related. (This result is as expected since the regression approach already yielded the same conclusion.) Figure 12.5 shows the two alternative hypotheses that are tested in Table 12.8. Figure 12.5(a) shows the conclusion if the null hypothesis is accepted: a single distribution is viewed as appropriate for all managers since attitude and age are not related. Figure 12.5(b) shows the conclusion if the null hypothesis is rejected: each group has its own age distribution. The numerical values shown on the age axes are unbiased estimates in the two cases but are not specified as part of the hypotheses.

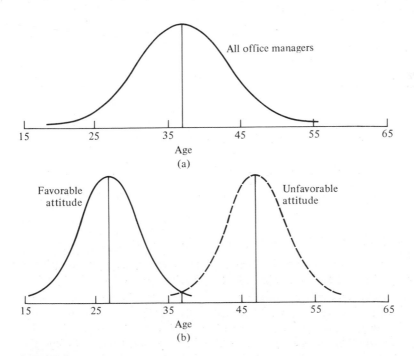

Fig. 12.5
Alternative conclusions for office managers' attitude–age problem;
(a) null hypothesis accepted, (b) null hypothesis rejected.

An alternative test of the null hypothesis is with Mahalanobis D^2 statistic. The simplified form of D^2 when there is only one independent variable is given by Eq. (12.14)[20]

$$D^2 = (n_1 + n_2 - 2)\frac{(\bar{x}_a - \bar{x}_b)^2}{W^2} \qquad (12.14)$$

where W^2 = within-group sum of squares, n_1 and n_2 = number of units in each group, and $\bar{x}_a$ and $\bar{x}_b$ = group means. Mahalanobis D^2 thus measures the distance between the two groups, adjusted by the amount of within-group dispersion. For the present problem, D^2 is equal to 2.6103.

$$D^2 = \frac{14(17.125)^2}{1572.88} = 2.6103.$$

This statistic when transformed is distributed according to the F-distribution. The transformation is given by Eq. (12.15) for the one-independent variable case.[21] For the present problem $F = 4(2.6103) = 10.44$.

$$F = \frac{n_1 n_2}{n_1 + n_2} \cdot D^2. \qquad (12.15)$$

The relevant degrees of freedom are m and $(n_1 + n_2 - 1 - m)$ where m is the number of independent variables. The numbers of degrees of freedom for the present problem are 1 and 14. Since the D^2-test and the F-test of Table 12.8 are mathematically equivalent, the results are identical. The null hypothesis is rejected: age and attitude are related.

The forces at work in D^2 and its related F-transformation may be identified by combining Eqs. (12.14) and (12.15) and forming three components.

$$F = \frac{(n_1 + n_1 - 2)(\bar{x}_a - \bar{x}_b)^2(n_1 n_2)}{W^2(n_1 + n_2)}$$

$$= (\bar{x}_a - \bar{x}_b)^2 \frac{1}{W^2/(n_1 + n_2 - 2)} \frac{n_1 n_2}{n_1 + n_2}.$$

(1) The greater the difference between the means $(\bar{x}_a - \bar{x}_b)$, the larger the F-value. If the sample groups differ by a large amount, the discriminant analy-

---

[20]Two forms of D^2 exist. The first is limited to two categories for the dependent variable and is given by

$$D^2 = (n_1 + n_2 - 2)\sum\sum a^{ij}(\bar{x}_{ai} - \bar{x}_{bi})(\bar{x}_{aj} - \bar{x}_{bj})$$

for any number of independent variables. The a^{ij} values refer to the appropriate entries from the inverse of the variance–covariance matrix. The second form is referred to as the Generalized Mahalanobis D^2 and applies regardless of the number of categories for the dependent variable. This form is discussed in the next section.

[21]For the more general case,

$$F = \frac{n_1 n_2 (n_1 + n_2 - m - 1)}{m(n_1 + n_2)(n_1 + n_2 - 2)} \cdot D^2,$$

where m = number of independent variables.

sis is likely to identify it as a "real" difference. A difference in mean age of 17 years is more convincing than a difference of five years would be. (2) The greater the within-group dispersion $[(W^2/(n_1 + n_2 - 2)]$, the smaller the F-value. If the amount of dispersion within each group is large, any difference between the means is less significant. The within-group standard deviation of 10.6—from $(1572.88/14)^{1/2}$—is more convincing evidence of a true difference between groups than a within-group standard deviation of 15 or 20 years would be. If the within-group standard deviation had been only four years, the mean difference of 17 years would have been even more impressive. (3) The larger the sample size and the more equally it is divided between the two groups, the larger the F-value. This factor, in contrast to the other two, is a function of the research design and is shown by the expression $n_1 n_2/(n_1 + n_2)$. The same substantive sample results would be even more convincing with a total sample of 50 rather than one of 16.

Completion of the confusion matrix requires a rule for predicting attitude from age. In general, discriminant analysis accomplishes this task by means of one or more discriminant functions. In the case of one independent variable, the calculation is superfluous since the midpoint between the two means establishes the critical value. However, the discriminant function is of the form $D^* = Ax$ with A determined by Eq. (12.16). $A = .01089$ for the present problem. Substituting

$$A = \frac{D(x)}{W^2} \tag{12.16}$$

where $D(x) = $ difference between group means, $W^2 = $ within-group sum of squared deviations.

The calculated value of A for the present problem is .01089. (See Table 12.9.) Substituting the mean age for each group yields the mean discriminant

Table 12.9
Discriminant Analysis Calculation for Attitude–Age Study. Two Groups.

1. Difference between groups $(D(x))$
$$D(x) = \bar{x}_a \text{ (unfavorable)} - \bar{x}_b \text{ (favorable)}$$
$$= 46.0 - 28.875$$
$$= 17.125.$$

2. Within-group sum of squared deviations (W^2)
$$W^2 = \Sigma(x_{ja} - \bar{x}_a)^2 + \Sigma(x_{jb} - \bar{x}_b)^2$$
$$= \frac{\sum_{j=a}^{b} x_j^2 - \sum_{j=a}^{b} (x_j)^2}{n_j}$$
$$= 17824 - \frac{(368)^2}{8} + 7347 - \frac{(231)^2}{8}$$
$$= 1572.88.$$

(continued)

Table 12.9
(continued)

3. Mahalanobis D^2

$$D^2 = \frac{(n_1 + n_2 - 2)\,[D(x)]^2}{W^2}$$

$$= \frac{14(17.125)^2}{1572.88}$$

$$= 2.6103.$$

4. Transformation of D^2 to F

$$F = \frac{D^2(n_1 n_2)}{n_1 + n_2}$$

$$= 2.6103 \,\frac{64}{16}$$

$$= 10.44\ (P < .01).$$

5. Calculation of discriminant function (D^*)

$$D^* = Ax.$$

$$A = \frac{D(x)}{W^2}$$

$$= \frac{17.125}{1572.88}$$

$$= .01089.$$

$$D^* = .01089x.$$

6. Mean discriminant score for each group

$$D^*(\text{favorable}) = .01089(28.875)$$
$$= .31445.$$
$$D^*(\text{unfavorable}) = .01089(46.0)$$
$$= .50094.$$

score for each group, .31445 for the favorable group and .50094 for the unfavorable group. Assignment or prediction is accomplished by calculating the discriminant score for the unit under question and assigning the unit to the group that has the closer mean score. For example, a unit with a discriminant score of .42471 (age 39) would be assigned to the unfavorable group since that score is closer to .50094 than to .31445. The confusion matrix generated by applying this rule to the 16 original units coincides precisely with that of Table 12.7, a mathematical necessity since the two approaches are equivalent. Table 12.9 summarizes the calculations involved in the discriminant approach to this problem.

Discriminant Analysis—Three Groups

If the number of nominal categories for the dependent variable is greater than two, regression is not a viable alternative to discriminant analysis. The deci-

sion maker's question, in this instance, is whether the independent variable discriminates among the *various* groups rather than between two groups. Since the dependent variable is nominally scaled, no ordering of them is inferred and certainly no concept of distance between them is implied.

Suppose we add the eight "neutral" office managers to our study of association between age and attitude toward computers. We now have three groups. Our general question is the same: "Does age discriminate among the groups?" Discriminant analysis considers the dependent variable to be truly nominal. The neutral group is not forced between the two extreme groups. Its age distribution, in the summary equations, may have the highest mean, the lowest mean, or its mean may lie between the other two. The objectives are precisely the same as in the two-group case: derivation of functions that discriminate among the groups and assignment (prediction) of group membership based on those functions.

Table 12.10 and Fig. 12.6 give the complete set of data for the 24 office managers. The mean age for the neutral managers is 39.875. This mean lies between the means for the other two groups but lies closer to that of the unfavorable group. Our concern is whether the three means (28.875, 39.875, and 46.0) differ by an amount sufficient to reject the null hypothesis. Our approach in the previous section compared only the two extreme groups; now we are looking at all three groups.

Isolation and comparison of extremes could indicate a significant difference whereas an analysis of the complete set of data shows no significant difference. Consequently, the decision maker must be extremely careful in identifying the appropriate groups to compare. A particularly troublesome problem occurs when the identification of extremes is accomplished within the

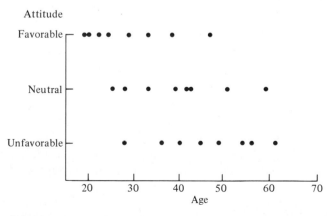

Fig. 12.6
Scatter diagram. Attitude of office managers toward computer by age of manager. Three groups.

Table 12.10
Attitude of Office Managers toward Computers by Age of Manager. Three Groups

Respondent	Age	Attitude	Predicted by discriminant analysis
1	19	Favorable	Favorable
2	45	Unfavorable	Unfavorable
3	38	Favorable	Neutral
4	20	Favorable	Favorable
5	47	Favorable	Unfavorable
6	61	Unfavorable	Unfavorable
7	28	Favorable	Favorable
8	54	Unfavorable	Unfavorable
9	22	Favorable	Favorable
10	56	Unfavorable	Unfavorable
11	40	Unfavorable	Neutral
12	27	Unfavorable	Favorable
13	36	Unfavorable	Neutral
14	49	Unfavorable	Unfavorable
15	24	Favorable	Favorable
16	33	Favorable	Favorable
17	42	Neutral	Neutral
18	27	Neutral	Favorable
19	59	Neutral	Unfavorable
20	33	Neutral	Favorable
21	39	Neutral	Neutral
22	51	Neutral	Unfavorable
23	43	Neutral	Unfavorable
24	25	Neutral	Favorable

research rather than distinct from it. In such a case, the testing process contains an element of circular reasoning.[22]

An F-test based upon among- and within-group variance is appropriate for testing significance of the difference between these three means. The results are presented in Table 12.11. The null hypothesis should be rejected, but the evidence is not as conclusive as it is when only the two extreme groups were included.

The next step is the establishment of rules for prediction or assignment in the confusion matrix. If we assume the conditional variances are equal within

---

[22]"Extreme value" tests avoid this circular reasoning. See, for example, Dixon and Massey, *op. cit.,* pp. 275–278.

Table 12.11
F-Test for Age Differences of Office Managers by Attitude. Three Groups

Source	Sum of squares	Degrees of freedom	Mean square	*F*-ratio
Among-groups	1204.75	2	602.38	5.04 ($P < .05$)
Within-group	2511.75	21	119.61	
Total	3716.50	23		

each of the three groups, the assignment rule is intuitively appealing. "Assign the manager to the group whose mean age is closest to that of the manager."[23] Using this rule, the individual assignments are shown in column 4 of Table 12.10 and the confusion matrix is given in Table 12.12.

Thirteen of the 24 managers (54 percent) are properly classified. This is a lower percentage of "hits" than is achieved when only the two groups were studied (75 percent), a result that is not too surprising. Even among the two extreme groups, the number of "hits" has decreased. Whereas 12 of 16 were properly classified before, only 11 of 16 are now properly classified. Respondent 11—an "unfavorable" manager—was properly classified before but now is assigned to the "neutral" group. With three alternative groups, there are two possible errors and only one correct assignment. As the number of groups increases, the assignment problem becomes increasingly difficult. As a result, percentage of "hits" as a summary statistic tends to be misleading when presented without information regarding the size of the confusion matrix.[24]

Examination of the predicted group for neutral office managers reveals a common difficulty in discriminant analysis. Figure 12.7 presents the assumed distributions for the three groups. The neutral group distribution overlaps the favorable group on one side and the unfavorable group on the other. For any

Table 12.12
Confusion Matrix for Attitude–Age Study. Three Groups

Predicted attitude	Favorable	Neutral	Unfavorable	Total
Favorable	6	3	1	10
Neutral	1	2	2	5
Unfavorable	1	3	5	9
Total	8	8	8	24

[23]Mathematical solution for the discriminant functions is unnecessary in the case of a single independent variable. This is true regardless of the number of groups. The solution and interpretation of the discriminant functions are relevant in cases involving multiple independent variables. This topic is covered in Chapter 13.

[24]See "Contingency Table Analysis of Confusion Matrices" (Chapter 13) that also discusses the necessity of considering the relative sizes of the groups.

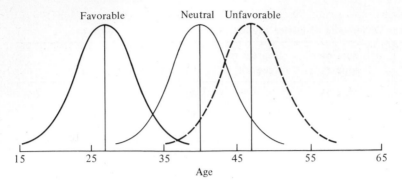

Fig. 12.7
Assumed population age distributions of office managers according to
attitude—null hypothesis rejected. Three groups.

given age, the probability that the manager comes from the neutral group is
confronted by significant probabilities from either one or the other group.
This results in a decrease in the number of managers classified as neutral—
only five in contrast to nine as unfavorable and ten as favorable. "Neutral" is
predicted only if age falls between 34.38 and 42.94. If the favorable and unfavorable distributions approached the neutral distribution even more closely, the
percentage assigned to the neutral group would be even smaller. Only if the
percentage of respondents toward the central tendency is very large would this
low assignment to middle groups be overcome. If within-group dispersion is
extremely small relative to dispersion among the group means (the ideal situation yielding good discrimination), the overlap is minimized and the problem
is reduced.

   An alternative test of the "no association" hypothesis is Mahalanobis
Generalized D^2. This statistic, in contrast to D^2 for two groups, is distributed
approximately as Chi Square. The number of degrees of freedom is equal to
$m(g - 1)$ where m equals the number of independent variables and g equals
the number of categories for the dependent variable. Therefore the present
problem has two degrees of freedom: $1(3 - 1)$. The generalized D^2 is computed (for the one independent variable case) by Eq. (12.17).

$$\text{Generalized } D^2 = (n - g) \frac{\sum\limits_{j=1}^{g} n_j(\bar{x}_j - \bar{\bar{x}})^2}{W^2} . \qquad (12.17)$$

The distinction between this statistic and the restricted D^2 for two categories of
Eq. (12.14) lies in the distance measured. Equation (12.14) refers to the distance between two means; Eq. (12.17) compares the mean of each group to the
composite mean based on all observations. The within-group variances in the

two equations are similar in concept but differ in terms of degrees of freedom.[25]

Computation of the Generalized D^2 for the present problem is given by

$$D^2 = 21\left[8(28.875 - 38.25)^2 + 8(39.875 - 38.25)^2 + 8(46 - 38.25)^2\right] \div 2511.75$$
$$= 10.07.$$

The Chi Square distribution, with two degrees of freedom, indicates that the null hypothesis should be rejected for these data. Attitude and age are not independent.

Conditional Distribution

The nature of the conditional distribution and the assumptions involved are somewhat obscured by the output of discriminant analysis. The use of the mid-point between group means as a critical value rests on the assumption of homoscedasticity. This critical value is established by using a linear function for the discriminant equation(s). A nonlinear equation would establish the critical value at a location other than the midpoint between means and would rest on different assumptions regarding the nature of the separate distributions.

The discriminant function is not truly a conditional distribution: it does not yield an estimate of the dependent variable. The function is merely a step toward the estimate. Substitution of the value of the independent variable in the function yields a discriminant score. A prediction can be made only after this score is compared with other scores. This comparison may be expressed in terms of alternative probabilities,[26] but the eventual estimate is the assignment of each unit to one of k categories: ($k = 2$ is merely a special case).

The use of the confusion matrix as a measure of association in no way corresponds to the usual concept of reduction in variance. It is possible, however, to compute a correlation ratio (η) from the within and among variances generated in the ANOVA approach.[27] If the dependent variable is dichotomous, the square of the correlation ratio is also the coefficient of determination. These percentage reductions in variance measures are often not cited in

---

[25]With more independent variables the Generalized D^2 employs the inverse of the variance–covariance matrix in place of the within-group variance and a series of cross-products in place of squared deviations from the composite mean. See Donald F. Morrison, 1967, *Multivariate Statistical Methods* (New York: McGraw-Hill).

[26]In Chapter 13, we shall discuss the conversion of discriminant scores into probabilities and their use in making assignments or predictions.

[27]For example, η for Tables 12.8 and 12.11 is .65 and .57, respectively. The percentage reduction in variance is, of course, the square of these numbers: 43 percent and 32 percent.

discriminant analysis, but the percentage of hits should not be confused with regression type measures of association.

Overview of Discrimination Analysis

A summary of discriminant analysis in the one-independent variable case is presented in Table 12.13.[28] The null hypothesis of no association is tested with Mahalanobis D^2. Two forms exist: one for the two-group dependent variable and a Generalized D^2 for more than two groups. Both must be transformed in order to perform a statistical test, the first into an F-ratio and the second into Chi Square. An alternative test uses a typical ANOVA approach.

The mean values for the various groups serve as the basis for estimates or classifications. Each unit is simply assigned to the group whose mean is most similar to its own score on the independent variable. No true conditional distribution equation is derived, and no summary relationship is determined.

Table 12.13
Discriminant Analysis Summary. One-Independent Variable

1. Test statistic: Mahalanobis D^2 with
   a) F-distribution for two groups
   b) χ^2 distribution for more than two groups
   c) ANOVA as an alternative

2. Estimate based on:
   a) Total percentage if H_0 is accepted
   b) Nearest mean score if H_0 is rejected

3. Summary of relationship, if any
   a) No true conditional distribution established
   b) Modal estimate from comparison with selected critical values

4. Measure of association
   a) Confusion matrix
   b) Correlation ratio squared (η^2)
   c) Coefficient of determination (r^2) for two-group case

5. Form of discriminant functions(s):
   a) Prior specification
   b) Linearity incorporated in use of midpoint between means

6. Criterion for "best" equation(s):
   a) Minimization of squared deviations on a 0/1 coding of dependent variable
   b) Subject to stated constraints
      i) Cost of misclassification
      ii) Prior probability of group membership

[28]See Table 13.20 for a more general summary involving two or more independent variables.

The confusion matrix shows the percentage of correct classifications and the distribution of incorrect classifications. These are not comparable to a percentage reduction in variance concept and must not be compared with that general measure of association.

Complications are introduced when the cost of misclassification is unequal for different errors or when there are unequal probabilities of group membership. These considerations as well as the determination and interpretation of the discriminant function(s) are postponed until the next chapter in which the case of multiple independent variables is considered.

SUMMARY

Regression and discriminant analysis deal with intervally scaled independent variables. Regression handles those cases in which the dependent variable is also intervally scaled, and discriminant analysis handles those cases in which the dependent variable is nominally scaled.

The standard regression approach establishes a linear conditional distribution [E $(y|x) = a + bx$] by the method of least squares. The existence of association is determined by testing whether the sample regression coefficient (b) is significantly different from zero. If the null hypothesis is rejected, the regression line is the basis upon which point estimates are made for the dependent variable. Interval estimates for individual observations are established by using the conditional standard deviation in conjunction with the point estimates. Interval estimates for conditional means are also possible by using conditional standard errors.

A summary measure of linear association is given by the coefficient of determination (r^2)—the percentage reduction in variance by measuring dispersion around the regression line instead of around the mean. The coefficient of correlation (r) is merely the square root of r^2, but it carries a sign indicating the direction of association.

Discriminant analysis, in the two-variable case, predicts the nominally scaled dependent variable by establishing one or more critical values for the intervally scaled independent variable. In the case of a dichotomous dependent variable, a single critical value is established at the midpoint between the means of the two groups. Elements below this value are assigned to one category of the dependent variable, and elements above that value are assigned to the other category. The null hypothesis of no association is tested by use of Mahalanobis D^2 statistic, which is a measure of distance between means, adjusted for within-group dispersion. Since discriminant analysis is primarily used with sets of independent variables rather than a single independent variable, the major development of the role of the discriminant functions is postponed until the next chapter.

EXERCISES AND PROBLEMS

1. Distinguish among the terms within each of the following sets.
   a) Regression and correlation
   b) A discriminant function and a conditional distribution
   c) Regression coefficient and standardized regression coefficient
   d) Confusion matrix and degree of association
   e) Generalized D^2 and two-group D^2
   f) Standard error of estimate and standard error of conditional mean
   g) Extrapolation and interpolation
   h) The symbols r^2, ρ^2, and $\overset{*}{\rho}{}^2$
   i) The symbols r and η

2. How does regression–correlation answer each of the following objectives?
   a) Prediction of a target variable
   b) Summary measure of degree of association
   c) Indicator of incremental effect of independent variable

3. Discuss the meaning of "explained" and "unexplained" variance and how they are used in measuring correlation. Is this the same as measuring regression? Why?

4. What assumptions are involved in using linear regression in a study of association? Are these assumptions necessary for all of the objectives of such a study?

5. A research worker concluded that two variables were associated in the universe. Another research worker, using the same data, was unwilling to conclude that the two variables were associated in the universe. Does this situation suggest that one of the individuals was more competent than the other? Why or why not?

6. Table E12.6 contains data collected from the Lightfield Department Store on seven "nonholiday season" Saturdays. They show x = number of persons entering the store (in 100's) and y = total sales (in $1,000).

Table E12.6

x	y
3	6
5	7
6	9
5	8
2	5
3	7
6	10

a) What is your best estimate of total sales volume on a Saturday if information about the number of persons entering the store is not available?

b) Establish a 99 percent confidence interval for your estimate in part (a).

c) What is your best estimate of total sales volume on a Saturday when 600 persons entered the store? when 1,000 persons entered the store?

d) Establish 99 percent confidence intervals for your estimates in part (c).

e) What percentage of the variance in Saturday total sales volume was explained by the number of persons entering the store?

f) What is your best estimate of the population correlation coefficient between these two variables?

g) The data employed for this problem were rounded to the nearest 100 or $1,000. Do you think this was a wise procedure? Why?

7. A least-squares linear regression and correlation analysis was performed on data from a simple random sample of 102 salespeople of a large textile firm. The following results were obtained.

$$E(y|x) = -9.8 + 1.1x$$
$$x = \text{age in years}$$
$$y = \text{annual commission (\$1,000)}$$
$$x \text{ range} = 29 \text{ to } 53$$
$$s_y = 5.2; \; s(y|x) = 3.1$$

a) What is the meaning, specifically in terms of this problem, of each of the numerical values given above (-9.8, $+1.1$, 5.2, and 3.1)?

b) Can you state the conditional equation that would result if both variables were expressed in standard scores? Explain, including the equation if it can be determined.

c) Would you be willing to use the equation above for estimating the annual commission of a 40-year-old sales person of this textile firm? Why or why not?

d) Would you give the same answer for estimating the annual commission of a 40-year-old sales person with another textile firm? Discuss.

e) You have been asked to classify individual annual commissions of the firm's salespeople as "typical," "unusually high," or "unusually low." Would the equation derived be useful? A 35-year-old salesperson received commissions of $25,000. How would you classify the sales person's commissions (either with or without the equation)?

8. Would you consider the problems given in Exercises 6 and 7 problems for regression analysis or correlation analysis? Why? Of what practical significance is your answer?

9. A sample of 12 shoppers in a record store was asked to rate a new release on a score of 1 to 10. The results, along with the age of the shopper, are given in Table E12.9.

Table E12.9

Respondent	Age	Rating
1	15	9
2	22	6
3	19	7
4	38	4
5	16	8
6	21	5
7	14	9
8	43	6
9	22	10
10	15	8
11	17	9
12	16	5

a) Do the age figures pose any difficulty if a regression approach is contemplated? Discuss.

b) Disregard your answer to part (a) if necessary. Determine a least-squares regression line for the data above, using age as the independent variable and rating as the dependent variable.

c) In the rating scale employed, high values are more favorable than low values. Suppose the reverse were true, how would this influence your calculations in part (b) or the use of the resulting equation?

d) Do you believe the data above warrant a conclusion that age and rating are associated?

e) Could the data be used in determining an equation to be used in predicting age, given rating? Why or why not?

f) Another researcher seeing the data made the following statement, "These figures provide additional evidence that musical taste varies with age." Assuming no arithmetic errors, do you think the statement is justified? Why?

10. A third research worker, seeing the data in Exercise 9, questioned the use of regression. She said that the rating values might not be intervally scaled but only ordinally scaled. She suggested that discriminant analysis be employed, dividing rating into only two categories: "favorable" if 8 or higher and "unfavorable" if 7 or lower.

a) How would you respond to her suggestion?

b) Perform the discriminant analysis suggested.

c) Did you obtain a conditional distribution in part (b)? Discuss.

d) Calculate the confusion matrix associated with your analysis in part (b). What does it tell you?

   e) Can you calculate the percentage reduction in variance achieved by your analysis? Discuss and make the calculation if appropriate.

   f) Would it be possible to establish three categories for the rating variable and perform a discriminant analysis with the data in that form? If possible, would it be desirable? Discuss.

   g) Do the values of the age variable pose any problem for discriminant analysis or its interpretation? Would they pose a problem in either contingency analysis or ANOVA? Discuss.

11. Draw rough graphs for each of the following situations.

   a) High inverse linear association

   b) Low direct linear association

   c) No association

   d) High curvilinear association with no reversal

   e) Low curvilinear association with one reversal

12. Compare contingency analysis, ANOVA, regression–correlation analysis, and discriminant analysis with respect to each of the following:

   a) Functional form of the conditional distribution

   b) *A priori* specification of conditional distribution

   c) Measure of association

   d) Test statistic for null hypothesis

   e) Approach to estimating confidence intervals

13. Refer to Exercise 6 of Chapter 9.

   a) Could these data be used for a discriminant analysis, using expenditures on small appliances as a basis for estimating donor status? Why?

   b) What, if any, additional information would you need in order to perform a discriminant analysis? If no additional data are required, perform the analysis. If additional data are required, indicate the steps involved in obtaining the required information.

14. Analyze, criticize, and explain:

   a) The variance around the regression line will be less than the variance around the mean of the dependent variable except in the unusual case of a perfect curvilinear relation.

   b) A bivariate linear regression analysis was performed and yielded a coefficient of determination of .64 and a regression coefficient of $+.3$. If a second linear regression equation is computed with the independent and dependent variables interchanged, one cannot know with certainty whether the coefficient of determination will be the same, greater, or less than that obtained in the first analysis. (Assume the same data are used in both analyses.)

   c) The random sampling distribution of the regression coefficient can be used in testing either $\beta = 0$ or $\rho = 0$ since the two tests must yield the same result (assuming both are tested at the same level of significance).

of product sales according to color of package is an example of the latter; the number of colors possible may be many, but only one characteristic (color) is being considered. The addition of package size and package shape would bring us into the case of multiple independent variables.

Bivariate ANOVA has a general estimating equation of the form $E(y|x) = \bar{y} + a_1 x_1 + a_2 x_2 + \cdots + a_n x_n$. Here $\bar{y}$ is the grand mean of the dependent variable, for example, product sales for all package colors. The individual a_i values would be the coefficients associated with the different package colors. The x_i's designate the various colors and have only two possible values, 0 or 1.

The extension of ANOVA to include package size and package shape requires a more complex estimating equation of the form given in Eq. (13.1).

$$\begin{aligned}
E(y|x_1, x_2, \cdots x_n) = \bar{y} &+ a_1 x_{11} + a_2 x_{12} + \cdots \\
&+ a_i x_{1i} + b_1 x_{21} + b_2 x_{22} + \cdots \\
&+ b_j x_{2j} + c_1 x_{31} + c_2 x_{32} + \cdots \\
&+ c_k x_{3k} + \cdots .
\end{aligned} \qquad (13.1)$$

How does Eq. (13.1) differ from the bivariate conditional distribution? The unconditional mean ($\bar{y}$), the point of reference against which revisions are made, again appears in the equation. The first subscript of the x's refers to the specific independent variable, and the second subscript refers to the specific category within that variable. For example, x_{32} means the second category of the third independent variable. The a-coefficients apply to the first independent variable; the b-coefficients, to the second; etc. The expression, c_k, thus refers to the kth category of the third independent variable. If $c_k = -2.0$, the estimate of the dependent variable would be decreased by two units for those elements within the kth category of the third independent variable. Estimates for these elements would be further modified according to their classification with respect to the remaining independent variables. For the multivariate equation, the number of nonzero entries in any estimate would coincide with the number of independent variables, the specific nonzero entries being determined by the relevant categories for the particular element in question.

ANOVA with multiple classifications seeks to determine which if any of the independent variables are related to the dependent variable and introduces only those variables into the prediction equation. Note that Eq. (13.1) says that the effect of each independent variable is not influenced by the values of any of the other independent variables—they are assumed to be "independent" of each other. ANOVA goes beyond this equation; it also tests for interactions among the independent variables.

The more independent variables we wish to consider and the greater the number of categories for each, the larger our sample must be in order to run the analysis. Consider the problem of product sales related to package color, size, and shape. If we wish to test four colors (red, blue, yellow, and white), three sizes (small, medium, and large), and two shapes (square side panels and rectangular side panels), we need at least 24 observations for a factorial design.[1] Twenty-four observations would not yield a measure of variation within the various treatments. Repeated measures (replications) are required in order to secure an estimate of this random variation, but added replications drive up sample size and cost.

The data in Table 13.1 show two complete replications for the package test considering only color and size of package. The analysis tests whether the observed differences in sales by package color and by package size are indicative of true differences in the universe or whether the observed differences merely reflect the inherent variability to be expected in repeated applications with packages that have the same ability to generate sales.

Table 13.2 analyzes the observed deviations among the 24 applications of the test. The arithmetic mean for the 24 observations is equal to 15. The unit of measure does not influence the analysis but must be defensible in terms of the company objectives; for this problem the measure was in hundreds of dollars of sales.[2] We wish first to determine the variance of the 24 observations around this grand mean of 15. The total sum of squared deviations is shown in Table 13.2 as 436.

We must now decompose this total sum of squares into its component parts; the denominator of the F-ratio used for the test will be our estimate of sampling variability when the null hypothesis is true. The null hypothesis states that neither package color nor package size nor their interaction produces any effect on sales. Variation in sales would exist even if these three factors have

Table 13.1
Sales Test of Package Color and Size

Color	Size			Total
	Small	Average	Large	
Red	12, 16 (28)	13, 14 (27)	19, 22 (41)	96
Blue	8, 10 (18)	11, 8 (19)	15, 14 (29)	66
Yellow	18, 16 (34)	16, 19 (35)	24, 21 (45)	114
White	12, 12 (24)	10, 13 (23)	19, 18 (37)	84
Total	104	104	152	360

[1] See "Factorial Design" in Chapter 3.

[2] Dollar sales may be biased in favor of the large package if the test period is short. A longer test period would permit repurchases for the smaller packages, leading to higher values than might appear with a short test period.

Table 13.2
Multiple Classification Analysis of Variance. Sales Test of Package Color and Size

Source of variation	Sum of squares	Degrees of freedom	Mean square	F-ratio
Treatment effect:	400	11		
Color	204	3	68.00	22.67 ($P < .01$)
Size	192	2	96.00	32.00 ($P < .01$)
Interaction	4	6	.67	0.22 ($P > .1$)
Within-cell	36	12	3.00	
Total	436	23		

$$\text{Total} = (12 - 15)^2 + (16 - 15)^2 + (13 - 15)^2 + \cdots$$
$$+ (18 - 15)^2 = 436.$$
$$\text{Within-cell} = (12 - 14)^2 + (16 - 14)^2 + (13 - 13.5)^2 + \cdots$$
$$+ (18 - 18.5)^2 = 36.$$
$$\text{Color} = 6\left[(16 - 15)^2 + (11 - 15)^2 + (19 - 15)^2 + (14 - 15)^2\right] = 204.$$
$$\text{Size} = 8\left[(13 - 15)^2 + (13 - 15)^2 + (19 - 15)^2\right] = 192.$$
$$\text{Treatment} = 2\left[(14 - 15)^2 + (13.5 - 15)^2 + \cdots + (18.5 - 15)^2\right] = 400.$$

no effect. The best indication of this variation is shown by the fact that sales are not identical even when package color and package size are held constant as in each of the 12 cells of Table 13.1. We wish to use this within-cell variability as the criterion for appraising other variations within the experiment in the same way we used within-column variance as a criterion when dealing with only one independent variable.

Each of the 12 cells has a mean. For example the red–small combination has a mean of 14 (28/2). The within-cell sum of squares is determined by comparing the two observations of each cell against their mean, squaring, and summing over all 12 cells. This result is 36.

The difference between the within-cell sum of squares (36) and the total sum of squares (436) is produced by either color, size, or their interaction. The sum of squared deviations among the four colors is determined by comparing the mean for each color against the grand mean. The mean for red packages is 16; for blue, 11; for yellow, 19; and for white, 14. The squared deviation for each of these means is weighted by the number of observations making up each mean—six in this example. The resulting color sum of squares is 204. The size sum of squared deviations is calculated in precisely the same manner using the three means of 13 for small, 13 for average, and 19 for large. Each of these squared deviations is again weighted by the number of observations contributing to each mean (8). The required calculations yield a result of 192.

We have skipped over the first entry of Table 13.2 because this did not occur in the bivariate analysis of variance. It is a composite and labeled "treatment." This designation means that it embraces the sum of squared deviations produced by all factors other than the random variability within cell. It could be calculated by a simple subtraction process, but we shall calculate it directly by comparing the mean of each cell against the grand mean. As already indicated, the mean for red–small is 14. It differs from the grand mean by one unit; its squared deviation is also one. Since the mean of 14 is based on two observations, the contribution of this cell to the treatment sum of squares is two (2×1). Similar calculations for the other 12 cells when combined yield a total of 400.

The treatment sum of squares is produced by three factors: color, size, and their interaction. The interaction sum of squares is most easily determined by subtraction.[3] Since color and size produce a combined sum of squares of 396, the interaction figure is 4 ($400 - 396$).

The number of degrees of freedom is determined in the same manner as that discussed in Chapter 11 except for the number of degrees of freedom associated with the interaction term. This figure may be obtained either by a subtraction process or by calculating the product of the number of degrees of freedom associated with the two factors that may be interacting. In either case, the number of degrees of freedom for the interaction term in this problem is six. The mean square for each term is determined in the usual manner by dividing the sum of squares by the number of degrees of freedom. No entry is made for the treatment term since that is a composite and we wish to determine which, if any, of the separate factors should be included in our estimating equation.

The F-ratios calculated in Table 13.2 reveal that sales levels differ according to both the size and color of the package, but that there is no interaction between the two. Each of the three tests has a different critical value for F because the number of degrees of freedom is different in each case, even though α is kept constant. The appropriate estimating equation can be determined directly from Table 13.1 and is given by

$$E(y|x_1, x_2) = 15.00 + 1.00x_{1r} - 4.00x_{1b} + 4.00x_{1y}$$
$$- 1.00x_{1w} - 2.00x_{2s} - 2.00x_{2m} + 4.00x_{2l};$$
$$x_{ij} = 0 \text{ or } 1, \qquad \sum_j x_{ij} = 1.$$

If the null hypothesis for either color or size had been accepted, that factor would have been excluded from the equation. The specifications regarding the x_{ij}'s in the equation simply indicate that each is nominally scaled and that each element must be in one and only one category for each variable. The equation is used for prediction in precisely the same way as the analogous equation for bivariate ANOVA is used. For example, predicted sales for the product in a large, red package would be

$$E(y|x_1, x_2) = 15 + 1(1) - 4(0) + 4(0) - 1(0) - 2(0) - 2(0) + 4(1)$$
$$= 15 + 1 + 4 = 20.$$

---

[3]We shall show its calculation by using a conditional distribution such as Eq. (13.1) later in the chapter.

Therefore the unbiased estimate of sales would be $2,000. (Note the estimate is not read directly from Table 13.1 in which the cell value is $2,050.)

Interaction Terms

The test for interaction should be made before testing for the individual effects, also referred to as main effects. If the null hypothesis with respect to interaction is rejected, we conclude that the variables do interact. Their individual effects depend on the value of the other variable. In this situation, we should refrain from answering a general question such as, "What impact does a red package have on sales?" All we can say is, "The impact is different, depending on the package size." If interaction exists, our conditional estimating equation should specify the 12 individual cells and the appropriate coefficient for each cell instead of relying on the separate main effects indicated by the various categories of the two independent variables.

Further insight into the nature of interaction can be observed in Table 13.3 that gives a direct calculation of the interaction sum of squares. If there is no interaction, the cell means could be computed directly from the estimating equation using only main-order effects. The means estimated from the equation and the observed means from the raw data are shown in the table. The interaction sum of squares is computed by comparing the observed cell mean with the calculated cell mean. A large value for the interaction sum of squares will result if the main-order effects equation yields poor estimates and will cast doubt on the null hypothesis of no interaction.

A problem exists when we have only a single replication for the analysis. In this situation, there is no measure of variability within a cell to serve as the basic measure of sampling variability in the denominator of the F-ratio. In such a situation we must estimate sampling variance by an alternative

Table 13.3
Interaction Sum of Squares. Sales Test of Package Color and Size

	Size					
	Small		Medium		Large	
Color	Calculated sales†	Observed sales	Calculated sales†	Observed sales	Calculated sales†	Observed sales
Red	14	14	14	13.5	20	20.5
Blue	9	9	9	9.5	15	14.5
Yellow	17	17	17	17.5	23	22.5
White	12	12	12	11.5	18	18.5

†Calculated sales by $E(y|x_1, x_2) = 15 + x_{1r} - 4x_{1b} + 4x_{1y} - x_{1w} - 2x_{2s}$
$- 2x_{2m} + 4x_{2l}$.

Interaction sum of squares $= 2\left[(14 - 14)^2 + (14 - 13.5)^2 + \cdots + (18 - 18.5)^2\right]$
$= 2(0 + .25 + \cdots + .25) = 2(2) = 4.$

approach that involves certain assumptions. The usual assumption is that the highest order of interaction in the table is the best estimate of such sampling variability.

If we have three main factors in our test, adding shape of package to color and size, the possible interactions among these independent variables are increased from one term to four terms. We have (1) color–size interaction, (2) color–shape interaction, (3) size–shape interaction, and finally (4) color–size-shape interaction—the last is a three-factor interaction term. The sum of squared deviations for each of these interaction terms would be calculated in a manner analogous to that of Table 13.3. In each case a theoretical cell value is calculated from a conditional distribution that includes only main effects. Three-term interaction compares the observed cell value (based on a table using three independent variables) with the corresponding values calculated from the estimating equation that contained each of the three variables. Two-term interactions are analyzed by combining all cells in which the two variables of interest are similar and comparing those results with the theoretical results derived from the conditional distribution that contained the main effects of the two variables of concern.

The data in Table 13.4 present a highly simplified problem involving knowledge of market offerings by eight individuals classified on three variables: sex, occupation (clerical and labor), and interest in shopping. The table

Table 13.4
Three-factor Analysis of Variance Data. Knowledge of Market Offerings

| Sex | Occupation | Interest in shopping | | |
		High	Low	Total
Male	Clerical	88	80	168
	Labor	89	77	166
	Male subtotals	177	157	334
Female	Clerical	90	85	175
	Labor	87	76	163
	Female subtotals	177	161	338
Interest subtotals		354	318	672

$$\text{Overall mean} = \frac{672}{8} = 84.00.$$

$$\text{Male mean} = \frac{334}{4} = 83.50. \qquad \text{Clerical mean} = \frac{343}{4} = 85.75.$$

$$\text{Female mean} = \frac{338}{4} = 84.50. \qquad \text{Labor mean} = \frac{329}{4} = 82.25.$$

$$\text{High interest mean} = \frac{354}{4} = 88.50.$$

$$\text{Low interest mean} = \frac{318}{4} = 79.50.$$

also shows the overall mean of 84.0 and the various means for each main-fac-
tor category. The objective of the analysis is to determine which of these differences are statistically significant and also to determine whether any of the
interactions are statistically significant.

Table 13.5 presents this analysis, identifying each possible source of variation. In the absence of a within-cell measure in variance, the highest order
interaction (three-factor) variance is used as the denominator for the F-ratios.

Summary figures in the upper portion of Table 13.5 show that only the
interest factor is associated with knowledge of market offerings. None of the
other five F-ratios is large enough to reject the null hypothesis of independence
at the .05 level. The estimating equation for this problem would therefore have
only three terms: the grand mean for all eight observations as the first and constant term (84.0) and the two terms representing the different interest levels
with the appropriate coefficients ($+4.5$ for the high-interest category and
-4.5 for the low-interest category).

$$E(y|x_I) = 84.0 + 4.5x_{IH} - 4.5x_{IL}.$$

Since the null hypothesis is accepted for the other main factors and for all
three of the two-factor interactions, none of these terms appears in the estimating equation.

An indirect and much less laborious method for calculating the sums of
squares associated with each source of variation is shown in the lower portion

Table 13.5
Multiple Classification Analysis of Variance. Knowledge of Market Offerings

Variation	Sum of squares	Degrees of freedom	Mean square	F-ratio
Main effects				
Interest	162.0	1	162.0	324.0 ($P < .05$)
Occupation	24.5	1	24.5	49.0
Sex	2.0	1	2.0	4.0
Two-factor interactions				
Interest–occupation	12.5	1	12.5	25.0
Interest–sex	2.0	1	2.0	4.0
Occupation–sex	12.5	1	12.5	25.0
Three-factor interaction	0.5	1	0.5	
Total	216.0	7		

$$\text{Correction factor } (C) = \frac{(\text{Grand total})^2}{n} = \frac{(672)^2}{8} = 56{,}448.$$

$$\text{Total sum of squares} = \Sigma (\text{Individual observations})^2 - C$$
$$= (88)^2 + (80)^2 + \cdots + (76)^2 - 56{,}448$$
$$= 56{,}664 - 56{,}448 = 216.0. \qquad \textit{(continued)}$$

Interest sum of squares $(I) = \dfrac{\Sigma \,(\text{Interest subgroup totals})^2}{\text{Size of interest subgroups}} - C$

$$= \frac{(354)^2 + (318)^2}{4} - 56{,}448$$

$$= 56{,}610 - 56{,}448 = 162.0.$$

Occupation sum of squares $(O) = \dfrac{\Sigma \,(\text{Occupation subgroup totals})^2}{\text{Size of occupation subgroups}} - C$

$$= \frac{(343)^2 + (329)^2}{4} - 56{,}448$$

$$= 56{,}472.50 - 56{,}448 = 24.5$$

Sex sum of squares $(S) = \dfrac{\Sigma \,(\text{Sex subgroup totals})^2}{\text{Size of sex subgroups}}$

$$= \frac{(334)^2 + (338)^2}{4} - 56{,}448$$

$$= 56{,}450 - 56{,}448 = 2.0.$$

Interaction terms sum of squares

Interest-occupation $= \dfrac{\Sigma \,(\text{Interest-occupation subgroup totals})^2}{\text{Size of interest-occupation subgroups}} - C - I - O$

$$= \frac{(178)^2 + (165)^2 + (176)^2 + (153)^2}{2} - 56{,}448 - 162 - 24.5$$

$$= 56{,}647 - 56{,}634.5 = 12.5.$$

Interest-sex $= \dfrac{\Sigma \,(\text{Interest-sex subgroup totals})^2}{\text{Size of interest-sex subgroups}} - C - I - S$

$$= \frac{(177)^2 + (157)^2 + (177)^2 + (161)^2}{2} - 56{,}448 - 162 - 2$$

$$= 56{,}614 - 56{,}612 = 2.0.$$

Occupation-sex $= \dfrac{\Sigma \,(\text{Occupation-sex subgroup totals})^2}{\text{Size of occupation-sex subgroups}} - C - O - S$

$$= \frac{(168)^2 + (166)^2 + (175)^2 + (163)^2}{2} - 56{,}448 - 24.5 - 2$$

$$= 56{,}487 - 56{,}474.5 = 12.5$$

Three-factor $=$ Total $- \Sigma(\text{Main effects}) - \Sigma(\text{Two-factor interactions})$
$= 216.0 - 188.5 - 27.0 = 0.50.$

of Table 13.5. This procedure uses the square of each cell value or the square of a total associated with a subgroup of observations along with a correction factor. This correction factor must be introduced because the raw scores are not deviations from means but deviations from zero.[4] Each of the squared terms has as its denominator the number of observations making up the sum that has been squared. Interaction sums of squares follow the same pattern with somewhat more complicated correction factors due to the fact that the sum of squares associated with each of the main effects involved must also be deducted from the initial calculation. The three-factor sum of squares is theoretically calculated in an analogous manner, but may be calculated more directly by the simple process of subtraction.

There are many marketing situations in which interaction terms are significant. This is the case in which synergistic effects are produced by appropriate combinations of different elements in either the total marketing mix or elements of a promotional mix. For example, the most desirable advertising copy may depend on the magazine employed. What is effective copy for one magazine may be totally ineffective in another magazine. When the analysis reveals significant interactions among the factors, the decision maker must gauge his or her behavior in accordance with these interaction terms rather than being led astray by reliance on the main effects. Only a test for interaction terms will prevent the possible misapplication of analyses that examine only the main effects.

Another tendency that must be resisted is that of being satisfied with the identification of the *one* most important factor. This is frequently the case in market segmentation problems. The mere fact that family income is more closely associated with buying behavior (for a particular product) should not blind the marketing manager to the possibility of defining a particularly attractive market segment based on family income plus another variable such as family size. The definition may be based on a simple two-variable linear model or an interaction model. Unless interaction is tested, the decision maker cannot know which model is appropriate.

Form of Conditional Distribution

The form of the conditional distribution is determined by the data. The relationship between estimates of the dependent variable, given different values of the independent variables, is unconstrained both with respect to magnitude and direction. This is simply an extension of what we saw in bivariate analysis of variance.

The basic form of Eq. (13.1) assumes independence among the independent variables. It calculates the combined effect of several independent variables as the sum of their separate effects. The simple model of Eq. (13.1) is thus properly classified as a "main-effects additive model."

---

[4]This is precisely the same correction factor that appears in many of the formulas for calculating the standard deviation.

Modification of Eq. (13.1) for interaction terms retains the basic unconstrained features of the initial formulation. The direction and magnitude of interaction effects is dictated by the data, including the possibility of no interaction effects. The basic model allows all forms of interactions from two-factor terms up to m-factor terms where m is the number of independent variables.

The conditional distribution possesses one very significant limitation. It yields estimates for only those values of the independent variables included in the experiment. Assume an experiment on message recall of a spot TV commercial yields the following equation:

$$E(y|x_1, x_2) = 78 + 6.2x_{11} - 4.3x_{12} - 1.9x_{13} + 1.3x_{21} + 7.4x_{22} - 8.7x_{23}.$$

Here x_{1i} refers to three different program types (x_{11} for musicals, x_{12} for sports features, and x_{13} for drama), and x_{2i} refers to time placement (x_{21} beginning, x_{22} middle, and x_{23} end). Estimates of message recall can be made for only the three types of programs tested and for only the three time placements included.

The results are even more limited if interactions are significant. In this case the estimates of the main effects are not valid. In the experiment above, the conditional equation would be revised to incorporate interaction effects and would be appropriate only for the nine cells of the original experiment. Estimates of the main effects of either independent variable would be invalid. The researcher does not know how time location will effect message recall when the ad is used with a documentary. The researcher should be extremely reluctant to estimate the interaction, having already discovered that timing has differential impact among the three types of programs tested.

Interval Estimates

Interval estimates from multiple classification ANOVA are made in precisely the same way as they are with bivariate ANOVA. The conditional variance, estimated from the within-cell variance, is the basic input in establishing the width of the interval. The t-distribution gives the required coefficient to use.

What is the 90 percent confidence interval of dollar sales for a large, yellow package (data in Table 13.1)? The point estimate from the equation derived is $2,300. The unbiased estimate of the universe conditional standard deviation is $173 (Table 13.2). The appropriate t-value is 1.78. Why? The standard deviation is assumed appropriate for all conditional estimates; homoscedasticity is assumed. Therefore, there are 12 degrees of freedom. Why is the t-value read from the .95 column instead of the .90 column? Applying 1.78, the resulting confidence interval is

$$2300 \pm 1.78(173),$$
$$2300 \pm 308,$$
$$\$1992 \text{ to } \$2608.$$

The 90 percent confidence interval for mean sales would be smaller since we are now dealing with the *standard error* of a conditional mean. This interval is based on the number of replications, modified by the number of categories for each variable.[5] The resulting interval is $2,145 to $2,455.

Computer Printouts

Analysis of variance computation can become quite laborious. The data in Table 13.5 show involved calculations although the total sample size is only eight. The availability of electronic computers plus the development of statistical packages have brought almost complete reliance on canned computer programs for multivariate statistical analysis.

Three of the more widely used sets of programs are the Biomedical Computer Programs (BMD), the Statistical Analyses System (SAS), and the Statistical Package for the Social Sciences (SPSS).[6] Each canned package requires input data in a certain form and specifies the control cards needed to use the program. We are concerned at this point with the form in which the programs present the results to the user—the output or the printout.

The analysis of response rates to mail questionnaires using different incentives illustrates the application of a canned ANOVA program. The experiment discussed in Chapter 5 was run in three different years: 1962, 1965, and 1970.[7] Therefore, we have two independent variables, year and incentive. Any attempt to order incentives or place them on an interval scale must proceed on dubious assumptions. ANOVA, using a nominal scale, assigns no order to the different incentives. The least stringent procedure with the three years is to consider time as nominal also. Three of the incentives were identical in all three years: sending a box of saltwater taffy with the questionnaire, promising a small gift for completion of the questionnaire, and thanking the respondent. All other incentives were varied over the time periods covered. The data are presented in Table 13.6.

A portion of the output from the SAS/ANOVA program is given in Table 13.7.[8] The first line of the table gives the mean and coefficient of variation for the dependent variable. The mean response rate over all 18 observations is 41 percent, and the coefficient of variation (σ/μ) is 20.58 percent. The next two

---

[5]The standard error of the conditional mean is equal to [(within-cell mean square) $(r + c - 1)/krc]^{1/2}$ where r and c are the number of categories and k is the number of replications.

[6]Descriptions of these programs are given in W. J. Dixon and M.B. Brown (eds.), 1977, *Biomedical Computer Programs,* P-Series (Berkeley, Calif.: University of California Press); Anthony James Barr and James Howard Goodnight, 1972, *A User's Guide to the Statistical Analysis System* (Raleigh, N.C.: Sparks Press); and Norman H. Nie, C. Hadlai Hull, Jean G. Jenkins, Karin Steinbrenner, and Dale H. Bent, 1975, *Statistical Package for the Social Sciences* (New York: McGraw-Hill).

[7]See "An Experiment in Various Incentives" in Chapter 5.

[8]Barr and Goodnight, *op. cit.,* pp. 138–154.

Table 13.6
Response Rates to Mail Questionnaire. Three Incentives and Three Different Years†

	Year		
Incentive	1962	1965	1970
Saltwater taffy sent	48, 58	42, 64	50, 46
Small gift promised	34, 58	32, 38	47, 46
Thank you given	28, 30	26, 22	31, 38

†The two entries in each cell represent the results from two different areas, one urban and one suburban. In order to simplify the example, they are treated as two observations from the same universe. Exercise 4 of this chapter investigates the justification of this procedure.

portions of the table give the separation of the total sum of squares into its component parts and the tests of the individual null hypotheses.

The total sum of squares is separated into four parts: two main effects, interaction, and residual. The two main effects are the differences in the incentives (labeled "INCENT") and the differences in the dates of the surveys (labeled "YEAR"). Their interaction is labeled "INCENT*YEAR." The residual term is the within-cell contribution. Degrees of freedom and mean square are computed in the usual way.

Each of the three tests uses the residual mean square as the denominator of an F-ratio. The table shows the probability of an F-ratio as large as the one observed if the null hypothesis is true. These probabilities exceed .5 for two tests: interaction and year. The probability is less than .01 for incentives.

The interaction test should be considered first. Acceptance of the null hypothesis means that incentive and year do not interact. Either may have its own effect, but the effects are independent of each other. The probability of .6298 indicates that the two, incentive and year, do not interact. Therefore, it is appropriate to consider the main effects.

The two tests of the main effects reveal that the various incentives have differential impacts but the various dates do not. Acceptance of the null hypothesis for YEAR is the equivalent of stating that the differences in the response rates for the three dates are simply reflections of inherent random fluctuations. The differentials produced by the various incentives may be determined from Table 13.6.[9] The individual means associated with the different incentives are 51.3 percent for the sending of the saltwater taffy, 42.5 percent for the promise of a small gift, and 29.2 percent for the thank you. These are the unbiased estimates for the separate incentives. None of the other variations within the table are viewed as significant; they are accepted as evidence of normal random fluctuations.

[9]The output from SAS includes the mean for each incentive as well as the mean for each year. That output has not been reproduced here.

Table 13.7
Computer Printout from SAS/Analysis of Variance

ANALYSIS OF VARIANCE FOR VARIABLE RESPS   MEAN   41.0000000   C.V.   20.5837218 %

SOURCE	DF	SUM OF SQUARES	MEAN SQUARE
INCENT	2	1494.33333	747.166667
YEAR	2	121.33333	60.666667
INCENT*YEAR	4	191.33333	47.833333
RESIDUAL	9	641.00000	71.222222
CORRECTED TOTAL	17	2448.00000	144.000000

TESTS SOURCE	DF	SUM OF SQUARES	MEAN SQUARE	F VALUE	PROB F
NUMERATOR: INCENT	2	1494.33333	747.166667	10.49064	0.0048
DENOMINATOR: RESIDUAL	9	641.00000	71.222222		
NUMERATOR: YEAR	2	121.33333	60.666667	0.85179	0.5386
DENOMINATOR: RESIDUAL	9	641.00000	71.222222		
NUMERATOR: INCENT*YEAR	4	191.33333	47.833333	0.67161	0.6298
DENOMINATOR: RESIDUAL	9	641.00000	71.222222		

Overview of Multiple Classification ANOVA

ANOVA with several independent variables differs little from bivariate ANOVA. The principal aspects are summarized in Table 13.8. Only the potential for interactions among the independent variables provides a significant differentiation from the bivariate ANOVA.

A measure of association is not usually included in the ANOVA output, regardless of whether the analysis is based upon a single independent variable or several independent variables. This lack is based on two main considerations. (1) The sample data usually represent a conscious selection of particular values of the independent variables—a type of "regression" approach rather than the "correlation" approach required for measuring degree of association. (2) The analysis is uniquely dependent on the categories established for the research. Changes in the number of categories or their definitions might lead to totally different results. In those situations in which a measure of association is appropriate, the correlation ratio (η) or its square is the appropriate measure, as is the case in bivariate ANOVA.

The researcher should be particularly conscious that ANOVA imposes no constraints on the form of the conditional distribution, either in the main effects (assuming no interaction) or in the individual cell estimates (assuming interaction). A second major feature of ANOVA is its assumption of homoscedasticity. This assumption is included in ANOVA's tests but also influences any confidence interval estimates. Pooled within-cell variance serves as the basis for both the F-tests and confidence interval estimates. The existence of unequal within-cell variances would destroy the appropriateness of this approach.

Table 13.8
Multiple Classification ANOVA Summary

1. Test statistic: F-ratio for each main effect and each interaction
2. Estimate based on:
   a) Grand mean if H_0 is accepted
   b) Conditional mean if H_0 is rejected
3. Summary of relationship, if any:
   a) Read directly from table
   b) May be irregular jumps
4. Measure of association: Correlation ratio (η)
5. Form of conditional distribution:
   a) No prior specification
   b) No constraints
   c) May or may not have interactions, depending on data

MULTIPLE REGRESSION

Multiple regression is the logical extension of bivariate regression, addressing itself to the problem of a single dependent variable that is measured on an interval scale and any number of independent variables that are also measured on interval scales. The multiple regression equation is of the form given in Eq. (13.2).

$$E(y|x_1, x_2, \ldots, x_n) = a + b_1x_1 + b_2x_2 + \cdots + b_nx_n. \qquad (13.2)$$

If it is a situation that can be properly identified as "correlation" rather than "regression," it is also appropriate to compute a multiple coefficient of determination (R^2). As was the case with only two variables, the multiple coefficient of determination measures the percentage reduction in variance by measuring dispersion of the observations around the estimating equation rather than around the mean of the dependent variable.

Interpretation of Coefficients

The a-coefficient of Eq. (13.2) has precisely the same interpretation as it had in two-variable regression. It is the calculated value for the dependent variable when all of the independent variables are equal to zero. As was the case in two-variable regression, this calculation is almost always an extrapolated value, and its use in decision making is suspect. Consider the following equation.

$$E(y|x_1, x_2, x_3) = 32.5 + 12.0x_1 + .2x_2 - 3.4x_3$$

$$y = \text{annual expenditures on product A}$$
$$\text{(in dollars)}$$
$$x_1 = \text{family discretionary income (in \$1,000)}$$
$$x_2 = \text{gregariousness score on ABC Test}$$
$$x_3 = \text{tenure in SMSA (in years).}$$

Taken at its face value, the a-value implies that a family with no discretionary income, a score of zero in gregariousness, and just arrived in the standard metropolitan area (a tenure of zero) would be expected to spend $32.50 on the product under consideration. The raw data upon which the equation is based (see Table 13.9) indicate family discretionary income in excess of $1,000 for all ten observations; tenure values observed fall between one year and ten years; and gregariousness scores are 60 or higher for all observations. The extrapolation is greatest for gregariousness. However, all three are clearly extrapolated, and the joint effect of three extrapolations may be considerably magnified.

The regression coefficients are also interpreted in a way quite similar to that used in two-variable regression. The only distinction is that each coefficient shows the effect of its particular variable when the other independent variables of the equation are held constant. For example, the 12.0 value associated with family discretionary income is designed to show the net effect of

Table 13.9
Multiple Regression. Expenditures on Product A versus Family Discretionary Income, Gregariousness Score, and Tenure

Expenditures on product A (y) ($)	Family discretionary income (x_1) ($1,000)	Gregariousness score (x_2) (raw score)	Tenure in SMSA (x_3) (years)
58	2.5	73	3
105	6.1	65	7
75	1.8	79	2
62	3.4	81	5
83	4.7	75	3
43	2.1	60	4
95	4.3	84	1
48	1.1	74	5
65	3.6	79	4
53	3.8	82	10
687	33.4	752	44

Sum of squares   Cross-products

$\Sigma y^2 = 50,959$ $\Sigma x_1 y = 2508.4$ $\Sigma x_1 x_2 = 2513.7$

$\Sigma x_1^2 = 131.86$ $\Sigma x_2 y = 51,824$ $\Sigma x_1 x_3 = 155.5$

$\Sigma x_2^2 = 57,078$ $\Sigma x_3 y = 2915$ $\Sigma x_2 x_3 = 3292$

$\Sigma x_3^2 = 254$

$$\Sigma y = na + b_1 \Sigma x_1 + b_2 \Sigma x_2 + b_3 \Sigma x_3$$
$$\Sigma x_1 y = a\Sigma x_1 + b_1 \Sigma (x_1)^2 + b_2 \Sigma x_1 x_2 + b_3 \Sigma x_1 x_3$$
$$\Sigma x_2 y = a\Sigma x_2 + b_1 \Sigma x_1 x_2 + b_2 \Sigma (x_2)^2 + b_3 \Sigma x_2 x_3$$
$$\Sigma x_3 y = a\Sigma x_3 + b_1 \Sigma x_1 x_3 + b_2 \Sigma x_2 x_3 + b_3 \Sigma (x_3)^2$$
$$E(y|x_1, x_2, x_3) = 32.5 + 12.0x_1 + .2x_2 - 3.4x_3$$
$$(2.7) \qquad (.5) \quad (1.5)$$

changes in discretionary income on expenditures for Product A while holding both gregariousness and tenure constant. The effect of each variable is isolated even though the experiment does not hold two variables constant while changing the third. The method of calculating the equation is a simultaneous solution for all constants rather than a sequential attempt of first changing one variable and then another.

The first and most obvious conclusion from the equation is that family discretionary income and gregariousness are both positively associated with expenditures on product A while tenure is inversely associated with these expenditures. These statements come directly from observation of the signs of the various coefficients. Second, we can interpret the meaning of the specific values of the coefficients. A change of $1,000 in family discretionary income on the average is accompanied by a change in expenditures on product A of $12.00 in the same direction—as discretionary income goes up, expenditures on product A usually go up. A change of one point in the gregariousness score is associated on the average with a change of $.20 in annual expenditures for product A (again in the same direction). A change for one year in tenure is associated on the average with a change of $3.40 in annual expenditures in the opposite direction.[10]

The calculation of the regression equation is an extension of the method employed in bivariate regression. The method of least squares is used, choosing the linear equation for which the sum of squared deviations is a minimum. This line is determined by the simultaneous solution of a system of equations. The number of equations is equal to the number of constants to be determined. The appropriate equations for the present problem are shown in Table 13.9.[11]

Is There Association?

The question of association in multiple regression is a series of questions rather than a single question. Each separate question asks whether the dependent variable is associated with a particular independent variable. Just as ANOVA tested for each main effect separately, multiple regression tests for each independent variable separately. This is done with a t-test for each regression coefficient.

The null hypothesis in each test is that the particular independent variable is not associated with the dependent variable. If the null hypothesis is rejected, the variable should be included in the equation; but if the null hypothesis is accepted, the variable should be deleted from the equation. In this way, the estimating equation is not complicated by the inclusion of variables whose relationship to the dependent variable have not been substantiated. Each regression coefficient has a standard error.[12] A t-test is appropriate for testing each null hypothesis, and uses the ratio of the calculated regression coefficient to its own standard error. The standard errors for our regression problem are shown in parentheses under each regression coefficient in Table 13.9.

The regression coefficient for discretionary income is about 4.4 times its own standard error, and the regression coefficient for tenure is 2.3 times its own standard error. The number of degrees of freedom for the test is six (ten

---

[10]A more precise interpretation of each of these coefficients would indicate that the other two independent variables are being held constant.

[11]The equations are determined by defining algebraically the squared deviation, summing, taking partial derivatives, and setting each partial derivative equal to zero.

[12]Calculation of these standard errors without access to the computer is an extremely tedious and long operation. Indeed, multiple regression itself is extremely tedious without a computer. Most "canned" regression programs yield the standard errors as part of the output, and the reader is advised to employ this approach as the most efficient procedure.

observations minus the four constants of the equation). Referring to Appendix Table A.3, the null hypothesis in respect to discretionary income should be rejected at even the .01 level of significance. The null hypothesis for tenure would be rejected at the .1 level but not at the .05 level. The coefficient for gregariousness is less than half its standard error. At any reasonable level of significance, we should conclude that expenditures on product A and gregariousness are not associated.[13]

Sometimes a decision maker will use any of the independent variables that exceed their own standard errors—in so doing the decision maker is relying much more on unbiased point estimates than on either interval estimates or tests of hypotheses. Each of the regression coefficients in the equation of Table 13.9 has two properties: (1) it describes the average linear relationship found *within the sample* and (2) it is an unbiased estimate if the sample has been selected in an unbiased manner of the average linear relationship to be found in the universe.

Regression Coefficients: Multivariate versus Bivariate

It should be noted that the regression coefficients shown in Table 13.9 are not the same as the coefficients that would be obtained by three separate bivariate problems. The coefficients that would be obtained in separate regressions are $+10.5$, $+0.3$, and -1.5. All are of the same general order of magnitude, but the numerical differences are not trivial. These differences are produced because the three independent variables are not independent of each other in the sample employed. In the gross (bivariate) equations, the magnitude of the relationships is either understated or overstated, depending on the correlations that exist among the independent variables.[14]

The coefficients of the multiple regression equation are often referred to as "net" coefficients. They are net in the sense that they show the relationship between a specific independent variable and the dependent variable after adjusting for the remaining independent variables *of the equation*. They obviously have not been adjusted for other variables. The coefficient in a bivariate equation is not adjusted for any other variables and shows a "gross" relationship.

Multicollinearity

If the independent variables are related to each other and not truly independent of each other, *multicollinearity* is said to exist. The task of determining the contribution of each of the variables is difficult in such a case. Consider

---

[13]The test of association does not actually test for association between the stated independent variable and the dependent variable; rather it tests for the net relationship after adjusting for the effects of the other independent variables in the analysis. Thus it can be thought of as a comparison of two models or equations, one including all variables except the one specified and the other including all variables of the analysis.

[14] The more usual situation is one in which the absolute magnitude of the coefficients is overstated in the bivariate equation.

the question of whether earnings level within a particular occupation is associated with amount of formal education and score on a particular aptitude test. If the amount of formal education and the score on the aptitude test are very highly correlated with each other, it is impossible to isolate the separate effect of each of these variables on earnings.

The data in Table 13.10 illustrate the extreme case. All persons with 12 years of education receive $19,000 income, and each additional year of education adds $1,000 in income. However, it is also true that an aptitude test score of 60 is associated with a $19,000 income and income rises $1,000 for every three points on the aptitude scale. Education and aptitude score are perfectly correlated. It is impossible to identify the separate effect of each variable on income. Multicollinearity exists among the independent variables and regression cannot uniquely identify their separate effects.

If we are more interested in making a prediction of the dependent variable than in identifying the separate contributions of each independent variable, multicollinearity is a less serious problem. In the prediction problem, we wish to estimate the dependent variable. The point estimate comes from the total equation, and its reliability is shown by the conditional standard deviation (standard error of estimate). If we wish to estimate the contribution of each separate independent variable, our attention is focused on the separate regression coefficients and their respective standard errors. If multicollinearity exists, the "confusion" of the equation appears in large standard errors of the regression coefficients rather than a large conditional standard deviation. Modification of multiple regression or preliminary treatment of the input data is designed to cope with this problem.[15]

Table 13.10
Earnings, Education, and Aptitude Test Score with Extreme Multicollinearity

Worker	Income	Education	Aptitude score
A	$25,000	18	78
B	19,000	12	60
C	23,000	16	72
D	20,000	13	63
E	23,000	16	72
F	19,000	12	60
G	21,000	14	66
H	19,000	12	60

[15]Two distinct approaches to multicollinearity exist: (1) stepwise regression that guards against the inclusion of independent variables that are redundant and (2) factor analysis that attempts to isolate the common "factors" possessed by correlated independent variables. The first is discussed in Chapter 14 and the second in Chapter 16.

Multiple Coefficient of Determination

The sample coefficient of determination will increase with the addition of each independent variable to the equation. As has already been explained, this is a descriptive measure for the sample rather than an unbiased estimate of the corresponding universe measure. An unbiased estimate of the universe coefficient of determination is obtained by Eq. (13.3). The factor $(n - 1)/(n - k)$ is the necessary adjustment for degrees of freedom.

$$\bar{R}^2 = 1 - (1 - R^2)\frac{(n - 1)}{(n - k)}. \tag{13.3}$$

Here n refers to the number of observations in the sample, and k refers to the number of constants in the regression equation. As was the case in the bivariate problem, a coefficient of determination or a coefficient of correlation is appropriate only if the data represent a problem in correlation rather than a problem in regression. If the data in Table 13.9 were generated from a simple random sample from the universe rather than individuals selected according to their values with respect to the independent variables, R^2, R, $\bar{R}^2$, and $\bar{R}$ are appropriate for calculation. The data in Table 13.9 yield the following results:

$$R^2 = .78$$
$$R = .88$$
$$\bar{R}^2 = 1 - (1 - .78)\ \frac{9}{6}$$
$$= 1 - .22 \times \frac{3}{2} = 1 - .33$$
$$= .67$$
$$\bar{R} = .82.$$

The interpretation of these results is analogous to the interpretation of the corresponding bivariate measures. The variance in expenditures on product A is 78 percent less when measured around the regression line than when measured around the mean expenditure. Variance in both cases is limited to the ten sample observations. The only distinction between this interpretation and the one for the bivariate case is that the regression equation contains more independent variables. The multiple coefficient of correlation ($R = .88$) is merely the square root of R^2. The numerical result of $\bar{R}^2 = .67$ provides an estimate of the percentage reduction in variance in the universe—in contrast to that in the sample. $\bar{R}$ is the estimate of the coefficient of correlation for the universe. Again it is the square root of the percentage reduction in variance.

Note that the sample coefficient of correlation is presented as .88, seeming to imply a positive multiple correlation. In multiple correlation the coefficient of correlation is always assigned a positive sign, but this is completely arbitrary. In our problem, the sample regression coefficients were positive in two instances and negative in the third. The positive sign for R carries no implication whatsoever of whether the relationship is positive, negative, or mixed. The same statements apply to the estimate of the universe coefficient of correlation ($\bar{R}$ = .82). The null hypothesis of no universe association is tested by comparing R with its own standard error. An alternative but equivalent test compares "explained" and "unexplained" variance via an F-test. Using this approach with the current data, the null hypothesis is rejected.[16]

It is a mathematical necessity that the sample coefficient of determination cannot decrease with the addition of more independent variables to the regression equation. This is not necessarily the case for unbiased estimates of universe coefficients of determination—the correction for degrees of freedom making the difference.

Partial Coefficients of Determination

Multiple correlation can also measure the degree of association between the dependent variable and each of the individual independent variables. These measures are called *partial coefficients of determination*. Each is computed from a different base, the variance about a regression line before introducing the particular variable.

Consider the data in Table 13.9. Three different equations with two independent variables could be computed: equations based upon discretionary income–gregariousness, gregariousness–tenure, and discretionary income–tenure could each be calculated. The partial coefficients of determination show the percentage reduction in variance by adding each of these three independent variables as the third variable. $R^2_{yx_i,\ x_ax_b}$ denotes the partial coefficient of determination between dependent variable y and independent variable x_i, net of variables x_a and x_b. It is defined by Eq. (13.4).

$$R^2_{yx_i,\ x_ax_b} = 1 - \frac{S^2(y|x_ix_ax_b)}{S^2(y|x_ax_b)}. \tag{13.4}$$

Table 13.11 shows the calculation of the partial R^2 values for the income-tenure-gregariousness data. The unconditional variance with respect to expenditures is 376.21. Each of the two independent variable equations reduces this variance, the income-tenure equation reducing it the most. The total equation has a final unconditional variance of 81.02. The partial R^2 values compare this final unconditional variance with the three unconditional variances based on the two independent variable equations.

Using Eq. (13.4), the partial R^2 values are 77.1 percent for discretionary income, 1.4 percent for gregariousness, and 45.0 percent for tenure. The sum of these three percentages (123.5) is meaningless since each is calculated from a different base. Partial coefficients of *correlation* may also be computed by

---

[16]The data are presented later in the chapter in the section "Computer Printouts."

Table 13.11
Calculation of Partial Coefficients of Determination

Reference point	Variance
Expenditure mean	376.21
Two independent variable equations	
Income-gregariousness	147.30
Gregariousness-tenure	353.66
Income-tenure	82.21
Three independent variable equation	81.02

Partial R^2

Income: $1 - \dfrac{81.02}{353.66} = .771$

Tenure: $1 - \dfrac{81.02}{147.30} = .450$

Gregariousness: $1 - \dfrac{81.02}{82.21} = .014$

extracting square roots. These results would be .878, .118, and .671. As was the case with r, R, and $\bar{R}$, partial coefficients of correlation should never be referred to as percentages.

Which Estimating Equation to Use

We have at least three options in selecting the appropriate estimating equation: (1) the total equation derived from all independent variables submitted in the analysis ($32.5 + 12.0x_1 + .2x_2 - 3.4x_3$); (2) the equation derived by option (1), excluding all variables for which the null hypothesis is accepted ($32.5 + 12.0x_1 - 3.4x_3$ or $32.5 + 12.0x_1$ depending on the level of significance employed); (3) a recalculated equation, excluding all variables for which the null hypothesis is rejected. This equation will be of the same form as option (2), but it will have different numerical values.

The use of the total equation is sometimes advised when the purpose is prediction of the dependent variable. The argument in favor of this option views the situation as an estimation problem. The total equation provides unbiased point estimates. The conditional standard deviation establishes the appropriate intervals, wide or narrow depending on the closeness of the overall association between the dependent variable and the *set* of independent variables. Following this procedure, the total equation of Table 13.9 would be employed.

The second option uses only a portion of the total equation. The logic of this position is that the retention of independent variables that are not associated with the dependent variable is superfluous. According to this position, the appropriate equation for the data in Table 13.9 (at $\alpha = .1$) would include discretionary income and tenure but not gregariousness. The regression coefficients would be 12.0 (discretionary income) and -3.4 (tenure) since these are the values showing their net effects. The logic breaks down at this point—the net effect after adjusting for two variables, one of which has no effect, is suspect. A net effect would seem more appropriate if adjustments are made for only independent variables that are associated with the dependent variable. A second and more serious difficulty in this option is the Y-intercept. If the means of all the independent variables are substituted in the regression equation, the calculated value is the mean of the dependent variable. The Y-intercept is the adjusting factor that produces this result. If one or more independent variables are excluded from the equation, retention of the original Y-intercept has no theoretical justification. In fact, its retention produces biased predictions.

The third option starts with the same logic as the second: do not retain independent variables for which the null hypothesis has been accepted. It differs by asking for the calculation of a new equation, using only the retained independent variables. The recalculated equation by this procedure would be

$$E(y|x_1, x_3) = 44.0 + 12.0x_1 - 3.5x_3.$$

One regression coefficient is identical, and the other differs by only .1. The Y-intercept, however, is drastically different. These results are typical. Net regression coefficients should be approximately the same since the only difference is whether a variable unassociated with the dependent variable has been included. The difference in Y-intercepts is necessary to accomplish an intersection of means; a different adjustment is necessary depending on the specific variables employed.

Estimates of the Dependent Variable

Whichever option is selected, the regression equation yields point estimates for expenditures on product A. Values must be supplied for all independent variables within the equation. Suppose we use the third option and the revised equation. A point estimate for a family with discretionary income of \$4,200 and tenure of three years is given by

$$y = 44.0 + 12.0(4.2) - 3.4(3)$$
$$= 84.2.$$

The point estimate for expenditures on product A is \$84.20.

An interval estimate can be made by using the conditional standard deviation. An unbiased estimate of the universe conditional standard deviation, rather than the sample result should be used; and the t-distribution is the appropriate model.[17] An unbiased estimate of the universe variance is given by $s^2(y|x_1,x_3)$ times $n/n\text{-}k$ where k is the number of constants in the regression equation. Its square root is the required conditional standard deviation and is equal to 10.8. Since there are seven degrees of freedom ($k = 3$ for the equation used), the appropriate coefficient for 95 percent confidence is 2.36. (See Appendix Table A.3.) The interval estimate is

$$84.2 \pm 2.36(10.8)$$

$$84.2 \pm 25.5$$

$$\$58.70 \text{ to } 109.70.$$

The mean for the given values of the independent variables can be estimated with greater reliability. Here the standard error of the conditional mean is used instead of the conditional standard deviation. This standard error ($\overset{*}{\sigma}_{\bar{y}|x_1,x_3}$) is equal to 3.4. Substituting, the 95 percent confidence interval for the desired conditional mean is

$$84.2 \pm 2.36(3.4)$$

$$84.2 \pm 8.0$$

$$\$76.20 \text{ to } \$92.20.$$

Interval Estimates for Regression Coefficients

Estimates of the incremental effect of the independent variables on the dependent variable are given by the individual regression coefficients. Interval estimates for these incremental effects can be established by using the appropriate t-coefficients with the standard errors of the relevant regression coefficient. The t-coefficient is again based on seven degrees of freedom. A 90 percent confidence interval for discretionary income regression coefficient is given by

$$12.0 \pm 1.90(2.7)$$

$$12.0 \pm 5.1$$

$$6.9 \text{ to } 17.1.$$

A difference of \$1,000 in discretionary income is accompanied, on the average, by a difference in expenditures of between \$6.90 and \$17.10—estimated with 90 percent confidence.

The 90 percent confidence interval for the tenure regression coefficient follows a similar format but uses a different standard error (1.5). This interval is

$$-3.4 \pm 1.90(1.5)$$

$$-3.4 \pm 2.8$$

$$-6.2 \text{ to } -0.6.$$

---

[17]Use of the t-distribution of course assumes that the distribution of observations around the regression line conforms to the normal curve.

This interval, compared with the prior interval, emphasizes two things. (1) The sign is extremely important. Higher discretionary income is associated with *higher* expenditures on product A, although the precise amount is uncertain. Longer tenure is associated with *smaller* expenditures on product A, although again the precise amount is uncertain. (2) The width of the interval depends on the magnitude of the standard error of the regression coefficient, not on the degree of association or on the magnitude of the regression coefficient.

Computer Printouts

The solution of multiple regression problems is extremely tedious. Simultaneous solution of systems of equations is involved and laborious. Rounding errors are involved at each succeeding step. Table 13.12 gives a portion of the computer printout from the SAS/multiple regression program.[18] This output first tests whether the regression equation (using all three independent variables) reduces variance significantly. This test separates total variance into explained and unexplained variance, labeled "regression" and "error." The regression "sum of squares" is based upon the dispersion among the values predicted for the ten original observations, using the regression equation and the given values for the three independent variables. The error "sum of squares" measures the dispersion of the original observations from these predicted values. An F-test compares the two variances (using the appropriate degrees of freedom) in order to determine whether the regression variance is merely a reflection of the inherent variability (error variance) within the data. The calculated F-ratio of 7.29 is large enough to reject the null hypothesis at an α of .05, shown by the column "PROB > F" of .0206. The sample coefficient of determination (R^2) is shown as .78 in the column "R-SQUARE."

The regression equation appears in the third section of Table 13.12 under the first two columns. The three independent variables are named in the first column along with the Y-intercept. Their numerical values appear in the second column labeled "B VALUES"; for example, the regression coefficient for family discretionary income is shown as "FAMDI 11.960 . . .". The third column of this section gives the result of the t-test for each constant estimated in the regression, including the Y-intercept. The null hypothesis tested in each case is that the universe constant is zero. The probability of a t as large as the one observed (if the null hypothesis is true) is given in the next column labeled "PROB > |T|". These probabilities indicate that the null hypothesis should be rejected for discretionary income. The decision with respect to tenure is less certain; the probability is greater than the traditional .05. The standard error of each constant is also given in this third section of the table.

The last column of the third section presents the standardized regression coefficients.[19] The intercept standardized value of 0.0 will always occur,

---

[18]Barr and Goodnight, *op. cit.*, pp. 94–107.

[19]See "Standardized Regression Coefficients" in Chapter 12.

Table 13.12
Computer Printout from SAS/Multiple Regression Analysis

MULTIPLE REGRESSION ANALYSIS

ANALYSIS OF VARIANCE TABLE , REGRESSION COEFFICIENTS , AND STATISTICS OF FIT FOR DEPENDENT VARIABLE EXPEND

SOURCE	DF	SUM OF SQUARES	MEAN SQUARE	F VALUE	PROB > F	R-SQUARE	C.V.
REGRESSION	3	2951.91097081	983.97032360	7.28697	0.0206	0.7846447	16.91456 %
ERROR	6	810.18902919	135.03150486			STD DEV	EXPEND MEAN
CORRECTED TOTAL	9	3762.10000000				11.62030571	68.70000

SOURCE	DF	SEQUENTIAL SS	F VALUE	PROB > F	PARTIAL SS	F VALUE	PROB > F
FAMDI	1	2251.72342396	16.67554	0.0065	2726.38646282	20.19074	0.0041
GREGSCR	1	37.33759837	0.27651	0.6179	11.92571640	0.08832	0.7763
TENURE	1	662.84994848	4.90885	0.0686	662.84994848	4.90885	0.0686

SOURCE	B VALUES	T FOR HO:B=0	PROB > |T|	STD ERR B	STD B VALUES
INTERCEPT	32.49431798	0.81351	0.4470	39.94344315	0.0
FAMDI	11.96016191	4.49341	0.0041	2.66171103	0.87864349
GREGSCR	0.15116183	0.29718	0.7763	0.50864814	0.05660820
TENURE	-3.43377920	-2.21559	0.0686	1.54982373	-0.43508656

OBS NUMBER	OBSERVED VALUE	PREDICTED VALUE	RESIDUAL	LOWER 95% CL FOR INDIVIDUAL	UPPER 95% CL FOR INDIVIDUAL
1	58.00000000	63.12829885	-5.12819885	32.43200046	93.82439724
2	105.00000000	91.24037027	13.75962973	54.12038133	128.36035921
3	75.00000000	59.00683570	15.90316430	26.76316138	91.43051003
4	62.00000000	68.23408081	-6.23408081	37.42114567	98.04701596
5	83.00000000	89.74287872	-6.74287872	57.80980719	121.67595026
6	43.00000000	52.94525107	-9.94525107	16.87421518	89.01628696
7	95.00000000	93.18682885	1.81317115	58.26388456	128.10977314
8	48.00000000	39.66757559	8.33242441	6.15100288	73.18414830
9	65.00000000	73.75756874	-8.75756874	43.49255216	104.02258532
10	53.00000000	56.00041139	-3.00041139	18.26511504	93.73570774

showing that substitution of the means for the independent variables yields the mean for the dependent variable. The standardized value for discretionary income is .8786 . . . meaning that a difference of one standard deviation in discretionary income is associated with a difference of .8786 . . . standard deviations in expenditures on product A—in the same direction since the sign is positive. The standardized score for gregariousness indicates a difference of one standard deviation in gregariousness (over seven points) is associated with a difference of only .0566 . . . of a standard deviation in expenditures (about $1). These results are implicit in the original constants, but the standardized values correct for any arbitrariness in the units chosen for the problem.

The last section of Table 13.12 presents the original sample values, the corresponding predicted values, the residuals, and the upper and lower bounds for a 95 percent confidence interval. The program has a dual option for this portion of the output. (1) The confidence coefficient may be 90, 95, or 99 percent. (2) The interval may be established for individual elements or for the conditional mean.

The residual entries permit the study of dispersion around the regression line. Four are positive, and six are negative. Residuals with the same sign show a slight tendency to occur together: one negative, two positive, three negative, two positive, and two negative. Any tendency toward "bunching" of similar signs or marked departure from an even division should lead to an examination for possible causative factors. "Bunching" would be particularly significant in a time series.[20]

The second section of the table presents the incremental reduction in the sum of squares for each independent variable. The left-hand portion shows the sequential reduction as first discretionary income is introduced (with a reduction of 2252), followed by the gregariousness score (a further reduction of 37), and finally tenure (a reduction of 663). The sequence in this program is arbitrary, being determined by the initial ordering of the variables.[21] The entries in the right-hand portion are partial sums of squares, each based upon the sum of squares remaining after adjusting for the effects of the other two independent variables.[22]

The tenure sums of squares are of course the same in the two portions since they refer to identical calculations: reduction after the other two independent variables have been employed. The two entries for discretionary income are atypical. In the usual situation, an independent variable would produce a greater reduction in the sum of squares when used as the first variable than it would when used as the last. The usual pattern is shown in the comparison of the gregariousness entries, a larger reduction when used as the second variable than when used as the third.

---

[20]A test for "bunching" of similar signs can be made with a runs test. See Chapter 18.

[21]Stepwise regression uses a sequential approach, but the sequence is determined by the data. This technique is discussed in Chapter 14.

[22]See "Partial Coefficients of Determination" earlier in this chapter.

Structure of the Conditional Distribution

Regression introduces severe constraints on the form of the conditional distribution. All relationships determined by Eq. (13.2) are assumed to be linear. If the true relationships are nonlinear, use of this form will understate the degree of association, overstate the width of confidence intervals, and of course yield less accurate point estimates. No interaction terms are involved in Eq. (13.2). Regression could incorporate interaction terms, but the researcher would have to specify the precise algebraic form of that interaction. Regression does not "search" for interactions. Finally, multiple linear regression assumes homoscedasticity. This assumption obviously affects interval estimation, but it is also involved in the determination of the regression equation itself. If the dispersion is greater for certain portions of the sample, those portions will have greater weight in determining the equation.

Overview of Multiple Regression

Multiple regression differs little from bivariate regression. The main distinction is the existence of two types of results in multiple regression. The first is the total relationship between the dependent variable and a set of independent variables. The second is the relationship between the dependent variable and each individual independent variable. Table 13.13 presents a summary of the principal features of multiple regression.

Table 13.13
Multiple Regression Summary

1. Test statistics:
   a) F-ratio or $t = R/\dot{\sigma}_R$ for total equation
   b) $t = b/\dot{\sigma}_b$ for individual independent variables

2. Estimate based on:
   a) Grand mean if H_0 is accepted
   b) Mathematical linear equation if H_0 is rejected
      i) Total equation including all independent variables or
      ii) Equation including only independent variables for which $H_0 (\beta_i = 0)$ is rejected

3. Summary of relationship, if any:
   a) Regression equation for relationship
   b) Individual regression coefficients for incremental relationship to each independent variable

4. Measure of association:
   a) Coefficient of determination (R^2) for aggregate of all independent variables
   b) Partial coefficients of determination ($R^2_{yx_i, x_a \ldots}$) for each independent variable

5. Form of conditional distribution:
   a) Prior specification
   b) Linear: $y = a + b_1 x_1 + b_2 x_2 + \cdots + b_n x_n$
   c) No interaction unless specified as a revision of 5(b)

6. Criterion for "best" equation: minimization of squared deviations

A series of "no association" hypotheses exist: one analyzing the dependent variable against the set of independent variables and an additional hypothesis for each independent variable separately. The first test may be made with an F-ratio along an ANOVA approach of explained and unexplained variance. An alternative test compares the sample coefficient of multiple correlation to its own standard error. The tests for relationships with the separate independent variables are made with a series of t-tests comparing the separate regression coefficients to their respective standard errors.

Estimates of the dependent variable employ either the total regression equation derived or a truncated form that retains only those independent variables which are "significantly" related to the dependent variable. The nature of the various relationships is shown by either the total equation or the individual coefficients. The measure of association is the relevant coefficient of determination, either total or partial.

The form of the conditional distribution and the criterion for "best" fit follow the pattern established in bivariate regression. Linearity is specified in advance, and the least-squares criterion is employed. Interaction among the independent variables is not usually included in the regression equation. If it is included, the precise structure of the interaction must be specified. It is not determined by the data!

DISCRIMINANT ANALYSIS

Multiple discriminant analysis is very similar to multiple regression analysis; the difference is the nature of the dependent variable—one is nominally scaled and the other is intervally scaled. Any number of categories for the dependent variable may be employed in discriminant analysis. We shall illustrate the procedure initially with only two categories.

The data of Table 13.9 would be appropriate for multiple discriminant analysis if the respondents were classified on expenditures into either high or low rather than precise measurements of expenditures on an interval scale. The task of the analysis is to use the three independent variables in a linear function that best discriminates between the two classes of individuals. With this procedure, measurement of the dependent variable has been relaxed from an interval scale to a nominal scale. In the more typical case, the researcher either does not have confidence in his or her ability to measure on an interval scale or believes the basic characteristic is best defined nominally rather than intervally. Table 13.14 uses the three independent variables that were employed in the multiple regression example; but the dependent variable is membership in the local civic organization—with membership coded 1 and nonmembership coded 0.

Note the comparisons between the means for members and the means for nonmembers on the three independent variables. It appears that members tend to have lower discretionary incomes, to be more gregarious, and to have longer

Table 13.14
Multiple Discriminant Analysis of Civic Organization Membership versus Family Discretionary Income, Gregariousness Score, and Tenure

Civic membership (y)	Family discretionary income (x_1)	Gregariousness score (x_2)	Tenure in SMSA (x_3)
No (0)	2.5	73	3
No (0)	6.1	65	7
Yes (1)	1.8	79	2
Yes (1)	3.4	81	5
No (0)	4.7	75	3
No (0)	2.1	60	4
No (0)	4.3	84	1
Yes (1)	1.1	74	5
Yes (1)	3.6	79	4
Yes (1)	3.8	82	10
5	33.4	752	44
Means			
Members	2.74	79.0	5.2
Nonmembers	3.94	71.4	3.6

Resulting discriminant function: $- .09065x_1 + .00230x_2 + .03204x_3 = y_c$

Assignment rule: If $y_c > .01116$, predict member,
        if $y_c < .01116$, predict nonmember.

tenure. Only one of the ten individuals in the sample possesses characteristics on all three variables that are consistent with nonmember status; the fifth person listed in Table 13.14 is above average in income, below average in gregariousness, and below average in tenure. The fifth person is in a nonmember status, consistent with the scores on all three characteristics. No one in the sample has scores on all three characteristics that are consistent with member status. The task of the discriminant analysis is to combine these three scores in a manner that will facilitate prediction of membership or nonmembership.

The discriminant function is established by solving the system of equations given by Eq. (13.5).

$$A\Sigma x_1^2 + B\Sigma x_1 x_2 + C\Sigma x_1 x_3 = \bar{x}_{1M} - \bar{x}_{1N}$$
$$A\Sigma x_1 x_2 + B\Sigma x_2^2 + C\Sigma x_2 x_3 = \bar{x}_{2M} - \bar{x}_{2N}$$
$$A\Sigma x_1 x_3 + B\Sigma x_2 x_3 + C\Sigma x_3^2 = \bar{x}_{3M} - \bar{x}_{3N}. \tag{13.5}$$

The right-hand side of Eq. (13.5) employs a series of differences between the two subgroups on the various independent variables. Solution of Eq. (13.5) yields coefficients for the different independent variables for the discriminant function. The function established for the data found in Table 13.14 is

$-.09065x_1 + .00230x_2 + .03204x_3 = y_c$. The next step is to determine a critical value that will be the basis for predicting membership or nonmembership. The average score for each subgroup is established by substituting the mean for the group on each of the independent variables. This substitution results in a mean value for members of .09993 and a mean score for nonmembers of $-.07760$.

Members $(-.09065)(2.74) + .00230(79) + .03204(5.2) = .09993$.

Nonmembers $(-.09065)(3.94) + .00230(71.4)$
$+ .03204(3.6) = -.07760$.

If we wish to predict membership status of an individual not in our sample, we should substitute the individual's values on the three independent variables and calculate a single number by the discriminant function. If that value is greater than .09993, the proper prediction is membership. If the calculated value is less than $-.07760$, the proper prediction is nonmembership. What of intermediate values? Are we more concerned with errors of one type than the other? What do we assume about the dispersion in each of the two groups with respect to calculated values on the discriminant function?

When we compared two groups with respect to a single intervally scaled independent variable, we assumed the two groups had equal dispersions: we assumed homoscedasticity.[23] If we also assume that each kind of error is equally serious, the critical point for assignment will be the midpoint between the two calculated means (.01116 in this instance). Thus we should predict a status of member for any individual whose calculated score is above that value and a status of nonmember for any individual whose calculated score is below that figure. Application of this critical value for the ten individuals in our sample results in the confusion matrix presented as Table 13.15. The table reveals that seven of the ten individuals are properly placed and three are improperly placed.

The signs of the coefficients associated with the three independent variables indicate the direction of their relationship to the dependent variable and

Table 13.15
Confusion Matrix. Discriminant Analysis of Civic Organization Membership

Actual	Prediction		Total
	Member	Nonmember	
Member	4	1	5
Nonmember	2	3	5
Total	6	4	10

---

[23]This assumption was made in both Chapter 9 in testing for the difference between two-sample means and in Chapter 12 where bivariate discriminant analysis was considered.

are completely consistent with the relationships previously observed between the means for the two groups. The negative sign associated with family discretionary income indicates that membership tends to decline with increases in income. The positive signs for the other two variables indicate that greater gregariousness is associated with a higher probability of membership and that a longer tenure is also associated with a higher probability of membership.

The magnitude of the individual coefficients reveals the effect of a one-unit change in the independent variable on the calculated score of the discriminant function. The relationships among these magnitudes does not necessarily reveal the relative importance of each of the variables since these magnitudes depend on the unit in which the independent variable is expressed. Importance is more likely to be shown by converting these coefficients into standard scores: this is accomplished by multiplying each coefficient by its own standard deviation. When expressed in standard scores, the coefficient shows the change in the calculated value of the discriminant function for each change of one standard deviation in the independent variable. Performing this calculation with the present data reveals standard score coefficients of $-.131$ for discretionary income, $.083$ for tenure, and $.016$ for gregariousness.

Implicit in the expression of coefficients in standard scores is the thought that a change of one standard deviation in the first independent variable should be equated in some sense to a change of one standard deviation in every other independent variable. If the independent variables are endogenous variables, the marketing manager is attempting to control for a desired result. The cost and ease of obtaining a change of one standard deviation may not be equal across all independent variables. If this be the case, it might be better to express the coefficient in terms of equal costs rather than simple standard scores.[24]

The essence of discriminant analysis with two categories of the dependent variable and two intervally scaled independent variables is shown by Fig. 13.1. A group of investors were classified according to their primary investment goal: either "safety" or "growth." Age and income were also determined for each investor. The open circles in Fig. 13.1 represent growth-oriented investors, and the closed circles represent safety-oriented investors. The two-variable mean for each group is also shown. The task of the discriminant function is to determine the line in the plane that will partition the total sample and minimize the number of observations falling on the wrong side of that line (labeled "Boundary line" in Fig. 13.1.) The discriminant function will be perpendicular to the boundary line and is shown by the broken line in Fig. 13.1. Each investor to be classified is projected onto this discriminant function that is a single dimension, corresponding neither to age nor income. If that projection is in a northwesterly direction from the boundary line of Fig. 13.1, the

---

[24]In the case of endogenous variables, the calculation of a standard deviation is always highly suspect. With historical data, the standard deviations simply reflect company past practice in variations with respect to the independent variables. In the case of a planned experiment, the standard deviations may again represent an arbitrary selection of values for these variables.

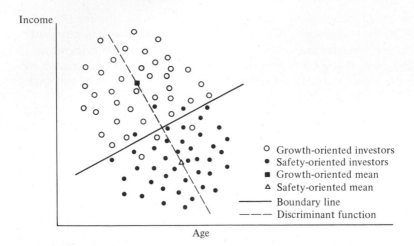

Fig. 13.1
Graphic representation of two-way discriminant function with two independent variables: age and income of investors.

investor should be predicted as growth-oriented; if the projection is southeast of the boundary line, the prediction is safety-oriented. According to Fig. 13.1 only six persons are improperly classified, and each of them is fairly close to the boundary line.

When the situation is expanded to include three independent variables, the graph is in three dimensions. This relationship can be generalized: with n independent variables, the boundary is a hyperplane in $n - 1$ dimensions. With only two groups, the discriminant function is a line in each case. It condenses information on n variables into a single dimension.

If the dependent variable consisted of three groups, the approach would be as shown in Fig. 13.2. Consider the audiences of three different television programs, defined so that each respondent is a viewer of one and only one program. Household size and income are also obtained from each subject. Figure 13.2 shows the location of each respondent and the three discriminant functions obtained—one for the viewers of each program.[25]

The task is to assign each respondent to the program that best fits his or her household size–income characteristics. The location of each respondent is shown, as are the means for the viewers of each program. The boundary lines represent lines of equal probability for a pair of programs; for example, boundary ac represents equal probability for programs A and C. In order to determine appropriate assignments in a prediction problem, the independent

---

[25]The discriminant function in Fig. 13.1 could be thought of as two separate functions, each one terminating at the boundary line. In this way they could be thought of as two rays each originating at the boundary line and together forming a single line.

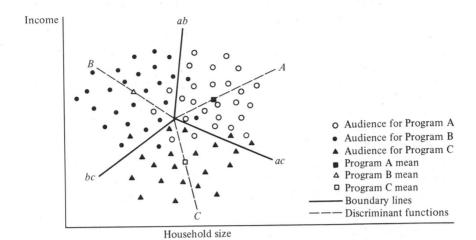

Fig. 13.2
Graphic representation of three-way discriminant function with two independent variables. Income and household size for viewers of three television programs.

variable scores for each respondent are tried in each of the discriminant functions. The group whose function provides the best fit is the group to which the respondent should be assigned.[26]

The confusion matrix based upon Fig. 13.2 is given in Table 13.16. Sixty-three of 73 viewers are correctly predicted. As mentioned in Chapter 12, the confusion matrix yields a biased estimate of the accuracy of the discriminant function in making assignments. A better estimate of its accuracy would be

Table 13.16
Confusion Matrix. Discriminant Analysis for Viewers of Three Television Programs

	Program predicted			
Program viewed	A	B	C	Total
A	22	2	2	26
B	2	23	1	26
C	2	1	18	21
Total	26	26	21	73

[26]The mathematics and probability tests for discriminant functions go beyond what is appropriate for an elementary text in marketing research. The interested reader is referred to Donald F. Morrison, 1967, *Multivariate Statistical Methods* (New York: McGraw-Hill); T.W. Anderson, 1958, *Introduction to Multivariate Statistical Analysis* (New York: Wiley); and Donald G. Morrison, 1969, On the interpretation of discriminant analysis, *Journal of Marketing Research* **6** (May).

obtained by a split-half approach. In this procedure, the equation or equations are determined from only half of the observations. The confusion matrix is then generated by applying the equation(s) to the other half of the observations. Thus there is no forced fit which introduces an upward bias in the calculation of accuracy.[27]

The percentage of correct classifications is an even more misleading index of accuracy when the observations in the sample are not equally divided among subgroups. For example, suppose the marketing manager of a consumer-products company wished to discriminate between innovators and the rest of the population. If the sample included only 10 percent who are classified as "innovators," the manager could generate a confusion matrix that had proper classification of 90 percent by assigning everyone to the category "noninnovator." Proper classification must be evaluated against the expected results due to chance alone. This is true even when a split-half approach is employed. One way of testing the accuracy of assignment is with Chi Square in a contingency table analysis. We shall illustrate this in the next section.

Contingency Table Analysis of Confusion Matrices

The confusion matrix for a two-category dependent variable falls very neatly into a 2 × 2 contingency table. Consider the data in Table 13.17 in which the marketing manager attempted to categorize respondents as either innovators or noninnovators using a three-variable discriminant function. First we see that 471 out of 500 are properly classified—94.2 percent which seems rather good. But is 94.2 percent still "good" when it is compared against the fact that 89.4 percent are known to be in the noninnovator category. Calculating Chi Square in the usual manner reveals that the discriminant function is better than chance (the calculated Chi Square is over 250 and the null hypothesis would be

Table 13.17
Contingency Table Analysis of Discriminant Confusion Matrix for Innovator-noninnovator Classification

	Discriminant classification		
True status	Innovator	Noninnovator	Total
Innovator	41	12	53
Noninnovator	17	430	447
Total	58	442	500

$\chi^2 = 252.2$

$P(\chi^2 > 252.2; \quad df = 1) < .005$

---

[27]See Ronald E. Frank, William F. Massy, and Donald G. Morrison, 1965, Bias in multidiscriminant analysis, *Journal of Marketing Research:* **2** 250–258. A "jackknifed" approach is another procedure for dealing with bias. See Table 13.19 and the accompanying discussion.

rejected at even a .005 level of significance).[28] Over 70 percent of those classified as "innovator" by the discriminant function are in this category. This is reasonably good, but the marketing manager must be careful concerning the claims made for the discriminant function and its ability to "discriminate."

When the dependent variable has three categories, the analysis is more complex. The data presented in Table 13.18(a) refer to brand preference data and identify not only errors but the kinds of errors present in prediction. This format is appropriate for Chi Square only if we wish to compare each cell against its theoretical probability. The null hypothesis associated with the 3 × 3 table is that the percentage distribution of brand preference is the same regardless of the brand predicted. Even if this hypothesis is rejected, it would not indicate whether the discriminant analysis yielded accurate predictions.

Table 13.18
Contingency Table Analysis of Discriminant Confusion Matrix for Brand Preference from Socioeconomic Variables

	(a) Original data Brand predicted			
Brand selected	A	B	C	Total
A	42	23	35	100
B	29	59	37	125
C	39	38	98	175
Total	110	120	170	400

	(b) Collapsed data Brand predicted		
Correct/incorrect	A	B	C
Correct	42	59	98
Incorrect	68	61	72
Total	110	120	170

$$\chi^2 = \frac{(27.5 - 42)^2}{27.5} + \frac{(82.5 - 68)^2}{82.5} + \frac{(37.5 - 59)^2}{37.5} + \frac{(82.5 - 61)^2}{82.5}$$
$$+ \frac{(74.375 - 98)^2}{74.375} + \frac{(95.625 - 72)^2}{95.625}.$$

$\chi^2 = 41.5$.
$P(\chi^2 > 41.5;$ $df = 3) < .01$.

---

[28]The statistical tests given in Tables 13.17 and 13.18 assume the confusion matrices are based on a "jackknifed" approach. See Table 13.19 and Note 31.

The percentage distributions could be quite dissimilar without a high percentage of accuracy. Useful descriptive statements are possible from the 3×3 table, but it is not well constructed for hypothesis testing.

The format in Table 13.18(b) collapses the data, for each brand predicted, into the number of correct and the number of incorrect predictions, combining the two types of incorrect answers. The theoretical cell values calculated in (b) do not refer to a common marginal distribution across all three brands. Each theoretical cell value is based on the market share of the particular brand; 25 percent for brand A, 31.25 percent for brand B, and 43.75 percent for brand C. Since brand A has a market share of 25 percent, chance alone would produce correct assignment for $.25(110) = 27.5$ of the individuals predicted for brand A. The discriminant function was correct for 42, however. The remaining calculations are also shown in Table 13.18. The resulting Chi Square indicates that the discriminant function does much better than chance (probability less than .01). There are three degrees of freedom for this analysis because the cell values are generated separately for each column, one degree of freedom resulting from each column.

Distance between Centroids

Discriminant analysis is based on the distance between the means of the groups compared. With several independent variables, these means involve as many measures as there are variables. These multidimensional means are called *centroids*. One possible approach to the problem would be a series of *t*-tests comparing each centroid against every other centroid. Such a procedure might be extremely cumbersome, and the proper interpretation of the aggregate analysis would be dubious. Mahalanobis Generalized D^2 provides a summary distance measure based on the comparison of each separate centroid against the composite centroid for all groups.

Mahalanobis Generalized D^2 is computed by Eq. (13.6).

$$D^2 = \sum_{a=1}^{m} \sum_{b=1}^{m} (S_{ab}^{-1}) \sum_{j=1}^{g} n_j \left[\left(\bar{x}_{ja} - \bar{\bar{x}}_a \right) \left(\bar{x}_{jb} - \bar{\bar{x}}_b \right) \right]. \tag{13.6}$$

S_{ab}^{-1} is the appropriate entry from the inverse of the pooled variance–covariance matrix, serving the same role as the within-group variance adjustment does when a single independent variable is involved. The matrix is square, covering all pairs of variables. The expression in the brackets shows the distance of each particular centroid from the grand mean and is weighted by the number of observations in the group. Since the summation is over g, the number of groups, Eq. (13.6) is an aggregate measure for the entire sample.

Mahalanobis Generalized D^2 is distributed as Chi Square (assuming normality) with $m(g - 1)$ degrees of freedom. The null hypothesis tested is that the mean values are the same in all g groups for the m variables.

Computer Printouts

The BMD, SAS, and SPSS statistical packages all have multivariate discriminant programs. Table 13.19 gives a portion of the output from BMDP7M.[29] This output refers to a study of supermarket patronage in which the dependent variable is regular supermarket shopped and the independent variables are age of female head of household, tenure in SMSA, and advertising awareness. The study covered three different supermarkets: Friendly, Nationwide, and Thrifty. Since there are three groups within the dependent variable, three discriminant functions are determined.

The three functions are presented in the first portion of Table 13.19. The function for Nationwide patrons is

$$-17.31 + .35x_2 + .26x_3 + .22x_4$$

x_2 = age in years

x_3 = tenure in years

x_4 = point score in advertising awareness.

These functions are used for assigning the individual observations to one of the three categories. This is accomplished by substituting the independent variable values for each individual observation and solving all three functions. The group whose function yields the highest calculated value is the group to which the individual is assigned.

Comparison of the coefficients of the various functions reveals the effect of the different independent variables. For example, the age coefficient is largest for the Nationwide function. Thus the older the age, net of other variables, the more likely an individual will be a patron of Nationwide. The same conclusion applies to tenure. Greater advertising awareness, all other things equal, is more likely to be associated with a Thrifty patron; this again is shown by the fact that the largest coefficient for advertising awareness is found in the function for Thrifty patrons.

The coefficients for Friendly are between those of Nationwide and Thrifty for all three functions. Thus large values of any single independent variable are not associated with Friendly patrons. The Y-intercept of the Friendly function also has interesting implications since it is larger than those of the other two. The calculated value of its function will be greater than that of Nationwide unless age and/or tenure are sufficiently large to overcome the initial difference. By similar reasoning the calculated value of the Friendly function will be greater than that of Thrifty unless advertising awareness is large enough to overcome the initial difference.

The confusion matrix is shown in the second portion of Table 13.19. Ten of the 18 observations are properly classified by the discriminant functions, an

---

[29]*Biomedical Computer Programs, op. cit.*, pp. 711–734.

Table 13.19
Computer Printout from BMDP7M Discriminant Analysis

CLASSIFICATION FUNCTIONS

VARIABLE	GROUP =	NATIONWD	FRIENDLY	THRIFTY
2 AGE		0.34870	0.21995	0.15618
3 TENURE		0.25593	0.14811	0.03389
4 ADVAW		0.21711	0.22284	0.29328
CONSTANT		-17.31123	-11.98268	-14.24168

CLASSIFICATION MATRIX

GROUP	PERCENT CORRECT	NUMBER OF CASES CLASSIFIED INTO GROUP -		
		NATIONWD	FRIENDLY	THRIFTY
NATIONWD	83.3	5	1	0
FRIENDLY	33.3	2	2	2
THRIFTY	50.0	1	2	3
TOTAL	55.6	8	5	5

JACKKNIFED CLASSIFICATION

GROUP	PERCENT CORRECT	NUMBER OF CASES CLASSIFIED INTO GROUP -		
		NATIONWD	FRIENDLY	THRIFTY
NATIONWD	66.7	4	2	0
FRIENDLY	33.3	2	2	2
THRIFTY	50.0	1	2	3
TOTAL	50.0	7	6	5

overall result of 55.6 percent correct. The "percent correct" shown for the individual rows uses as its base the number who are patrons of the specific store; for example, 83.3 percent of Nationwide patrons are classified as Nationwide patrons by the analysis.[30] The "jackknifed classification" matrix is an attempt to correct for the upward bias caused because the same observations are used in determining the functions and in determining the accuracy of the functions.[31]

The final portion of Table 13.19 presents the individual observations and their assignment (using the "jackknifed" approach). These figures identify the

---

[30]An alternative procedure would ask how many classified as Nationwide patrons are truly Nationwide patrons. The percentage correct with this approach would be 62.5 percent for Nationwide, 40 percent for Friendly, and 60 percent for Thrifty.

[31]This procedure excludes the element being classified in the determination of the functions. With 18 original observations, each set of functions is based on 17 observations, and 18 different sets of functions are employed for the confusion matrix. The three functions presented as a summary of the analysis are thus not actually used in that form in the jackknifed confusion matrix.

Table 13.19
(continued)

		INCORRECT CLASSIFICATIONS	MAHALANOBIS D–SQUARE FROM AND POSTERIOR PROBABILITY FOR GROUP –	
GROUP NATIONWD		NATIONWD	FRIENDLY	THRIFTY
CASE				
1		3.3 0.832	7.3 0.116	8.9 0.053
3	FRIENDLY	12.3 0.243	10.1 0.750	19.3 0.007
7		0.8 0.542	2.0 0.295	3.2 0.163
10		4.3 0.899	9.3 0.075	11.4 0.026
11	FRIENDLY	8.6 0.017	1.4 0.646	2.7 0.337
15		0.2 0.503	0.9 0.352	2.7 0.146
GROUP FRIENDLY		NATIONWD	FRIENDLY	THRIFTY
CASE				
2	THRIFTY	7.3 0.030	3.4 0.207	0.8 0.763
6	NATIONWD	2.3 0.781	5.3 0.176	8.2 0.042
9		3.5 0.185	1.9 0.411	1.9 0.404
14	NATIONWD	26.2 1.000	48.9 0.000	48.1 0.000
16	THRIFTY	6.6 0.033	3.4 0.167	0.2 0.800
18		2.4 0.223	0.8 0.496	1.9 0.260
GROUP THRIFTY		NATIONWD	FRIENDLY	THRIFTY
CASE				
4	FRIENDLY	8.1 0.042	2.4 0.746	4.9 0.212
5		2.8 0.200	1.5 0.378	1.3 0.422
8	FRIENDLY	3.2 0.122	0.3 0.528	1.1 0.350
12	NATIONWD	2.5 0.627	4.2 0.263	5.9 0.110
13		11.9 0.007	5.0 0.224	2.6 0.769
17		11.4 0.020	7.6 0.134	3.9 0.846

misclassifications and give the basis upon which the classification is made. The first entry in each column is a Mahalanobis type of distance measure, measuring the distance between the specific case and the centroid for each group.[32] Each case is assigned to the group for which the distance is least. The first observation (Case 1) is properly classified. Its distance measures are 3.3 to Nationwide, 7.3 to Friendly, and 8.9 to Thrifty. The smallest distance is for Nationwide; therefore it should be assigned to Nationwide.

The second entry in each column is the probability that the case should be assigned to a specific group. This probability is calculated in a two-step process. First, g discriminant scores are calculated for each case, the scores for

---

[32]The formula for this measure is given by

$$\sum_{a=1}^{m} \sum_{b=1}^{m} (S_{ab}^{-1})(x_{ra} - \bar{x}_{ja})(x_{rb} - \bar{x}_{jb})$$

where r designates the case under review and j is the group against which it is compared.

the case on each discriminant function. Second, each score is transformed into a probability by Eq. (13.7).

$$P_i = \frac{e^{f_i - \max f_i}}{\Sigma e^{f_i - \max f_i}}; \qquad i = 1, \ldots, g. \qquad (13.7)$$

The sum of these probabilities over all g groups is 1.0.[33]

According to Table 13.19, the probabilities for Case 1 are 83.2 percent for Nationwide, 11.6 percent for Friendly, and 5.3 percent for Thrifty. Individual cases, particularly where misclassified, can be examined in this portion of the output. Case 14 illustrates a very difficult assignment problem. This individual is far removed from all three groups, as shown by the distance measures (26.2, 48.9, and 48.1). Assignment to Nationwide (an error) is made only because the other two functions are so poor, rather than because the Nationwide assignment is so good.

Overview of Multiple Discriminant Analysis

A summary of multiple discriminant analysis is presented in Table 13.20. The null hypothesis of no association is tested with Mahalanobis Generalized D^2. This test compares within group variance with total variance, based on $m(g - 1)$ degrees of freedom. Estimation is not obtained directly from a conditional equation but in a two-step process. A series of discriminant scores are calculated for each desired unit, a separate score from each discriminant function. The group whose function best "fits" (yields the highest score) the unit is the best prediction for the unit.

Discriminant analysis does not yield a summary statement of the relationship between the dependent variable and the set of independent variables. Instead one must compare the coefficients for a given independent variable across discriminant functions. The greater the differences among the coefficients, the more that particular variable discriminates among the groups. Given large differences, a positive sign indicates a direct relationship between the variable and group membership while a negative sign indicates an inverse relationship.

The degree of association between the dependent variable and the set of independent variables can be observed in the confusion matrix. However, the percentage of correct "hits" is not a "reduction of variance" concept. Therefore it cannot be interpreted as, nor compared with, a coefficient of determination. It is even a biased estimate of "accuracy" in the limited sense of percentage of "hits." This bias can be removed and tested for by submitting the data from a confusion matrix to a contingency table analysis.

A correlation ratio based upon within-group variance and total variance is an alternative approach to the measurement of association. This approach

---

[33]See C.R. Rao, 1965, *Linear Statistical Inference and Its Applications,* (New York: Wiley) or Donald F. Morrison, 1967, *Multivariate Statistical Methods,* (New York: McGraw-Hill) for further discussion.

Table 13.20
Multiple Discriminant Analysis Summary

1. Test statistic: Mahalanobis Generalized D^2 distributed as Chi Square

2. Estimate based on:
    a) Total percentage if H_0 is accepted
    b) Discriminant function yielding highest score if H_0 is rejected

3. Summary of relationship, if any:
    a) No true conditional distribution established
    b) Sign and magnitude of coefficients reveal direction of relationships and relative importance of the individual independent variables

4. Measure of association:
    a) Confusion matrix
    b) Correlation ratio squared (η^2)

5. Form of discriminant functions:
    a) Prior specification
    b) Linear via assumed homoscedasticity

6. Criterion for "best" equations:
    a) Minimization of squared deviations after converting independent variables to standard scores
    b) Subject to stated constraints
        i)   Cost of misclassification
        ii) Prior probability of group membership

would introduce no new concepts except the calculation of variance in m dimensions (m independent variables). In order to remove unequal or arbitrary weighting of the independent variables, transformation into standard scores should precede the calculations.

The form of the conditional distribution and the criterion for "best" fit are analogous to the situation with only one independent variable. Linear equations are employed, and the fit is by "least squares." This approach assumes the independent variables have a multinormal distribution and that the groups have equal variances (homoscedasticity).

MULTIVARIATE CONTINGENCY TABLES

The multivariate contingency table is little used in marketing problems. This is true for several reasons. (1) It rapidly loses its power in testing a null hypothesis as the number of variables increases. (2) Both regression and discriminant analysis can be modified to incorporate nominally scaled independent variables. When thus modified, both the structuring of the problem and the interpretation of the results are easier than with a contingency table. (3) The contingency table is uniquely structured to test the hypothesis that all variables under investigation are independent of each other; very rarely is this a practical marketing question. We shall limit our discussion of the multivariate contingency table to a problem involving only three variables. This establishes the framework and procedures that are appropriate for any number of variables.

A professor of theology wished to determine whether "interest in religion" is associated with marital status and education. If the theoretical frequencies under the null hypothesis are calculated by the product of the three marginal distributions, the null hypothesis being tested is that the three variables are independent of each other. An appropriate table for testing this hypothesis is given with hypothetical data as Table 13.21.

The calculation of theoretical frequencies can be illustrated by the expected number of married high school graduates with a low interest in religion: 600(405/600)(300/600) (150/600) that results in a figure of 50.625. Forty respondents were in this category; thus the first entry in the calculation of Chi Square is based on the comparison of these values. The total value of Chi Square is 18.5, large enough to reject the null hypothesis of independence among the three variables at the .01 level of significance. But that is not really the question that the theology professor wanted to test—whether marital status and education were related to interest in religion. The professor did not wish to incorporate the relationship between marital status and education as part of the hypothesis.

In order to test the hypothesis of interest, the professor should examine interest in religion holding both marital status and education constant. That could be done by comparing the four rows of Table 13.21 against the overall

Table 13.21
Contingency Table for Marital Status, Education, and Interest in Religion

Marital status	High school graduate	Interest in religion			Total
		Low	Moderate	High	
Married	Yes	40	95	65	200
	No	60	110	35	205
Single	Yes	20	50	30	100
	No	30	45	20	95
Total		150	300	150	600

Marginal distributions

Low interest	150	High school graduate	300	Married	405
Moderate interest	300	Nongraduate	300	Single	195
High interest	150				

$$\chi^2 = \frac{(50.625 - 40)^2}{50.625} + \frac{(101.25 - 95)^2}{101.25} + \cdots$$

$$= 18.5$$

$$P(\chi^2 > 18.48; \quad df = 7) < .01.$$

distribution of interest in religion: 150, 300, and 150 or a distribution of 25, 50, and 25 percent. The theoretical values for the individual cells are changed slightly for this second hypothesis, and result in a calculated Chi Square value of 18.31. The number of degrees of freedom also increases with this second hypothesis, from 7 to 8, and the critical value for Chi Square with a .01 level of significance is increased to 20.09. These two changes bring about an acceptance of the second null hypothesis (at $\alpha = .01$).[34] Is $\alpha = .01$ too demanding?

If the number of variables is increased above three, the contingency table is very difficult to construct in a way that facilitates understanding of the data. It also becomes less likely that the decision maker is really interested in a null hypothesis that simply states there is no relationship among the n variables. Often the marketing problem reduces to a case somewhat similar to either regression or discriminant analysis but with both intervally scaled independent variables and nominally scaled independent variables. We shall consider this problem in the next chapter.

SUMMARY

The analytic techniques of analysis of variance (ANOVA), regression and correlation, and discriminant analysis each can be extended to include several independent variables in establishing functional relationships with a single dependent variable. All three are logical extensions of the proposition, "If one independent variable improves control over or prediction of a dependent variable, more than one should improve control or prediction even more."

The simple conditional equation of bivariate relationships [$E(y|x)$] is replaced by $E(y|x_1, x_2, \ldots)$. In its linear form, this merely adds more variables to the right-hand side of the equation; $y = a + bx$ is replaced by $y = a + b_1x_1 + b_2x_2 + \ldots$. The three techniques thus address the same general question. They differ according to the scales used for the variables as shown in the following diagram.

	Independent variables	
Dependent variable	Nominal	Interval
Nominal		Discriminant
Interval	ANOVA	Regression

---

[34]The number of degrees of freedom is equal to the number of cells minus the number of independent constraints imposed by the hypothesis. For the first hypothesis of independence among all three variables, there are five independent constraints. These are established by the grand total of 600 observations, plus one less than the number of categories in each of the three variables: one for marital status, one for education, and two for interest in religion. There are thus seven degrees of freedom: 12 cells minus five constraints. For the second hypothesis, there is one independent constraint for each of the four separate groups; therefore there are eight or (12 − 4) degrees of freedom.

The contingency table occupied the empty cell for bivariate analysis. It does not follow the general pattern in multivariate analysis since it is typically concerned with whether all the variables are associated without regard to a dependent–independent structure.

Multivariate analysis of variance (ANOVA) tests each independent variable for association with the dependent variable through a series of F-tests. It also tests for possible interactions among the independent variables. The main-effects model, using the sum of the individual independent variable contributions, should be employed only if no interactions exist. Unbiased point estimates may be obtained from the cell means when interaction is present or from the marginal figures if no interaction exists. Confidence intervals are generated by the same techniques discussed in earlier chapters.

Association between the individual independent variables and the dependent variable is tested in regression by a series of null hypotheses with respect to the individual regression coefficients. These tests employ the t-distribution, comparing the individual coefficients to their own standard errors. Each coefficient shows the net effect of a particular independent variable on the dependent variable, after adjusting for the other variables in the equation. If interest centers on the identification of those independent variables associated with the dependent variable and the measure of the relationship, the final equation should include only those variables for which the null hypothesis is rejected. If prediction of the dependent variable is the focus of interest, the total equation may be retained or the nonsignificant variables may be deleted.

The multiple coefficient of determination (R^2) measures the overall association between the dependent variable and the linear combination of all independent variables of the regression equation. Its limits, like those of r^2, are 0 and 1; and it shows the percentage reduction in variance by measuring dispersion around the regression line instead of the mean of the dependent variable. As is the case with two variables, it is appropriate to calculate R^2 only if the observations are a simple random sample from the relevant universe. The multiple coefficient of correlation (R) is simply the square root of R^2 but, contrary to the bivariate case, is always assigned a positive sign. Partial coefficients of determination measure the net contribution of each independent variable, indicating the percentage of variance uniquely eliminated by that variable after adjusting for all other independent variables in the regression equation.

We have considered only linear regression in this chapter. If the relationship is nonlinear, the equations of this chapter will understate the magnitude of the relationships and will at best yield linear approximations of the true form. The conditional standard deviations will also overstate the dispersion from the true line of relationship. Nonlinear regression is considered in Chapter 14.

Discriminant analysis, like regression, determines whether the separate independent variables are associated with the dependent variable through the coefficients determined for each variable. The relative importance of various independent variables is often judged by converting the coefficients into standard scores (each coefficient is multiplied by the standard deviation of the corresponding variable). This adjustment does not take account of costs, however, and it assumes the standard deviations are based upon random samples.

The confusion matrix of discriminant analysis compares predictions by the discriminant function(s) with the true classification of those elements. It thus shows "hits" and "misses." An upward bias exists if the matrix is based on the same data used to generate the discriminant function(s). Care must also be exercised in the accuracy claims derived from the confusion matrix. Its accuracy should be judged against the division among categories in the population—90 percent accuracy loses most of its impressiveness when 85 percent of the population is in a single category. Contingency table analysis can be used to test a null hypothesis of no discrimination power.

Assignment of elements in the prediction problem is based upon a single critical value of the discriminant function in the two-category case. If costs of the two types of "misses" are equal and the groups are equal in size, this critical value is the midpoint between the means (centroids) of the two groups. In the case of more than two categories, n discriminant functions are determined, one for each group. Assignment in the prediction problem is then based upon comparison of the fit given by testing each element in the various functions.

Computer packages for the various multivariate techniques exist. Three of the more widely used are the Statistical Analysis System (SAS), the Statistical Package for the Social Sciences (SPSS), and the Biomedical Computer Programs (BMD). Sample computer output was included in the chapter.

EXERCISES AND PROBLEMS

1. Distinguish among the terms within each of the following sets.
   a) Regression coefficient and partial coefficient of correlation
   b) Treatment effect and interaction
   c) Discriminant score and assignment–prediction
   d) Residual variance and highest-order interaction variance
   e) Net regression coefficient and standardized regression coefficient
   f) Interval estimate for item and interval estimate for mean
   g) Centroid and mean

2. Briefly explain the meaning and significance of each of the following terms.
   a) Multicollinearity
   b) "Jackknifed" approach
   c) Homoscedasticity
   d) Variance decomposition

e) Interaction

f) Main effects

g) Confusion matrix

3. Compare and contrast the conditional equations derived from ANOVA and regression–correlation with respect to each of the following.

a) Possible values of the independent variables

b) *A priori* specification

c) Number of terms

4. Use the data in Table 13.6 in which the first entry of each cell refers to an urban area and the second refers to a suburban area.

a) Test for each main effect (incentive, year, and urban–suburban) and for interactions.

b) What variance did you use for the denominator of the F-ratios in (a)? Does this pose any limitation on your analysis? Why?

c) Present the conditional equation you think should be employed for this problem.

d) Would you be willing to use the equation of (c) in estimating response rates in a suburban area in 1980? Why or why not?

e) Is it possible to calculate the percentage reduction in variance achieved in this analysis? Why? If it is possible, make the calculation.

5. An insurance company wished to examine the relationship between the amount of life insurance held by the principal family wage earner, income, and size of family. The data collected from 12 families are given in Table E13.5.

Table E13.5

Family	Amount of life insurance ($1,000)	Income ($1,000)	Family size
A	14	8	3
B	50	30	3
C	33	18	5
D	23	16	3
E	26	16	3
F	45	24	7
G	27	20	6
H	15	12	3
I	30	18	4
J	60	32	5
K	30	16	4
L	25	15	4

a) Determine the linear multiple regression equation with income and family size as the independent variables.

b) Are you willing to conclude that each independent variable is associated with amount of life insurance?

c) What are the meanings of the net regression coefficients—specifically in the units and terms of this problem?

d) Calculate the sample multiple coefficient of determination. What is its meaning?

e) What is your unbiased estimate of the population multiple coefficient of determination?

f) Establish the 95 percent confidence interval for the regression coefficient for income.

6. The insurance company in Exercise 5 is a subsidiary of a conglomerate that also operates a personal finance company. The 12 families have been classified as "good" or "poor" risks, as shown below.

Good: B, C, F, G, I, J

Poor: A, D, E, H, K, L

a) Determine a discriminant function(s) that can be used for classifying families as "good" or "poor" risks, given information on amount of life insurance, income, and family size.

b) Which, if any, of the independent variables appear to have the most significance in discriminating between "good" and "poor" risks? Explain the basis for your answer.

c) Do you think the function(s) in (a) discriminate well? Quantify your result.

d) Can you test a null hypothesis with respect to the discriminatory power of the function(s)? If yes, make the test. If no, explain why no test is possible.

7. A manufacturer of industrial supplies developed the following model for predicting the number of sales per month within its various sales regions.

$$Y = 41 + .3X_1 + .05X_2 - 7X_3 + 10X_4$$

where

Y = number of sales per month
X_1 = number of manufacturing firms with 25 or more employees
X_2 = number of wholesale and retail firms with 25 or more employees
X_3 = number of competing firms
X_4 = number of full-time company salespeople

Input data are regional figures.

a) Explain the correct interpretation of all numbers in the equation.

b) The conditional standard deviation is 3. What does that number tell you? Do you think it is large or small?

c) R is equal to $+.7$. What does that figure mean? Include reference to the positive sign.

d) Which independent variable is most important? Why?

e) Partial R^2 values are .21 for X_1, .15 for X_2, .17 for X_3, and .26 for X_4. What do these values tell you?

f) Are the figures given in (e) consistent with the figure given in (c)? Discuss.

g) How many sales would you predict for a region with five salespeople, seven competitors, 41 manufacturing firms, and 107 wholesalers and retailers? How much confidence do you have in your answer? How could you increase your confidence?

h) Would ANOVA, discriminant analysis, or contingency analysis be appropriate for analyzing these relationships? Explain.

8. Formulate original marketing problems in which each of the specified techniques would be appropriate. Clearly indicate the variables, how each variable is measured, and the dependent–independent status of each variable.

a) Multiple regression

b) Multiple discriminant analysis

c) Contingency analysis

d) Multiple classification ANOVA

9. Present a set of possible results for both 8(a) and 8(b).

10. Supply a small set of original data for both 8(c) and 8(d). Perform the appropriate analyses.

11. Present a small set of original data in which multicollinearity would be serious. (Hypothetical data are acceptable.) Explain why the data show multicollinearity.

12. The price data for sugar in Table E13.12 are available from four competing super-markets within a large SMSA. The two numbers represent data collected one month apart, but for the same date for each chain.

a) Transform the data into units that will be appropriate for testing whether there is

i) a store effect

ii) a size effect

iii) an interaction effect

b) Use ANOVA to test for the effects enumerated in (a).

Table E13.12

Size	Chain			
	A	F	J	K
2-pound bag	.79	.69	.89	.85
	.75	.79	.85	.85
5-pound bag	1.49	1.45	1.55	1.69
	1.59	1.49	1.55	1.59
10-pound bag	2.99	2.89	3.19	3.29
	3.19	2.99	3.15	3.29

Refer to Table 13.12.

a) Why are the F-values and the corresponding probabilities identical with respect to tenure but not for the other two variables?

b) Do you see any evidence that the errors in prediction are larger for either the high or low values of the dependent variable? Discuss the implication of your answer.

c) Should the difference between "LOWER 95% CL FOR INDIVIDUAL" and "UPPER 95% CL FOR INDIVIDUAL" be the same for all estimates? Why?

d) Is Table 13.12 consistent with your answer in (c)? What does this imply?

14. Analyze, criticize, and explain:

a) The main effects determined by ANOVA should not be employed in making estimates unless either the null hypotheses regarding interactions have been accepted or the sample is representative of the universe.

b) Interpolation is impossible with ANOVA because the independent variable categories are neither ordinal nor interval in scale. Subjective but dubious estimates might be made if an interval scale could be assumed.

c) The degree of association in ANOVA can be shown by the correlation coefficient if a simple random sample has been used. Otherwise, the F-ratio is the best measure of percentage reduction in variance.

d) If the null hypothesis for a particular regression coefficient is accepted, the coefficient should be changed to zero and the equation should be used in that form.

e) Standardized coefficients with the independent variables are preferable to the raw coefficients in both regression and discriminant analysis, but the standardized coefficients are even more necessary in discriminant analysis.

f) Net regression coefficients show the true impact of each independent variable after adjusting for any factor that accounts for as much as 5 percent of the variance in the dependent variable (using $\alpha = .05$).

g) The null hypothesis in multiple regression is not a single hypothesis but a series of hypotheses.

h) Mahalanobis D^2 measures average distance between all possible pairs of centroids. This is superior to the "jackknifed" approach which measures average distance of the group centroids from the overall centroid for the entire sample.

i) ANOVA has a distinct advantage over regression and discriminant analyses since it can incorporate and test for interactions.

j) Multicollinearity is less of a problem in predicting values of the dependent variable than it is in ascertaining the incremental effects of the individual independent variables.

13. Refer to Table 13.12.

  a) Why are the F-values and the corresponding probabilities identical with respect to tenure but not for the other two variables?

  b) Do you see any evidence that the errors in prediction are larger for either the high or low values of the dependent variable? Discuss the implication of your answer.

  c) Should the difference between "LOWER 95% CL FOR INDIVIDUAL" and "UPPER 95% CL FOR INDIVIDUAL" be the same for all estimates? Why?

  d) Is Table 13.12 consistent with your answer in (c)? What does this imply?

14. Analyze, criticize, and explain:

  a) The main effects determined by ANOVA should not be employed in making estimates unless either the null hypotheses regarding interactions have been accepted or the sample is representative of the universe.

  b) Interpolation is impossible with ANOVA because the independent variable categories are neither ordinal nor interval in scale. Subjective but dubious estimates might be made if an interval scale could be assumed.

  c) The degree of association in ANOVA can be shown by the correlation coefficient if a simple random sample has been used. Otherwise, the F-ratio is the best measure of percentage reduction in variance.

  d) If the null hypothesis for a particular regression coefficient is accepted, the coefficient should be changed to zero and the equation should be used in that form.

  e) Standardized coefficients with the independent variables are preferable to the raw coefficients in both regression and discriminant analysis, but the standardized coefficients are even more necessary in discriminant analysis.

  f) Net regression coefficients show the true impact of each independent variable after adjusting for any factor that accounts for as much as 5 percent of the variance in the dependent variable (using $\alpha = .05$).

  g) The null hypothesis in multiple regression is not a single hypothesis but a series of hypotheses.

  h) Mahalanobis D^2 measures average distance between all possible pairs of centroids. This is superior to the "jackknifed" approach which measures average distance of the group centroids from the overall centroid for the entire sample.

  i) ANOVA has a distinct advantage over regression and discriminant analyses since it can incorporate and test for interactions.

  j) Multicollinearity is less of a problem in predicting values of the dependent variable than it is in ascertaining the incremental effects of the individual independent variables.

CHAPTER 14

DUMMY VARIABLES AND ANALYSIS OF COVARIANCE
THE CASE OF MIXED INDEPENDENT VARIABLES

A marketing manager may wish to appraise both the effect of different advertising media and the effect of the size of the advertising expenditure. One variable is nominally scaled and the other is intervally scaled. Another problem may address the relationship between product usage and age, income, sex, and occupation. Again the set of independent variables contains a mixture of scales. A third problem may be concerned with testing alternative in-store promotions. If the test is run in different stores, part of the difference in results may reflect differences in store size or store traffic at the time of the test. An attempt to adjust for the effect of the uncontrolled variable and measure the effects of the various promotions encounters the same difficulty—mixed scales for the independent variables.

Regression and discriminant analysis handle the mixed scale problem by the *dummy variable* technique. ANOVA is changed into the analysis of covariance (ANCOVA) in order to deal with the problem. Both approaches result in a conditional equation containing both nominally and intervally scaled variables. The two techniques are conceptually equivalent, but the problems from which they arise are usually different.

THE DUMMY VARIABLE

A nominally scaled variable can be thought of as 0/1 variable: 0 if the unit does not possess the characteristic and 1 if it does possess the characteristic. The *dummy variable* is placed into what is ordinarily an interval scale format but has only two possible values (0 and 1). The conditional distributions associated with ANOVA incorporate this 0/1 concept. Each coefficient indicates the amount to be added or subtracted to some base figure, depending on the particular classification for the various elements. Incorporation of this approach along with intervally scaled independent variables in a regression (or discriminant) format permits a simultaneous solution for the net effect of each variable although a mixed scale situation is present.

The procedure is illustrated by the product manager of Dyna Kleen who wished to get a better "feel" of the factors making for high and low volume in various retail outlets. The manager's dependent variable was number of cases of Dyna Kleen sold per week. Size of store, shelf space allocated to Dyna Kleen, and store traffic were all potential intervally scaled independent variables. Other potential independent variables were nominally scaled: various ways of classifying the store neighborhood, independent or chain operation, and finally whether the store in question carried a private brand that competed with the manager's product. We illustrate the procedure, using only one intervally scaled independent variable and one nominally scaled independent variable: shelf space allocated and presence or absence of a competing private brand. The data are given for 12 stores in Table 14.1.

A portion of the SAS computer output is presented in Table 14.2.[1] The equation describing the relationship is

$$y = 3.90 + 1.31x_1 - 4.79x_2$$

where

x_1 is number of feet of shelf space,
x_2 is presence of private brand competition
(0 = No, 1 = Yes), and
y is number of cases sold.

Table 14.1
Dyna Kleen Sales versus Shelf Space and Private Brand Competition. Data for Regression with Dummy Variable

Store sales (number of cases)	Shelf space (number of feet)	Private brand competition (No = 0, Yes = 1)
20	10	0
4	6	1
12	6	0
15	12	1
7	4	0
17	8	0
6	6	1
15	10	1
11	6	0
6	4	1
22	16	0
9	8	1
144	96	6

[1] A. J. Barr and J. H. Goodnight, 1972, *A User's Guide to the Statistical Analysis System*, (Raleigh, N.C., Sparks Press), pp. 118–119.

This equation indicates (1) a positive relationship between sales and shelf space allocated to the product and (2) an inverse relationship between sales and the presence of a competing private brand. The only difference between this equation and previous regression equations is a slight modification in the interpretation of the coefficient associated with the dummy variable (presence of a competing private brand). The modification comes about because of the meaning of one unit in the dummy variable; one unit corresponds to a difference in categories rather than a measured difference on an interval scale. What then does -4.8 convey? It compares expected sales of two stores, equal in shelf space allocation. One store carries a competing private brand and the other does not. The expected sales of Dyna Kleen are 4.8 cases less for the store carrying a competing private brand.

The equation given assumes that the amount of shelf space allocated and the presence or absence of a competing private brand do not interact in their effect on sales. The regression coefficient for shelf space is the same (1.31) regardless of the value of x_2. Similarly the coefficient for the presence of a competing brand (-4.79) is the same regardless of the value of x_1.[2] Graphically, the equation can be shown as two parallel lines, 4.8 units apart. (See Fig. 14.1). The lower line refers to stores in which there is a competing private brand, and the other line refers to stores in which there is no competing private brand.

The dummy variable technique can be extended to any number of dummy variables mixed with any number of intervally scaled variables. The technique can also be applied to discriminant analysis. The right-hand side of the equa-

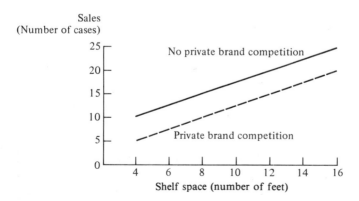

Fig. 14.1
Graphic representation of regression results with dummy variable. Dyna Kleen problem.

---

[2]The dummy variable technique does not *introduce* the assumption of no interaction. It was present in our earlier discussion of regression as well. The linear additive model assumes no interaction regardless of the scales involved.

Table 14.2
Computer Printout from SAS/Regression with Dummy Variable

REGRESSION WITH DUMMY VARIABLE

ANALYSIS OF VARIANCE TABLE , REGRESSION COEFFICIENTS , AND STATISTICS OF FIT FOR DEPENDENT VARIABLE SALES

SOURCE	DF	SUM OF SQUARES	MEAN SQUARE	F VALUE	PROB > F	R-SQUARE	C.V.
REGRESSION	2	328.09900990	164.04950495	29.58750	0.0003	0.86798680	19.62240 %
ERROR	9	49.90099010	5.54455446			STD DEV	SALES MEAN
CORRECTED TOTAL	11	378.00000000				2.35468776	12.00000

SOURCE	DF	SEQUENTIAL SS	F VALUE	PROB > F	PARTIAL SS	F VALUE	PROB > F
SHELF	1	259.88235294	46.87164	0.0001	231.76567657	41.80060	0.0001
PRIVBRD	1	68.21665696	12.30336	0.0066	68.21665696	12.30336	0.0066

SOURCE	B VALUES	T FOR HO: B=0	PROB > |T|	STD ERR B	STD B VALUES
INTERCEPT	3.90099010	2.00558	0.0759	1.94506792	0.0
SHELF	1.31188119	6.46534	0.0001	0.20290992	0.76689731
PRIVBRD	-4.79207921	-3.50761	0.0066	1.36619313	-0.42691235

OBS NUMBER	OBSERVED VALUE	PREDICTED VALUE	RESIDUAL	LOWER 95% CL FOR INDIVIDUAL	UPPER 95% CL FOR INDIVIDUAL
1	20.00000000	17.01980198	2.98019802	11.21565119	22.82395277
2	4.00000000	6.98019802	-2.98019802	1.17604723	12.78434081
3	12.00000000	11.77227723	0.22772277	5.91992505	17.62462941
4	15.00000000	14.85148515	0.14851485	8.76384816	20.93912214
5	7.00000000	9.14851485	-2.14851485	3.06087786	15.23615184
6	17.00000000	14.39603960	2.60396040	8.64049386	20.15158534
7	6.00000000	6.98019802	-0.98019802	1.17694723	12.76434881
8	15.00000000	12.22772277	2.77227723	6.37537059	18.08007495
9	11.00000000	11.77227723	-0.77227723	5.81992505	17.62462041
10	6.00000000	4.35643564	1.64356436	-1.63819569	10.35106698
11	22.00000000	24.89108911	-2.89108911	18.14666783	31.63551039
12	9.00000000	9.60396040	-0.60396040	3.84841466	15.35950614

SUM OF RESIDUALS   =   0.00000000

SUM OF SQUARED RESIDUALS   =   49.90099010

SUM OF SQUARED RESIDUALS - ERROR SS   =   0.00000000

FIRST ORDER AUTOCORRELATION OF RESIDUALS   =   -0.60176367

tion, encompassing the independent variables, requires precisely the same modifications in both models.

Except for the interpretation of the regression coefficient concerning the dummy variable, the entries of Table 14.2 have the same meaning as the corresponding entries in the standard regression program. R^2 is equal to 87 percent, indicating that variance around the regression line is 87 percent less than it was around the mean; this calculation describes the sample and is not an estimate of the universe value. The F-value of 29.5875 (with a probability of .0003) indicates that the null hypothesis for the total equation should be rejected. Evaluation of the separate variables is shown by the individual "Prob > T-values" or the "Prob > F-values." Both are significant at the .01 level of significance. The upper and lower limits for 95 percent confidence intervals have the usual meaning.

The entries at the bottom of the table reveal several items with respect to the residuals (the differences between the actual observations and the predicted values). First, positive and negative deviations precisely balance each other; the algebraic sum of 0.0. This is a necessary result of the least-squares solution and will always be 0.0 except for possible rounding errors. Second, the sum of the squared residuals equals the error sum of squares; this again is a check. The final entry, "First-order autocorrelation of residuals," is the coefficient of correlation among the residuals of successive observations. This calculation has potential significance only if the order of the observations has significance. For this particular problem the order is completely arbitrary. If a time series were involved, this would not be the case.[3]

The procedure is only slightly more complex when the nominally scaled independent variables have more than two categories. Consider the case of the same product manager who is now investigating the relationship between store sales and shelf space plus the relationship between store sales and membership in various chains. Suppose there are four different chains under investigation (W, X, Y, and Z). The number of dummy variables introduced into the equation is one less than the number of categories. This is consistent with the preceding problem in which one independent variable was introduced for private brand although there were two categories.

A possible result is given by the equation

$$y = .3 + 1.3x_1 + 0.5x_2 + 1.6x_3 - 0.8x_4$$

where

$$x_2 = 1 \text{ for Chain W,}$$
$$x_3 = 1 \text{ for Chain X, and}$$
$$x_4 = 1 \text{ for Chain Y.}$$

This equation actually gives four parallel lines, one for each chain. Only the Y-intercepts differ among the four chains; these intercepts become .8 for

---

[3]Autocorrelation in time series will be considered in Chapter 15.

Chain W (.3 as given in the equation plus the coefficient of .5 for x_2), 1.9 for Chain X, $-.5$ for Chain Y, and .3 for Chain Z. It is of course immaterial which chain seems to be missing from the equation. Chain Z is the base from which the values are computed for the other chains in the stated equation, but any of the other three could have served equally well. For example, designating $x_5 = 1$ for Chain Z, an equivalent equation is

$$y = .8 + 1.3x_1 + 1.1x_3 - 1.3x_4 - .5x_5.$$

Chain W provides the base in this equation. Comparison of the two equations underlines the interpretation of the coefficients. Only the coefficient of x_1 remains the same; this has the usual interpretation of showing the average relationship between shelf space and sales, net of any chain effects. The other coefficients change because they must be interpreted as differences from Chain Z in the first equation but differences from Chain W in the second.

To be sure you have followed the logic in dummy variables, consider the following problem. How many different variables would be stated in an equation with four intervally scaled independent variables, two nominally scaled independent variables with two categories each, one nominally scaled independent variable with three categories, and one nominally scaled independent variable with four categories? First, it is clear that the answer is not eight, the number of independent variables. This would be the correct answer only if each nominally scaled independent variable possessed two categories. The correct answer to this problem is 11. Why?

ANALYSIS OF COVARIANCE

The analysis of covariance (ANCOVA) provides an alternative approach to handling mixed scales among the independent variables, but the problem setting is typically different. ANCOVA most often arises with a problem that starts as ANOVA. Consider a factorial design in which the researcher identifies three types of "deals" and chain/independent status as the test variables, each to be evaluated for their impact on product sales. ANOVA is obviously appropriate. However, the researcher fears that the impact of the test variables may be obscured in the experiment by additional independent variables that are beyond control. In this case, the researcher believes that both mean neighborhood income and square feet of selling space may have significant effects. ANCOVA makes a statistical adjustment for the uncontrolled variable(s) so that the net effect of the test variables can be appraised.

Important uncontrolled variables may also distort the test by producing a high level of variability in the experiment. Even though no bias is introduced, the high variability leads to a high measure of residual variance, making it difficult to identify the effects of the test variables.

Consider a test designed to show the relative effectiveness of manufacturer's coupon versus retailer's coupon. If the dependent variable is unit sales and the test is run with stores of vastly different sizes, the variability in sales will be great. Even if the test balances the assignment of stores so that the results are not biased toward either type of coupon, the high dispersion among observations may obscure any underlying difference between the effectiveness of the two types of coupons. ANCOVA, by adjusting for the effect of the uncontrolled variable(s), reduces the residual variance and permits a better identification of any effects of the test variables.

Alternatively, a significant uncontrolled variable may be correlated with a test variable. Unless the analysis adjusts for the extraneous variable, the results run the risk of improperly attributing observed differences to the test variable. Suppose one of the test variables is occupation and the dependent variable relates to expenditures on leisure activities. Since income levels vary with occupation, a straight ANOVA without adjusting for income runs the risk of attributing effects to occupation that should be attributed to income.[4]

The analysis of covariance is illustrated by Tables 14.3 and 14.4. The data refer to a study proposed by the sales manger of the Clark Wholesale Company who wants to know whether the differences in the sales levels of Clark's salespeople are associated with differences in their levels of formal education. "Formal education" is here defined as one of three categories: nongraduate, high school graduate, or college graduate. The amount of selling experience is included as an uncontrolled variable that may also influence the level of sales.

Mean sales for high school graduates are $25,000 per month, for nongraduates $21,000, and for college graduates only $16,800. Application of

Table 14.3
Salespeople's Sales versus Amount of Formal Education and Years of Selling Experience. Data for Analysis of Covariance. Clark Wholesale Company.

	Amount of formal education					
	Nongraduate		High school graduate		College graduate	
	Sales†	Experience	Sales†	Experience	Sales†	Experience
	23	7	32	16	18	3
	16	2	19	5	20	7
	28	10	28	7	14	4
	20	5	24	12	10	1
	18	11	22	8	22	5
Totals	105	35	125	48	84	20
Means	21.0	7.0	25.0	9.6	16.8	4.0

†Sales are expressed in $1,000 per month.

[4]The marketing manager may settle for market segmentation strategies based on occupation, but should recognize that it is being used as a proxy variable for income—assuming the analysis reveals this distinction.

Table 14.4
Computer Printout from SAS/Analysis of Covariance

ANALYSIS OF COVARIANCE

ANALYSIS OF VARIANCE TABLE , REGRESSION COEFFICIENTS , AND STATISTICS CF FIT FOR DEPENDENT VARIABLE SALES

SOURCE	DF	SUM OF SQUARES	MEAN SQUARE	F VALUE	PROB > F	R-SQUARE	C.V.
REGRESSION	3	292.26693122	97.42231041	6.67000	0.0081	0.64527583	18.25693 %
ERROR	11	160.66640212	14.60603656			STD DEV	SALES MEAN
CORRECTED TOTAL	14	452.93333333				3.8217844 7	20.93333

SOURCE	DF	SEQUENTIAL SS	F VALUE	PROB > F	PARTIAL SS	F VALUE	PROB > F
EXPER	1	276.13240472	18.90536	0.0012	124.13359788	8.49879	0.0141
SCHOOL	2	16.13452650	0.55232	0.5950	16.13452650	0.55232	0.5950

SOURCE	B VALUES	T FOR H0:B=0	PROB > |T|	STD ERR B	STD B VALUES
INTERCEPT	14.71155203	6.25680	0.0001	2.35129102	0.0
EXPER	0.90608466	2.91527	0.0141	0.31080665	0.64530294

OBS NUMBER	OBSERVED VALUE	PREDICTED VALUE	RESIDUAL	LOWER 95% CL FOR INDIVIDUAL	UPPER 95% CL FOR INDIVIDUAL
1	23.00000000	21.00000000	2.00000000	11.78542329	30.21457671
2	16.00000000	16.46957672	-0.46957672	6.64065680	26.29849664
3	28.00000000	23.71825397	4.28174603	14.27790607	33.15840096
4	20.00000000	19.18733069	0.81216931	9.87223608	28.50342529
5	18.00000000	24.62433862	-6.62433862	15.01205797	34.23661928
6	32.00000000	30.79894180	1.20105820	20.59715454	41.00072906
7	19.00000000	20.83201058	-1.83201058	11.09493386	30.56908730
8	28.00000000	22.64417989	5.35582011	13.25951691	32.02884288
9	24.00000000	27.17460317	-3.17460317	17.81490609	36.53430026
10	22.00000000	23.55026455	-1.55026455	14.27090970	32.82961940
11	18.00000000	15.89391534	2.10608466	6.65398062	25.13385007
12	20.00000000	19.51825397	0.48174603	10.07790697	28.95860096
13	14.00000000	16.80000000	-2.80000000	7.58542329	26.01457671
14	10.00000000	14.08174603	-4.08174603	4.64139904	23.52209303
15	22.00000000	17.70608466	4.29391534	8.46614993	26.94601938

SUM OF RESIDUALS = 0.00000000

SUM OF SQUARED RESIDUALS = 160.66640212

SUM OF SQUARED RESIDUALS - ERROR SS = 0.00000000

ANOVA reveals that these differences are statistically significant. The sales manager who relies on ANOVA would conclude that high school graduates achieve higher sales levels than either college graduates or those who have not completed high school.[5] The company's former practice of shunning college graduates and giving a plus to high school graduates seems to have been correct. Recent departures from these practices seem to have been poorly advised.

Table 14.3 also reveals that the high school graduates have the most selling experience—9.6 years compared to 7.0 for nongraduates and 4.0 for college graduates. The analysis of covariance attempts to determine whether the conclusion from ANOVA is still appropriate after adjusting for experience.

Suppose the net regression coefficient between sales and years of experience is 1.1 (later calculations yield a slightly lower estimate). The analysis of covariance asks whether the relationship summarized by this coefficient is sufficient to explain the observed differences among the mean sales of the three groups. Figure 14.2 summarizes this first approximation to the relationship between sales and years of experience, forcing the line to pass through the intersection of the two means. It also identifies the location of the three groups of salespeople. The college graduates, having the least experience, would be expected to achieve the lowest average sales. But the graph shows them even lower than the sales–experience line indicates. The actual results and the predicted results for the three groups are

	Actual	Predicted	Difference
College graduate	16,800	17,800	− 1,000
High school graduate	25,000	23,900	+1,100
Nongraduate	21,000	21,100	− 100

These differences between the predicted and actual figures are produced by one of two causes: either (1) they are the effects of differences in educational levels or (2) they are produced by random forces. The second explanation is asserted in the null hypothesis and tested. Only if it is rejected should the sales manager conclude that differences in formal education levels affect sales.

Table 14.4 presents a portion of the computer output from the SAS analysis of covariance program.[6] The table contains four distinct but related results: (1) the test of the combined effect of all the independent variables, (2) separate tests for the effect of each independent variable, (3) the regression equation for the uncontrolled variable, and (4) predictions for the individual observations.

---

[5]The application of ANOVA of course assumes that the data constitute samples from appropriate universes. If the data are universe values, no tests are needed; the universe means are known. Alternatively, even a complete enumeration of present salespeople might be considered as a sample from a theoretical universe of potential sales persons.

[6]Barr and Goodnight, *op. cit.*, pp. 114–117.

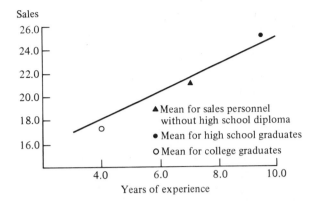

Fig. 14.2
Adjustment of salespeople data for amount of experience. Analysis of covariance concept.

The most significant portion for the sales manager's question is the second portion that examines the independent variables separately.

The program generates tests for the separate variables in two ways, shown at the left by the column SEQUENTIAL SS and at the right by the column PARTIAL SS. The sequential approach corresponds more closely to our conceptualization of the problem. It says to first determine the relationship between sales and experience by a linear regression. The portion of the initial sum of squares removed by this linear regression is 276.13. This reduction is highly significant ($F = 18.9$ and a probability of .0012).

We now ask how much of the remaining variance is removed by the variable formal education (labeled SCHOOL). The printout gives the answer in terms of a sum of squares although the F-test uses variance. Formal education removes only 16.13 of the remaining sum of squares. The F-ratio is .55, and the null hypothesis should be accepted (probability .595). Sales level is not associated with level of formal education, at least not for the Clark Company as defined in this problem. The observed differences between the mean sales for the three groups and the values predicted for them (based on mean experience) are considered random deviations.

The PARTIAL SUM OF SQUARES column approaches the analysis on a "net" basis. The contribution of each separate variable is appraised, after the effects of the other variables have been incorporated. The result for formal education is the same (partial and sequential) because the question is the same: How much of the variance is eliminated by formal education after adjusting for experience first? The result for experience is slightly different since we now evaluate its effect after (rather than before) introducing education. The probability on a net basis is .0141 whereas the probability was only .0012 on a gross basis. *A priori* specification of both the test (net or gross) and alpha is critical in this instance; otherwise we run the risk of attempting to prove our predispositions instead of testing them.

The first portion of Table 14.4 evaluates the combined effect of both experience and formal education (labeled "REGRESSION"). Together they account for 64.5 percent of the variance in sales (R-SQUARE). The hypothesis of no association should clearly be rejected ($F = 6.67$ has a probability of less than .01). This portion of the output, as well as the fourth portion, is appropriate for use only if interest is centered on the total equation. If the primary emphasis is on the evaluation of the treatment variable(s), the second portion of the table accomplishes this purpose.

The linear regression between sales and experience is given in the third portion of the table: $y = 14.7 + .9x$. This is a net relationship, after adjusting for formal education. The complete equation used for the predictions within the table and upon which R^2 is based includes dummy variables for education.[7]

Table 14.5 presents another set of data used in an ANCOVA problem. These data give store sales of a new product using three different in-store promotions: a low introductory price, a special display rack, and in-store distribution of samples. The product manager thought the results of the promotions would be clearer if adjustment were made for store traffic. The differences in mean sales according to the promotion are not significant (using ANOVA); the

Table 14.5
Store Sales versus In-store Promotion Campaign and Traffic Count. Data for Analysis of Covariance

	Promotion campaign					
	Introductory price		Special rack		Samples given	
	Sales	Traffic	Sales	Traffic	Sales	Traffic
	56	37	37	23	43	20
	24	17	66	42	29	13
	59	48	25	15	72	31
	43	28	54	36	58	24
Totals	182	130	182	116	202	88
Means	45.5	32.5	45.5	29.0	50.5	22.0

[7]The dummy variable coefficients indicate differentials of 3.13 for high school graduates and 1.48 for nongraduates over college graduates. Use of the total equation or the dummy variable coefficients is suspect since we have concluded that formal education and sales are not associated.

respective means are 50.5 when samples are given and 45.5 for the other two promotions.

Adjusting for store traffic isolates the net effect of the respective promotions. In this case adjusting for the uncontrolled variable has the opposite effect of that in the preceding illustration. The theoretical calculation using only the relationship between sales and store traffic show large deviations from the actual sales. The summary table for the analysis is given in Table 14.6. Both the relationship between sales and store traffic and the net relationship between sales and type of promotion are significant. The latter is the item of concern to the product manager, but it was discerned only by adjusting for store traffic. The estimating equation, in a dummy variable format, shows the special rack as 5.2 units better than the low introductory price and the sample distribution as 11.5 units better than the low introductory price.

Table 14.6
Analysis of Covariance. Store Sales versus Promotion with Store Traffic as a Covariate

Source	Sum of squares†	Degrees of freedom	Mean square	F-ratio‡
Promotion	757.23	2	378.62	9.98 ($P < .01$)
Traffic	1788.95	1	1788.95	47.16 ($P < .01$)
Residual	303.49	8	37.94	
Total	2849.67	11		

†The sums of squares figures are based on a sequential partitioning—first traffic and then promotion.
‡F-ratios are based on mean squares carried to more decimals than shown in table.

The sums of squares shown in Table 14.6 are based on a sequential partitioning of the total. If we were interested in studying the effect of traffic, net of type promotion employed, the reverse sequence would be required. Simultaneous solution and use of partial sums of squares are appropriate if the net effect of each variable is desired.[8]

These two sets of data illustrate the two different types of adjustments possible with analysis of covariance. In the first case, the covariate (experience) was correlated with the treatment variable (education); adjustment for the covariate eliminated the apparent effect of the treatment variable. In the second case, the covariate (traffic) was correlated with the response variable (sales); adjustment for the covariate revealed the previously hidden effect of the treatment variable (promotion) on sales.

[8]Use of partial sums of squares will not yield a neat partitioning of the total sum of squares since the entries show only the removal by each variable when it is the last variable added. The reductions at the prior stages do not appear in the figures. In most cases the sum of the partial sum of squares will be less than the sum of sequential sum of squares.

Dummy Variable or Analysis of Covariance

The dummy variable technique and the analysis of covariance both consider the problem of mixed scales for the independent variables. They usually arise in different contexts: the dummy variable format arising when one is interested in evaluating the effects of both intervally scaled and nominally scaled variables and the analysis of covariance arising when one believes adjustment for an uncontrolled intervally scaled variable will permit a better evaluation of treatment variables in an ANOVA design. Despite these differences, the two techniques yield identical conditional estimating equations when solved by simultaneous least squares.[9]

The similarity can be best seen by reviewing the interpretation of some of our results. The dummy variable approach yields parallel estimating equations for the different categories. Use of a constant regression coefficient for the uncontrolled variable in the analysis of covariance produces precisely the same result. The location of the estimating line is shifted for different categories, but the same slope is maintained. The similarity is further evident in the test of the null hypothesis. The explained variance is tested against the unexplained variance by an F-ratio—precisely the same in each technique. In fact if the same data were submitted, the numerical results would be identical because the initial variance is the same, the estimating equations the same, and the dispersion around the equation the same.

Why Parallel Lines?

Should we assume parallel lines for all categories? Might not the relationship between the dependent variable and one or more intervally scaled independent variables differ among groups? The effect of store traffic may interact with the in-store promotion employed; years of selling experience may have a different impact on sales depending on the amount of formal education. The basic procedures we have used assume the regression coefficients are equal. This assumption could be tested, asserting in the null hypothesis that the regression coefficients are equal for all categories.

If the null hypothesis is rejected, separate equations that depend on the specific values of the nominal variables must be used. This is the same conclusion we reached in multiple classification ANOVA. If interaction exists, the estimating equation employed should not be a main-effects model. Instead the estimates should be made at the level at which interactions are significant.[10]

---

[9]An argument can be made that the estimating equation for the typical ANCOVA problem should be determined in two steps: (1) the covariate(s) against the dependent variable and (2) the treatment variables against the residuals of step (1). This approach would show net effects for the treatment variables but a gross relationship for the covariate(s). In actual practice, a simultaneous solution for all independent variables is almost always employed.

[10]See Wilfrid J. Dixon and Frank J. Massey, Jr., 1957, *Introduction to Statistical Analysis* (New York: McGraw-Hill), pp. 216–219, for the test of this and related assumptions.

This procedure can be illustrated by referring to the dummy variable problem of Table 14.1: store sales versus shelf space and presence of a competing private brand. The regression coefficient for shelf space was 1.3. Suppose shelf space has a greater effect when there is a competing private brand than when there is not.[11] What steps should now be taken? One equation (sales versus shelf space) should be determined for stores with a competing private brand and another for stores without a private brand. These results might be $y = -7.8 + 12.1x_1$ for stores with one or more competing private brands, and $y = 5.3 + 1.3x_1$ for stores without competing private brands. These lines are shown in Fig. 14.3.

The equations of Fig. 14.3—in contrast to the parallel lines of Fig. 14.1—show that a large amount of shelf space produces almost equal sales, regardless of whether a competing brand is present. However, the sales resulting with low shelf space vary considerably, depending on whether a competitive private brand is stocked.

Several more complicated models might be suggested by such a result. Is it the mere presence of a competing private brand, or is it the shelf space devoted to the private brand? Alternatively, should a new independent variable be defined in terms of shelf space devoted to the company's brand versus shelf space devoted to the private brand? Either a ratio or the absolute difference might provide an acceptable new variable.[12]

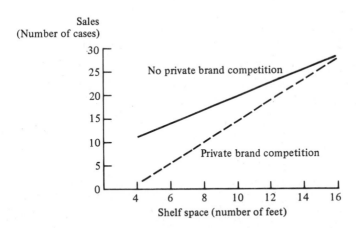

Fig. 14.3
Graphic representation of regression results, dummy variable, and interaction term.

---

[11]The null hypothesis of equality should be tested along the lines indicated by Dixon and Massey, *loc. cit.* The data in Table 14.1 do not suggest that any interaction exists.

[12]These modifications may introduce problems with respect to multicollinearity and the need of transformations. Both problems are considered in Chapter 15.

Dummy Variable Approach versus Use of Intervally Scaled Variable

The sales manager for the Clark Wholesale Company defined three different educational levels for the analysis of salespeople's performance. Since education could be defined on an interval scale, it might be argued that the three levels of nongraduate, high school graduate, and college graduate should use only one independent variable instead of two dummy variables. The difficulty with this argument is two-fold.

First, the researcher must assign interval locations to each of the three categories. A 1, 2, 3 assignment is no less arbitrary or subjective than any other assignment. The computation of the conditional distribution will neither question nor test the appropriateness of the interval scale values. The mathematical equation that summarizes the relationship makes it easy to forget the subjective decisions upon which it rests. The dummy variable approach does not require such arbitrary decisions.

Second, the use of a single variable forces a linear relationship upon the data. Not only may the true relationship be nonlinear but it may have reversals. This is the case with the Clark data. Although not statistically significant, the high school graduates recorded higher sales than either the college graduates or those who had not graduated from high school. Use of a linear regression with education as a single intervally scaled variable would not permit such a summary.

SUMMARY

The marketing problems encountered in practice often present the analyst with a mixture of intervally scaled and nominally scaled independent variables. Regression and discriminant analysis can cope with this situation by using *dummy variables*. ANOVA solves the problem by using the analysis of covariance (ANCOVA).

Nominally scaled variables may be converted into dummy variables by coding them into a 0/1 system, thus permitting their inclusion in regression and discriminant analysis. This procedure permits the inclusion of independent variables measured on either interval or nominal scales. The regression coefficients of the dummy variables show expected differences among the various categories of the nominally scaled variables—in contrast to the per unit interpretation associated with intervally scaled variables. The number of dummy variables added for each nominally scaled variable is one less than the number of categories. Thus nominally scaled variables decrease the number of degrees of freedom more rapidly than intervally scaled variables.

The analysis of covariance also deals with the problems of mixed scales for the independent variables and yields precisely the same estimating equation and significance tests results as the dummy variable approach. Covariance analysis typically arises from a desire to adjust for uncontrolled variables in an ANOVA design. The rationale is to first discover how the uncontrolled variable affects the dependent variable and then to analyze the way in which the treatment variables "produce" departures from the results expected because of the uncontrolled variable(s).

The typical "canned" computer programs do not test for interactions, either with dummy variables or in the analysis of covariance. The results impose linear functions on the relationships although the dummy approach preserves the unordered properties of the nominal scale. The summary statistics available from the analyses and the interpretation of them are similar to those discussed in the preceding chapters.

EXERCISES AND PROBLEMS

1. Distinguish between the terms within each of the following pairs.
   a) Analysis of covariance and regression with dummy variable
   b) Sequential sums of squares and partial sums of squares
   c) Four intervally scaled independent variables and one nominally scaled independent variable with four categories

2. Briefly explain the meaning and significance of each of the following terms.
   a) Dummy variable
   b) Covariate
   c) 0/1 variable
   d) Sum of residuals

3. How many coefficients will be obtained from a regression equation based upon each of the following?
   a) Two intervally scaled independent variables, one nominally scaled independent variable with three categories, and one nominally scaled independent variable with four categories.
   b) Three intervally scaled independent variables, four nominally scaled independent variables with two categories each, and one nominally scaled independent variable with three categories.
   c) Four intervally scaled independent variables and one nominally scaled variable with an unknown number of categories.

4. Both regression with dummy variables and the analysis of covariance yield parallel lines to be used in making estimates.
   a) What does the distance between the parallel lines represent?
   b) Why is the distance between the lines measured in a direction parallel to the axis of the dependent variable rather than perpendicular to the parallel lines?
   c) What would be the implication if the lines were not parallel?

5. An analysis of covariance may reveal a treatment effect where none appeared in ANOVA. It is also possible that an analysis of covariance may reveal no treatment effect where ANOVA revealed a treatment effect. Briefly discuss the underlying situation for each of these cases.

6. a) Define an original problem in which analysis of covariance would be an appropriate technique. Be sure to specify how each variable is measured.

    b) Could the problem be analyzed by regression with dummy variables? Why?

7. Provide a small set of hypothetical data for the problem specified in Exercise 6, and perform the required analysis.

8. A nonprofit consumer affairs organization wished to examine relationships between interest in consumer affairs, television viewing, and newspaper readership. The data presented in Table E14.8 were obtained from a small pilot project, but treat the data as though they represent a simple random sample. Newspaper readership is in minutes/day.

Table E14.8

Respondent	Interest in consumer affairs	TV viewing (hrs per wk)	Newspaper readership	Newspaper read
1	82	27	40	B
2	50	25	5	C
3	91	9	75	A
4	46	35	30	C
5	73	15	15	B
6	95	6	60	B
7	70	22	10	B
8	58	30	25	C
9	81	10	35	A
10	75	16	20	C
11	86	8	45	A
12	77	12	15	A
13	65	16	15	C
14	68	15	20	B
15	85	14	30	A

a) Determine the constants of a least-squares regression line that will yield estimates for interest in consumer affairs, given TV viewing, newspaper readership, and newspaper read.

b) Test a null hypothesis of no association for each independent variable.

c) Is the small sample size a source of difficulty with this analysis? Why or why not?

d) Suppose the organization wishes to recruit additional support and members. What, if any, guidance would your analysis offer?

9. A large chemical company has been concerned that its salespeople may be calling on customers with greater frequency than necessary. It therefore designs an experi-

ment to test whether decreased frequency will have an adverse effect on dollar sales. Since lost sales is a critical matter, it wishes to keep the experiment small but still reliable and unbiased. The data in Table E14.9 are based upon a simple random sample of accounts, each account assigned to its "frequency" category by random methods. The research director, believing other variables may be large, wants to adjust for such disturbances. Number of production employees is suggested as a variable that may capture some of these exogenous factors. The data obtained are presented below with sales in $1,000 for a six-month period and number of production employees in 100's.

Table E14.9

		Frequency			
Two weeks		Four weeks		Six weeks	
Sales	Number of employees	Sales	Number of employees	Sales	Number of employees
5	3.3	4	2.4	5	3.5
4	2.1	3	1.6	8	7.1
10	7.7	12	8.5	2	1.5
8	6.1	7	5.9	6	5.4
3	1.4	5	3.6	4	2.5

a) Perform an ANOVA on the sales figures. What is your conclusion?

b) Perform an ANCOVA using number of employees as the covariate.

c) Do your two analyses, (a) and (b), yield the same conclusion? Why or why not?

d) Draw a graph, showing the conditional distribution obtained in part (b).

e) Does your graph in (d) incorporate the concept of interaction? Why or why not?

f) Do you think the experimental design and the variables incorporated in it are adequate? (Disregard sample size.) Why or why not?

10. Three versions (A, B, and C) of a new product were presented to three different groups in a simulated laboratory purchase situation. The mean expenditure on the product and mean purchases of the product type within the past six months are given in Table E14.10.

Table E14.10

	A	B	C
Mean expenditure on new product (coupon points)	45.2	49.3	36.4
Mean purchase of product type (units)	3.62	3.57	3.65

a) Do you think an analysis of covariance, using mean purchases of product type as the covariate, should be recommended? Why?

b) What additional data would you need before deciding whether the mean expenditures on the three versions are significantly different? Explain precisely.

c) Could the data be analyzed by a regression approach with a dummy variable? Why or why not?

11. Analyze, criticize, and explain:

a) The coefficient of determination computed from a typical analysis of covariance is useless because it is not germane to the decision problem.

b) The regression coefficient associated with a dummy variable must be between 0.0 and 1.0 because a dummy variable by definition must be either 0 or 1.

c) Interaction in ANCOVA can be seen subjectively by computing separate regression equations for each subgroup and determining whether the lines are parallel.

d) Both regression with dummy variables and the analysis of covariance deal with problems in which the independent variables contain a mixture of intervally, ordinally, and nominally scaled measurements.

e) The separate net "sums of squares" calculated from an analysis of covariance will sum to the total sum of squares, but the sum with a sequential approach will usually be less than the total.

CHAPTER 15

SEARCH TECHNIQUES
A HALF-STRUCTURED HYPOTHESIS PLUS DATA
EQUALS A STRUCTURED MODEL

Many research projects fall between the extremes of exploratory research—a vague inquiry about a general topic—and a completely structured, well-defined, specific hypothesis. Such projects employ *search* techniques in establishing the specific descriptive relationships. These search techniques incorporate a "trial-and-error" approach. What "works" is retained, and what doesn't is discarded. Search techniques fall into two general categories: (1) those designed to select which of a large number of independent variables should be incorporated in the conditional equation and (2) those designed to select the appropriate structural form for the relationship.

A small manufacturer of computer peripheral equipment wishes to classify various firms in terms of their purchase potentials. A vast array of variables is considered as possible independent variables: Standard Industrial Classification (SIC), size as measured under several alternative definitions, age of firm, geographic location, characteristics of key personnel within the firm, plus a variety of financial and operational data. The application of search techniques is an appropriate way to sort out a small group of variables with high predictive power.

Voting preference in an upcoming election is thought to be related to age and income. The researchers are unwilling to assume a linear relationship for either variable. They are willing to go a step further and consider the possibility of reversals. They believe that three or four categories may be enough for each of the independent variables, but they would like to avoid the imposition of their own guesses concerning the appropriate class limits. Again search techniques offer approaches by which the researchers can let the data guide the analysis.

Search techniques possess two principal dangers. First, since the data generate the model and the hypotheses, the standard probability statements cannot be applied to the conclusions presented. Second, since the model and hypotheses are generated by a sequential procedure, the result at any step may be suboptimal. Despite these dangers, search techniques offer powerful tools for screening data when the researcher is a step removed from a final, clearly articulated hypothesis.

We shall consider search techniques in this chapter in the multivariate format with a single dependent variable.[1] We shall discuss two principal techniques: (1) stepwise solutions and (2) transformations. Stepwise solutions are sequential procedures in which one independent variable is added (or subtracted) at each step. Transformations represent an alternative approach in which the usual linearity assumption is relaxed, allowing the researcher to incorporate various nonlinear relationships. Regardless of which approach is used, the objective is the reduction of residual ("unexplained") variance.

Our discussion in this chapter will focus on three specific techniques: (1) stepwise regression, (2) selected transformations, and (3) the Automatic Interaction Detector (AID). The first applies the stepwise approach to a technique we have already considered—regression. The second applies the transformations approach to the same technique. The third applies a stepwise approach, a different concept of transformations, and the incorporation of interaction terms—thus yielding a new technique.

STEPWISE REGRESSION

Marketing research studies often involve a large number of potential independent variables as predictors for one or more critical dependent variables. With a limited database, the number of degrees of freedom may be exhausted (or at least radically depleted) if all of these variables are included in the estimating equation. A step-by-step generation of the equation is an alternative approach in which the database is "searched" for successive variables to introduce into the equation.

A second motivating force for the stepwise approach is the frequently encountered problem of multicollinearity. The independent variables may be correlated with each other, leading to large standard errors of the regression coefficients since it is difficult to isolate the net effect of each separate variable. An alternative is to introduce the variables one at a time, adding only those variables that make unique contributions and refusing to add those that are redundant.

The motivation leading to stepwise solutions is understandable, but the solutions have distinct drawbacks. First, the meaning and appropriateness of probability statements are highly suspect. If the final equation retains two or three independent variables out of a large number of candidates, chance alone may be responsible for their inclusion. A level of significance of .05 identifies in advance one's willingness to reject the null hypothesis *when it is true* 5 per-

---

[1]Other search techniques will be considered in Part IV.

cent of the time. If there are 50 candidate variables, the expected number of rejections of the null hypothesis is 2.5 even if none of the 50 is associated with the dependent variable.[2] Second, the set of independent variables included is not necessarily the optimal set. Each variable is added sequentially because *at that step* it reduces variance more than any of the other candidates. Another equation with the same number of variables (or fewer) may reduce the total variance by a larger amount. For both of these reasons, inferences based on the results of a stepwise routine must be carefully qualified. Nevertheless, the technique offers a powerful tool for handling a large volume of data, particularly with a large number of intercorrelated independent variables.

The stepwise regression approach first asks which of the independent variables will remove the largest amount of total variance. A simple two-variable regression equation is then computed using that independent variable. At the next stage, the question is which of the *remaining* independent variables will eliminate the largest amount of variance—variance unexplained by the first variable. This second variable is combined with the first variable in establishing a regression equation with two independent variables.[3] The process is repeated at each succeeding step, always asking which of the remaining independent variables (not in the previous equation) will remove the largest amount of unexplained variance. Most of the stepwise regression routines incorporate a "significance level for staying in." Variables introduced at earlier steps may lose a portion of their net contribution as other variables are added. The programs test each variable at each stage, permitting deletion of variables if they become redundant.

We illustrate stepwise regression with the data set from Chapter 13—expenditures on product A as the dependent variable and family discretionary income, gregariousness, and tenure in the SMSA as the candidate independent variables. Table 15.1 presents the output from the SAS stepwise multiple regression program.[4] This is a very compact summary of the results. The BMD output, in contrast, supplies detailed data concerning the equation and the separate variables at each step.[5]

Table 15.1 shows that family discretionary income is the first variable entered. R^2 after step 1 is 59.9 percent, and the F-ratio concerning the reduction in variance for step 1 is significant at the .01 level. Tenure is entered at step 2 with R^2 increased to 78.1 percent. The F-ratio concerning the net contri-

---

[2]Here, as in many other marketing research problems, the split-half technique can be applied. The model structure is determined, using only half the data. That structure is then tested, using the other half of the data.

[3]The regression equation is recomputed using two independent variables. Thus the regression coefficient associated with each independent variable will change with each successive step.

[4]A. J. Barr and J. H. Goodnight, 1972, *A User's Guide to the Statistical Analysis System* (Raleigh, N.C.: Sparks Press), pp. 127–137.

[5]W. J. Dixon and M. B. Brown (eds.), 1977, *Biomedical Computer Programs, P-Series* (Berkeley, Calif.: University of California Press), pp. 697–710.

bution of tenure is significant at the .05 level. The printout also shows that the *net* contribution of discretionary income is significant at step 2; the *F*-ratio based on the partial sum of squares is 23.39 with a probability of less than .01.

The program does not add gregariousness to the equation as a third step. Instead the routine is terminated at step 2. The SAS program adds variables, one at a time, only if the specified "significance level for entry" is met. The specified level for Table 15.1 is .1. Since the *F*-ratio for gregariousness does not qualify, the appropriate solution is obtained at step 2. The program also stipulates a "significance level for staying in." A variable previously entered may lose some of its net impact as other variables are added. The deletion criterion makes it possible to drop variables that no longer make sufficient net contributions.

The final equation is shown at the bottom of the table in the usual way with the coefficients, the *t*-statistics, probability associated with each *t,* the standard errors of the coefficients, and the coefficients expressed in standard score units. The final equation of $y = 43.95 + 11.99x_1 - 3.48x_3$ can be used for point estimates either for individual persons or for conditional means.

Care must be exercised in interpreting the results of a stepwise program, particularly with respect to the variables excluded. A variable may be excluded because it is highly correlated with a variable that has already entered the equation even though it is associated with the dependent variable. Suppose a publisher of textbooks were studying the market for book sales and included among the potential independent variables the following three variables: number of students in the school system, number of high school graduates last year, and number of graduates entering college this year. These variables may be so highly correlated with each other that only one (or at most two) would enter a stepwise regression solution. This does not justify the conclusion that the excluded variables are not associated with the dependent variable. It merely indicates that their contribution to the estimating equation is negligible—after the other variable has been included.

The stepwise procedure also highlights a warning mentioned earlier: analytic results cannot uniquely identify causative factors. We talk about the "effect" of the independent variables, but no analysis can really establish cause and effect. Consider the three variables cited in the preceding paragraph (number of students in school system, number of high school graduates last year, and number of graduates entering college this year) and assume that only one (high school graduates last year) is included in the final estimating equation. Use of that single variable may be satisfactory in making esimates, but the publisher should not conclude that the other two variables are unrelated to sales. The coefficient for high school graduates probably embraces the net relationships of the other variables as well as its own.[6] The regression coeffi-

---

[6]Even if a unique association could be established, the direction of causation—which is cause or which is effect—would be lacking. See the discussion "Research and the Philosophy of Science" in Chapter 2 and "Causation" in Chapter 3.

Table 15.1
Computer Printout from SAS/Stepwise Regression

STEPWISE REGRESSION

STEPWISE REGRESSION PROCEDURE FOR DEPENDENT VARIABLE EXPEND

NUMBER IN MODEL	R-SQUARE	VARIABLES IN MODEL
1	0.59852833	FAMDI
2	0.78147451	FAMDI TENURE

THE VARIABLES IN THE MODEL ABOVE HAVE ALL BEEN DEEMED SIGNIFICANT AT THE 0.1000 SIGNIFICANCE LEVEL

ANALYSIS OF VARIANCE TABLE , REGRESSION COEFFICIENTS , AND STATISTICS OF FIT FOR THE MODEL ABOVE

SOURCE	DF	SUM OF SQUARES	MEAN SQUARE	F VALUE	PROB > F	R-SQUARE	C.V.
REGRESSION	2	2939.98525442	1469.99262721	12.51644	0.0054	0.78147451	15.77468 %
ERROR	7	822.11474558	117.44496365				
CORRECTED TOTAL	9	3762.10000000					

SOURCE	DF	SEQUENTIAL SS	F VALUE	PROB > F	PARTIAL SS	F VALUE	PROB > F
FAMDI	1	2251.72342396	19.17258	0.0036	2747.58724117	23.39468	0.0023
TENURE	1	688.26183046	5.86029	0.0447	688.26183046	5.86029	0.0447

SOURCE	B VALUES	T FOR H0:B=0	PROB > |T|	STD ERR B	STD B VALUES
MEAN	43.95212453				
FAMDI	11.99495418	4.83680	0.0023	2.47993357	0.88119947
TENURE	-3.48074352	-2.42080	0.0447	1.43784602	-0.44103730

cient summarizes the way in which two variables tend to vary together. The basic factors that produce this common pattern are not revealed by the equation. Any regression coefficient shows a *gross* relationship with respect to variables not in the equation; the *net* aspect refers only to other variables in the equation.

A stepwise procedure may also be employed with discriminant analysis. Consider the case of a producer of office supplies who wishes to divide the market into "prime" targets and "all others." The producer has data on 25 different characteristics plus classification as "prime" or "other." The stepwise procedure selects from among these characteristics the one that best discriminates between the two groups—that is the characteristic for which percentage reduction in variance is the greatest. Suppose this characteristic is number of clerical employees. At step two, a second characteristic is selected from among the remaining 24. Again the criterion is which variable shows the greatest percentage reduction in variance, but now the point of reference is variance remaining after step 1 rather than initial variance.

Any variables that are highly correlated with number of clerical employees are not likely to be entered at the second step. Their potential contributions were included in step 1. Instead an uncorrelated variable such as tenure in office of purchasing agent may be entered at step 2. The procedure continues step by step until the potential contribution of the remaining variables is less than the specified critical level.[7]

TRANSFORMATIONS

Two assumptions appear over and over in multivariate analyses: (1) the relationship between the expected value of the dependent variable and the independent variable is linear and (2) the variance of the observations around the conditional distribution is constant for all levels of the independent variable—homoscedasticity is present. If these assumptions are suspect, transformation of the original data may produce new variables for which the assumptions are more valid. Neither assumption is removed by the transformation, but the researcher believes the assumptions are more valid for the transformed data.

The most common types of transformations in marketing research are logarithmic and exponential. Logarithmic transformations are particularly useful when one or both of the variables are appropriately analyzed in terms of percentage changes. Exponential transformations are most useful in compressing or amplifying the significance of large deviations from some base value.

---

[7]The critical level is specified in terms of the *F*-test. See Norman H. Nie, C. Hadlai Hull, Jean G. Jenkins, Karin Steinbrenner, and Dale H. Bent, 1975, *Statistical Package for the Social Sciences* (New York: McGraw-Hill), Chapter 23, for a very complete description.

Our discussion of transformations will be illustrative and far from exhaustive. Each individual problem must be considered on its own in terms of logic, fit, and the range for which description is desired.[8]

Logarithmic Transformations

The basic rationale for a logarithmic transformation is that the percentage rate of change in one variable displays a constant relationship to equal changes in the other variable. Figure 15.1 illustrates one type of situation in which the log transformation could change a nonlinear relationship between the original variables into a linear relationship between the original dependent variable and the log of the independent variable.

The plot in Fig. 15.1 (a) suggests that the independent variable (advertising expenditures) has a diminishing effect on the dependent variable (sales). A logarithmic transformation on advertising expenditures compresses the scale much more for the high values than for the low values. The resulting graph in Fig. 15.1 (b) shows a relationship that is much closer to linearity.

The data in Table 15.2 also illustrate a situation in which the logarithmic transformation yields a better fit. Total income is the independent variable, and the dependent variable is monthly expenditures on a "basic-necessity" product category. The motivation for a logarithmic transformation stems from two sources: (1) the theoretical expectation that expenditures on a necessity would increase less rapidly as income levels increase and (2) inspection of the data that suggested that equal *percentage differences* in income might be accompanied by *constant dollar differences* in expenditures.

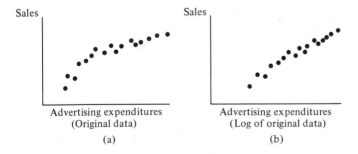

Fig. 15.1
Original data suggesting logarithmic transformation; (a) before transformation, (b) after transformation.

---

[8]An excellent discussion of various types of transformations, their rationale, and their results is given in Ronald E. Frank, 1966, Use of transformations, *Journal of Marketing Research* 3(August): 247–253.

Table 15.2
Monthly Expenditures on a "Basic-Necessity" Product
Category versus Annual Income

Monthly expenditures ($)	Annual income ($1,000)
70	17.2
82	23.5
61	12.6
51	9.5
65	14.3
56	10.8
47	8.3
57	11.7
59	12.4
72	16.5
60	11.4
75	19.6

A linear regression without transformation ($y = 31.35 + 2.26x$) accomplishes a large reduction in variance ($R^2 = .96$). With a logarithmic transformation on the independent variable, R^2 is slightly larger (.985). Examination of the residuals provides an added argument in favor of the log transformation: the estimating equation computed with the original data tends to overestimate expenditures associated with low and high incomes and understate expenditures associated with middle incomes. The distribution of residuals is shown in Table 15.3, with the income values arranged in order of magnitude in order to facilitate inspection. Five of the seven negative residuals occur among the lowest and highest incomes.

The distribution of the residuals with the logarithmic equation reveals no systematic pattern. Thus the equation based on the original data yields biased estimated with the bias depending on the level of income. Table 15.3 also reveals that the magnitude of the residuals is lower for the logarithmic equation than it is for the original data equation: the mean deviation (absolute value) is .85 versus 1.53.

One frequent argument against transformations is that their interpretation is obscure. Difficulties may be introduced, but a simple incorrect explanation is not preferrable to a slightly more complex correct explanation. Let us examine the log equation resulting from the data of Table 15.2.

$$y = -23.73 + 76.9 \log (x).$$

A one-unit change in log (x) is associated with a change of $76.90 in y. But what is a one-unit change in log x? A difference of 1.0 in the logs of two num-

Table 15.3
Residuals for Expenditure–Income Data. Original and Logarithmic Equations

Annual income ($1,000)	Monthly expenditures ($)	Residuals	
		Original equation	Logarithmic equation
8.3	47	−3.09	+0.05
9.5	51	−1.79	−0.46
10.8	56	+0.27	+0.26
11.4	60	+2.92	+2.45
11.7	57	−0.76	−1.41
12.4	59	−0.34	−1.35
12.6	61	+1.21	+0.11
14.3	65	+1.37	−0.12
16.5	72	+3.40	+2.11
17.2	70	−0.18	−1.28
19.6	75	−0.59	−0.36
23.5	82	−2.40	+0.29
Mean absolute residual		1.53	0.85

bers (log to the base 10) means that one number is ten times the other number; for example, $2,000 income and $20,000 income. Differences of this magnitude do not appear in the table. Switching to a difference of .1 in log x, we calculate an expected difference of $7.69 in y. A difference of .1 between logs converts to approximately a 25 percent difference. Therefore, a difference in incomes of 25 percent is associated with an expected difference of $7.69 in expenditures. Proper interpretation simply requires a small amount of care.

For other problems, transformation of the dependent variable would be appropriate. This is often the case when reasonably strong relationships exist and the assumption of homscedasticity is suspect. If absolute dispersion is larger for large values of the dependent variable, the assumption of homoscedasticity is unwarranted. Such a situation is quite common. The dispersion about the regression line is much greater for a predicted value of $175 than it is for a predicted value of $35. The dispersion may be much more uniform when expressed as a percentage. A log transformation on the dependent variable yields a conditional standard deviation with exactly that interpretation.

Log transformations have also been proposed for response functions to marketing mix formulations. These models often visualize the response functions in terms of elasticities, a constant percentage response in the dependent variable for a given percentage change in the various independent variables. Double log transformations produce this type of relationship.[9]

[9]See for example Philip Kotler, 1965, Competitive strategies for new product marketing over the life cycle, *Management Science* **12**(December): 104–119.

Exponential Transformations

Numerous studies of retail trading areas have employed modifications of Newton's Law of Gravitation.[10] These models employ exponential transformations of the form $(X)^a$ or $(X - k)^a$ where X is the original observation. The constants a and k may be either specified in advance or solved for in the research. The data in Table 15.4 are illustrative of the general gravitational model approach.

Table 15.4 presents data for 15 families, giving the proportion of food expenditures made in a particular shopping center and the distance between the shopper's residence and the shopping center. A linear equation between the two variables, without any transformation, yields an inverse relationship with $R^2 = 62.6$ percent. The resulting equation is

$$y = 62.8 - 7.0x.$$

This equation suggests that patronage decreases evenly, a most unlikely situation and not borne out by the data. The data indicate that the dependent

Table 15.4
Proportion of Food Expenditures in Given Shopping Center versus Distance from Shopping Center

Proportion of food expenditures (y)	Distance (miles) (x)
73	1.3
30	4.3
37	2.4
15	7.3
46	2.2
27	2.7
52	1.8
20	5.7
23	3.3
19	4.6
12	8.1
21	6.1
48	4.3
62	2.4
34	3.7

[10]See Rom J. Markin, Jr., 1971, *Retail Management: A Systems Approach* (New York: Macmillan), Chapter 9, for a discussion of some of the gravitational models as well as other approaches.

variable seems to level off at about the 20 percent figure with only small decreases thereafter. Calculations using the equation yield negative estimates for any person nine miles or more from the center. While such calculations go beyond the range of the data, they clearly indicate that the equation does not capture an adequate description of the overall relationship.

An exponential transformation will yield an equation of the form $y = a + b(x)^a$ or $y = a + b(x - k)^a$. We choose the first form (or $k = 0$), assuming that distance from the shopping center is the appropriate variable rather than that distance compared to some arbitrary value. We substitute $a = -2$ to coincide with Newton's Law of Gravitation and Reilly's original work on retail patronage.[11] The resulting equation is

$$y = 21.5 + 97.9(1/x^2).$$

The fit for this equation is slightly improved ($R^2 = 67.5$ percent), and it possesses some theoretical properties that are more satisfactory. It incorporates the idea that the proportion of expenditures at the shopping center decreases less rapidly as the distance from the center increases. The parameters of the equation still pose some difficulties, however. The Y-intercept (21.5) is the lower limit of the equation. No matter how far an individual lives from the center, the estimated proportion cannot be less than 21.5 percent (21.5 is an asymptote, as $x \to \infty$, $y \to 21.5$). The result is that the equation does not fit the data very well for the larger distances. There are also some difficulties for the lower distances; these difficulties refer to theoretical calculations more than goodness of fit although the estimate is poor for one of the lower values. Substitution of any distances less than 1.12 mile yields a calculation in excess of 100 percent.

Three different approaches are possible in attempting to secure a better fit or to deal with the upper and lower limits. (1) Exponents other than two could be tried. The larger the exponent, the more the X-axis is compressed. (2) The expression $(X - k)$ could be tried with selected values for k, both positive and negative. (3) A Y-intercept value could be imposed on the equation. This approach is frequently based on a logical analysis of the relationship; for example, using zero or some arbitrarily small number in conjunction with the data in Table 15.4.

The first two approaches are "search" procedures. The result that gives the "best" fit is the "best" description. The number of alternatives tried is limited only by the researcher's creativity and persistence. Even if the alternatives are specified at the outset of the research, the standard probability statements are appropriate for each separate hypothesis and should not be presented in isolation with only the best fit. Specification of a single value at the

---

[11]William J. Reilly, 1929, *Method for the Study of Retail Relationships* (Research Monograph No. 4, University of Texas Bulletin No. 2944, Bureau of Business Research, Austin: University of Texas Press), p. 16.

outset of the research—for example an exponent of two or a *Y*-intercept of zero—does not pose this difficulty. The researcher and decision maker have merely structured a particular functional form in the hypothesis to be tested.

Polynomials

Nonlinear relationships can sometimes be fit by polynomials:

$$y = a + bx + cx^2 + dx^3 + \cdots.$$

Such functions are extremely flexible, adding the possibility of reversals in the relationship. This flexibility is simultaneously their weakness—unless strong *a priori* consideration dictates the precise form of polynomial employed. Reversals in the equation may be produced by erratic behavior in the data caused by uncontrolled variables rather than reversals in the nature of the relationship.

The polynomial may be considered a linear additive model of the original variable plus various transformations of the original variable. The equation $y = a + bx + cx^2$ embraces both the ordinary linear component (x) and the transformed variable (x^2). Each will influence predicted values of the dependent variable in their usual way, and the total equation calculates their combined effect as the sum of their separate contributions.

The relationship between annual income and monthly expenditures on a basic necessity (Table 15.2) might be described by a polynomial, using only the first- and second-degree terms. This will produce a curvilinear relationship, the amount and type of curvature being determined by the data rather than a prespecification in the original hypothesis. In this particular case, the coefficient associated with the square term would be negative since expenditures tend to increase less rapidly at higher incomes. (Exercise 10 considers these data and the results with different equations.)

AUTOMATIC INTERACTION DETECTOR

The Automatic Interaction Detector (AID)[12] is a technique that has certain similarities to stepwise procedures. AID uses a single dependent variable that may either be dichotomous or intervally scaled. The independent variables may either be nominal, ordinal, or interval in scale although the technique converts them into either nominal or ordinal scales, depending on the instructions given. AID, like stepwise regression, proceeds in sequential steps. It is basically a search routine whose steps are ordered by the data. Like stepwise regression, the criterion for choosing among alternatives is the reduction in variance. Unlike stepwise regression, the structure of the estimating equation

---

[12]See J. A. Sonquist and J. N. Morgan, 1964, *The Detection of Interaction Effects* (Monograph No. 35, Survey Research Center, University of Michigan); and J. A. Sonquist, E. L. Baker, and J. N. Morgan, 1971, *Searching for Structure* (Survey Research Center: University of Michigan).

is unspecified. Stepwise regression uses an additive linear model; AID is completely open.

All of the dangers and risks of stepwise regression apply to AID plus others. AID is strictly a search routine with the results descriptive of the sample data; no inferential statements with accompanying probability specification are employed. Therefore, AID must be considered exploratory research. It can lead to hypotheses, but it does not test hypotheses. Despite these inherent weaknesses, AID offers a very flexible search routine that yields a structured view of the data.

AID successively partitions the sample into dichotomies. At the first step the entire sample is split into two groups. At the next stage these two groups are considered independently, and each is further split into two groups—not necessarily on the basis of the same independent variable or with the same partitioning even if the same variable serves as the basis for partitioning.

The following example uses AID to establish market segments defined according to consumption of cola beverages. The example is based on a sample of only 186 and was drawn from members of a club. The independent variables under consideration are age, sex, education, political conservatism score, religious preference, frequency of shopping, number in household, IQ, frequency of "dining out," and distance from nearest shopping center. Several of these are measured on interval scales. The first task is to change these interval scales into a series of categories, thus transforming them into ordinal scales. The usual procedure is to limit the number of categories for each variable to six or seven, and fewer if possible.

Our set of independent variables now consists of four ordered categories for age, two categories for sex, four ordered categories for education, five ordered categories for political conservatism, seven nominal categories for religious preference, etc. The researcher must specify whether order can be disregarded in the partitioning or whether order must be preserved. With four categories for age (under 25, 25–40, 40–60, and over 60), there are three ways of dichotomizing if order is preserved, but there are seven if order is not preserved.[13]

The number of possible two-way splits with only ten different variables would be quite large. AID calculates the total within group sum of squares (on the dependent variable) for each possible two-way grouping. Since the objective is to reduce variance as much as possible, the dichotomy with the smallest within-group variance serves as the basis for the first split. In our example (Fig. 15.2) age accomplishes this objective with 40 as the division point.

---

[13]The three splits with order preserved use 25, 40, and 60 as the possible division points. The additional four groupings that ignore order are (1) under-25 combined with 40–60, (2) under-25 combined with over 60, (3) under-25 combined with both 40–60 and over-60, and (4) under-25 combined with 25–40 and over-60. Specification of the complementary groupings is implicit in these four; for example, establishment of the 25–40 category as a separate group is accomplished by the third specification.

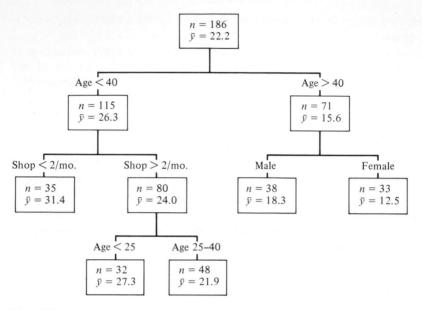

Fig. 15.2
Tree diagram of AID sequence.

The next step subdivides further the groups established at the first step. AID repeats the same procedure at each step, applying it to the newly formed groups. In our illustration, the group under 40 is dichotomized on every possible basis, including age (under 25 versus 25–40). The dichotomy reducing variance by the greatest amount at this stage employs frequency of shopping with an ordered division point at two per month. The group over 40 is also dichotomized, but the basis for division is chosen independently of the basis employed with the other group. Sex accomplishes the greatest reduction in variance for this group. We now have four groups: (1) under 40 shopping less than twice per month, (2) under 40 shopping two or more times per month, (3) over 40 and male, and (4) over 40 and female. Each of these four groups is now examined for further subdivision.

The process generates the tree diagram of Fig. 15.2. The basis for dichotomizing is shown, and each box gives the size of the group and the group mean. Each branch of the tree is further dichotomized until one of several stopping rules is violated. Examples of possible stopping rules are:

1. Minimum sample size of 25 for any group.

2. Each step must reduce the group sum of squares by at least 10 percent.

3. No group shall be subdivided unless the subdivision accounts for at least 5 percent of the initial sum of squares.

The first stopping rule—a minimum sample size of 25 per group—is the critical constraint with the data of Fig. 15.2. This is not unexpected with a total sample size of only 186. Note that age is also the cutting variable at a later step in this example, further dividing the under 40 group into under 25 and 25–40. Because of the small sample size, there is no opportunity to observe whether the variables in one branch appear later in the other branch.

What can AID reveal that other stepwise procedures would not? Non-linearity is a standard claim. The ability to identify unique types of interaction is another. The data in Fig. 15.2 demonstrate both features. Frequency of shopping may have a discontinuous effect. Twice per month may be a critical level that differentiates. More frequent shopping may have litle impact, as may less frequent shopping. Remember the criterion for selection is the minimization of within-group variance. Shopping frequency may differentiate among younger persons (under 40) but not among older (over 40). In the same way sex may differentiate among only the older group. With a larger sample, more groups would be generated and more elaborate segmentation ideas could be interwoven. Any or all of the ideas can then be tested by use of a validation sample and a structured hypothcsis testing model.[14]

SUMMARY

Search techniques represent procedures whereby the researcher can generate a tentative model rather than tcst an *a priori* model. These search techniques are not appropriate for open-ended exploratory research in which only a vague subject has been specified. Search routines employ an existing database and are thus analytic procedures. The search retains that which works or looks promising, and discards the rest.

Two principal types of questions are considered by search techniques. (1) Which of a number of variables should be incorporated in the equation summarizing the relationship? This question typically arises if the number of candidate variables is large or if these variables are correlated with each other. In either case, the search attempts to select those that are most helpful in "explaining" the dependent variable. (2) What functional form best describes the relationship between the variables? This question arises when a linear equation is not a satisfactory approximation. The search combines logical considerations and data plots in generating alternative forms. The objective of the search in each case is to present a model that reduces the variance as much as possible—and thus yields a good "fit." Stepwise procedures, transformations, and the Automatic Interaction Detector (AID) are specific techniques that are illustrative of search procedures.

Stepwise routines proceed sequentially using the criterion of maximum reduction in variance as a basis of choosing the appropriate step. The steps

---

[14]See Ronald E. Frank, William F. Massy, and Yoram Wind, 1972, *Market Segmentation* (Englewood Cliffs, N.J.: Prentice-Hall), pp. 144ff.

depend on the data, not on *a priori* logic. Stepwise regression routines include *F*-ratios and hypothesis testing, but the probability statements tend to mislead. With a large number of candidate variables, chance alone may be responsible for the relationships discovered among a few variables. The results are also heavily dependent on the variables introduced early in the routine. Other variables, correlated with them, are not likely to appear in the equations because their contribution would be redundant. The high dependence of each step on the preceding steps also means that the final equation may be nonoptimal; there is no assurance that the equation derived removes more of the initial variance than any other equation with the same number of independent variables.

The linearity and homoscedasticity assumptions of multivariate techniques are sometimes violated by the nature of marketing research data. Transformations of the original variables may make these assumptions more reasonable. Any transformation can be employed by the researcher; among the more commmon are logarithmic, exponential, and polynomial. Transformations do not drop the assumptions of multivariate techniques; they attempt to change the form of the data so that the assumptions are met. In appraising the appropriateness of a given transformation the researcher should consider the logical nature of the resulting equation, the goodness of the fit, and the range within which it will be employed.

The theoretical and inferential base for AID is weaker than that of stepwise regression, but it has greater flexibility. Its structure is completely open, and it is able to search for various types of interactions. As part of this interaction, it admits the possibility that a variable may be significant for some subgroups but not for others. It also admits the possibility that a variable may be significant for some portions of its range but not for others. This flexibility offers a great advantage in exploratory work but requires validation before the results can be a accepted as definitive conclusions.

EXERCISES AND PROBLEMS

1. Distinguish among the terms within each of the following sets.
   a) Search techniques, exploratory research, and structured hypothesis tests
   b) Gross and net coefficients
   c) Nonlinearity and interaction
   d) AID stopping rules and regression *F*-ratios

2. Briefly explain the meaning and significance of each of the following terms in search procedures.
   a) Stepwise approach
   b) Transformations
   c) Deletion of variables
   d) Homoscedasticity
   e) Multicollinearity

3. AID is said to avoid some of the more restrictive assumptions of regression analysis.

   a) State the principal assumptions that AID avoids.

   b) Discuss how AID's approach avoids those assumptions.

   c) What, if any, price is paid for avoiding those assumptions?

4. Search techniques are often viewed as a way of coping with a large number of potential independent variables.

   a) Why is this a problem?

   b) How do search techniques cope with this problem?

   c) What, if anything, is lost by this approach?

5. The Boise Electronics Company has a ten-week training program for its newly hired electrical engineer/sales personnel. Part of the program includes spot assembly of products for demonstration purposes. Over the past few months Boise has timed various trainees at different points in their training. The data are presented in Table E15.5. No trainee was timed more than once. Two different trainees were timed at each time point.

Table E15.5

Training week (x)	Assembly time in minutes (y)
1	47.6, 51.2
2	45.0, 31.8
3	27.6, 35.7
4	29.1, 33.6
5	32.7, 26.3
6	27.5, 36.8
7	26.0, 26.4
8	24.5, 36.0
9	28.4, 21.3
10	21.7, 29.4

The training director would like to obtain an estimating equation for appraising the progress and standing of future trainees. The director is trying to decide which of the following two models to use.

$$y = a + bx.$$
$$y = a + \frac{b}{x}.$$

   a) Discuss the relative advantages and disadvantages of the two models. Consider the scatter diagram of the data, the meaning of constants in the equation, and the logical maximum and minimum values.

   b) Solve for the constants in each model.

   c) Do any of the numerical values in (b) strengthen or weaken your appraisal in (a)?

6. The data in Table E15.6 refer to advertising expenditures and profits before taxes of 15 proprietary drug firms. All data are in millions of dollars.

Table E15.6

Firm	Advertising (x)	Profits before taxes (y)
1	4	2
2	3	5
3	16	4
4	8	11
5	17	8
6	2	3
7	11	9
8	6	7
9	25	3
10	3	4
11	6	6
12	5	2
13	3	3
14	21	3
15	2	3

a) Plot these data in a scatter diagram.

b) Would you be willing to fit a linear function to these data? Why or why not?

c) Two alternative models have been proposed.

$$y = a + bx + cx^2.$$
$$y = a + b \log x.$$

Discuss the relative advantages and disadvantages of these models against $y = a + bx$.

d) Which of the three alternative models yields the best fit?

7. A large, hospital-supply company wishes to build a model for predicting dollar sales to hospitals with various characteristics. The number of potential independent variables is large, and a research consultant has suggested that stepwise regression be employed. The three variables showing the largest bivariate relationship to dollar sales are number of beds, annual budget, and distance from the company's corporate office. The bivariate coefficients of correlation (with dollar sales) are .76 (number of beds), .72 (annual budget), and .41 (distance from corporate office). The bivariate coefficients among the independent variables are .95 (number of beds and annual budget), .13 (number of beds and distance), and .09 (annual budget and distance).

a) Which of these three independent variables would be entered into a stepwise regression first? Why?

b) Which of these three would you expect to be entered at the second step? Why?

8. Collect data on the following characteristics from a small sample (15 to 25): dollar expenditures on a frequently purchased consumer nondurable, age, income, years of formal education, size of household, and two or three intervally scaled variables of your own choice. Collect the data in a format suitable for regression analysis. Be sure to state a time interval for the expenditure data.

a) Determine a conditional equation for estimating dollar expenditures on your selected product, using a stepwise approach.

b) Explain the meaning of "significance level for entry" in terms of your problem.

c) Which variables are not included in your final equation? Why were these variables not included; i.e., what are their relationships to the dependent variable and the other independent variables?

d) How strong is the relationship between the dependent variable and the independent variables in the final equation? **Note:** Retain these data for the exercises in Chapter 17.

9. Suppose you wish to analyze the data of Exercise 8 by AID.

a) Would the sample size permit such an analysis? Why?

b) Are the variables defined and measured in a manner that could be employed in AID?

c) AID requires certain adjustments to intervally scaled variables. What procedures or adjustments would you recommend for this problem? Be specific in your recommendations.

d) Marital status and sex are suggested as additional variables by another consultant. How would these variables be handled in the two techniques, i.e., stepwise regression and AID.

10. Refer to the data in Table 15.2.

a) Determine the constants of a second-degree polynomial

$$\left(y = a + bx + cx^2\right).$$

b) Compare the "fit" yielded by the model of part (a) with the "fit" yielded by the log transformation discussed within the chapter.

c) Which model seems better in terms of the logic of the two models? Why?

d) In view of your answers in parts (b) and (c), which would you prefer to use in making predictions? Discuss briefly.

11. Analyze, criticize, and explain:

a) Transformations are not really search procedures. They are simply alternative ways of making the assumptions of the techniques more reasonable.

b) A danger in a stepwise approach is that a single independent variable will be credited (or blamed) for a greater "effect" than it alone produces.

c) AID can handle nominal scales only if they are dichotomous. If more than two categories exist, the variable must be treated as ordinal.

d) "Automatic Interaction Detector" is a misnomer. The technique permits non-linear relationships, discontinuities, and even reversals; but it does not reveal interactions.

e) Stepwise regression is a convenient way of "searching" a large number of potential independent variables. If the total number of variables were included in a single simultaneous solution, multicollinearity might show few if any of the regression coefficients as significant.

f) The linearity assumption of least-squares regression is a frequent source of difficulty in real-world problems. Transformations permit the removal of this assumption.

g) The claim that search procedures negate the possibility of including probability statements is erroneous. F-tests and t-tests can still be applied to the results with their standard interpretations.

CHAPTER 16

TIME SERIES
DOES THE PASSAGE OF TIME PRODUCE CHANGE?

A recurring problem for the marketing manager is how to predict. What will sales be for a particular product next year? What will the Gross National Product (or a regional counterpart) be? What will be the size of particular market segments in five years? in ten years?

All of these questions introduce the time dimension. If we know the values of these characteristics at the present time and the way in which they have evolved over time, can we make better estimates of their future values? Will the study of the dependent variable over time help the marketing manager make better predictions, and will better predictions enable him or her to make better decisions and plans?

Our previous discussion of techniques for studying the association between a dependent variable and one or more independent variables has ignored the time dimension. We have assumed that the timing of the observations is immaterial. This approach implies that the pattern of association revealed by the data should be accepted as appropriate for the decision, regardless of its time dimension. No marketing manager believes this to be true and does not act that way in making decisions. The marketing manager raises questions about "universes past, present, and future" and whether the universe studied is relevant. But the appraisal is subjective. We now consider ways in which changes over time might be quantified and used as a basis of predicting future values. Most of the techniques lack strong theoretical justification. Despite this weakness, they are employed because the prediction problem is an integral part of marketing management. It is not a question of *whether* to forecast but *how* to forecast.

A *time series* is a sequence of measurements arranged in chronological order. When these measurements refer to a dependent variable that is to be predicted, one approach is to examine the series for past patterns of change. Any patterns discovered can then be incorporated in forecasts for the future. If unit sales have grown at an average of 8 percent per year for the past ten years, we might forecast an increase of 8 percent per year over the next two years. If 35 percent of our sales usually occur in the fourth quarter, we might be willing to forecast that 35 percent of 1981 sales will be in the fourth quarter. The summary of the observed patterns may be simple or complex; the actual data may reveal high consistency or low consistency with respect to the pattern. But our first alternative in a time-series model is to assume that the variable to be forecast will change in the future in the same way it has in the past—this approach uses time as the independent variable.

A second alternative is to establish a lead–lag relationship. Advertising and sales are associated, but they should not refer to the same period. Advertising in one month is expected to generate sales in the following month. If housing permits turn up in October, lumber sales should start to recover in March. This model is superficially very similar to the association models already considered, but new issues are raised. First, different time coordinates are used for the dependent variable and the independent variable. Second, if different time coordinates are to be used, how should the relationship between the time coordinates be determined? The advertising–sales model uses a one-month lag. The building permit–lumber sales model uses a five-month lag.

TIME AS AN INDEPENDENT VARIABLE

A time-series model, in which time is treated as an independent variable, states that the dependent variable can be predicted from a knowledge of time alone. Time may be expressed as historical dates (1952–1977) or as elapsed time from some starting date such as a product introduction or most recent cyclical trough.

Two factors complicate the analysis of a time series. First, the problem of uniform definitions and procedures is even more acute than in the analysis of data collected at the same point in time. New classification schemes may be adopted; products are born and die; clerical procedures are modified; and new staff are hired. All of these changes raise questions concerning the comparability of data within the series. If monetary units are employed, questions with respect to price inflation or deflation must be considered. Second, a time series can only describe the changes. It does not identify the factors that have produced the changes. These factors may not be constant throughout the period covered, and the dominant factors of the future may be totally different. Prediction of the future path of a time series assumes that the pattern established by the past can be extrapolated into the future; any significant changes in procedures or the environment must reduce the likelihood that the model will yield accurate forecasts.

Time-series models with time as the independent variable state $y = f(t)$ where t is time and y is the characteristic of interest. The functional form of the equation is constrained only by the researcher's imagination. Two general approaches can be employed in predicting the value of the series for a particular time period: (1) the most recent observation serves as the base and is modified by the general pattern of change found in the historical data and (2) the historical pattern serves as the basis for a prediction without giving special significance to the most recent period. The first approach would use 1979 sales of $550,000 as a base, apply the historical average increase of 7 percent, and predict 1980 sales to be $588,500. The second approach would establish a general equation describing how sales have changed over time and predict 1980 sales from that general equation. Sales in 1979 would enter into the determination of the equation but would not serve as a starting point in the prediction process.

A second distinction among methods for analyzing time series concerns whether the functional form of the pattern is constrained. One approach specifies the mathematical form of the pattern: for example, linear, parabolic, etc. and whether the original data are used or transformed. The most common transformation in time-series equations is a logarithmic transformation. This approach is analogous to regression and discriminant analyses that impose the functional form of the relationship on the data. The second approach merely describes the data. Reversals, changing rates of growth, lower limits, and other features are determined by the data. This approach is analogous to contingency analysis and ANOVA where the functional form is unconstrained.

The establishment of patterns or summary descriptions is essential if a time-series analysis is to be used for predictions. Historical descriptions that defy projections are of no aid to a decision maker; the results can be used in planning only when generalizations emerge. For this reason, we will first consider several types of mathematical functions. The mathematically derived equations have been used most often in long-range forecasting. Our examples are designed to illustrate the approach; only simple equations will be used. In actual practice, the equations could be more complex. Next, we will turn to a *decomposition* approach that separates a time series into trend, cycle, seasonal, and irregular compenents. Each of the components is defined according to its duration, and each has its own description and functional form.[1] Exponential smoothing will be considered as a third approach that has been derived from the moving average methods used in decomposition techniques.

Linear Trends

A frequent first step in analyzing a time series is to ask, "What has been the average change per year?" Such a question, perhaps without meaning to, says to describe the historical pattern with a linear equation. The resulting linear equation will not determine whether past changes have been stable! It tells what the change would have been had stability been present.

What has been the average increase per year in sales of the Crovel Fastener Company between 1969 and 1979 (Table 16.1)? There are at least

---

[1]A mathematic function as descriptive of the trend might be employed as a first step in a decomposition approach.

four possible answers to this seemingly direct question. Each answer corresponds to a different concept of average, and two separate issues are involved. (1) Should the average be expressed in dollars or as a percentage? (2) Are the first and final years of special significance or is an overall description desired?

An average dollar increase, if used in prediction, assumes that the focus should be on the *amount* of increase. This approach expects the absolute levels of change to be approximately the same at all levels of the series. An average percentage increase assumes that larger dollar increases should be expected at higher sales levels than at lower sales levels. The choice between these two models is typically based on two criteria: (1) actual historical experience—which model "fits" better? and (2) the manager and/or researcher's perception of logical patterns for the particular series.

Emphasis on the first and final years stresses the $60,000 figure for 1969 and the $200,000 figure for 1979. Intermediate years might be completely ignored in the calculations although they might be considered in appraising how well the model describes the data. The alternative is to include all observations in the determination of the model as well as in appraising the "goodness of fit."

Equations (16.1) and (16.2) yield constant amounts of change. The first is based upon only two observations,[2] and the second uses a least-squares crite-

Table 16.1
Sales of the Crovel Fastener Company

Year	Sales ($1,000)
1969	60
1970	75
1971	90
1972	120
1973	100
1974	125
1975	140
1976	130
1977	180
1978	160
1979	200

[2]Calculation of the arithmetic mean of the annual amounts of change yields the same answer as Eq. (16.1). Thus an apparent attempt to use all of the data fails to consider any except the first and the final observations. This result can be seen in the algebra involved:

$$(y_1 - y_0) + (y_2 - y_1) + \cdots + (y_{n-1} - y_{n-2}) + (y_n - y_{n-1}) = y_n - y_0.$$

rion. Equation (16.2) uses all of the data and employs a transformation of t (time) so that $\Sigma t = 0$. This transformation shifts the time axis so that the zero point is at the midpoint of the time period analyzed: 1974 for the data in Table 16.1.

$$b = \frac{y_n - y_o}{n}. \tag{16.1}$$

$$b = \frac{\Sigma yt}{\Sigma t^2}. \tag{16.2}$$

Application of Eqs. (16.1) and (16.2) yield average changes of \$14,000 and \$12,500, respectively. The two equations each with $t = 0$ in 1974 are $y = 130 + 14t$ and $y = 125.5 + 12.5t$. The Y-intercept of the least-squares equation (using a transformation so that $\Sigma t = 0$) is the arithmetic mean of the series. Thus the total solution is given by Eq. (16.3).[3]

$$b = \frac{\Sigma ty}{\Sigma t^2},$$

$$a = \frac{\Sigma y}{n}. \tag{16.3}$$

Figure 16.1 presents the original data and the two trend equations.

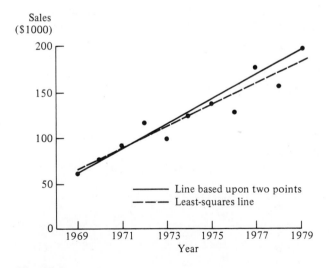

Sales ($1000)

Fig. 16.1
Crovel data with two linear trend lines.

[3]Of course the usual equations for least-squares regression could be used without a transformation of t. The result in this case would yield the same b-value but a drastically different Y-intercept. This intercept would correspond to an extrapolated value for the year zero.

Which is a better description of the data? If "a better description" means from which is the sum of the squared deviations less, the least-squares fit will always be a better description. If the sum of the absolute differences (rather than their square) is the criterion, we must make the calculation. Neither approach establishes the equation by minimizing this value. For the current data, the least-squares line has a mean deviation of $9,600 against $9,800 for the simpler approach based on Eq. (16.1)—not a very large difference in this instance.

The least-squares approach possesses two general properties that add to its attractiveness. *First*, the positive and negative deviations balance. The least-squares line will cut through the series with equal portions above and below it. The trend line based upon Eq. (16.1) may have an imbalance. For the Crovel data, the negative deviations total $29,000 while the positive deviations total $79,000. This difference is seen in Fig. 16.1 by the positioning of the line; it is relatively high on the chart while the least-squares line occupies a more central position. The distinction is particularly apparent in the latter portion of the period. *Second,* the least-squares line is based upon all of the data. All of the observations contribute to the determination of the trend line. Judicious selection of the first and last dates permits a strong advocate to "prove" any point he or she wishes, when Eq. (16.1) is used. Opposing political candidates have been known to present completely divergent "facts," each using Eq. (16.1) but with slightly different dates. A sales manager wishing to "push" the sales force may select dates that yield a high "average" increase, but the same sales manager may select two other dates when talking to superiors about the base used in calculating his or her bonus. This potential problem and high subjectivity mean the researcher must be extremely cautious in using it.

Equations (16.4) and (16.5) yield the appropriate answers concerning average percentage change. Eq. (16.4) employs only the first and final observations and is subject to the same type of hazards discussed for Eq. (16.1).

$$1 + r = \sqrt[n]{y_n/y_0} \; . \tag{16.4}$$

This equation is actually the reduced form of the geometric mean of relatives where r is the average percentage change.[4] Equation (16.5) gives the pair of equations needed for a least-squares fit to the logs with a time transformation so that $\Sigma t = 0$.

$$b = \frac{\Sigma t \log(y)}{\Sigma t^2}.$$

$$a = \frac{\Sigma \log(y)}{n}. \tag{16.5}$$

---

[4] A relative is defined as the ratio between two numbers. The series of relatives $(y_1/y_0)(y_2/y_1) \cdots (y_n/y_{n-1})$ reduces to y_n/y_0. An arithmetic mean of these relatives yields a figure that has an upward bias: if it were applied successively to y_0 for n periods, the result would exceed y_n. The geometric mean yields a mathematically consistent result. In the limiting case where the percentage change is constant for the entire series, the arithmetic mean and geometric mean are equal.

The average percentage rate of change associated with Eq. (16.5) is given by one minus the antilog of b.

Applying Eq. (16.4) to the Crovel data we have

$$1 + r = \sqrt[10]{200/60}$$
$$= \sqrt[10]{3.33}$$
$$= 1.128$$
$$r = .128 \text{ or } 12.8\%.$$

An annual increase of 12.8 percent would yield a total growth from \$60,000 to \$200,000 in ten years. Equation (16.4) incorporates the principle of compounding. Each successive percentage change is based on a different level of operations. In this particular example, we are using one-year intervals and are assuming annual compounding. The n of Eq. (16.4) gives the number of periods involved in the compounding.

The least-squares solution, using Eq. (16.5), yields

$$\log(y) = 2.073094 + .045903t$$
$$t = 0 \text{ in } 1974$$
$$t \text{ is in one-year units.}$$

If this equation is converted into the equivalent exponential equation, by taking antilogs, the result is

$$y = 118.3(1.111)^t.$$

Thus the annual percentage change, according to a least-squares fit to the logs, is 11.1 percent.

Figure 16.2 presents the Crovel data, using a log scale for sales, and the two trend lines with constant percentage changes.[5] Although the slope is greater for the geometric mean of relatives [Equation (16.4)], that trend line is lower than the least-squares line for the entire 1967–1977 period. As was the case with constant amounts of change, the least-squares line bisects the data with equal deviations above and below the line.[6] The geometric-mean approach is lower than the actual data for seven of nine years (not considering the first and last observations which must coincide with the geometric mean trend line). Both Figs. 16.1 and 16.2 suggest that the 1969 sales figure of \$60,000 was a somewhat depressed value. Use of it as a starting point thus leads to a higher "average" rate of change.

The mean deviation for the least-squares logarithmic equation is \$10,600 while the simpler approach has a mean deviation of \$12,600. Both are larger

---

[5] If the trend lines were plotted against an arithmetic scale, they would of course be curvilinear and concave.

[6] The least-squares fit with logs minimizes the sum of the squared deviations in terms of logarithms. There is no assurance that least squares gives a "better" fit in terms of dollar sales. There is also no assurance that the resulting equation will balance positive and negative deviations when expressed in the original units.

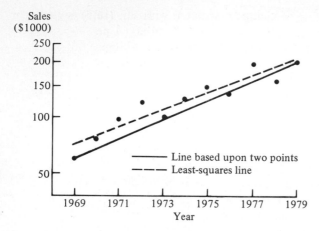

Fig. 16.2
Crovel data with two linear trends to logarithms.

than the corresponding figures for the earlier models for the Crovel data, but the results depend on the specific series under study. The large deviations for the geometric mean result principally from the atypical nature of the initial value of $60,000 in 1969. This starting point not only generates an inflated rate of increase but it also results in a poor description for most of the period.

Prediction by Linear Trends

The marketing manager of Crovel is concerned with the immediate problem of predicting sales for 1981 and planning activities accordingly. The four models derived in the preceding section yield four different predictions, and two additional predictions are available with a slightly modified approach. As a practical person, the marketing manager believes he or she has too much information, which is almost worse than not having enough.

The critical questions are (1) should the forecast take 1979 sales as a base or should it use the total equation,[7] (2) which of the summary average rates of change should be applied, and (3) should any further adjustments be applied—based on predicted unusual forces in 1981. Both the marketing manager and the research manager agree that a linear equation is suspect for long-range forecasting, but they think a linear model will be satisfactory for a two-year forecast. They believe, however, that 1981 is far enough in the future that they have no knowledge of special forces that will be working at that time. Therefore, no special adjustments will be made for that year.

The question of whether to use 1979 sales or the total equation as a base hinges on the perceived influence of 1979 sales on 1981 sales. If the two dates

---

[7]This question is of course unnecessary for the two equations that are based on only the first and last observations in the series.

are so close together that the unusually high (or low) level of sales in 1979 will carry over into 1981, then the base should be 1979 sales. (A perceived inverse relationship could also be incorporated into the forecast if appropriate.) If the 1979 sales level is not of particular significance, then the total equation should be used as the base for the forecast.

Table 16.2 presents the actual annual changes in the Crovel data, both in absolute and percentage terms. These changes are extremely erratic, suggesting little carry-over from one year to the next or indeed from one year to two years hence. Figures 16.1 and 16.2 give the same impression. Thus the two managers agree to base their prediction on the overall equation with the best fit.

If "best fit" is defined in terms of the minimization of squared deviations, each least-squares equation must give the best fit for its form. It is not a mathematical necessity that the least-squares equations yield the smallest mean deviation, but this is the usual result—and it is true for the Crovel data. The manager's principal problem is in choosing between the two least-squares lines. The mean deviation is smaller for the constant amounts equation ($9,600 versus $10,600). Other considerations, however, may be more critical. The logarithmic equation starts higher in 1969 and 1970, falls below the natural numbers equation from 1971 through 1977, and then rises above the natural numbers equation for 1978 and 1979. This pattern is shown in Table 16.3. Extrapolated values beyond 1979 will be larger for the logarithmic equation and the differences will be greater with each succeeding year.[8] The marketing manager is convinced that the constant percentage growth embodied in the

Table 16.2
Absolute and Percentage Changes. Crovel Company Data

Year	Sales ($1,000)	Absolute change	Percentage change
1969	60	—	—
1970	75	+ 15	+ 25.0
1971	90	+ 15	+ 20.0
1972	120	+ 30	+ 33.3
1973	100	− 20	− 16.7
1974	125	+ 25	+ 25.0
1975	140	+ 15	+ 12.0
1976	130	− 10	− 7.1
1977	180	+ 50	+ 38.5
1978	160	− 20	− 11.1
1979	200	+ 40	+ 25.0

[8]This is the typical result, but it is not a mathematical necessity. The logarithmic equation could yield lower predictions for short-range forecasts although it is not the typical situation, and it would become increasingly unlikely with forecasts further in the future.

Table 16.3
Trend Equation Values for Two Least-squares Lines. Crovel Company Data

Year	Sales ($1,000)	Trend values	
		Natural numbers	Log equation
1969	60	63.0	69.8
1970	75	75.5	77.5
1971	90	88.0	86.2
1972	120	100.5	95.8
1973	100	113.0	106.5
1974	125	125.5	118.3
1975	140	138.0	131.5
1976	130	150.5	146.2
1977	180	163.0	162.5
1978	160	175.5	180.6
1979	200	188.0	200.7

logarithmic equation is the correct perspective and sets plans for the $248,000 forecast by that equation. The research manager, being more conservative by nature, suggests a pooling of estimates from the two models ($213,000 and $248,000 for an average of $230,500).

The reader will note the "search" characteristics of this problem. Various approaches are tried, the results are examined, and a conclusion is reached. The criteria for the decision are not always well articulated, and a clear concept of hypothesis testing is missing. It is possible to start the process with a single model and determine the appropriate parameters from the data available. However, the usual starting point is at least a visual inspection of the data in order to determine which model is suggested.

Time Series and Linear Regression

Least-squares fitting with time-series data should consider the theoretical justification of the model. It has the form of the regression models used in earlier chapters. How do they differ?

Recall that correlation is addressed to problems in which both the dependent and the independent variables may be considered as observations from a random sample. Certainly we are not dealing with correlation in a time series! Time is not a random variable; the observations are made at stated intervals, determined in advance or simply dictated by availability.

Regression concerns problems in which the observations of the dependent variable can be considered samples from the various conditional distributions.

A time series may fall into this classification when dealing with physical problems such as the law of falling bodies. But can a marketing or economic time series be considered in the same light? Can we visualize several different results at $t = 4$—with a particular distribution around the calculated value? The expression $t = 4$ for the law of falling bodies usually means four seconds after the object is dropped. The physicist "expects" approximately the same result each time with some experimental error around this result. The expression $t = 4$ for the Crovel data means 1978. In this context, are sales a random variable with a distribution of possible results? Even if we visualize a distribution of possible results for 1978, do we think the distribution follows the normal curve? Most often, the theoretical foundation of regression is missing in marketing data. Sales for a particular year are unique or at least deviate from the trend line in a nonrandom manner. Therefore, use of the model must be on a pragmatic basis—"It seems a reasonable way to describe the series and it fits the data." If we can make this statement, we use the model. If we cannot, we should reject the model. Even when the model is used, the probability properties of the regression model should not be assumed.

We have applied these four simple models to the Crovel data for several reasons despite their inherent weaknesses. (1) These simple approaches are widely used in practice. The student should understand their assumptions and the differences among them. (2) They provide a convenient framework in which to illustrate differences in focus: percentage changes versus amounts of change and consideration of appropriate criteria for a good fit. (3) They provide a point of departure for considering more complex models.

Parabolic Trend Lines

The next step in complexity beyond a linear equation is a second-degree polynomial or a parabola. Its general form is given by Eq. (16.6), with the two forms corresponding to fitting against the original data or their logs.

$$y = a + bt + ct^2 \quad \text{or} \quad \log y = a + bt + ct^2. \tag{16.6}$$

The precise shape of the curve is determined by the data and is revealed by the constants of the equation. Four general patterns are possible from Eq. (16.6): (1) an increasing series whose rate of growth is diminishing, (2) an increasing series whose rate of growth is also increasing, (3) a decreasing series whose rate of decline is slowing, and (4) a decreasing series whose rate of decline is accelerating. The rates involved are either amounts of change or percentage changes depending on which form of Eq. (16.6) is chosen.

The second-degree equation adds two important modifications to the first-degree (linear) equation. First, the rate of change may vary over time. Second, a reversal of direction is permitted. The idea of a variable rate of change is usually more in conformity with our logical models than is a constant rate, but the flexibility possible with a parabola is severely limited. The reversal possibility is fine as far as the logic is concerned, but predictions using a precise dating of that reversal usually cause more problems than they solve. This is particularly true when the timing of the reversal is a forecast.

The sign of the b-coefficient indicates the basic direction of the series within the time period covered: positive for an increasing series and negative for a decreasing series.[9] The c-coefficient produces the curvature in the equation; if c were zero, a linear relation would result.

The set of equations in (16.7) applies the least-squares criterion for a parabolic trend.

$$\Sigma y = na + b\Sigma t + c\Sigma t^2$$
$$\Sigma yt = a\Sigma t + b\Sigma t^2 + c\Sigma t^3$$
$$\Sigma yt^2 = a\Sigma t^2 + b\Sigma t^3 + c\Sigma t^4. \tag{16.7}$$

If t is transformed so that $\Sigma t = 0$, the set of equations in (16.8) can be employed.

$$b = \Sigma yt/\Sigma t^2$$
$$\Sigma y = na + c\Sigma t^2$$
$$\Sigma yt^2 = a\Sigma t^2 + c\Sigma t^4. \tag{16.8}$$

Logarithmic transformation of the dependent variable merely requires substitution of log y for y in the equations. The trend line then focuses on percentage changes rather than absolute changes. Using Eq. (16.8) with logs, the resulting trend line for the Crovel data is

$$\log y = 2.096285 + .045903t - .002319t^2.$$

Taking the antilogs the equation is

$$y = 124.8(1.111)^t(.9947)^{t^2}.$$

Comparison of the linear and parabolic exponential equations reveals how the addition of the t^2 term changes the description of the trend. The b-coefficient in the log equation and its antilog are precisely the same in each equation—the overall average percentage change is 11.1 percent per year. This is not the best description of the trend, however. The percentage changes are larger in the early portion of the period, gradually diminishing over time. This is shown by the negative c in the log equation and the base of t^2 in the exponential equation. This base is less than unity, thus dampening the rate of increase. The factor $(.9947)^{t^2}$ becomes increasingly significant the further we move into the future.

Prediction of 1981 sales by this equation yields an estimate of only $201,000—lower than the predictions from any of the four simple linear models. Thus, although the base of t^2 seems very close to unity, it has a sub-

---

[9]This statement assumes that time has been transformed so that $t = 0$ is about the midpoint of the data.

stantial impact on the various calculated values. The total trend line (Fig. 16.3) seems to show only a slight departure from linearity, but the impact of this departure is significant. The percentage increase in the calculated trend is 17 percent for 1969 to 1970 but only 6 percent for 1978 to 1979. This rate continues to decrease until the line reaches its maximum value in 1984. The reversal of the line at this point and the rapid deceleration prior to that point caused the two managers to reject its use as a basis for forecasting despite its relatively good fit for the 1969–1979 data.

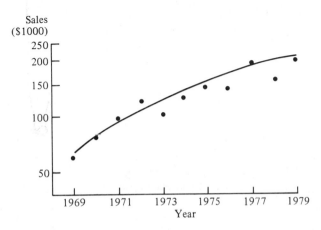

Fig. 16.3
Crovel data with parabolic trend to logarithms.

Other Growth Curves

Much marketing literature and many forecasting models are concerned with a *product life cycle*. The product life cycle views the development of a product over time as divisible into distinct stages. The typical stages are (1) introduction, characterized by slow growth; (2) rapid growth, a period of large increases; (3) maturity, a period of slower growth with ultimately a period of stability; and (4) decline. The first three stages can be described mathematically by several different S-curves.

Three of the more commonly used S-type of growth curves are the Gompertz, logistic, and the modified exponential. These curves are more complex than those discussed in the preceding sections, but they incorporate properties that may be more desirable. Instead of reaching a point of reversal, these curves introduce upper or lower limits as asymptotes. The series need not be characterized with continually decreasing rates of change. The more typical product life cycle with increases in the rates of change in the first two stages followed by decreases in the rates of change in the maturity stage may emerge.[10]

The properties of the various curves are quite flexible and can be constrained or unconstrained depending on the analyst's desires. These curves are usually reserved for long-run forecasts in which the underlying trend is the principal interest.[11] The forms of the equation are more involved than those discussed thus far, but this additional complexity produces an equation with properties that have more ready acceptance. We illustrate with a Gompertz equation fitted to the Crovel data.

The general form of the Gompertz equation is given by Eq. (16.9)

$$\log y = \log k + (\log A)B^t \tag{16.9}$$

which can be expressed as Eq. (16.10).

$$y = kA^{B^t}. \tag{16.10}$$

The symbol k is the upper limit of the equation, and B is the dampening factor. The resulting equation for the Crovel data [in the form of Eq. (16.9)] is

$$\log y = 2.66448 + (-.88633)(.91471)^t$$

$$t = 0 \text{ in } 1969.$$

The upper limit of this trend line is \$462,000 (log 2.66448 with sales in \$1,000). The factor $(.91471)^t$ produces the deviations from this upper limit; the larger t is, the smaller the deviation. The results in this equation are typical: $\log A < 0$ and $0 < B < 1$. Other results lead to totally different interpretations; for example, $\log A > 0$ yields k as a lower limit.[12] Use of the Gompertz equation for predicting Crovel 1981 sales yields a value of \$229,000.[13]

Decomposition

The *decomposition* approach to time-series analysis assumes that the series is generated by several different forces working simultaneously. The long-run trend component is viewed as gradual unidirectional, supplying the foundation about which forces of a shorter duration produce deviations. Cyclical fluctua-

---

[10]A parabola fitted to the logs usually follows this pattern with respect to the amounts of change when b is positive and c is negative. The Crovel parabolic trend to logs reveals this pattern. Although the percentage rate of increase declines continuously, the absolute increases accelerate slightly in the first portion of the period and then diminish in the latter portion. However, while the parabola has a reversal, the S-curves have asymptotes as upper limits.

[11]See F. E. Croxton and D. J. Cowden, 1960, *Applied General Statistics,* (3rd ed.), (Englewood Cliffs, N.J.: Prentice-Hall, pp. 582–599.

[12]*Ibid.,* pp. 590–595.

[13]The equation derived was fitted by the method of selected points that forced the trend line through the initial, middle, and final observations. A least-squares fit is also possible but not often used.

tions are reversible but relatively smooth, alternating between upward and downward movements. Their duration varies depending on the specific series, but it is rarely less than two to three years. Seasonal variations are repetitive fluctuations that are a year or less in duration. Typically the seasonal variations are much more predictable than the cycles, but this is not a part of their definitions. The fourth component encompasses the remaining forces of a time series and is designated as irregular movements or simply as the residual component, depending on the analyst's preference. Prediction of this component is almost impossible since its pattern is highly erratic.

The most common decomposition model is multiplicative as shown by Eq. (16.11).

$$O = (T)(C)(S)(R) \qquad\qquad (16.11)$$

where

O = original data,

T = secular trend,

C = cyclical fluctuations,

S = seasonal movements, and

R = residual component.

This formulation uses one of the components in an absolute sense and the other three in relative forms; for example, the seasonal component might be shown as a seasonal index of .92 meaning that seasonal forces for a particular month are expected to produce a reduction of 8 percent. The trend component may be established along the lines already discussed in this chapter or by a moving average approach.

A moving average uses the same number of observations for each calculated value, constantly moving forward or backward and using different observations for the calculations. For example, a seven-month moving average would use data for January through July for an observation centered on April. The next observation would use data from February through August with centering in May. This approach allows the data to establish the form of the trend equation; it need not be linear and any number of reversals is possible. With the trend established in one of these two manners, the other three components are typically analyzed and summarized by deviations from the established trend lines. The mechanics underlying the procedures and the rationale are relatively simple although a wide variety of details and steps are available. For the marketing manager facing a prediction problem, the chief question arises with respect to how the given descriptions can be extrapolated and whether such extrapolations are warranted.

Forecasts involving a few months' lead time are used constantly in market plans, and they are often quite accurate. This is particularly true with strong seasonal patterns. The incorporation of the cycle in such forecasts has also been successful during the recovery and early recession phases. Turning points of the cycle are notoriously difficult to pinpoint.[14]

Crovel's marketing manager is concerned about detailed plans for 1980 as well as a prediction for 1981. The manager is focusing on the last half of the year in particular, and wants to plan activities by quarters. The seasonal indices established for the third and fourth quarters are 1.15 and 1.05, respectively—Crovel's business is somewhat better in the second half of the year than in the first. Leading indicators suggest that Crovel has passed the peak of its cyclical activity but has not really entered a recession. A subjective estimate of cyclical forces calls for "5 percent above normal" during the last half of 1980. No other significant factors have been identified for the target period.

Annual sales estimates must be converted into quarterly figures using Eq. (16.11). The annual trend figure for Crovel is taken as \$220,000 or \$54,000 per quarter. Substituting in Eq. (16.11), the two managers arrive at an estimate of \$65,200 for the third quarter.

$$O = 54,000(1.05)(1.15) = 65,200.$$

Does the trend estimate seem appropriate? Why? Using, this trend estimate, what should the marketing manager plan for sales in the fourth quarter?

Exponential Smoothing

An increasingly popular method for short-range forecasting is *exponential smoothing*, a type of weighted moving average. The technique has advantages over both the simple moving average approach and mathematically derived equations when short-range forecasting is required. Its superiority over the moving average is two-fold: (1) it is more sensitive to recent developments, and (2) it yields calculated values for the most recent periods.[15] The superiority of exponential smoothing over mathematical equations is also two-fold: (1) again it is more sensitive to recent developments, and (2) it does not assume steady and consistent changes. Even if this stability is appropriate for long-range forecasts, it is dubious for short-range forecasts.

The formula for exponential smoothing is given by Eq. (16.12).

$$\overset{*}{z}_t = \alpha y_t + (1 - \alpha)\overset{*}{z}_{t-1}. \tag{16.12}$$

The $\overset{*}{z}$-figures are calculated estimates that replace the actual observations that may be unduly distorted by unusual conditions, but they still permit heavy weighting of recent observations. Equation (16.12) indicates that the weights

---

[14]Details of the decomposition approach, including the use of moving averages, are given in most elementary statistics texts: Morris Hamburg, 1970, *Statistical Analysis for Decision Making* (New York: Harcourt, Brace, and World), pp. 539–579 or Richard C. Clelland, John S. de Cani, and Francis E. Brown, 1973, *Basic Statistics with Business Applications* (New York: Wiley), pp. 541–574.

[15]The greater the number of periods in a moving average, the more the calculated values lose currency. An n-period moving average loses $n - 1$ observations, half at the beginning of the series and half at the end.

are divided between the most recent observation (with weight α) and the exponentially smoothed calculation for the prior period with weight $(1 - \alpha)$. The larger α is, the heavier the weight assigned to the most recent observations. The smaller α is, the more the earlier observations influence the calculation.

Equation (16.12) can be shown to be equal to Eq. (16.13).

$$\overset{*}{z}_t = \alpha \sum_{j=1}^{t-1} (1 - \alpha)^j y_{t-j} + (1 - \alpha)^t \overset{*}{z}_0. \tag{16.13}$$

The term $\overset{*}{z}_0$ is either an initial weighted or unweighted moving average or some arbitrary value. The process has continued for t periods beyond that initial period. Each observation in the series is weighted by $\alpha(1 - \alpha)^j$ with j designating the number of periods prior to the current period. Suppose our smoothing constant is $\alpha = .4$. The weights for the various observations are

$$\alpha(1 - \alpha)^0 = .4$$
$$\alpha(1 - \alpha)^1 = .24$$
$$\alpha(1 - \alpha)^2 = .144$$
$$\alpha(1 - \alpha)^3 = .0864$$

$$\vdots \qquad \vdots$$

The weights applied to the various observations decrease as we go back in time. Larger values of α would give even greater weights to the more recent observations, and the earlier observations would receive less weight. Smaller values of α would have the opposite effect, although the most recent observation would still receive the most weight.

Exponential smoothing has been applied in Table 16.4 to the Crovel Fastener data, using two different values of α, (.4 and .6). An arbitrarily selected $\overset{*}{z}$ of 60 is assigned to 1968. With a series of this type that has such a strong upward trend, the calculated $\overset{*}{z}$-values understate the series in almost every instance. Even larger values of α would improve the fit, but the assignment of any weight to the earlier observations produces a downward bias. Use of monthly data, adjusted for seasonal variations if appropriate, might be an even better procedure.

The determination of the correct numerical value for α is a major problem with exponential smoothing. Its value is usually determined on a trial-and-error basis, choosing the α that yields the best fit for the data. More elaborate formulations permit the analyst to incorporate elements of a decomposition model.[16] Exponential smoothing in its simplest form yields a $\overset{*}{z}$-value for the

---

[16]A full discussion of the technique and its modifications is presented in R. G. Brown, 1959, *Statistical Forecasting for Inventory Control* (New York: McGraw-Hill) and R. G. Brown, 1963, *Smoothing, Forecasting, and Prediction* (Englewood Cliffs, N.J.: Prentice-Hall).

Table 16.4
Exponential Smoothing of Crovel Fastener Company Data

Year	Sales ($1,000)	αy_i	$\overset{*}{z}_i$	$(1 - \alpha)\overset{*}{z}_i$	αy_i	$\overset{*}{z}_i$	$(1 - \alpha)\overset{*}{z}_i$
		$\alpha = .4$			$\alpha = .6$		
1968			60.0	36.0		60.0	24.0
1969	60.0	24.0	60.0	36.0	36.0	60.0	24.0
1970	75.0	30.0	66.0	39.6	45.0	69.0	27.6
1971	90.0	36.0	75.6	45.4	54.0	81.6	32.6
1972	120.0	48.0	93.4	56.0	72.0	104.6	41.8
1973	100.0	40.0	96.0	57.6	60.0	101.8	40.7
1974	125.0	50.0	107.6	64.6	75.0	115.7	46.3
1975	140.0	56.0	120.6	72.4	84.0	130.3	52.1
1976	130.0	52.0	124.4	74.6	78.0	130.1	52.0
1977	180.0	72.0	146.6	88.0	108.0	160.0	64.0
1978	160.0	64.0	152.0	91.2	96.0	160.0	64.0
1979	200.0	80.0	171.2		120.0	184.0	

most recent date, but it does not supply a forecast. As seen in Table 16.4, a forecast for 1980 must adjust the $\overset{*}{z}$ of 1979 (either $171,200 or $184,000 depending on which is used).

The virtue of exponential smoothing is observed most readily by inspection of Fig. 16.4 that presents the Crovel data and the two $\overset{*}{z}$-series of Table

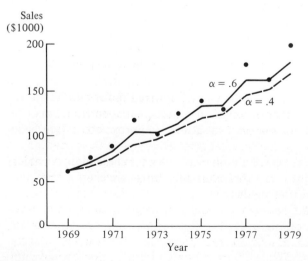

Fig. 16.4
Crovel data with two exponentially smoothed series.

16.4. The twin desires are (1) a series that follows the data but (2) does not display large erratic movements. The selection of α indicates the compromise reached between these two desires. A large α value gives a better fit while a smaller α gives a smoother line. Figure 16.4 vividly shows the principal weakness of exponential smoothing: it consistently yields underestimates for a series with a strong growth trend.

LEAD–LAG RELATIONSHIPS

Our discussion of multiple regression made no mention of the way in which the variables were related in timing. Assume company sales levels by region are related to various endogenous and exogenous variables within the region. Some of the variables might be the firm's advertising, sales force size, and price levels; competitor's marketing mix activities; and the region's unemployment rate and construction activity. Should all of these variables refer to the same time period? Both logic and empirical evidence are relevant in answering this question. But raising the question introduces a new theoretical model for our conditional equations. This model is given by Eq. (16.14) where the subscripts $t - i$ and $t - j$ permit differences in the timing of the dependent variable and the independent variables.

$$y_t = f(x_{t - i}, z_{t - j}, \ldots). \tag{16.14}$$

The model does not specify that the timing of the dependent variable must differ from that of the independent variable: i could equal zero. Nor does the model state that the timing of the dependent variable must follow that of the independent variable: i could be negative. The model is useful for predictive purposes, however, only when the lead–lag relationship has the dependent variable occurring after the independent variables.

Cross-sectional versus Time-series Data

The difference in timing in Eq. (16.14) poses no additional problems over the typical regression situation—as long as the data are *cross sectional* rather than *time series*. Cross-sectional data are data collected from different units of the pertinent universe, with the same timing for all units. Cross-sectional data for a multiple regression of company sales by region against several independent variables would require collection of data from all regions at the same time. A modification that the time specification for certain independent variables apply to prior periods would not invalidate the appropriateness of the procedure.

Suppose, however, the data refer to the same region, collected as time-series data for the various variables. Even if no theoretical problems occur, differences in the interpretation of the regression coefficients must be recognized. With cross-sectional data, the appropriate interpretation should compare two regions that differ by one unit with respect to a particular independent variable.

Consider the regression equation obtained from a study of the ages of husbands and wives.

$$y = 4.07 + 1.03x$$

where

$$x = \text{age of wife and}$$

$$y = \text{age of husband.}$$

The regression coefficient means, "Given two wives who differ in age by one year, we expect their husbands to differ in age by 1.03 years." It does not mean that the average husband ages by 1.03 years when the wife ages by one year (although such a finding might explain the greater life expectancy of women).

The distinction between cross-sectional and time-series data exists whether similar timing of the variables is employed or whether different timing is employed. Many managerial problems are concerned with the possible introduction of changes in the independent variable in order to produce changes in the dependent variable—a time-series concept although the experiment run may be cross sectional in nature.

Consider an experiment to determine demand elasticity with respect to price. Double log transformation (transforming both price and demand) would yield an equation of

$$\log D = a + b \log P$$

with b typically negative. Estimates of demand are made, given price data collected from several test cities. The equation is not designed for estimating changes in demand associated with specific price changes for the same city. A marketing manager will frequently use a model based upon cross-sectional data for time-series predictions, but the manager should recognize that he or she is assuming the two approaches will yield equivalent results.[17]

Lead–lag Example

Let us examine a typical two-variable, lead–lag regression equation. The units involved in the study are retail outlets. The dependent variable is number of cases purchased and the independent variable is exposure to promotion. The following is a possible result:

$$y_t = 12.3 + 10.4x_{t-1}$$

where y is number of cases purchased and x is promotional expenditure in dollars.

---

[17]Time-series analysis that focuses on the relationship between *changes* in the independent variable of a specific element and *changes* in the dependent variable of that element can employ a *first-difference* approach. This procedure is discussed later in the present chapter.

The model is formulated in terms of a one-month, lead–lag relationship. Dollar expenditures on promotional material in one month are analyzed against purchases in the following month. The unit of analysis is the individual retailer. The input data refer to promotional expenditures directed to a particular retailer[18] and that retailer's purchases in the following month. The data are cross sectional since the sample consists of many different retailers.

The selection of a one-month, lead–lag relationship could be *a priori,* or it could be selected on a trial and error approach, using the time period that yielded the best fit. Consideration of many different lead–lag periods and use of the best fit invite the usual difficulty associated with search techniques and the presentation of the best fit as "the" relationship. The use of probability concepts in testing hypotheses or making interval estimates is invalid. The split-half approach of using half of the data to generate the model and the other half for testing is the recommended procedure.

The marketing manager can use this equation for several different kinds of decisions. First, it can be used for predictions. These predictions can then help in inventory and distribution planning. Second, the equation can provide a basis for identifying retailers that make unusually high or low purchases, given the level of promotion reaching them. The next step is to identify reasons for these deviations, incorporating the most effective procedures and avoiding the ineffective in future plans. Finally, the equation can be helpful in choosing levels of promotion and its allocation.

More complex functions, with additional independent variables, their interaction, possible transformations, and upper or lower limits would make the relationship more realistic and would yield more explicit recommendations.[19] The application of the lead–lag concept and its utility would be precisely the same; only the specific functional form would change.

Time Series and Autocorrelation

If two time series are both increasing, are they associated together? From a strictly historical and descriptive perspective, the answer must be affirmative. The smaller values of one series coincide in timing with the smaller values of the other, and the larger values of the two series also have similar timing. Is this an association that is useful for prediction purposes?

Crovel sales are positively associated with attendance at professional football games. To facilitate the prediction problem, we might introduce a lead–lag relationship: Crovel sales in t and professional football attendance in $t - 1$. Again a high degree of association would be found. But should Crovel's manager use such a relationship in prediction? It seems rather risky!

---

[18]Personal calls by the sales person, telephone calls, and direct mail are the typical items falling within this category.

[19]See David B. Montgomery and Glen L. Urban, 1969, *Management Science in Marketing* (Englewood Cliffs, N.J.: Prentice-Hall), pp. 102–108, for an interesting formulation of bivariate advertising response functions.

Regression compares the similarity of the standard scores of two (or more) variables for the units analyzed. In time-series analysis the unit of analysis or unit of association refers to the time period. If a particular unit or time period has a small standard score on variable *y*, does it also have a small standard score on *x*? Using a 30-year time series of automobile sales (*y*), gross national product (x_1), and population (x_2), we could determine a linear equation $y = a + b_1x_1 + b_2x_2$. All three series have experienced substantial growth during this period. Both regression coefficients would be positive. How useful would the equation be for making predictions? The crux of the answer hinges on autocorrelation.

Autocorrelation exists when successive observations of a single series are correlated with each other. If each of two series reveals a high degree of autocorrelation, the two series must be correlated with each other—directly or inversely depending on the patterns within the two series.[20] Potential problems exist in regression analyses based on time-series data because autocorrelation leads to predictive models that seem better than they really are. Thus a false sense of confidence may be generated. An exaggerated optimism is produced in two distinct areas. (1) The standard errors of the regression coefficients are understated. (2) The observed relationships may reflect similar patterns without any logical linkage between the variables. While all association models are based on similar covariance rather than causal links, the danger of spurious conclusions is particularly likely with time-series data in which there are strong long-run trends. Strong autocorrelation in effect reduces the number of *independent* observations in the sample since the successive readings are "dependent" on each other.

Three approaches to the problem of autocorrelation have been proposed. (1) Econometric models based upon systems of equations—with "staged" relationships and various assumptions or transformations of the residuals—can be employed. (2) A regression based upon first differences instead of the original observations can be employed. (3) The relationship can be used despite the presence of autocorrelation. The third procedure relies on the fact that any prediction assumes that the same environmental conditions will continue through the period for which the prediction is required and emphasizes that the equation is descriptive of the relationship during the period covered. This approach essentially ignores the existence of autocorrelation, assuming that past relationships will hold in the future regardless of whether there has been any logical or causal chain.

A simple first step to an econometric model might be as shown by Eq. (16.15). This equation adds to Eq. (16.14), which permits differential timing

---

[20]The terms autocorrelation, serial correlation, and lag correlation are sometimes used interchangeably and are sometimes differentiated. The concepts may also refer to the relationship between successive observations or successive residuals. We shall not consider the technical aspects of these differences. See Taro Yamane, 1967, *Statistics: An Introductory Analysis* (2nd ed.) (New York: Harper & Row), pp. 866–867.

between the dependent variable and the independent variables, the value of the dependent variable at a preceding time.

$$y_t = a + b_1 x_{1(t - i)} + b_2 x_{2(t - j)} + \cdots + c y_{t - k}. \qquad (16.15)$$

A series with a strong underlying trend will show a strong relationship between y_t and $y_{t - k}$. The model shows the relationship between y_t and the other independent variables on a net basis with this trend removed. Multicollinearity among $y_{t - k}$ and the other independent variables may result with Eq. (16.15) and additional modifications or complexities may be required. These modifications typically involve systems of equations rather than a single equation.[21]

The first-difference approach can be illustrated with the data of Table 16.5, relating sales and advertising of Crovel. These data also illustrate (1) the general problem of autocorrelation and (2) the alternatives of simultaneous timing versus lead–lag relationships. The first-difference approach asks whether *changes* in advertising expenditures are associated with *changes* in sales. Therefore the regression equation is based on the data in the third and fifth columns instead of the second and fourth. The equation derived also uses a one-year lag of sales against advertising. Only nine observations are employed since one data point is lost by using changes instead of the original data and another is lost because of the difference in timing.

Table 16.5
Sales and Advertising of Crovel Fastener Company

Year	Sales ($1,000) Level	Change	Advertising ($100) Level	Change
1969	60.0		25	
1970	75.0	+15.0	36	+11
1971	90.0	+15.0	43	+ 7
1972	120.0	+30.0	51	+ 8
1973	100.0	−20.0	61	+10
1974	125.0	+25.0	70	+ 9
1975	140.0	+15.0	73	+ 3
1976	130.0	−10.0	91	+18
1977	180.0	+50.0	103	+12
1978	160.0	−20.0	118	+15
1979	200.0	+40.0	130	+12

[21]See J. Johnston, 1963, *Econometric Methods* (New York: McGraw-Hill). Clelland, deCani, and Brown, *op. cit.*, pp. 614–618, provide a short discussion of one type of model.

The least-squares regression is determined in the usual manner by solving two equations simultaneously. Denoting sales by y and advertising by x, the equations to solve are

$$\Sigma(\Delta y_t) = na + b\Sigma(\Delta x_{t-1}) \quad \text{and}$$
$$\Sigma(\Delta y_t)(\Delta x_{t-1}) = a\Sigma(\Delta x_{t-1}) + b\Sigma(\Delta x_{t-1})^2.$$

The resulting equation is

$$\Delta y_t = -21.77 + 3.45(\Delta x_{t-1}).$$

Using this equation to predict 1980 sales is accomplished in two steps. (1) The predicted change in sales is $-21.77 + 3.45(12) = 19.6$ (or \$19,600). (2) Total sales are then predicted as \$219,600 since 1979 sales were \$200,000. Thus the predicted change in sales uses the entire equation; it is not dependent on b alone.

The a-constant indicates that sales would be expected to decline by \$21,800 if the level of advertising remained constant for two years. Failure of the "causative" factor to increase in the future will not result in a "holding" of sales; it will result in a decrease. The value $\Delta x = 0$ is an extrapolation for this particular series and possesses all of the dangers inherent in extrapolation. The value of the a-constant, of course, depends on the particular series. It need not be negative, and it could be approximately zero. Regardless of its value, great care should be exercised whenever $\Delta x = 0$ involves extrapolation.[22]

If a least-square regression equation were calculated with the original data, using a one-year lead–lag timing, an entirely different mental model would exist. This model would yield the same estimate of sales for two successive years with the same level of advertising—since the value of the independent variable would be the same in each calculation. The equation, using the original data, is

$$y_t = 47.80 + 1.25x_{t-1}.$$

The estimate of 1980 sales, using known advertising of \$13,000 in 1979 ($x = 130$), is \$210,300. If 1980 advertising remained at the same level, the estimate of 1981 sales would again be \$210,300. Thus this is a mental concept that is entirely different from the first-difference approach that says the change in advertising is crucial for determining the change in sales.

The first difference approach is often helpful in distinguishing between two situations: (1) two series that have strong and similar trends but whose short-run fluctuations show little similarity and (2) two series that are similar in both long- and short-run patterns. Regression based on the original observations will infer that a strong relationship exists in each instance, but the first-difference approach will claim a relationship in only the second.

---

[22]This example is presented to illustrate the rationale and interpretation of first-difference equations. The substantative results cannot be generalized.

The problem of autocorrelation in the Crovel data can be observed by comparing the two r^2 values calculated from the two advertising/sales equations. The r^2 based upon the original data (with a one-year lag) is .91; r^2 based on the first-difference equation is only .35. The artificially high value with the original data suggests a much higher association than is warranted.[23]

SUMMARY

A time series is the chronological arrangement of a series of observations on one or more variables. A prime problem of marketing managers is the prediction of such variables at future points in time. Several predictive models are based on the assumption that the current level of the variable and/or pattern by which it has evolved have a bearing on its future values. These models treat time as an independent variable. Other alternative models assume that relationships exist between one or more separate independent variables and the emerging value of the dependent variable at a latter point in time—lead–lag models.

The models that treat time as an independent variable fall into two groups: mathematical equations whose properties are specified *a priori* by the analyst and more flexible descriptions whose forms are determined by the data. Mathematical equations vary from simple linear functions to S-curves. The more complex curves are usually reserved for long-run forecasts of the trend component. The simple linear functions summarize the average amount of change (linear to the original data) or the average percentage change (linear to the logs), and are rarely useful for more than short-range forecasts.

Mathematic functions are usually determined by either of two approaches: forcing the equation to pass through arbitrarily selected points or a least-squares fit to the entire data. Predictions also employ two different approaches. (1) The most recent observation is modified by the pattern of change stated in the equation. This approach focuses on short-run forecasts and assumes that the most recent experience establishes the base from which those short-run changes will develop. (2) The total equation is the basis for predictions. This approach focuses on long-run forecasts and assumes that any present deviation from the equation is a short-run phenomenon.

The most frequently used nonmathematical approaches are (1) decomposition models and (2) exponential smoothing, a special type of moving average. Decomposition models separate a time series into the four component parts of trend, cycle, seasonal, and irregular (or residual). Each is defined in terms of its duration and properties, and predictions require the combination of the separate components. Exponential smoothing is a weighted moving average

---

[23]The appropriate test for autocorrelation is the Durbin–Watson test. One of the better short descriptions is found in Yamane, *op. cit.*, pp. 809–813 and 866–868. See also J. Durbin and G. S. Watson, 1950, Testing for serial correlation in least-squares regression, *Biometrika* **37**: 409–428.

approach that assigns the greatest weight to recent observations. It is most useful in very short-range predictions, retaining a sensitivity to recent developments while introducing a smoothing of the series. Since simple exponential smoothing possesses a downward bias for series with strong growth trends, the technique is not useful for even short-range predictions unless more complex adjustments are made.

Lead–lag models are very similar to ordinary regression equations with the exception that all variables need not refer to the same time. As long as cross-sectional data are employed, no special problems arise—*cross-sectional data* referring to data gathered from a sample of units from the relevant universe. If time-series data are employed observations are made on a single unit at different times. The potential problem arising with time-series data is that successive observations within the same series may be correlated with each other: *autocorrelation* may exist.

The presence of autocorrelation leads to two potential difficulties. First, the observed relationship between two series may result from similar long-run trends. If two series have strong upward trends, they are moving together. This similarity may be a poor basis for prediction unless there is a logical link between the variables. Any change in the environment of either variable may lead to the disappearance of the relationship. Second, the existence of autocorrelation leads to an understatement of the sampling variance. Thus the results suggest greater reliability and may lead to greater confidence than is warranted.

There are three usual approaches to the problem of autocorrelation, differing successively in their sophistication. First, econometric models provide a sound theoretic approach and yield the best understanding of the underlying relationships. Second, the use of first differences attempts to adjust for underlying trends and compares *changes* of the two series. The third approach simply proceeds with the regression despite the presence of autocorrelation, defending its use with the argument that all prediction assumes stability of environmental conditions. This approach, as is the case in using time as an independent variable, relies on the goodness of fit and the analyst's subjective confidence in its continuity rather than relying on a well-established theoretical foundation.

EXERCISES AND PROBLEMS

1. Distinguish among the terms within each of the following sets.
    a) Regression with time as an independent variable and lead–lag regression
    b) Time series to logs and geometric mean of relatives
    c) Exponential smoothing and moving average
    d) *S*-curve, parabola, and linear to logs
    e) Asymptotes and reversals
    f) Decomposition, moving average, and mathematical equation

g) Lead–lag model and first-difference model

h) Cross-sectional data and time-series data

i) Autocorrelation and multicollinearity

2. Briefly explain the similarities and differences among the four simple linear time-series models.

3. Explain briefly the features that distinguish between the following time-series components.

   a) Seasonal and cycle

   b) Trend and cycle

   c) Seasonal and residual

4. Obtain population figures for your hometown from 1920 to date.

   a) Would it be necessary to use all figures available to determine the trend? Why?

   b) Would it be advisable to use all figures available? Why?

   c) Using the data you think should be used and the model you think is most appropriate, determine the trend in population for your hometown.

5. Sales of International Multifoods Corporation for the period 1971–1979 are presented in Table E16.5.

Table E16.5

Year	Sales (million $)
1971	439
1972	459
1973	530
1974	740
1975	828
1976	801
1977	847
1978	823
1979	931

   a) Plot the data.

   b) Is exponential smoothing appropriate for these data? The objective is short-run forcasting. Discuss.

   c) Using $\alpha = .6$ and $.3$, prepare two exponential smoothings of these data. Do the results substantiate your answer in (b)? Explain.

   d) Which α yields a better fit? Does your answer illustrate a general principle? Explain.

   e) Would you be willing to use these data for establishing a mathematical trend line? Why?

f) What type of mathematical trend line would yield the best fit for these data? Why? (Disregard your answer to (e) if necessary.)

6. Sales of the Minnesota Mining and Manufacturing Company are presented in Table E16.6.

Table E16.6

Year	Sales (million $)
1959	501
1960	550
1961	614
1962	700
1963	813
1964	904
1965	1000
1966	1153
1967	1243
1968	1451
1969	1613
1970	1687
1971	1829
1972	2114
1973	2546
1974	2937
1975	3127
1976	3514
1977	3980
1978	4662

a) Plot the data.

b) Determine the annual percentage change in sales between 1959 and 1978, using data for only the first and last observations.

c) Determine the average increase in dollar sales per year, again using only the first and last observation.

d) Show the results of (b) and (c) as linear functions on the appropriate graphs. Which one seems a better fit? Explain.

e) Would you expect linear functions determined by least squares to yield better fits than your results of (b) and (c)? Discuss for these data.

f) It has been proposed that least-squares equations be determined by using data for 1961, 1966, 1971, and 1976. Do you think this would be an appropriate procedure? Why?

g) An alternative suggestion is to use five-year averages centered on 1961, 1966, 1971, and 1976. How would this be any different from (f)? Would it be advantageous—both as a general procedure and for the Minnesota Mining and Manufacturing data? Why?

h) Would a parabolic trend line be appropriate for these data, either to the logs or to the original data? Why?

i) Determine the trend equations that you believe are the most appropriate for these data for short-run forecasts and for long-run forecasts.

j) What is your estimate of Minnesota Mining and Manufacturing sales for 1980?

7. An economics student viewing the data of Exercises 5 and 6 hypothesized that International Multifoods sales have a one-year lag relationship to Minnesota Mining and Manufacturing sales.

a) Determine the constants of a linear regression equation that corresponds to this hypothesis. Use all of the data presented in the two exercises that are appropriate.

b) Are the two series related according to the one-year lag proposed? What evidence leads you to this conclusion?

c) Another student, on viewing the data, suggested that the existence of a relationship be checked by fitting a regression line to the first differences. Again a one-year lag is to be used. Determine the results of a linear regression that corresponds to this model.

d) Would you think it appropriate to estimate International Multifood sales by using the equation obtained in (c)? Why?

8. Gross capital expenditures for International Multifoods Corp. for the period 1970–1979 are presented in Table E16.8.

Table E16.8

Year	Gross capital expenditures (million $)
1970	4.8
1971	7.2
1972	5.1
1973	9.9
1974	16.8
1975	10.6
1976	13.2
1977	16.6
1978	18.6
1979	22.6

It has been suggested that there is a lead–lag relationship between gross capital expenditures and sales. However, the strong possibility of autocorrelation might make the relationship appear stronger than it really is. The following model is, therefore, proposed: sales in year (t) are a function of both gross capital expenditures in year ($t - 1$) and sales in year ($t - 1$).

a) Using the data shown in Tables E16.5 and E16.8 determine the linear regression equation that corresponds to the proposed model.

b) Would you conclude that gross capital expenditures are related to sales—with a one-year lag? Why?

9. The second-degree trend equation to the profits of a construction firm is log y = $4.02313 + .05184t - .00182t^2$ where $t = 0$ in 1972 and t is expressed in one-year intervals. Profits (y) are in \$100.

a) Express the trend equation in terms of y instead of log y.

b) Interpret the meaning of the constants of your answer in (a).

c) When does the trend equation indicate a reversal? Would this have any bearing on your willingness to use the equation for forecasting? Why?

10. The Gompertz equation is superficially similar in appearance to a simple linear function. However, the general nature of the trend described is quite different. Discuss the constants found in a Gompertz, indicating the role played by each in determining the trend.

11. Present the model employed in the decomposition approach to time-series analysis. Be sure to include reference to

a) how one factor must be established as a base,

b) the multiplicative nature of the model,

c) a numerical example of its use.

12. Analyze, criticize, and explain:

a) A trend equation based upon the average annual amount of change is a simplified model of the first-difference approach.

b) Long-run forecasts normally are based on a trend equation alone. Short-run forecasts, however, usually use the most recent observation(s) as a base to be adjusted by applying appropriate relationships or patterns.

c) A lead–lag relationship to time-series predictions has all of the advantages of a standard regression plus the future orientation incorporated in the "lead" concept.

d) Autocorrelation is an inherent difficulty with almost all time-series data. Cross-sectional data do little to help the situation since the managerial problem usually involves a time orientation.

e) The major difficulty with sophisticated analytic approaches to time-series analysis is the focus. They ask whether assumptions are met and whether forecasts are justified. The marketing manager must forecast. Therefore it is immaterial whether the assumptions are met.

f) The treatment of time as an independent variable falls within the regression concept. Therefore the analyst must refrain from using the coefficient of determination. But all other summary measures and hypothesis-testing aspects of regression/correlation are appropriate.

g) Long-run forecasts and extrapolation are most defensible when nonmathematical trend lines are employed.

h) The arithmetic mean of relatives supplies a more conservative approach than does the geometric mean of relatives. Thus even though the arithmetic mean might contain a theoretic bias, it involves less risk.

i) Exponential smoothing requires a careful choosing of the appropriate α-value. If α is too large, the calculated values will exceed the actual values. If α is too small, the calculated values will be lower than the actual values.

RECENT ANALYTIC
DEVELOPMENTS

Part IV continues our study of techniques addressed to nominally and intervally scaled variables and introduces specific techniques employed with ordinal data. Chapter 17 deals with relationships among a set of variables where no specific dependent variable has been identified. The question is thus one of summarizing relationships or collapsing the number of variables rather than one of prediction. Factor analysis and clustering consider this situation from two different perspectives. Chapter 18 introduces the case of multiple dependent variables. Relationships between two sets of variables are examined rather than relationships with a single target variable. Canonical correlation is emphasized in this context although both analysis of variance and analysis of covariance can be extended to the multiple dependent variable problem. Chapter 19 considers a number of nonparametric tests designed for ordinal data, an area neglected by many marketing researchers. The possibility of deriving interval results without interval scale input is introduced in Chapter 19 and extended in Chapter 20, which is addressed to multidimensional scaling and conjoint measurement. Chapter 21 shifts our focus to the future of marketing research, discussing current needs and weaknesses in order to identify the most likely directions of future developments.

The areas covered in Part IV represent tremendous potential for the marketing researcher and marketing manager. The techniques offer new approaches to complex problems. Our objective is to familiarize the reader with the subject matter and basic concepts of these growing fields. Since the mathematical complexity and sophistication involved are greater than those of Parts I through III, our approach will not address the details of the various techniques beyond the level needed for intelligent use of their results.

CHAPTER 17

COLLAPSING THE NUMBER
OF VARIABLES

MANY NUMBERS: CONFUSION OR INFORMATION?

The techniques considered in the preceding chapters partition the variables into two sets: dependent and independent. For prediction problems, the independent variables are given and provide the basis upon which the value of the dependent variable is predicted. We now consider a different type of problem: the variables are not partitioned but are considered as a single group.

National retail chains may consider "social class" as a relevant concept in their approach to market segmentation. But just what is social class? How is it defined? Warner combined occupation, source of income, house type, and dwelling area into a single index number.[1] His weighting schemes are largely subjective. Other variables and weights are certainly possible. *Factor analysis* provides an approach that reduces a set of variables into one or more underlying variables. The technique groups together those variables that seem to belong together and simultaneously supplies the weighting scheme. The same technique can be applied to the identification of the factors that make up the image of a brand or store. One or more composite performance measures for salespeople might be generated in the same way.

A companion question exists to the "factor" question: which individuals, brands, or stores have similar factor profiles? If social class is a good basis for market segmentation, how can the segments be identified? If store images can be defined on two or three factors, which stores have similar images? *Cluster analysis* provides an approach to these questions.

Factor analysis has two principal aims, either of which may be dominant in a particular problem. (1) A large set of variables should be reduced to a smaller number of underlying factors. A battery of 50 attitudinal questions, yielding 50 separate variables, is cumbersome. Factor analysis may reduce this

---

[1] W. Lloyd Warner, Marcia Meeker, and Kenneth Eells, 1949, *Social Class in America* (Chicago: Science Research Associates).

number to a manageable few. (2) The substantive meaning of a large set of variables is best discerned by combining those that are similar. The battery of 50 attitudinal questions does not reflect 50 attitudes but no more than five or six. Factor analysis will aid in the identification of relevant and separate concepts.

Cluster analysis is concerned with *objects* rather than *variables*. Very often these objects are customers, and market segmentation is desired. This is true whether the objects are individual customers or geographic locations such as census tracts, cities, or even countries. Alternatively, the objects might be products and management's concern may be product positioning.

Both factor analysis and cluster analysis are attempts to find system when the decision maker is overwhelmed by mountains of data that seem to have no central message. They are general techniques that approach the same data set from two different perspectives. Consider a research project that has collected information concerning 20 retail chains on 35 different characteristics. Factor analysis would attempt to compress the 35 variables into a few dimensions, perhaps labeled service orientation, quality level, width of assortment, etc. Clustering would attempt to form two or three groups of chains—the chains within each group being as similar as possible on the characteristics. In general, the analyst starts with a group of n units or objects and m variables, as shown below.

	Variables			
Objects	1	2	. . .	m
1				
2				
3				
.				
.				
.				
n				

Factor analysis attempts to reduce the number of columns, and clustering attempts to reduce the number of rows.

Factor analysis and cluster analysis are both "search" techniques. The researcher–decision maker does not typically have a clear *a priori* structure of the number of factors or clusters to be identified. Cutoff points with respect to stopping rules for the analyses are often ad hoc as the output becomes available. Even where the procedures and rules are stipulated in advance, the results are more descriptive than inferential.

FACTOR ANALYSIS

Factor analysis seeks to identify one or more underlying dimensions, given a set of variables. The basic approach relies on the following argument: "Variables that are highly correlated are getting at a common concept." Factor analysis combines correlated variables into new variables or factors. It proceeds sequentially, identifying first one factor and then proceeding to another.

Let us start with a simple illustration with only two variables, height and weight. Factor analysis is interested in summarizing these two variables into a single factor, retaining as much of the original information as possible. This is not a regression problem in which one variable is being estimated from knowledge of the other. Factor analysis, if successful, will substitute an overall measure of "size" in place of the two original variables of height and weight.

Figure 17.1 shows a scatter diagram of height and weight for ten persons. Our task is to establish a line on that graph which will minimize the dispersion of the points from the line. The least-squares criterion is typically used, but we now measure dispersion perpendicular to the line—neither variable is the dependent variable on which dispersion is minimized. The projections of the points onto the line also indicate the appropriate location of each individual for the new factor "size."

If height and weight were perfectly correlated, the ten points would lie on a single line. The ten individuals would occupy the same rank with respect to each of the variables. This is not the case. C is second in height but fifth in weight; I is lowest in weight but sixth in height. Each individual is uniquely

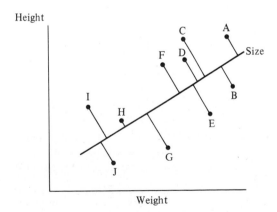

Fig. 17.1
Scatter diagram. Height and weight and the resulting factor of size.

placed with respect to the new dimension: C is third and I is ninth in this combined concept of size.

If a third variable of bone structure were introduced, factor analysis would attempt to combine all three into a single factor. This would, of course, require a three-dimensional graph to illustrate. Our concern with the output would be whether the three variables should be considered aspects of a single factor. This in turn would be shown by two considerations: (1) the comparison of the initial dispersion among all ten points (in three dimensions) and the dispersion of the points from the derived factor equation and (2) the extent to which all three variables are important in computing a score on the new factor. If more than one factor were derived from the data, we would revise our considerations slightly by determining whether each of the original variables were uniquely associated with one and only one factor.

The term "factor analysis" embraces a variety of techniques. Our discussion focuses on one procedure: principal-components analysis.[2] Interval scales are assumed for all variables; and the factors derived from the analysis are expressed as linear equations. These linear equations are of the form shown by Eq. (17.1)

$$F_i = a_{1i}x_1 + a_{2i}x_2 + a_{3i}x_3 + \cdots + a_{mi}x_m. \tag{17.1}$$

The i-factors are derived, and each variable appears in each equation. The a-coefficients indicate the importance of each variable with respect to a particular factor—a coefficient of zero indicating the variable is of no significance for that factor. In principal-components analysis, the factors are derived sequentially, using the criteria of maximum reduction in variance and noncorrelation among factors.[3]

The Data Matrix

A specific example will help explain factor analysis and the various parts of its output. A manufacturer of fabricating parts is interested in identifying the determinants of a successful salesperson. The manufacturer has on file the information shown in Table 17.1 for all of the salespeople and has used some of these variables in screening applicants in the past. An associate recently raised the question of whether some of these variables might not be expressions of the same underlying factor. The seven variables form a nonpartitioned set: none is a target dependent variable that is of major concern to the manager as important in and of itself. Factor analysis is an appropriate technique to use

---

[2]The reader interested in a technical analysis of the various procedures is referred to H. H. Harmon, 1960, *Modern Factor Analysis* (2nd ed.) (Chicago: University of Chicago Press), Paul Horst, 1965, *Factor Analysis of Data Matrices* (New York: Holt, Rinehart and Winston), and Donald F. Morrison, 1967, *Multivariate Statistical Methods* (New York: McGraw-Hill).

[3]When factors are uncorrelated, they are said to be orthogonal. Some procedures do not impose the criterion of uncorrelated factors.

Table 17.1
Data Matrix for Factor Analysis of Seven Variables (14 Salespeople)

Salesperson	Height (x_1)	Weight (x_2)	Education (x_3)	Age (x_4)	Number of children (x_5)	Size of household (x_6)	IQ (x_7)
1	67	155	12	27	0	2	102
2	69	175	11	35	3	6	92
3	71	170	14	32	1	3	111
4	70	160	16	25	0	1	115
5	72	180	12	36	2	4	108
6	69	170	11	41	3	5	90
7	74	195	13	30	1	2	114
8	68	160	16	32	1	3	118
9	70	175	12	45	4	6	121
10	71	180	13	24	0	2	92
11	66	145	10	39	2	4	100
12	75	210	16	26	0	1	109
13	70	160	12	31	0	3	102
14	71	175	13	43	3	5	112

in order to determine whether these seven variables can be reduced to two or three factors.

Looking at Table 17.1, we might first attempt to discover a single underlying factor for all seven variables. Such an attempt would meet with very limited success because the variables do not possess uniformly high correlations with one another or with some single underlying factor. Nevertheless factor analysis would attempt to determine a single linear equation that did the best job possible. A better approach might be to permit two, three, or more factors. Intuition might suggest the presence of at least three primary factors: physical size as shown by height and weight, a maturity factor revealed in age/children/size of household, and intelligence or training as revealed by education and IQ. An ideal solution for the data in Table 17.1 using three factors would be

$$F_1 = 1.0x_4 + 1.0x_5 + 1.0x_6,$$
$$F_2 = 1.0x_1 + 1.0x_2,$$
$$F_3 = 1.0x_3 + 1.0x_7,$$

with all coefficients other than those presented equal to zero. With actual data, this ideal solution would not be obtained and each factor would possess seven coefficients all of which are nonzero and nonunity.

The first factor identified by principal-component analysis is selected on the criterion of reducing variance as much as possible. Thus one cannot know with certainty the general nature of the first factor that will be identified. The first factor derived from a somewhat similar set of data for an analogous sample could be totally different. Similarity of factors is evident from the similarity of coefficients rather than from the fact that it was the first factor derived. Another consequence of the criterion of reducing variance means that the coefficients need not approach zero or unity. They may have intermediate values of $+.4$, $-.5$, etc. Such coefficients complicate the interpretability of the factor since variables may be partially in one factor and partially in another. In such situations, it may be difficult to articulate and label the nature of the various factors derived. Further processing may be required to yield results that are more easily interpreted.

Another possibility, using the variables of Table 17.1, is that one of the variables is not reflected in any of the first three factors. For example, IQ might be missing. In this case the coefficient associated with x_7 would be small for all three factors.

Factor Analysis Results

The overriding concern in factor analysis is, "What are the factors?" The factor equations summarize this result. The number of equations clearly shows the number of factors derived, and the coefficients indicate which variables are most important for the various factors. Several other terms help identify various aspects of the results of factor analysis.

Factor loadings. The coefficients in the factor equations are called the "factor loadings." These loadings have a lower limit of -1.0 and an upper limit of $+1.0$.[4] The absolute value shows the strength of the relationship; the sign merely aids in assigning a name to the factor.

Communality. In the ideal solution, the factors derived will explain 100 percent of the variance in each of the original variables. "Communality" measures the percentage of the variance in the original variables that is captured by the combination of factors in the solution. Thus a communality is computed for each of the original variables. Each variable's communality might be thought of as showing the extent to which it is revealed by the system of factors.

Variance summarized. Factor analysis employs the criterion of maximum reduction of variance—variance found in the initial set of variables. Each factor contributes to the reduction. The percentage of the initial variance associated with (or removed by) each factor is shown under the label "variance summarized."

---

[4] These limits apply only if the calculations are based upon a data matrix of correlation coefficients.

Factor scores. Numerical values can be computed on each factor for the individual units by substituting in equations of the form Eq. (17.1). The calculated values will show the extent to which each unit possesses each factor. These factor scores, rather than the original variables, can then serve as the appropriate input data in other analyses.

The use of factor scores instead of the original variables accomplishes two purposes. (1) It reduces the number of variables. This both simplifies the computations and facilitates the interpretation of results. (2) It avoids the problem of multicollinearity since the factors are uncorrelated.

Interpretation of Numerical Results

Good research procedure focuses on *possible* research results in the planning stage. Let us consider several possibilities for the salespeople data; three are presented in Table 17.2. Three-factor equations are given in each section.

Table 17.2(a) reveals a perfect solution, each variable having a factor loading of 1.0 on one factor and 0.0 on the other two factors. The communality is 1.0 for each of the seven variables, and the total variance summarized is 100 percent. The negative factor loadings for Factor I suggest that the factor is youth rather than maturity, but the negative signs in no way detract from the perfect solution. We trust that the opposite signs for education and IQ are an unlikely result, but it would mean that they are inversely correlated. Factor I, made up of three variables, summarizes a larger portion of the variance than the other two factors (43 percent versus 29 percent for both II and III).

Table 17.2
Hypothetical Results of Factor Analysis with Seven Variables.
Salespeople Characteristics

Variable	Factor			Communality
	I	II	III	
Height	0	1	0	1
Weight	0	1	0	1
Education	0	0	−1	1
Age	−1	0	0	1
Number of children	−1	0	0	1
Size of household	−1	0	0	1
IQ	0	0	1	1
Sum of squares	3	2	2	1
Variance summarized	.4286	.2857	.2857	1.0000
		(a)		

(continued)

Table 17.2
(continued)

| | Factor | | | |
Variable	I	II	III	Communality
Height	+ .12	+ .92	− .05	.8633
Weight	+ .05	+ .87	+ .02	.7598
Education	− .07	+ .04	+ .96	.9281
Age	+ .85	+ .15	+ .21	.7891
Number of children	+ .73	− .06	− .07	.5414
Size of household	+ .61	+ .02	− .03	.3734
IQ	− .13	+ .07	+ .25	.0843
Sum of squares	1.6662	1.6363	1.0369	
Variance summarized	.2380	.2338	.1481	.6199

(b)

| | Factor | | | |
Variable	I	II	III	Communality
Height	+ .03	− .95	− .02	.9038
Weight	+ .01	− .97	+ .03	.9419
Education	− .02	+ .04	+ .85	.7245
Age	+ .86	− .07	− .04	.7461
Number of children	+ .75	− .03	+ .02	.5638
Size of household	+ .93	+ .01	− .01	.8651
IQ	− .02	− .04	+ .77	.5949
Sum of squares	2.1688	1.8525	1.3188	
Variance summarized	.3098	.2646	.1884	.7629

(c)

The principal difference between Table 17.2(b) and (c) appears in Factor III. In Table 17(b), only education has a heavy factor loading on this factor while in Table 17(c) both education and IQ have relatively large loadings. The results of Table 17(b) also show that none of the factors reflect IQ to any appreciable extent and that most of the variation in size of household in the original data remains even after introducing the three factors (a communality of only 37.34 percent). The amount of variance summarized by the three factors of Table 17.2(b) is approximately 62 percent, with factor I accounting for 23.8 percent of that variance.

Table 17.2(c) shows a total of 76 percent of the variance summarized by the three factors and a communality of over 50 percent for each of the seven variables. The results of (c) also show factor loadings that are uniformly closer to unity or zero than was the case in (b). The negative coefficients for height and weight in Factor II have no significance except in the label assigned to the factor. In (b) this label might be physical size while in (c) the label might be lack of physical size.

Alternative Data Inputs

Factor equations can be derived either from the data in their original units or from standard scores. Use of the original units has the potential disadvantage of giving greater weights to variables for which the absolute dispersion is the greatest—regardless of how arbitrary the units might be and regardless of how noncomparable the units of the different variables might be.[5] Conversion of all variables to standard scores eliminates much of this difficulty since all units are then in number of standard deviations above or below the mean. Most computer programs accept the data in the original units, transforming them into standard scores prior to the factor analysis.[6]

The salespeople data have been analyzed by the SAS program.[7] This program accepts data in the original units, automatically transforming them into standard scores. The results are presented in the next section.

Principal-component Factors

The three factors derived from the salespeople data by a principal-components analysis (SAS program) are presented in Table 17.3. Factor I accounts for 51.6 percent of the total variance (of the seven variables); Factor II, for 26.4 percent; and Factor III, for 16.5 percent. Together the three factors "explain" almost 95 percent of the variance, and the communality is over 85 percent for every variable. Thus the three factors seem to capture the underlying dimensions involved in these variables—not perfectly but better than either of the two nonperfect sets of hypothetical results.

The meaning of the individual factors is not at all clear, however. In this respect, the actual results are inferior to the hypothetical results. None of the variables have near zero loadings on Factor I. In its present form it is a conglomerate, almost defying interpretation. The largest factor loadings apply to age, number of children, and size of family. But education has a loading of .8, and both height and weight have loadings of approximately .5. Factor II is also

---

[5]Different factor equations would result by switching one of the variables to meters instead of inches because the absolute dispersion would be changed. Also, while composite measures of dispersion using inches, pounds, dollars, and a few other units can be computed, the appropriateness of such measures is suspect.

[6]Use of a correlation matrix as input data yields the same factor equations as does use of standard scores. The choice between the two is largely determined by convenience, preliminary analyses performed, and programming ease.

[7]Anthony James Barr and James Howard Goodnight, 1972, *A User's Guide to the Statistical Analysis System* (Raleigh, N.C.: Sparks Press), pp. 201–207.

Table 17.3
Three-factor Results with Seven Variables. Salespeople Characteristics

	Factor			
Variable	I	II	III	Communality
Height	.59038	.72170	−.30331	.96140
Weight	.45256	.75932	−.44273	.97738
Education	.80252	.18513	.42631	.86006
Age	−.86689	.41116	.18733	.95564
Number of children	−.84930	.49247	.05883	.96730
Size of household	−.92582	.30007	−.01953	.94756
IQ	.28761	.46696	.80524	.94918
Sum of squares	3.61007	1.85136	1.15709	
Variance summarized	.51572	.26448	.16530	.94550

a mixture. No loadings are as much as .8, but only education falls below .2. Factor III is only slightly less confusing.

Principal-components analysis makes no attempt to establish factor equations that have loadings that are near unity or near zero. It merely solves for a first factor that reduces variance as much as possible. If variables are correlated, they tend to appear in the same factor equations even if the correlations and conceptual similarities are limited. Interpretability of factors is facilitated when individual factor loadings are either high or low. The rotation of axes, after a principal-components analysis has been performed as a first step, is designed to yield this result.

Rotation of Axes[8]

The interpretability problem is illustrated in Fig. 17.2 that shows the factor loadings for eight variables on two factors. Each of the eight variables has moderately large loadings on each of the two factors (I and II). If the axes are rotated to positions I' and II', the variables now show large loadings for only one factor and near zero loadings on the other factor.

SAS uses a varimax rotation which retains the communality of each variable although the portion of variance accounted for by the separate factors is modified.[9] This is an obvious result since the amount of variance a factor

---

[8]An excellent short discussion of varimax and quartimax rotations is included in a series of papers in David A. Aaker, 1971, *Multivariate Analysis in Marketing: Theory and Application* (Belmont, Calif.: Wadsworth), pp. 205–257.

[9]H. F. Kaiser, 1958, The varimax criterion for analytic rotation in factor analysis, *Psychometrika* **23:** 187–200.

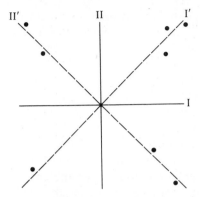

Fig. 17.2
Scatter diagram before and after rotation in factor analysis.

accounts for will be revised depending on the number of variables with high
loadings after the rotation.

Table 17.4 gives the SAS output for the salespeople data after the axes
have been rotated. Six of the seven variables are now uniquely associated with
a single factor. The factors are very similar to those hypothesized: Factor I for
maturity and Factor II for physical size. Factor III does not capture as much
of education as expected although the loading for IQ is quite high. Education
also poses a problem by the moderate loadings on Factors I and II. The rotation has reduced the portion of variance summarized by Factor I (52 percent to

Table 17.4
Rotated Factor Matrix. Salespeople Characteristics

Variable	Factor		
	I	II	III
Height	.16278	.94616	.19922
Weight	.03855	.98669	.04832
Education	.55183	.26358	.69719
Age	−.96809	−.12943	.04105
Number of children	−.98308	.00303	−.03414
Size of household	−.94266	−.13835	−.19953
IQ	−.06694	.08517	.96822
Variance summarized	.44703	.28306	.21546

45 percent) while increasing the portion summarized by the other two factors. Principal-components analysis selected Factor I so that it eliminated as much variance as possible. Rotation tried to establish more easily interpretable factors, preserving the total variance summarized but not concerned for how much was associated with each separate factor.

Factor scores for each individual sales person may be obtained by substituting standard scores on the seven original variables into the three equations of Table 17.4. The calculated factor scores (1) enable comparison of individuals on these three factors and (2) provide input data as potential independent variables in predicting performance by salespeople on various characteristics. Use of these factor scores as independent variables eliminates the problem of multicollinearity since the factor analysis solution yields factors that are uncorrelated.[10]

Assume we have two salespeople with the standard scores indicated in Table 17.5. Sales person 15 has a factor score on Factor I of $.16278(1.3) + .03855(0.9) + .55183(0.4) - .96809(-1.5) - .98308(-1.3) - .94266(-1.6) - .06694(0.7) = 4.6586$ and a factor score on Factor II of $.94616(1.3) + .98669(0.9) + .26358(0.4) - .12943(-1.5) + .00303(-1.3) - .13835(-1.6) + .08517(0.7) = 2.6946$. What is sales person 15's factor score on Factor III? What are sales person 16's three factor scores? These new scores as well as the analogous scores for the other 14 salespeople could serve as three independent variables for use in predicting sales performance. The dependent variable (sales performance) is not a part of this factor analysis but would come from some other source.

Table 17.5
Input Data in Standard Scores for Two Salespeople

	Sales person 15	Sales person 16
Height	+1.3	-0.2
Weight	+0.9	+0.1
Education	+0.4	-1.2
Age	-1.5	+0.8
Number of children	-1.3	+0.9
Size of household	-1.6	+0.5
IQ	+0.7	-0.9

[10]Nonorthogonal factors are derived in some programs. Such factors might then be further factor analyzed in higher order analyses. See Y. Wind, P. E. Green, and A. K. Jain, 1973, Higher order factor analysis in the classification of psychographic variables, *Journal of the Market Research Society* **15**: 224–232.

Subjective Issues

There are many aspects of factor analysis that are more an art than a science. Among the various questions that must be answered in a rather subjective manner are the following. (1) How many factors should be employed in attempting to reduce the data? This question involves not only how many factors should be employed, but also what criterion should be used in establishing that number. Should the number of factors bear some relationship to the number of original variables? Should factors be added until the percentage of variance explained reaches a stated level? (2) Should factor rotation be employed? A principal-component solution may be somewhat ambiguous with respect to the meaning of the factors discerned. Various types of rotation may be employed in order to clarify these underlying factors. Since several types of rotation are available, the selection of the appropriate rotation is largely subjective. Closely related to this decision is the question of whether the factors should be independent of each other or whether one might permit nonzero correlation among the factors.[11] (3) The labeling of the factors is purely intuitive and subjective. If three variables have high loadings on the same factor, the analyst must "intuit" what is common and therefore identify the nature of the underlying factor. What is a proper name for age, number of children, and size of household? (4) What are the proper input data? Our discussion has stressed input data of standard scores. Alternatively the input data could be in the original units. Since the criterion for solution is reduction of variance, this would mean that variables with the larger variances would be given greater weight in the determination of the solution.

These issues are present in every factor analysis and must be answered before a solution can be obtained. Disagreements exist among practitioners, and what is appropriate for one problem may be inappropriate for another. The solution obtained is appropriate only if one is convinced that the right subjective decisions have been made among alternative courses.

The factor equations derived by principal components are unaffected by the addition of other factors. This is not true of the factor equations determined after the rotation of axes. Thus the meaning of the factors, their loadings, and factor scores are all dependent upon the answers to these highly subjective questions.

Perfect or near perfect reduction of a set of variables to a few factors does not assure relevance of those factors for a marketing manager. The manager's interest in selecting good salespeople, products, or territories may or may not be improved by a reduction of m variables to k factors. The testing of the factors, perhaps using factor scores, must be made against the appropriate dependent variable—sales performance in the case of the salespeople.

[11]L. L. Thurstone, 1947, *Multiple Factor Analysis* (Chicago: University of Chicago Press) and David A. Aaker, *loc. cit.*

Introduction of sales performance as an eighth variable to be used in factor analysis would be an inappropriate procedure. Such a procedure would be addressed to the question of which other variables have loadings on the same factor as the criterion variable. The answer to this question might give some additional insight to the prediction and screening problem, but it is not a well-structured problem permitting the prediction or estimation of a designated dependent variable. The problem would be even more complicated if the loading factors did not approach zero and unity.

Hypothesis Testing and Factor Analysis

Factor analysis, although basically a search procedure, can incorporate elements of hypothesis testing. The testing normally requires a creative approach and uses the results of the factor analysis as input into a subsequent analysis. But the pessimistic note of, "Factor analysis is . . . an exploratory technique, to be used when one happens to know nothing about the subject matter,"[12] is much too sweeping.

Readership or viewing behavior may be studied by factor analytic methods in an attempt to identify "types" of articles, programs, or advertisements. If no *a priori* hypotheses are proposed or no testing procedures are established, the results must of necessity be purely descriptive. If the researcher provides no research design or test, we should not be surprised to find that the analysis implies a lack of knowledge concerning substantive matters—none of that knowledge (if it existed) was incorporated in the design. But this need not be the case!

Jones and Siller studied audience exposure to the specific content of a particular newspaper, testing their hypothesized model by factor analysis.[13] The thrust of their thesis is that newspaper exposure is selective rather than general. They hypothesized that portions of the newspaper having similar content would have their highest loadings on the same factor. They divided the newspaper into sections, retaining only four in their experiment: business, public affairs, sports, and women's sections. Each page within these stated sections was divided into quarters, and only those quarters that matched the section in content analysis were used for the research. Seventy-four quarter pages were retained. Respondents reported whether they had looked at each quarter page. These responses were then subjected to a factor analysis with rotation.

Four factors were extracted, each a 74-variable linear function. The number of factors was based on the *a priori* classification into four sections. A portion of the factor loadings is presented in Table 17.6.

---

[12]A. S. C. Ehrenberg, 1968, On methods: the factor analytic search for program types, *Journal of Advertising Research* **8**: 58.

[13]Vernon J. Jones and Fred H. Siller, 1978, Factor analysis of media exposure data using prior knowledge of the medium, *Journal of Marketing Research* **15**: 137–144.

Table 17.6
Comparison of *A Priori* and Empirical Assignment to Factors. Newspaper Exposure†

Quarter page number	*A priori* classification	Factor loadings			
		Factor I	Factor II	Factor III	Factor IV
1	Sports	− .24	− .16	.65(S)	− .12
2	Sports	− .23	− .17	.62(S)	− .09
3	Business	− .64(B)	− .02	.20	.04
4	Business	− .74(B)	− .11	.19	.02
5	Business	− .59(B)	− .16	.16	.05
.					
.					
.					
10	Public affairs	− .33	− .41(P)	.08	.16
.					
.					
.					
20	Business	− .27	− .48(B)	.15	.02
.					
.					
.					
74	Women's pages	− .01	− .18	.04	.75(W)

†Source: Vernon J. Jones and Fred H. Siller, 1978, Factor analysis of media exposure data using prior knowledge of the media, *Journal of Marketing Research* **15**: 137–144.

The critical question is the largest factor loading for each quarter page. For example, Factor III received the largest loading from the first quarter page (*a priori* classification of sports). The overall results from the 74 variables showed the following.

Factor	Number of variables with largest loading
I	26 (all business)
II	23 (all except two public affairs)
III	15 (all except one sports)
IV	10 (all women's pages)

The factor analysis demonstrates that four distinct patterns exist among readers in their exposure to the newspaper content, corresponding to both the structure established by the newspaper itself and that hypothesized by Jones and Siller. The actual test of the hypothesis employed a series of 2×2 contingency tables.[14] The significance of the results, according to the authors, is that newspaper audience measures are too gross. They argue that meaningful exposure should be calculated according to the separate sections of the paper.

A second general problem that can be tested within a factor-analysis approach is the comparison of two groups. Such studies could apply to the underlying factors that make up attitudes or that comprise purchasing motives. Anderson and Engledow have compared United States and German subscribers to product-testing magazines.[15] Their basic approach was to use essentially the same data collection instrument on each group and to factor analyze both sets of data.[16] The resulting factors for the two groups were then compared. Herein lies the crux of whether a valid test is performed or whether data descriptions are obtained. If ad hoc procedures are adopted after inspecting the data, no valid inferences are possible.

Anderson and Engledow compared the United States and German factors by computing coefficients of congruence for the seemingly similar factors.[17] Their general conclusion is that "there is considerable evidence of similarity in cognitive structure" although "the groups are far from identical." Out of 60 total variables, 47 loaded significantly in Germany versus 38 in the United States. Brand and brand reputation occupy more important roles in the United States. In Germany, advertising is perceived as part of the external information source while it is a separate source in the United States.

The split-half approach as a way of turning a search technique into an inferential base can be applied even when only one group is involved. Care must be exercised, however, that a proper basis for testing or comparing be established in advance. Some version of the contingency table, and often the 2×2 variety, can usually be constructed with a little forethought.

One procedure is to classify each variable with respect to the magnitude of its loading factor on a particular function; for example, greater than .5 or not. A 2×2 contingency table can then be constructed for pairs of factors—one from each of the two split halves. The resulting tables would be similar to that given as Table 17.7. This table indicates that five of the 20 variables had factor loadings in excess of .5 for the factor function in question (first half of

---

[14]*Ibid.* The actual research employed two separate panels, thus replicating the experiment. All eight contingency tables rejected the null hypothesis at the .001 level of significance. The portion of total variance removed by the four factors was 50.4 percent and 44.9 percent for the two panels.

[15]Ronald Anderson and Jack Engledow, 1977, A factor analytic comparison of United States and German information seekers, *Journal of Consumer Research* 3: 185–196.

[16]Their approach was a two-step factor analysis. Approximately 20 factors were derived at the first step. These first-order factors were then reduced to seven second-order factors at the second step. Our discussion is limited to the second-order factors.

[17]See Anderson and Engledow, *op. cit.*, and Bard Korth and L. R. Tucker, 1975, The distribution of chance congruence coefficients from simulated data, *Psychometrika*: **40**: 361–372.

Table 17.7
Contingency Table for Testing Factor Similarity by Split-half Approach

First half	Second half	
	Factor loading > .5	Factor loading < .5
Factor loading > .5	4	1
Factor loading < .5	2	13
	6	14

sample). Four of these five variables also had factor loadings in excess of .5 using the second half of the sample. Two other variables that did not exceed .5 in the first half of the sample reached that mark in the second half.

A separate table would be prepared for each pair of functions although the number of variables to be classified would be the same for each table. Of course an element of subjectivity remains in matching the functions into pairs since the analysis does not uniquely identify or name the various functions. There is also the possibility that the functions derived from the two halves are dissimilar.

CLUSTER ANALYSIS

Whereas factor analysis seeks for similarity among variables or a reduction in the number of variables, cluster analysis seeks for similarity among the units or subjects studied. Graphically, factor analysis reduces variance among points in n-dimensional space by projecting the points onto a series of lines (the factor equations). Clustering takes the same points in n-dimensional space and places them into subgroups with each subgroup as homogeneous as possible—homogeneity being determined by how close the points within each subgroup are to each other.

Let us start with a simple two-variable problem. An investment analyst selects a sample of ten securities, determining the current yield (annual dividend/market price) and the growth rate (average annual change in earnings per share) for each security. The resulting scatter diagram is shown in Fig. 17.3. Three subgroups are formed, three securities in groups A and B and four securities in C. The clusters consist of securities that are as similar as possible on both variables simultaneously. Subgroup C contains securities that have high yields but low growth rates. Subgroup A is made up of low yield/high growth securities, and subgroup B securities occupy intermediate positions in both variables.

Cluster analysis can be considered as somewhat analogous to stratification in sampling. Differences *among* subgroups should be large, and differ-

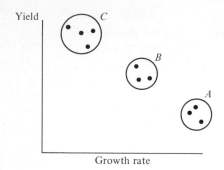

Fig. 17.3
Scatter diagram. Yields and growth
rates and the resulting clusters.

ences *within* subgroups should be small. In stratification within- and among-
stratum differences are measured by variance on a *single* variable; in cluster
analysis, the differences are measured simultaneously on more than one variable. The rationale and steps in clustering are precisely the same as in stratification: (1) a central tendency for the entire group is the reference point from
which differences among subgroups is determined and (2) a series of central
tendencies—one for each subgroup—comprises the reference points from
which within-subgroup differences are determined. The arithmetic mean is the
appropriate reference point concept for one dimension. The centroid—an
n-dimensional mean—is the appropriate reference point for *n* dimensions.

Euclidean distance in *n*-dimensional space is given by Eq. (17.2) where d_{ij}
is the distance between point i and point j, v refers to a particular variable, and
m is the number of variables.

$$d_{ij} = \left[\sum_{v=1}^{m} (x_{iv} - x_{jv})^2 \right]^{1/2} \tag{17.2}$$

For the ten-security problem of Fig. 17.3, m is two. Comparisons would be
made with respect to both yield and growth rate, v referring first to one and
then to the other. Several relevant distances would be obtained by Eq. (17.2):
(1) distance of the points (securities) within each subgroup from the centroid
of the respective subgroups, (2) distance of the subgroup centroids from the
total group centroid (all ten points combined), (3) distance between any two
points, and (4) distance of the individual points from the total group centroid.

The overall effectiveness of the clustering is determined by comparing the
sum of the within-cluster variances with the original total variance.[18] The

---

[18]Alternative measures of distance could be employed if deemed appropriate. "City-block" distance uses the absolute value of differences rather than squared differences. Quite dissimilar measures are required with noninterval scales. These measures are discussed later in the present chapter.

measure of homogeneity is obviously dependent on the units in which the original variables are expressed and the choice of those variables. As in factor analysis, standard scores can be employed instead of the original units. In this procedure, each variable will be given approximately the same weight in determining the overall variance.

Clustering of salespeople, using the data from Table 17.1, would attempt to group together those salespeople who are most similar with respect to the seven variables under consideration. How many groups should we use? The two extremes are a single group containing all 14 salespeople and 14 separate groups, each containing a single sales person. Neither extreme requires further data manipulation, but neither one yields any additional insight. Clustering, dealing as it does with nonpartitioned data, does not introduce a dependent variable that could serve as the criterion for appropriateness of the subgroups. Therefore the question simply asks which of many possible cluster arrangements results in the most homogeneous groupings—using these seven variables.

A variety of criteria and procedures exists for the formation of clusters. The hierarchical methods are intuitively appealing and permit useful discussion of cluster analysis in general.[19] Application of the BMDP2M program[20] (a hierarchical approach) to the salespeople data of Table 17.1 starts with 14 points corresponding to the 14 salespeople. The next step is to calculate interpoint distances between each pair of points, 91 such distances in the present example. These distances are given as a portion of the BMDP2M output (see Table 17.8).

The two points that are the closest together in this seven-dimensional space are placed together as the first step in the program: salespeople 6 and 2 in this case with a distance of 1.122. Line 1 of Table 17.9 shows the result of this amalgamation. The first two columns of the table identify that this first step in the program has an interpoint distance of 1.122. Columns 3 through 9 give the coordinates of the seven-dimensional centroid for this group of two, showing the mean with respect to each variable. The last column indicates the number of points that have been joined to form the subgroup at this stage—two for the first step.

The next step in the program may either (1) join a third point to the initial subgroup or (2) form a second subgroup of two. The criterion in determining which alternative to select is again interpoint distance. As shown by Table 17.9, the second step is a new cluster based upon two points. The interpoint

---

[19]Other approaches and criterion are discussed later. Detailed discussion is found in G. H. Ball and D. J. Hall, 1968, Background information on clustering techniques, Working Paper, Stanford Research Institute, Menlo Park, California.

[20]W. J. Dixon and M. B. Brown (eds.), 1977, *Biomedical Computer Programs, P-Series* (Berkeley, Calif.: University of California Press), pp. 322–336.

Table 17.8
Computer Printout from BMDP2M/Cluster Analysis—Interpoint Distances

INITIAL DISTANCES BETWEEN CASES

CASE NUMBER	1	2	3	4	5	6	7
1	0.0	3.87	2.60	2.82	3.46	3.89	4.04
2	3.87	0.0	3.48	5.33	2.52	1.12	4.43
3	2.60	3.48	0.0	2.17	1.70	3.56	2.13
4	2.82	5.33	2.17	0.0	3.83	5.40	3.30
5	3.46	2.52	1.70	3.83	0.0	2.60	2.19
6	3.89	1.12	3.56	5.40	2.60	0.0	4.58
7	4.04	4.43	2.13	3.30	2.19	4.58	0.0
8	2.91	4.44	1.85	1.93	3.25	4.49	3.66
9	5.23	3.39	3.70	5.57	2.76	3.36	4.46
10	2.52	3.82	2.54	3.11	3.09	4.02	2.90
11	2.86	2.81	3.71	4.97	3.51	2.44	5.26
12	5.17	5.92	3.50	3.69	4.05	6.09	2.20
13	1.51	3.21	1.71	2.85	2.33	3.22	3.11
14	4.32	2.73	2.54	4.55	1.61	2.59	3.44

	8	9	10	11	12	13	14
1	2.91	5.23	2.52	2.86	5.17	1.51	4.32
2	4.44	3.39	3.82	2.81	5.92	3.21	2.73
3	1.85	3.70	2.54	3.71	3.50	1.71	2.54
4	1.93	5.57	3.11	4.97	3.69	2.85	4.55
5	3.25	2.76	3.09	3.51	4.03	2.33	1.61
6	4.49	3.36	4.02	2.44	6.09	3.22	2.59
7	3.66	4.46	2.90	5.26	2.20	3.11	3.44
8	0.0	4.15	3.78	4.02	4.55	2.83	3.33
9	4.15	0.0	5.68	3.95	6.24	4.47	1.48
10	3.78	5.68	0.0	4.46	3.41	2.07	4.43
11	4.02	3.95	4.46	0.0	6.93	2.89	3.53
12	4.55	6.24	3.41	6.93	0.0	4.46	5.10
13	2.83	4.47	2.07	2.89	4.46	0.0	3.37
14	3.33	1.48	4.43	3.53	5.10	3.37	0.0

distance between these two points is 1.475. Reference to Table 17.8 shows that salespeople 9 and 14 differ by this amount. The first five steps with the salespeople data each result in the formation of two-person subgroups. At step 6, a three-person subgroup is formed. At step 8, two subgroups of three each are combined into a six-person subgroup. The process continues until all 14 are combined at the last step.

Table 17.9
Computer Printout from BMDP2M/Cluster Analysis—Amalgamation Order

EACH ROW CONTAINS THE VALUES OF VARIABLES FOR THE CLUSTER FORMED BY THE AMALGAMATION OF THE GIVEN ORDER. (THE LAST COLUMN REPRESENTS THE SUM OF CLUSTER CASE WEIGHTS.)

AMALGAMATION ORDER	DIST.	HT	WT	ED	AGE	CHILD	SIZE	IQ	
1	1.122	-0.494	0.022	-0.994	0.693	1.124	1.267	-1.512	2.000
2	1.475	0.116	0.172	-0.221	1.576	1.481	1.267	1.034	2.000
3	1.509	-0.698	-0.882	-0.479	-0.630	-1.021	-0.507	-0.414	2.000
4	1.699	0.523	0.172	0.037	0.105	0.051	0.084	0.335	2.000
5	1.929	-0.494	-0.731	1.583	-0.704	-0.664	-0.802	1.034	2.000
6	1.987	0.863	0.573	0.037	-0.091	-0.068	-0.211	0.485	3.000
7	2.182	-0.359	-0.430	-0.307	-0.876	-1.021	-0.605	-0.747	3.000
8	2.411	0.252	0.072	-0.135	-0.483	-0.545	-0.408	-0.131	6.000
9	2.394	0.065	-0.129	0.295	-0.538	-0.575	-0.507	0.160	8.000
10	2.574	-0.901	-0.530	-1.166	0.742	0.885	0.971	-1.213	3.000
11	2.934	-0.494	-0.249	-0.788	1.076	1.124	1.089	-0.314	5.000
12	3.124	-0.150	-0.175	-0.122	0.082	0.079	0.107	-0.022	13.000
13	4.269	0.000	0.000	0.000	0.000	0.000	0.000	0.000	14.000

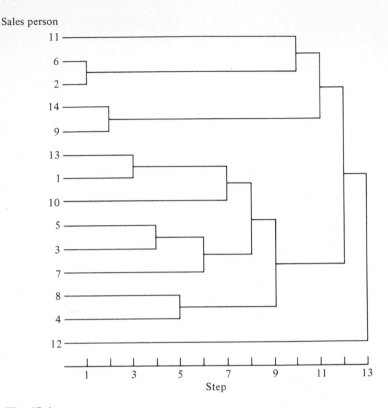

Fig. 17.4
Sequence of cluster formation.

The order of amalgamation is shown in Fig. 17.4, with the final step accomplished by joining sales person 12 to the subgroup of the other 13 salespeople. At next to the last step (step 12) these 13 were placed into a single group by combining a group of five (salespeople 11, 6, 2, 14, and 9) with a group of eight (salespeople 13, 1, 10, 5, 3, 7, 8, and 4).

The common question in clustering is how to describe the subgroups that exist at any stage in the process. The answer comes from two potential sources: (1) examination of the coordinates of the centroids or (2) impressionistic views concerning the members of the various subgroups. Let us illustrate the first approach by comparing the group of five salespeople with the group of eight.

Where are these two groups most dissimilar? Inspection of the centroids of Table 17.9 (as shown in lines 9 and 11 for these two subgroups) supplies the appropriate information. They differ by over 1.5 standard deviations on three variables (age, number of children, and household size) and by over 1.0 standard deviation on education. The group of eight is younger, has fewer children, has smaller households, and has more formal education. The relationship between this result and the result of the factor analysis is not coincidental. The variables with heavy loadings on the first factor are the most important in the establishment of clusters.

Should clusters be established primarily on the basis of a single factor, even if several variables manifest themselves in that factor? An alternative approach is to establish clusters using factor scores instead of the original variables. In the present illustration, centroids and distances would be computed using three dimensions—the three factors determined earlier. With this approach, the number of variables with heavy loadings on a single factor is not significant; each factor is weighted equally.

Critical Issues in Cluster Analysis

Cluster analysis, like factor analysis, is not a single technique but a variety of techniques. Therefore, the researcher cannot simply determine that cluster analysis is appropriate for the particular problem; the researcher must also select the specific set of procedures to be employed. The specific procedural questions must often be answered on rather arbitrary bases. The principal issues the researcher must consider are (1) the selection of relevant variables, (2) the transformation of input data, (3) the adoption of a distance or similarity measure, (4) the procedure for forming subgroups, and (5) "stopping rules."

The selection of relevant variables. The variables or factors selected for inclusion must reflect characteristics that have some relevance in the problems faced by the decision maker. Clustering has no dependent variable, but unless the clusters established differ in some respect that has decision-making implications, it is merely an academic exercise. Therefore it is important to anticipate how the clusters derived can be useful in future decisions. Unless potential logical links can be formed between the variables employed and future actions, the research is nothing more than a "fishing" expedition.

Cluster analysis concerned with potential market segments should stress those variables hypothesized as useful in that endeavor. If the marketing manager uses all the information on file—financial data, operating statistics, plus a variety of personal and historical data—clusters will be formed, but they will be formed on the basis of that diverse information. The utility of such clusters for marketing decisions may be suspect. Unless the manager can visualize how and why the input variables have relevance for the operations, the groups formed may lack action implications.

The transformation of input data. At least three main alternatives exist with respect to input data (even if all of the variables are intervally scaled): the original data, standard scores, or factor scores. The clusters identified often differ depending on which input is used. The original data are expressed in units that apply to each particular variable; dollars, inches, pounds, worker-weeks, etc. These units may be arbitrarily chosen, but a decision to use a week rather than a month may have a profound impact on the ultimate measure of distance. Most clustering does not base the analysis on the original units.

Both standard scores and factor scores overcome the arbitrary weighting of the original units. The choice between them depends on whether the researcher wishes equal weighting for each variable or for each factor. Standard scores correspond to the first, and factor scores correspond to the second. An input of factor scores also deals with the problem of correlated variables, but the researcher must determine whether that is a problem.

Assume a merchandising manager is concerned with store image and the identification of which stores have similar images. Thirty-five different variables are chosen for the analysis. A factor analysis reveals six main factors, but ten of the variables load heavily on a single factor labeled "Quality." A cluster analysis with standard score input will rely heavily on quality variables in establishing the clusters. A cluster analysis with factor score input will treat quality as no more important than the other five factors. The clusters resulting from the two analyses may be quite dissimilar.

Yet another problem occurs in the input data if some or all of the variables are nominally or ordinally scaled. Since Euclidean distances are not appropriate with such data, alternative measures of similarity or dissimilarity must be calculated, measures that are appropriate for the given data. The question at issue is not so much "what input data?" as "what proximity measure?" Preprocessing of data is necessary when the original data contain a mixture of scale types. Interval-scale data can always be downgraded to ordinal or nominal. Upgrading of lower scales may also be possible although the researcher must always be conscious of the additional assumptions introduced.

The adoption of a distance or similarity measure.[21] The usual distance measure with interval scale data is Euclidean distance.[22] This answer is not nearly as straightforward as it seems. The various axes may be either consciously or unconsciously weighted. We have already indicated the arbitrary weighting implicit when the original units are employed. A failure to extract all factors (using factor scores) introduces a system of 0/1 weighting; "1" for those factors extracted and "0" for the rest.

The usual justification for truncating the number of factors is that the first few are the only significant factors since they account for a large share of the initial variance. But they do not account for all the variance nor does each factor account for the same portion of that variance. If truncating the number

---

[21]See R. B. Cattell, 1952, The three basic factor analytic research designs—their interrelationships and derivatives, *Psychological Bulletin* **49:** 449–520; and William Stevenson, 1953, *The Study of Behavior* (Chicago: University of Chicago Press).

[22]Mahalanobis D^2 can also be utilized. See J. E. Overall, 1964, Note on multivariate methods for profile analysis, *Psychological Bulletin* **61:** 195–198.

of factors is rejected, two contrasting approaches are possible: (1) extract all factors and assign them all equal weights and (2) extract all factors but assign them unequal weights. Differential weights may be empirically derived (usually corresponding to the portion of variance summarized) or subjectively determined if a satisfactory *a priori* rationale has been established.

An alternative distance measure with interval scales is "city-block" distance. This approach uses the first power of differences rather than the square. The result is that large differences on isolated measures do not dominate the calculation as much as they do in Euclidean distance.

Inverse or *Q-type* factor analysis represents yet another approach to clustering. Ordinary or *R*-type factor analysis examines for similarity or correlation among variables. *Q*-type factor analysis examines for similarity among objects. Factor loadings are determined for each object with respect to each function extracted. Those objects with heavy loadings on the same function are judged to be similar, and they are placed together in distinct clusters. This procedures does not supply an output that actually makes the assignment; rather the researcher must make the assignment based on inspection of the results with ad hoc assignment rules where the proper assignment is ambiguous.

Interpoint distances can be computed only if input data are intervally scaled. With ordinal or nominal scales an alternative similarity measure is necessary. Bivariate correlation coefficients offer one alternative[23]—an alternative that is also possible with intervally scaled data. Nominal-scale input is usually handed in cluster analysis by a matching score based upon the degree of agreement.[24]

Consider the three firms in Table 17.10. Data have been collected on ten attributes. Some data were initially measured on interval scales and others on nominal scales. All have been reduced to dichotomous nominal classifications. A "1" within the table indicates that the firm possesses the given characteristic; a "0" indicates the absence of the characteristic.

One similarity measure is simply a count of the number of characteristics on which the firms "match." These measures are

$$\text{A \& B: } \frac{5}{10} = .5,$$

$$\text{A \& C: } \frac{6}{10} = .6, \text{ and}$$

$$\text{B \& C: } \frac{3}{10} = .3.$$

---

[23]See Chapter 19 for a general discussion of nonparametric methods and ordinal data.

[24]Interpoint distances can be calculated from nominal input with appropriate transformations, but attribute matching is the more typical approach. See J. C. Gower, 1966, Some distance properties of latent root and vector methods used in multivariate analysis, *Biometrika* **53**: 325–338.

Table 17.10
Attribute Similarity for Three Manufacturing Firms

	Firm		
Attribute	A	B	C
Corporate organization	1	1	1
Sales over $10 million	1	0	1
More than 200 employees	1	0	1
Operates a foreign office	1	0	0
Organized before World War II	0	0	1
More than three domestic plants	1	1	1
Return on investment over 15%	1	1	0
Shares traded on New York Stock Exchange	0	0	1
Earnings trend up 1973–1978	0	1	0
Separate president and board chairperson	1	0	1

An alternative approach is to emphasize possession of the characteristic and de-emphasize nonpossession of the characteristic. The resulting scores for Table 17.10 are .3 for A & B, .5 for A & C, and .2 for B & C.[25] This approach requires the researcher to defend the precise wording of the characteristic since the significance of a "1" is not interpreted as merely a rephrasing of the complementary statement. Since alternative similarity measures do not yield the same results, the researcher must carefully weigh the substantive implications of the various alternatives.[26]

The procedure for forming subgroups.[27] Our discussion has followed the *hierarchical* approach in forming subgroups. This approach uses a treelike structure, successively joining branches together as shown in Fig. 17.4. There are two distinct methods within the hierarchical approach: starting with the individual points and sequentially forming larger clusters (Fig. 17.4) or starting with the total and sequentially partitioning into smaller clusters. The criterion for partitioning is a measure of average within-cluster distance. Those clusters

---

[25]A variety of matching measures is available. See T. Joyce and C. Channon, 1966, Classifying market survey respondents, *Applied Statistics* **15**: 191–215, and R. R. Sokal and P. H. A. Sneath, 1963, *Principles of Numerical Taxonomy* (San Francisco: Freeman).

[26]A comparison of ten proximity measures and the empirical results obtained using a common data bank are given in Paul E. Green and Vithala R. Rao, 1969, A note on proximity measures and cluster analysis, *Journal of Marketing Research* **6**: 359–364.

[27]G. H. Ball and D. J. Hall, *op. cit.* The various procedures are discussed as are many modifications although the terminology is slightly different from that used here.

that are the best candidates for partitioning are those with the highest within-cluster variability, that is, the ones that are the least homogenous. The process proceeds until all points are identified as unit clusters.

Nonhierarchical methods These methods select one or more cluster centers as the starting points. Objects are then assigned to particular clusters using either minimum threshold distances or making assignments to the center nearest each object. In contrast to the hierarchical methods where the data determine the cluster centers, the researcher selects the centers in the nonhierarchical methods. Some programs using the nonhierarchical method assign objects to centers on a tentative basis subject to later revision while others remove the object from further processing once an assignment is made.

Connectivity methods Unlike either hierarchical or nonhierarchical methods, connectivity methods are based exclusively on interpoint distances between *objects* without regard to the centroids of the clusters. An object is added to a cluster if its distance from any member of the cluster is less than some threshold distance. Clusters are thus formed by "connecting" each new object to an object that has already been assigned to a cluster although the new object's connection with other members of the cluster may be strained.

High profile similarity methods These methods place objects that have high scores on the same characteristics or dimensions in the same clusters. Q-type factor analysis is illustrative of this approach. Clusters might also be formed from similarity measures like those discussed for Table 17.10. These methods are often highly subjective, and different researchers may reach different conclusions from the same data.

"Stopping rules" How many clusters should be established within a particular study? Should the number of objects within each cluster be uniform? These two questions establish the "stopping rules" for any particular cluster analysis.

The number of clusters may be stated directly or else some cutoff rule may be established that makes the number of clusters a function of the data. For example, a maximum average within-cluster distance could be established. No objects would be added to a cluster if their addition resulted in the violation of this cutoff. Increasing the number of clusters will automatically lower the average within-cluster distance. Therefore one must be cautious in claiming homogeneity of clusters—an obvious trade-off is implicit in the stopping rules established by the researcher.

Specification of an equal number of objects per cluster will produce a larger average within-cluster distance than will a procedure that explicitly minimizes that average (given the same number of clusters). The rationale for an equal number of objects per cluster lies in a model that divides the set of objects into groups of equal size. The researcher, if applying this rule, must defend the logic of this position in contrast to one that stresses a measure of maximum within-cluster homogeneity. Cluster programs based on clusters of equal size also tend to produce final clusters that are heterogeneous.[28]

Clustering and Segmentation

Clustering appears to be an attractive procedure addressed to market segmentation problems. However, it is all too obvious that market segmentation should not be established without reference to the product or service of interest. *A priori* establishment of the variables relevant for segmentation is only as good as the analyst's or decision maker's prior judgments.

Inclusion of the potential dependent variable as one of the nonpartitioned variables submitted for clustering poses the same hazard that it does in factor analysis. Assume that five potential variables (or factors) are submitted to a clustering program along with a dependent variable of product usage. The dependent variable is only one of six variables serving as the bases for establishing the clusters. There is no assurance that the resulting clusters will differ significantly in product usage. A much better method is to use a partitioned approach, recognizing that the problem falls into the mold of the techniques discussed earlier. Clustering on the basis of location in five-dimensional space against the dependent variable is one possible approach.

The critical question in market segmentation is "Which basis for grouping potential customers is most closely associated with differential response to the product–service offering?" Morrison has suggested that the variables used in clustering be weighted according to their importance, importance being judged subjectively by the decision maker.[29] He argues rather persuasively that the conscious introduction of weights is better than the naive assumption that each variable is equally important, even if an element of great subjectivity is present in the weights introduced. Testing whether different cluster groupings are generated by different weighting schemes would reveal how sensitive the results are to changes in the weights. The different clusterings could also be tested against product use or attitudes. This procedure is more of a search than an analysis, but any of the techniques discussed in earlier chapters would be appropriate depending on the type of scale assumed in the clustering and the measurement of the dependent variable.

Statistical Inferences

Attempts to draw statistical inferences from cluster analysis are made on very dubious theoretical bases. This weakness stems from two principal sources. First, valid statistical inference requires a specific null hypothesis. The general

---

[28]See Ronald E. Frank and Paul E. Green, 1968, Numerical taxonomy in marketing analysis: a review article, *Journal of Marketing Research* **5**: 83–94, for a helpful discussion of some of these issues.

[29]Donald G. Morrison, 1967, Measurement problems in cluster analysis, *Management Science* **13** (August): 775–780.

working hypothesis in cluster analysis seems to be that the data can be divided into homogeneous subgroups. This is possible with any set of data; thus it is not a hypothesis. Second, the clusters are established on the basis of the data, not specified apart from the data. A description generated by the data cannot be tested by the same data.

The researcher might perform tests for consistency in clusters generated by alternative clustering programs. This approach can take either of two forms. (1) Different proximity measures or different programs could be applied to the same data set.[30] (2) Ad hoc tests can be established in which results are obtained from subsets of the data. These subsets may be based upon partial coverage either of the objects or of the variables. The test compares the resulting clusters for consistency. The researcher must be careful in the interpretation of the result because inherent differences between the subsets may limit the appropriateness of the test.

The marketing manager–researcher is well advised to consider cluster analysis as a search technique, most useful in exploratory studies and for descriptions. The technique is capable of aiding in the formulation of classification schemes. It is not at present well suited to the testing of those schemes.

Cluster Analysis as Preprocessing

A number of studies have used cluster analysis as an initial stage in marketing research studies. This approach establishes clusters as homogeneous groups and then determines whether these groups differ significantly on other characteristics that have marketing significance to a specific firm or group of firms. Yet another area of application for cluster analysis has appeared in the design of marketing experiments and surveys.

Greeno, Sommers, and Kernan combine cluster analysis with ANOVA in studying the relationship between personality and behavior.[31] Housewives are sorted into six clusters based on their self-image toward 38 different products. These clusters are identified as Homemakers, Matriarchs, Variety Girls, Cinderellas, Glamour Girls, and Media-conscious Glamour Girls. Personality differences (using the Gordon Personal Profile) among clusters are then tested by ANOVA. Differences among those characteristics are also tested across clusters, using diverse techniques.

Claxton, Fry, and Portis follow a somewhat similar approach in a study of prepurchase information gathering.[32] Clusters are formed on the bases of

---

[30]Green and Rao, *op. cit.*

[31]Daniel W. Greeno, Montrose S. Sommers, and Jerome B. Kernan, 1973, Personality and implicit behavior patterns, *Journal of Marketing Research* **10**: 63–69. The study is more valuable for its methodology in combining cluster analysis with subsequent tests than it is for its substantive results that are largely conjectural.

[32]John D. Claxton, Joseph N. Fry, and Bernard Portis, 1974, A taxonomy of prepurchase information gathering patterns, *Journal of Consumer Research* **1**: 35–42.

prepurchase search activity, using both city-block distance with dichotomous data and Euclidean distance with interval scale data. The resulting clusters are then compared on demographic variables, search motivation, and selected behavioral variables. The study analyzes separately furniture buyers and appliance buyers, noting similarities and differences in the results.

Marketing experiments must guard against two dangers: (1) large, random forces because the test objects are dissimilar and (2) nonrepresentativeness because the test objects are drawn from a unique subgroup. Day and Heeler propose cluster analysis as a means of avoiding both extremes. They cluster the test objects (stores in their case) on relevant variables and then sample from each cluster, the sample size from each cluster corresponding to the number of treatments to be tested.[33]

SUMMARY

In this chapter we have considered only nonpartitioned data, data for which the variables are not separated into independent variables and dependent variables. A data matrix of the following type has been considered.

Objects	Variables			
	1	2	. . .	m
1	x_{11}	x_{21}		x_{m1}
2	x_{12}	x_{22}	. . .	x_{m2}
.	.	.		.
.	.	.		.
.	.	.		.
n	x_{1n}	x_{2n}	. . .	x_{mn}

Two different types of questions have been raised. (1) Can the number of variables be reduced to a few factors without unduly sacrificing the amount of information provided? (2) Can the objects be placed into homogeneous subgroups, thereby permitting the analysis of the groups instead of requiring detailed study of each object?

The first question asks whether some of the columns are redundant and can be combined, thus collapsing the data matrix. A reduction of this type has two possible benefits: the data can be handled more expeditiously and the nature of the underlying system may be better comprehended. The second

---

[33]George S. Day and Roger M. Heeler, 1971, Using cluster analysis to improve marketing experiments, *Journal of Marketing Research* **8:** 340–347. See also Paul E. Green, Ronald E. Frank, and Patrick J. Robinson, 1967, Cluster analysis in test market selection, *Management Science* **13:** B387–400.

question asks whether the data matrix can be reduced by combining rows. Factor-analysis techniques attempt to reduce m variables to k factors ($k < m$). If m variables are summarized by two factors, the resulting two factors can be expressed in the form of the following equations:

$$F_1 = a_{11}x_1 + a_{21}x_2 + \cdots + a_{m1}x_m.$$
$$F_2 = a_{12}x_1 + a_{22}x_2 + \cdots + a_{m2}x_m.$$

The a-coefficients are the factor loadings—indicating the degree to which each variable manifests a particular factor. The most desirable situation in terms of interpretation occurs when all of these factor loadings are close to unity or zero and when the factor loading for each variable is near unity on a single factor only. The labeling of the factor is a matter of substantive nature determined by what the analyst or decision maker conceives to be the underlying force common to those variables with high factor loadings on that factor. Factor scores may be computed for each object on each of the factors by substituting the values of the variables into the factor equations.

The input data for factor analysis may be either the original data, their standard scores, or a correlation matrix. The latter two yield identical results and are used in most computer programs since the units of the original data are normally noncomparable and arbitrary. The transformed variables also correspond more closely to an equal weighting concept.

The problem of multicollinearity among variables is eliminated in most factor-analysis programs by imposing the condition that the factors derived are uncorrelated. Thus factor scores can serve as input data to standard association techniques without concern for multicollinearity. The degree to which the set of factors preserves the variability of the original variables is shown by the *communality* of the individual variables and the *variance summarized* by the total set of factors.

Interpretability of factors is often unclear in a principal-components analysis since the various factor loadings may be moderate (.3 to .7). *Rotation* of axes may be performed in order to secure a better assignment of the individual variables to unique factors. Most computer programs incorporate a rotation, thus yielding factor loadings that are closer to unity or zero.

Several clustering techniques exist for establishing homogeneous subgroups of respondents. Closeness, as shown by distance in n-dimensional space, is the usual basis for forming these subgroups. Various programs have different starting points, but the general objective is to maximize distances (variance) among clusters and minimize distances (variance) within clusters.

Adoption of cluster analysis by the researcher is accompanied by the need to answer five procedural issues. These issues are (1) the selection of relevant variables, (2) the transformation of input data, (3) the adoption of a distance or similarity measure, (4) the procedure for forming subgroups, and (5) "stopping rules." The procedures chosen are partially constrained by the nature of the problem and the accompanying data, but a number of alternatives exist.

Familiarity with the various options makes the arbitrary choice at least an "informed" choice.

Both factor analysis and clustering should be thought of as search procedures rather than analytic techniques capable of yielding statistically valid inferences. They are primarily data summaries, often using ad hoc rules. Rough checks such as the split-half technique or submission of the data to alternative programs using different algorithms are helpful and yield added confidence, but the techniques conform more to exploratory research than to explanatory research.

EXERCISES AND PROBLEMS

1. Distinguish among the terms within each of the following sets.
    a) Partitioned data and nonpartitioned data
    b) Factor analysis and cluster analysis
    c) Factor equation, factor loading, and factor score
    d) Communality and variance summarized
    e) Euclidean distance, city-block distance, and similarity measures
    f) Hierarchical methods, nonhierarchical methods, and connectivity methods

2. Briefly explain the meaning and significance of each of the following terms.
    a) Rotation of axes
    b) Orthogonal
    c) Stopping rules
    d) Factor labeling
    e) Interpoint distance
    f) Transformation of input data

3. A factor analysis of seven store characteristics yielded the two-factor equations presented in Table E17.3. The results shown were obtained by a principal-components solution.

Table E17.3

Variable	Factor I	Factor II
Fashion	− .42	+ .58
Price	− .86	− .49
Quality	+ .75	+ .47
Size	+ .35	+ .14
Parking	+ .37	+ .43
Assortment	+ .43	+ .39
Modern	− .29	+ .19

a) Determine the communality for each variable. Explain the meaning of the figures calculated.

b) Determine the variance summarized by each factor and by the two factors combined.

c) Plot the factor loadings.

d) Do you think a rotation of axes would improve the interpretability of the two factors? Why?

e) Propose labels for the two axes and explain your rationale.

4. Ilustrative data on magazine readership is given in Table E17.4(a) for 12 members of a consumer panel. The scores have been double centered, i.e., all columns and all rows total zero.

Table E17.4(a)

	Magazine					
Panel member	Business Week	Reader's Digest	Popular Mechanics	Time	Better Homes and Gardens	Sports Illustrated
1	+1.4	−1.3	−0.3	+0.9	−1.4	+0.7
2	−0.6	+1.0	−0.8	+0.3	+0.9	−0.8
3	+0.2	+0.7	−0.4	−0.2	+0.5	−0.8
4	−0.7	+0.8	+0.9	−0.8	−0.1	−0.1
5	+0.7	−1.6	+0.2	+0.4	−0.5	+0.8
6	−0.5	+0.8	−0.4	−0.7	+0.6	+0.2
7	+1.0	−0.7	0.0	+1.2	−1.5	0.0
8	+0.9	−0.3	+0.4	+0.8	−0.8	−1.0
9	−0.7	−0.4	+1.3	−1.2	+0.6	+0.4
10	+0.4	−0.1	−0.3	+0.5	−1.4	+0.9
11	−1.3	+0.6	−0.4	−0.8	+1.6	+0.3
12	−0.8	+0.5	−0.2	−0.4	+1.5	−0.6

a) Perform a principal-components factor analysis on these data.

b) What proportion of the total variance is recovered by each of the first two factors?

c) Rotate the axes by means of a varimax rotation. How would you interpret each of the factors?

d) Compute the factor scores for each panel member on the first factor.

e) Do the factor scores obtained in (d) show any association with interest in a monthly business letter? The interest indices are shown in Table E17.4(b).

Table E17.4(b)

Panel member	Interest index
1	73
2	35
3	51
4	42
5	61
6	25
7	83
8	75
9	46
10	65
11	36
12	53

f) Do you think factor scores on another factor would be a better indicator of interest? Why?

g) An alternative suggestion is multiple regression, with interest in the monthly business letter as the dependent variable and the factor scores on all factors as the independent variables. Do you think this suggestion has merit?

h) Would the suggestion in (g) be any different from an ordinary multiple regression with the seven individual magazine scores as the independent variables? Discuss.

5. Refer to and use the data of Exercise 4.

a) Determine the interpoint distances between all possible pairs of the 12 panel members.

b) Submit the data to a hierarchical clustering program.

c) What would you accept as the appropriate clustering for these data? Why?

d) How would you describe the clusters obtained?

e) Do any of these clusters represent meaningful market segments? If yes, for whom?

6. Direct mail offers of free gifts to persons visiting a large, real estate resort development were sent to names on a purchased list. All persons visiting the office were asked to complete a short questionnaire. Data from a sample of 20 persons are given in Table E17.6.

Table E17.6

Respondent number	Sex†	Age‡	Income§	State	Occupation‖
1	M	I	I	PA	I
2	F	IV	III	DEL	III
3	M	III	II	MD	V
4	M	III	III	NJ	III
5	F	IV	I	NJ	IV
6	M	III	IV	PA	II
7	F	I	I	DEL	I
8	M	III	II	PA	V
9	M	IV	III	MD	VI
10	M	IV	IV	MD	II
11	F	III	II	PA	I
12	F	II	III	DEL	I
13	M	II	IV	PA	III
14	M	IV	I	MD	VII
15	M	I	II	NY	V
16	F	IV	III	DEL	VII
17	M	III	III	PA	IV
18	M	IV	IV	MD	III
19	F	II	II	NJ	VII
20	M	III	IV	PA	III

†Sex code: M = Male, F = Female
‡Age code: I = Under 30, II = 30–44, III = 45–60, IV = over 60
§Income code: I = Under $15,000; II = $15,000–24,999; III = $25,000–39,999; IV = $40,000 and over
‖Occupation code: I = sales, II = professional, III = managerial, IV = clerical, V = skilled or semiskilled labor, VI = retired, VII = other

   a) Convert each of the five variables into a dichotomous variable. Explain your rationale for the cutoff points or groupings.

   b) Which two respondents are most similar?

   c) Can you form clusters of respondents that are similar? If yes, how would you proceed? If no, why not?

   d) Could these data be converted and used in a hierarchical clustering routine? Why?

7. Use the data collected by you in Exercise 8 of Chapter 15.

   a) Do you believe multicollinearity exists among the independent variables? Between which variables is it greatest?

  b) How would factor analysis help deal with multicollinearity?

  c) How many factors would you hypothesize are present? Identify the variables that you think will have the largest factor loadings on each factor.

  d) Solve for the number of factors specified in (c) by principal-components and a varimax rotation.

  e) Compare the result to your hypothesis in (c). Comment on any differences.

  f) What proportion of the total variance is recovered by the factors in (d)? Does this seem a large or a small proportion? Why?

8. Submit the data of Exercise 7 (and Exercise 8 of Chapter 15) to the cluster program of your choice.

  a) Discuss the nature of the clusters obtained.

  b) Which two clusters are most similar to each other? least similar to each other? Cite the evidence that leads you to this conclusion.

9. What information is given by Fig. 17.4 that is not revealed by Table 17.9?

10. Find (in current marketing journals) two research studies that employ factor analysis. For each study discuss the benefit, if any, of rotating axes; the need for using factor analysis in the given problem; whether the conclusions reached are justified.

11. Find (in current marketing journals) two research studies that employ cluster analysis. For each study discuss the way in which similarity or distance is measured; the procedure and criterion for forming clusters; and whether the conclusions reached are justified.

12. Analyze, criticize, and explain:

  a) The number of factor equations derived in a factor analysis should be increased in a stepwise fashion until each variable is uniquely associated with one and only one factor.

  b) The principal-components approach has three main advantages:
  i) All factors derived are multicollinear.
  ii) Reduction in variance is maximized at each step.
  iii) Interpretability is facilitated.

  c) When the same number of objects is placed in each cluster, total within-cluster homogeneity will be decreased. As an offset to this disadvantage, no single cluster will show high heterogeneity.

  d) Factor analysis and cluster analysis both use a basic $n \times m$ matrix, where n is the number of variables and m is the number of objects. Factor analysis attempts to reduce the number of variables to $k(k < n)$. Cluster analysis, on the other hand, attempts to combine objects.

  e) Both factor analysis and cluster analysis are concerned with nonpartitioned data. This means that the introduction of a dependent variable at a later stage of the research violates the assumptions of the first-stage analysis.

  f) If similar data are collected from a series of communities and factor equations are derived, the factor loadings in the first-factor equations should be roughly similar for all communities.

g) Factor analysis and cluster analysis both should be classified as search procedures. The only way to overcome this difficulty is to specify procedures and
stopping rules before the data are collected.

h) The use of factor scores as input data in cluster analysis is preferable to the use
of either the orginal data or the original data transformed into standard scores.
Either of the latter two inputs assigns weight to the various factors in a highly
arbitrary manner, corresponding roughly to the number of variables with high
loadings on each factor.

CHAPTER 18

MULTIPLE DEPENDENT VARIABLES
THE ANALYSIS OF MULTIPLE GOALS

Multiple goals exist more often than single goals. A sales person is expected to open new accounts, retain existing accounts, generate high dollar sales, and realize large profits. A good product is characterized by long life, freedom from breakdown, ease of maintenance, and multiple uses. In each case, the target or dependent variable is a complex of several variables. Arbitrary weights can be assigned to the individual goals—thus defining a new dependent variable. If defensible, this index can be employed with any of the techniques discussed earlier. In multivariate problems, candidate independent variables can be tested for their predictive power against the index. Alternatively, it may be preferable to allow the data to determine both the appropriate weighting scheme(s) within the multiple goals and relationships against the independent variables.

Other marketing situations exist in which two sets of variables are to be compared, but the focus is on the relationship without establishing an independent–dependent dichotomy. Personality profiles and the pattern of media exposure may run in either direction, depending on the research purpose and contemplated use. A technique that avoids stipulating which is dependent and which is independent merely determines how one set of variables is related to the other set. Information processing and decision making illustrate two other sets of variables of frequent concern to the marketing manager. Marketing research can aid by identifying how various composites from one set of variables are related to composites from the other set.

Canonical correlation is designed to deal with precisely these kinds of problems. It represents an extention of multiple correlation, replacing the univariate dependent variable with the multivariate although the technique does not require a designation of which variables are dependent and which are independent. Canonical correlation can be likened to running separate factor analyses on two sets of nonpartitioned data followed by a correlation analysis on the factor scores taken in pairs.[1] The analysis seeks to determine (1) the underlying factors from each set of variables and (2) the degree of relationship between specific pairs of factors.

ANOVA can also be extended to include multiple dependent variables. Where ANOVA tests for differences among means on a single dependent variable, multivariate analysis of variance (MANOVA) tests for differences among centroids on a set of dependent variables. The addition of a covariate leads to multivariate analysis of covariance (MANCOVA).

Canonical correlation, MANOVA, and MANCOVA are all addressed to problems dealing with data sets that have been partitioned into two sets, with both sets multivariate. In its simplest form, both sets are intervally scaled in canonical correlation. In MANOVA, the dependent set is intervally scaled and the independent set is nominally scaled. MANCOVA extends the situation to include both intervally scaled and nominally scaled independent variables. Our exposition of the three techniques will be in this format although each technique can be modified to include mixed sets by the dummy variable technique.

The techniques discussed in this chapter provide the fourth step in our study of estimation. This study has proceeded in the following sequence:

1. Unconditional estimates of a single variable—univariate procedures.

2. Conditional estimates of a single variable, given knowledge of one additional variable—bivariate procedures.

3. Conditional estimates of a single variable, given knowledge of more than one additional variable—multivariate procedures.

4. Conditional estimates of a composite variable, given knowledge of more than one additional variable—double multivariate procedures.[2]

CANONICAL CORRELATION

Canonical correlation offers potential aid to the marketing manager in three principal spheres. *First,* it permits the manager to ascertain whether a relationship exists between the *underlying factors* of a set of independent variables and the *underlying factors* of a set of dependent variables. *Second,* it provides a basis for identifying which variables contribute most to relationships between the sets. *Third,* it yields estimating equations that can be used in making predictions. We shall stress the first. It logically precedes the others, and the interpretation of the results is less subject to debate.

---

[1]See Harold Hotelling, 1963, Relations between two sets of variates, *Biometrika* **28:** 321–377.

[2]The term "multivariate" is not applied uniformly to either step three or four in existing literature. Sometimes it refers to both steps while at other times it is used for only step four; for example, the designation MANOVA is reserved for step four while the designation ANOVA may apply to either step two or three.

Pairs of Functions

Canonical correlation yields pairs of linear functions and determines the degree of relationship between them. The linear functions of each pair are maximally correlated with each other and uncorrelated with the functions derived in the other pairs. The maximum number of pairs derived equals the number of variables in the smaller of the two data sets.

Equation (18.1) shows the form taken by the pairs of linear functions.

$$\overset{*}{y}_1 = a_{11}y_1 + a_{12}y_2 + \cdots + a_{1p}y_p \qquad (18.1)$$
$$\overset{*}{x}_1 = b_{11}x_1 + b_{12}x_2 + \cdots + b_{1q}x_q$$

$$\cdot$$
$$\cdot$$
$$\cdot$$

$$\overset{*}{y}_i = a_{i1}y_1 + a_{i2}y_2 + \cdots + a_{ip}y_p$$
$$\overset{*}{x}_i = b_{i1}x_1 + b_{i2}x_2 + \cdots + b_{iq}x_q$$

where

p = number of variables in the first set,

q = number of variables in the second set,

$\overset{*}{y}_i$ = canonical score for the first set of variables (*i*th function).

$\overset{*}{x}_i$ = canonical score for the second set of variables (*i*th function).

The maximum number of pairs is equal to p or q, whichever is smaller. The $\overset{*}{y}_i$ and $\overset{*}{x}_i$ values are based on a different number of terms except where $p = q$. Both $\overset{*}{y}_i$ and $\overset{*}{x}_i$ (the canonical scores or canonical variates) are calculated values; they do not refer to actual observations.

The proper label for each canonical variate is a matter of conjecture and is analogous to the situation in factor analysis although the equations are not derived by a factor-analytic procedure.[3] Canonical correlation has as its criterion of "best fit" maximum correlation between $\overset{*}{y}_i$ and $\overset{*}{x}_i$. This is not equivalent to the correlation between the original sets of variables—a potential source of difficulty in interpretating the results that will be discussed later in the chapter. A separate canonical correlation coefficient (R_c) applies to each pair of functions, and each can be tested for statistical significance.

Canonical correlation, like factor analysis, proceeds sequentially. The first pair of linear equations uses the criterion of maximum correlation. The next pair selected must be uncorrelated with the first pair. Subject to this constraint, the second pair again is selected with maximum correlation. The pro-

---

[3]Hotelling has shown that canonical analysis is the equivalent of independent principal-components analyses with rotation to produce maximum correlation. See Harold Hotelling, *op. cit.*

cess continues through as many pairs as the analyst wishes, but no more than the lesser of p or q where p is the number of variables in the first set and q is the number of variables in the second set.

Numerical Example

The salespeople data of the previous chapter offer an opportunity to examine the results of canonical analysis and an opportunity to compare factor-analysis results with those of canonical correlation. The sales manager is concerned with sales person performance. He or she must add appropriate measures of performance to the seven characteristics in the personnel file. The manager chooses four: dollar volume of sales, dollar profit on sales, number of new accounts, and number of calls made. These data, along with the seven personal characteristics, are presented in Table 18.1.

The data are partitioned into two sets: four dependent variables and seven independent variables although they need not be so designated. The sales manager gives the data to the research analyst asking whether these seven variables are related to job performance. If the answer is affirmative, the manager also wants to know the nature of the relationship and how that information can be used in future screening of applicants.

The research analyst runs a canonical analysis on the data. Four pairs of functions can be derived. Why? The first two sets of canonical coefficients (a's and b's of Eq. (18.1)) are presented in Table 18.2 along with other relevant statistics.

Are the two sets of variables related? R_c (correlation between the canonical scores) is .98 for the first pair of functions. Therefore 96.04 percent of the variance in $\overset{*}{y}_1$ is associated with the variance in $\overset{*}{x}_1$. As shown in Table 18.2, the observed correlation is significant at $\alpha = .10$. R_c equals .857 for the second pair, but this value is not statistically significant.[4]

The manager is justified in concluding that the two sets of variables are related (using $\alpha = .1$). The next question is "How?" Inspection of the canonical coefficients is required to answer this question.

The canonical variates of Table 18.2 illustrate a typical situation. Neither the dependent nor the independent composite can be readily interpreted as a single underlying factor. The three factors of physical size, maturity, and mental capacity (found in the factor analysis) do not appear in that form in the salespeople characteristic equations. In fact, opposite signs for the variables making up these factors are present. Height and weight possess opposite signs while the three variables that contributed to "maturity" also have mixed signs. The performance variables do not yield simple concepts either. Moderate weights are assigned to all four variables, with two positive signs and two negative. This new variable shows positive performance on sales and number of calls but poor performance on new accounts and profits.

---

[4]Tests of significance for R_c are discussed later in the chapter.

Table 18.1
Salespeople Characteristics and Performance

Sales person	Sales (in $1,000) (y_1)	Number of new accounts (y_2)	Profit (in $1,000) (y_3)	Number of calls (y_4)	Height (x_1)	Weight (x_2)	Education (x_3)	Age (x_4)	Number of children (x_5)	Size of household (x_6)	IQ (x_7)
1	32	4	2.0	12	67	155	12	27	0	2	102
2	37	1	3.5	22	69	175	11	35	3	6	92
3	26	1	3.0	24	71	170	14	32	1	3	111
4	29	4	2.3	15	70	160	16	25	0	1	115
5	21	2	1.5	16	72	180	12	36	2	4	108
6	52	1	6.0	19	69	170	11	41	3	5	90
7	27	3	2.4	14	74	195	13	30	1	2	114
8	45	0	4.9	17	68	160	16	32	1	3	118
9	49	0	5.1	27	70	175	12	45	4	6	121
10	30	5	2.5	14	71	180	13	24	0	2	92
11	34	3	3.3	20	66	145	10	39	2	4	100
12	24	6	3.1	21	75	210	16	26	0	1	109
13	39	3	3.4	19	70	160	12	31	0	3	102
14	41	2	3.9	29	71	175	13	43	3	5	112

Table 18.2
Canonical Analysis Results.
Salespeople Characteristics and Performance

Variables	Canonical coefficients	
	First pair	Second pair
Performance		
Sales	.743	1.122
New accounts	− .718	− .542
Profit	− .849	− 1.966
Calls	.514	− .183
Characteristics		
Height	.352	.989
Weight	− .522	− 1.314
Education	.174	− 1.222
Age	− .145	− 2.428
Number of children	− .333	.902
Size of household	1.508	.626
IQ	.370	.925
Roots (λ)	.9604	.7344
Canonical R (R_c)	.9800	.8570
Wilks lambda (Λ)	.0061	.1535
χ^2	40.80	14.99
Degrees of freedom	28	18
Probability	< .10	> .5

Canonical variables, in which several variables have moderate coefficients, have ambiguous meaning because the same score can be generated by widely divergent inputs. For example, the first performance canonical variate would yield the same value with any number of different combinations: high sales and average performance on the other three variables; a low number of new accounts and average performance on the other variables; low profit, high sales, high number of calls, and an average number of new accounts; and many other possibilities. The existence of both positive and negative coefficients is particularly troublesome when all variables in the dependent set are desirable to management. Both high profitability and a large number of new accounts are aspects of good performance. The first canonical performance function is increased in value by low scores on both of these variables.

The first canonical variate for personal characteristics assigns a large weight to a single variable. The coefficient for household size is approximately three times that of any other variable. Thus household size is the most significant variable in determining scores on this variate. An underlying factor—such as maturity—has not emerged.

Canonical variates are not defined by their utility in decision making. They are determined by the data. The original set of dependent variables is normally selected for its practical relevance, but the combinations defined by the canonical equations reflect patterns in the data, not in the decision maker's model. Canonical correlation is more a tool for uncovering and understanding relationships than it is a quantification of an explicit model. It should be classified as a "search" technique rather than as a basis for testing hypotheses. It can *generate* hypotheses. The sales manager in the current problem might hypothesize that salespeople with large households stress sales volume and many calls with little regard for profitability or the generation of new business.

What of the second pair of canonical variates? R_c is .857. This may seem reasonably large, but it is not statistically significant. The second pair of functions should be ignored by the sales manager; whatever it shows may well be the result of chance fluctuations in the data.

Significance Test for Canonical Correlation

The canonical correlation coefficient (R_c) is calculated as a simple bivariate coefficient of correlation. It is the correlation between the two sets of canonical scores. A separate correlation measure applies to each pair of functions, and the magnitude of the canonical correlation must decrease with each successive pair. The coefficients of determination (R_c^2) are employed in canonical correlation, but they are referred to as either the *characteristic roots* or the *eigenvalues* (λ's).

The appropriate test for canonical correlation uses Wilks lambda (Λ).[5] Lambda involves the proportion of unexplained variance—by all pairs of canonical equations beginning with the pair being evaluated. Its formula is given by Eq. (18.2).

$$\Lambda_i = \prod_{k=i}^{p} (1 - \lambda_k); \qquad p < q \qquad (18.2)$$

where

p and q = number of dependent and independent variables, respectively.

In the salespeople problem, there are four dependent variables and seven independent variables. Therefore, p is four. Lambda for the first pair of canonical equations is based on the product of four terms; the number of terms in testing other pairs would be reduced by one with each succeeding pair. The usual sta-

---

[5]See M. S. Bartlett, 1941, The statistical significance of canonical correlations, *Biometrika* **32**: 29-38.

tistical test uses a Chi Square approximation that is computed as part of most computer programs.[6] The transformation is given by Eq. (18.3).

$$\chi^2 = - N[-.5(p + q + 1)]\ln \Lambda. \qquad (18.3)$$

The lack of significance with the salespeople data—only the first pair of functions is significant at .1—occurs because of the small number of observations, the large number of variables (relative to the number of observations), and the unconstrained two-way search for the best fit.

Caveats against Canonical Correlation

Several questions regarding the interpretation and use of canonical results do not have uniformly clear answers.[7] Other questions regarding the assumptions of the technique also deserve specific mention. Two of the more significant questions in interpretation and use are (1) how best to judge the importance of individual variables, and (2) what is the proper indicator of the strength of the relationship between the set of independent variables and the set of dependent variables. Other questions concerning assumptions focus on linearity, normality, and equal variances (homoscedasticity). A final issue, already mentioned briefly, is the relevance of the canonical variates for decision making.

The importance of individual variables in the linear equations is often discussed in terms of their coefficients in the canonical functions. These *canonical coefficients* are expressed in terms of standard scores. An alternative approach is to use the *canonical structure correlations*. Canonical structure correlations show the correlation between the various individual variables and the canonical variates to which they contribute.[8] This approach shows importance by the magnitude of gross correlation. Still another alternative, discussed by Alpert and Peterson, for measuring importance is the percentage distribution of the squares of canonical structure correlations.[9] This approach yields the same rankings as the structure correlations, but with different measures of importance. Alpert and Peterson's measure also standardizes so that the sum of the weights is 100 percent.

Canonical structure correlations are based on the premise that the importance of a particular variable to its canonical composite is best shown by its correlation with that composite. It is a gross rather than a net concept. Differ-

[6]Anthony James Barr and James Howard Goodnight, 1972, *A User's Guide to the Statistical Analysis System* (Raleigh, N.C.: Sparks Press), pp. 179–189.

[7]Lambert and Durand illustrate certain difficulties with empirical data from replicated research studies. See Zarrel V. Lambert and Richard M. Durand, 1975, Some precautions in using canonical analysis, *Journal of Marketing Research* 12: 468–475.

[8]See William A. Cooley and Paul R. Lohnes, 1971, *Multivariate Data Analysis* (New York: Wiley).

[9]Mark I. Alpert and Robert A. Peterson, 1972, On the interpretation of canonical analysis, *Journal of Marketing Research* 9: 187–192.

ences between canonical coefficients and structure correlations as measures of importance occur when multicollinearity is present. The canonical coefficients attempt to show the net relations after adjusting for all other variables in the equation; the structure correlations show the gross relations without regard for other variables. Table 18.3 presents the structure correlations and the canonical coefficients for the four performance characteristics, using the first performance canonical function.

The results in Table 18.3 dramatize the possible differences between structure correlations and canonical coefficients, but such results are not typical. The sign for profits is reversed, and the rankings in importance (shown in parentheses and based on absolute values) are almost completely reversed. Structure correlations show new accounts (negative relation) and calls as the most important; the canonical coefficients show profit (negative relation) and sales as the most important. Such dramatic differences are more likely in situations such as the present case in which a number of variables have moderate coefficients of approximately the same magnitude.

The *strength of the relationship* between the sets of variables is overstated if one accepts R_c (or λ) as the appropriate measure. These measures are based on the relationship between the linear composites of variables rather than the relationship between the variables themselves. Stewart and Love have proposed a *redundancy index* to assess variance shared by the two *sets* of variables.[10] This index is based upon the variance in the original variables, variance as measured in n-dimensional space. The index is also defined so that it copes with the asymmetric nature of the initial variance, thus yielding two measures. One measure shows the percentage of variance in the dependent variables associated with variability in the independent variables and the other has the opposite focus—the percentage of variance in the independent variables associated with variability in the dependent variables.

Table 18.3
Structure Correlations and Canonical Coefficients for First-performance Canonical Function. Salespeople Data

Variable	Structure correlations	Canonical coefficients
Sales	.609 (3)	.743 (2)
New accounts	− .890 (1)	− .718 (3)
Profit	.528 (4)	− .849 (1)
Calls	.694 (2)	.514 (4)

[10]Douglas Stewart and William Love, 1968, A general canonical index, *Psychological Bulletin* **70**: 160–163.

A convenient way of calculating the redundancy index $(\bar{R}_p^2 \cdot_q)$ involves the structure correlations and is given by Eq. (18.4)

$$\bar{R}_p^2 \cdot_q = \frac{\sum_{i=1}^{p} r_{p \cdot y_i}^2}{p} \left(R_c^2 \right) \tag{18.4}$$

where $r_p^2 \cdot_{y_i}$ is the structure correlation between dependent variable i and the dependent canonical variate (p and R_c^2 as previously defined). $\bar{R}_q^2 \cdot_p$ is defined in an analogous manner and is based on the variance in the independent variable set.

The redundancy index indicates the proportion of variance in one set of variables that is shared by the other set. This results in a much more conservative claim than the canonical correlation measure. Application of Eq. (18.4) to the salespeople data yields the following measures of relationship: $\bar{R}_p^2 \cdot_q = .46$ and $\bar{R}_q^2 \cdot_p = .34$. Forty-six percent of the variance in the set of dependent variables is associated with variation in the independent variables, considerably less than R_c^2 of 96 percent. Reversing the focus to the set of independent variables, the percentage relationship is only 34 percent—illustrating the asymmetric nature of the redundancy index.

All relationships developed in canonical correlation assume linearity in two phases: the canonical variates are formed by linear equations and the maximization of correlation is performed in terms of linear relation between the canonical variates. Transformations of the original variables are of course possible, but the final fit must be linear. In actual practice, transformations are rarely performed. This is readily understandable since the meaning of a linear equation with various transformations may be obscure and the selection of the proper transformations may be arbitrary.

The assumption of multinormality underlies most of the statistical tests although canonical correlation as a descriptive device does not assume multinormal distributions. However, use of the least-squares technique has its basis in the assumption of equal variance about the conditional distributions. The researcher should consciously consider the validity of these various assumptions before using canonical correlation.

Two final warnings should be weighed as one employs canonical correlation. First, canonical coefficients are subject to considerable instability from sample to sample. In multiple regression, this instability would be shown by the standard error of the regression coefficients. Lambert and Durand discuss this problem, suggesting either replication of studies or variations of the split-half approach.[11] Second, the use of canonical correlation as a predictive device implies that the researcher has some goal or set of goals in mind. The canonical

---

[11] Lambert and Durand, *op. cit.*

variate formed from the dependent variables will assign specific weights to the individual variables (differing weights in each pair of functions). There is no assurance that these weights will define an index that has practical significance for a marketing manager. This may be particularly true when the signs suggest that the canonical variate is generated by the presence of some desirable characteristics and the absence of others.

Product Use and Market Segmentation

Canonical correlation is a logical technique to consider when one is interested in consumption patterns for a group of products. The researcher is concerned with consumption of several items, whether competing brands within a specific product category or items over a range of categories. If interest centers on a series of dependent variables each of which is to be studied separately, it is not a case for canonical correlation. But if the researcher wants to determine patterns across several products, canonical correlation is an appropriate technique.

Many buyer–behavior models include personality as a partial determinant of attitudes toward products and buyer behavior.[12] Canonical correlation can approach this situation by employing two sets of variables, one for personality traits and the other for buying behavior or attitudes. The truncated equations of Table 18.4 are taken from a study of personality traits and product use by Sparks and Tucker.[13]

The first product-use equation shows the use of alcoholic beverages, cigarettes, and possibly fashion adoption. Personality traits associated with these products are sociability, emotional stability, and irresponsibility (negative responsibility). The second product–use equation shows the use of headache remedies, mouthwash, and again fashion adoption. The principal personality traits associated with these products are cautiousness and lack of emotional stability.

Further discussion of the substantive findings is contained in the original article.[14] Our present purpose is to illustrate the potential of canonical correlation in this type of problem. Table 18.4 shows emotional stability with fairly large coefficients in each pair of functions but with a different sign. Sociability appears in both pairs but with the same sign. Sociability plus emotional stability leads to one set of products; sociability minus emotional stability leads to a

---

[12]See, for example, John A. Howard and Jagdish N. Sheth, 1969, *The Theory of Buyer Behavior* (New York: Wiley), and Frederick E. Webster, Jr. and Yoram Wind, 1972, *Organizational Buying Behavior* (Englewood Cliffs, N.J.: Prentice-Hall).

[13]David L. Sparks and W. T. Tucker, 1971, A multivariate analysis of personality and product use, *Journal of Marketing Research* **8**: 67–70. Seventeen products and eight personality traits are included in the original study.

[14]*Ibid.*

Table 18.4
Canonical Coefficients. Product Use and Personality Traits†

Variables	Canonical coefficients	
	First pair	Second pair
Product use		
Headache remedy	− .01	.44
Mouthwash	− .16	.45
Alcoholic beverages	.46	− .31
Cigarettes	.41	− .06
Fashion adoption	.32	.40
Personality traits		
Responsibility	− .51	− .08
Emotional stability	.43	− .64
Sociability	.61	.36
Cautiousness	− .29	.60
Canonical correlation	.61	.55

†Adapted from David L. Sparks and W. T. Tucker, 1971, A multivariate analysis of personality and product use, *Journal of Marketing Research* **8**: 67–70. Only variables for which at least one coefficient is .40 or more are included in the table. Signs of the second set have been reversed to facilitate the interpretability.

different set. A type of interaction can be identified while using a linear additive model that contains only the individual variables. The same variable can contribute to different patterns of the dependent variables by appearing with different coefficients and/or signs in the various linear equations.

Frank and Strain employ canonical correlation in an attempt to form market segments based on the relationship between the use of two product types and sociodemographic variables.[15] The two-variable dependent set results in two linear functions, one with positive coefficients for each product type and the other with opposite signs for the two product types. The set of independent variables contains 151 different items. The items with large coefficients differ considerably between the two independent canonical variates.[16]

Farley and Ring use canonical correlation along with AID in testing and modifying the Howard–Sheth buyer-behavior model.[17] Using 11 endogenous

---

[15]Ronald E. Frank and Charles E. Strain, 1972, A segmentation research design using consumer panel data, *Journal of Marketing Research* **9**: 385–390.

[16]A somewhat similar approach, using 18 food products and 27 household characteristics, is reported in Ronald E. Frank, 1972, Predicting new product segments, *Journal of Advertising Research* **12**: 9–13.

[17]John U. Farley and L. Winston Ring, 1974, Empirical specification of a buyer-behavior model, *Journal of Marketing Research* **11**: 89–96; and Howard and Sheth, *op. cit.*

cally adjust for such variables when they either are not or cannot be controlled experimentally. MANOVA can similarly yield more useful results by adjusting for one or more covariates.

The *n*-dimensional graph of MANOVA considers the location of the centroids. The extension to covariance (MANCOVA) adjusts the location of the centroids for the effects of uncontrolled variables. The distances among the adjusted centroids then serves as the basis for evaluating the treatment effects or their interactions.

The failure of MANOVA to reveal significant differences in the ad theme/coupon experiment could reflect the acceptance of a false null hypothesis. The experiment could be redesigned in order to make it more sensitive since within-cell variability is rather large. First, more observations per cell would increase the reliability of both the individual cell estimates and the main effects estimates. Second, the introduction of a covariate might explain the large within-cell variability. Newspaper circulation is a potentially useful covariate. BMD12V allows for the incorporation of a covariate, including a test for its effect and the adjustment of the centroids for that effect. The computer printout follows the format of Table 18.6 and also incorporates a test for each covariate.

Table 18.7 is adapted from a study of the effectiveness of TV commercials by Wind and Denny.[21] Seven separate measures of the "effectiveness" of a particular commercial comprise the set of dependent variables. This set pos-

Table 18.7
Effectiveness of TV Commercial. Multivariate Analysis of Covariance†

Source of variation	Log (generalized variance)	Approximate *F*-ratio
Test versus control	33.29	0.69
Brand users versus nonusers	33.75	18.33‡
Interaction	33.30	1.21
Covariates§		
TV watching	36.21	2.55‡
Liking for program (before)	34.71	1.25
.	.	.
.	.	.
.	.	.

†Adapted from Yoram Wind and Joseph Denny, 1974, Multivariate analysis of variance in research on the effectiveness of TV commercials, *Journal of Marketing Research* **11** (May): 136–142.
‡*F*-ratio significant at $\alpha = .05$.
§A total of eight covariates was included in the analysis.

[21]Yoram Wind and Joseph Denny, 1974, Multivariate analysis of variance in research on the effectiveness of TV commercials, *Journal of Marketing Research* **11**: 136–142.

variables and 17 exogenous variables, five significant pairs of canonical variates result. The authors use their results as a basis for validating the Howard–Sheth model. Relationships are placed into one of three categories: (1) original relationship verified, (2) original relationship not verified, and (3) new relationship suggested.

MULTIVARIATE ANALYSIS OF VARIANCE

The analysis of variance (ANOVA) tests for differences among means on a single dependent variable. The introduction of a multiple dependent variable replaces the mean of a single dimension with a centroid in *n*-dimensions.[18] The analysis asks whether the centroids examined represent significant departures from one overall centroid. Multivariate analysis of variance (MANOVA) resembles cluster analysis in this sense; it asks whether the subgroups differ enough to be treated as "truly" different.

The subgroups to be compared in MANOVA are specified by the experimental design. For example, the marketing manager might wish to test three variations of a particular cake recipe, two package shapes, and two package colors. The 12 subgroups are defined by these specifications. The dependent variables, also specified by the marketing manager, may be ratings on "uniqueness" and ease of preparation plus a preference score. MANOVA compares the subgroups with respect to their centroids on these dependent variables. Cluster analysis, in contrast, forms subgroups based upon the data. No prior specification of subgroups is involved; nor are the variables partitioned into independent and dependent.

MANOVA differs from canonical correlation in the nature of the independent variables. Canonical correlation employs interval scales for all variables; thus a plot of the data matrix would require *p* plus *q* dimensions where *p* is the number of dependent variables and *q* is the number of independent variables. MANOVA requires only *p* dimensions, with the various combinations of the *q* variables determining the number of centroids to be plotted in *p* dimensions.

MANOVA possesses the same application difficulty as canonical correlations: the derived dependent variable must have decision-making relevance. Differences among the *n*-dimensional centroids in MANOVA raise the familiar problem of measurement and the appropriate unit of measure. The usual procedure employs standard scores with respect to the various dependent variables in Euclidean space. If the dependent variables do not deserve equal weight, a single dependent variable derived with arbitrary weights assigned could be employed in a straight ANOVA.

[18]See Cooley and Lohnes, *op. cit.*

Table 18.5
Ad Theme and Coupon Experiment. Responses from Males and Females.†

| Ad theme | Coupon type | | Mean |
	Without questions	With questions	
Economy	(22, 17)	(37, 25)	(28.75, 19.50)
	(27, 16)	(29, 20)	
Prestige	(31, 12)	(26, 20)	(30.00, 19.75)
	(42, 25)	(21, 22)	
Beauty	(10, 21)	(19, 34)	(17.25, 31.50)
	(15, 31)	(25, 40)	
Mean	(24.50, 20.33)	(26.17, 26.83)	(25.33, 23.58)

†Cell entries give number of males first and number of females second.

Table 18.5 presents data appropriate for MANOVA. The data refer to an experiment with three different ad themes—economy, prestige, and beauty—and two types of coupons, one type with questions and one without. Thus there are two nominally scaled independent variables, one with two categories and one with three. The dependent variables are number of respondents, one for number of males and one for number of females. The experiment consists of 12 observations, with two observations per cell. Each observation consists of two entries, one for males and one for females. Table 18.5 shows that the mean response—the centroid for the entire experiment—is 25.33 males and 23.58 females. The questions to be tested are whether (1) the responses differ among ad themes, (2) the responses differ by type of coupon, and (3) there is interaction among ad theme and coupon type. The centroids for the main-effects analysis are shown by the marginal figures of the table.

Figure 18.1 shows the location of the overall centroid for the data of Table 18.5 and the two sets of main-effect centroids. The ad theme centroids reveal greater differences than do the coupon-type centroids. The "beauty" theme produced more female respondents and fewer male respondents than the other two themes. The coupon with questions produced more respondents of both sexes, but the gain was greater among females.

The differences cited are descriptive of the sample studied. Are they large enough to justify rejection of the null hypothesis? The appropriate test is based on the *U*-statistic which is a three-parameter distribution involving Wilks lambda.[19] The BMD12V program[20] uses an *F*-test based upon a trans-

---

[19]T. W. Anderson, 1958, *Multivariate Statistical Methods* (New York: Wiley), Chapter 8.

[20]W. J. Dixon (ed.), 1974, *Biomedical Computer Programs* (Berkeley, Calif.: University of California Press), pp. 751–764. More recent labeling refers to the program as BMDX69.

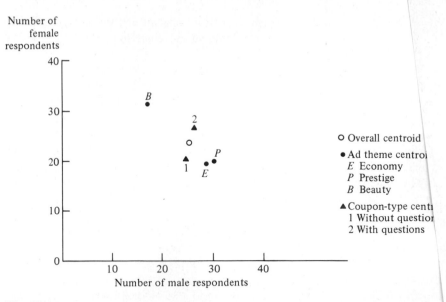

Fig. 18.1
Location of centroids for ad theme and coupon experiment.

formation of *U*. A portion of the results for the ad theme/coupon experimen is given in Table 18.6. The final two columns show the *F*-ratios and the number of degrees of freedom. Despite the differences suggested by Fig. 18.1, none are statistically significant.

Table 18.6
Multivariate Analysis of Variance Results. Ad Theme and Coupon Experiment

Source	Log (generalized variance)	*U*-statistic	Degrees of freedom	Approximate *F*-statistic†	Degrees of freedom
Coupon type	8.94	0.043	2, 1, 2	11.08	2, 1
Ad theme	10.60	0.008	2, 2, 2	5.02	4, 2
Interaction	8.76	0.052	2, 2, 2	1.70	4, 2
Replicates	7.96				

†None of the differences are statistically significant.

MULTIVARIATE ANALYSIS OF COVARIANCE

The existence of uncontrolled variables in a research design is always a potential source of problems. The determination of net regression coefficients and the analysis of covariance are but two examples of analytic devices that statisti-

sesses the usual difficulties encountered in such problems: no one "best" measure can be defended, the several measures are intercorrelated, but inconclusive and/or inconsistent recommendations stem from separate analyses of the individual dependent variables. The problem is further complicated by the potential effects of uncontrolled variables such as amount of TV watching and liking for the particular program. Wind and Denny included eight covariates in their study.

The experiment involved four subgroups defined by a 2 × 2 table: test group versus control group and brand users versus nonusers. Separate tests for the seven dependent variables reveal significant differences for only "intention to buy"—test group versus control group. Management should use the commercial only if it can defend "intention to buy" as the critical measure. MANCOVA simultaneously avoids the conflicting recommendations of the seven separate tests and adjusts for the possible effects of covariates by using centroids based on all seven measures, adjusted for the eight covariates. The analysis shows no significant difference between the test group and the control group. This result led the authors to recommend against use of the commercial.

Table 18.7, however, does reveal significant differences between brand users and nonusers. The direction of this difference is not shown in the table but must be ascertained from the coordinates of the two centroids. The user group is more favorable to the product in each of the seven dimensions. Table 18.7 also reveals that the interaction term is nonsignificant and identifies whether the various covariates are significant. The only significant covariate is the amount of TV watching.

MANCOVA is appropriate for testing the results of any marketing mix or advertising mix strategy where multiple objectives exist. The significance of each sample difference is determined by a single test—applied to an n-dimensional centroid. This is a neat unambiguous test of a specific hypothesis (equality of centroids), but the final interpretation may not always be as unambiguous as was the case with Wind and Denny's TV commercial. What recommendation is forwarded to the manager if the coordinates of the centroids reveal conflicting superiority? Suppose the centroids differ significantly, but the test-group coordinates are superior on five variables and inferior on three. It is hoped this will not be the case, but the researcher should recognize it as a possibility.

Comparison of Canonical Correlation and MANOVA

Both canonical correlation and MANOVA address the problem of multiple dependent variables, but they differ considerably in both their approach and the type of situations addressed. These differences are summarized in Table 18.8. Underlying all of these differences is the specific *a priori* hypothesis test versus search distinction: MANOVA involves precise hypotheses and canonical correlation involves a search procedure.

Table 18.8
Comparsion of Canonical Correlation and MANOVA

MANOVA
  Dependent variable: Centroid based on set of dependent variables
  Independent variables: Nominal scale specified in design of experiment
  Analysis results: 1) Each independent variable tested separately
                    2) Each interaction among independent variables tested separately
                    3) Each covariate tested separately if extended to multiple analy-
                       sis of covariance (MANCOVA)
Canonical correlation
  Dependent variates: Linear equations determined by data
  Independent variates: Interval scale linear equations determined by data
  Criteria for determining equations: 1) Maximum correlation between equations—
                                          by pairs
                                       2) Zero correlation with equations from other
                                          pairs
  Analysis results: 1) Correlation between linear equations—in pairs with signifi-
                       cance tests.
                    2) Derived canonical equations and structure correlations
                    3) Redundancy indices

Dependent variable. MANOVA combines the set of dependent variables into a series of centroids in n-dimensional space where n is equal to the number of dependent variables. Separate centroids are computed and compared for the various subgroups of interest. Canonical correlation uses the set of dependent variables to form a series of new variables termed dependent variates. Each variate is a linear composite of the original dependent variables. The precise form of the variates is determined by the data; neither the researcher nor the decision maker has any input in establishing the form taken by these composites. In MANOVA the location of the centroids is determined by the data, but each variable is weighted equally by converting to standard scores.

Independent variables. In canonical correlation, the independent variables are treated in precisely the same way as the dependent variables. In fact, canonical correlation proceeds without distinguishing between which set is dependent and which is independent. The independent variables are specified in the experimental design for MANOVA; this includes both the variables and the specific categories within each variable. The MANOVA independent variables are nominal in scale while the canonical independent variables are interval.

Criteria for determining equations. The linear equations in canonical correlation are determined in pairs, applying two criteria. (1) The coefficients are chosen to maximize the correlation between the canonical scores calculated

variables and 17 exogenous variables, five significant pairs of canonical variates result. The authors use their results as a basis for validating the Howard–Sheth model. Relationships are placed into one of three categories: (1) original relationship verified, (2) original relationship not verified, and (3) new relationship suggested.

MULTIVARIATE ANALYSIS OF VARIANCE

The analysis of variance (ANOVA) tests for differences among means on a single dependent variable. The introduction of a multiple dependent variable replaces the mean of a single dimension with a centroid in n-dimensions.[18] The analysis asks whether the centroids examined represent significant departures from one overall centroid. Multivariate analysis of variance (MANOVA) resembles cluster analysis in this sense; it asks whether the subgroups differ enough to be treated as "truly" different.

The subgroups to be compared in MANOVA are specified by the experimental design. For example, the marketing manager might wish to test three variations of a particular cake recipe, two package shapes, and two package colors. The 12 subgroups are defined by these specifications. The dependent variables, also specified by the marketing manager, may be ratings on "uniqueness" and ease of preparation plus a preference score. MANOVA compares the subgroups with respect to their centroids on these dependent variables. Cluster analysis, in contrast, forms subgroups based upon the data. No prior specification of subgroups is involved; nor are the variables partitioned into independent and dependent.

MANOVA differs from canonical correlation in the nature of the independent variables. Canonical correlation employs interval scales for all variables; thus a plot of the data matrix would require p plus q dimensions where p is the number of dependent variables and q is the number of independent variables. MANOVA requires only p dimensions, with the various combinations of the q variables determining the number of centroids to be plotted in p dimensions.

MANOVA possesses the same application difficulty as canonical correlations: the derived dependent variable must have decision-making relevance. Differences among the n-dimensional centroids in MANOVA raise the familiar problem of measurement and the appropriate unit of measure. The usual procedure employs standard scores with respect to the various dependent variables in Euclidean space. If the dependent variables do not deserve equal weight, a single dependent variable derived with arbitrary weights assigned could be employed in a straight ANOVA.

---

[18]See Cooley and Lohnes, *op. cit.*

Table 18.5
Ad Theme and Coupon Experiment. Responses from Males and Females.†

| | Coupon type | | |
Ad theme	Without questions	With questions	Mean
Economy	(22, 17)	(37, 25)	(28.75, 19.50)
	(27, 16)	(29, 20)	
Prestige	(31, 12)	(26, 20)	(30.00, 19.75)
	(42, 25)	(21, 22)	
Beauty	(10, 21)	(19, 34)	(17.25, 31.50)
	(15, 31)	(25, 40)	
Mean	(24.50, 20.33)	(26.17, 26.83)	(25.33, 23.58)

†Cell entries give number of males first and number of females second.

Table 18.5 presents data appropriate for MANOVA. The data refer to an experiment with three different ad themes—economy, prestige, and beauty —and two types of coupons, one type with questions and one without. Thus there are two nominally scaled independent variables, one with two categories and one with three. The dependent variables are number of respondents, one for number of males and one for number of females. The experiment consists of 12 observations, with two observations per cell. Each observation consists of two entries, one for males and one for females. Table 18.5 shows that the mean response—the centroid for the entire experiment—is 25.33 males and 23.58 females. The questions to be tested are whether (1) the responses differ among ad themes, (2) the responses differ by type of coupon, and (3) there is interaction among ad theme and coupon type. The centroids for the main-effects analysis are shown by the marginal figures of the table.

Figure 18.1 shows the location of the overall centroid for the data of Table 18.5 and the two sets of main-effect centroids. The ad theme centroids reveal greater differences than do the coupon-type centroids. The "beauty" theme produced more female respondents and fewer male respondents than the other two themes. The coupon with questions produced more respondents of both sexes, but the gain was greater among females.

The differences cited are descriptive of the sample studied. Are they large enough to justify rejection of the null hypothesis? The appropriate test is based on the U-statistic which is a three-parameter distribution involving Wilks lambda.[19] The BMD12V program[20] uses an F-test based upon a trans-

---

[19]T. W. Anderson, 1958, *Multivariate Statistical Methods* (New York: Wiley), Chapter 8.

[20]W. J. Dixon (ed.), 1974, *Biomedical Computer Programs* (Berkeley, Calif.: University of California Press), pp. 751–764. More recent labeling refers to the program as BMDX69.

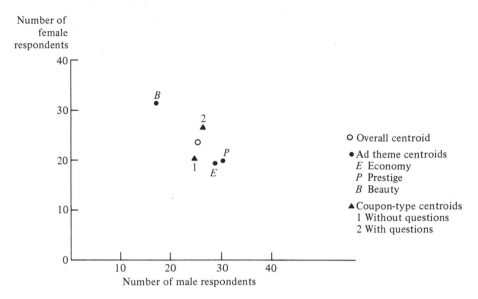

Fig. 18.1
Location of centroids for ad theme and coupon experiment.

formation of U. A portion of the results for the ad theme/coupon experiment is given in Table 18.6. The final two columns show the F-ratios and the number of degrees of freedom. Despite the differences suggested by Fig. 18.1, none are statistically significant.

Table 18.6
Multivariate Analysis of Variance Results. Ad Theme and Coupon Experiment

Source	Log (generalized variance)	U-statistic	Degrees of freedom	Approximate F-statistic†	Degrees of freedom
Coupon type	8.94	0.043	2, 1, 2	11.08	2, 1
Ad theme	10.60	0.008	2, 2, 2	5.02	4, 2
Interaction	8.76	0.052	2, 2, 2	1.70	4, 2
Replicates	7.96				

†None of the differences are statistically significant.

MULTIVARIATE ANALYSIS OF COVARIANCE

The existence of uncontrolled variables in a research design is always a potential source of problems. The determination of net regression coefficients and the analysis of covariance are but two examples of analytic devices that statistically adjust for such variables when they either are not or cannot be controlled experimentally. MANOVA can similarly yield more useful results by adjusting for one or more covariates.

The n-dimensional graph of MANOVA considers the location of the centroids. The extension to covariance (MANCOVA) adjusts the location of the centroids for the effects of uncontrolled variables. The distances among the adjusted centroids then serves as the basis for evaluating the treatment effects or their interactions.

The failure of MANOVA to reveal significant differences in the ad theme/coupon experiment could reflect the acceptance of a false null hypothesis. The experiment could be redesigned in order to make it more sensitive since within-cell variability is rather large. First, more observations per cell would increase the reliability of both the individual cell estimates and the main effects estimates. Second, the introduction of a covariate might explain the large within-cell variability. Newspaper circulation is a potentially useful covariate. BMD12V allows for the incorporation of a covariate, including a test for its effect and the adjustment of the centroids for that effect. The computer printout follows the format of Table 18.6 and also incorporates a test for each covariate.

Table 18.7 is adapted from a study of the effectiveness of TV commercials by Wind and Denny.[21] Seven separate measures of the "effectiveness" of a particular commercial comprise the set of dependent variables. This set pos-

Table 18.7
Effectiveness of TV Commercial. Multivariate Analysis of Covariance†

Source of variation	Log (generalized variance)	Approximate F-ratio
Test versus control	33.29	0.69
Brand users versus nonusers	33.75	18.33‡
Interaction	33.30	1.21
Covariates§		
TV watching	36.21	2.55‡
Liking for program (before)	34.71	1.25
.	.	.
.	.	.
.	.	.

†Adapted from Yoram Wind and Joseph Denny, 1974, Multivariate analysis of variance in research on the effectiveness of TV commercials, *Journal of Marketing Research* **11** (May): 136–142.
‡F-ratio significant at $\alpha = .05$.
§A total of eight covariates was included in the analysis.

[21]Yoram Wind and Joseph Denny, 1974, Multivariate analysis of variance in research on the effectiveness of TV commercials, *Journal of Marketing Research* **11**: 136–142.

from the equations. (2) Each successive pair of equations is uncorrelated with all preceding equations. MANOVA does not require a corresponding step, employing the centroids in the analysis.

Analysis results. MANOVA tests three types of hypotheses: main effects, interactions, and tests for covariates if MANCOVA is employed. These tests are analogous to similar tests from ANOVA although the test statistic in MANOVA uses the *U*-statistic derived from Wilks lambda. Canonical correlation tests for the significance of the correlation between each pair of linear equations. Other results are descriptive of the sample, rather than inferential for the universe. The importance of each original variable may be presented as either the canonical coefficients or the structure correlations. Finally, the redundancy indices give a measure of "shared" variance. They are better indicators of the strength of the relationship between the *sets* of variables than are the canonical correlations (or their corresponding eigenvalues).

SUMMARY

The extension of association techniques to include multiple dependent variables leads into canonical correlation in the case of regression and into MANOVA in the case of analysis of variance. The two techniques are similar only in the sense that each deals with relationships between two *sets* of variables. Canonical correlation combines the original variables into linear composites of the form $\overset{*}{y}_i = a_{1i}y_1 + a_{2i}y_2 + \cdots$ and $\overset{*}{x}_i = b_{1i}x_1 + b_{2i}x_2 + \cdots$. MANOVA tests for differences among centroids whose coordinates are given by the dependent variables. The nominally scaled independent variables define the experimental design in MANOVA and identify the subgroups whose centroids are to be compared.

Canonical correlation solves for pairs of linear equations, selected so that the correlation between the two canonical variates is a maximum. The pairs are determined sequentially, subject to the condition that the equations are not correlated with the equations derived previously. The meaning of the canonical variates hinges on the canonical coefficients of the variables in the equations. They have the potential of reflecting common factors, but unique meaning is not assured.

Canonical correlation can aid the decision maker in two ways. First, the resulting pairs of equations may reveal systems of relationships that are obscured in simpler approaches. Second, the equations permit prediction or control for specific canonical variates, provided these variates have managerial significance. Care must be exercised that excessive claims not be made with respect to canonical results. The canonical R_c's refer to the relationship between the canonical variates—the base for calculation is not variance in the original variables. The redundancy index is perhaps a better indicator of the degree of association.

MANOVA and multivariate analysis of covariance (MANCOVA) test for differences in centroids in the same way that the simpler techniques test for differences in means. The tests in the multiple procedures use Euclidean distance and involve standard scores. The results, therefore, assume that this type of equal weight is appropriate for the decision maker. Interpretation of the results must rely on the specific coordinates and the meaning of the individual variables. Preferred locations in n-dimensional space, of necessity, rely on the meaning of the individual axes.

EXERCISES AND PROBLEMS

1. Distinguish among the terms within each of the following sets.
   a) Canonical correlation, MANOVA, and MANCOVA
   b) MANOVA and ANOVA
   c) Canonical correlation coefficient, redundancy index, and canonical structure correlation
   d) Canonical correlation and ordinary least-squares multiple correlation
   e) MANOVA and cluster analysis
   f) Canonical variates and the variables of the canonical functions

2. Canonical correlation is of potential aid to a marketing manager for three different types of questions. Name and briefly describe them.

3. Canonical correlation solves for pairs of functions.
   a) How does the technique select these functions? Explain the criterion or criteria applied.
   b) Discuss how managerial utility is assured and obtained.

4. The proper indicator of the importance of individual variables in canonical correlation is a matter of debate. Three different methods are presented in the text.
   a) What are the essential similarities and differences among them?
   b) Will they always yield similar rankings?

5. Collect the following data from a small sample (at least 15): expenditures on four or five products of your choice, income, size of household, and two or three additional variables. Define the variables so that canonical correlation can be employed.
   a) How, if at all, did the fact that canonical correlation was to be employed influence the variables chosen and their definitions? Discuss briefly.
   b) Determine at least two pairs of canonical functions.
   c) What is the maximum number of pairs of functions that could be obtained? Why?
   d) What is the best way of summarizing the degree of association found? Present your result(s) and explain its(their) meaning in terms of this problem.

    e) How is your result in (d) superior to alternative measures?

    f) Discuss the meaning of the functions derived.

6. A second analysis of your data in Exercise 5 is to be performed with the expenditure variables as a set of dependent variables. Choose three of the other set as independent variables to be used in MANOVA. Redefine the independent variables if necessary.

    a) Was a redefinition necessary? Why?

    b) Do the data conform to a satisfactory research design for MANOVA? Why or why not?

    c) Add additional observations if necessary to provide a satisfactory research design, and perform a MANOVA analysis. Present the summary results.

    d) Which, if any, of the independent variables or interactions are associated with the dependent variable? Cite evidence for your conclusion.

    e) Would the centroids found have managerial significance for any firm? (Disregard statistical significance if necessary.) Discuss.

7. Refer to the data in Tables 18.1 and 18.2. An executive of the firm said the second pair of canonical functions confirmed a general feeling that had long been within the firm—namely that older salespeople were more concerned with company profit. Do you concur? Why?

8. The multivariate analysis of covariance results included in Table 18.7 indicate two significant F-ratios. How is it possible with statistically significant differences to recommend against use of the commercial?

9. Find (in current marketing journals) a research study that employs canonical correlation. Discuss

    a) the interpretability of the canonical variates,

    b) the number of pairs solved for and whether high association is present between the last pair included,

    c) whether the conclusions reached are justified.

10. Find (in current marketing journals) a research study that employs MANOVA. Discuss

    a) whether the research design is balanced,

    b) the advantages and disadvantages of a composite dependent variable versus a single dependent variable,

    c) whether the conclusions reached are justified.

11. Analyze, criticize, and explain:

    a) Canonical correlation deals with multicollinearity by choosing pairs of functions that are uncorrelated. It, thus, is a possible alternative approach to stepwise regression.

    b) The artificially high canonical correlation coefficients are not really a problem because the statistical test of the null hypothesis automatically adjusts for this upward bias. If one is still concerned, it is always possible to use the characteristic roots which will be numerically smaller than R_c.

c) MANOVA and canonical correlation have distinct advantages over subjectively weighted indices. The weights determined are the same regardless of the researcher, and operational significance is assured by the nature of the input data.

d) Cluster analysis might be an appropriate step preceding MANOVA. The subgroups established in cluster analysis can provide the appropriate bases for the data collection required in MANOVA.

e) The redundancy index may be a better measure of degree of association than is the canonical correlation coefficient, but it loses much of its superiority because two measures (rather than one) are derived for each pair of functions.

CHAPTER 19

ORDINAL SCALES—USES AND TRANSFORMATIONS
WHEN IS RANKING GOOD ENOUGH?

Decision making is often based on an expected yield over a period of time. This expected yield in turn is determined by estimates of dollar revenues and dollar costs. All of these estimates require measurements, and measurements require interval scales. Nominal scales frequently become relevant as the number of individuals within a particular category is considered—often modified by the application of assumed mean dollar figures from a second source. Since the typical marketing manager works in the framework established by these considerations, the techniques discussed in previous chapters have employed either nominal or interval scales or a combination of the two.

Ordinal scales work with ranks and the accompanying relationships of more than and less than, but these scales do not address the questions of how much more or how much less.[1] Measurements of differences are not given nor are they possible. Thus ordinal-scaled data fall short of the decision maker's usual requirements.

Despite the inherent weaknesses of ordinal data, the decision maker often finds that the data available are properly classified as ordinal. Preference rankings of six brands as one through six can hardly be treated as an interval scale. If questionnaire responses on a seven-point scale of strongly agree, agree, mildly agree, neutral, mildly disagree, disagree, and strongly disagree are considered to be seven equidistant locations on an interval scale, the results may be a considerable distortion of the true facts. Asymmetric options, for example, five positive and only two negative alternatives, pose even greater problems. An assumption of an interval scale is almost certainly wrong.

The question to be considered, given the availability or necessity of ordinal data, is how they can be useful to the decision maker. All too often, the data have not been used in ordinal form. Either they have been upgraded, assuming the ordinal scale is the equivalent of an interval scale, or they have

---

[1]See "Scales and Measurements" in Chapter 4 for a discussion of various types of scales.

been downgraded to nominal data by establishing a limited number of categories. The first is usually unwarranted, and the conclusions derived must be suspect. The second discards information and suffers a loss of analytic power. Both are unfortunate procedures because ordinal data can be used in their existing form.

The popularity of ordinal data stems from two different causes. First, it is easier for most people to rank than to measure. This is partially due to the unwillingness of respondents to exert the required effort, but it may also reflect a difficulty in thinking in numerical terms. Second, an interval scale demands a clear definition of the appropriate unit of measure. The collection of such data requires that the researcher–decision maker (1) establish an unambiguous definition and (2) communicate that definition to the respondent. In many instances, the most that can be claimed for data of the attitudinal-opinion-preference type is an ordinal scale even when an interval scale is attempted.

Given the prevalence of ordinal data, their analysis falls into two general categories. *First*, the data are analyzed as ordinal data, using appropriate procedures for either hypothesis testing or estimation. These procedures fall into the general province of *nonparametric statistics*—the name stemming from the fact that they make no assumptions concerning the distribution of the population from which the observations are drawn.[2] A wide variety of analyses can be performed with ordinal data: two or more groups can be compared; a single group can be compared against hypothesized values; measures of association can be derived; indeed most questions asked of interval data have their counterparts for ordinal data. *Second*, the implicit interval values contained in ordinal data may be recovered. This process must not be confused with the assumption that ordinal data may be treated simply as interval data.

Ordinal data, like interval data, may be analyzed as univariate, bivariate, or multivariate data. Our coverage will be illustrative rather than exhaustive, presenting some of the more common procedures in the present chapter and moving to multidimensional scaling and conjoint measurement in the next.

THE MEDIAN

The median is an ordinal concept. It is the central item of a series arrayed by size.[3] The median can be identified with both ordinal and interval data, but its greatest utility occurs with ordinal data where an arithmetic mean cannot be calculated. The median can also be determined with interval scale data where

---

[2]Nonparametric statistics are not restricted to ordinal-scaled data. Contingency table analysis also falls within nonparametric statistics as do certain tests using interval data. Our principal concern at the present is ordinal data. See Sidney Siegel, 1956, *Nonparametric Statistics for the Behavioral Sciences* (New York: McGraw-Hill).

[3]Two distinct conventions exist for locating the median with an even number of observations. One places the median midway between the two central items. The other places the median at the location where the cumulative distribution first exceeds 50 percent. The distinction is trivial for most practical problems.

the first or last class is open-ended. Ordinal data, with the median as a measure of central tendency, might also be employed in order to reduce costs even though the characteristic under study is conceptually interval in nature.

The median, with truly ordinal data, is not measured; it is merely located. The presentation of a median income of $15,349 states that the basic scale is interval. The use of the median rather than the mean is often forced by the lack of measured data for all observations. Income may be thought of as interval in scale, but precise numerical values may not be available for all individuals. If the observations can be placed in order of magnitude, it is necessary to record a numerical measurement for only the middle observation in order to know the median value. Such a procedure may reduce the data collection task considerably. Another situation in which the median may be preferred over the mean occurs when a "representative value" is desired. The mean is influenced by the numerical values of the most extreme observations while the median is merely the value of the middle item in the array. Thus in extremely skewed distributions, the mean might be highly unrepresentative while the median gives more of a central tendency.

The median can be used as a point of demarcation in testing whether two groups differ in their central tendencies. It can be used for this purpose regardless of whether the raw data come from an ordinal scale or an interval scale, but it is the best alternative if an ordinal scale is involved.[4]

The median test with ordinal data, using the median as a point of division, can be illustrated by a problem faced by a national research firm. The firm has obtained local interviewers through two "temporary-help" firms (Ace and G&K). These two firms have supplied interviewers for the same community. The supervisor of the field staff believes the interviewers provided over the past few months can be ranked but is unwilling to quantify the ratings. Twenty-four interviewers have been supplied by Ace and 20 by G&K. The data can be placed into the standard 2×2 contingency table, using the median as the dividing point. Table 19.1 presents the relevant data. The median is located for the total group of 44 interviewers.

Sixty-five percent of the G&K interviewers are above the median while only 38 percent of the Ace interviewers are above this mark. Chi Square is used

Table 19.1
Interviewer Quality from Ace and G&K

Firm	Number below median	Number above median	Total
Ace	15	9	24
G&K	7	13	20
Total	22	22	44

---

[4]The mode as a measure of central tendency is possible for some problems, but analyses based on the median have greater analytic power.

to test whether this difference is large enough to conclude that G&K interviewers are superior. The results yield $\chi^2 = 3.30$; with $\alpha = .05$, the null hypothesis should be accepted. The supervisor is not justified in concluding that G&K is supplying higher quality interviewers, using the median as the point of demarcation.[5]

The same type of test could be extended to any number of groups, generating a $k \times 2$ table where k is the number of groups. The median is obtained from the pooled data, and each sample unit is classified as above or below that reference point. The technique can be further extended with other points of demarcation; for example, quartiles or thirds.

The test presented above does not use all of the information available with ordinal data. The rankings are lost in the table, in effect reducing the data to two nominal categories. Even when several categories are established by using various ordinal locations as reference points, a contingency table analysis reduces the ordinal data to a nominal scale since order is not relevant in the Chi Square test. In the next section we illustrate several tests that retain the rank information.

RANK TESTS

The rationale of most rank tests is straightforward and intuitively appealing. The principal difficulties are encountered in the tests of significance that usually involve special statistics whose significance can be evaluated only with specially constructed tables (appropriate and useful only for that particular statistic). We will give only a few illustrations and include the necessary tables in the Appendix.[6]

First, let us examine the field supervisor's rankings of the 44 interviewers provided by Ace and G&K. These rankings, identified only by firm, are presented in Table 19.2. Intuitively the mean or median ranks seem likely statistics to compare. Both statistics show lower figures for G&K: 18.3 versus 26.0 for the means and 16.5 versus 27.5 for the medians.

The appropriate test statistic is the Mann–Whitney U, where U is equal to the smaller of the two values calculated from Eq. (19.1).

$$U_i = n_1 n_2 + \frac{n_i(n_i + 1)}{2} - R_i. \tag{19.1}$$

The test statistic U yields a test of the null hypothesis that the two samples have been drawn from the same population. The R values in the formula refer to the sum of the ranks (624 and 366 in Table 19.2); the inclusion of the sample sizes

---

[5]Separate medians could be computed for Ace and G&K, with the difference tested against the standard error of the difference between medians. Such a procedure is not nonparametric, involving as it does assumptions concerning the two population distributions.

[6]Siegel, *op. cit.*, contains extensive discussion and examples of many other nonparametric tests, including some for interval scale data.

Table 19.2
Rankings of Interviewers from Ace and G&K

Ace	3, 5, 7, 9, 12, 16, 17, 20, 23, 24, 26, 27, 28, 30, 31, 32, 34, 36, 37, 39, 40, 41, 43, 44

Σ ranks = 624; $\bar{x}$ rank = 26.0;   Median rank = 27.5

G&K 1, 2, 4, 6, 8, 10, 11, 13, 14, 15, 18, 19, 21, 22, 25, 29, 33, 35, 38, 42

Σ ranks = 366; $\bar{x}$ rank = 18.3;   Median rank = 16.5

$$U_1 = n_1 n_2 + \frac{n_1(n_1 + 1)}{2} - R_1$$

$$= (20)(24) + \frac{20(21)}{2} - 366$$

$$= 480 + 210 - 366 = 324$$

or $$U_2 = n_1 n_2 + \frac{n_2(n_2 + 1)}{2} - R_2$$

$$= (20)(24) + \frac{24(25)}{2} - 624$$

$$= 480 + 300 - 624 = 156$$

$$U = 156$$

$$\mu_U = \frac{n_1 n_2}{2} = \frac{20(24)}{2} = 240.$$

$$\sigma_U = \left[\frac{n_1 n_2(n_1 + n_2 + 1)}{12}\right]^{1/2} = \left[\frac{20(24)(45)}{12}\right]^{1/2}$$

$$= 42.43.$$

$$z = \frac{U - \mu_U}{\sigma_U} = \frac{156 - 240}{42.43} = -1.98.$$

(n_1 and n_2) automatically adjusts for the number of observations. If no differences existed in the mean ranks of the two groups, U_1 and U_2 would have the same value (240 in the present case). This value is given by Eq. (19.2).

$$U = \frac{n_1 n_2}{2}. \qquad (19.2)$$

Extensive tables have been compiled by Mann and Whitney for testing differences in ranks where neither group is larger than 20.[7] They have also demonstrated that the sampling distribution of U rapidly approaches normal

[7]H. B. Mann and D. R. Whitney, 1947, On a test whether one of two random variables is stochastically larger than the other, *Annals of Mathematical Statistics* **18**: 50–60. These tables are also reproduced in Siegel, *op. cit.*

as n_1 and n_2 increase in size.[8] Equation (19.2) gives the mean of the distribution, and Eq. (19.3) gives its standard deviation. The test statistic is of course $(U - \mu_U)/\sigma_U$.

$$\sigma_U = \left[\frac{n_1 n_2 (n_1 + n_2 + 1)}{12} \right]^{1/2}. \tag{19.3}$$

Applying Eqs. (19.2) and (19.3) to the present data yields a z of 1.98.[9]

$$z = \frac{156 - 240}{42.43} = -1.98.$$

The observed difference, using rank data, is significant at the .05 level. The supervisor is now justified in concluding that G&K interviewers are superior to those of Ace. Individual rank data—in contrast to a contingency table based on the median as a reference point—supply a more powerful approach.

Analysis of Variance

Marketing research is often concerned with the evaluation of alternative marketing mixes. This evaluation is often performed by a sample of individuals from the target group. Suppose the individuals can rank the alternatives but find difficulty in assigning numerical values. An analysis of variance using rank data is possible.

A sample of 20 students was asked to compare four alternative formulations of a proposed new entry to the soft drink field, ranking them one through four in preference. The company has decided on the base for the beverage; the four formulations differ in the added ingredient—lemon, vanilla, cherry, or none (plain). A portion of the data and relevant totals are presented in Table 19.3. What conclusions are justified? The null hypothesis is that the four are equally preferred.

Friedman uses a statistic denoted by χ_r^2 to test whether the rank totals (R_i) differ significantly. This statistic is defined by Eq. (19.4) and is approximated by Chi Square with $k - 1$ degrees of freedom.[10]

$$\chi_r^2 = \frac{12}{Nk(k + 1)} \sum_{i=1}^{k} (R_i)^2 - 3N(k + 1) \tag{19.4}$$

where

$$N = \text{number of row,}$$
$$k = \text{number of columns, and}$$
$$R_i = \text{sum of ranks in } i\text{th column.}$$

---

[8]Mann and Whitney, *op. cit.*

[9]Either value of U from Eq. (19.1) can be substituted when the normal approximation with Eqs. (19.2) and (19.3) is employed. The special tabulations for small samples require use of the lower of the two values computed in Eq. (19.1).

[10]M. Friedman, 1937, The use of ranks to avoid the assumption of normality implicit in the analysis of variance, *Journal American Statistical Association* **32**: 675–701.

Table 19.3
Student Rankings of Four Alternative Soft Drink Formulations

Student	Formulation (added to base)			
	Lemon	Vanilla	Cherry	None (plain)
1	4	1	3	2
2	4	3	2	1
3	3	1	2	4
.				
.				
.				
20	3	2	1	4
Total (R_i)	69	32	47	52

$$\chi_r^2 = \frac{12}{20(4)(5)} \left[(69)^2 + (32)^2 + (47)^2 + (52)^2 \right] - 3(20)(5)$$

$$= 320.94 - 300 = 20.94.$$

Applying Eq. (19.4), the value of χ_r^2 is 20.94, with three degrees of freedom. The company should certainly reject the hypothesis that the four are equally preferred. Inspection of the table reveals the preferences. Vanilla added to the base ranked highest. The formulation with lemon is ranked lowest. Cherry and plain are ranked second and third.

Ranking methods, along with other nonparametric techniques, are sometimes the most appropriate to use even when the data are measured on an interval scale. None of the ranking methods assume anything about the form of the underlying distribution. A comparison of two means, using a t-test, assumes normality. The U-test makes no such assumption. A researcher might downgrade interval data to ordinal when the data do not satisfy the necessary conditions for the statistical test. In the same way ordinary ANOVA assumes both homoscedasticity and normality. ANOVA with ranked data assumes neither.

We must be careful in applying ranking methods and other nonparametric tests to recognize the specific nature of the null hypothesis. For example, ANOVA with ranks does not test for equality of means or totals. Nor does it test for equality in the number of first-place rankings. It tests whether the ranks assigned the various treatments came from the same population. Means can be equal although rankings are different. Overall rankings may balance out although the number of first (or last) place ranks differ. No statistical test can identify similarities or differences unless the sample data use the relevant measures. The need for careful definition of the research problem and pertinent characteristics is present in all aspects of research; ordinal data and the associated tests are merely another aspect of it.

Rank Correlation

Association studies using interval scaled variables rely on strong assumptions: linearity and normality being particularly significant. Summary measures of association, such as r^2, and tests of their statistical significance may be considerably distorted if these assumptions are not met. These assumptions are dropped if the degree of association between two characteristics is determined by rank correlation. Thus rank correlation may be appropriate in either of two situations: (1) one or both characteristics are ordinally (not intervally) scaled or (2) the data do not meet the assumptions of linear least-squares correlation.

An ad agency wanted to determine whether a company's image in social responsibility varied with its return on investment. The agency made a small pilot study, obtaining rankings for ten companies on social responsibility. Return on investment was calculated from accounting records over a four-year period. The ranks on each characteristic are given in Table 19.4. Three different conclusions are possible: (1) the ranks are positively correlated, (2) the ranks are negatively correlated, or (3) the ranks are independent.

Spearman's rank correlation coefficient is defined by Eq. (19.5),[11] where D equals the difference in ranks and n equals the number of items ranked.

$$r_\mathrm{s} = 1 - \frac{6\Sigma D^2}{n^3 - n}. \tag{19.5}$$

The coefficient of rank correlation is $-.58$ for the social responsibility/return on investment data of Table 19.4. The two rankings are negatively correlated in the sample; higher rankings on one tend to occur with lower rankings on the other.

The coefficient of rank correlation (r_s) can be tested against the null hypothesis by the t-distribution (given $n \geq 10$). The appropriate standard error is given by Eq. (19.6).

$$\sigma_{r_\mathrm{s}} = \left[\frac{1 - r_\mathrm{s}^2}{n - 2} \right]^{\frac{1}{2}}. \tag{19.6}$$

Application of the test yields a t of 2.01. Is this a one-tailed test or a two-tailed test? If the ad agency's *a priori* hypothesis suspected a negative relation, the formulation would be

$$H_0 : r_\mathrm{s} \geq 0;$$
$$H_1 : r_\mathrm{s} < 0.$$

As a one-tailed test, the result is large enough to reject H_0—the two characteristics are inversely correlated ($\alpha = .05$).

This finding would not establish any necessary causal relationship between return on investment and social responsibility image. Once more, as

---

[11]C. Spearman, 1904, The proof and measurement of association between two things, *American Journal of Psychology* **15**: 72–101.

Table 19.4
Social Responsibility Image versus Return on Investment

| Company | Rankings | | D^2 |
	Social responsibility image	Return on investment	
A	4	7	9
B	7	2	25
C	2	10	64
D	5	1	16
E	9	5	16
F	1	6	25
G	10	3	49
H	3	9	36
I	6	8	4
J	8	4	16
			260

$$r_s = 1 - \frac{6(260)}{1000 - 10} = 1 - \frac{1560}{990} = -.58.$$

in the case of linear least-squares correlation, the findings show whether the characteristics tend to vary together. The ad agency, however, might be concerned about a possible link in the public's mind between the two variables. It might wish to identify and define variables that make up social responsibility apart from the financial success of the enterprise.

Spearman's coefficient of rank correlation, like the standard r, has a lower limit of -1.0 and an upper limit of $+1.0$. It coincides with the result that would be obtained if r were computed by the usual methods using ranks as input data. Unlike r, the possible results for r_s are greatly constrained with small samples. For example, only four different numerical results are possible with $n = 3$: -1, $-\frac{1}{2}$, $+\frac{1}{2}$, and $+1$. Special tables have been prepared for appraising statistical significance when $n < 10$.[12]

If ranks on more than two characteristics are to be compared, one approach would be to compute all possible r_s values and find their mean. Another approach is to define a new statistic which equals 1.0 if all rankings are the same and 0.0 if there is a complete lack of agreement. Kendall's coefficient of concordance (W) is such a measure.

The data in Table 19.5 refer to preference rankings given by six panel members to five brands of ice cream. If there were complete uniformity in

---

[12]See Siegel, *op. cit.*, p. 284.

Table 19.5
Preference Rankings of Ice Cream Brands

Panel member	Ice cream brand				
	Baker	Cool	Delishas	Presto	Treat
Armstrong	2	5	1	3	4
Frank	3	4	2	1	5
Goodman	2	4	1	3	5
Green	1	3	2	4	5
Robertson	2	3	1	5	4
Wind	1	5	3	2	4
Total (R_i)	11	24	10	18	27

preference, the sums of the ranks would be 6, 12, 18, 24, and 30—in general, $k, 2k, \ldots$ where k = number of judges. If there were overall lack of conformity, the total of each column would be 18—$k(n + 1)/2$ where n = number of brands. The greater the dispersion among the totals, the closer the agreement. Equation (19.7) gives the formula for W.[13]

$$W = \frac{s}{(k^2/12)(n^3 - n)} \tag{19.7}$$

where

s = sum of squared deviations of R_i from mean of R_i.

The sum of squared deviations for the data of Table 19.5 is

$$s = (11 - 18)^2 + (24 - 18)^2 + (10 - 18)^2$$
$$+ (18 - 18)^2 + (27 - 18)^2$$
$$= 230.$$

W, then, is equal to .64, as shown below:

$$W = \frac{230}{(36/12)(125 - 5)} = .64.$$

The degree of agreement among the six panel members is 64 percent of perfect agreement. The denominator is the maximum value of s, achieved only if there is perfect agreement.

Is 64 percent agreement significant? The answer depends on the number of judges and the number of objects compared. For small samples, the test requires a listing of the sampling distribution when the null hypothesis is true. Appendix Table A.6 gives the required values of s at two levels of significance

---

[13]M. G. Kendall, 1948, *Rank Correlation Methods* (London: Griffin).

for up to seven objects and for selected numbers of judges up to 20. Referring to this table, we see that the critical values of s are 136.1 ($\alpha = .05$) and 176.1 ($\alpha = .01$). The test results from Table 19.5 are significant. These judges show similarity in the rankings they assign the five brands of ice cream. Delishas and Baker are the preferred brands. Treat ranks at the bottom, and Cool is not much better. Presto is in the middle.[14]

A large or significant W is an indication of agreement among the judges. In certain instances the consensus may serve as a standard, but agreement need not indicate "correct" results. Perception, image, and many similar opinion or attitude measurements are often lacking in valid external criteria. The marketing researcher, in examining these topics, should carefully distinguish between a consensus and an objectively defined external measure.

Signed-rank Tests

Many marketing experiments assign different treatments to matched pairs. The effect of product endorsement by a public figure may be tested in a laboratory situation by comparing simulated purchase behavior of two matched samples. The results of such an experiment, using nine matched pairs of individuals, are shown in Table 19.6.

The standard test for these data would be a t-test, but for either of two reasons its appropriateness might be questioned. First, the normality assump-

Table 19.6
Simulated Purchase Behavior with and without Endorsement by a Public Figure. Matched Pairs

Pair	Simulated purchases		Difference (d)	Rank of (d)
	With endorsement	Without endorsement		
1	22	11	11	6
2	15	14	1	1
3	27	19	8	5
4	32	35	− 3	2 (−)
5	10	15	− 5	3 (−)
6	26	11	15	7
7	41	23	18	9
8	36	30	6	4
9	45	29	16	8

[14]For larger samples, the statistical significance of W can be tested with a Chi Square distribution with the following transformation: $\chi^2 = k(n - 1)W$ with $n - 1$ degrees of freedom.

tion might be dubious. Second, the simulated purchase measure might not be interval in scale. If the researcher is able to rank the nine pairs from most simi- lar to least similar, the Wilcoxon matched-pairs, signed-rank test can be employed. This test uses the data in the last column of Table 19.6 that rank the nine pairs from most similar (pair 2) to least similar (pair 7). The insertion of (−) indicates pairs in which simulated purchase was greater without endorse- ment by a public figure.

If endorsement has no effect, the sum of the ranks with a positive sign should be approximately the same as the sum of the ranks with a negative sign. This is not the case! The sum is 40 for the positive signs and only five for the negative signs. The Wilcoxon test defines T as the smaller of the two summed ranks: five in our example.

Our sample is only nine, fairly small. Appendix Table A.7 provides the critical values of T for samples from size six through 25.[15] Three significance levels are provided. The present results meet the first level ($\alpha = .025$ for a one- tailed test), but not the other two. Endorsement by a public official has a fav- orable effect—as long as we are not testing H_0 at a lower level of significance.

SIGN AND RUNS TESTS

Less powerful nonparametric tests simply ask which is larger or whether there is a bunching of similar results. The first is a sign test. For example, we might ask whether individuals receiving three requests for contributions have more or less favorable attitudes than those receiving only two requests. The second is a runs test. Data gathered over a period of time might be affected by changes in the environment. A runs test, in such a case, would indicate that the data should not be pooled as a picture of a constant universe.

Sign Test

The development officer for a public charity selected 25 matched individuals from a file. One member of each pair had received three requests for contribu- tions, and the other had received two requests. Several attitudinal questions toward the charity were included in a telephone interview. The key question to the development officer concerned reaction to current communications. The results showed a more favorable response by 14 who received only two re- quests, a more favorable response by eight who received three requests, and three ties.

---

[15]For larger samples, T approaches normality with

$$\mu_T = \frac{n(n + 1)}{4} \quad \text{and} \quad \sigma_T^2 = \frac{n(n + 1)(2n + 1)}{24} .$$

Ignoring ties, we have 22 observations distributed 14 and eight.[16] The binomial distribution is appropriate for testing the null hypothesis of equal division ($p = q = \frac{1}{2}$). The desired probability is a cumulative value: the probability of eight *or less* if the null hypothesis is true. Thus nine separate values must be calculated: $P(0) + P(1) + \cdots + P(8)$. Extensive tables for the binomial (or sign test) have been prepared. They are typically included in handbooks of tables.[17] For a sample size 22, the critical value for a one-tailed test at $\alpha = .05$ is six. If the respondent who received three requests was more favorable in six or fewer comparisons, the null hypothesis would be rejected. Therefore, the development officer is not justified in concluding that a difference in attitude exists between the groups who received two and three requests. (As is always the case, larger samples and more precise measuring instruments might lead to other conclusions.)

The binomial distribution is always the correct model for the sign test. Two alternative tests may be used as approximations with large samples. The first is a 1×2 contingency table. The theoretical frequencies are provided by the hypothesized $p = q = \frac{1}{2}$.[18] The second alternative is to use the normal curve as an approximation.

Runs Test

The runs test is concerned with the distribution of observations over time. For example, is a change in quality or preference discernible? Quarterly surveys of customer opinion have been made by the Collins Clothing Company for a number of years. One of the more important questions to management concerns the stability of Collins rating over time. The percentage of number one rankings received in the last 20 surveys is given in Table 19.7. The median percentage attained by Collins in these 20 surveys is 38.5 percent. Each of the 20 observations is compared to the median, $(+)$ indicating a result above the median and $(-)$ indicating a result below the median.

The runs test examines the time sequence of signs, determining when changes occur. The first change occurs at observation 3, from $(+)$ to $(-)$. The series changes back to $(+)$ at the next observation, continuing at $(+)$ until observation 6. In all there are 11 changes, yielding 12 "runs" of observations

---

[16]The proper treatment of ties poses a problem in many of the tests mentioned in this chapter. In the case of ranked data, the usual procedure is to assign each tied observation the average of the ranks involved. Adjusting factors are then necessary in testing for statistical significance. See the noted references for the modifications required. In the case of the sign test, the existence of ties decreases the power of the test.

[17]See, for example, *Handbook of Tables for Probability and Statistics,* 1968, William H. Beyer (ed.) (Cleveland: Chemical Rubber Company).

[18]Use of a contingency table for the present problem yields a Chi Square of 1.64 with one degree of freedom. The binomial test is more appropriate although neither test shows a significant difference.

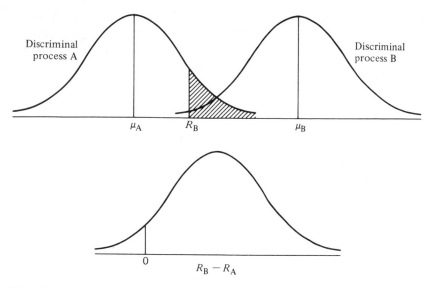

Fig. 19.1
Thurstone's law of comparative judgment. Two objects.

two distributions are normally distributed, $R_B - R_A$ would also be normally distributed. If we assume (1) the discriminal dispersions are equal for all of the original distributions and (2) the correlations between the paired judgments are zero,[22] the conversion from paired comparisons to interval data is further simplified. Incorporation of these assumptions lead to what Thurstone identifies as Case V.[23]

Price perceptions, using paired comparison data, are given in Table 19.8 for four supermarkets. The data show the percentage of respondents rating the column store higher in price than the row store. For example, 35 percent of the respondents rate Thrifty higher than Lucky; the complement of course is that 65 percent rate Lucky as higher than Thrifty.

The next step is to convert the percentage figures to a z-value on the normal curve. The appropriate z-values are read directly from Appendix Table A.2. We ask what z-value divides the normal curve into the specified percentage distributions. A z-value of .39 yields a 65/35 percentage division. Thus both Thrifty–Lucky comparisons receive a z of .39. The lower percentage receives the negative sign while the other receives the positive sign. Table 19.9 presents the appropriate z-values for all six paired comparisons.

---

[22]As shown by Mosteller, one need only assume equal correlations. Frederick Mosteller, 1951, Remarks on the method of paired comparisons, *Psychometrika* **16**: 3–11.

[23]L. L. Thurstone, 1959, *The Measurement of Values* (Chicago: University of Chicago Press).

Table 19.8
Respondent Ratings of Supermarket Prices. Paired Comparisons

		First store†		
Second store	Lucky	Thrifty	A&D	X-Cel
Lucky	—	35	10	20
Thrifty	65	—	22	33
A&D	90	78	—	56
X-Cel	80	67	44	—

†Table entries show percentage rating first store higher than second store.

The standard deviation of the $R_B - R_A$ distribution, assuming zero correlation, is given by Eq. (19.8). The second step assumes the two variances are equal.

$$\sigma_{R_A - R_B} = \left(\sigma_{R_A}^2 + \sigma_{R_B}^2\right)^{1/2} \tag{19.8}$$
$$= \left(2\sigma_R^2\right)^{1/2} = \sigma_R \sqrt{2}.$$

The individual values for the paired comparisons may be expressed according to Eq. (19.9).

$$z_{BA} = \frac{R_B - R_A}{\sigma_{R_B - R_A}} = \frac{R_B - R_A}{\sigma_R \sqrt{2}} \tag{19.9}$$

Conversion into standard scores sets $\sigma_R = 1$ and yields the following relationship, Eq. (19.10).

$$R_B - R_A = z_{BA} \sqrt{2}. \tag{19.10}$$

Table 19.9
z-values and Derived Scale for Supermarket Price Perceptions

		First store		
Second store	Lucky	Thrifty	A&D	X-Cel
Lucky	—	− .39	− 1.28	− .84
Thrifty	.39	—	− .77	− .44
A&D	1.28	.77	—	.15
X-Cel	.84	.44	− .15	—
Σz	2.51	.82	− 2.20	− 1.13
Scale values	.89	.29	− .78	− .40

If we hold B constant and sum over all stores we obtain

$$nR_B - \Sigma R_i = \sqrt{2}\Sigma z_{Bi}.$$

Since we are assuming an interval scale rather than a ratio scale, we can select any zero point. We set $\Sigma R_i = 0$ and obtain Eq. (19.11).

$$R_B = \frac{\sqrt{2}}{n}\Sigma z_{Bi}. \tag{19.11}$$

We can now use Eq. (19.11) to compute price ratings for the four stores on an interval scale. This is accomplished most simply by multiplying the column sums of Table 19.9 (Σz) by .3536 which is the value of $\sqrt{2}/4$. The placement of the four stores is as shown on Table 19.9: Lucky as the highest (.89), Thrifty second highest (.29), X-Cel next ($-.40$), and A&D lowest ($-.78$). X-Cel and A&D are more similar in perceived price level than are any other two stores since the difference in their scale values is least. The other two adjacent pairs are almost equidistant: .60 between Lucky and Thrifty and .69 between Thrifty and X-Cel.

Goodness of Fit

If the interval scale derived by the law of comparative judgment is implicit in the paired comparisons, we should be able to work back to the original data from the interval scale. The resulting estimates, when compared to the original data, will be an indication of how well the results fit the input data. The better

Table 19.10
Goodness of Fit for Supermarket Price Perceptions

Second store	First store			
	Lucky	Thrifty	A&D	X-Cel
Lucky				
Original	—	35	10	20
Calculated	—	34	12	18
Thrifty				
Original	65	—	22	33
Calculated	66	—	22	31
A&D				
Original	90	78	—	56
Calculated	88	78	—	60
X-Cel				
Original	80	67	44	—
Calculated	82	69	40	—
Mean discrepancy†	1.7	1.0	2.0	2.7

†Overall mean discrepancy = 1.8.

the fit, the more confidence we can place in the scale as a valid description of the price perceptions.

The check on the fit reverses the solution steps. Equation (19.10) is solved for z, given $R_B - R_A$. $R_B - R_A$ for the Lucky–Thrifty comparison is .60. Dividing by $\sqrt{2}$ yields a z-value of .42—a percentage of 66 percent against the original input of 65 percent. Table 19.10 gives similar calculations for the remaining paired comparisons. The overall mean discrepancy is only 1.8 percentage points and the mean discrepancy for each store is under 3 percentage points. The largest single discrepancy is 4 percentage points in the X-Cel–A&D comparison.

If an alternative way of estimating an interval scale gave a better fit, it would be a prime candidate as a better description of price perceptions. Alternatively if a better fit in two dimensions were possible, that description might be accepted and price perception might be considered as composed of two concepts rather than one. We shall consider some of these thoughts in the next chapter.

SUMMARY

Ordinal scales are less demanding on both the respondent and the researcher. Responses correspond to more than or less than without regard to "how much" more or less. The principal advantages of ordinal data over interval data are two-fold: (1) the data are usually easier (and less costly) to collect and (2) statistical tests based on order do not require knowledge of the population distribution. Thus the continual warnings concerning the normality assumption of t, ANOVA, regression, etc. are not relevant.

Statistical tests of ordinal data fall into the general category of nonparametric tests. Despite their attractiveness for the reasons stated above, the decision maker and researcher should be aware of two principal weaknesses. (1) The tests do not always address the problem of concern. The null hypotheses refer to ranks, medians, similarity of distribution, sign of comparisons, etc. Marketing decisions are more likely to depend on means or totals. The researcher must be familiar with the alternatives and guide the decision maker in structuring decisions. (2) The tests of ordinal data do not have as much "power" as the corresponding tests of interval data. Larger sample sizes with ordinal data will offset this difficulty, but the possibility of a larger sample must exist.

There are a multitude of specialized tests with ordinal data. We have discussed only a few in order to provide readers with a "feel" for their nature and to acquaint them with some of the more widely used tests. The median test with a contingency table, the Mann–Whitney U-test, ANOVA with rank data, rank correlation, the coefficient of concordance, the signed-ranks test, the sign test, and the runs test have all been presented. Many of these tests have special statistics associated with them, statistics that are used for only one specific technique. The originators and refiners of the techniques have usually investigated the sampling distributions of the particular statistic and have provided ιne necessary tables for evaluating statistical significance. The need for special tables presents a slight inconvenience, but most of the more widely used tables are available in special handbooks.

A second important use of ordinal data is as a means of deriving interval data. If the ordinal data are viewed as generated by an underlying continuum, the ordinal relationships may imply more precise measurements. Thurstone's law of comparative judgment, using paired comparisons, is one such technique. The test of the output is in the ability of the results to reconstruct the initial input. The law of comparative judgments assumes a single scale exists. In the next chapter, we will extend the investigation to multiple dimensions.

EXERCISES AND PROBLEMS

1. Distinguish among the terms of each of the following sets.
   a) Coefficient of rank correlation and coefficient of concordance
   b) Signed-ranks test and sign test
   c) Sign test and runs test
   d) Contingency table based on median as critical value and Mann–Whitney U
   e) Median, mean, and mode
   f) Ordinal scales, interval scales, and nominal scales

2. Briefly explain the meaning and significance of each of the following terms.
   a) Nonparametric test
   b) Cumulative binomial
   c) Paired comparisons
   d) Median
   e) Rank correlation

3. A manufacturer of labels, tags, and related small equipment surveyed a sample of its customers concerning receptivity to various changes in billing and pricing policies. A portion of the survey asked for a preference ranking of four alternatives: (1) prepaid freight, net 30; (2) 2/10, net 30; (3) 1/15, net 60; and (4) freight split 50/50, net 60. The distribution of answers in Table E19.3 was obtained.

Table E19.3

	Prepaid freight, net 30	2/10, net 30	1/15, net 60	Freight 50/50, net 60
Rank 1	8	7	3	2
Rank 2	6	8	4	2
Rank 3	4	4	8	4
Rank 4	2	1	5	12
	20	20	20	20

a) Calculate the coefficient of concordance for these data.

b) What hypothesis would be tested by your answer in (a)? State it clearly in terms of this problem.

c) Would you be willing to reject your hypothesis in (b)? Cite the evidence upon which you reach this conclusion.

d) Would a contingency analysis with x^2 have been equally appropriate? Why or why not?

e) Suppose only ten judges had been involved. Would it be appropriate to compute a coefficient of concordance? a x^2 with a contingency table analysis? Discuss.

f) Would it be possible to analyze the data by the analysis of variance for rank data? If yes, make the analysis and compare the result with your earlier conclusion. If no, explain why not?

4. Two ad campaigns, one with a colonial theme and one with a sports theme, were given extensive testing, using several different criteria. Ten matched groups of three subjects each were used. The results presented in Table E19.4 are mean scores, based on unweighted means for the various criteria. The research team does not want to assume that the scores are normally distributed.

Table E19.4

Group	Colonial theme	Sports theme
1	27	5
2	15	12
3	36	25
4	18	41
5	3	16
6	8	23
7	21	2
8	18	16
9	21	14
10	39	29

a) Analyze the data by a nonparametric test that you are willing to defend.

b) Present your defense of the procedure.

c) What is your conclusion? Cite appropriate evidence.

d) Is your conclusion consistent with the subjective impression given by a visual inspection of the data? Discuss.

e) Could the data be analyzed by another nonparametric test? Discuss.

5. An independent rating service has been asked to rate two large motel chains. They have selected 20 locations of Chain H and 14 locations of Chain R. These 34 locations have been placed in rank order in Table E19.5.

Table E19.5

Rank	Chain	Rank	Chain	Rank	Chain
1	H	13	H	24	R
2	H	14	H	25	R
3	R	15	R	26	H
4	H	16	R	27	H
5	R	17	H	28	R
6	H	18	R	29	H
7	H	19	R	30	R
8	H	20	H	31	H
9	R	21	R	32	H
10	H	22	H	33	H
11	R	23	H	34	R
12	H				

a) What do you think would be the best way to analyze the above data? Why?

b) Would you be willing to conclude that either Chain H or Chain R deserves a better rating? Cite the evidence that justifies this conclusion.

c) Would a 2 × 2 contingency table analysis, using the median as a division point, lead to the same conclusion?

6. The marketing research director of a manufacturer of small electrical appliances has been asked to compare advertising expenditures of various companies and the perceived aggressiveness of the companies' marketing managers. The director chooses to express advertising expenses as a percentage of sales and perceived aggressiveness on an ordinal scale generated by a panel of six judges.

a) Do you think the director showed good judgment in the decisions made concerning the two variables? Why?

b) The data on advertising expenditures have been converted to an ordinal scale. The data collected are presented in Table E19.6. Do you think the two variables are related? If yes, quantify your estimate.

c) If a third variable (percentage rate of increase in sales) were added to the analysis, would it be possible to calculate a summary measure of association for the three variables? Why or why not?

Table E19.6

Company	Advertising expenditures rank	Perceived aggressiveness rank
A	3	4
B	10	11
C	5	2
D	1	3
E	8	6
F	11	10
G	2	5
H	4	1
I	7	9
J	6	7
K	9	8

7. Membership in a local YMCA and expenditures on promotion are shown in Table E19.7.

Table E19.7

Year	Membership	Expenditures on promotion
1970	722	$500
1971	745	515
1972	793	575
1973	815	585
1974	826	600
1975	858	650
1976	870	660
1977	883	665
1978	915	700
1979	925	710

a) Fit a linear trend line to the data for each series.

b) Classify each observation as either above or below the trend line.

c) Would you be willing to conclude that the two series show a positive relationship with respect to the direction of their deviations from the trend lines?

d) Is there any evidence that the deviations from the membership trend line are bunched together? Use a specific test rather than a subjective appraisal.

CHAPTER 20

MULTIDIMENSIONAL SCALING AND CONJOINT ANALYSIS
GETTING MORE BUT ASKING LESS

Marketing managers must know how their products are perceived relative to competition. Unless managers know "where they are," they cannot know which way to move. Current product position is the foundation from which decisions emerge.

Multidimensional scaling is addressed to the product positioning question. It has as its goal *spatial representation*. In the typical marketing application, the goal is spatial representation of buyer perceptions and preferences. Which cold cereals are similar to each other and which are dissimilar? Which product attributes are most important in differentiating automobiles? Can residential housing buyers be segmented according to "benefit bundles" sought? How do objectively measured computer performance characteristics compare to the derived axes of a perceptual map? Which retail outlets compete for which market segments? Perceptual and preference issues exist within all industries and for all products and services. Religious institutions, countries, entertainers, and political candidates face the same question: "How are we perceived (and rated) by our existing customers, members, constituencies, etc. and by those we wish to cultivate in the future?"

All of the multivariate techniques discussed in the preceding chapters require the specification of the variables to be employed. Even factor analysis and clustering start with a set of variables that the technique attempts to reduce. In the cases of data that are partitioned into independent–dependent sets, both the dependent and independent variables are specified. This seems so logical that the reverse may sound implausible. Yet, that is the approach of multidimensional scaling.

Multidimensional scaling starts with response data on a single variable, overall perception or preference. From this starting point, the technique attempts to identify the underlying variables that are responsible for these perceptions and preferences—without the respondents' mentioning them.[1]

---

[1] Supplementary questioning, apart from multidimensional scaling, may be employed as an aid in labeling the axes.

This approach has two principal advantages. First, the researcher does not restrict or impose his or her view of the relevant dimensions. Second, the respondent need not articulate nor rationalize the decision process employed. The net result is that descriptive data are gathered without the introduction of a normative setting.

Multidimensional scaling can be applied to either metric data (intervally scaled or stronger) or nonmetric data (usually ordinal). More recent applications have stressed the use of nonmetric input data with metric output. This "boot-strapping" has been accomplished with a variety of algorithms and several different forms of input data. Many different computer programs are available, most of which are highly sophisticated. Our objective in this chapter is to familiarize the reader with the general subject area and to highlight some of the more pervasive concepts.[2]

Conjoint analysis is a related technique addressed to the determination of partial utilities for the separate attributes of multivariate offerings. It is similar to ANOVA in research design but does not demand an intervally scaled dependent variable. A bank contemplating some of the newer mortgage ideas could ask respondents to rank several alternatives, each alternative containing a different mix of the features to be tested. A manufacturer of vacuum cleaners could simultaneously determine the value of different brand names, various warranties, and the design of a new attachment.

MULTIDIMENSIONAL SCALING

Mapping of alternatives by multidimensional scaling (MDS) reveals either (1) the degree of similarity (or dissimilarity) between and among alternatives, (2) relative preference for the various alternatives, or (3) both. We will start with the first that requires only perceptual data. Respondents are asked to compare alternative offerings; for example, competing brands of detergent, alternative retail outlets, or opposing political candidates. Then we will examine preference data, comparing both the input and output of the two types of analyses.

Critical research design issues are involved with both types of data. What alternatives should be compared? How should the alternatives be presented—physically, by names, by descriptions, etc? Should responses be for total offering or by individual attributes? If for individual attributes, by

---

[2]The reader desiring operational competence should refer to the literature of psychometrics, measurement theory, and their business applications. The literature is extensive, both with respect to the theoretical basis, computer programs, and applications. C. H. Coombs, 1964, *A Theory of Data* (New York: Wiley) is an excellent example of the first as is W. S. Torgerson, 1960, *Theory and Methods of Scaling* (New York: Wiley). Discussions of various computer programs and specific examples may be found in Paul E. Green and Vithala R. Rao, 1972, *Applied Multidimensional Scaling: A Comparison of Approaches and Algorithms* (New York: Holt, Rinehart and Winston). Another work in the same vein, with particular stress on applications to marketing is Paul E. Green and Yoram Wind, 1973, *Multiattribute Decisions in Marketing: A Measurement Approach* (Hinsdale, Ill.: Dryden). Current issues of professional journals are also likely to have recent developments.

whom are they selected—respondent or researcher—and by what mechanism? Should responses refer to specific scenarios? If yes, which one or ones? These and similar issues are part of the problem definition. Analytical results, as is always the case, are appropriate only if the specific design is relevant for the manager's problem.[3]

The precise format for the subjects' responses is particularly important for MDS. The possibilities range from precise interval data on a series of specified attributes to various types of ordinal data for the total offerings. Once the data format has been determined, the program options available are constrained. Therefore this step is even more critical than in other research problems.

All MDS relies on the concept of a good fit, or alternatively the concept of a poor fit as measured by the *stress*. The measure of stress is based upon the comparison between the derived configuration and the relationships expressed in the original input data. The smaller the stress, the better the fit and the more satisfactory the mapping.

Similarities Data

Given a group of n objects, similarities data ask which of the items are most similar to each other and which are the most dissimilar. This information may be asked in a variety of formats.[4] Probably the three most common are (1) comparisons among triads, (2) ranking of paired items according to similarity, and (3) comparison against an anchor point.

Comparisons among triads. These involve the presentation of three items. The respondent is asked to select which two are the most similar and which two are the least similar. A particular attribute may be specified for the comparison or the comparison may address the total of all attributes.

Within each group of three candidates, which two are the most similar? the least similar?

   a) Carter, Jackson, Kennedy

   b) Brown, Jackson, Kennedy

   c) Carter, Harris, Brown

.

.

.

The presentation of all possible triads establishes constraints for possible positioning of the various candidates. MDS seeks to determine a mapping that is consistent with the input data.

---

[3]An excellent discussion of these issues, particularly as they pertain to multidimensional scaling, is given in Paul E. Green and Yoram Wind, *op. cit.*, pp. 26–31.

[4]Our discussion will focus on nonmetric input data since that approach is less demanding of respondents. Metric input is, of course, possible. Algorithms exist for both types of data.

Ranking of paired items according to similarity. This is illustrated by the data in Table 20.1. Five cold cereals are compared. The ranking of similarity is shown by the cell entries. Wheaties and Sugar Flakes are perceived as the most similar, and Granola and Shredded Wheat are perceived as the least similar. These rankings are derived from the two-dimensional mapping of Fig. 20.1 (based on eight cereals). We will use this graph as the basis for a short intuitive discussion of the issues involved in MDS.

Figure 20.2 represents a first try at placement of the *five* cereals ranked in Table 20.1. The typical MDS requires an initial configuration, supplied either by the researcher or a preprocessing step that is part of the computer program. The placement in Fig. 20.2 (our initial configuration) places Granola and Shredded Wheat at the endpoints because they are perceived as the least similar. Wheaties and Sugar Flakes are placed closest together. Other placements focus mainly on the fact that Total, Sugar Flakes, and Wheaties rank 1 through 3 in pairwise similarities—therefore they should be bunched together while their distances from Granola and Shredded Wheat should be greater.

Table 20.1
Cold Cereal Data. Ranking of Pairs by Similarity

Brand	Sugar Flakes	Total	Granola	Wheaties	Shredded Wheat
Sugar Flakes	—	3	8	1	5
Total		—	4	2	9
Granola			—	7	10
Wheaties				—	6
Shredded Wheat					—

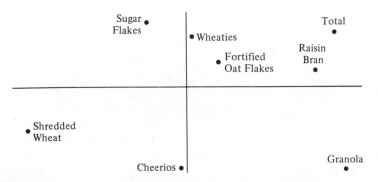

Fig. 20.1
Two-dimensional map of eight cold cereals.

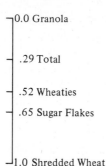

0.0 Granola

.29 Total

.52 Wheaties

.65 Sugar Flakes

1.0 Shredded Wheat

Fig. 20.2
Trial placement of five cold cereals on a single dimension.

Table 20.2
Derived Distances and Ranks for Cold Cereal Data†

Brand	Sugar Flakes	Total	Granola	Wheaties	Shredded Wheat
Sugar Flakes	—	.36 (5)	.65 (8)	.13 (1)	.35 (4)
Total		—	.29 (3)	.23 (2)	.71 (9)
Granola			—	.52 (7)	1.00 (10)
Wheaties				—	.48 (6)
Shredded Wheat					—

†Based on Fig. 20.2.

Table 20.2 presents the derived distances between the ten pairs and their ranks. Only three discrepancies exist between Table 20.2 and the input ranks of Table 20.1: Sugar Flakes–Total, Sugar Flakes–Shredded Wheat, and Total–Granola. A MDS program would ask at this point how to change the configuration in order to secure a better fit.

A better fit can be obtained either by moving points within the existing dimensions or by adding a new dimension. MDS programs typically keep the number of dimensions constant in this initial step. Perfect agreement can be achieved within the current problem without adding a second dimension. An increase in the scale value of Total to .33 will achieve a perfect fit. A change in the scale value of Sugar Flakes to .57 would also yield perfect agreement.

A single tightly constrained solution is not imposed by the current data. Note that a perfect fit is obtained in a single dimension despite the fact that the original mapping is in two dimensions. What would happen if we added a sixth cereal from Fig. 20.1? Five more ranks would be generated, moving from 10 to 15. More constraints and less "freedom" exist within the acceptable mapping. If all eight cereals are used, a total of 28 rankings are generated. The rapid increase in the number of constraints provides the basis by which MDS can generate a metric mapping with nonmetric input data. Ranking of pairs yields $n(n - 1)/2$ ranks. Even if the number of dimensions is increased as additional stimuli are added, the number of rankings increases faster than the number of dimensions.

Comparison between the horizontal axis of Fig. 20.1 and the derived perfect solution is instructive. The ordinal placement of the five cereals is in perfect agreement with their ordinal placement on the horizontal axis of Fig. 20.1. However, the metric distances differ considerably—particularly with respect to relationships against Total. These discrepancies exist because Total is perceived as similar to Granola in the horizontal axis (nutrition) but not in the vertical axis (texture). The derived single axis is a composite of the two characteristics and does not distinguish between them. The opposite effect is displayed by the comparison of Total with Sugar Flakes and Wheaties: the three are perceived as similar in texture but not in nutrition. The initial configuration placed Total close to Sugar Flakes and Wheaties, and there was not enough additional information in the ten rankings to overcome that aspect of the mapping.

The mapping on Fig. 20.1 is based upon data for all eight cereals and the 28 ranks. The identification and labeling of the axes is subjective and must be based upon substantive knowledge. Similarities data may be supplemented by additional questions concerning the objects under study, allowing the respondents to identify the relevant attributes or requesting ratings on attributes specified by the researcher. Another alternative is to submit the spatial mappings to the respondents, asking them to name the axes.

The horizontal axis seems to refer to perceived nutritional content. The vertical axis is not as clear but seems to involve physical texture. The difficulty in interpreting this axis illustrates the assumption that the scales are interval in nature. If physical texture is nominal, there is no way in which multidimensional scaling can yield a meaningful spatial plotting. Truly nominal variables violate the concept of closeness. Only if the nominal categories can be ordered on some explicit or implicit basis can MDS yield a useful output.

Addition of a third dimension for the cold cereal data would produce a still better fit. The question of whether it would be worthwhile hinges on two considerations: (1) how much better the fit would be and (2) how difficult the result would be to interpret and use. The first question depends on the calculation of agreement.[5] Since no statistical test has been devised as yet, the conclusion rests on the descriptive measures. Difficulties in interpretability and ability to visualize increase rapidly beyond two dimensions. Physical presentation in three dimensions requires either a three-dimensional model or a set of two or three graphs, each of which is in two dimensions. Beyond three dimensions, a single pictorial presentation is virtually impossible and the number of graphs in a set of two-dimensional figures becomes unwieldy.

---

[5]"Stress" as a measure of fit is discussed later in the chapter.

Comparison against an anchor point. This approach is illustrated by a study of eight Philadelphia retail stores. The data are presented in Table 20.3 where the technique is employed. Each of the eight stores served sequentially as the reference point, with each of the remaining stores ranked in terms of similarity to the anchor point. Row one compares the seven stores to B. Altman. John Wanamaker is perceived as most similar to it, and Two Guys is perceived as least similar. Comparison among rows is not implied by any of the data. The entries within Table 20.3 represent a consensus formed from individual data supplied by 14 persons.

The perceptual mapping of the retail stores was solved by the NMSCL program of MAP.[6] Table 20.4 gives the coordinates for the solution in two dimensions, and Fig. 20.3 gives the mapping for these coordinates. Supplementary questions concerning prestige, values, style, assortment, and quality suggest that Axis 1 coincides with a "Prestige" concept and Axis 2 coincides with "Assortment." Axis 2 is actually the complement of assortment in this instance; low values mean greater perceived assortment.

The mapping shows Korvette (K) and Two Guys (2G) as the most similar, closely followed by John Wanamaker (JW) and Strawbridge & Clothier (SC). Dispersion on the prestige axis is much greater than that perceived on the assortment axis. J. C. Penney (JCP) and Sears Roebuck (SR) exemplify a distinct pair—in comparison with the other six stores. JCP and SR are very similar in prestige but at opposite extremes in assortment. Competition between these stores, thus, depends on the relative importance given to these two dimensions, the degree of market segmentation present, and the stability of the perceptual space across different purchase decisions. These matters will be considered later in the chapter after we have addressed measurement and computational aspects of the aggregate solution given in Fig. 20.3.

Table 20.3
Similarities Data for Eight Retail Stores. Rotating Anchor Point

Anchor point	Ranking in similarity
B. Altman (BA)	JW, SC, GB, JCP, SR, K, 2G
Gimbel Bros. (GB)	SC, JW, BA, SR, JCP, K, 2G
Korvette (K)	2G, JCP, SR, GB, SC, JW, BA
J. C. Penney (JCP)	SR, K, 2G, GB, SC, JW, BA
Sears Roebuck (SR)	JCP, GB, K, 2G, SC, JW, BA
Strawbridge & Clothier (SC)	JW, GB, BA, SR, JCP, K, 2G
Two Guys (2G)	K, JCP, SR, GB, SC, JW, BA
John Wanamaker (JW)	SC, BA, GB, SR, JCP, K, 2G

[6]Terry C. Gleason, December 1976, Multivariate analysis package, The Wharton School (Unpublished).

Table 20.4
Two-dimensional Solution for Retail Store Mapping†

Store	Axis 1	Axis 2
B. Altman	4.74	0.69
Gimbel Bros.	1.68	0.12
Korvette	−4.61	−0.02
J. C. Penney	−1.78	1.56
Sears Roebuck	−1.23	−1.33
Strawbridge & Clothier	2.69	−0.36
Two Guys	−4.95	−0.10
John Wanamaker	3.45	−0.56

Stress (Kruskal formula 1) = .0041

Stress (Kruskal formula 2) = .0072

†Solved by NMSCL program of MAP. Terry C. Gleason, December 1976, Multivariate analysis package, The Wharton School (Unpublished).

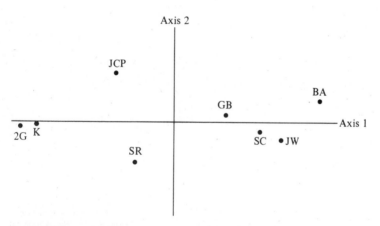

Fig. 20.3
Two-dimensional map of eight retail stores. (Derived from Table 20.4.)

Stress

Perfect agreement between the derived configuration and the input data will rarely be achieved. Such agreement would suggest complete internal consistency by the respondents on all ratings, the existence of a well-structured perceptual map by them, and the use of the proper number of dimensions in the MDS program. If individual data are employed, it would further require homogeneity of perceptual maps across individuals. These conditions cannot be expected in the real world. Kruskal has proposed a measure of stress as an appraisal of the fit achieved.[7] This measure is a logical development based on the following rationale. (1) Compute the distance between the various pairs of items according to the derived plotting. Call the distance between item i and item j, d_{ij}. These calculations correspond to the distances in Table 20.2. (2) Designate by δ_{ij} the original input ranks. These numbers are the rankings of Table 20.1. (3) Define a new measure of the distance between i and j, implicit in the δ_{ij} rankings. Call this new measure $\hat{d}_{ij}$. Any numerical values are permitted for $\hat{d}_{ij}$ as long as $\hat{d}_{ij} \leq \hat{d}_{kl}$ if $\delta_{ij} < \delta_{kl}$. Subject to this constraint choose $\hat{d}_{ij}$ as close to d_{ij} as possible. For the data of Tables 20.1 and 20.2 the corresponding entries are shown in Table 20.5. (4) Kruskal's stress measure (S) is computed by Eq. (20.1) or (20.2).

$$S(1) = \left[\frac{\sum_{i \neq j}(d_{ij} - \hat{d}_{ij})^2}{\sum_{i \neq j} d_{ij}^2} \right]^{\frac{1}{2}} \tag{20.1}$$

$$S(2) = \left[\frac{\sum_{i \neq j}(d_{ij} - \hat{d}_{ij})^2}{\sum_{i \neq j}(d_{ij} - \bar{d})^2} \right]^{\frac{1}{2}} \tag{20.2}$$

where $\bar{d}$ = mean distance between pairs.

The numerator of S will be small if the d_{ij} values approximate their corresponding $\hat{d}_{ij}$ values and would be zero if they were uniformly identical. If the ranks of the d_{ij}'s coincide perfectly with the ranks of the δ_{ij}, stress will be zero since there are no restrictions concerning the form of transformation applied in generating the $\hat{d}_{ij}$ values.[8] The numerator for each equation is the sum of the squared discrepancies between the two metric distances (d_{ij} and $\hat{d}_{ij}$). The denominators are standardizing values to permit comparisons across dimensions. The results from Table 20.5 are .0023 [Eq. (20.1)] and .0106 [Eq. (20.2)].

A large stress value indicates that either one or both of two additional steps should be attempted. First, a different mapping of the points in the same number of dimensions may be attempted. With this approach, the d_{ij} values are revised and then $\hat{d}_{ij}$'s are recomputed to give the lowest possible value for S. Second, the number of dimensions may be increased. With mapping permitted in more dimensions the fit must be the same or better.

[7] Joseph B. Kruskal, 1964, Multidimensional scaling by optimizing goodness of fit to a nonmetric hypothesis, *Psychometrika* **29**: 1–27.

[8] Detailed discussion of Kruskal's multidimensional scaling program, M–D–SCAL is found in Joseph B. Kruskal and Frank J. Carmone, 1969, *How to Use M–D–SCAL (Version SM) and Other Useful Information* (Murray Hill, N.J.: Bell Telephone Laboratories); and Joseph B. Kruskal, *op. cit.*

Table 20.5
Basic Figures Needed for Calculation of Stress. Cold Cereal Data.†

Pair	d_{ij}	δ_{ij}	$\hat{d}_{ij}$
Wheaties—Sugar Flakes	.13	1	.13
Wheaties—Total	.23	2	.23
Total—Granola	.29	4	.29
Sugar Flakes—Shredded Wheat	.35	5	.35
Sugar Flakes—Total	.36	3	.28
Wheaties—Shredded Wheat	.48	6	.48
Wheaties—Granola	.52	7	.52
Sugar Flakes—Granola	.65	8	.65
Total—Shredded Wheat	.71	9	.71
Granola—Shredded Wheat	1.00	10	1.00

†Basic data taken from Tables 20.1 and 20.2.
‡The $\hat{d}_{ij}$'s given in the table are for illustrative purposes only; i.e., the $\hat{d}_{ij}$ for Sugar Flakes–Total was reduced to .01 less than the $\hat{d}_{ij}$ for Total–Granola. The actual calculation would involve minimization of the sum of squares with a monotone regression.

Improving the Configuration[9]

A better configuration can be produced only if the computer program has a procedure to follow. The basic objective is to find the direction of movement that will reduce stress most rapidly. The "method of steepest descent" determines the desired direction of movement by evaluating the partial derivatives of S. This procedure determines the simultaneous effect on all distances when a given point is moved in a specific direction. This is evaluated by the effect on $\Sigma(d_{ij} - \hat{d}_{ij})^2$.

A second related question is how far to move in the indicated direction. Clearly it is possible to move so far in the given direction that stress is increased rather than decreased. The rationale incorporated in the program is that the distance should be proportional to the size of the discrepancy being corrected. Alpha (α), the step size, specifies the proportion of the average discrepancy that is to be corrected in a given step of the iterative procedure. This value is supplied by the researcher. A small value means that the iterations improve very slowly, but a large α may mean that the solution moves too rapidly in a given direction. Rapid movement in a given direction either over-

---

[9]This discussion, as well as other sections in this chapter, is on an intuitive rather than on a mathematical level. The reader should consult the documentation for any particular program; for example, Kruskal and Carmone, *op. cit.*

compensates or focuses on gains from movement of a particular point while ignoring gains that might be realized by movement of other points.[10]

Preference Data

Preference data identify which locations in a spatial mapping are most desired. This "joint-space" shows perceptual and preference data simultaneously. Distances again designate degree of preference or closeness to the most preferred location. Two types of preference are possible with MDS: (1) points and (2) vectors. An *ideal point* specifies a particular location as the most preferred spot. Alternatives are evaluated in terms of their closeness to this ideal point: those closest are the best. A *preference vector* specifies the trade-off between the attributes and the direction of preference—whether more or less of each attribute is preferred. Alternatives are most preferred when their projections on these vectors have the greatest distance from the origin. The two types are illustrated by Figs. 20.4 and 20.5.

Figure 20.4 presents the perceived spatial locations of 12 automobiles on two dimensions, identified as sportiness and economy.[11] The 12 automobiles are widely dispersed. Which location is the best? According to whom? Individual respondents must indicate their preference. Ideal points may be determined by considering 13 automobiles: the 12 listed plus a hypothetical ideal. Assume respondents A and B have supplied such input data, resulting in their respective ideals as shown in Fig. 20.4. Among the 12 alternatives listed, A prefers Cadillac. He would prefer something a little more sporty and a little more luxurious. VW, closely followed by Dart, are the least acceptable to him, despite their relative acceptability in sportiness. Their economy ratings rule them out. B rates Firebird as the most preferred although she is almost equally drawn to Corvette. Mercedes is the least acceptable to her.[12]

Figure 20.5 illustrates a case in which preference is indicated by a vector. Five toothpastes are mapped with respect to decay prevention and whitening action. Both features are desired and the higher a brand is in both, the better its rating. The question is the trade-off between the two attributes. If a brand is inferior to a competitor in both dimensions, it is not worthy of consideration—unless of course it is superior on a third dimension that should be

---

[10]The solution obtained by various MDS algorithms is dependent on the particular steps taken, their sequence, the stopping rules chosen, and the critical levels established for those rules. Despite differences in approach and algorithms, Green and Rao conclude that the 17 different approaches employed by them on the same basic database yield configurations that are "rather closely related to each other." Green and Rao, *op. cit.,* p. 138.

[11]This example is adapted from Franko M. Nicosia and Yoram Wind (eds.), 1975, *Behavioral Models of Market Analysis: Foundations for Market Analysis* (Hinsdale, Ill.: Dryden).

[12]Figure 20.4 assumes that A and B have the same perceptions of the 12 automobiles but different preferences. Perceptions, as well as preferences, may differ among individuals.

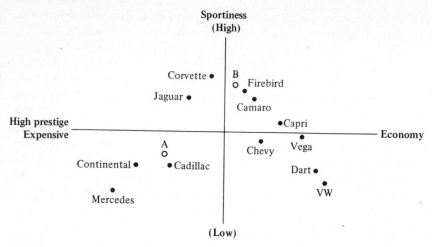

Fig. 20.4

Two-dimensional configuration of 12 automobiles with ideal points. (Adapted from Franco M. Nicosia and Yoram Wind (eds.), 1975, *Behavioral Models of Market Analysis: Foundations for Market Analysis*. Hinsdale, Ill.: Dryden.)

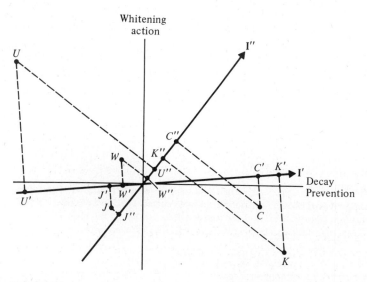

Fig. 20.5

Two-dimensional configuration of five toothpastes with ideal vectors.

included in the appraisal. Using only the two dimensions, brand J is inferior to brand W.

Preference vectors are shown for two individuals. I' shows the vector for a person who is principally concerned with decay prevention. Brand K is his preference, indicated by the perpendicular projection of K onto the vector as K'. Distance from the vector is not of concern; C, W, and J are all closer to the indicated vector than is K, but are not preferred to it.[13] The second individual gives almost equal weight to each characteristic, slightly more to whitening action since the angle is a little over 45°. This person prefers brand C. Despite its high rating on whitening action, brand U is rated lower than either C or K since it is grossly inferior in decay prevention. U would rate first in preference only if the preference vector gave almost all weight to whitening action.

Preference Input Data

What is the proper format for collecting preference data, and how are they incorporated in the determination of the preference mapping? Data collection falls into two distinct types: (1) preference among existing products with the ''ideal'' inferred and (2) explicit comparison of existing products against the respondent's ideal. The determination of the preference map involves the selection of either the ideal point or preference vector approach and the actual placement of ''preference'' on a perceptual map.

The procedure requiring the fewest new ideas is the use of $(n + 1)$ stimuli with n existing products plus the respondent's ideal. The same procedures discussed under similarities data can be employed; the only distinction is in the interpretation of the results. We have already considered Fig. 20.4 in this respect.

The principal difficulty with this approach concerns the ability of respondents to conceptualize an ideal and to maintain a constant frame of reference for all responses. (1) If the ''ideal'' is not on the market, the task of visualizing that product may be beyond the ability of most respondents. Many persons find it easier to evaluate specifics. This is essentially the reason prototype testing is often viewed as mandatory in new product research. (2) The instability of reference points may be particularly likely as respondents move from similarity data to preference data. Subjects may assign different weights to the perceptual axes (or even use different axes) as they change from one task to the other. This can happen as they play an evaluative role as opposed to a passive observer role.

A second alternative data collection procedure is the fitting of an ideal point or preference vector onto an existing perceptual map. This procedure

---

[13]Convention has the vector going through the origin that is often the intersection of the two means. Preference could be determined by using any line parallel to the indicated vector. Most programs are written in terms of the directional cosine of the angle that uniquely indicates the angle and the slope of the vector.

separates the two steps, both in data collection and the determination of the joint-space (spatial mapping of both perceptions and preferences). The first step considers only the similarities data. The second step requires preference data related to the existing products and fits the preference data onto the existing perceptual map. The placement of the preference data may be either as an ideal point or as a preference vector.[14]

The study of the eight retail outlets included preference data as well as perceptual data. The simple rank-order consensus data are given in Table 20.6. The basic question is how to portray these preferences on the perceptual map of Fig. 20.3. A perfect fit can be obtained by using either an ideal point or a preference vector. In addition, either solution has a certain amount of looseness; that is, the preference input data do not determine a unique result.[15] Assuming that more prestige and greater assortment are preferred, a preference vector approach is employed. The result is shown in Fig. 20.6. The projections of the eight stores onto this vector show the perfect fit obtained (see Table 20.6). The angle of the vector indicates almost equal weight for prestige and assortment with a slightly greater weight to prestige.

A third alternative is to use preference data alone as the input data. Existing products are judged in paired comparisons or ranked in preference. The

Table 20.6
Consensus Rank-order Preference.
Eight Retail Outlets

Store	Rank
John Wanamaker	1
B. Altman	2
Strawbridge & Clothier	3
Gimbel Bros.	4
Sears Roebuck	5
J. C. Penney	6
Korvette	7
Two Guys	8

---

[14]Carroll-Chang PREFMAP includes four phases, each of which addresses a different aspect of this general question. J. Douglas Carroll and Jie Jih Chang, 1969, *Relating Preference Data to Multidimensional Scaling Solutions via a Generalization of Coombs's Unfolding Model* (Mimeographed) (Murray Hill, N.J.: Bell Telephone Laboratories), and J. Douglas Carroll, Individual differences and multidimensional scaling, in R. N. Shepard, A. K. Rommey, and S. Nerlove, (eds.), 1972, *Multidimensional Scaling: Theory and Application in the Behavioral Sciences* (New York: Seminar Press).

[15]Additional constraints via metric preference data or additional stores and comparisons would yield a "tighter" fit.

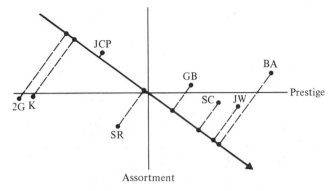

Key: BA = B. Altman   SR = Sears Roebuck
       GB = Gimbel Bros.   SC = Strawbridge & Clothier
       K = Korvette   2G = Two Guys
       JCP = J. C. Penney   JW = John Wanamaker

Fig. 20.6
Two-dimensional joint perception and preference map. Eight
retail stores.

various algorithms derive a mapping that includes both perceived similarities
and an indication of preference via either an ideal point or a preference
vector.[16]

Distance Measures

Our discussion has assumed that the proper measure of distance is Euclidean.
This is the same issue that we mentioned in conjunction with clustering.[17]
Alternative measures of distance can be computed by the general formula of
Eq. (20.3).

$$d_{ij} = \left[\sum^k |x_{ik} - x_{jk}|^r \right]^{1/r} \tag{20.3}$$

If $r = 2$, we are in Euclidean space and distance. If $r = 1$, we have the
alternative of "city-block" distances. Distance in this case would be measured
by the sum of the absolute differences on the various dimensions.

The measure of distance and the value of r are imposed upon the MDS
solution. These choices depend on the researcher's perception of how the respondents visualize the mapping and how they compute proximity. Many of
the computer algorithms available are equipped to handle MDS with various
metrics, but most of the applications have been limited to Euclidean distance.

---

[16]For example MDPREF and M-D-SCAL 5. Jie Jih Chang and J. Douglas Carroll, 1969, *How to
Use MDPREF: A Computer Program for Multidimensional Analysis of Preference Data* (Murray
Hill, N.J.: Bell Telephone Laboratories), and Kruskal and Carmone, *op. cit.*

[17]See "The Adoption of a Distance or Similarity Measure" in Chapter 17.

Segmentation

Market segments may differ in either preference or in perception. Different buyers may perceive the same stimuli in different ways. These differences may refer to at least four different aspects of MDS: (1) perceptions of products may differ among buyers although the same axes are used, (2) different characteristics or axes may be viewed as relevant for the perceptual space, (3) the preferred location may differ among buyers, and (4) some buyers may have a preferred location (ideal point) while others may prefer maximization or minimization of various characteristics (preference vector). Each market segment would consist of a subgroup whose members possess (1) similar perceptions of the stimuli and (2) similar preferences whether they be ideal points or preference vectors.

Figure 20.4 shows a situation in which perceptions are similar but preferences are different. A and B might represent two substantial segments. A third market segment might stress economy and have little concern for "sportiness." These three segments could agree on which automobiles are most similar but not on which are preferred.

The critical question is whether the market should be treated as a single entity or whether it should be divided into segments. Segmentation always hinges on the grouping together of homogeneous units; in this case that homogeneity refers to the perceptual map or the joint perceptual–preference map. The appropriate measure must deal with distances among groups in contrast to distances within groups. If groups are formed *a priori,* it is appropriate to test the reduction in variance achieved by forming subgroups. If groups are formed via clustering routines, the results are a forced fit and merely descriptive of the data.[18]

If grouping is based upon *a priori* segmentation, the researcher merely establishes a different mapping for each group. No new methodological issues are involved. If grouping is based upon perceptual or preference data, MDS must first deal with the data for individual respondents rather than aggregate data. We shall consider how MDS deals with individual differences after a brief discussion of scenario dependent maps, a special type of segmentation.

Scenario Dependent Maps

The perception evoked may be situation-dependent. Consumers may view ice cream when thinking of a snack in a way quite different from the way they view it when thinking of a dessert. Computers may be perceived differently for a statistical analysis than for an accounting function. The relevant attributes for a first car may differ from those considered for a second car. Perceptual

---

[18]See Yoram Wind, 1978, Issues and advances in segmentation research, *Journal of Marketing Research* 15: 317–337 for a brief discussion of alternative procedures for classifying segments as well as coverage of many other segmentation issues.

data obtained in an unstructured format are very likely to differ from those obtained in a highly specific situation.

The scenario issue mixes with the segmentation issue. The marketing manager must know not only the competition within a particular market segment but the competition within that segment in meeting specific situations or needs. The favorite store of upper middle-class housewives may differ according to the product purchased or the occasion. A wedding gift for a favorite niece will probably evoke thoughts different from those involving the purchase of a last minute Christmas card for the newspaper vendor. Salience of dimensions and even the dimensions themselves may vary.

The scenario issue can be handled in MDS by several different methods. Separate mappings can be generated for each scenario and the results can be compared. This approach is essentially the same as *a priori* segmentation on any other basis. The issue may be more complex and require analysis of differences among individual respondents as well as differences among scenarios.

Individual Differences

Market segmentation must recognize and deal with individual differences. If perception and preference vary simultaneously, the result is a mixture that stymies the marketing manager unless he or she has external data or assumptions that identify the contribution of each. The typical approach with MDS has been to deal with the two issues sequentially, first perception and then preference.

Carroll and Chang's INDSCAL program takes a modified position.[19] It works with perceptual data, assumes a common perceptual mapping, but permits individual differences in the salience of the various dimensions. These salience measures can serve as a basis for combining individuals into segments, and a separate perceptual map, if appropriate, can be generated for each segment. Preference data can then be added to yield a joint perceptual–preference map.

Green and Rao's study of bakery items illustrates this sequential approach.[20] Segments were formed on both an *a priori* basis (sex and scenario) and by applying INDSCAL to the perceptual data without prior subgrouping. Three dimensions were obtained: snack type–meal type, sweet–nonsweet, and breadlike–cakelike.

The dimensional saliences for males and females were approximately the same with highest salience given to the snack–meal dimension. Thus this

---

[19]J.Douglas Carroll and Jie Jih Chang, 1970, Analysis of individual differences in multidimensional scaling via an *N*-way generalization of "Eckart-Young" decomposition, *Psychometrika* **35**: 283–319.

[20]Paul E. Green and Vithala R. Rao, 1972, Configuration synthesis in multidimensional scaling, *Journal of Marketing Research* **9**: 65–68. The same study provides the empirical basis for much of the material in Green and Rao, *Applied Multidimensional Scaling: A Comparison of Approaches and Algorithms.*

dimension received the greatest weight in determining overall perceived differences among 15 different bakery products.[21] However, the saliences accompanying various preference scenarios were quite varied. The bread–cake dimension received high salience in conjunction with a heavy breakfast and almost none in conjunction with the snack scenario. Sweetness was prominent for all scenarios but rarely received the greatest weight.

Use of INDSCAL without imposing an *a priori* basis of segmentation yielded two distinct groups—based upon within-group perceptual similarity. Both segments placed five sweet products in close proximity: jelly donut, glazed donut, Danish pastry, cinnamon bun, and coffee cake. The segments differed in their approach to the other products. One segment (A) perceived toast items as similar while the other (B) grouped bread products together.

Preference data led to a further segmentation of each of the two initial segments. Within group A, one segment preferred the toast items while the other was oriented away from them and toward the sweet products. The results were not as clear within B. The two-dimensional solution may even suggest the need for a new product that adds just a touch of the breadlike quality to some of the existing sweet products. This is clearly not achieved by toast and marmalade or buttered toast and jelly which are placed in a totally different quadrant.

PREFMAP permits study of market segmentation and offers three alternatives with respect to preference: ideal points, preference vectors, or negative ideals. The latter is an "anti-ideal"; the farther an item is from such a point, the more it is preferred. PREFMAP classifies each individual as possessing one of the three preference orientations.[22] This classification is based on whichever one gives the best fit to the data. Segments are formed from the individual classifications by ad hoc decisions or by clustering rules.

Marketing Strategy

Joint perceptual–preference maps provide the marketing manager with important information, but the correct strategy may not be obvious. At least four alternatives exist, both before and after studying the joint map: (1) reposition the company brand to a new location, (2) maintain the present location, (3) add a new brand, and (4) withdraw from the market. The manager must be extremely careful in his or her deliberations to distinguish between perceived dimensions and objective dimensions. It is not enough to determine the location desired for the brand; the manager must take actions that will place the brand at that location in *perceptual* space. The achievement of that goal may depend on credible communication as much as it does on product design. Add to the dilemma the two pervasive marketing facts that competing products will

---

[21]The products studied included various combinations with toast, two types of donuts, different types of muffins with assorted additions, specific kinds of buns or cake, toast pop-ups, etc.

[22]Carroll, *op. cit.*

bombard the target market with their own messages and that consumer preferences will undoubtedly change over time.

The first task facing the researcher and marketing manager as they examine the joint map is the labeling of axes. Substantive familiarity with the field is a strong ally, but supplementary data can also be helpful. The labeling of the two axes in the study of Philadelphia retailers relied on respondent rankings on five specific characteristics. Since prestige and assortment rankings agreed perfectly with positions on the two axes, these labels were assigned to the axes. This procedure has the added advantage that the same respondents generate both the mapping and labeling. Yoram Wind, in a slightly different context, suggests that respondents be asked to rate five to ten different product benefits.[23]

Physicians' perceptions and preferences for brands of ethical pharmaceuticals revealed the existence of two market segments, differing both in perception and preference.[24] Two dimensions were sufficient to give a satisfactory fit, and supplementary questions provided the labels of "potency" and "side effects." Segment 1 preferred medium potency and few side effects. (See Fig. 20.7.)[25] No brand was perceived as close to this ideal point. Segment 2 preferred both low potency and low side effects. This segment perceived that two

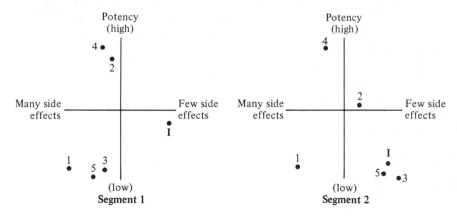

Fig. 20.7
Joint perceptual–preference mappings for two physician segments. (Adapted from Lester A. Neidell, 1969, The use of nonmetric multidimensional scaling in marketing analysis, *Journal of Marketing* **33**: 42.)

[23]Yoram Wind, 1973, A new procedure for concept testing, *Journal of Marketing* **37**: 2–11.

[24]Lester A. Neidell, 1969, The use of nonmetric multidimensional scaling in marketing analysis, *Journal of Marketing,* **33**: 37–43.

[25]It might be argued that the logical preference would call for minimization of side effects rather than a precise level. With the existing maps, such a change would not result in differences in possible strategies.

brands (3 and 5) were near this ideal. Segment 1 perceived both of these brands to be much higher in side effects.

What strategy is appropriate, given the mappings of Fig. 20.7? The field is wide open in segment 1—if the segment generates a sufficient volume of sales. None of the five brands is close enough to the ideal to pose a threat if a firm can truly produce the type drug desired *and* convince the market that it has done it. Brand 1, while not at a great competitive disadvantage, is so far-out that either it should be drastically changed or withdrawn from the market. Before adopting either strategy, the firm should check whether another market segment exists that has a more favorable perception of its products. Brand 2 would be in an attractive position if segment 2 had the same ideal point as segment 1 or if segment 1 perceived it as segment 2 does. A strong educational program might be aimed to achieve both goals simultaneously. What strategies would you recommend for the other brands?

Limitations

MDS is clearly addressed to important marketing questions. But the answers provided must be valid. The issues that must be satisfied are many and varied. In this respect MDS is no different from research in general. However, a few of the more pervasive problems should be highlighted lest they be ignored in the complications of computer programs and voluminous printouts.

The set of products is typically prescribed by the researcher. The presence of additional items could change the perceptual mental set, eliciting different dimensions as well as changing the locations of existing items. Removal of one or more items from the constrained set could have similar effects.[26]

If *overall* perceptions or preferences are obtained, the proper interpretation of results may be unclear. It can also be argued that buying decisions are not made in a general or average situation; each decision is made for a specific buying scenario. Unique specification of one or several scenarios, however, generates information for only those specifics. Nothing is known of additional situations. The more specific the setting, the clearer the interpretation, but simultaneously the usefulness may be impaired because of its idiosyncratic nature.

Consumer-behavior experts have recently started discussing the variety syndrome and portfolios of brands. The preferred brand need not be purchased with 100 percent probability. The second brand purchased may act as a complement to the first rather than as a substitute for it. Unless data are collected in a format that conforms to the reality of the purchase environment, the data can hardly be relied on as a guide in marketing decisions.

A number of data collection techniques and formats plus a variety of algorithms are available for generating the MDS mappings. To some extent the

---

[26]See Paul E. Green and Yoram Wind, *op. cit.,* pp. 9–13 for a more complete discussion of this issue as well as several others.

result depends on the alternative chosen. Several authors have studied the extent of differences produced by different collection methods or different programs.[27] Despite well-designed studies and significant amounts of analyses, the findings are far from definitive. Current studies suggest that results are more sensitive to alternative data collection methods than to alternative algorithms, but much additional study is needed before firm conclusions are available.

MDS describes the data; it does not test hypotheses. The researcher specifies acceptable stress levels, maximum number of iterations, the size of steps, and the initial configuration (or alternatively how the configuration will be determined). At the very least, the user of MDS should be familiar with these concepts and choose among alternatives in a knowledgeable way. Reliance on default options or specification of other numerical values without a clear understanding of their meaning can have a strong influence on the resulting maps. The underlying "sampling" distributions and associated reliability of results and/or procedures lie at the core of some of these issues. They demand difficult and expensive research studies, and their investigation is only in the beginning stages.

These are but a sampling of the problems associated with MDS. Competent researchers are making new applications, refining existing techniques, investigating the sensitivity of solutions, and developing broad decision models from MDS.[28] Current practitioners in the field seem to fluctuate between seeing MDS as another fad and seeing it as the marketing manager's panacea.[29]

CONJOINT ANALYSIS

Conjoint analysis is addressed to the measurement of the joint and separate contributions of two or more independent variables on some target variable. How much does the addition of a new safety feature improve the utility of last year's power mower? What effect does a decorator box have on the perceived value of a box of tissues? Is obtaining a master's degree worth the effort? What effect does it have on potential employers?

---

[27]See Green and Rao, *op. cit.*, for extensive comparisons of different programs. Thomas W. Whipple, 1976, Variation among multidimensional scaling solutions: an examination of the effect of data collection differences, *Journal of Marketing Research* 13: 98–103 and Walter A. Henry and Robert V. Stumpf, 1975, Time and accuracy measures for alternative multidimensional scaling collection, *Journal of Marketing Research* 12: 165–170 both discuss alternative data collection approaches and the resulting differences.

[28]Allan D. Shocker and V. Srinivasen, 1974, A consumer-based methodology for the identification of new product ideas, *Management Science* 20: 921–937, and Edgar A. Pessemier and H. Paul Root, 1973, The dimensions of new product planning, *Journal of Marketing* 37: 10–18.

[29]See Paul E. Green, 1978, Marketing applications of MDS: assessment and outlook, *Journal of Marketing* 42: 24–31 for a balanced discussion.

The basic model for conjoint measurement, in its simplest form, is a linear additive equation. Total utility of the complete offering is determined by Eq. (20.4)—the usual linear model.

$$U = a_i X_i + a_j X_j + \cdots + b_k Y_k + b_l Y_l + \cdots +$$
$$c_m Z_m + \cdots. \tag{20.4}$$

X, Y, and Z designate the different characteristics while the subscripts designate the various levels employed. The distinction in conjoint measurement is that the input data need not be intervally scaled. This applies to both the independent variables and the dependent variable. Conjoint measurement, like MDS in general, "bootstraps"—massaging ordinal data with sufficient constraints from the input interrelationships and recovering the implicit interval scales.

Conjoint analysis is similar to MDS in that the respondent supplies a single global response to a multiattribute offering. It differs from MDS with respect to how the multiattribute nature of the offerings has been structured. MDS leaves the offerings in a completely unstructured format—alternatives are presented as totalities. MDS does not identify the attributes possessed by the various offerings although the analysis may be supplemented by questions with respect to these attributes. Conjoint analysis utilizes a careful structure of the experiment with respect to the attributes possessed by the various offerings. Indeed conjoint analysis has as its objective the determination of the separate utilities of the attributes that are built into the design. They must be both identified and controlled in order to realize this objective.

Design of the Experiment

Consider a refrigerator manufacturer who wishes to derive the relative importance to the consumer of the frost-free feature, the ice maker, and adjustable shelves. The manufacturer further wants to evaluate each at two different levels: (1) completely frost free (refrigerator and freezer compartment) and refrigerator only, (2) ice dispenser on the exterior of the refrigerator and internal ice maker, and (3) one or two adjustable shelves. A complete factorial experiment with each level of each variable paired with all possibilities would require 27 observations: $3 \times 3 \times 3$. Evaluations of all interactions would require at least 54 observations.

A managerial decision in which a large number of attributes are to be evaluated, each of which may be present or absent (or present at various levels) requires an extremely large experiment. *Experimental design,* as a distinct topic, is concerned with establishing guides in how to allocate the test treatments to a restricted number of observations. A crucial consideration is the "balancing" of this allocation so that the results that seem to reflect a particular treatment are not contaminated by overrepresentation or underrepresentation of other variables. A variety of designs are available; we shall illustrate only a few relatively simple ones—starting with the Latin square.[30]

The Latin square design achieves measurement of all main effects while neglecting all interactions. This design requires that all variables be tested on the same number of levels, a condition met by the refrigerator manufacturer's problem. Table 20.7 presents the allocation as it applies to the manufacturer's problem. Each of the levels for each of the variables occurs once with each level of the other two factors. A total of nine observations is required for this problem.

Table 20.7
Latin Square Design for Refrigerator Problem†

| | Frost-free | | |
Ice maker	No	Refrigerator	Complete
No	0	2	1
Interior	1	0	2
Exterior dispenser	2	1	0

†Table entries show the number of adjustable shelves.

The Greco-Latin square design is a combination of two Latin square designs. The experiment would then involve a fourth independent variable, also tested at three levels. Suppose the fourth variable is color: white, yellow, or brown. Table 20.8 indicates the appropriate assignment of the treatments to the nine observations. No level appears with the same level of another variable

Table 20.8
Greco-Latin Square Design for Refrigerator Problem†

| | Frost-free | | |
Ice maker	No	Refrigerator	Complete
No	0, White	2, Yellow	1, Brown
Interior	1, Yellow	0, Brown	2, White
Exterior dispenser	2, Brown	1, White	0, Yellow

†Table entries show the number of adjustable shelves and the color of the refrigerator.

[30]B. J. Winer, *Statistical Principles in Experimental Design,* 1973 (New York: McGraw-Hill) gives a detailed development of the general topic of experimental design. See also "Experimental Designs" in Chapter 3.

more than once, and it appears with each precisely once. It is completely balanced although it yields no measure of interaction.

Both the Latin square design and the Greco-Latin square design are fractional factorial designs. In place of the complete factorial designs requiring 27 and 81 observations for the present example, the required number of observations has been reduced to nine. Both designs may use either ordinal or interval data for the dependent variable. Our present interest with conjoint measurement is particularly concerned with ordinal data. We shall proceed with the refrigerator problem before considering other more complex experimental designs.

Utility Derivation

Our task in the refrigerator problem is to estimate the utility associated with the various alternatives, separately and in combination. MONANOVA, an algorithm developed by Kruskal, yields estimates of the main effects of the additive model (Eq. 20.4).[31] This algorithm accepts ordinal data from either complete or fractional factorial designs. The fitting minimizes the stress factor discussed earlier in conjunction with MDS. The rankings of the nine observations for the refrigerator problem are given in Table 20.9.

MONANOVA output gives interval scale utility ratings for all levels of the independent variables. The ratings are given in Table 20.10, showing that the frost-free features have the most utility. Adjustable shelves, according to these data, possess greater utility than either version of the ice maker, but the

Table 20.9
Rankings for Nine Alternatives. Refrigerator Problem

Frost-free	Ice maker	Number of adjustable shelves	Rank†
No	No	0	9
No	Interior	1	8
No	Exterior dispenser	2	7
Refrigerator	No	2	5
Refrigerator	Interior	0	6
Refrigerator	Exterior dispenser	1	2
Complete	No	1	3
Complete	Interior	2	1
Complete	Exterior dispenser	0	4

†Rank 1 indicates the most preferred.

[31]Joseph B. Kruskal, 1965, Analysis of factorial experiments by estimating monotone transformations of the data, *Journal of the Royal Statistical Society* (Series B) **27**: 251–263.

Table 20.10
Utility Values for Independent Variables. Refrigerator Problem

Variable	Level	Utility
Frost-free	Complete	3.667
	Refrigerator	2.705
	No	0.000
Ice maker	Exterior dispenser	0.942
	Interior	0.471
	No	0.000
No adjustable shelves	2	1.412
	1	1.412
	0	0.000

addition of a second adjustable shelf makes no contribution beyond the first.[32] Care must be exercised in interpreting these results since the zero point is arbitrary. The focus should be on differences among levels of the same variable, not on the absolute values. (Interval scales are involved, not ratio scales.)

Experimental Designs of Greater Complexity

Fractional factorial designs of greater complexity are often desirable as the number of independent variables increases. Consider a pudding mix with five potential attributes: high vitamin content, few calories, convenient to prepare, economical, and high protein content.[33] Thirty-one possible formulations are possible, excluding the null set that contains none of the components. All main effects can be estimated with a fractional factorial of only 15 combinations: all pairs and all quadruples. This design is obviously balanced, with each component appearing in eight combinations and with each other component four times.

The design along with the rankings of the different combinations is given in Table 20.11. Kruskal's MONANOVA again is appropriate for deriving the main effects. The derived utilities for the five components are high vitamin content (1.6), convenient to prepare (1.2), high protein content (0.7), few calories (0.5), and economical (0.3).

As the number of potential attributes increases, fractional factorials become even more appealing. A manufacturer of pocket calculators might attempt to estimate the utilities for a number of different functions; for example, square roots, polar transformations, log transformations, trigono-

---

[32]The stress factor for this fit is only .003. A portion of this good fit is due to the small number of observations and the wide differences in perceived utility for some of the features. The result is that a wide variation in the precise utility values would still yield a good fit.

[33]This example is taken from Yoram Wind, A new procedure for concept testing, *op. cit.*

Table 20.11
Fractional Factorial Design. Pudding Mix with Five Possible Components†

Combination (components included)‡	Rank
ab	8
ac	5
ad	9
ae	7
bc	11
bd	15
be	13
cd	12
ce	10
de	14
abcd	3
abce	1
abde	4
acde	2
bcde	6

†Source: Yoram Wind, 1973, A new procedure for concept evaluation, *Journal of Marketing* **37**: 2-11.
‡Letters refer to the following components:

a High vitamin content	d Economical
b Few calories	e High protein content
c Convenient to prepare	

metric functions, reciprocals, standard deviations, and many other possibilities. If there were nine potential functions, a complete factorial design would generate 512 different combinations. A balanced design of only 16 of these combinations will yield estimates for all main effects. The 16 would consist of nine five–attribute combinations, six three–attribute combinations, and a combination in which all attributes are present. In this design each attribute appears four times with every other attribute.[34]

Presentation of Alternatives

One of the practical questions arising in conjoint analysis is how to present the alternatives to the subjects. This is more a relevance issue than it is a research question. The determination of partial utilities requires that the alternative

---

[34]A design of this type is called an orthogonal array. See Paul E. Green, 1974, On the design of choice experiments involving multifactor alternatives, *Journal of Consumer Research* **1**: 61–68 for a discussion of orthogonal as well as incomplete block designs (both balanced and partially balanced).

offerings be articulated in some manner. Three main approaches are readily seen: (1) presentation of the physical alternatives, (2) listing of the alternatives by their brand or model names, and (3) oral or written description of the alternatives.

A presentation of the alternatives physically has one principal advantage. The respondent is responding to the product and not to the researcher's articulation of it. However, the researcher's analysis must supply a specification of the relevant attributes and identify the levels involved. Therefore, the researcher must properly classify each alternative. This approach obviously requires that the researcher be able to make a physical presentation. Nonexisting products, complex or extremely large products, and service-based offerings are either impossible or extremely difficult and costly to present. The result is that this approach is appropriate for only a very limited number of product types.

The listing of alternatives by their brand or model names can be used only with existing products that are reasonably well known to the respondents. This approach again avoids the potential bias that might be introduced by the articulation of the alternatives. But it still requires the researcher to specify attributes and their levels in the analysis stage. The establishment of an appropriate research design is particularly troublesome here since the real world of the marketplace seldom generates a "balancing" of alternatives.

The third approach has been used most often in marketing applications. The researcher enumerates the characteristics possessed by each alternative. The choice of descriptions is an obvious source of bias, and the results apply to the articulation rather than its implementation in a real product. If this is kept firmly in mind, conjoint analysis offers extremely useful insights.

Individual Differences

Conjoint analysis can be applied to individual data as well as to aggregate data. Separate stress measures can be calculated for each individual in order to determine whether the underlying model is appropriate for all subjects.[35] Practical interest in individual data usually stems from a consideration of segmentation possibilities. The typical approach is to establish segments on some external basis and then to compare the derived utilities of the different segments, building up the segment summaries from individual data.

Individual differences in conjoint results may occur because (1) subjects attach different utilities to various attributes and their levels although all employ the simple additive model of Eq. (20.4), (2) at least some subjects employ a more complex model than Eq. (20.4), and (3) at least some subjects are inconsistent in their ratings of the alternatives. Stress levels for the individual subjects can be used as a check for the first possibility against the other two. Low individual stress values indicate the functional form is appropriate. Inter-

---

[35]See, for example, Green and Wind, *op. cit.*, pp. 137–158.

subject differences may be discerned by differences in the coefficients (utilities) for the individual respondents. Differences will also be indicated by larger stress values for the aggregate function than for the individual respondents.[36] The application of clustering techniques to the individual utility results is another approach to the segmentation question.[37]

High stress values for all or selected individual respondents indicate a poor fit. More complex models with interaction terms or nonunity exponents may be investigated by fitting the individual (and ultimately group) data to other models.[38] High stress values may also be indicative of inconsistent respondent evaluations. Only a trial of alternative models can aid in determining which reason has produced the high stress result.

Aggregate data for segments established on an *a priori* basis can of course be determined by combining the relevant individual data. In this way product benefits sought by particular market segments can be studied. A further aid in establishing market segments is the use of supplementary questions. Such questions may ask the respondent to specify a preference model by a direct approach in which salience weights are assigned to the named characteristics. While the approach is somewhat redundant, utilities derived from conjoint analysis can be checked against these "self-explicated" models.

Limitations

Many of the limitations of conjoint analysis are general limitations that apply to a number of research techniques. They should, however, be kept firmly in view as the marketing manager uses the output in making marketing decisions. These limitations can be conveniently placed in three different categories: (1) data collection relevance, (2) inferential weakness, and (3) operational translation.

Data collection relevance requires that the input data correspond to a valid marketplace situation. The characteristics incorporated in the experiment and the levels employed are fixed for any specific trial. Unless the characteristics rank high in salience and the respondents are sensitive to differences among the *chosen* levels, the utilities derived may show no significant patterns or, worse yet, may mislead. The environmental conditions and the response format may be artificial and contrived. Even when the collection procedure

---

[36]The hypothesis to be tested is that the same parameters apply to all individuals. The properties of the relevant sampling distribution have not been demonstrated in the general literature at this writing.

[37]Yoram Wind, John F. Grashof, and Joel D. Goldhar, 1978, Market-based guidelines for design of industrial products, *Journal of Marketing* **40**: 27–37. This study is discussed in "Marketing Applications" later in this chapter.

[38]Carroll and Chang's PREFMAP can be employed to deal with polynomial functions. See footnote 14.

stresses the proper features, subjects may not react as they would in a buying situation. The laboratory–research environment may generate a more rational calculated response than would exist in the marketplace.

Conjoint analysis and the utility measures derived must currently be viewed as *descriptive*. Goodness of fit measures suffer the same limitations they do in MDS. The sampling distributions of stress measures and of partial utility measures have not been investigated fully at this point. Rank correlations between input data and predictions of various models are possible, but the hypotheses associated with such comparisons do not correspond to the typical management problem.

The *operational translation* of conjoint results is the familiar one of bridging the gap between objective product characteristics and psychological perceptions of related characteristics. This is particularly true when the input data are based upon verbal communication as opposed to a physical product. This problem exists in the identification of the characteristics but is even more troublesome as one specifies the levels to be tested. Use of yes–no dichotomies and quantification of specific values may simplify the research endeavor but fail to disclose the buyers' psychological reactions. The use of "few repairs needed" as a dichotomy may facilitate the research but convey diverse (and unknown) messages to respondents. Unless the meaning of the attribute is clear, its incorporation in the product is impossible.

Marketing Applications

The number of conjoint applications cited in the open literature is limited. Green and Rao cited potential uses in their expository article, but they used synthetic and hypothetical data for their illustrations.[39] In 1972, Green, Carmone, and Wind published the results of an empirical conjoint analysis.[40] This study investigated consumers' utilities for various aspects of discount cards. Three different aspects of discount cards were studied, each at three different levels. The analysis was subsequently expanded to five factors. Both analyses identified "size of discount" as the most important factor with "initial cost" ranking second.

Wind, Grashof, and Goldhar's study of scientific and technical information services represents a large-scale study that combines conjoint analysis and clustering in order to identify several market segments.[41] The total study covered 12 different factors, and the number of levels ranged from two to nine. The relative importance of each factor was estimated by expressing its range in

---

[39]Paul E. Green and Vithala R. Rao, 1971, Conjoint measurement for quantifying judgmental data, *Journal of Marketing Research* **8**: 355-367.

[40]Paul E. Green, Frank J. Carmone, and Yoram Wind, 1972, Subjective evaluation models and conjoint measurement, *Behavioral Science* **17**: 288-299.

[41]Wind, Grashof, and Goldhar, *op. cit.*

situation. Both issues ask if the single mapping conceals a heterogeneous population that can be presented more relevantly as two or more separate maps—each to be addressed separately (or avoided) by the manager.

Conjoint measurement, like MDS, attempts to decompose a single response variable into its constituent parts. Unlike MDS, the constituent parts are built into the research design. The general design is similar to that employed with ANOVA. Conjoint analysis takes the overall evaluation by the subjects and solves for the partial utilities of the various factors at each specified level. Segmentation possibilities for the total market can be investigated by either *a priori* specifications or by ad hoc bases that differentiate among individual results.

A number of computer programs are available for both MDS and conjoint measurement. Before proceeding with research in either area, the researcher should check carefully the input data requirements: first, with respect to the substantive considerations of the decision problem; and second, with respect to the input data format required for the computer program. The computer program should be determined by the problem, not the reverse.

Several important limitations pertain to both MDS and conjoint analysis despite their obvious pertinence to important marketing decisions. First, they offer data descriptions; they have not as yet reached the inferential hypothesis testing state. Second, the problem presented to the respondent may be highly restricted or artificial. Both MDS and conjoint analysis require extensive input data for even a small problem. Therefore, the marketing manager must avoid global acceptance of results that are highly specific. Third, the marketing manager must make a double translation—from perceptual characteristics to proposed operational changes and back again to the anticipated perceptual results of the proposed changes. These limitations are significant, but they do not apply uniquely to MDS and conjoint measurement. Research techniques offer valuable help; but translation of results, the ultimate decisions, and their implementation remain with the operational manager.

EXERCISES AND PROBLEMS

1. Distinguish among the terms within each of the following sets.
   a) Conjoint analysis and multidimensional scaling
   b) Multidimensional scaling and factor analysis
   c) Conjoint analysis and ANOVA
   d) Comparison among triads, rotating anchor point, and ranking of paired similarities
   e) Perceptual mapping and joint perceptual–preference space
   f) Ideal point, preference vector, and anti-ideal
   g) Factorial design and fractional factorial design

2. Briefly explain the meaning and significance of each of the following terms as used in multidimensional scaling and conjoint analysis.

   a) Stress

   b) Distance measure

   c) Scenario dependence

   d) Boot strapping

   e) Partial utility

   f) Method of steepest descent

3. Multidimensional scaling programs require that the researcher choose the number of dimensions to be obtained in the solution.

   a) Discuss the issues involved and the criteria that should be employed in this choice.

   b) How do ordinal input data place constraints on the solution, and how are constraints related to the number of dimensions?

4. Refer to Fig. 20.7 which contains the joint perceptual–preference mappings of five ethical pharmaceuticals by two market segments. Assume there are no other market segments and each is approximately the same size.

   a) What advice would you give to brand 1? Why?

   b) What advice would you give to brand 3? Why?

5. A producer of games wishes to determine how the public views games, which games are most similar, etc. Multidimensional scaling is a possible approach. The ranking of pair similarities for seven popular games has been provided by a sample of customers. The aggregate matrix of rankings is given in Table E20.5. The most similar pair is designated by "1," and the least similar is designated by "21."

Table E20.5

	Scrabble†	Monopoly†	Pit†	Chinese Checkers	Dominoes	Parcheesi†	Mille Bornes†
Scrabble		17	21	7	20	15	5
Monopoly			14	12	18	2	3
Pit				19	6	10	16
Chinese Checkers					9	8	4
Dominoes						11	13
Parcheesi							1
Mille Bornes							

†Registered trade names.

A first attempt in one dimension is suggested with Pit and Scrabble as two end-points since this pair is assigned rank "21." The proposed sequence for the other five is Dominoes, Monopoly, Parcheesi, Chinese Checkers, and Mille Bornes. This sequence is based on the pairwise rankings involving Scrabble. The seven games are placed at intervals roughly equivalent to the Scrabble pairwise rankings. The resulting initial configuration is Pit, 0.00; Dominoes, 0.07; Monopoly, 0.25; Parcheesi, 0.36; Chinese Checkers, 0.74; Mille Bornes, 0.86; and Scrabble, 1.00.

a) From your own familiarity with games, do you think this sample of seven games is representative of the population of games? What is the implication of your answer on the utility of any results obtained from the study?

b) Determine the interpoint distances between the 21 pairs according to the proposed configuration, and rank these calculated distances.

c) How would the calculation of stress aid in evaluating the adequacy of the initial configuration?

d) At an intuitive level, do you think the initial configuration is a good fit? Cite illustrative evidence.

e) Discuss how the fit could be improved.

f) Submit the data and the initial configuration to a computer multidimensional program. Solve for solutions in one and two dimensions.

g) Propose labels for the two dimensions of the two-dimensional solution.

h) Does the plotting give a better grasp of perceptions and similarities than the original data do? Discuss, indicating any groupings that are observable.

i) Stress calculated from the aggregate data is much smaller than stress calculated using the individual data and the configuration derived. What does this indicate? Discuss its implications for management.

6. Two respondents provided the preference data in Table E20.6 for the games studied in Exercise 5. (Rank 1 is most preferred.)

a) Refer to the two-dimensional solution obtained in Exercise 5. Are the preferences recorded above more consistent with an ideal point or a preference vector? Answer separately for each respondent and place the appropriate preference indicators on the perceptual map.

Table E20.6

Rank	Respondent 1	Respondent 2
1	Chinese Checkers	Pit
2	Mille Bornes	Parcheesi
3	Scrabble	Monopoly
4	Parcheesi	Mille Bornes
5	Monopoly	Dominoes
6	Dominoes	Chinese Checkers
7	Pit	Scrabble

b) Do your preference data yield a good fit with the perceptual maps? Cite evidence that justifies this conclusion. (It is not necessary to compute stress.)

7. Collect similarities data with respect to a product category of your choice, for example, automobiles, political candidates, local stores, magazines, or a frequently purchased consumer nondurable.

   a) Process the data into an appropriate format, summarizing the group response.

   b) Submit the data to a multidimensional scaling program of your choice.

   c) Divide the group into two potential market segments. Repeat steps (a) and (b) for each segment.

   d) Do your results indicate that the two segments have different perceptual maps? Discuss.

8. Refer to Tables 20.3 and 20.4 for the eight Philadelphia retail stores.

   a) Calculate the three pairwise interpoint distances between Gimbel Brothers, Strawbridge & Clothier, and John Wanamaker.

   b) Are these calculations consistent with the input data? Explain.

   c) Apart from the comparisons in (a), do you think the fit of the solution in Table 20.4 reproduces the input data of Table 20.3 perfectly? Why? (It should not be necessary to calculate all interpoint distances.)

9. Refer to Tables 20.9 and 20.10 for the refrigerator problem.

   a) Do the utilities presented in Table 20.10 yield a perfect reproduction of the input data of Table 20.9?

   b) What does your answer to (a) suggest with respect to the solution obtained?

10. A producer of pocket calculators wishes to decide the perceived utilities for various features. Five features are of most concern: rechargeable, programmable, log transformations, trigonometric functions, and alternative display modes (scientific, engineering, and standard). All five are 0/1 variables, i.e., present or missing.

    a) How many alternatives would have to be tested in a complete factorial design?

    b) Would the design proposed in Table 20.11 be satisfactory for this test? Discuss what, if anything, is lost and what, if anything, is gained.

    c) Collect rank data for this experiment from a small group. Use the design of Table 20.11. Prepare a summary ranking for the entire group, and submit the data to MONANOVA.

    d) What problems did you encounter in preparing a summary ranking? Are you satisfied with the input data submitted? Discuss.

    e) Discuss the substantive results of your analysis.

11. Select from a current marketing journal a study in which MDS is employed. Discuss

    a) the format of the data input,

    b) the labeling of the derived axes,

    c) whether the substantive conclusions are justified.

12. Select from a current marketing journal a study in which conjoint analysis is employed. Discuss

   a) the research design,

   b) whether interactions might be a problem,

   c) whether the substantive conclusions are justified.

13. Analyze, criticize, and explain:

   a) Multidimensional scaling achieves a "boot-strapping" effect because the number of paired rankings increases rapidly as the number of items to be compared increases. The same effect is achieved whether the input data are ordinal or nominal.

   b) MDS output allows a business firm to identify its closest competitors and gaps in the marketplace even if the axes derived are not easily interpretable.

   c) Conjoint analysis and a perceptual map of MDS possess a similar disadvantage. Since both fail to provide a preference concept, their value is limited. Firms know where they are but not whether they should move.

   d) Scenario specification makes MDS more valuable. Without it, the decision maker may be looking at average results that pertain to no individual situations.

   e) Conjoint analysis, as usually employed, yields estimates of partial utilities via a linear additive model. The coefficients or utilities obtained may be interpreted as ratio scaled—a definite advantage over typical regression coefficients.

   f) "Stress" is basically a measure of "badness of fit." It uses total variance as the base for calculations and shows the percentage of variance remaining in the final solution.

   g) Application of a small α applied with the method of steepest descent tends to avoid overcorrection for discrepancies. However, the small α has the accompanying disadvantage that progress toward a solution is slow.

   h) The best way to determine whether an ideal point or a preference vector should be employed is by direct questioning of the respondents. Reliance on data analysis runs the risk that both approaches yield equally satisfactory results.

   i) A high stress value often results because perceptions across individuals are homogeneous but preferences are not.

CHAPTER 21

FUTURE DIRECTIONS IN MARKETING RESEARCH
FINDING AND FILLING THE GAPS

Marketing research has added techniques and analytic sophistications since Pharaoh relied on Joseph to guide the Egyptians through the seven years of plenty followed by the seven years of drought. But the basic goal remains the same: deliver the right product to a willing customer at an appropriate location and price. What new techniques and analytic sophistications are on the horizon that will enhance the role of marketing research in helping the marketing manager realize this goal? The answers are speculative and uncertain, but consideration of the basic forces that shape the role of marketing research should be helpful.

The future directions of marketing research depend on many factors but four will underlie the changes that emerge. (1) The past inadequacies of marketing research will generate efforts designed to correct them. (2) Technical advances in data manipulation will open new opportunities in marketing research. (3) The increased availability of competent and knowledgeable personnel will increase both the quality and quantity of marketing research. (4) Theoretical developments in marketing per se and the behavioral sciences in general will be incorporated in the analytic techniques and models used by marketing research. Consideration of these four forces in conjunction with the five steps of marketing research permits a sketching of the probable directions in which marketing research will move over the next few years. Our time horizon is short, and many of the developments are already evident. Therefore, our task is not overly ambitious. Nevertheless, our discussion is merely suggestive and illustrative. Table 21.1 presents this framework with examples of probable changes.

PAST INADEQUACIES OF MARKETING RESEARCH

Marketing research, like any other product, must meet a need. Where the needs are not met satisfactorily, there is a drive to change the product. Marketing research supplies information and recommendations stemming from that

Table 21.1
Future Directions in Marketing Research

Underlying factor	Marketing research step				
	Problem definition	Research design	Data collection	Data analysis	Interpretation
Past inadequacies of marketing research	More comprehensive questions More emphasis on "bottom line"	Less tolerance of "case study" sampling Identification and control of more variables	Use of alternative measures Greater use of continuous monitoring	Further stress on multivariate analyses Demand for reliability measures	Timeliness Better communication between researcher and decision maker
Technical developments in data handling	Ability to handle larger quantities of data	Ability to recall previously stored data	New ways of collecting data	Rapid solution of complex models	Immediate visual display of results
Availability of competent research personnel	Better communication between researcher and decision maker	Designs to measure several critical relationships simultaneously	Better quality control	Testing of alternative models	Better management understanding of results
Developments in behavior science and marketing	Incorporation of psychometric concepts Concern for market segmentation	Study of sequential steps in buying Test–retest reliability	Greater use of A-I-O (attitude-interest-opinion) Greater use of unobtrusive methods	Use of mixed DMU's Greater use of mixed scales	Recommendation extending beyond usual marketing lines

information. The possible inadequacies of information are the same regardless of the area of application: misleading, nonrelevant, out of date, too expensive, carrying a false sense of confidence, and just plain inaccurate.

More Comprehensive Questions

The areas mentioned in Table 21.1 are by no means exhaustive, but they indicate vast needs and opportunities. Taken together they decry the inadequacies of simple models. The marketplace is an interrelated phenomenon of actions, reactions, and interactions. A simple univariate or bivariate analysis must at best obscure a clear understanding of the complex forces and at worst distort and mislead.

The manager who asks, "What is the effect of price changes on . . . ?" invites disaster. An accurate answer must be conditional. If the rest of the marketing mix is . . . , if the general economy is . . . , if competitors . . . . Unless the answer is thoroughly hedged, it is as likely to be inappropriate as to be appropriate for the specific situation facing the manager. If the answer is carefully hedged, it may be as useless as advice to buy a stock when it is at its low point.

The use of simple models stems from an understandable desire for clarity and precision. On occasions this clarity and precision have come at the expense of relevance. But an approximate answer to a significant question is preferable to a precise answer to an insignificant one. We must expect and strive for the more comprehensive questions since that is the world in which marketing decisions are made. Five major levels exist: (1) the integrated marketing mix for a particular product, (2) total company decisions—including both marketing and nonmarketing decisions, (3) industry-wide decisions involving competitors' decisions as well as intracompany decisions, (4) the total domestic economic and political scene, and (5) the corresponding international scene. All need not be incorporated in any particular research endeavor, but the sophisticated marketing manager of the future will rarely be interested in a univariate or bivariate result.

The more comprehensive questions at the problem definition step have their counterparts in the research design and analysis steps. The researcher must observe and/or control all relevant variables, assure sufficient coverage of all appropriate levels of each variable, and have the proper analytic techniques to cope with the data involved. The wave is also felt in the second and third lines of Table 21.1 High-speed computers and personnel trained in both computers and analysis are needed. Advances have occurred in all these areas and are continuing—thus the movement toward greater complexity will accelerate.

Greater reliance and stress on model building are the natural outcomes of more comprehensive questions. The model does not evolve of itself. The manager and researcher must jointly articulate and structure its form. The variables must be enumerated, the mathematical function must be specified, and the existence or nonexistence of interactions must be incorporated. This calls for greater dialogue between the researcher and the decision maker. Therefore, each must have an understanding of the other's area of expertise.

"Bottom-line" Emphasis

States of mind, opinions, predispositions, attitudes, and other prebehavioral concepts are significant to the marketing manager only when and if they are translated into sales and profits. We must expect "hardheaded" business executives to tolerate research only if its advice leads to "bottom-line" performance. The future of marketing research will cope with this issue in two ways: (1) the use of sales and profits as explicit dependent variables and (2) the incorporation of alternative definitions of prebehavior variables within the same research project.

Sales and profits data as explicit variables have traditionally come from market tests. This will no doubt continue but with decreased reliance. Market tests are expensive and as run in the past violate the "comprehensive model" movement since expense grows exponentially if several variables are to be tested. The laboratory experiment remains a viable alternative, but technical developments offer an even more promising alternative. Remote TV or computer consoles with selective exposure and/or trial no longer fall into the realm of "blue-sky" thinking. Future marketing research no doubt will use such devices for a variety of purposes.

Alternative definitions and measures of related concepts allow the determination of how sensitive results are to the particular definition employed. "Sensitivity analysis" is broader than this particular issue, but its use in this area will indicate whether the manager should proceed with confidence or caution. If the result is highly dependent on the precise form of the question or measurement, further testing and probing are required before the manager can rely on one specific result. Another area that will receive greater attention is the study of relationships between various prepurchase states of mind or behavior and ultimate purchase behavior.

Unrepresentative Samples

Excessive use of unrepresentative "case study" samples has made the validity of "research" suspect to many marketing managers. Even when disclaimers and caveats are included, they often go unheeded. Only the results are recalled. The researcher would do the client a service if he or she refused to tabulate the results of pretests. Perhaps greater training in research will reduce the manager's tendency to rush to conclusions, but much needs to be done. The author recently had the unhappy experience of having a client reach a conclusion on the basis of a pretest conducted on only one of eight strata planned for the total project. Let us hope it was not the feared "unrepresentative sample."

Future marketing research will have less justification for the case study approach. The trained researcher will know better, and alternative collection schemes will lessen the cost attractiveness of a case study approach.

The unrepresentative sample has been particularly prevalent in two areas. (1) College and university classroom research encourages the use of unrepresentative samples by stressing the "learning experience" or the "demonstration of analytic techniques." Substantive results are minimized in the rhetoric, but they still seem to be disseminated and widely known. The reader need go no further than the present text which has a number of such examples. (2) Time- and cost-conscious commercial enterprises settle for less than optimal sample plans. Universe lists are not available; national samples are expensive. This pervasive problem must decrease in significance; marketing managers cannot afford to base decisions on such research.

Demand for Reliability Measures

Clustering, AID, multidimensional scaling, and factor analysis must at present be considered descriptive rather than inferential. Good measures of reliability or the related concept of confidence are not available. This stems basically from lack of knowledge concerning the relevant sampling distributions and/or ad hoc sequential procedural and stopping rules. Should a marketing manager make important economic decisions on results of unknown reliability—even if they seem intuitively plausible? Surely we can do better than that!

Marketing research will find indicators of reliability for these extremely useful techniques. At least three avenues offer help in this problem. (1) The split-half approach divides the sample into two groups and runs a similar analysis on each. The two results are then compared—the extent of similarity providing an indication of the degree of reliability. This approach could of course be extended, dividing the sample into more than two subgroups. (2) Various types of sensitivity analysis can be performed. These approaches can vary the processing rules or parameters employed in the programs. Alternatively, input data from a variety of sources can be submitted to the same program. In either case, reliability is indicated by the extent of agreement among the results. Both the first and second approach attempt to measure reliability by obtaining a partial empirical sampling distribution, albeit small. (3) A mathematical investigation of the relevant sampling distributions, including the determination of the relevant parameters, will serve as a basis for a more formal approach to reliability and hypothesis testing.

The difficulty encountered on this issue is a pragmatic one. All three approaches require time and money. Commercial establishments are concerned with today's decisions rather than theoretical research. The most likely source for reliability investigations is the academic community.

Timeliness and Cost

The marketing manager must react quickly to developments. It is more frustrating than useful to be given the correct information three weeks after the decision has been made. Time delays and added expense are expected as the research and analytic procedures become more complex. This is where advances in both computer hardware and software come into focus.

Remote interactive consoles, data banks with continuous input of both internal and external information, and the development of new multivariate packages will considerably reduce turn-around time between the manager's questions and the researcher's answer. Better understanding and communication of each other's perspectives, problems, and expertise will further improve the situation. The cost side will also improve as advances in hardware and software reduce both computer and personnel costs.

The availability of continuing panels will also improve the timeliness of marketing research data. Lead-in time for assembling universe lists, selecting samples, training interviewers or respondents, and establishing procedures for processing data will be minimal. Commercial firms will have these problems under control, and the necessary revisions for a particular survey will be routine. One word of warning, however! We must not assume—without checking—that *all* firms will be equally competent.

TECHNICAL DEVELOPMENTS IN DATA HANDLING

The electronic computer has made complex multivariate analyses available to the smallest company. No longer must the marketing manager settle for univariate means and standard deviations. The comprehensive models referred to in the previous section have been made possible by the computer. The future will bring greater speed, the availability of "canned" programs for more complex analyses, and new breakthroughs in communication.

The storage capacity of the computer provides immediate access to three principal types of information: raw and partially processed data, programs to execute various statistical analyses, and a package of relevant models. The first two are obvious but their contribution to marketing research—past and future—should not be understated. The third has not been utilized as much in marketing research as in other disciplines. But its role in the future will be that much greater, partially as a result of its past neglect.

Accounting and control have developed a large number of models that can be used in different companies. Payroll, accounts receivable and payable, and inventory control are three prime examples. Marketing and marketing research have similarly repetitive problems that are common to various organizations. Consumer behavior, brand switching, new product decisions, advertising allocation, and competitive reaction models are illustrative of specific marketing models that have been developed. They have not, however, been incorporated into a general arsenal available at a simple EXECUTE instruction.

The future of marketing research will bring to each organization a group of the models that is most relevant to its operations. The typical package of models will include several that are addressed to the same problem area. In this way the researcher and manager can compare the results of related models, testing for sensitivity and examining the logical strengths and weaknesses of the different approaches. Consideration of these models will have the oft-repeated benefit: participants in model building and its critique obtain a better understanding of the problem when they are forced to articulate and structure their views.

The computer also offers a new and interesting mode for data collection. Many of the more complex multivariate techniques and nonmetric methods require respondents to supply significant quantities of nonroutine types of data. Complete rankings and paired or triad comparisons are not within the daily considerations of most consumers—at least not in the structured format of the usual questionnaire schedule. As a result, the groups used for these techniques have been highly unrepresentative and unusually cooperative. If the substantive results are to be applicable to real-world problems, samples that are more representative are a necessity.

Sequential presentations of individual questions via computer consoles or cable TV provide a new and interesting experience for the respondent. With the proper format, this collection technique will be much less threatening and formidable. Data collection through these methods will free respondents from some of the burdensome paperwork and record keeping. These benefits should foster greater willingness to participate in continuing panels, thus making them more representative. The operation of such a panel by a single firm will also permit lower per unit costs for all participating firms.

The increasing use of the telephone interview, accompanied by good quality control, is yet another way of countering two dilemmas. The resulting sample can be more representative, covering the appropriate geographic areas and dealing more adequately with the "not-at-home" issue. Creative ways of combining the telephone with the computer and/or cable TV are certain to emerge. The simple procedure of unattended mechanical recording devices with input to a computer is an obvious possible direction.

The feedback of results to the manager is a natural with remote consoles. Hardcopy paper output or video display addresses both the timeliness issue and the comprehensibility issue. Much has already been done with respect to graphic presentation of results. Much is yet needed, but it is a start.

The interactive feature of manager-computer communication is an additional plus that makes marketing research more palatable to the marketing manager. The movement toward English (or any other spoken language) as the mode of interaction will further accelerate the acceptability of the computer to the manager.

AVAILABILITY OF COMPETENT RESEARCH PERSONNEL

The educational process is a great ally in the future of marketing research. This holds true both on the research side and on the management side. Gone is the day when a marketing researcher was competent by virtue of knowing or having access to encyclopedic reams of data. Gone also is the day when competence was achieved by virtue of the ability to construct appropriate data collection instruments and supervise their administration. These abilities are still necessary, but the competent marketing researcher of today and tomorrow must be able to wed the required research design and analyses to these other talents. The marketing manager of the future must recognize research as an ally, not as an antagonist. In order to do this, the manager must know enough about research to know what it can and what it cannot offer, and the researcher must be able and willing to communicate with the manager. The progressive companies of the future will insist that their researchers and managers have this required training and perspective. Educational institutions must construct their programs to that end.

Paradoxically, the higher level of analytic ability required will have one of its most obvious impacts in data collection. "Garbage In—Garbage Out" will become more apparent. The remedy is in more careful preparation of data collection schedules, instruction and training in their use, and continuous supervision in order to assure adequate quality control. Companies are learning that it is false economy to rely on their sales personnel or part-time clerical force for data collection. The use of such personnel for this task results in poor data and simultaneously takes the individuals away from their areas of expertise.

Better quality control of the interview comes from the use of trained personnel. Here the company faces the "make-or-buy" decision. Unless the company will have a continuing need for such personnel, the training cost may be excessive. In such a case an external firm with the required staff can handle the data collection task more effectively and efficiently.

The increased use of computer, cable TV, and telephone further facilitates quality control. The possibility of monitoring the collection process allows the early correction of improper procedures and protects against cheating. On-line monitoring allows supervision and observation of the data collection process rather than examination of its result. The existence of this monitoring reduces the probability of cheating, whether from fraudulent returns or slovenly work.

The development of more comprehensive models will have a synergistic effect on data analysis. Mixed models with both ordinal data and interval data will encourage alternative analytic techniques. The addition of nominally scaled data and the use of dependent variables expressed on a 0/1 probability continuum will further encourage the use and investigation of alternative analytic models. Prebehavioral and postbehavioral variables plus greater use of "bottom-line" considerations will lead to greater concern for time-lag relationships and the possibility of two-stage equations. The greater recognition that interactions are a part of the real world will lead to experimentation with alternative ways of expressing interaction and examination of differences in the results produced by the alternative approaches.

Theoretically competent and broad-gauge personnel are required for the investigation of the differences produced by alternative models. As the technical level of marketing researchers is raised, both theoretically oriented and applied researchers will be drawn to these questions. This attraction will be felt because the comparisons have economic significance as well as intellectual challenge.

Analytic techniques involving nonlinear relationships will also become more prevalent. This will involve both transformations and the use of alternative forms of interaction. Greater stress on sequential application of different techniques can also be expected; for example, factor analysis followed by the use of the derived factor scores in regression or discriminant analysis. Widespread and creative use of analytic techniques is possible only as the competence level of marketing researchers rises. This is clearly the wave of the future.

DEVELOPMENTS IN BEHAVIORAL SCIENCE AND MARKETING

New marketing theories and reclassifications of existing concepts offer new opportunities as well as challenges for marketing research. Similarly, developments in the various behavioral science areas have potential relevance for marketing decisions. Every development offers several new directions for marketing research. We shall discuss only a few; the reader can expand the number indefinitely.

Psychographics and psychometrics are areas with great potential for marketing decisions. Personality, life-style, attitudes, and similar dimensions offer new ways of describing consumers. The theoretical study of scales—symmetric versus nonsymmetric, equal versus unequal intervals, bipolar adjectives versus labels for each category, rotations, stretching of axes, and a variety of technical and substantive issues—impinge on the marketing practitioner. What, if any, utility do they lend to the available "bag of tricks"? How, if useful to the practitioner, can the marketing researcher incorporate the relevant developments in the research?

Human behavior concepts cannot be summarily rejected. They have been used in the past, albeit with mixed results. But mixed results have also been obtained from demographic variables. The future will see greater incorporation of nondemographic variables in problem definition, if only to test their significance. The addition of psychological concepts will be joined by variables from the other social sciences—thus making the research questions posed even more comprehensive.

Psychological variables pose an additional problem because they are not directly observable. Their measurement may be both unreliable and unstable over time. The psychologist has typically addressed this dilemma with exten-

2. Briefly explain the meaning of each of the following terms and indicate how each poses a challenge to marketing research

   a) Decision Making Unit (DMU)

   b) Data quality control

   c) Interactive computer terminal

   d) Testing of alternative models

   e) Attitude-interest-opinion (A-I-O) data

   f) Sensitivity analysis

3. Choose a company with which you are familiar. Company size is of no concern. Illustrate how the future directions indicated in Table 21.1 would be manifest within the company chosen. Four or five cells are sufficient, but be sure to identify the cells you are discussing.

4. The factors chosen in Table 21.1 and the use of a $n \times m$ format are subjective and arbitrary. Present an alternative basis for discussing "Future Directions in Marketing Research." The discussion need not be pursued; only an indication of the approach and general format is needed.

5. Identify a recent marketing research project that was reasonably well done.

   a) What developments within the past 10 to 12 years made this project either possible or at least easier to accomplish?

   b) Do you think the developments are indicative of developments in the future? Discuss.

6. Marketing managers should possess some knowledge of marketing research, but they clearly do not need the same degree of expertise as the marketing research director.

   a) Prepare two lists, one of topics and/or concepts in which marketing managers should have knowledge of marketing research and the other of topics and/or concepts in which marketing managers need not have knowledge. The lists should be illustrative rather than comprehensive—six to ten items on each list.

   b) How, if at all, would a common acceptance of such lists be helpful within a company? Why?

APPENDIX

Table A.1
Random Digits

Line	(1)	(2)	(3)	(4)	(5)	(6)	(7)	(8)	(9)	(10)	(11)	(12)	(13)	(14)
1	10480	15011	01536	02011	81647	91646	69179	14194	62590	36207	20969	99570	91291	90700
2	22368	46573	25595	85393	30995	89198	27982	53402	93965	34095	52666	19174	39615	99505
3	24130	48360	22527	97265	76393	64809	15179	24830	49340	32081	30680	19655	63348	58629
4	42167	93093	06243	61680	07856	16376	39440	53537	71341	57004	00849	74917	97758	16379
5	37570	39975	81837	16656	06121	91782	60468	81305	49684	60672	14110	06927	01263	54613
6	77921	06907	11008	42751	27756	53498	18602	70659	90655	15053	21916	81825	44394	42880
7	99562	72905	56420	69994	98872	31016	71194	18738	44013	48840	63213	21069	10634	12952
8	96301	91977	05463	07972	18876	20922	94595	56869	69014	60045	18425	84903	42508	32307
9	89579	14342	63661	10281	17453	18103	57740	84378	25331	12566	58678	44947	05585	56941
10	85475	36857	53342	53988	53060	59533	38867	62300	08158	17983	16439	11458	18593	64952
11	28918	69578	88231	33276	70997	79936	56865	05859	90106	31595	01547	85590	91610	78188
12	63553	40961	48235	03427	49626	69445	18663	72695	52180	20847	12234	90511	33703	90322
13	09429	93969	52636	92737	88974	33488	36320	17617	30015	08272	84115	27156	30613	74952
14	10365	61129	87529	85869	48237	52267	67689	93394	01511	26358	85104	20285	29975	89868
15	07119	97336	71048	08178	77233	13916	47564	81056	97735	85977	29372	74461	28551	90707
16	51085	12765	51821	51259	77452	16308	60756	92144	49442	53900	70960	63990	75601	40719
17	02368	21382	52404	60268	89368	19885	55322	44819	01188	65255	64835	44919	05944	55157
18	01011	54092	33362	94904	31273	04146	18594	29852	71585	85030	51132	01915	92947	64951
19	52162	53916	46369	58586	23216	14513	83149	98736	23495	64350	94738	17752	35156	35749
20	07056	97628	33787	09998	42698	06691	76988	13602	51851	46104	88916	19509	25625	58104
21	48663	91245	85828	14346	09172	30168	90229	04734	59193	22178	30421	61666	99904	32812
22	54164	58492	22421	74103	47070	25306	76468	26384	58151	06646	21524	15227	96909	44592
23	32639	32363	05597	24200	13363	38005	94342	28728	35806	06912	17012	64161	18296	22851
24	29334	27001	87637	87308	58731	00256	45834	15398	46557	41135	10367	07684	36188	18510
25	02488	33062	28834	07351	19731	92420	60952	61280	50001	67658	32586	86679	50720	94953

26	81525	72295	04839	96423	24878	82651	66566	14778	76797	14780	13300	87074	79666	95725
27	29676	20591	68086	26432	46901	20849	89768	81536	86645	12659	92259	57102	80428	25280
28	00742	57392	39064	66432	84673	40027	32832	61362	98947	96067	64760	64584	96096	98253
29	05366	04213	25669	26422	44407	44048	37937	63904	45766	66134	75470	66520	34693	90449
30	91921	26418	64117	94305	26766	25940	39972	22209	71500	64568	91402	42416	07844	69618
31	00582	04711	87917	77341	42206	35126	74087	99547	81817	42607	43808	76655	62028	76630
32	00725	69884	62797	56170	86324	88072	76222	36086	84637	93161	76038	65855	77919	88006
33	69011	65795	95876	55293	18988	27354	26575	08625	40801	59920	29841	80150	12777	48501
34	25976	57948	29888	88604	67917	48708	18912	82271	65424	69774	33611	54262	85963	03547
35	09763	83473	73577	12908	30883	18317	28290	35797	05998	41688	34952	37888	38917	88050
36	91567	42595	27958	30134	04024	86385	29880	99730	55536	84855	29080	09250	79656	73211
37	17955	56439	90999	49127	20044	59931	06115	20542	18059	02008	73708	83517	36103	42791
38	46503	18584	18845	49618	02304	51038	20655	58727	28168	15475	56942	53389	20562	87338
39	92157	89634	94824	78171	84610	82834	09922	25417	44137	48413	25555	21246	35509	20468
40	14577	62765	35605	81263	39667	47358	56873	56307	61607	49518	89686	20103	77490	18062
41	98427	07523	33362	64270	01638	92477	66969	98420	04880	45585	46565	04102	46880	45709
42	34914	63976	88720	82765	34476	17032	87589	40836	32427	70002	70663	88863	77775	69348
43	70060	28277	39475	46373	23219	53416	94970	25832	69975	94884	19661	72828	00102	66794
44	53976	54914	06990	67245	68360	82948	11398	42878	80287	88267	47363	46634	06541	97809
45	76072	29515	40980	07391	58745	25774	22987	80059	39911	96189	41151	14222	60697	59583
46	90725	52210	83974	29992	65831	38857	50490	83765	55657	14361	31720	57375	56228	41546
47	64364	67412	33339	31926	14883	24413	59744	92351	97473	89286	35931	04110	23726	51900
48	08962	00358	31662	25388	61642	34072	81249	35648	56891	69352	48373	45578	78547	81788
49	95012	68379	93526	70765	10592	04542	76463	54328	02349	17247	28865	14777	62730	92277
50	15664	10493	20492	38391	91132	21999	59516	81652	27195	48223	46751	22923	32261	85653

Page 1 of *Table of 105,000 Random Digits*, Statement No. 4914, May, 1949, File No. 261-A-1, State Commerce Commission, Washington, D.C.

Table A.6
Critical Values of s in the Kendall Coefficient of Concordance

| k | \multicolumn{5}{c}{N} | \multicolumn{2}{c}{Additional values for $N = 3$} |
	3	4	5	6	7	k	s
\multicolumn{8}{c}{$\alpha = 0.05$}
3			64.4	103.9	157.3	9	54.0
4		49.5	88.4	143.3	217.0	12	71.9
5		62.6	112.3	182.4	276.2	14	83.8
6		75.7	136.1	221.4	335.2	16	95.8
8	48.1	101.7	183.7	299.0	453.1	18	107.7
10	60.0	127.8	231.2	376.7	571.0		
15	89.8	192.9	349.8	570.5	864.9		
20	119.7	258.0	468.5	764.4	1,158.7		
\multicolumn{8}{c}{$\alpha = 0.01$}
3			75.6	122.8	185.6	9	75.9
4		61.4	109.3	176.2	265.0	12	103.5
5		80.5	142.8	229.4	343.8	14	121.9
6		99.5	176.1	282.4	422.6	16	140.2
8	66.8	137.4	242.7	388.3	579.9	18	158.6
10	85.1	175.3	309.1	494.0	737.0		
15	131.0	269.8	475.2	758.2	1,129.5		
20	177.0	364.2	641.2	1,022.2	1,521.9		

Adapted from M. Friedman, 1940. A comparison of alternative tests of significance for the problem of m rankings. *Ann. Math. Statist.* **11:** 86–92, with the kind permission of the author and the publisher.

Table A.7
Critical Values of *T* in the Wilcoxon
Matched-pairs, Signed-ranks Test

	Level of significance for two-tailed test		
N	.05	.02	.01
6	1	—	—
7	2	0	—
8	4	2	0
9	6	3	2
10	8	5	3
11	11	7	5
12	14	10	7
13	17	13	10
14	21	16	13
15	25	20	16
16	30	24	19
17	35	28	23
18	40	33	28
19	46	38	32
20	52	43	37
21	59	49	43
22	66	56	49
23	73	62	55
24	81	69	61
25	90	77	68

Adapted from Table 2 of Frank Wilcoxon and Roberta A. Wilcox, 1964. *Some Rapid Approximate Statistical Procedures.* New York: American Cyanamid Company, p. 28, with the kind permission of The American Cyanamid Company.

INDEX

prior specification of functional form, 262

selection of functional form, 261–265

summary of relation, 254

See also Analysis of variance, Contingency table, Discriminant analysis, and Regression

Athey, K. R., 122

Attitudes, 42, 87, 88, 90, 100, 101, 146, 530, 539

A-I-O (Attitude-Interest-Opinion), 600

Audimeters, 111

Audits and Surveys, 133

Autocorrelation, 400, 455

Automatic Interaction Detector (AID), 426–429, 518

market segments, 427

stopping rules, 428

tree diagram, 428

stopping rules, 428

Baker, E. L., 426

Balanced designs, 68, 72, 73

Ball, G. H., 487, 494

Banks, Seymour, 58

Barr, James, 354, 368, 396, 404, 417, 477, 514

Bartlett, M. S., 513

Behavioral science, 517, 599

Bent, Dale H., 354, 420

Beyer, William H., 541

Bias, 8, 16, 91–98, 168

interviewer, 122

in lists, 86, 96

nonresponse, 125

role playing, 122

See also Data collection, Research design, and Sampling

Biomedical Computer Programs (BMD), 354, 381, 382, 417, 487, 488, 489, 521, 522

Bipolar adjectives, 101

"Black box" model, 270

"Blowup" factor, 175, 211

BMD, *see* Biomedical Computer Programs

Boyd, Harper W., Jr., 9, 122

Brand preference, 63, 95, 379

Brown, Francis E., 306, 450, 457, 606

Brown, M. B., 354, 417, 487

Brown, R. G., 451

Bureau of Census, 109

Business Enumeration Districts, 221

Buyer behavior, 6, 40–43, 82, 87, 94, 111, 133, 136, 517

awareness, 33

motives, 88, 94

See also Decision-making unit

Cannell, Charles L., 122

Canonical correlation, 507, 508–519

canonical coefficients, 512

canonical correlation coefficient, 509, 510

canonical scores, 509, 510

canonical structure correlations, 514

characteristic roots, 512, 513

compared with MANOVA, 523–525

functions, 509

limitations, 514–517

market segmentation, 517–519

product use, 517–519

redundancy index, 515

significance test, 513

Wilks lambda, 512, 513

Carmone, Frank J., 563, 564, 569, 583

Carroll, J. Douglas, 568, 569, 571, 572, 582

Carry-over effect, 71

Cattell, R. B., 492

Causation, 52, 53, 268

Central Limit Theorem, 178

Centroids, 380, 486, 519

Chang, Jie Jih, 568, 569, 571, 582

Channon, C., 494

Characteristic of interest, 12, 29, 40–43

stability, 11

versus unit of analysis, 43

Chi Square

analysis of variance (rank data), 534

canonical correlation, 512

coefficient of concordance, 539

contingency coefficient, 281

contingency table, 241, 276

discriminant analysis, 334, 380

one-sample problem, 244

table, 609

two-tailed versus one-tailed tests, 245

Churchman, C. West, 31, 33, 52, 269

Coombs, C. H., 556
Correlation, 268, 321
  rank, 536
  See also Regression
Correlation ratio (η), 293, 320, 335
Covariance, see Analysis of covariance
Covariation, 52, 268
  See also Association
Cowden, Dudley J., 263, 448
Cox, Gertrude, 70
Criterion variable, 258
Cross-sectional, 15, 54, 253
Croxton, Frederick E., 263, 448
Cyclical fluctuations, 449

Data analysis, 18
  techniques, classification of, 19
  See also Analysis of variance,
    Analysis of covariance,
    Contingency tables, Clus-
    ter analysis, Discriminant
    analysis, Factor analysis,
    Conjoint analysis,
    Multidimensional scaling,
    Regression, and Time series
Data collection, 15, 79–113, 119–138
  communication media, 120–125
  costs, 122, 124, 128, 133, 135
  definition, 79
  disguised questions, 87
  fieldwork, 119–138
    See also Cluster sampling
  instrument design, 82–113
  interviewer selection and training,
    136–138
  nonresponse problem, 125–127
  versus problem definition, 79
  questionnaire construction, 92
  roles, 80
  structured questions, 82
  task, 80
  UAW test, 81, 95
  unstructured questions, 82
Day, George S., 498
deCani, John S., 306, 450, 457, 606
Decision making, 8
  alternative actions, 30
  as hypothesis testing, 21–25
  relation to dummy tables, 107

relation to scales, 104
research problem versus decision
  problem, 12
Decision-making unit (DMU), 34, 600
Decision maker, 4, 27, 30
Deduction, 31
Degrees of freedom, 178, 245
  analysis of variance, 289, 347
    ranked data, 534
  canonical correlation, 512
  conditional standard deviation, 311
  contingency tables, 243, 244, 276
  discriminant analysis, 328, 334
  F-ratio, 289
  regression, 317, 360
    multiple coefficient of
      determination, 363
  stepwise regression, 416
  t-distribution, 178
Deitsch, Morton, 50
Deming, William Edwards, 159
Demographic variables, 41
Denny, Joseph, 522
Dependent variable, 19, 61
  definition, 258
  scales and analytic techniques, 267
Depth interview, 7, 81
Dichotomous questions, 84
Discriminant analysis, 268, 323–337,
    372–385
  boundary lines, 375
  centroids, 380
    distance between, 380
  computer printouts, 381–384
  confusion matrix 326, 333, 374, 378,
    382
    bias, 377–378
  contingency analysis, 378–380
  discriminant functions, 329, 373, 375,
    381, 384
  graphs, 327, 334
  "jackknifed" approach, 378, 379, 382
  kinds of errors, 374, 380
  Mahalanobis D^2, 328, 334
  three groups, 330–335
  two groups, 326–330
Disguised questions, 87
Dixon, Wilfrid J., 179, 294, 319, 332,
    354, 408, 409, 417, 487, 520

Class limits, 97
  exhaustive, 98
  mutually exclusive, 98
Claxton, John D., 497
Clelland, Richard C., 306, 450, 457, 606
Cluster analysis, 469, 485–498
  amalgamation, 489, 490
  centroids, 486
  "city-block" distance, 486, 493
  computer printouts, 488, 489
  connectivity, 495
  data input, 487, 491
  distance measures, 486, 492
  Euclidean distance, 486, 492
  forming subgroups, 494
  hierarchial methods, 487, 494
  high profile similarity, 495
  interpoint distance, 487, 488
  market segmentation, 491, 496
  nonhierarchical methods, 495
  selection of variables, 491
  similarity measures, 492
  statistical inference, 496–497
  stopping rules, 495
Cluster sampling, 163–165, 216–219
  compared to stratification, 165–166
  costs, 217
  intraclass correlation, 216
  multistage, 164
  number of clusters, 164
  optimal allocation, 218
  reliability, 216
  sample selection, 164
  worksheet for sample size, 219–220
Cochran, William, 70
Coefficient of determination, 316
  See also Regression
Coefficient of variation
  definition, 208–209
  use in sample size determination,
    209–211
Coleman, Joan, 122
Comparative judgment, law of, 543–546
Computer printouts
  analysis of covariance, 403
  analysis of variance, 354, 356
  cluster analysis, 488, 489
  discriminant analysis, 381, 382
  dummy variable, 398

regression, 368, 369
  stepwise regression, 419
Concordance, coefficient of, 537
  table, 612
Conditional distribution, 255–264, 343
  a priori specification, 262
  analysis of variance, 294, 352
  contingency tables, 282
  regression, 307, 358, 365, 371
  versus unconditional distribution, 255
Confidence interval, see Interval
    estimation
Conjoint analysis, 556, 575–584
  experimental design, 576–580
    Greco–Latin square, 73, 577
    Latin square, 577
  individual differences, 581
  limitations, 582
  marketing applications, 583
  stress, 582
  utility derivation, 578
Consumer characteristics, 256
  classification, 41–43
  general inferred, 42
  general objective, 41
  situation specific inferred, 42
  situation specific objective, 42
Contingency coefficient, 281, 284
Contingency tables, 267, 275–287,
    385–387
  Chi square, 241
  contingency coefficient, 281
  degrees of freedom, 276
  dependent/independent variable
    classification, 282
  effect of sample size, 243
  interval estimates, 279
  measure of association, 279–281
  multivariate, 385–387
  one versus several samples, 283
  ordering of categories, 285
  Phi coefficient, 280
  $r \times c$, 277–279
  sampling considerations, 283
  $2 \times c$, 276
  2×2, 241–244
Control group, 57, 58, 61–63
Cooley, William A., 514, 519
Cook, Stuart W., 50

"Don't know" answers, 98, 105
Dummy report, 108
Dummy tables, 65, 106, 285–286
Dummy variable, 395–401, 408
    computer printouts, 398
    definition, 395
    interaction, 397
    versus interval scales, 410
Dunn & Bradstreet, 112
Durand, Richard M., 514, 516
Durbin, J., 459

Econometric models, 456
Eells, Kenneth, 469
Ehrenberg, A. S. C., 482
Endogenous variables, 256, 375
Engledow, Jack, 484
Environmental conditions, 8, 44,
    256
    producer–product, 53
Errors, 23–25, 184
    power curve, 187, 230
    See also Hypothesis testing
Estimation, see Point estimation and
    Interval estimation
Exogenous variables, 6, 256
Experimental design, 8, 14, 49, 62–74,
    576–580
    cross-sectional, 15, 253
    experimental group, 61, 63
    exploratory research, 49, 50
    factorial, 65–68, 345
    4-group, 6-study, 63
    Greco–Latin square, 73, 577
    versus hypothesis testing, 50
    Latin square, 68, 577
    random assignment, 168
    time series, 453
    typical approaches, 51
Explanatory research, 50
Exploratory research, 50
Exponential transformations, 424
    modified exponential, 447
Extrapolation, 315

F-ratio
    analysis of covariance, 405, 407
    analysis of variance, 288, 346
    discriminant analysis, 328

multivariate analysis of covariance,
    522
multivariate analysis of variance, 520,
    521
    regression, 319
    table, 610
Factor analysis, 469, 471–485
    communality, 474
    data input, 477, 481
    data matrix, 472
    factor loadings, 474
    factor scores, 475, 480
        use in managerial decisions,
        481–482
    interpretation, 475
    labeling, 481
    principal components, 472, 477
    Q-type, 493, 495
    rotation of axes, 478–480
    subjective issues, 481
    use in hypothesis testing, 482–485
    variance summarized, 474
    varimax rotation, 478
Factorial designs, 65–67, 345
Farley, John U., 518
Ferber, Robert, 131, 132
Field experiment, 14
Fieldwork, see Data collection
Finite multiplier, 156
    with two samples, 238
Fisher, Sir Ronald A., 70, 608,
    609
Fisz, Marck, 242
Fixed location interview, 131
Focus group interview, 86
Fortune (magazine), 110
Frank, L. K., 87
Frank, Ronald, 35, 41, 378, 421, 429,
    496, 498, 518
Freund, John E., 174
Friedman, M., 534, 612
Fry, Joseph N., 497
Functional forms
    imposed versus determined, 262

Gale Research Corp., 110
Geometric mean, 264, 440
Gleason, Terry C., 561–562
Goldhar, Joel D., 582, 583

Gompertz S-type growth curve equation, 448
Goodnight, James Howard, 354, 368, 396, 404, 417, 477, 514
Gower, J. C., 493
Grashof, John F., 582, 583
Greco-Latin square design, 73, 577
Green, Paul E., 480, 494, 496, 497, 498, 556, 557, 565, 571, 574, 575, 580, 581, 583, 584
Greeno, Daniel W., 497
Greyser, Stephen A., 93

Haire, Mason, 91
Hall, D. J., 487, 494
Hamburg, Morris, 306, 450
Hanson, Morris H., 151, 209, 211, 216
Hanson, Robert H., 122
Harmon, H. H., 472
Hartley, H. O., 610
Heeler, Roger M., 498
Henry, Walter H., 575
Homoscedasticity, 291, 313, 335, 371, 374, 420, 423,
Horst, Paul, 472
Hotelling, Harold, 508, 509
Howard, John A., 517, 518
Hull, C. Hadlai, 354, 420
Hurwitz, William N., 151, 209, 211, 216
Hypothesis
  definition, 21
  sets, 21–25
Hypothesis testing, 173, 183–193, 228–233
  arithmetic mean, 188–189
  one-sample versus two-sample, 230–231
    pooled variance, 232
    sample percentages, 231
  one-tail versus two-tail, 189
  percentage, 184–187
    alternative hypotheses, 184
    null hypothesis, 184
    power curve, 186–187
    Type I error, 185
    Type II error, 186
  "shifty alpha," 233

  two-sample case, 228–233
    power curve, 230
    sample means, 228
  two-step process, 23

In-product distribution of mail questionnaire, 131
Incentives, 128–130
Independence
  sample selection, 57, 154, 229, 240
  See also Independent variable, Interaction, and Multicollinearity
Independent variable, 19
  definition, 258
  scales and analytic techniques, 267
INDSAL, 571, 572
Induction, 31
Inference, 173
Interaction, 66, 67, 344, 346, 348
International Business Machines (IBM), 112
Interval estimation, 173, 177–183
  association statistics, 265
  confidence coefficient, 177
  interpretation, 179
  level of confidence, 177, 181
  relation to standard error, 177
  use of unit normal, 177
  See also Conditional distribution
Interview, 7
  depth, 86
  focus group, 86
  group, 131
  See also Interviewers
Interviewers, 84, 136
  cheating, 123
  selection and training, 136
  See also Interview
Irregular movements, 449

"Jackknifed" approach, 378, 379, 382
Jackson, Robert W. B., 281, 291, 320
Jahoda, Marie, 50
Jain, A. K., 480
Jenkins, Jean G., 354, 420
Johnson, Palmer O., 281, 291, 320
Johnston, J., 457
Joint-space mapping, 568, 569, 573

Jones, Vernon J., 482, 483
Joyce, T., 494

Kahn, Robert L., 122
Kaiser, H. F. 478
Kendall, M. G., 538
Kerlinger, Fred N., 6
Kernan, Jerome B., 497
Korth, Bard, 484
Kotler, Philip, 423
Kruskal, Joseph B., 562, 563, 564, 569, 578

Laboratory experiment, 12, 72, 135
Lambert, Zarrel V., 514, 516
Landon, Alfred, 39
Latin square designs, 68–70, 577
   carry-over design, 71–72
Lavidge, Robert J., 43
Lead–lag relationships, 453–459
Leading questions, 93
Least squares, method of, 308, 360, 471
Literary Digest, 39
Logarithmic transformations, 263, 320, 421
Logistic equation, 263, 447
Lohnes, Paul R., 514, 519
Longitudinal study, 15
Love, William, 515

M-D PREF, 569
M-D-SCAL, 563, 569
Madow, William G., 151, 209, 211, 216
Mahalanobis D^2, 308, 380, 383, 492
Mail questionnaire, 124–125
   advantages, 132
   disadvantages, 132
MANCOVA, see Multivariate analysis of covariance
Mann, H. B., 533, 534
Mann–Whitney U, 532
MANOVA, see Multivariate analysis of variance
MAP (Multivariate Analysis Package), 561, 562
Market Research Corporation of America, 111, 133

Market segments, 15, 18, 92, 106, 284–285, 352, 427, 496, 517, 570
Marketing, definition of, 5
Marketing concept, 6
Marketing mix
   interaction, 263, 352
   response function, 423, 523
   See also individual elements
Marketing research
   "bottom-line" emphasis, 594
   definition, 5–9
   future directions, 591–601
   past inadequacies, 591
   process, 9–20
Marketing strategy, 572–574
Matched-pairs, signed-ranks test, 539
   table, 613
Markin, Rom J., 424
Marks, Eli S., 122
Massey, Frank J., Jr., 179, 294, 319, 332, 408, 409
Massy, William F., 35, 41, 378, 429
Matched pairs, 539
MDS, see Multidimensional scaling
Median, 104, 530–532
Meeker, Marcia, 469
Mode, 104
Modified exponential, 263, 447
MONANOVA, 578, 579
Montgomery, David B., 455
Moody's, 110
Morgan, J. N., 426
Morrison, Donald F., 335, 377, 384, 472
Morrison, Donald G., 377, 378, 496
Mosteller, Frederick, 544
Moving average, 449
Multichotomous questions, 84
Multicollinearity, 361, 457
Multidimensional scaling (MDS), 555, 556–575
   distance measures, 569
   Euclidean distance, 569
   ideal point, 565, 566
   individual differences, 571
   joint space, 568, 569, 573
   limitations, 574
   perceptual mapping, 558, 572

Reilly, William H., 425
Reitman, Audrey, 122
Replications, 14, 68, 345
Research, characteristics, 6–9
Research design, 13, 50–74
  components, 58–61
    history, 58
    maturation, 59
    selection, 58
    testing, 58
    treatment, 58
  See also Experimental design
Residual component, 449
Response format, 82, 84, 96
Response rates, 127–128
  call-backs, 127
  incentives, 128
Retail trading area, 424
Ring, L. Winston, 518
Robinson, Patrick J., 498
Role playing, 135
  See also Bias
Romney, A. K., 568
Root, H. Paul, 575
Roshwalb, Irving, 210
Runs test, 541–543

S-type growth curves, 447
Sales Management (magazine), 110
Sample, 10
  bias, 146
  reliabiltiy, 146, 155–158
    and sample size, 195–223
  representative, 7, 145, 166
  standard error, 155
  unrepresentative, 594
  See also Sampling
Sample size
  effect of reliability, 156
  See also Sample size required, Sample,
    and Sampling
Sample size required, 195–223
  clustering, 216
  confidence level, 196–200
  difference between means, 237
  difference between proportions,
    235–237
  disproportional stratification, 214–215

effect of specified reliability and
    confidence, 199
  estimation for subgroups, 207
  estimation of totals, 205
  means, 201
  percentages
    effect of sample result, 196, 197
    finite population, 199
  proportional stratification, 211–214
  required precision, 195
  sequential sampling, 204
  worksheets, 203, 219, 239
Sample statistic, 175
Sampling, 145–169
  cluster, 163–165, 216–219
  comparison of alternative designs,
    220–223
  nonprobability, 166–168
  sampling error, 18
  sequential sampling, 204
  simple random sample, 147–155
  stratification, 159-163, 211–216
  systematic, 158
Sampling fraction
  definition, 156
  effect on reliability, 156
SAS, *see* Statistical Analysis System
Scales, 99–105
  interval, 101
  mixed, 395–411
  nominal, 99
  ordinal, 100, 529–548
  ratio, 102
  two-step ordinal, 102
  zero point, 102
Scatter diagram, 307
Schaeffer, Francis A., 32
Search techniques, 415–429
Seasonal movement, 449
Self-selection bias, 54, 58, 62, 133, 168
Self-weighting, 158, 215
Selltiz, Claire, 50
Search techniques, 415–430
Secondary data, 17, 108–112
  commercial data services, 110
  internal, 109
  published external, 109
  sources, 109

Semantic differential, 101
Sensitivity analysis, 496–497, 595
Sequential sampling, 204
Serial correlation, 456
Shephard, R. N., 568
Sheth, Jagdish N., 517, 518
Shocher, Allan O., 575
Siegal, Sidney, 281, 530, 532, 533, 537
Sign test, 540
Signed-ranks test, 539
Siller, Fred H., 482, 483
Similarities data, 557
Simmons, W. R., and Associates, 111
Simple random sampling, 147–155
Smith, Gail, 43
SMSA, *see* Standard Metropolitan Statistical Area
Sneath, P. H. A., 494
Socioeconomic variables, 41
Sokal, R. R., 494
Sommers, Montrose S., 497
Sonquist, J. A., 420
Sorting box, 136
Space coordinates, 12, 35
Sparks, David L., 517, 518
Spearman, C., 536
Spitz, Lawrence K., 584
Split-half technique, 270, 320, 378, 417 455, 484–485, 516
SPSS, *see* Statistical Package for the Social Sciences
Srinivasen V., 575
Standard & Poor, 110
Standard deviation, 152
Standard error
  general definition, 155
  See also Point estimation, Interval estimation, Hypothesis testing, *and specific techniques*
Standard error of estimate, 311
Standard Industrial Classification Code, 112, 415
Standard Metropolitan Statistical Area (SMSA), 28, 417
Standard score, 104, 316, 477, 487
Starch, 59, 111
States of nature, 21

Statistical Abstract of the United States (publication), 110
Statistical Analysis System (SAS), 354, 355, 356, 368, 381, 396, 398, 404, 413, 417–418, 477, 478–479, 514
Statistical Package for the Social Sciences, 354, 381, 420
Steepest descent, method of, 564
Steinbrenner, Karin, 354, 420
Steiner, Gary A., 43
Stewart, Douglas, 515
Strain, Charles E., 518
Stratification, 159–163, 211–216
  disproportional, 214–216
    optimal allocation, 215
  with estimates of proportions, 213
  gain over simple random sampling, 162
  pooled within-stratum variance, 212
  proportional, 211–214
    gain in reliability, 211
  reliability, 161
  sample selection, 162
  self-weighting, 160
  strata, 160
  versus subgroup estimation, 212
  worksheet for sample size, 219–220
Stress, 560, 562, 582
Student *t*-distribution, *see t*-distribution
Stumpt, Robert V., 575
Subgroup estimates, 212
Suci, George J., 101
Sufficient conditions, 268
Survey of Current Business, 110
Systematic sampling, 158

t-distribution, 178
  table, 608
  use in regression, 313
Tang, Jerry, 122
Tannenbaum, Perry H., 101
TAT, 90
Tchebycheff inequality, 179
Telephone interview, 123124
  advantages, 132
  disadvantages, 132
Test–retest reliability, 106
Thematic Apperception Test (TAT), 90
Thurstone, L. L., 481, 544

Thurstone's law of comparative
   judgment, 543–546
Time coordinates, 10, 35
Time series, 15, 54, 435–460
   autocorrelation, 455–459
   versus cross-sectional, 453
   decomposition, 448–450
      cycle, 448
      irregular, 449
      residual, 449
      seasonal, 449
      trend, 448
   definition, 435
   econometric models, 456
   exponential smoothing, 450–453
   first differences, 454, 456
   geometric mean, 440
   lead–lag, 453–459
   linear trends, 437–445
   logarithmic equations, 441, 446
   moving average, 449
   multicollinearity, 457
   parabolic, 445–447
   relation to linear regression, 444
   S-type growth curves, 447
   time as an independent variable,
      436
Torgerson, W. S., 556
Transformations, 320, 420–426
   double log, 423, 454
   exponential, 424–426
   logarithmic, 105, 421–423
   polynomials, 426
Trend, 448
Tucker, L. R., 484
Tucker, W. T., 517, 518
TV viewing, 111, 133
Type I error (alpha), 185
Type II error (beta), 186

UAW test, 81
   See also Data collection
Undisguised questions, 87
Unit normal distribution, 177
   graph, 178
   table, 606
   use in regression, 313
Unit of analysis, 10, 33–35

Universe, 10, 28, 33–39
   list, conceptual, 36
   list, enumerative, 36
   parameter, 175
   problem universe, 11, 37–39
   research universe, 11, 37–39
   size, 39
Unobstrusive techniques, 18
Urban, Glen, L., 455

Variables
   dependent, 40
   endogenous, 40
   exogenous, 40
   independent, 40
Variance, 152
   explained, 318, 408
   among strata, 161
   within stratum, 161
   unbiased estimator, 175
   unexplained, 318, 408
   See also Analysis of variance
Verdoorn, P. J., 131, 132
van Pechmann, F., 91

Warner, W. Lloyd, 469
Wasserman, Paul, 110
Watson, F. S., 459
Webster, Frederick E., Jr., 91, 517
Westfall, Ralph, 9, 122
Whipple, Thomas W., 575
Whitney, D. R., 533, 534
Wilcox, Roberta A., 613
Wilcoxon, Frank, 540, 613
Wide Area Telephone Service (WATS),
   123
Williams, J. Allen, Jr., 122
Wind, Yoram, 35, 41, 429, 480, 517,
   522, 556–557, 565–566, 570,
   573–574, 579, 581–584
Winer, B. J., 294, 577
Wording of individual questions, 82, 92
   rephrasing, 83, 121

Yamane, Taro, 456, 459
Yates, Frank, 608

Zeisel, Hans, 133